# THE SUBLIME READER

# THE SUBLIME READER

*Edited by Robert R. Clewis*

BLOOMSBURY ACADEMIC
LONDON • NEW YORK • OXFORD • NEW DELHI • SYDNEY

BLOOMSBURY ACADEMIC
Bloomsbury Publishing Plc
50 Bedford Square, London, WC1B 3DP, UK
1385 Broadway, New York, NY 10018, USA

BLOOMSBURY, BLOOMSBURY ACADEMIC and the Diana logo are trademarks of Bloomsbury Publishing Plc

First published in Great Britain 2019

Cover design by Irene Martinez Costa
Cover Image: Guo Xi, Early Spring © The Picture Art Collection / Alamy Stock Photo

A catalogue record for this book is available from the British Library.

A catalog record for this book is available from the Library of Congress.

ISBN: HB: 978-1-3500-3015-2
PB: 978-1-3500-3016-9
ePDF: 978-1-3500-3014-5
eBook: 978-1-3500-3017-6

Typeset by Deanta Global Publishing Services, Chennai, India
Printed and bound in Great Britain

To find out more about our authors and books visit www.bloomsbury.com and sign up for our newsletters.

# CONTENTS

# LIST OF ILLUSTRATIONS

# PREFACE

In the years in which I was preparing my book, *The Kantian Sublime and the Revelation of Freedom* (2009), I realized that, although there were anthologies on aesthetics, beauty, or collections of eighteenth-century texts on the sublime, there were no anthologies explicitly devoted to reprinting texts from the extensive history of the sublime. True, excerpts on the sublime were occasionally included in anthologies on aesthetics, art, or the history of philosophy, but the excerpts were included as if in passing (that is, the sublime was not the focus of the anthology), or the anthologies were limited in period (for example, to the eighteenth century) or in scope (for instance, to contemporary art). This absence of an anthology on the sublime surprised me, since the sublime was one of the central concepts in the history of aesthetics—especially during the modern period, when aesthetics came into its own as an academic discipline—and since in the western tradition the sublime has roots going back to ancient Greek thought. In twentieth-century francophone philosophy, the sublime was of utmost significance; in addition, the possibility of the sublime has been the subject of debate in recent anglophone aesthetics. Since the time of my initial surprise (more than a decade ago), no anthology in the English language has appeared.

We sometimes hear that the sublime is dated and outmoded—an historic relic, a concept of little use today. This judgment has rarely struck me as fitting. This volume's contemporary selections from various academic disciplines and intellectual traditions provide ample evidence to the contrary. Psychologists are carrying out more and more studies of the sublime (using the term "awe"), creating a body of empirical research that could be of interest to theoretically inclined scholars and writers; the latter, in turn, might be able to guide and collaborate in future studies. The sublime has been criticized for being "gendered"—with the sublime supposedly associated with masculinity and domination, beauty with femininity, and so on. While some authors such as Edmund Burke unquestionably present their theories by drawing on concepts of gender (and race), the women voices represented in this volume would seem to indicate that the situation is more complex than a preoccupation with writers like Burke would initially suggest. The sublime has been accused of being "western" and even "anti-environmental." This volume's texts from India, China, and Japan, and the discussions of the sublime and the natural environment, respectively, suggest that these charges are at the very least questionable.

In short, it is my humble hope that this volume will grant the sublime the focused attention it deserves, revise our understanding of it, and invigorate and sustain interest in the sublime.

# SOURCES

The publisher and editor gratefully acknowledge the permission granted to reproduce the copyright material in this book:

Longinus, *On Sublimity*, from *Ancient Literary Criticism: The Principal Texts in New Translations*, edited by Donald Andrew Russell and Michael Winterbottom. Copyright © 1972 Oxford University Press. Reprinted with the permission of the publisher.

Bharata-Muni, *The Nāṭyaśāstra Ascribed to Bharata-Muni*, translated by Manomoha Ghosh. Copyright © 1951 Asiatic Society of Bengal. Reprinted with permission of the publisher.

Guo Xi, from *The Interest of Lofty Forests and Springs*, translated by Jonathan Johnson. Published here for the first time with the permission of the translator.

Zeami Motokiyo, "Notes on the Nine Levels," from *On the Art of the Nō Drama: The Major Treatises of Zeami*, translated by J. Thomas Rimer and Yamazaki Masakazu. Copyright © 1984 Princeton University Press. Reprinted with the permission of Princeton University Press; permission conveyed through Copyright Clearance Center, Inc.

Petrarch, "The Ascent of Mont Ventoux," from *Renaissance Philosophy of Man*, edited by Paul Oskar Kristeller, Ernst Cassirer, and John Herman Randall, Jr. Copyright © 1948 University of Chicago Press. Reprinted with the permission of the publisher.

Nicolas Boileau Despréaux, "Preface to his Translation of Longinus on the Sublime," from *Selected Criticism*, edited by Ernest Dilworth. Copyright © 1965 Bobbs-Merrill.

Giambattista Vico, "On the Heroic Mind," in *Social Research: An International Quarterly* 43, no. 4 (Winter 1976): 886–903. Copyright © 1976 The New School. Reprinted with permission of Johns Hopkins University Press.

Moses Mendelssohn, "On the Sublime and Naive in the Fine Sciences," from *Philosophical Writings*, edited and translated by Daniel Dahlstrom, 1997. Copyright © 1997 Cambridge University Press, reproduced with permission.

Immanuel Kant, from *Observations on the Feeling of the Beautiful and Sublime*, translated by Paul Guyer, and *Anthropology from a Pragmatic Point of View*, translated by Robert B. Louden. In *Anthropology, History, Education*, edited by Günter Zöller and Robert B. Louden, 2007. Copyright © 2007 Cambridge University Press, reproduced with permission.

Immanuel Kant, *Critique of the Power of Judgment*, edited by Paul Guyer and translated by Paul Guyer and Eric Matthews, 2000. Copyright © 2000 Cambridge University Press, reproduced with permission.

Friedrich Schiller, "On the Sublime (Toward the Further Development of Some Kantian Ideas)," translated by Daniel Dahlstrom, from *Essays*, edited by Daniel Dahlstrom and Walter Hinderer. Copyright © 1998 Continuum. Reprinted with permission.

William Wordsworth, "The Sublime and the Beautiful," in *The Prose Works of William Wordsworth*, edited by W. J. B. Owen and Jane Worthington Smyser. Copyright © 1974 Clarendon Press. Reprinted with the permission of the publisher.

# Sources

# ACKNOWLEDGMENTS

I have shared the ideas for this project with many individuals—far more than space allows me to recognize here. At a conference in the spring of 2014, Paul Guyer gave me the encouragement to publish this book, making concrete a project that I had long been envisioning. Stefan Bird-Pollan, Camilla Caporicci, Noël Carroll, Richard Eldridge, Susan Feagin, Serena Feloj, David Kim, Stefan Micali, Lara Ostaric, Andrei Pop, and Bart Vandenabeele gave excellent advice on the project as a whole or on specific texts, as did anonymous reviewers consulted by Bloomsbury. My understanding of the sublime also profited from discussions or correspondence with Uygar Abaci, Henry E. Allison, Allen Carlson, Rick Clewis, Richard Kearney, Robert B. Louden, Samantha Matherne, Elisa Schwab, Sandra Shapshay, Susan Shell, John Zammito, as well as with the members of the Philadelphia area Aesthetics Reading Group, including Sally Banes, Noël Carroll, John Carvalho, Richard Eldridge, Susan Feagin, Kristin Gjesdal, Espen Hammer, Lara Ostaric, and Mary Wiseman. I likewise owe a debt of gratitude to colleagues (in addition to some of the ones just mentioned) who made helpful suggestions and comments regarding the selection of texts: Peter Adamson, Betsy Chapin, Tom Hanauer, Patrick Messina, Mohammed Rustom, and Yuriko Saito. Joseph Margolis has been a wonderfully stimulating interlocutor about the sublime and aesthetics in general.

I am grateful to those who have invited me to talk about the sublime at their universities, in particular, Kimberly Blessing (Buffalo State University), Serena Feloj (University of Pavia), Des Hogan (Princeton University), Erik Schmidt and Ted di Maria (Gonzaga University), and Günter Zöller (University of Munich). For invaluable discussion or comments on my essay (chapter 37) in this volume, I am grateful to many individuals, including but not limited to: Emily Brady, Elanna Dructor, Abigail Friel, Norbert Gratzl, Rebecca Gullan, Vladimir Konečni, Cornelia Kroiss, J. Colin McQuillan, Patrick Messina, Lara Ostaric, Amanda Pirrone, Amanda Wortham, and David B. Yaden.

I have benefited from many discussions with students. In particular, Elanna Dructor, Abigail Friel, and Amanda Wortham patiently helped with the preparation of this book during its various phases, making suggestions regarding selections and reading versions of the manuscript. Abigail Kennedy and Mikhail Melknik also helped with proofreading.

Robert Garber and Anne Marie Mullen at Gwynedd Mercy University provided indispensable administrative support, and I am likewise grateful to the university library staff, especially to Donna Wallace and Patricia Smith.

This project has been in part supported by the Alexander von Humboldt Foundation: I completed the final stages of the book in the summer of 2017 during a research stay at the University of Munich. I am grateful to my host Günter Zöller for both his hospitality and advice regarding readings, and to Kristina Maschek for administrative support.

I am grateful to Lisa McGarry, Dean of the School of Arts and Sciences at Gwynedd Mercy University, and to Frank E. Scully, Jr. and Mary Van Brunt, Vice Presidents for Academic Affairs. Lisa McGarry awarded this project a Dean's Discretionary Fund (made possible by a gift from Dick and Kathy Target) and helped offset some of the costs of the permissions fees. I am indebted to the philosophy chairperson, Patrick Messina, who has encouraged me in this project and (inter alia) shared his knowledge of medieval philosophy.

I would like to thank Liza Thompson and Frankie Mace at Bloomsbury for their support of this project as well as their assistance obtaining some of the permissions.

I am grateful to my family for putting up with me as I worked on this project: This book is dedicated to them.

# NOTE ON THE TEXTS

This anthology contains "selections"—not only have I selected which texts to include, but I have also redacted some of the texts and have therefore selected which parts to retain and reprint. In those cases where I have made cuts and omissions, it should be clear why I have done so. For considerations of space, I have occasionally deleted a reading's sections that seemed inessential to the argument or topic. I indicate when this occurs by using an ellipsis as follows: "[. . .]".

The early and late modern printed style, as Dabney Townsend has noted, was idiosyncratic at times, and in the course of the century the accepted practices of style and printing were modified. The way of capitalizing, use of italics, and spelling practices changed over time. In the Note on the text at the beginning of each selection, I indicate how I handled such matters.

When a text was originally printed with editorial notes, I have usually included a version of the notes, although I have omitted them if they seemed unnecessary in light of the anthology's aims. (For instance, editorial footnotes comparing textual variants between two editions of Giambattista Vico's "On the Heroic Mind" have been omitted.) Notes that appear in the original have been numbered and (re)positioned as endnotes; however, if an original text made a distinction between different types of notes, I have tried to preserve a version of it.

Whereas text written by me here conforms to US English style, in editing selections I generally follow the style and format of the original text or translation (allowing texts written in British English to remain that way). Unless otherwise noted, I have silently corrected typographical errors or obvious misprints, however.

To be most useful, these selections must be accessible to as wide an audience as possible while providing a reliable text within the constraints of space, time, and funding. The specialist to whom textual variants matter should probably consult the original texts or facsimiles of them. I hope that the selections collected here will suffice for the kind of intellectual, historical, cultural, and critical work that this collection is intended to promote.

# EDITOR'S INTRODUCTION
*Robert R. Clewis*

This anthology is the first comprehensive, historical reader in English on the sublime. It includes selections from Longinus to today, presenting texts from the Greek, Indian, Chinese, and Japanese traditions and including authors from the ancient, postclassical, modern, late modern, and contemporary periods.[1]

## The sublime

But first, what is the sublime? The sublime (or sublimity) is difficult to define, and its meaning has changed over time. While eluding precise definition, the sublime can be described as a complex feeling of intense satisfaction, uplift, or elevation, felt before an object or event that is considered to be awe-inspiring. Although the sublime is sometimes characterized as a complex combination of satisfying and discomforting elements, it is on the whole a positive and pleasant experience: perceivers typically desire the experience to continue. Related concepts are elevation, wonder, reverence, awe, and admiration—perhaps one could think of the sublime as a kind of "aesthetic" awe. An example of the feeling of the sublime would be the exaltation or excitement felt before a vast or powerful object, a natural wonder like the Grand Canyon, or a work of architecture such as the Great Pyramid of Giza. Contemporary psychologists have sometimes studied the sublime under another name, "awe." (They have identified some of the bodily or physiological changes that take place in people experiencing this emotion: goose bumps, dropped jaw, raised inner eyebrows, and widened eyes.[2] It is an exciting time for research in this area of positive psychology, and there may be potentially beneficial results.) In contrast, philosophers, theologians, and other theoretically oriented authors typically prefer the words "sublime" and "sublimity." But I take them to be writing about nearly the same experience or concept, even if the details of awe–sublimity relation need to be worked out (and some of the contributors to this volume may even disagree on those details). If so, scholars and students of the humanities and social sciences may very well profit from reading each other's work on this topic.[3]

There is, however, an ambiguity in theories of the sublime, an ambiguity that may well be unavoidable. The sublime can refer to a person's or subject's feelings and experiences, and it can be applied to the *object* that elicits those responses. Typical examples of such objects include waterfalls, icebergs, raging storms, deep ravines, the starry sky, mountain ranges, and some artworks or artifacts, including cathedrals, dams, and ancient ruins.

The object has properties (e.g., vastness, power) that can awaken fear. In fact, if one were not experiencing the sublime, these features might very well elicit fear. But one cannot actually be afraid of the powerful storm or volcano, when one is having a positive "aesthetic" experience of it. Thus, a viewer feeling the sublime is typically in a position of safety or at some distance from the vast or powerful object. (Whether or not this condition is met is an empirical matter—it depends on the person experiencing it.) If the sublime is an "aesthetic" experience, it can be more easily switched off than can the other fundamental emotions, which differentiates the sublime from plain, uncontrollable fear.

Perhaps it would be useful to offer more examples of what is considered sublime. Here is a short list (many more examples are found throughout this anthology): Haydn's *Creation*, Beethoven's Ninth symphony, and Wagner's *Lohengrin*; the poetry of Homer, Shakespeare, Milton, Wordsworth, Coleridge, Leopardi, Baudelaire,

Edgar Allan Poe, Walt Whitman, or Nikki Giovanni; natural wonders such as the Grand Canyon; the starry sky unaffected by light pollution; an image of a black hole or a photo of the Milky Way; the Himalayas or Alps; the sculptures of Richard Serra; the paintings of Caspar David Friedrich, J. M. W. Turner, and Barnett Newman; the tragedies of Sophocles or Schiller; Werner Herzog's film *Aguirre: The Wrath of God* and many a scene from natural disaster and doomsday films; St. Peter's in Rome, and the churches at Chartres, Milan, or Ulm.

To say these are considered "sublime" is not to use the term as an epithet for "excellent" but is to indicate that the objects are likely or disposed to elicit a sublime response (or at least a response lying on that continuum). Some on the aforementioned list are large objects viewed from the right distance (pyramids, mountains, cathedrals). Some speakers and writers, following Longinus, use the word to describe speech, rhetoric, and poetry. Sometimes the word refers to a work of painting or music. (I think it is best not to be too restrictive about using the word.) The term might even be applied to *small* things if they are perceived in a certain way—such as through a microscope—just as it can be applied to vast things that appear small to the unaided eye (e.g., stars in the sky). If the sublime is an aesthetic experience, whether or not something is considered sublime in part depends on the observer, on factors such as the perceiver's perspective and mood, and on the circumstances in which the object or event is perceived (imagined, remembered).

I have suggested that the sublime can be considered an "aesthetic" experience. (We need not insist that it is *only* an aesthetic experience, of course.) To understand what this means, it would be useful to know more about aesthetics. Viewed as a scholarly discipline, aesthetics is the study of the nature and value of properties (or experiences) such as beauty, ugliness, grandeur, and sublimity (among other states and qualities), and the investigation of how we enjoy, interpret, appraise, or use art. Aesthetics investigates humor, irony, satire, style, metaphor, and the features and role of genres (e.g., horror, comedy, tragedy). It explores the characteristics and merits of the various fine arts (poetry, music, dance, etc.), works of fiction, film, comic books, and folk art and crafts. In addition to making use of conceptual analysis, the methods of aesthetics can sometimes make use of work in empirical fields such as psychology, neuroscience, and the cognitive sciences. After all, the word is etymologically related to the Greek *aisthēsis*, which means perception, sensation. Understood as the philosophy of art, the discipline called aesthetics raises questions about how to understand, recognize, interpret, judge, and evaluate artworks. Since aesthetics examines aesthetic value(s), it is sometimes thought of as a kind of "value theory"—a broader field that would also include the study of ethical value, namely, ethics. Aesthetics is neither art history nor art criticism, but it can pose questions about these. It can also ask questions about the relation between the beautiful and the good or between aesthetic and moral values. The field can be understood widely so as to include environmental aesthetics and even the aesthetics of everyday life. So, where does the sublime fit in? The sublime is certainly not the central topic studied in aesthetics, but it is still an important one and it has been studied across the centuries. The sublime can be examined by aesthetics in at least one of its large branches—that is, in the more psychologically oriented branch, or in the philosophy of art branch (both of which can make use of conceptual analysis). (In the present anthology, Burke provides a good instance of the psychological approach, and Danto of the philosophy of art perspective.) To say that the experience of the sublime is an "aesthetic" one is first and foremost to say what it is *not*. An aesthetic experience is neither an ordinary, day-to-day experience nor a moral one. In an aesthetic experience, the world (or object) strikes us as unfamiliar yet interesting—peculiar and novel, but worthy of careful attention. But the sublime differs from curiosity, since the latter aims at learning, knowing, and the formation or confirmation of beliefs, while the sublime contains an intense affective or sensory element, an emotional punch. Due to its unique emotional intensity, the sublime can be distinguished from more intellectual subjective states such as wonder and curiosity, although the relation between wonder and sublimity merits more study and discussion. Aesthetic experiences, at least on one view, necessarily involve and engage our capacity for pleasure or displeasure. The pleasure-displeasure element in an aesthetic experience lies somewhere on a spectrum containing exuberance, exhilaration, enjoyment, satisfaction, contentedness, disquiet, discomfort, and pain. In any case, an aesthetic experience has to *feel* a certain way. The sublime is a mixed experience, containing both elements of exhilaration and elements of discomfort.

The line between sublime responses and religious feelings is sometimes fuzzy. John Dennis, Hegel, and other writers consider God to be the best source of the sublime. Some eighteenth-century British writers likewise interpreted the experience of sublimity as evidence of the power of a divine creator. Writers as diverse as Augustine,[4] William James,[5] and Rudolf Otto[6] examine a religious feeling, which, even if not identical to the sublime, can be considered to be an allied subjective state. In the end, however, it seems best not to identify the sublime and religious feeling. If, like Otto (1917), we follow the Kantian framework, then the aesthetic and the religious experience lie in different spheres. Indeed, more than 125 years after the publication of Kant's *Critique of the Power of Judgment* (1790), Otto drew parallels between the numinous religious feeling and the sublime. In the end, however, the sublime remained an *analogy* of the religious feeling.[7]

Insofar as the sublime is conceived as aesthetic, it is not a kind of moral feeling, either. Yet the line between the moral and the sublime (aesthetic) is not always so clear, or at least needs to be described carefully. We can feel sublimity in response to a great, extraordinary moral act, such as a person's noble demonstration of self-sacrifice. (Cato's suicide upon learning of the victory of Julius Caesar and the consequent loss of the Roman republic has been a traditional example of such an admirable act. Cato's act was supposedly virtuous, and we onlookers or readers are the ones feeling the sublime or awe.) Moral content (symbols, exemplars, illustrations of virtue) can certainly be represented in paintings and in other forms and works of art. In principle, such artworks could elicit the sublime: a vast (or somehow great) work of art could represent moral content in a striking, stirring way that has the negative-positive structure of the sublime response. In short, a key part of the distinction between the morality and sublimity has to do not simply with differences in how they feel (their phenomenology), but also with the characteristics and features of the persons experiencing them, that is, with what they are trying to do or accomplish, their ability to switch off attention from the matter at hand, the extent to which they have something at stake, and so on. In addition, the kind of object eliciting the experience (vast object, versus duty) is also relevant, even if some overlap is possible.

In any case, as mentioned, one need not insist that the sublime is only or exclusively an "aesthetic" experience. The concept of the sublime (or "sublimes") could be examined relative to political, moral, or religious contexts as well. The relation of sublimity to these other spheres is perhaps best left open here, allowing readers to pursue this topic for themselves.

Finally, the sublime can be called an "aesthetic quality" or aesthetic predicate. Other aesthetic qualities include the beautiful, picturesque, ugly, disgusting, and the grotesque. Theorists handle the relation between the sublime and related aesthetic qualities in different ways. The relation between sublimity and beauty merits special attention. Some theorists (Plotinus, Shaftesbury, Hegel, Ruskin, Croce, A. C. Bradley, Konečni, and many more) understand the sublime as a form of beauty. Characterizing sublimity as a mode of beauty (albeit of a stirring, intense sort and elicited by a vast or powerful object) may have its merits. However, in organizing this anthology, I have followed the Burkean and Kantian line, which separates and distinguishes beauty and sublimity. I have been motivated chiefly by practical reasons, since including beauty would have excessively broadened this anthology's size and scope. (There may also be compelling conceptual reasons for distinguishing beauty and sublimity, but I cannot defend these here.)

## Inclusions and exclusions

This anthology includes texts from the Chinese, Indian, Japanese, and Greco-Roman-based traditions, and a range of periods from the ancient or classical to the contemporary. It presents a range of representative texts while, as much as possible, revising the canon and introducing the reader to some lesser known texts and arguments. Naturally, this is quite a balancing act.

Not everyone who uses the term "sublime" has *the* sublime in mind. It is often used as a term of praise. Food vendors have extolled their espresso and brownies in such glorious terms. There was an American ska punk band called Sublime. The food vendors and band members hardly employ the term in a Longinian or Kantian sense. Even within the sublime's own long and complicated history (or histories), it has been used in various contexts, for instance, to discuss rhetorical devices, the natural environment, art, even alchemy.[8] In addition, not all writers who use the word have the same concept in mind. The term has been applied to rhetorical style, natural wonders, works of art, subjective states, the mind or reason itself, ideas of reason, and even the Ideal or Absolute (Hegel). This volume showcases the plurality of uses and meanings of the sublime.[9] To complicate matters further, some philosophical texts touch on what falls under (at least one strand of) the sublime, though they do so without being explicit about it. Consider the conclusion of Wittgenstein's *Tractatus Logico-Philosophicus*. "Whereof one cannot speak, thereof one must be silent."[10]

In selecting texts, I have adopted the principle that an author need not use the word "sublime" in order to be in this collection.[11] Samuel Monk's comment on his analysis of Ann Seward's letters is apt here. "These statements are made on the assumption that when Miss Seward speaks of 'the terrible graces' she is referring to the sublime, an assumption that is amply borne out by the most casual reading of her letters."[12] As Sandra Shapshay points out in her contribution to this volume, an author can describe a sublime response without explicitly utilizing the term. Some theorists of what I would consider the sublime never use the word "sublime" (nor *Erhabene, il sublime, lo sublime, le sublime, hypsous,* Возвышенное), but related terms such as the Latin *admiratio*. (In English, words that have been used to indicate or refer to the "sublime" include "awe," "admiration," "ecstasy," and "transport.") The experience of sublime, I submit, can also be discussed using words from languages such as Sanskrit, Chinese, and Japanese (e.g., *yūgen*, or mysterious profundity). Writers in these traditions describe the sublime, or at least something like it, such as the *rasa* associated with astonishment, terror, and the marvelous. (Guo Xi discusses getting into the appropriate position to view, and even paint, mountain scenery so as to elicit aesthetic effects and responses reminiscent of the sublime.) The sublime is arguably not just a word, but a whole range of ideas, meanings, and experiences that are embedded in conceptual and experiential patterns.[13] If that is correct, and if a conceptual and experiential pattern hospitable to the sublime is in place, then a person can write and talk about the sublime without using that exact term. The writings by Bharata, Zeami, and Guo Xi reveal that something similar to the sublime (astonishment, mysterious profundity, the impression of towering heights) was theorized by several intellectual traditions around the globe.

In selecting texts, I aimed to show that our canon could be different. I wished to move beyond reprinting only the well-studied and familiar texts such as Longinus's *Peri Hypsous*, Burke's *Enquiry*, or Kant's *Critique of the Power of Judgment* (although each of these texts deserves and receives a place in this volume). Significantly, I wished to include many more women writers than are usually represented in historical anthologies.

The following readings were selected with the following aims or criteria in mind. Very few selections meet all of these, and some readings meet some criteria better than other criteria. Not necessarily in order of importance, the main selection criteria are the following:

1. The reading will have primarily conceptual or theoretical content (rather than poetic–literary).
   Readings should tend to be more discourses *on* the sublime than discourses *of* the sublime

(literary-poetic responses to the sublime experience).[14] (Thankfully, some of the readings, by quoting from literary-poetic and religious texts, partially make up for omissions resulting from the application of this criterion.)

2. Possibly in tension with the first aim, the selections should (collectively) cover various disciplinary perspectives and not be restricted to philosophy and philosophical aesthetics. After all, the discipline of aesthetics has a complicated history, and the boundaries between aesthetics, philosophy, psychology, theology, history, rhetoric, and criticism have not always been as delineated as they seem today.

3. The selections should highlight new or previously excluded or underrepresented voices—a purposely revisionary aim. One outcome of this aim is that a text or author already known or widely anthologized may not be found in the present anthology, in order to make room for underrepresented theories or authors.[15]

4. Ideally, the theories (to the extent that they achieve the first aim above) would be insightful, viable, and plausible. Likewise, a reading should not be a mere rehashing of previous ideas or tropes.

5. The selection should have historical significance and influence. To be sure, this can come into tension with the two previous goals. (If a tradition or group has been traditionally underrepresented, it makes it harder for it to be influential; moreover, not all of the influential theories are insightful and plausible.) The reading should make (or be of sufficient quality to make) a contribution to our understanding of the sublime.

6. It is an exemplary representative of an approach or method. For instance, an entire volume devoted exclusively to the postmodern sublime in francophone philosophy is possible (and in fact, already exists).[16] Yet, space allows for only one or two readings from this tradition to be reprinted.

7. The reading should lend itself to study, learning, and teaching: it should be readable and accessible (as much as possible), though without sacrificing rigor. In some cases, of course, readability may be hard to achieve (Hegel).

8. The reading can be seen to have relevance today or connected to current debates and questions. I hope that the sublime shows itself to be, not an outmoded and dated category suited for only a particular period in art history (e.g., Romanticism), but a topic of interest to contemporary scholars across the humanities and social sciences.

It would no doubt be tiresome to run through how each of the selections fares in terms of these criteria; readers are certainly invited to come up with their own assessments if they so choose. As noted in 5, tension between selection criteria is possible. For instance, revising the canon to make room for underrepresented voices can come into conflict with making a lasting or significant influence on the history and reception of the sublime. For it is precisely because the underrepresented writers have been overlooked that they have not made the lasting influence they deserve.

Feminist writers have tended to be suspicious of the sublime. For instance, Judy Lochhead warns against letting "such terms as the sublime, the ineffable, the unpresentable . . . mask sedimented gender binaries that will keep the feminine in the ground."[17] In a similar vein, Barbara Claire Freeman argues that the eighteenth-century sublime is a masculine discourse aiming at articulating and ultimately controlling the experience of otherness in the sovereign subject.[18] The approach I propose in my own chapter may be more conducive to the goals of feminism, however. If we do not conceive of the sublime as a response to the ineffable or unpresentable (or completely other), then perhaps such criticisms can be avoided. Bonnie Mann raises a related but slightly different objection. She notices work touching on the sublime written by Luce Irigaray, Barbara Claire Freeman, Sheila Lintott, Christine Battersby, and Carolyn Korsmeyer, and comments, "This is to say that while male philosophers have been explicitly writing about sublime experience for well over three hundred years, women seem to have entered this discussion only when feminist interest in the sublime emerged explicitly three decades ago!"[19] But the texts here anthologized—including seven women authors from the seventeenth and eighteenth centuries—suggest that this conclusion may be too hasty. For instance, Anna Aikin advanced a compelling explanation of the pleasures in the sublime, emphasizing the activity and stretching of the imagination.

I would like to return for a moment to an issue mentioned under criterion 2 (i.e., on the porous boundaries between aesthetics and allied fields), which is admittedly in some tension with criterion 1. The distinction between the various arts-related disciplines is artificial in those cases where neither philosophy nor literary theory (etc.) had been segregated into discrete academic fields.[20] However, the distinction between philosophy (or theory) on the one hand and, on the other, literature (poetry, fiction, etc.) and sacred texts, provides a rough-and-ready distinction that justifies excluding the poetry of Li Po,[21] or Milton, Wordsworth, Coleridge, P. B. Shelley, H. D. Thoreau, Leopardi, and Nikki Giovanni ("Ego Tripping"), as well as religious writings and sacred texts (e.g., *Psalms* 8, 90, 104; *Bhagavad Gita*; *Upanishads*, the writings of Rumi or Meister Eckhart), which might otherwise have been considered for this anthology. This anthology could well have emphasized texts such as this from the *Tao te Ching*:

> Look, and it can't be seen. / Listen, and it can't be heard. / Reach, and it can't be grasped. / Above, it isn't bright. / Below, it isn't dark. / Seamless, unnamable, / it returns to the realm of nothing. / Form that includes all forms, / image without an image, / subtle, beyond all conception. / Approach it and there is no beginning; / follow it and there is no end. / You can't know it, but you can be it, / at ease in your own life. / Just realize where you come from: / this is the essence of wisdom.[22]

Or this passage from another Taoist text, *Zhuangzi*:

> The earl of the Ho said, "Whether the subject be what is external or internal in things, how do we come to make a distinction between them as noble and mean, and as great or small?" Zo of the Northern Sea replied, "When we look at them in the light of the Tao, they are neither noble nor mean. Looking at them in themselves, each thinks itself noble, and despises others. Looking at them in the light of common opinion, their being noble or mean does not depend on themselves. Looking at them in their differences from one another, if we call those great which are greater than others, there is nothing that is not great, and in the same way there is nothing that is not small. We shall thus know that heaven and earth is but as a grain of the smallest rice, and that the point of a hair is as a mound or a mountain;— such is the view given of them by their relative size."[23]

In addition, the aforementioned distinction allows me to leave out and redact some of the many literary examples cited by theorists such as Longinus, Dennis, and Mendelssohn. In this anthology, I have not tried to include representative poetry or literary responses to the sublime experience. In similar fashion, I have not aimed to include texts written in order to *evoke* the sublime.

Selections are generally long enough to give readers a sense of the reading's content, method, and style, but (I hope) not so long as to scare readers away or to prevent the inclusion of other deserving texts and authors. In choosing and editing this collection, I have been guided by the thought of what would be most useful to the student of the sublime or to the scholar desiring a reasonably comprehensive introduction and overview of the subject. Some of the texts, for instance Burke's *Enquiry* or Kant's "Analytic of the Sublime" are readily available in inexpensive editions, and serious students probably have easy access to them. But omitting Burke and Kant here would have given an unbalanced picture of the history and reception of the sublime. Alongside Longinus, in my estimation, Burke and Kant offer what have (hitherto) been the most influential theories of the sublime.

It would likewise be a mistake (if one applies my criteria) to omit John Dennis and Jean-François Lyotard, even though their texts have already been anthologized.[24] I have, however, had to omit some worthwhile texts on the sublime such as those of Joseph Priestley, John Baillie, David Hume, Alexander Gerard, Joseph Addison, Archibald Alison, Frances Reynolds, Thomas Reid, and Shaftesbury (and many others), in order to make room for other worthy authors and texts from other periods; thankfully, these writings can be readily found elsewhere. There are a number of texts such as the correspondence and notes (e.g., by British men and women from the 1700s and 1800s, including Coleridge's drafts on the sublime) that would have added literary, cultural, or historical perspective to this volume.[25] In the end, however, such writings contribute relatively little in terms of theory or philosophical content, or are too provisional and insufficiently developed. Finally, one could plausibly argue that the sublime is found in and discussed by pre-Longinian Greek thinkers such as Plato (who discusses *hupsos* as well as the *kalon*)[26] and even Aristotle, and thus that this anthology should begin with them. Although this view is reasonable enough, it is at least just as reasonable to expect an anthology on the sublime to begin (as this one does) with the author of the first significant, extant treatise on the topic: Longinus.

Due to the aforementioned constraints and limited space and resources, several relatively recent texts could not be included, and I owe these authors at least a mention. Here I have in mind writings employing a psychoanalytic or literary approach (Paul de Man, Neil Hertz, Jacques Lacan, Thomas Weiskel, Slavoj Žižek), or influenced by the French and German continental philosophical traditions (Theodor Adorno, Gilles Deleuze, Jacques Derrida, Richard Kearney, Jean-Luc Nancy, Jacques Rancière, Marc Richir), or taking up ecological or environmental themes (Christopher Hitt, Ronald Hepburn) or matters concerning technology (David Nye, Mario Costa, Leo Marx), or works which discuss or employ psychological or cognitivist methods (Dacher Keltner and Jonathan Haidt, John Onians, Alan Richardson) or which adopt feminist perspectives (Christine Battersby, Barbara Freeman, Sheila Lintott, Bonnie Mann, Patricia Yaeger, Joanna Zylinska). To offset these omissions, this anthology includes texts written by authors exemplary of the foregoing approaches or traditions: Julia Kristeva (psychoanalytic), Jean-François Lyotard (francophone continental), Emily Brady (environmental), Fredric Jameson (technological-postmodern), Vladimir Konečni (pscyhological), and Meg Armstrong (postcolonial-feminist). This is not to reduce the value of these contributions to their membership in a certain "category," but simply to say that (in light of this book's aims) they stand among the best exemplars of their tradition, method, or approach.[27]

## Organization of this book

Texts are placed into one of five groups: ancient, postclassical, modern, late modern, and contemporary. To be sure, the book could have been organized in another way (e.g., according to themes or geographical regions), but the chronological organization has the advantage of bringing out the developmental history of the sublime. Within one of the five groups, moreover, the selections appear in (approximately) chronological order.

All but one of the terms ("postclassical") should be fairly self-explanatory. I prefer the former to "medieval" or "Renaissance" since it allows room for the texts from India, China, and Japan. (Today, of course, authors and scholars from these geographical regions may very well be influenced by the Burkean, Kantian, and contemporary interpretations of the sublime.)[28]

Not all the texts gathered herein are currently part of the "canon" of the history of the sublime. Some of the texts were written in epistolary form (e.g., Petrarch, Seward, Carter) or speeches (Vico) or are unpublished literary remains (e.g., Wordsworth), and as noted, this anthology highlights the work of modern women writers. And even if Kant deserves to be amply represented in such an anthology due to his undeniable influence on later accounts of the sublime, this volume avoids an "all-roads-lead-to-Kant" approach. The editors of an anthology of eighteenth-century British texts on the sublime, Ashfield and de Bolla, justifiably criticize Monk's otherwise excellent study (*The Sublime*) on just these grounds.[29]

## Using this book

This collection presents perspectives of the sublime (or sublimes) from various fields and traditions. It brings together a number of texts dealing with the sublime in aesthetics and the philosophy of art, literary theory, psychology, philosophy of education, political theory, environmental studies, theology, and allied fields. The selections should be of interest to a wide range of users—students, teachers, and scholars of art history, film and visual studies, architecture, music, theater, religion and theology, classics, literature, feminist studies, gender and cultural studies, to name a few. It is also intended for readers and students (of various levels) who wish to pursue an interest in the sublime. They may find it useful in giving an overview of the sublime, perhaps finding a selection that they desire to examine or study more closely.

Readers can jump in and read a selection as they please. To facilitate such reading at will, brief introductory material has been placed just before a selection rather than tucked away in an Afterword or in this Introduction. Readers looking for basic insight into the topic of the book and descriptions of the experience of the (natural) sublime would do well to begin with the accessible excerpts written by Elizabeth Carter, Helen Maria Williams, or Francesco Petrarca.

The book may be read with certain themes in mind, such as global traditions or female voices, the natural environment, the arts, or politics.

- The seventeenth- and eighteenth-century women contributors to this volume are Carter, Aikin, Wollstonecraft, Seward, Radcliffe, Williams, and Shelley.

- Authors who discuss (in varying degrees) the natural environment include Guo Xi, Petrarch, Mendelssohn, Carter, Williams, Kant (1790), Schiller, Radcliffe, Wordsworth, Schopenhauer, Mary Shelley, Konečni, Shapshay, Brady, and Clewis.

- Authors who consider or discuss the arts include Longinus, Bharata, Guo Xi, Zeami, Boileau, Vico, Dennis, Mendelssohn, Kant (1764), Aikin, Seward, Schiller, Radcliffe, Hegel, Schopenhauer, Shelley, Wagner, Nietzsche, Otto, Newman, Lyotard, Jameson, Danto, Konečni, Clewis, and Freeland. In terms of art forms and media, one could group them roughly as follows, allowing for some overlap and different degrees of emphasis: poetry (Longinus, Boileau, Vico, Dennis, Kant [1764], Seward, Hegel), fiction (Aikin, Radcliffe, Shelley), theater or dance (Bharata, Zeami, Mendelssohn, Schiller, Nietzsche), music or opera (Mendelssohn, Schopenhauer, Nietzsche, Wagner, Otto, Konečni), painting (Guo Xi, Newman, Lyotard, Danto), architecture (Otto, Jameson), and film (Freeland, Clewis).

- Political themes are raised by Wollstonecraft, Williams, Jameson, and the chapter headnotes to Burke and Kant (1790).

Each selection is preceded by the editor's headnotes containing background information and by a "Note on the text" containing bibliographic information and editorial remarks. The selection is followed by "Further reading" and "Questions" to promote and assist study, discussion, and reflection. (Most of the recommended studies for "Further reading" will be works written in English.)

## Overview

I cannot pretend to cover the venerable history of the concept of the sublime in this brief Introduction. Moreover, I refrain from giving a chapter-by-chapter summary here, since one is found at the end of this book. *Readers unfamiliar with the sublime may prefer to skip this Overview and to read the chapter summaries at the end of the book and/or any background information found in a chapter's headnote.*

Although I prefer to let readers construct their own histories of the sublime, an Introduction should nonetheless contain a few words about the general trajectory of the sublime. Many, but not all, of the following authors or texts are covered in this volume.*

The *Nāṭyaśāstra* ("treatise on drama") is an ancient (ca. 200 BCE–200 CE) Sanskrit manual in stagecraft, a canonical text in the Indian aesthetic tradition. It describes—though without philosophical analysis—various emotional flavors or *rasa* ("sentiments") represented on a theatrical stage. For the purposes of this anthology, the handbook's (brief) remarks on the terrible, marvelous, and the heroic sentiments are the most relevant. The treatise also describes "dominant" states such as "terror" and "astonishment"—passions or emotions readily associated with (even if not identical to) the sublime.

In his treatise, Guo Xi (ca. 1000–1090) discusses three perspectives that can be taken when viewing mountains; they are different modes of perception that can prompt the viewer to have an experience bordering on the sublime. The experience can be attained through positioning oneself at a particular level or distance with respect to large objects (mountains), as well as through using very specific painting techniques to convey these levels or distances on a flat surface. Guo Xi examines not so much the rhetorical aspect of the sublime as natural sublimity and its depiction in scenic art. His painting, *Early Spring* (detail on this book's front cover), also takes up a distinct strand of the sublime—the transcendent. The latter is represented by blank spots or absences, specifically, mists amid the mountains.

Zeami Motokiyo (1363–1443) characterizes nine different levels of mastering the Japanese theatrical art of nō. The highest level ("the art of the flower of peerless charm") can be associated with the strand of the sublime that emphasizes unknowability and transcendence. Zeami's conception of "peerless charm" is intended to bring to mind the experience of enjoying the unique grace of the greatest nō theater performers. In describing the second highest level ("the art of the flower of profundity"), he draws attention to our perception and interaction with a vast and striking object: a mountain (Mount Fuji).

The remainder of this overview proceeds (roughly) chronologically and, given the foregoing discussion, is limited to the western tradition rooted in Greco-Roman thought.[30]

It was through the reception of Longinus's first-century CE (or perhaps third-century CE) work of rhetoric, *On the Sublime*, and modern translations of that treatise, that the concept became influential in rhetoric, aesthetics, philosophy, and related fields.[31] For Longinus, the sublime referred to that inspiring or overwhelming quality in great literary works or rhetoric. It was what made "elevated" speech elevated, or "lofty" speech lofty. His examples of what elicits the sublime tended to come from poetry (though he mentioned Mount Etna; the Nile, Danube, and Rhine rivers; and "above all the Ocean"). The treatise by Longinus remained largely unknown until translations of *On the Sublime* appeared in the mid-1500s. Boileau's French translation (1674) is perhaps the most well-known translation in modernity; however, it was by no means the first translation into a European vernacular language, being preceded by (among others) Italian and English translations.

---

*For the sake of readability and space, I have not given bibliographic references for every author mentioned in this Introduction, which is not intended to be exhaustive. References for many of these authors can be found in the bibliography at the end of this book.

In fact, consideration of the sublime predates even the rediscovery of Longinus. As noted, Augustine's experience of the divine can be seen as an analogue of the sublime and a feeling of (religious) awe:

> When first I knew you, you raised me up [*assumpsisti*] so that I could see that there was something to be seen, but also that I was not yet able to see it. I gazed on you with eyes too weak to resist the dazzle of your splendor. Your light shone upon me in its brilliance, and I thrilled with love [*amore*] and dread [*horrore*] alike.[32]

One finds the sublime addressed more explicitly in the writings of medieval authors such as St. Bonaventure and St. Thomas. In his work of theology, *The Journey of the Mind to God*, the Franciscan theologian Bonaventure writes: "Man therefore, who is called a microcosm, has five senses that serve as five doors, through which the cognition [*cognitio*] of all things existing in the sensible world enters his soul. For through vision enter bodies sublime [*sublimia*] and luminous and the other colored things, but through touch enter solid and terrestrial bodies."[33] Perhaps one should not dwell too much on *sublimia* in this passage, since the word in classical Latin was also used for the air—a usage which persists in the English verb "to sublimate" (i.e., to vaporize). In another passage, however, Saint Bonaventure's theory undoubtedly discusses the transcendent or ineffable strand of the sublime, that is, the one concerned not so much with aesthetic play and emotion as with the failure to capture a truth or to be adequate to a reality, above all, God. Bonaventure cites a passage from Dionysius the Areopagite that does not shy away from paradoxical formulations.

> O Trinity super-essential and super-divine and super-excellent guardian of the divine wisdom of the Christians, direct us into the super-unknown and super-luminous [*superincognitum et superlucentem*] and most sublime [*et sublimissimum*] height of mystical speech [*eloquiorum*]; where the new and absolute and unspeakable [*inconversibilia*] mysteries of theology are, according to the super-luminous darkness of an instructing silence, secretly hidden in the most obscure [*in obscurissimo*].[34]

Writing around the same time, Aquinas uses the word *admiratio* to describe a mode of fear resulting from the apprehension of the sublime truth (ultimately, for him, God). "Admiration is a species of fear following upon the apprehension of something exceeding our faculty. Hence, admiration is an act following the contemplation of the sublime truth [*sublimis veritatis*]. It has been said that contemplation is terminated in affection."[35] Admiration involves the intellect's contemplation of the "sublime truth" lying beyond the intellectual faculty. But an ambiguity lies in the claim that in admiration we apprehend a truth that exceeds us. Although Aquinas is clearly among theorists who interpret the sublime in terms of contemplation and truth, it is not clear how much he thinks the intellect falls short and fails, or instead how much that truth is embraced and comprehended. Nor is he very clear about the roles of the will ("affection") and the intellect in such "contemplation" and embracing.

In Petrarch's "The Ascent of Mont Ventoux" (1336), too, we find accounts of what one could consider the sublime. The text is structured as a "letter" and was written during the Renaissance, before the Latin and vernacular translations appearing in the middle of the sixteenth century inaugurated a new epoch in the sublime's history. Incidentally, it is also one of the first essays in alpinism and mountaineering. In his letter recounting his (spiritual and physical) ascent, Petrarch quotes from a mixture of sources—the Christian Bible, Saint Augustine's *Confessions*, and Latin poets.

During the modern period, literary, artistic, intellectual, and cultural phenomena influenced theorization of the sublime.[36] For writers from the British tradition in particular, the King James Bible[37] and Milton's *Paradise Lost* provided literary and theological sources of texts thought likely to exhibit or elicit the sublime.

In the period after Boileau's French translation (1674), there was (broadly speaking) a growing tendency in the anglophone world to adopt psychological perspectives and to focus on nature rather than on rhetoric or style (as Longinus and Boileau had done). In British writings, the sublime became (in general) associated more with a response to natural marvels than to texts and speech. One can discern a transitional phase in the work of John Dennis (1704): his examples of the sublime come from poetry, and he locates the paradigmatic source of the sublime in religion and, ultimately, God. On the continent, however, this transition took place more slowly. The Italian humanist Vico (1732) considers the sublime in terms of the liberating ascent of the soul made possible by a formation in grammar, rhetoric, philosophy, and history, a study which is intended to draw students and scholars closer to God.

The European Enlightenment was a particularly fruitful time for theories of the sublime.[38] Burke's empirical account and Kant's transcendental theory were among the most influential of all. According to Burke (1757), the sublime is a delightful terror induced by a vast or powerful object. He also gives physiological and psychological descriptions of this experience, drawing from his understanding of the science of his day. Mendelssohn (1761), who was familiar with Burke's empirical account, draws from his own German scholastic philosophical tradition to discuss the admiration felt before an object or person exhibiting a kind of "perfection." Something that is intensively (rather than extensively) immense is said to be "strong," and when that strength is a matter of a perfection, it is said to be "sublime." He defines the sublime in art as a "sensuously perfect representation" of something immense, capable of inspiring awe, which is a debt we owe to the extraordinary spirit or genius creating the work. Toward the beginning of his academic career, Kant wrote a popular treatise on the sublime (1764) in which he mingled aesthetic claims with non-aesthetic ones—claims we might say today belong to the sphere of social science, and which have been widely criticized for propagating gender, ethnic, and racial stereotypes. Kant is thus better known for his analysis of the sublime in the *Critique of the Power of Judgment* (1790), where he maintains that the feeling of the sublime is based on one's power of reason, and, on one reading, involves reflection on and awareness of one's rational faculties.[39] In a relatively neglected work, *Kalligone* (1800), Johann Gottfried Herder unfavorably responds to Kant's aesthetics while offering a theory of the sublime in the form of a naive naturalism that combines aspects of theories of Burke and Kant.[40] In her contribution to this volume, Meg Armstrong (1996) analyzes Burke's and Kant's reliance on alleged gender and racial differences. She criticizes their use of bodies of color and gender in establishing their theories of the sublime. Armstrong pays particular attention to Burke's reference to the purported, and supposedly natural and immediate, "effects of blackness."

A letter by Elizabeth Carter (1762) to Elizabeth Montagu offers a noteworthy yet overlooked instance of writing on the sublime in nature. Anna Aikin (1773) addresses the question of why we would take pleasure in something that is unpleasant—as we appear to do in the experience of the sublime. The contributions by Mary Wollstonecraft, Anne Seward, Helen Maria Williams, and Ann Radcliffe were written during the turbulent 1790s, which witnessed the French Revolution and the Reign of Terror. Wollstonecraft (1790) identifies weaknesses in Burke's theory of the sublime (and beautiful). In a 1792 letter, the Romantic author Seward maintains that the poetry of "Ossian," the purported author of epic poetry published by James Macpherson beginning in 1760, evokes experiences of the sublime. Like Carter (and many other writers), Seward thinks that the intense experience of the sublime can be endured only briefly. British author Helen Maria Williams (1798), an avid supporter of the French Revolution, describes the "swelling" of the imagination in response to "sublime objects" of nature, and draws connections between the aesthetic, moral, and political spheres. Ann Radcliffe's descriptions of the sublime in nature reveal how the sublime was employed in an influential early work of Gothic literature (1794).

Developing this trend, Mary Shelley's *Frankenstein* (1818)—written by the daughter of Mary Wollstonecraft—showcases a blending of philosophy and literature in a text that became exemplary of the

Gothic sublime. Her descriptions of the creation of the monster, and of the confrontation between the creator and the monster, are paradigmatic descriptions of sublimity on many fronts—psychological, theological, natural, and technological. Based on Wordsworth's poetry, John Keats referred to Wordsworth's version of the sublime as the "egotistical sublime." But in a prose piece reprinted here—an unfinished essay presumably written around 1810—Wordsworth presents a theory that may call into question Keat's characterization. The sublime feeling, Wordsworth thinks, is found more in natural landscape than in artificial gardens. Wordsworth locates the sublime in the play between variety and intense unity, emphasizes the repetition of "individual form," and (unlike Kant) attributes a key role to color in eliciting the experience of the sublime.

Schiller (1793), a poet, tragedian, and philosopher, offers a Kant-inspired theory, but he departs from Kant by considering artworks and applying the sublime to dramatic tragedy. Hegel (1835) criticizes theorists (like Kant—though one might add Schiller and Wordsworth) who view the sublime as a merely subjective state or emotion. Hegel views the sublime as a stage on the way to beauty, which he considers the more important aesthetic category. Given Hegel's enormous influence on nineteenth-century thought, this view would have significant consequences for the sublime. After Hegel, the sublime had a diminished role in aesthetics and the philosophy of art.

Schopenhauer (1818), like Schiller, examines the sublime in both nature and art, in particular tragic drama. Schopenhauer's philosophy influenced the ideas and writings of the composer and author Richard Wagner (1870), who discusses the sublime in the music of Beethoven. Like some of Beethoven's music, Wagner's works (e.g., the "Rheingold" Prelude) are sometimes mentioned in discussions of the musical sublime.[41] In various writings (1872, 1882, 1883–85), Nietzsche, a onetime devotee of Wagner, resists Kantian versions of the sublime. Commenting on Greek tragedy, Nietzsche characterizes the sublime as a form of inspired enthusiasm: the sublime can be found in the shared, ecstatic Dionysian element in Greek culture. Remarkably, Nietzsche also develops the concept of the sublime into that of sublimation (*Sublimisierung*), introducing a noteworthy shift in the history of the sublime. Sublimation is a socially accepted expression of otherwise hidden psychological drives and forces. Thus, instead of the higher or elevated (the sublime), Nietzsche analyzes the hidden and lower (the sublimated).

It is perhaps above all in work of Freud, however, that we recognize the concept of sublimation as the socially acceptable expression of hidden drives. Through the process of sublimation, we adjust and redirect desires that might be socially alarming or harmful if acted upon. (Since some uses of the term "sublimation" do not directly pertain to the aesthetic experience of the sublime, the reader might wonder what connections, beyond etymological links, exist between sublimation and the sublime. Here is one attempt at an answer. Sublimation contains an uplifting or elevating element. By taming and rechanneling impulses, an individual is uplifted or raised into civilized society—which can be ennobling.) In another context, Freud discusses a feeling of something "unbounded" or oceanic; he refers to it as the "oceanic feeling."[42] Since it is a feeling of something limitless and of oneness with the universe, the quasi-mystical feeling bears some similarities with the feeling of the sublime, despite their differences. In any case, Freud explains this experience of oneness as a remnant of an earlier psychic stage of the ego. As noted, Otto (1917) also draws an analogy between the feeling of (religious) awe and the aesthetic experience of the sublime, though with aims quite different from Freud's.

A Freud-inspired concept of the sublime and sublimation can be found in the work of Lacan, Žižek,[43] and (reprinted here) Julia Kristeva (1980). The Marx-inspired cultural critic Jameson (1984) describes what can be called the technological sublime, that is, the sublime in response to various (increasingly more powerful) forms of modern technology—today, one thinks of the expansiveness and ever-growing reach of the internet and social media. Jameson's view has affinities with that of Lyotard, a member of a francophone tradition that devoted much attention to the sublime in the 1980s and 1990s. The sublime, for Lyotard (1985), suggests or gestures at the limits of representation in its attempt to represent what cannot be represented (i.e., the "unrepresentable"). According to Lyotard, the (contemporary) sublime does not hint at the unrepresentable in a "nostalgic" way, as if it were a kind of longing for a world out of reach. Rather, the limits of representation are shown or indicated by abstract works of art such as the paintings of Barnett Newman, author of an influential yet brief essay, "The Sublime is Now" (1948). The art critic and philosopher Arthur Danto (2003) also draws on Newman's work in his discussion of the sublime in artworks—from the Getty spiral to abstract expressionist paintings and the Sistine Chapel. In her Kant-inspired contribution, Freeland (1999) discusses the relevance of the sublime to understanding and appreciating film. Konečni (2005) introduces the notion of an "aesthetic trinity" in order to account for peak aesthetic responses lying on a spectrum ranging from thrills and chills to the "aesthetic awe" typically induced by a sublime natural object or work of art.

More than a century ago, British philosopher and aesthetician E. F. Carritt wrote an essay critical of a contemporary theory of the sublime (though not necessarily of the sublime generally).[44] The Scottish philosopher Ronald Hepburn took an interest in the sublime as early as the 1980s. However, it was not until an article by Guy Sircello that analytic anglophone aesthetics began to give more sustained and careful attention to the sublime.[45] Jane Forsey (2007) probed Sircello's answers to his questions about the possibility of the sublime. Forsey deserves credit for renewing a recent debate about the very possibility of a theory of the sublime. Her article drew various responses, some of which are gathered here (Shapshay, Clewis, Brady). In short, recent work on the sublime discusses themes ranging from (e.g.) the environmental and political, to the cognitive and psychological, to the more theological, literary-artistic, and philosophical.

## Conclusion

I therefore hope that this historical anthology awakens and sustains an interest in the sublime and related emotions; reduces distances between cultural, philosophical, or intellectual traditions; and shapes our understanding of the sublime's history while guiding its future.

# PART I
## ANCIENT

# CHAPTER 1
## LONGINUS, FROM *ON SUBLIMITY*

Given its historical and cultural influence and its particular importance for this anthology, it seems worthwhile to sketch the publication and translation history of *Peri Hypsous* as well as to outline the reception of this first-century (or possibly third-century) work.

The treatise *On Sublimity* combines ideas appropriated from the rhetorical tradition of literary criticism with ideas drawn from philosophy. Its topic is great or excellent writing or discourse. Some parts of the text (largely omitted here) discuss matters such as figures of speech and word-order, that is, topics regularly studied in rhetorical schools.[1] Longinus is writing to rebut the views of Caecilius of Caleacte, a rhetorical theorist whose life spanned the first century BCE and the first century CE.[2] Longinus locates five "most productive" sources of sublimity: great thoughts, strong and inspired emotion, lofty figures, noble diction, and elevated word-arrangement.

The title of the treatise has been translated in English in various ways, including *On the Sublime* (W. R. Roberts, 1899), *On Great Writing* (G. M. A. Grube, 1957), *Of the Height of Eloquence* (John Hall, 1652), and *A Treatise of the Loftiness or Elegancy of Speech* (Pulteney, 1680).

*Peri Hypsous* is thought to have been written in the first century CE, although its origin and authorship remain uncertain.[3] At one time, the author was held to be the third-century CE writer Cassius Longinus, but this is now widely disputed; various alternatives have been proposed over the years, including the rhetorician Dionysius of Halikarnassos. Given this uncertainty, the author of the treatise has been variously referred to as Dionysius Longinus, Longinus, and pseudo-Longinus. (The present volume will simply refer to the author as "Longinus.")

According to one scholar, the "oldest and best" of all the manuscripts of *Peri Hypsous*, and the one from which all the rest derive directly or indirectly, is a tenth-century manuscript in the Bibliothèque Nationale in Paris.[4] The (apparently) first publication (*editio princeps*) of the Greek treatise appeared in 1554 in Basel, prepared by Francisco Robortelli (Robortello), followed by that of Paulo Manuzio (Manutius) (Venice, 1555),[5] although a Latin version is conjectured by some scholars[6] to have appeared around this time, even before 1550 (which would, if true, grant it the title of earliest publication). A Latin translation by Pizzimenti came out in 1566. Additional versions in Greek and in Latin were produced in that century and the stream of publication further swelled in the 1600s and 1700s.

The Greek treatise was widely translated into various European languages. Giovanni da Falgano (Florence, 1575) produced an Italian translation. According to our present state of knowledge, the first English translation appeared in 1652 (by John Hall),[7] that is, twenty-two years before Nicolas Boileau Despréaux's influential French translation (Paris, 1674). A widely reprinted and influential English translation appeared in 1739 (by William Smith). Another translation worthy of mention, in Italian and by Anton Gori, appeared around 1732.

Serious study of the treatise's authorship, content, and underlying manuscripts appears to have picked up only in the 1700s. A famous letter by the prefect of the Vatican Library, Girolamo Amati, was published in Benjamin Weiske's 1809 edition of *De Sublimitate*. Amati noted an equivocation in the attribution in the table of contents of the tenth-century manuscript: Dionysius "or" Longinus. Amati thus put into question the authorship of the *De Sublimitate*, stimulating debates about the work's dating and composition.

In short, it would be a mistake to think that interest in the sublime began as only a result of the publication of Boileau's important French translation published in 1674 (see also Boileau's Preface, in the present volume).[8] Nor was the sublime's impact limited to rhetoric and literature, for it also extended to the visual arts and architecture, theater, philosophy, and religion.[9] A wave of increased interest in the sublime came in the eighteenth century (and a corresponding absorption into the intellectual and even public cultures)—in some ways comparable to the mixed reception and influence of Sigmund Freud[10] on the first half of the twentieth century.

## Note on the text

Source: Excerpted from Longinus, "On Sublimity." In *Ancient Literary Criticism: The Principal Texts in New Translations,* edited by Donald Andrew Russell and Michael Winterbottom, 462–95. Oxford University Press, 1972.

The following reading includes chapters 1–2, 6–10, 13–15, and 33–36. Footnotes are composed by Oleg Bychkov and Anne Sheppard. The translation's format, spelling, and style are reproduced, with occasional modifications. The chapter divisions, which derive from the sixteenth century, are listed as headers, with each section given in square brackets in the main body text.

## On sublimity, *1–2*

1

[1] My dear Postumius Terentianus,

You will recall that when we were reading together Caecilius' monograph *On Sublimity,*[11] we felt that it was inadequate to its high subject, and failed to touch the essential point. Nor indeed did it appear to offer the reader much practical help, though this ought to be a writer's principal object. Two things are required of any textbook: first, that it should explain what its subject is; second, and more important, that it should explain how and by what methods we can achieve it. Caecilius tries at immense length to explain to us what sort of thing 'the sublime' is, as though we did not know; but he has somehow passed over as unnecessary the question how we can develop our nature to some degree of greatness. [2] However, we ought perhaps not so much to blame our author for what he has left out as to commend him for his originality and enthusiasm.

You have urged me to set down a few notes on sublimity for your own use. Let us then consider whether there is anything in my observation which may be thought useful to public men. You must help me, my friend, by giving your honest opinion in detail as both your natural candour and your friendship with me require. It was well said that what man has in common with the gods is 'doing good and telling the truth'.

[3] Your education dispenses me from any long preliminary definition. Sublimity is a kind of eminence or excellence of discourse. It is the source of the distinction of the very greatest poets and prose writers and the means by which they have given eternal life to their own fame. [4] For grandeur produces ecstasy rather than persuasion in the hearer; and the combination of wonder and astonishment always proves superior to the merely persuasive and pleasant. This is because persuasion is on the whole something we can control, whereas amazement and wonder exert invincible power and force and get the better of every hearer. Experience in invention and ability to order and arrange material cannot be detected in single passages; we begin to appreciate them only when we see the whole context. Sublimity, on the other hand, produced at the right moment, tears everything up like a whirlwind, and exhibits the orator's whole power at a single blow.

## 2

[1] Your own experience will lead you to these and similar considerations. The question from which I must begin is whether there is in fact an art of sublimity or profundity. Some people think it is a complete mistake to reduce things like this to technical rules. Greatness, the argument runs, is a natural product, and does not come by teaching. The only art is to be born like that. They believe moreover that natural products are very much weakened by being reduced to the bare bones of a textbook.

[2] In my view, the arguments can be refuted by considering three points:

 i. Though nature is on the whole a law unto herself in matters of emotion and elevation, she is not a random force and does not work altogether without method.

 ii. She is herself in every instance a first and primary element of creation, but it is method that is competent to provide and contribute quantities and appropriate occasions for everything, as well as perfect correctness in training and application.

 iii. Grandeur is particularly dangerous when left on its own, unaccompanied by knowledge, unsteadied, unballasted, abandoned to mere impulse and ignorant temerity. It often needs the curb as well as the spur.

[3] What Demosthenes[12] said of life in general is true also of literature: good fortune is the greatest of blessings, but good counsel comes next, and the lack of it destroys the other also. In literature, nature occupies the place of good fortune and art that of good counsel. Most important of all, the very fact that some things in literature depend on nature alone can itself be learned only from art.

If the critic of students of this subject will bear these points in mind, he will, I believe, come to realize that the examination of the question before us is by no means useless or superfluous. [...]

## 6–10

### 6

[1] At this stage the question we must put to ourselves for discussion is how to avoid the faults which are so much tied up with sublimity. The answer, my friend, is: by first of all achieving a genuine understanding and appreciation of true sublimity. This is difficult; literary judgement comes only as the final product of long experience. However, for the purposes of instruction, I think we can say that an understanding of all this can be acquired. I approach the problem in this way.

### 7

[1] In ordinary life, nothing is truly great which it is great to despise; wealth, honour, reputation, absolute power – anything in short which has a lot of external trappings – can never seem supremely good to the wise man because it is no small good to despise them. People who could have these advantages if they chose but disdain them out of magnanimity are admired much more than those who actually possess them. It is much the same with elevation in poetry and literature generally. We have to ask ourselves whether any particular example does not give a show of grandeur which, for all its accidental trappings, will, when dissected prove vain and hollow, the kind of thing which it does a man more honour to despise than to admire. [2] It is our nature to be elevated and exalted by true sublimity. Filled with joy and pride, we come to believe we have created what we have only heard. [3] When a man of sense and literary experience hears something many times over, and it fails to dispose his mind to greatness or to leave him with more to reflect upon than was contained in the mere words, but comes instead to seem valueless on repeated inspection, this is not true sublimity; it endures only for the moment of hearing. Real sublimity contains much food for reflection, is difficult or rather impossible

to resist, and makes a strong and ineffaceable impression on the memory. [4] In a word, reckon those things which please everybody all the time as genuinely and finely sublime. When people of different trainings, ways of life, tastes, ages and manners all agree about something, the judgement and assent of so many distinct voices lends strength and irrefutability to the conviction that their admiration is rightly directed.

## 8

[1] There are, one may say, five most productive sources of sublimity. (Competence in speaking is assumed as a common foundation for all five; nothing is possible without it.)

i. The first and most important is the power to conceive great thoughts; I defined this in my work on Xenophon.[13]

ii. The second is strong and inspired emotion. (These two sources are for the most part natural; the remaining three involve art.)

iii. Certain kinds of figures. (These may be divided into figures of thought and figures of speech.)

iv. Noble diction. This has as subdivisions choice of words and the use of metaphorical and artificial language.

v. Finally, to round off the whole list, dignified and elevated word-arrangement.[14]

Let us now examine the points which come under each of these heads. I must first observe, however, that Caecilius has omitted some of the five – emotion, for example. [2] Now if he thought that sublimity and emotion were one and the same thing and always existed and developed together, he was wrong. Some emotions, such as pity, grief, and fear, are found divorced from sublimity and with a low effect. Conversely, sublimity often occurs apart from emotion. Of the innumerable examples of this I select Homer's bold account of the Aloadae:

Ossa upon Olympus they sought to heap; and on Ossa
Pelion with its shaking forest, to make a path to heaven

and the even more impressive sequel –

and they would have finished their work ...[15]

[3] In orators, encomia[16] and ceremonial or exhibition pieces always involve grandeur and sublimity, though they are generally devoid of emotion. Hence those orators who are best at conveying emotion are least good at encomia, and conversely the experts at encomia are not conveyers of emotions. [4] On the other hand, if Caecilius thought that emotion had no contribution to make to sublimity and therefore thought it not worth mentioning, he was again completely wrong. I should myself have no hesitation in saying that there is nothing so productive of grandeur as noble emotion in the right place. It inspires and possesses our words with a kind of madness and divine spirit.

## 9

[1] The first source, natural greatness, is the most important. Even if it is a matter of endowment rather than acquisition, we must, so far as is possible, develop our minds in the direction of greatness and make them always pregnant with noble thoughts. [2] You ask how this can be done. I wrote elsewhere something like this: 'Sublimity is the echo of a noble mind.' This is why a mere idea, without verbal expression, is sometimes admired for its nobility just as Ajax's silence in the Vision of the Dead[17] is grand and indeed more sublime

than any words could have been. [3] First then we must state where sublimity comes from: the orator must not have low or ignoble thoughts. Those whose thoughts and habits are trivial and servile all their lives cannot possibly produce anything admirable or worthy of eternity. Words will be great if thoughts are weighty. [4] This is why splendid remarks come naturally to the proud; the man who, when Parmenio[18] said, 'I should have been content'[19]... the interval between earth and heaven. One might say that this is the measure not so much of Strife as of Homer.[20]

[5] Contrast the line about Darkness in Hesiod – if the *Shield* is by Hesiod:

Mucus dripped from her nostrils.[21]

This gives a repulsive picture, not one to excite awe. But how does Homer magnify the divine power?

As far as a man can peer through the mist,
sitting on watch, looking over the wine-dark sea,
so long is the stride of the gods' thundering horses.[22]

He uses a cosmic distance to measure their speed. This enormously impressive image would make anybody say, and with reason, that, if the horses of the gods took two strides like that, they would find there was not enough room in the world.

[6] The imaginative pictures in the Battle of the Gods are also very remarkable:

And the great heavens and Olympus trumpeted around them.
Aïdoneus, lord of the dead, was frightened in his depths;
and in fright he leapt from his throne, and shouted,
for fear the earth-shaker Poseidon might break through the ground,
and gods and men might see
the foul and terrible halls, which even the gods detest.[23]

Do you see how the earth is torn from its foundations, Tartarus laid bare, and the whole universe overthrown and broken up, so that all things – Heaven and Hell, things mortal and things immortal – share the warfare and the perils of that ancient battle? [7] But, terrifying as all this is, it is blasphemous and indecent unless it is interpreted allegorically; in relating the gods' wounds, quarrels, revenges, tears, imprisonments, and manifold misfortunes, Homer, or so it seems to me, has done his best to make the men of the Trojan War gods, and the gods men. If men are unhappy, there is always death as a harbour in trouble; what he has done for his gods is to make them immortal indeed, but immortally miserable.

[8] Much better than the Battle of the Gods are the passages which represent divinity as genuinely unsoiled and great and pure. The lines about Poseidon, much discussed by my predecessors, exemplify this:

The high hills and the forest trembled,
and the peaks and the city of Troy and Achaean ships
under the immortal feet of Poseidon as he went his way.
He drove over the waves, the sea-monsters gambolled around him,
coming up everywhere out of the deep; they recognized their king.
The sea parted in joy; and the horses flew onward.[24]

[9] Similarly, the law-giver of the Jews, no ordinary man – for he understood and expressed God's power in accordance with its worth – writes at the beginning of his *Laws*: 'God said' – now what? – '"Let there be light", and there was light; "Let there be earth", and there was earth.'

[10] Perhaps it will not be out of place, my friend, if I add a further Homeric example – from the human sphere this time – so that we can see how the poet is accustomed to enter into the greatness of his heroes. Darkness falls suddenly. Thickest night blinds the Greek army. Ajax is bewildered. 'O Father Zeus!', he cries,

> 'Deliver the sons of the Achaeans out of the mist,
> make the sky clear, and let us see;
> in the light – kill us.'[25]

The feeling here is genuinely Ajax's. He does not pray for life – that would be a request unworthy of a hero – but having no good use for his courage in the disabling darkness, and so angered at his inactivity in the battle, he prays for light, and quickly: he will at all costs find a shroud worthy of his valour, though Zeus be arrayed against him.

[11] In this passage, the gale of battle blows hard in Homer; he

> rages like Ares, spear-brandishing, or the deadly fire
> raging in the mountains, in the thickets of the deep wood.
> Foam shows at his mouth.[26]

In the *Odyssey*, on the other hand – and there are many reasons for adding this to our enquiry – he demonstrates that when a great mind begins to decline, a love of story-telling characterizes its old age. [12] We can tell that the *Odyssey* was his second work from various considerations, in particular from his insertion of the residue of the Trojan trouble in the poem in the form of episodes, and from the way in which he pays tribute of lamentation and pity to the heroes, treating them as person long known. The *Odyssey* is simply an epilogue to the *Iliad*:

> There lies warlike Ajax, there Achilles,
> there Patroclus, the gods' peer as a counsellor,
> and there my own dear son.[27]

[13] For the same reason, I maintain, he made the whole body of the *Iliad*, which was written at the height of his powers, dramatic and exciting, whereas most of the *Odyssey* consists of narrative, which is a characteristic of old age. Homer in the *Odyssey* may be compared to the setting sun: the size remains without the force. He no longer sustains the tension as it was in the tale of Troy nor that consistent level of elevation which never admitted any falling off. The outpouring of passions crowding one on another has gone; so has the versatility the realism, the abundance of imagery taken from the life. We see greatness on the ebb. It is as though the Ocean were withdrawing into itself and flowing quietly in its own bed. Homer is lost in the realm of the fabulous and incredible. [14] In saying this, I have not forgotten the storms in the *Odyssey*, the story of Cyclops, and a few other episodes; I am speaking of old age but it is the old age of a Homer. The point about all these stories is that the mythical element in them predominates over the realistic.

I digressed into this topic, as I said, to illustrate how easy it is for great genius to be perverted in decline into nonsense. I mean things like the story of the wineskin, the tale of the men kept as pigs in Circe's palace ('howling piglets', Zoilus[28] called them), the feeding of Zeus by the doves (as though he were a chick in the nest), the ten days on the raft without food, and the improbabilities of the murder of the suitors. What can we say of all this but that it really is 'the dreaming of a Zeus'?

[15] There is also a second reason for discussing the *Odyssey*. I want you to understand that the decline of emotional power in great writers and poets turns to a capacity for depicting manners. The realistic description of Odysseus' household forms a kind of comedy of manners.

## 10

[1] Now have we any other means of making our writing sublime? Every topic naturally includes certain elements which are inherent in its raw material. It follows that sublimity will be achieved if we consistently select the most important of these inherent features and learn to organize them as a unity by combining one with another. The first of these procedures attracts the reader by the selection of details, the second by the density of those selected.

Consider Sappho's treatment of the feelings involved in the madness of being in love. She uses the attendant circumstances and draws on real life at every point. And in what does she show her quality? In her skill in selecting the outstanding details and making a unity of them:

[2] To me he seems a peer of the gods, the man who sits
facing you and hears your sweet voice
and lovely laughter; it flutters my heart in my breast. When
I see you only for a moment, I cannot speak;
my tongue is broken, a subtle fire runs under my skin; my
eyes cannot see, my ears hum;
cold sweat pours off me; shivering grips me all over; I am
paler than grass; I seem near to dying;
but all must be endured …[29]

[3] Do you not admire the way in which she brings everything together – mind and body, hearing and tongue, eyes and skin? She seems to have lost them all, and to be looking for them as though they were external to her. She is cold and hot, mad and sane, frightened and near death, all by turns. The result is that we see in her not a single emotion, but a complex of emotions. Lovers experience all this; Sappho's excellence, as I have said, lies in her adoption and combination of the most striking details.

A similar point can be made about the descriptions of storms in Homer, who always picks out the most terrifying aspects. [4] The author of *Arimaspea*[30] on the other hand expects these lines to excite terror:

This too is a great wonder to us in our hearts:
there are men living on water, far from land, on the deep sea:
miserable they are, for hard is their lot;
they give their eyes to the stars, their lives to the sea;
often they raise their hands in prayer to the gods,
as their bowels heave in pain.

Anyone can see that this is more polished than awe-inspiring. [5] Now compare it with Homer (I select one example out of many):

He fell upon them, as upon a swift ship falls a wave,
huge, wind-reared by the clouds. The ship

is curtained in foam, a hideous blast of wind
roars in the sail. The sailors shudder in terror:
they are carried away from under death, but only just.[31]

[6] Aratus tried to transfer the same thought:

A little plank wards off Hades.[32]

But this is smooth and unimpressive, not frightening. Moreover, by saying 'a plank wards off Hades', he has got rid of the danger. The plank *does* keep death away. Homer, on the other hand, does not banish the cause of fear at a stroke; he gives a vivid picture of men one might almost say, facing death many times with every wave that comes. Notice also the forced combination of naturally uncompoundable prepositions: *hupek*, 'from under'. Homer has tortured the words to correspond with the emotion of the moment, and expressed the emotion magnificently by thus crushing words together. He has in effect stamped the special character of the danger on the diction: 'they are carried away from under death'.

[7] Compare Archilochus on the shipwreck, and Demosthenes on the arrival of the news ('It was evening …').[33] In short, one might say that these writers have taken only the very best pieces, polished them up and fitted them together. They have inserted nothing inflated, undignified or pedantic. Such things ruin the whole effect because they produce as it were, gaps or crevices, and so spoil the impressive thoughts which have been built into a structure whose cohesion depends upon their mutual relations. [...]

## *13–15*

### 13

[1] To return to Plato, and the way in which he combines the 'soundless flow' of his smooth style with grandeur. A passage of the *Republic* you have read makes the manner quite clear: 'Men without experience of wisdom and virtue but always occupied with feasting and that kind of thing naturally go downhill and wander through life on a low plane of existence. They never look upwards to the truth and never rise, they never taste certain or pure pleasure. Like cattle, they always look down, bowed earthwards and tablewards; they feed and they breed, and their greediness in these directions makes them kick and butt till they kill one another with iron horns and hooves, because they can never be satisfied.'[34]

[2] Plato, if we will read him with attention, illustrates yet another road to sublimity, besides those we have discussed. This is the way of imitation and emulation of great writers or the past. Here too, my friend, is an aim to which we must hold fast. Many are possessed by a spirit not their own. It is like what we are told of the Pythia at Delphi: she is in contact with the tripod near the cleft in the ground which (so they say) exhales a divine vapour, and she is thereupon made pregnant by the supernatural power and forthwith prophesies as one inspired.[35] Similarly, the genius of the ancients acts as a kind of oracular cavern, and effluences flow from it into the minds of their imitators. Even those previously not much inclined to prophesy become inspired and share the enthusiasm which comes from the greatness of others. [3] Was Herodotus the only 'most Homeric' writer? Surely Stesichorus and Archilochus earned the name before him. So, more than any, did Plato, who diverted to himself countless rills from the Homeric spring. (If Ammonius had not selected and written up detailed examples of this, I might have had to prove the point myself.)[36] [4] In all this process there is no plagiarism. It resembles rather the reproduction of good character in statues and works of art. Plato could not have put such a brilliant finish on his philosophical doctrine or so often risen to poetical subjects and

poetical language, if he had not tried, and tried whole heartedly, to compete for the prize against Homer, like a young aspirant challenging an admired master. To break a lance in this way may well have been a brash and contentious thing to do, but the competition proved anything but valueless. As Hesiod says, 'this strife is good for men'.[37] Truly it is a noble contest and prize of honour, and one well worth winning, in which to be defeated by one's elders is itself no disgrace.

## 14

[1] We can apply this to ourselves. When we are working on something which needs loftiness of expression and greatness of thought, it is good to imagine how Homer would have said the same thing, or how Plato or Demosthenes or (in history) Thucydides would have invested it with sublimity. These great figures, presented to us, as objects of emulation and, were shining before our gaze, will somehow elevate our minds to the greatness of which we form a mental image. [2] They will be even more effective if we ask ourselves 'How would Homer or Demosthenes have reacted to what I am saying, if he had been here? What would his feelings have been?' It makes it a great occasion if you imagine such a jury or audience for your own speech, and pretend that you are answering for what you write before judges and witnesses of such heroic stature. [3] Even more stimulating is the further thought: 'How will posterity take what I am writing?' If a man is afraid of saying anything which will outlast his own life and age, the conceptions of his mind are bound to be incomplete and abortive; they will miscarry and never be brought to birth whole and perfect for the day of posthumous fame.

## 15

[1] Another thing which is extremely productive of grandeur, magnificence, and urgency, my young friend, is visualization (*phantasia*). I use this word for what some people call image-production. The term *phantasia* is used generally for anything which in any way suggests a thought productive of speech; but the word has also come into fashion for the situation in which enthusiasm and emotion make the speaker *see* what he is saying and bring it *visually* before his audience. [2] It will not escape you that rhetorical visualization has a different intention from that of the poets: in poetry the aim is astonishment, in oratory it is clarity. Both, however, seek emotion and excitement.

> Mother, I beg you, do not drive them at me,
> the women with the blood in their eyes and the snakes –
> they are here, they are here, jumping right up to me.

Or again:

> O! O! She'll kill me. Where shall I escape?

The poet himself saw the Erinyes, and has as good as made his audience see what he imagined.[38]
[3] Now Euripides devotes most pains to producing a tragic effect with two emotions, madness and love. In these he is supremely successful. At the same time, he does not lack the courage to attempt other types of visualization. Though not formed by nature for grandeur, he often forces himself to be tragic. When the moment for greatness comes, he (in Homer's words)

> whips flank and buttocks with his tail
> and drives himself to fight.[39]

[4] For example, here is Helios handing the reins to Phaethon:

> 'Drive on, but do not enter Libyan air –
> it has no moisture in it, and will let
> your wheel fall through – '

and again:

> 'Steer towards the seven Pleiads.'
> The boy listened so far, then seized the reins,
> whipped up the winged team, and let them go.
> To heaven's expanse they flew.
> His father rode behind on Sirius,
> giving the boy advice: 'That's your way, there:
> turn here, turn here.'[40]

May one not say that the writer's soul has mounted the chariot, has taken wing with the horses and shares the danger? Had it not been up among those heavenly bodies and moved in their courses, he could never have visualized such things.

Compare, too, his Cassandra:

> Ye Trojans, lovers of horses …[41]

[5] Aeschylus, of course, ventures on the most heroic visualizations; he is like his own Seven against Thebes

> Seven men of war, commanders of companies,
> killing a bull into a black-bound shield
> dipping their hands in the bull's blood,
> took oath by Ares, by Enyo, by bloodthirsty Terror –[42]

in a joint pledge of death in which they showed themselves no mercy. At the same time, he does sometimes leave his thoughts unworked, tangled and hard. The ambitious Euripides does not shirk even these risks. [6] For example, there is in Aeschylus a remarkable description of the palace of Lycurgus in its divine seizure at the moment of Dionysus' epiphany:

> the palace was possessed, the house went bacchanal.

Euripides expresses the same thought less harshly:

> The whole mountain went bacchanal with them.[43]

[7] There is another magnificent visualization in Sophocles' account of Oedipus dying and giving himself burial to the accompaniment of a sign from heaven, and in the appearance of Achilles over his tomb at the departure of the Greek fleet.[44] Simonides has perhaps described this scene more vividly than anyone else; but it is impossible to quote everything.

[8] The poetical examples, as I said, have a quality of exaggeration which belongs to fable and goes far beyond credibility. In an orator's visualizations, on the other hand, it is the element of fact and truth which makes for success; when the content of the passage is poetical and fabulous and does not shrink from any impossibility, the result is a shocking and outrageous abnormality. This is what happens with the shock orators of our own day; like tragic actors, these fine fellows *see* the Erinyes, and are incapable of understanding that when Orestes says "Let me go; you are one of my Erinyes, you are hugging me tight, to throw me into Hell,"[45] he visualizes all this *because he is mad.*

[9] What then is the effect of rhetorical visualization? There is much it can do to bring urgency and passion into our words; but it is when it is closely involved with factual arguments that it enslaves the hearer as well as persuading him. 'Suppose you heard a shout this very moment outside the court, and someone said that the prison had been broken open and the prisoners had escaped – no one, young or old, would be so casual as not to give what help he could. And if someone then came forward and said, "This is the man who let them out," our friend would never get a hearing; it would be the end of him.'[46] [10] There is a similar instance in Hyperides' defence of himself when he was on trial for the proposal to liberate themselves which he put forward after the defeat. 'It was not the proposer,' he said, 'who drew up this decree: it was the battle of Chaeronea.'[47] Here the orator uses a visualization actually in the moment of making his factual argument, with the result that his thought has taken him beyond the limits of mere persuasiveness. [11] Now our natural instinct is, in all such cases, to attend to the stronger influence, so that we are diverted from the demonstration to the astonishment caused by the visualization which by its very brilliance conceals the factual aspect. This is a natural reaction: when two things are joined together, the stronger attracts to itself the force of the weaker.

[12] This will suffice for an account of sublimity of thought produced by greatness of mind, imitation, or visualization. [...]

## 33–36

### 33

[1] Let us consider a really pure and correct writer. We have then to ask ourselves in general terms whether grandeur attended by some faults of execution is to be preferred, in prose or poetry to a modest success of impeccable soundness. We must also ask whether the greater *number* of good qualities or the greater good qualities ought properly to win the literary prizes. These questions are relevant to a discussion of sublimity, and urgently require an answer.

[2] I am certain in the first place that great geniuses are least 'pure'. Exactness in every detail involves a risk of meanness; with grandeur, as with great wealth, there ought to be something overlooked. It may also be inevitable that low or mediocre abilities should maintain themselves generally at a correct and safe level, simply because they take no risks and do not aim at the heights whereas greatness, just because it is greatness, incurs danger.

[3] I am aware also of a second point. All human affairs are, in the nature of things, better known on their worse side; the memory of mistakes is ineffaceable, that of goodness is soon gone. [4] I have myself cited not a few mistakes in Homer and other great writers, not because I take pleasure in their slips, but because I consider them not so much voluntary mistakes as oversights let fall at random through inattention and with the negligence of genius. I do, however, think that the greater good qualities, even if not consistently maintained are always more likely to win the prize – if for no other reason, because of the greatness of spirit they reveal. Apollonius makes no mistakes in the *Argonautica*; Theocritus is very felicitous in the *Pastorals,* apart from a few passages not connected with the theme; but would you rather

be Homer or Apollonius? [5] Is the Eratosthenes of that flawless little poem *Erigone*[48] a greater poet than Archilochus, with his abundant, uncontrolled flood, that bursting forth of the divine spirit, which is so hard to bring under the rule of law? Take lyric poetry: would you rather be Bacchylides or Pindar? Take tragedy: would you rather be Ion of Chios or Sophocles? Ion and Bacchylides, are impeccable, uniformly beautiful writers in the polished manner; but it is Pindar and Sophocles who sometimes set the world on fire with their vehemence, for all that their flame often goes out without reason and they collapse dismally. Indeed, no one in his senses would reckon all Ion's works put together as the equivalent of the one play *Oedipus.*

## 34

[1] If good points were totted up, not judged by their real value, Hyperides would in every way surpass Demosthenes. He is more versatile, and has more good qualities. He is second-best at everything, like a pentathlon competitor; always beaten by the others for first place, he remains the best of the non-specialists. [2] In fact, he reproduces all the good features of Demosthenes, except his word-arrangement, and also has for good measure the excellences and graces of Lysias. He knows how to talk simply where appropriate; he does not deliver himself of everything in the same tone, like Demosthenes. His expression of character has sweetness and delicacy. Urbanity, sophisticated sarcasm, good breeding, skill in handling irony, humour neither rude nor tasteless but flavoured with true Attic salt, an ingenuity in attack with a strong comic element and a sharp sting to its apt fun – all this produces inimitable charm. He has moreover great talents for exciting pity, and a remarkable facility for narrating myths with copiousness and developing general topics with fluency. For example, while his account of Leto is in his more poetic manner, his Funeral Speech is an unrivalled example of the epideictic style.[49] [3] Demosthenes, by contrast, has no sense of character. He lacks fluency, smoothness, and capacity for the epideictic manner; in fact he is practically without all the qualities I have been describing. When he forces himself to be funny or witty, he makes people laugh at him rather than with him. When he wants to come near to being charming, he is furthest removed from it. If he had tried to write the little speech on Phyrne or that on Athenogenes,[50] he would have been an even better advertisement for Hyperides. [4] Yet Hyperides' beauties, though numerous, are without grandeur: 'inert in the heart of a sober man', they leave the hearer at peace. Nobody feels frightened reading Hyperides.

But when Demosthenes begins to speak, be concentrates in himself excellences finished to the highest perfection of his sublime genius – the intensity of lofty speech, living emotions, abundance, acuteness, speed where speed is vital, all his unapproachable vehemence and power. He concentrates it all in himself – they are divine gifts, it is almost blasphemous to call them human – and so outpoints all his rivals, compensating with the beauties he has even for those which he lacks. The crash of his thunder, the brilliance of his lightning make all other orators of all ages insignificant. It would be easier to open your eyes to an approaching thunderbolt than to face up to his unremitting emotional blows.

## 35

[1] To return to Plato and Lysias, there is, as I said a further difference between them. Lysias is much inferior not only in the importance of the good qualities concerned but in their number; and at the same time he exceeds Plato in the number of his failings even more than he falls short in his good qualities.

[2] What then was the vision which inspired those divine writers who disdained exactness of detail and aimed at the greatest prizes in literature? Above all else, it was the understanding that nature made man to be no humble or lowly creature, but brought him into life and into the universe as into a great festival, to be both a spectator and an enthusiastic contestant in its competitions. She implanted in our minds from the start an irresistible desire for anything which is great and, in relation to ourselves, supernatural.

[3] The universe therefore is not wide enough for the range of human speculation and intellect. Our thoughts often travel beyond the boundaries of our surroundings. If anyone wants to know what we were born for let him look round at life and contemplate the splendour, grandeur and beauty in which it everywhere abounds. [4] It is a natural inclination that leads us to admire not the little streams, however pellucid and however useful, but the Nile, the Danube, the Rhine, and above all the Ocean. Nor do we feel so much awe before the little flame we kindle, because it keeps its light clear and pure, as before the fires of heaven, though they are often obscured. We do not think our flame more worthy of admiration than the crater of Etna, whose eruptions bring up rocks and whole hills out of the depths, and sometimes pour forth rivers of the earth-born, spontaneous fire. [5] A single comment fits all these examples: the useful and necessary are readily available to man, it is the unusual that always excites our wonder.

## 36

[1] So when we come to great geniuses in literature – where, by contrast, grandeur is not divorced from service and utility – we have to conclude that such men, for all their faults, tower far above mortal stature. Other literary qualities prove their users to be human; sublimity raises us towards the spiritual greatness of god. Freedom from error does indeed save us from blame, but it is only greatness that wins admiration. [2] Need I add that every one of those great men redeems all his mistakes many times over by a single sublime stroke? Finally, if you picked out and put together all the mistakes in Homer, Demosthenes, Plato, and all the other really great men, the total would be found to be a minute fraction of the successes which those heroic figures have to their credit. Posterity and human experience – judges whose sanity envy cannot question – place the crown of victory on their heads. They keep their prize irrevocably, and will do so

so long as waters flow and tall trees flourish.[51]

[3] It has been remarked that 'the failed Colossus is no better than the Doryphorus of Polyclitus'.[52] There are many ways of answering this. We may say that accuracy is admired in art and grandeur in nature, and it is *by nature* that man is endowed with the power of speech; or again that statues are expected to represent the human form, whereas, as I said, something higher than human is sought in literature.

[4] At this point I have a suggestion to make which takes us back to the beginning of the book. Impeccability is generally a product of art; erratic excellence comes from natural greatness; therefore, art must always come to the aid of nature, and the combination of the two may well be perfection.

It seemed necessary to settle this point for the sake of our enquiry; but everyone is at liberty to enjoy what he takes pleasure in. [...]

## Questions

1. How might one achieve the high or lofty style today? Consider the five principal or most productive sources of sublimity identified by Longinus.

2. What is Longinus's view of the role of the emotions in the sublime? Who feels the emotion (more)—the speaker/writer, or the audience/reader?

3. Does Longinus focus more on the natural or on the rhetorical sublime? Explain, taking into account his references to the Nile, Danube, and natural wonders such as Mt. Etna.

4. How does Longinus use classical sources such as Homer, Demosthenes, and Plato? Do you agree with his assessment? Explain.

## Further reading

Abrams, Meyer H. *The Mirror and the Lamp*. New York: Norton, 1953.

Auerbach, Erich. *Literary Language and Its Public in Late Latin Antiquity and in the Middle Ages*. Princeton: Princeton University Press, 1993.

Grube, George Maximilian Anthony. *The Greek and Roman Critics*. Indianapolis: Hackett Publishing, 1995.

Longinus. *On the Sublime*, trans. James A. Arieti and John M. Crossett. New York: Edwin Mellen Press, 1985.

Monk, Samuel H. *The Sublime: A Study of Critical Theories in XVIII-Century England: With a New Preface by the Author*. Ann Arbor, MI: The University of Michigan Press, 1960.

Saint Girons, Baldine. *Le Sublime, de l'Antiquité à Nos Jours*. Paris: Desjonquères, 2005.

# CHAPTER 2
# BHARATA-MUNI, FROM *NĀṬYAŚĀSTRA*

Attributed to the thinker or sage called Bharata-Muni (or Bharata) but possibly the creation of more than one scholar, the *Nāṭyaśāstra*, or "treatise on drama," is a foundational text in the Indian aesthetic tradition. The handbook was probably compiled between the third century BCE and the second century CE. *Nāṭyaśāstra* (or *Natyasastra*) offers detailed instructions on theatrical performance, giving advice on issues ranging from the gestures of actors to the metrical features of the texts cited by actors. This manual of stagecraft contains treatments of the diverse arts embodied in the classical Sanskrit concept of drama, including dance, music, and poetics, or some combination of these. Like many canonical texts, the thirty-six-chapter primer has given rise to a venerable tradition of interpretation, including a commentary by Abhinavagupta (ca. 950–1016 CE).

The key concept for present purposes is *rasa*, discussed in Chapters 6 ("The Sentiments") and 7 ("The Emotional and Other States"). *Rasa* is the characteristic emotional flavor elicited by, or presented in, the drama, dance, music, or poetry. The idea of an emotional "flavor" or *rasa* is derived from the notion of savor in cooked food and spices. *Nāṭyaśāstra* identifies eight flavors or "sentiments [*rasa*] in drama": the erotic, comic, pathetic, furious, heroic, terrible, odious, and marvelous.[1] One *rasa* can ground or give rise to another *rasa*: "The result of the Heroic Sentiment is called the Marvelous, and that which is Odious to see results in the Terrible."[2] Indian commentators such as Abhinava later sometimes added a ninth *rasa*, "tranquility" or equanimity.[3]

For the purposes of this anthology, the manual's remarks on the terrible, marvelous, and the heroic sentiments are the most relevant. The treatise focuses on how we experience and judge what is represented on a theatrical stage—responses that bear similarities to the sublime. The manual offers advice to actors or dancers on how to represent a *rasa* and thus perhaps (by a kind of participation and identification) to elicit it in the audience. (The text describes "consequents," which are bodily effects and physiological changes associated with each state and which are represented by the actors.) There are further connections to the sublime. The treatise distinguishes between what it calls the dominant, temperamental, and transitory states. The "dominant" states include "terror" and "astonishment,"[4] which are passions or emotions associated (in various ways) with the sublime.

## Note on the text

Source: Excerpted from *The Nāṭyaśāstra Ascribed to Bharta-Muni*, translated by Manomohan Ghosh, 105–08, 114–17, 123–25, 142. Calcutta: Asiatic Society of Bengal, 1951.

Ghosh's parenthetical transcriptions of words have been largely omitted, although some are included in round brackets. The remarks in square brackets were also composed by Ghosh. Orthography (set in roman), style, and punctuation have been occasionally modified. In the present volume, "[…]" indicates omissions made by the volume editor.

Nāṭyaśāstra, 105–08

## The Sentiments explained

In that connection I shall first of all explain the Sentiments (*rasa*).[5] No meaning proceeds [from speech] without [any kind of] Sentiment. The Sentiment is produced from a combination of Determinants, Consequents, and Transitory states. Is there any instance [parallel to it]? [Yes], it is said that, as taste (*rasa*) results from a combination of various spices, vegetables, and other articles, and as six tastes (*rasa*) are produced by articles such as raw sugar or spices or vegetables, so the Dominant States, when they come together with various other States, attain the quality of the Sentiment (i.e., become Sentiment). Now one enquires, "What is the meaning of the word *rasa*"? It is said in reply to this [that *rasa* is so called] because it is capable of being tasted. How is *rasa* tasted? [In reply] it is said that just as well-disposed persons while eating food cooked with many kinds of spices enjoy its tastes (*rasa*) and attain pleasure and satisfaction, so the cultured people taste the Dominant States while they see them represented by an expression of the various States with Words, Gestures, and the Temperament and derive pleasure and satisfaction. Thus is explained [the Memorial Verse ending with] *tasman natyarasa iti*. For in this connection there are two traditional couplets:

32-33. Just as connoisseurs of cooked food while eating food which has been prepared from various spices and other articles, taste it, so the learned people taste in their mind the Dominant States (such as love, sorrow, etc.) when they are represented by an expression of the States with Gestures. Hence these Dominant States in a drama are called the Sentiments.

## The relation between the Sentiments and the States

Now one enquires, "Do the States come out of the Sentiments (*rasa*) or the Sentiments come out of the States?" On this point, some are of opinion that they arise from their mutual contact. But this is not so. Why?

"It is apparent that the Sentiments arise from the States and not the States from the Sentiments. For [on this point] there are [traditional] couplets such as:

34-35. The States are so called by experts in drama, for they cause to originate the Sentiments in connection with various modes of dramatic representation. Just as by many articles of various kinds auxiliary cooked food is brought forth, so the States along with different kinds of Histrionic [i.e., theatrical – Ed.] Representation will cause the Sentiments to originate.

36. There can be no Sentiment prior to [literally, without] the States and no States without the Sentiments [following it], and during the Histrionic Representation they are produced from their mutual relation.

37. Just as a combination of spices and vegetables imparts good taste to the food cooked, so the States and the Sentiments cause one another to originate.

38. Just as a tree grows from a seed, and flowers and fruits [including the seed] from a tree, so the Sentiments are the source [literally, root] of all the States, and likewise the States exist [as the source of all the Sentiments].

## The eight Sentiments from the four original ones

Now we shall describe the origins, the colours, the [presiding] deities, and examples of these Sentiments. Sources of these [eight] Sentiments are the four [original] Sentiments, e.g., Erotic, Furious, Heroic, and Odious.

39. The Comic [Sentiment] arises from the Erotic, the Pathetic from the Furious, the Marvelous from the Heroic, and the Terrible from the Odious.

40-41. A mimicry of the Erotic [Sentiment] is called the Comic, and the result of the Furious Sentiment is the Pathetic, and the result of the Heroic Sentiment is called the Marvelous, and that which is Odious to see results in the Terrible. […]

[…] We shall now enumerate the Dominant States in different Sentiments. […]

## *Nāṭyaśāstra*, 114–17

### The Heroic Sentiment

Now the Heroic Sentiment, relates to the superior type of persons and has energy as its basis. This is created by Determinants such as presence of mind, perseverance, diplomacy, discipline, military strength, aggressiveness, reputation of might, influence, and the like. It is to be represented on the stage by Consequents such as firmness, patience, heroism, charity, diplomacy, and the like. Transitory States in it are contentment, judgement, pride, agitation, energy (*vega*), ferocity, indignation, remembrance, horripilation [goose bumps – Ed.], and the like.
　　There are two Aryas [on these points]:

67. The Heroic Sentiment arises from energy, perseverance, optimism, absence of surprise, and presence of mind and [other such] special conditions [of the spirit].

68. This Heroic Sentiment is to be properly represented on the stage by firmness, patience, heroism, pride, energy, aggressiveness, influence, and censuring words.

### The Terrible Sentiment

Now the Terrible Sentiment has as its basis the Dominant State of fear. This is created by Determinants like hideous noise, sight of ghosts, panic, and anxiety due to [the untimely cry of] jackals and owls, staying in an empty house or forest, sight of death or captivity of dear ones, or news of it, or discussion about it. It is to be represented on the stage by Consequents such as trembling of the hands and the feet, horripilation, change of colour, and loss of voice. Its Transitory States are paralysis, perspiration, choking voice, horripilation, trembling, loss of voice, change of colour, fear, stupefaction, dejection, agitation, restlessness, inactivity, fear, epilepsy and death, and the like.
　　On these points there are two traditional Aryas:

69. The Terrible Sentiment is created by hideous noise, sight of ghosts, battle, entering an empty house or forest, offending one's superiors or the king.

70. Terror is characterised by looseness of the limbs, the mouth and the eyes, paralysis of the thighs, looking around with uneasiness, dryness of the drooping mouth, palpitation of the heart, and horripilation.

71. This is [the character of] natural fear; the artificially shown fear also should be represented by these conditions. But in case of the feigned fear all efforts for its representation should be milder.

72. This Terrible Sentiment should be always represented by tremor of the hands and the feet, paralysis, shaking of the body, palpitation of the heart, dryness of the lips, the mouth, the palate, and the throat.

## The Odious Sentiment

Now the Odious Sentiment has as its basis the Dominant State of disgust. It is created by Determinants like hearing of unpleasant, offensive, impure, and harmful things, or seeing them or discussing them. It is to be represented on the stage by Consequents such as stopping the movement of all the limbs, narrowing down of the mouth, vomiting, spitting, shaking the limbs [in disgust], and the like. Transitory States in it are epilepsy, delusion, agitation, fainting, sickness, death, and the like.

On these points there are two traditional Aryas:

73. The Odious Sentiment arises in many ways from disgusting sight, tastes, smell, touch and sound, which cause uneasiness.

74. This is to be represented on the stage by narrowing down the mouth and the eyes, covering the nose, bending down the head, and walking imperceptibly.

## The Marvelous Sentiment

The Marvelous Sentiment has as its basis the Dominant State of astonishment. It is created by Determinants such as sight of heavenly beings or events, attainment of desired objects, entrance into a superior mansion, temple, audience hall, a seven-storied palace and [seeing] illusory and magical acts. It is to be represented on the stage by Consequents such as wide opening of eyes, looking with fixed gaze, horripilation, tears [of joy] perspiration, joy, uttering words of approbation, making gifts, crying incessantly *ha, ha, ha,* waving the end of *dhoti* or *sari* [traditional dress of men and women – Ed.], and movement of fingers and the like. Transitory States in it are weeping, paralysis, perspiration, choking voice, horripilation, agitation, hurry, inactivity, death, and the like.

On this point there are two traditional Aryas:

75. The Marvelous Sentiment is that which arises from words, character, deed, and personal beauty.

76. This is to be represented on the stage by a gesture of feeling [sweet] smell, joyful shaking of limb, and uttering of *ha, ha, ha,* sounds, speaking words of approbation, tremor, choking voice, perspiration, and the like.

## The three kinds of the Erotic, the Comic, and the Terrible Sentiments

77. The Erotic Sentiment is of three kinds, namely, of words, dress, and action. And the Comic and the Terrible Sentiments are likewise of three kinds, namely, of limbs, dress, and words.

## The three kinds of the Pathetic Sentiment

78. The Pathetic Sentiment is of three kinds, namely, that rising from obstruction to lawful deeds, from loss of wealth, and from bereavement.

## The three kinds of the Heroic Sentiment

79. The Heroic Sentiment is likewise of three kinds, namely, that arising from making gifts, from doing one's duty (*dharma*) and from fighting [one's enemy].

## The three kinds of the Terrible Sentiment

80. The Terrible Sentiment is also of three kinds, namely, feigned fear, fear from a wrong action, and fear from an apprehension of danger.

## The three kinds of the Odious Sentiment

81. The Odious Sentiment is of three kinds, namely, nauseating, simple, and exciting. Of these the Sentiment from a sight of stool and worms is nauseating, and the sight of blood and similar objects is exciting.

## The three kinds of the Marvelous Sentiment

82. The Marvelous Sentiment is of two kinds, namely, celestial and joyous. Of these the celestial is due to seeing heavenly sights, and the joyous due to joyful happenings.

83. These are the eight Sentiments and their definitions, I shall hereafter speak of the characteristics of the States.

Here ends Chapter VI of Bharata's *Nāṭyaśāstra* which treats of the Sentiments.

## *Nāṭyaśāstra,* Chapter VII, 123–25

### Energy

Energy relates to persons of the superior type. It is caused the Determinants such as absence of sadness, power, patience, heroism, and the like. It is to be represented on the stage by Consequents such as steadiness, munificence [i.e., generosity – Ed.], boldness of an undertaking, and the like.

On this point there is a Sloka[6]:

21. Energy which has effort as its basis and which grows out of alertness and other such qualities should be represented on the stage by acts of vigilance and the like.

### Fear

Fear relates to women and persons of the inferior type. It is caused by Determinants such as acts offending one's superiors and the king, roaming in a forest, seeing an elephant and a snake, staying in an empty house, rebuke [from one's superiors], a dark rainy night, hearing the hooting of owls and the cry of animals that go out at night, and the like. It is to be represented on the stage by Consequents such as trembling hand and feet, palpitation of the heart, paralysis, dryness of the mouth, licking the lips, perspiration, tremor, apprehension [of danger], seeking for safety, running away, loud crying, and the like.

On this point there are Slokas:

22. Fear arises from an embarrassment due to offending one's superiors and the king, seeing terrible objects, and hearing awful things.

23. This is to be represented with trembling of the limbs, panic, drying up of the mouth, hurried movement, widely opened eyes, and other such gestures and actions.

24. Fear in men arising from terrifying objects should be represented on the stage by actors [literally, dancers] with slackened limbs and suspended movement of the eyes.

There is also an Arya on this point:

25. This (fear) should be represented on the stage with tremor of hands and feet, and palpitation of the heart, paralysis, licking the lips, drying up of the mouth, loosened limbs, and sinking body.

## Disgust

Disgust relates to women and persons of the inferior type. It is caused by Determinants such as hearing and seeing unpleasant things, and the like. It is to be represented on the stage by Consequents such as contracting all the limbs, spitting, narrowing down of the mouth, heartache, and the like.
On this point there is a Sloka:

26. Disgust is to be represented on the stage by covering the nose, contracting all the limbs, [general] uneasiness, and heartache.

## Astonishment

Astonishment is created by Determinants such as illusion, magic, extraordinary feats of men, great excellence in painting, artworks in parchment, and the like. It is to be represented on the stage by Consequents such as wide opening of the eyes, looking without winking of the eye, [much] movement of the eyebrows, horripilation, moving the head to and fro, the cry of "well, done," "well done," and the like.
On this point there is a Sloka:

27. Astonishment arising from joy due to extraordinary acts should be represented by means such as joy tears, fainting, and the like. […]

## Nāṭyaśāstra, Chapter VII, 142

## Fright

Fright is caused by Determinants such as flash of lightning, a meteor, thunder, earthquake, clouds, crying or howling of big animals, and the like. It is to be represented on the stage by Consequents such as shaking of narrow limbs, tremor [of the body], paralysis, horripilation, speaking with a choked voice, talking irrelevantly, and the like.
There is a Sloka on this point:

91. Fright is caused by a very terrible sound and the like. It should be represented on the stage by looseness of limbs and half-shut eyes. […]

## Questions

1. Explain your interpretation of *rasa* ("Sentiment"). How is a particular *rasa* evoked?

2. What in this text can be related to or associated with the sublime (or what Longinus called *hypsous*)? Explain. Which elements seem most relevant?

3. How might the characterization of fear and other emotions be compared to analyses of emotion in ancient Greek tragedy? In modern tragic plays?

4. How is this text like, or unlike, early modern European writings on "taste" and aesthetic judgment? Explain.

## Further reading

Chakrabarti, Arindam, ed. *The Bloomsbury Research Handbook of Indian Aesthetics and the Philosophy of Art*. London: Bloomsbury, 2016.

Gerow, Edwin. "Indian Aesthetics: A Philosophical Survey." In *A Companion to World Philosophies*, ed. Eliot Deutsch and Ron Bontekoe, 319–21. Malden, MA: Blackwell, 1997.

Pollock, Sheldon, trans. *A Rasa Reader: Classical Indian Aesthetics*. New York: Columbia University Press, 2016.

Schwarz, Susan L. *Rasa: Performing the Divine in India*. New York: Columbia University Press, 2004.

Thampi, G. B. Mohan. "Rasa as Aesthetic Experience." *The Journal of Aesthetics and Art Criticism* 24, no. 1 (1965): 75–80.

# PART II
## POSTCLASSICAL

# CHAPTER 3
## GUO XI, FROM *THE INTEREST OF LOFTY FORESTS AND SPRINGS*

Guo Xi (Kuo Hsi) (ca. 1000–90) was a leading Northern Song dynasty (960–1127) landscape artist and theorist of painting. A detail of his painting, *Early Spring*, is on the cover of the present volume. Guo Xi's paintings of winter and spring display the "empty space" or gap in many Chinese landscape paintings, such as those of Juran and other Chinese painters from the Northern Song dynasty. The blank or gap we find in some Chinese paintings fits in as something to be left untouched rather than removed; its empty spaces imply the presence of something that resists representation.[1]

His paintings provide insights into his treatise on depicting landscapes, *The Interest of Lofty Forests and Springs*, excerpted here. Both his paintings and writings were influential within classical Chinese aesthetics. His *Early Spring* allows the reader to see a visualization of his claims. In this painting, one can discern two strands of the sublime: the "natural" and the "transcendent." The natural strand is revealed by two figures on the lower-right side of the painting. They are admiring a waterfall above them and looking up at a monastery and other human dwellings. They appear to be feeling a mixture of awe and astonishment. The figure on the left looks enthralled and entranced, his gaze affixed; the figure to the right is lurching back as if in a mode of fear.

The transcendent or ineffable strand of the sublime can be found in the gaps and mists. Above the waterfall (not shown in the detail) is a mist that creates the empty space or gap, which could be taken to exemplify or illustrate transcendence. The painting hints at transcendence through a covering—a mist—an ongoing play of hiddenness and disclosure. "It is therefore the unique character of the Chinese sublime experience," according to Kin-yuen Wong, "that negation [that is, the gap] is both a means and an end." According to Wong, "The sublime experience manifests itself through an intersubjective relationship between the painting and the viewer, the content of which takes the form of an ideational activity motivated and controlled by blanks and negations."[2] In the monumental style of Northern Song, depicting mists became an artistic device to solve the problem of how to handle the relationship of near, middle, and far ground.[3]

In this "Three Distances" excerpt, Guo Xi develops the notions of high, deep, and level perspectives or distances. First, the "upward" view is respectful and deferential, and it is labeled as "lofty" or "high"—what strikes the viewer is the towering overwhelming stature of the high peaks. The reader must visualize an observer at the base of the peaks, which from such a position can only be observed in their looming verticality. According to the second (deep) perspective, the viewer looking before the mountains (whose overlapping forms occlude one another) may only glimpse, or spy, the range of mountain backs retreating from view into the atmospheric distance. This view is called "deep" perhaps in order to call attention to the "profound" expansiveness of the mountains. Third is the perspective of someone viewing other mountains from atop another mountain. It is called "level" because the observer is at the same height as other mountaintops.

Guo describes how each view looks—its appearance to the depicted viewer not only *in* the scene, but also of the scene itself (i.e., to us viewers). There is no clear and rigid distinction between the two kinds of appearances. Guo desires to evoke the feeling of the person in the scene, by means of the painted scroll. This participatory engagement with the work of art by reference figures is crucial to appreciating classical East-Asian landscapes. In Guo's text, the human being is peacefully placed within such an environment, that is, without any adversarial tension between humanity and nature. (At the same time, in *Early Spring* the figures appear to be moved, enthralled, or astonished by their surroundings.)

Guo explains that, according to the first perspective, figures at the base of the mountains should be clearly depicted—and thus "clearly understood" by an observer. "The appearance of lofty-distance is pure clarity." In the second perspective, figures in the deep distance must be painted with "fine pieces," that is, finely applied strokes of paint. It conveys a person in the midst of the vanishing depths. Third, the person who has obtained the heights is to be depicted as having obtained tranquility. The final clause in this excerpt gives technical-artistic advice toward achieving such depictions: the strokes for clarity are not abrupt, those for diminutive vagueness are not extended, and the person in tranquility should not have a large presence.

## Note on the text

Source: This English translation is based on the 1936 text, 美術叢書: 二集, 第七輯. 石印本. ed. 出版地缺: 神州國光社刊.

This original translation by Jonathan Johnson is here published for the first time.[4] The footnotes were composed by Johnson.

### The Interest of Lofty Forests and Springs (林泉高致)

| | |
|---|---|
| 山有三遠 | Mountains have three distances: |
| 自山下而仰山顛 | From below mountains one gazes upwards at mountain pinnacles, |
| 謂之高遠 | This is called lofty-distance; |
| 自山前而窺山後 | Before mountains one glimpses mountain ridges, |
| 謂之深遠 | This is called deep-distance; |
| 自近山而望遠山 | From near mountains gazing upon distant mountains, |
| 謂之平遠 | This is called level-distance.[5] |
| 高遠之色清明 | The appearance[6] of lofty-distance is pure clarity; |
| 深遠之色重晦 | The appearance of deep-distance is weighty obscurity; |
| 平遠之色有明有晦 | The appearance of level-distance has both clearness and obscurity. |
| 高遠之勢突兀 | Lofty-distance has the impression of towering heights; |
| 深遠之意重疊 | Deep-distance has the suggestion of thick overlapping; |
| 平遠之意沖融而縹縹紗紗 | Level-distance has the suggestion of harmonious fusions and misty indistinctness. |
| 其人物之在三遠也 | The portrayal of a person in the three distances is as follows: |
| 高遠者明瞭 | In lofty-distance clearly understood; |
| 深遠者細碎 | In deep-distance with fine pieces;[7] |
| 平遠者沖澹 | In level-distance awash in tranquility. |
| 明瞭者不短 | That which is clearly understood is not brief; |
| 細碎者不長 | That which is in fine pieces is not long; |
| 沖澹者不大 | That which is awash in tranquility is not large.[8] |
| 此三遠也 | Such are the three distances. |

## Questions

1. Where, if at all, would you locate an account of the sublime in this text? Explain.

2. How do Guo Xi's ideas compare with claims made in other theories of the sublime? Consider his references to "towering heights" and a "thick overlapping" of forms.

3. Compare and contrast the "deep" perspective with the "mysterious profundity" (*yūgen*) discussed in the second level in "Notes on the Nine Levels" by the Japanese author Zeami Motokiyo (reprinted in the present volume).

4. Compare and contrast the notion of a Chinese sublime of "transcendence" with the first level in Zeami's "Notes on the Nine Levels."

## Further reading and translations

Hu, Yunhua. *Chinese Penjing: Miniature Trees and Landscapes*. Hong Kong: Wan Li Book Co., Ltd., 1987.

Lin, Yutang. *The Chinese Theory of Art: Translations from the Masters of Chinese Art*, 72–80. New York: Putnam's Sons, 1967.

Mair, Victor H. *The Columbia Anthology of Traditional Chinese Literature*. New York: Columbia University Press, 1994.

Yang, Xiaoshan. *Metamorphosis of the Private Sphere: Gardens and Objects in Tang-Song Poetry*. Cambridge, MA: Harvard University Press, 2003.

# CHAPTER 4
## ZEAMI MOTOKIYO, "NOTES ON THE NINE LEVELS"

The Japanese essayist and playwright, Zeami Motokiyo (1363–1443) is considered a foremost dramatist and theorist of nō (or Noh), one of the world's great theater traditions.[1] His plays and treatises are largely responsible for transforming nō from a rustic form of entertainment into a high art. He is credited with having written 240 plays, approximately 100 of which still survive and are regularly performed. In addition, his treatises are regarded as a significant contribution not only to the dramatic arts, but also to Japanese aesthetics as a whole. In 1400, Zeami began writing his first treatise, *Fūshikaden* (*Style and the Flower*), to preserve and pass on the teachings of his father, likewise an actor and leader of a troupe. Zeami introduces the concept of *hana,* the flower—a metaphor that Zeami employs throughout his writings. As demonstrated in his plays and articulated in his treatises, Zeami infused nō with religious significance deriving from Zen Buddhism.

The term *yūgen* (profound grace, mysterious profundity) is first found in Chinese philosophical texts, where it has the connotation of "dark" or "mysterious."[2] Kamo no Chōmei, the author of *Hōjōki* ("An Account of my Hut," from the year 1212), considered *yūgen* to be important to the poetry of his time. Kamo no Chōmei offers the following as a characterization of *yūgen*: "It is like an autumn evening under a colorless expanse of silent sky. Somehow, as if for some reason that we should be able to recall, tears well uncontrollably."

According to one interpretation, *yūgen* emphasizes the role played by a cultivated and expanded imagination. For instance, a limitless vista created in imagination surpasses anything we can see clearly and distinctly. *Yūgen* concerns not so much a world beyond as the depth of the present world.

Zeami wrote a number of treatises on nō drama, in which *yūgen* figures as the highest principle. He associates it with the highly refined culture of the Japanese nobility, and in particular with refined speech. In addition, nō involves three Graces: that of music, the performance of different roles, and dance. Grace is something rare, attained only by the greatest actors in the tradition, and only after decades of dedicated practice of the art. Given its resistance to conceptualization, Zeami often resorts to imagery in trying to explain it: "Cannot the beauty of Grace be compared to the image of a swan holding a flower in its bill, I wonder?"[3]

A famous formulation appears at the beginning of Zeami's "Notes on the Nine Levels," excerpted here. "The meaning of the phrase Peerless Charm surpasses any explanation in words and lies beyond the workings of consciousness." This phrase alludes to and tries to capture the results of the rigorous discipline that informs many of the Japanese performing arts (broadly conceived to include the tea ceremony, calligraphy, and theater) and East-Asian martial arts. Nō is exemplary in this respect, since its forms of diction, gestures, gaits, and dance movements are all highly stylized.

In the following, Zeami characterizes the levels of learning and mastering the art of nō. The first level (the art of the flower of peerless charm) can be associated with the strand of the sublime that emphasizes unknowability, or at least it describes a "feeling that transcends cognition." The second level (the art of the flower of profundity) may also emphasize paradox and ineffability. (This is left for readers to decide.) In any case, it brings out the strand of the sublime that emphasizes our perception and interaction with a vast and striking object: a mountain (Mount Fuji).

## Note on the text

Source: Reprinted from Zeami, *On the Art of the Nō Drama: The Major Treatises of Zeami*, translated by J. Thomas Rimer and Yamazaki Masakazu, 120–25. Princeton: Princeton University Press, 1984.

The format and style of this translation have been reproduced, with occasional modifications. Comments in square or round brackets are composed by the translators, unless otherwise noted. Their editorial notes have been included, with occasional modifications.

## Notes on Nine Levels (*Kyūi*)

### *The flower of the upper three levels*

1. *The art of the flower of peerless charm*

   "In Silla, in the dead of the night, the sun shines brightly."[4]—The meaning of the phrase Peerless Charm surpasses any explanation in words and lies beyond the workings of consciousness. It can surely be said that the phrase "in the dead of night, the sun" exists in a realm beyond logical explanation. Indeed, concerning the Grace of the greatest performers in our art, there are no words with which to praise it, [as that Grace gives rise to] the moment of Feeling that Transcends Cognition, and to an art that lies beyond any level that the artist may have consciously attained. Such surely represents the level of the Flower of Peerless Charm.

2. *The art of the flower of profundity*

   "Snow covers a thousand mountains; why is there one peak that is not white?"[5]—In ancient days, someone said that "because Mount Fuji is so high, the snow there cannot melt." A man of T'ang [China] reproved him, saying, "it is rather because Mount Fuji is so deep." Indeed the greatest heights are equivalent to great depths. There are limits to heights. Yet the depths cannot be measured. Thus, cannot the image of depth conveyed by the one snowless peak amid a thousand mountains covered with snow serve to convey the sense of the Flower of Profundity?

3. *The art of the flower of tranquillity*

   "Piling up snow in a silver bowl."[6]—Piling snow in a silver bowl, the hues that derive from the pure, clean white light, an appearance that gives rise to a real sense of gentleness—can it not be said that such represents the Flower of Tranquillity?

### *The middle three levels*

4. *The art of the true flower*

   "In the bright mists the sun is setting, and all the mountains become crimson:"[7]—In the blue heavens, a spot of bright light: as far as the eye can see, the countless mountains stand revealed in utter clearness—such is the way of the True Flower. This level is superior to the way of Broad Skill and represents the moment when the actor begins to enter into the Realm of the Flower.

5. *The art of broad mastery*

   "To describe fully the spirit of the clouds on the mountains, the moon on the sea."[8]—When the essence of mountains ringed by clouds and the moon shining on the sea, indeed when all that the eye can absorb of the vast panorama of the green mountains can be fully recounted, then the stage of mastery appropriate to the Art of Broad Mastery has been achieved. At this level, the actor can move either forward or backward: the crossroads are here.

6. *The art of early beauty*

"What the world calls the Way is not the True Way."[9]—While first walking the True Way, the actor must follow the various other Ways as well. If he does so, he can show the beauty he has achieved since the beginning of his training. Thus, the Art of Early Beauty provides the first means to begin to master the nine levels.

## The bottom three levels

7. *The art of strength and delicacy*

"The shadow of the metal hammer moving; the cold gleam of the sacred sword."[10]—The moving shadow of the metal hammer represents an artistic appearance of strong movement. The cold gleam of the sacred sword represents a cold and restrained performance in which a certain delicacy also plays a part.

8. *The way of strength and crudeness*

"Three days after its birth, a tiger wants to eat an ox."[11]—A tiger three days after its birth can be said to show an energetic and forceful spirit. On the other hand, to eat an entire ox is merely coarse.

9. *The way of crudeness and leadenness*

"The five skills of the flying squirrel."—Confucius[12] said, "The flying squirrel has five skills. He can climb trees, swim in the water, dig holes, fly, and run. Yet in none of these talents does he exceed his lowly station."[13] In an art that does not show some Delicacy within Strength, the results will be coarse and leaden.

## The order in which to study the nine levels

It is commonly said that one should study first the middle three levels, next the upper three, and finally the lower three.

As a beginning toward learning the art of *nō*, the various aspects of the Two Arts must be thoroughly practiced, so as to achieve the level of Early Beauty. When this level has been thoroughly mastered through study, and when the actor has in turn developed the beauty he has gained since the beginning of his training, he is already in the realm of Broad Mastery. At this stage, all kinds of roles are studied thoroughly, and the actor broadens his art in every direction while still keeping the True Way [of the Two Basic Arts], so that all comes to fruition at the level of the True Flower. Thus, this level can be said to serve as the turning point at which the actor expands his mastery to the Three Role Types. This level is also the crucial crossroad where the actor attains the Flower of Perfect Fluency, and his enlightenment concerning the Way of his art can be manifested in his appearance. At this level, the actor can look below him at the levels of mastery he had previously achieved; now he occupies a position of the Highest Fruition, an ease that represents the Flower of Tranquillity.

Then, above this level still, the actor achieves the peerless art of Grace, and his performances can manifest that beauty that surpasses the difference between the adorned and the unadorned; such is the level called the Flower of Profundity. Then, still above this, exists that level that no words can describe, where the workings of the spirit and their manifestation in performance can no longer be divided: such is the Art of the Flower of Peerless Charm, which represents the highest reaches of our art.

In general, the point of departure for all three upper levels of our art rests in the Art of Broad Mastery. This level provides the basis for all the skills of the *nō* and serves as a means to nurture the seed of every artistic Flower, be it broad or delicate in scale. This level represents the crossroads from which these broad and delicate skills may either develop or wither away. Those who grow to gain real Flower will achieve the level of the Art of the True Flower. Those who cannot achieve this will sink down to the lower three levels.

The lower three levels represent the rapid currents of theatrical art; they can be divided from the rest and do not constitute an important element in our training. On occasion, when an actor has acquired the three middle levels and has gone on to master the upper three as well, and has achieved the level of Perfect Fluency and the Flower of Peerless Charm, he may then reverse himself and sometimes for his own amusement select the manner of the lower three levels; and should he perform on these levels of skill, something mild and approachable will be found in his performance. However, from the beginning there have been artists of great ability who, while they have mastered the upper three levels of the Flower, have declined to descend to make use of the lowest three levels in their own performances. Their choice might be likened to the old expression, "an elephant does not amuse himself by walking the path of a rabbit."[14] I know of no one other than my late father Kan'ami who was able to perform in all styles, from high to low. Apart from him, among all the heads of the various troupes, there were many who studied to achieve the level of Broad Mastery but were not able to ascend to the level of the True Flower, and so sank back to the three lowest levels of skill, thus never finally gaining a reputation in the capital. Indeed even today there are those who begin their study at the lower three levels in order to achieve their art. Such is not the proper way to proceed. So it is that many actors can never enter at all into the nine levels.

It can be said, therefore, that as a means to enter into the three lower levels, three possibilities are available. In the case of the superior actor who begins by learning his art at the middle levels, then proceeds to the higher levels and finally descends to the lower levels, he will give a superior performance by using the techniques of the three lower levels as well. An actor who begins at the level of Broad Mastery in the middle level and then descends to the lower levels can only exhibit the artistic strength appropriate to the Art of Strength and Delicacy, or Strength and Crudeness. In addition, those who vainly attempt to begin at the lower three levels can hardly be said to have entered into the nine levels in any fashion, as their art does not follow the proper path and cannot even be said to have a name. Such men, even though they yearn for the art of the three lower levels, cannot even achieve the skills appropriate to them. It is unthinkable that such actors could even reach the middle three levels.

## Questions

1. Can you locate a discussion of the "sublime" in this treatise? Explain. If so, which level or levels seem most relevant?

2. How do you understand the second level? Shouldn't unmelted snow be white? (Or is the point to create a paradox? If that is the case, explain how this mysterious profundity differs from the unknowability described in level one.) Explain the meaning of this passage: "Indeed the greatest heights are equivalent to great depths. There are limits to heights. Yet the depths cannot be measured."

3. What does this passage (quoted above) imply about our concepts of height and depth? What, if anything, does it entail regarding concepts in general, say, how concepts interact with or relate to each other? Explain.

4. Which images represent each of the nine levels of artistic achievement or excellence? How significant is it that, in the second level, Zeami discusses an object of nature—Mount Fuji? Explain.

5. How would you characterize Zeami on moral and aesthetic education, on virtue and art?

6. Compare and contrast the mysterious profundity of *yūgen* with the "deep" perspective of landscape painting discussed by Guo Xi (reprinted in the present volume).

## Further reading

Hume, Nancy G., ed. *Japanese Aesthetics and Culture: A Reader.* Albany: State University of New York Press, 1995.

Nagatomo, Shigenori. "Zeami's Conception of Freedom." *Philosophy East and West* XXXI, no. 4 (October 1981): 401–16.

Saito, Yuriko. "The Japanese Appreciation of Nature." *The British Journal of Aesthetics* 25, no. 3 (1985): 239–51.

Ueda, Makoto. "Zeami and the Art of the Nō Drama: Imitation, *Yūgen*, and Sublimity." In *Japanese Aesthetics and Culture: A Reader*, ed. Nancy G. Hume, 177–91. Albany: State University of New York Press, 1995.

# CHAPTER 5
## FRANCESCO PETRARCA, "THE ASCENT OF MONT VENTOUX" (1336)

Francesco Petrarca (1304–1374), or Petrarch, was an Italian Renaissance poet and scholar. His writings were influential on the formation of the modern Italian language, and his sonnets were commended as examples of lyrical poetry. The following reading has been interpreted (e.g., by Jakob Burkhardt) as an early piece of writing in the modern spirit, or at least as representative of a transition from the medieval to the modern periods. It has also been considered (e.g., by Ernst Cassirer) an early example of alpinism and environmental writing.

In this "letter," Petrarca describes the ascent of Mount Ventoux, which he undertook with his brother and two assistants. He uses the experience as an opportunity to confess his shortcomings and struggles. At the summit of the mountain (elevation 1,912 meters), he reads a passage from Augustine's *Confessions* (10.8.15): "And men go to admire the high mountains, the vast floods of the sea, the huge streams of the rivers, the circumference of the ocean, and the revolutions of the stars—and desert themselves." Petrarca reflects on the triviality of common, ordinary affairs and admires the greatness of the mind drawing closer to God. Freedom from everyday concerns, reflection on the mind's greatness, and (partial) unity with God are sources of the pleasure in the experience, rendering it on the whole positive. On his way down the mountain, he muses on these thoughts—with his group, yet in silence.

### Note on the text

Source: Reprinted from Petrarca, "The Ascent of Mont Ventoux." In *Renaissance Philosophy of Man*, edited by Paul Oskar Kristeller, Ernst Cassirer, and John Herman Randall Jr., 36–46. Chicago: University of Chicago Press, 1948.

The format and style of the translation as well as editorial notes have been reproduced here, with occasional modifications.

### "The Ascent of Mont Ventoux"

Letter to Francesco Dionigi de'Roberti of Borgo San Sepolcro, professor of theology in Paris. Malaucène, April 26, 1336.

(*Fam.*, IV, I, in *Le Familiari*, ed. V. Rossi, I, 153–61; *Opera* [Basel, 1581], pp. 624–27.)

*To Dionigi da Borgo San Sepolcro, of the Order of Saint Augustine, Professor of Theology, about his own troubles*:

Today I ascended the highest mountain in this region, which, not without cause, they call the Windy Peak.[1] Nothing but the desire to see its conspicuous height was the reason for this undertaking. For many years I have been intending to make this expedition. You know that since my early childhood, as fate tossed around human affairs, I have been tossed around in these parts, and this mountain, visible far and wide from everywhere, is always in your view. So I was at last seized by the impulse to accomplish what I had always wanted to do. It happened while I was reading Roman history again in Livy that I hit upon the passage where Philip, the king of Macedon—the Philip who waged war against the Roman people—"ascends Mount Haemus in Thessaly, since he believed the rumor that you can see two seas from its top: the Adriatic and the Black Sea."[2] Whether he was right or wrong I cannot make out because the mountain is far from our region, and the disagreement among authors renders the matter uncertain. I do not intend to consult all of them: the cosmographer Pomponius Mela does not hesitate to report the fact as true;[3] Livy supposes the rumor to be false. I would not leave it long in doubt if that mountain were as easy to explore as the one here. At any rate, I had better let it go, in order to come back to the mountain I mentioned at first. It seemed to me that a young man who holds no public office[4] might be excused for doing what an old king is not blamed for.

I now began to think over whom to choose as a companion. It will sound strange to you that hardly a single one of all my friends seemed to me suitable in every respect, so rare a thing is absolute congeniality in every attitude and habit even among dear friends. One was too sluggish, the other too vivacious; one too slow, the other too quick; this one too gloomy of temper, that one too gay. One was duller, the other brighter than I should have liked. This man's taciturnity, that man's flippancy; the heavy weight and obesity of the next, the thinness and weakliness of still another were reasons to deter me. The cool lack of curiosity of one, like another's too eager interest, dissuaded me from choosing either. All such qualities, however difficult they are to bear, can be borne at home: loving friendship is able to endure everything; it refuses no burden. But on a journey they become intolerable. Thus my delicate mind, craving honest entertainment, looked about carefully, weighing every detail, with no offense to friendship. Tacitly it rejected whatever it could foresee would become troublesome on the projected excursion. What do you think I did? At last I applied for help at home and revealed my plan to my only brother, who is younger than I and whom you know well enough. He could hear of nothing he would have liked better and was happy to fill the place of friend us well as brother.

We left home on the appointed day and arrived at Malaucène at night. This is a place at the northern foot of the mountain. We spent a day there and began our ascent this morning, each of us accompanied by a single servant. From the start we encountered a good deal of trouble, for the mountain is a steep and almost inaccessible pile of rocky material. However, what the Poet says is appropriate: "Ruthless striving overcomes everything."[5]

The day was long, the air was mild; this and vigorous minds, strong and supple bodies, and all the other conditions assisted us on our way. The only obstacle was the nature of the spot. We found an aged shepherd in the folds of the mountain who tried with many words to dissuade us from the ascent. He said he had been up to the highest summit in just such youthful fervor fifty years ago and had brought home nothing but regret and pains, and his body as well as his clothes torn by rocks and thorny underbrush. Never before and never since had the people there heard of any man who dared a similar feat. While he was shouting these words at us, our desire increased just because of his warnings; for young people's minds do not give credence to advisers: When the old man saw that he was exerting himself in vain; he went with us a little way forward through the rocks and pointed with his finger to a steep path. He gave us much good advice and repeated it again and again at our backs when we were already at quite a distance. We left with him whatever of our clothes and other belongings might encumber us, intent only on the ascent, and began to climb with merry alacrity. However, as almost always happens, the daring attempt was soon followed by quick fatigue.

Not far from our start we stopped at a rock. From there we went on again, proceeding at a slower pace, to be sure. I in particular made my way up with considerably more modest steps. My brother endeavored to reach the summit by the very ridge of the mountain on a short cut; I, being so much more of a weakling, was bending down toward the valley. When he called me back and showed me the better way, I answered that I hoped to find an easier access on the other side and was not afraid of a longer route on which I might proceed more smoothly. With such an excuse I tried to palliate my laziness, and, when the others had already reached the higher zones, I was still wandering through the valleys, where no more comfortable access was revealed, while the way became longer and longer and the vain fatigue grew heavier and heavier. At last I felt utterly disgusted, began to regret my perplexing error, and decided to attempt the heights with a wholehearted effort. Weary and exhausted, I reached my brother, who had been waiting for me and was refreshed by a good long rest. For a while we went on together at the same pace. However, hardly had we left that rock behind us when I forgot the detour I had made just a short while before and was once more drawing down the lower regions. Again I wandered through the valleys, looking for the longer and easier path and stumbling only into longer difficulties. Thus I indeed put off the disagreeable strain of climbing. But nature is not overcome by man's devices; a corporeal thing cannot reach the heights by descending. What shall I say? My brother laughed at me; I was indignant; this happened to me three times and more within a few hours. So often was I frustrated in my hopes that at last I sat down in a valley. There I leaped in my winged thoughts from things corporeal to what is incorporeal and addressed myself in words like these:

What you have so often experienced today while climbing this mountain happens to you, you must know, and to many others, who are making their way toward the blessed life. This is not easily understood by us men, because the motions of the body lie open, while those of the mind are invisible and hidden. The life we call blessed is located on a high peak. 'A narrow way'[6] they say, leads up to it. Many hilltops intervene, and we must proceed 'from virtue to virtue' with exalted steps.[7] On the highest summit is set the end of all, the goal toward which our pilgrimage is directed. Every man wants to arrive there. However, as Naso says: 'Wanting is not enough; long and you attain it.'[8] You certainly do not merely want; you have a longing, unless you are deceiving yourself in this respect as in so many others. What is it, then, that keeps you back? Evidently nothing but the smoother way that leads through the meanest earthly pleasures and looks easier at first sight. However, having strayed far in error, you must either ascend to the summit of the blessed life under the heavy burden of hard striving, ill deferred; or lie prostrate in your slothfulness in the valleys of your sins. If 'darkness and the shadow of death'[9] find you there—I shudder while I pronounce these ominous words—you must pass the eternal night in incessant torments.

You cannot imagine how much comfort this thought brought my mind and body for what lay still ahead of me. Would that I might achieve with my mind the journey for which I am longing day and night as I achieved with the feet of my body my journey today after overcoming all obstacles. And I wonder whether it ought not to be much easier to accomplish what can be done by means of the agile and immortal mind without any local motion "in the twinkling of the trembling eye"[10] than what is to be performed in the succession of time by the service of the frail body that is doomed to die and under the heavy load of the limbs.

There is a summit, higher than all the others. The people in the woods up there call it "Sonny,"[11] I do not know why. However, I suspect they use the word in a sense opposite to its meaning, as is done sometimes in other cases too. For it really looks like the father of all the surrounding mountains. On its top is a small level stretch. There at last we rested from our fatigue.

And now, my dear father [i.e., his confessor, Donigi – Ed.], since you have heard what sorrows arose in my breast during my climb, listen also to what remains to be told. Devote, I beseech you, one of your hours to reading what I did during one of my days. At first I stood there almost benumbed, overwhelmed by a gale such as I had never felt before and by the unusually open and wide view. I looked around me: clouds were gathering below my feet, and Athos and Olympus grew less incredible, since I saw on a mountain of lesser fame what I had heard and read about them. From there I turned my eyes in the direction of Italy, for which my mind is so fervently yearning. The Alps were frozen stiff and covered with snow—those mountains through which that ferocious enemy of the Roman name once passed, blasting his way through the rocks with vinegar if we may believe tradition.[12] They looked as if they were quite near me, though they are far, far away. I was longing, I must confess, for Italian air, which appeared rather to my mind than my eyes. An incredibly strong desire seized me to see my friend[13] and my native land again. At the same time I rebuked the weakness of a mind not yet grown to manhood, manifest in both these desires, although in both cases an excuse would not lack support from famous champions.

Then another thought took possession of my mind, leading it from the contemplation of space to that of time, and I said to myself: "This day marks the completion of the tenth year since you gave up the studies of your boyhood and left Bologna. O immortal God, O immutable Wisdom! How many and how great were the changes you have had to undergo in your moral habits since then." I will not speak of what is still left undone, for I am not yet in port that I might think in security of the storms I have had to endure. The time will perhaps come when I can review all this in the order in which it happened, using as a prologue that passage of your favorite Augustine: "Let me remember my past mean acts and the carnal corruption of my soul, not that I love them, but that I may love Thee, my God."[14]

Many dubious and troublesome things are still in store for me. What I used to love, I love no longer. But I lie: I love it still, but less passionately. Again have I lied: I love it, but more timidly, more sadly. Now at last I have told the truth; for thus it is: I love, but what I should love not to love, what I should wish to hate. Nevertheless I love it, but against my will, under compulsion and in sorrow and mourning. To my own misfortune I experience in myself now the meaning of that most famous line: "Hate I shall, if I can; if I can't, I shall love though not willing."[15] The third year has not yet elapsed since that perverted and malicious will, which had totally seized me and reigned in the court of my heart without an opponent, began to encounter a rebel offering resistance. A stubborn and still undecided battle has been long raging on the field of my thoughts for the supremacy of one of the two men within me.[16]

Thus I revolved in my thoughts the history of the last decade. Then I dismissed my sorrow at the past and asked myself: "Suppose you succeed in protracting this rapidly fleeing life for another decade, and come as much nearer to virtue, in proportion to the span of time, as you have been freed from your former obstinacy during these last two years as a result of the struggle of the new and the old wills—would you then not be able—perhaps not with certainty but with reasonable hope at least—to meet death in your fortieth year with equal mind and cease to care for that remnant of life which descends into old age?"

These and like considerations rose in my breast again and again, dear father. I was glad of the progress I had made, but I wept over my imperfection and was grieved by the fickleness of all that men do. In this manner I seemed to have somehow forgotten the place I had come to and why, until I was warned to throw off such sorrows, for which another place would be more appropriate. I had better look around and see what I had intended to see in coming here. The time to leave was approaching, they said. The sun was already setting, and the shadow of the mountain was growing longer and longer. Like a man aroused from sleep, I turned back and looked toward the west. The boundary wall between France and Spain, the ridge of the Pyrenees, is not visible from there, though there is no obstacle of which I knew, and nothing but the weakness of the mortal eye is the cause. However, one could see most distinctly the mountains of the province of Lyons to the right and, to the left, the sea near Marseilles as well as the waves that break against Aigues Mortes, although it takes several days to travel to this city. The Rhone River was directly under our eyes.

I admired every detail, now relishing earthly enjoyment, now lifting up my mind to higher spheres after the example of my body, and I thought it fit to look into the volume of Augustine's *Confessions* which I owe to your loving kindness and preserve carefully, keeping it always in my hands, in remembrance of the author as well as the donor.[17] It is a little book of smallest size but full of infinite sweetness. I opened it with the intention of reading whatever might occur to me first: nothing, indeed, but pious and devout sentences could come to hand. I happened to hit upon the tenth book of the work. My brother stood beside me, intently expecting to hear something from Augustine on my mouth. I ask God to be my witness and my brother who was with me: Where I fixed my eyes first, it was written: "And men go to admire the high mountains, the vast floods of the sea, the huge streams of the rivers, the circumference of the ocean, and the revolutions of the stars—and desert themselves."[18] I was stunned, I confess. I bade my brother, who wanted to hear more, not to molest me, and closed the book, angry with myself that I still admired earthly things. Long since I ought to have learned, even from pagan philosophers, that "nothing is admirable besides the mind; compared to its greatness nothing is great."[19]

I was completely satisfied with what I had seen of the mountain, and turned my inner eye toward myself. From this hour nobody heard me say a word until we arrived at the bottom. These words occupied me sufficiently. I could not imagine that this had happened to me by chance: I was convinced that whatever I had read there was said to me and to nobody else. I remembered that Augustine once suspected the same regarding himself, when, while he was reading the Apostolic Epistles, the first passage that occurred to him was, as he himself relates: "Not in banqueting and drunkenness, not in chambering and wantonness, not in strife and envying; but put ye on the Lord Jesus Christ, and make no provision for the flesh to fulfil your lusts."[20] The same had happened before to Anthony: he heard the Gospel where it is written: "If thou wilt be perfect; go and sell that thou hast, and give to the poor, and come and follow me, and thou shalt have treasure in heaven."[21] As his biographer Athanasius says, he applied the Lord's command to himself, just as if the Scripture had been recited, for his sake. And as Anthony, having heard this, sought nothing else, and as Augustine, having read the other passage, proceeded no further, the end of all my reading was the few words I have already set down. Silently I thought over how greatly mortal men lack counsel who, neglecting the noblest part of themselves in empty parading, look without for what can be found within. I admired the nobility of the mind, had it not voluntarily degenerated and strayed from the primordial state of its origin, converting into disgrace what God had given to be its honor.

How often, do you think, did I turn back and look up to the summit of the mountain today while I was walking down? It seemed to me hardly higher than a cubit compared to the height of human contemplation, were the latter not plunged into the filth of earthly sordidness. This too occurred to me at every step: "If you do not regret undergoing so much sweat and hard labor to lift the body a bit nearer to heaven, ought any cross or jail or torture to frighten the mind that is trying to come nearer to God and set its feet upon the swollen summit of insolence and upon the fate of mortal men?" And this too: "How few will ever succeed in not diverging from this path because of fear of hardship or desire for smooth comfort?[22] Too fortunate would be any man who accomplished such a feat—were there ever such anywhere. This would be him of whom I should judge the Poet was thinking when he wrote:

> Happy the man who succeeded in baring the causes of things
> And who trod underfoot all fear, inexorable Fate and
> Greedy Acheron's uproar ...[23]

How intensely ought we to exert our strength to get under foot not a higher spot of earth but the passions which are puffed up by earthly instincts."

Such emotions were rousing a storm in my breast as, without perceiving the roughness of the path, I returned late at night to the little rustic inn from which I had set out before dawn. The moon was shining all night long and offered her friendly service to the wanderers. While the servants were busy preparing our meal, I withdrew quite alone into a remote part of the house to write this letter to you in all haste and on the spur of the moment. I was afraid the intention to write might evaporate; since the rapid change of scene was likely to cause a change of mood if I deferred it.

And thus, most loving father, gather from this letter how eager I am to leave nothing whatever in my heart hidden from your eyes. Not only do I lay my whole life open to you with the utmost care but every single thought of mine. Pray for these thoughts, I beseech you, that they may at last find stability. So long have they been idling about and, finding no firm stand, been uselessly driven through so many matters. May they now turn at, last to the One, the Good, the True, the stably Abiding.

Farewell.

On the twenty-sixth day of April, at Malaucène.

## Questions

1. In your view, does Petrarca's experience count as an experience of awe and sublimity? Does it count as aesthetic (or rather moral or religious)? Explain.

2. What is the role of nature in his "ascent"? What is the source of the pleasure(s)? How are Petrarca's perceptions of space and time altered during his experience?

3. Discuss the relation between the inner ascension and outer ascent (climbing the mountain). To what extent could the mountain be understood as a metaphor? Explain.

4. Is it significant that Petrarca was not alone? Did other people affect this experience? Explain. Comment on the role of texts (the Christian Bible, Augustine's *Confessions*, Latin poetry).

5. Does this strike you as a *modern* piece of writing? Renaissance? Pre-Renaissance? Explain, citing specific examples from the text and commenting on the text's genre (a "letter"), plot, metaphors, or compositional structure.

## Further reading

Burckhardt, Jacob. *The Civilization of the Renaissance in Italy*, trans. S. G. C. Middlemore. New York: Macmillan, 1890.

Cassirer, Ernst, Francis R. Johnson, Paul Oskar Kristeller, Dean P. Lockwood, and Lynn Thorndike. "Some Remarks on the Question of the Originality of the Renaissance." *Journal of the History of Ideas* 4, no. 1 (1943): 49–74.

O'Connell, Michael. "Authority and the Truth of Experience in Petrarch's 'Ascent of Mount Ventoux.'" *Philological Quarterly* 62 (1983): 507–20.

Petrarch. "Familiar Letters." In *Petrarch: The First Modern Scholar and Man of Letters*, ed. and trans. James Harvey Robinson. New York: G.P. Putnam, 1898. [An alternate translation.]

# PART III
## MODERN

# CHAPTER 6
## NICOLAS BOILEAU DESPRÉAUX, FROM "PREFACE TO HIS TRANSLATION OF LONGINUS ON THE SUBLIME" (1674–1701)

Nicolas Boileau Despréaux's translation of Longinus's *Peri Hypsous* in *Traité du Sublime* (Treatise on the Sublime) and its Preface (1674, revised in 1683 and 1701) are justly recognized as playing a crucial role in the modern revival of the sublime. "Aesthetics" evolved and developed as an independent area of study or discipline only in the course of the eighteenth century, and Boileau (1636–1711) was writing decades before aesthetics was established as a field.[1] Thus, although we cannot delve into these details here, it would be helpful to bear in mind the intellectual, literary, and cultural contexts in which the French neo-classicist was writing.

Despite Boileau's important role in—intentionally or not—reinvigorating or even "inventing" the sublime, he did not single-handedly rescue the sublime from oblivion. It is not true that the sublime would have been forgotten had it not been for Boileau's translation and intellectual interest in the topic. As important as the sublime was to the British desire to be freed from the (perceived) confines of classical rule-following, there was interest in the sublime (though not necessarily using that term) in the anglophone world of letters before 1674. In other words, a series of editions and translations, into Latin and English, were produced in England before the publication of Boileau's *Traité du Sublime ou du Merveilleux dans le Discours* in 1674. Britain produced the largest and most varied group of editions, translations, and adaptations in the seventeenth century.[2] For instance, before John Hall's 1652 English translation, Longinus was quoted by George Chapman, the translator of Homer, in his *On Translating and Defending Homer* of 1611, and included in the ideal curriculum devised by Milton for the Christian poet in 1641–44.[3] Moreover, English writers were interested in the sublime of another author: Lucretius. Many English translations of Lucretius's *De rerum natura* were produced, although the majority circulated only in manuscript form.[4]

This is not to take anything away from either Boileau or Longinus, but rather should help us recall the presence and activity of other translators and authors (many of whom, for reasons of space, could not be included in this anthology), who were writing in various intellectual, social, artistic, and political[5] contexts.

In the following Preface, Boileau identifies the author of the text as the third-century rhetorician, Cassius Longinus. Since this identification is disputed (though critics G. M. A. Grube and Malcolm Heath defend it), some of the passages and anecdotes about Cassius Longinus have been omitted. Commenting on his translation, Boileau says that though he has followed "the rules of faithful translation," he has nevertheless allowed himself an "honest liberty." "It has seemed to me," he writes, "that what I was concerned with here was not merely translating Longinus, but offering the public a Treatise on the Sublime, which might be useful." In one of his comments on Longinus, Reflection XII, he offers a definition that identifies at least three sources of the sublime:

> The Sublime is a certain power in discourse able to lift and transport the soul, a power that springs either from the grandeur of the thought and the nobility of the feeling, or from the splendor of the words, or from the harmonious, poignant, and vivid turn of phrase; that is, from one of these things taken separately, or—which makes for the perfect Sublime—from these three things joined together.[6]

## Note on the text

Source: Excerpted from Nicolas Boileau Despréaux. "Preface to his Translation of Longinus on the Sublime," trans. In *Selected Criticism*, edited by Ernest Dilworth, 43–52. Indianapolis: Bobbs-Merrill, 1965.

Footnotes from Dilworth's edition have been included here, with occasional modifications. Textual omissions made by the volume editor are indicated using "[…]".

## "Preface to His Translation of Longinus on the Sublime"

This little treatise, the translation of which I offer to the public, is one piece that escaped the shipwreck suffered by several other works written by Longinus. Yet it has not come down to us complete. For though the volume is not very big, several parts of it are imperfect, and we have lost the Treatise on the Passions, of which the author had made a separate book as a natural sequel to this one. Nevertheless, disfigured as it is, enough of it is left to give us a very high opinion of its author, and to make us feel a real regret at the loss of his other works.

There was no small number of them. Suidas[7] reckons them at nine, of which only the titles remain, and they in a state of some confusion. They were all works of criticism. And certainly we can hardly exaggerate the loss to us of what, to judge by the present work, must have been nine masterpieces of good sense, erudition, and eloquence. I say eloquence, for Longinus was not content, like Aristotle and Hermogenes[8], to give us dry precepts, naked of ornament. He did not wish to fall into the same error as that for which he reproached Caecilius[9]—to have (as he says) written on the sublime in a low style. In speaking of the beauties of elocution,[10] he has made use of all the niceties of elocution. He often does what he teaches; and in speaking of the sublime, he is most sublime himself. Yet he does it in such a fitting way, and with so much art that one could not accuse him at any of these times of slipping out of the didactic style. That is what has given his book the high reputation it has won among scholars, who have all regarded it as one of the most precious relics of antiquity so far as matters of rhetoric are concerned. Casaubon[11] calls it a "Golden Book," wishing to call attention to the weight of this little work, which, despite what it lacks in size, may balance the hugest volumes.

Indeed no man has been more highly esteemed than Longinus, even in his own times.[12] The philosopher Porphyry,[13] who had been his pupil, speaks of him as of a prodigy. If we are to believe him, Longinus's judgment was the pattern of good sense; his decisions in literary matters passed for sovereign decrees; and nothing was good or bad except as Longinus approved or disapproved it. Eunapius, in his lives of the Sophists,[14] goes even further. To express the esteem in which he holds Longinus, he allows himself to be carried away in wild hyperbole; he is unable to make up his mind to speak in reasonable style of such extraordinary merit as that of our author.

[…]

By that we can see that Longinus was not only a clever rhetorician, like Quintilian and Hermogenes, but a philosopher, worthy to be set beside a Socrates and a Cato. There is nothing in his book to contradict what I say. The character of an upright man appears everywhere in it, and there is something about his sentiments that testifies not only to a sublime understanding, but to a mind of rare nobility. Thus, I do not at all regret having devoted some of my midnight labors to bringing to light so excellent a work, one that I may say has, until now, been understood by only a very small number of scholars. Muret[15] was the first to undertake to translate it into Latin, at the solicitation of Manutius;[16] but he did not complete the work, either because its difficulty discouraged him, or because death prevented him. Gabriel de Petra,[17] a good while afterwards, was more valorous, and it is to him that we owe the Latin translation we have. There are indeed two others, but they are so crude and clumsy that to name the authors would be to do them too much honor. And even the version of Petra, which is infinitely better than the others, is not a highly finished piece of work. For apart from the fact that in Latin he often talks Greek, there are several spots in which one can say he has not very well understood his author. Not that I should like to accuse so learned a man of ignorance, or establish my reputation on the ruins of his. I know what it is to be the first to unravel an author; and besides, I admit that his work has been very useful to me, as have the little notes of Langbaine[18] and of M. Lefebvre.[19] But I am very happy to excuse, by the faults of the Latin translation, those which may have escaped me in the French. I have, however, made every effort to render it as exact as possible. To tell the truth, I have had no small difficulty in doing so. It is easy for a Latin translator to manage, even in places he does not understand. He has only to translate the Greek word for word, and to deliver himself of language that people can at least suspect of being intelligible. In fact the reader, often unable to conceive of such a thing, will blame himself rather than the ignorance of the translator. This is not the way with translations into the vernacular. Here everything the reader fails to understand is called gibberish,[20] for which the translator is solely responsible. Everything is laid at his door, including the faults of his author; and in many passages he will have to rectify them, yet without daring to depart from them.

Small as the volume of Longinus is, I should not think I had made a small gift to the public if only I had given it a good translation of the book into our language. To this end I have spared myself neither care nor labor. Let no one expect, however, to find here a timid and precise translation of the words of Longinus. For though I have striven not to depart in a single instance from the rules of faithful translation, I have nevertheless allowed myself an honest liberty, above all in his quoted passages. It has seemed to me that what I was concerned with here was not merely translating Longinus, but offering the public a Treatise on the Sublime, which might be useful. Yet for all that, there will perhaps be some people who not only will disapprove of my translation but will not even spare the original. I am sure there are many who will decline to accept the jurisdiction of Longinus, who will condemn what he approves, and who will praise what he blames. This is the treatment he must expect from most of the judges of our century. These men who are accustomed to the intellectual debauches, to all the excesses, of modern poets; who, admiring only what they do not understand, do not think an author elevated unless they have lost sight of him altogether; these little minds, I say, will doubtless not be particularly struck by the judicious boldness of a Homer, a Plato, and a Demosthenes. They will often go seeking the sublime in the sublime, and perhaps they will ridicule the exclamations Longinus makes over passages that, though most sublime, are yet simple and natural, and rather seize upon the soul than blaze before the eyes. But however assured these gentlemen may be of the spotlessness of their understanding, I beg them to consider that what I offer them here is not the work of an apprentice but the masterpiece of one of the most learned critics of antiquity: and that if they do not see the beauty of these passages, the reason may quite as well be weakness of sight as feebleness of shine. At worst, I counsel them to blame the translation, since it is only too true that I have neither caught, nor been able to attain to, the perfection of these excellent originals. And I declare to them in advance that if there are some defects they can only be mine.

To finish this preface,[21] all that remains is to tell what Longinus means by the *sublime*. For as he wrote on this subject after Caecilius, who had devoted almost the whole of his book to showing what the sublime is, he did not think it incumbent on him to go over again what had already been only too thoroughly discussed by another. It should be understood, then, that by the *sublime*, Longinus does not mean what orators call the sublime style, but the extraordinary and the marvelous which strikes us in terms of language, and causes a work to carry away, ravish, transport us. The sublime style always calls for grand words, but the sublime may be found in a single thought, in a single image, in a single turn of phrase. A thing may be in the sublime style and yet not be sublime; that is, have nothing extraordinary or surprising about it. For example, "The sovereign arbiter of nature with but one word created light." There we have something in the sublime style; it is not sublime, however, for there is nothing very marvelous about it, and nothing one could not easily arrive at. But "God said, Let there be light: and there was light"—this extraordinary feat of expression, which so well shows the obedience of the Creature to the commands of the Creator, is truly sublime, and has in it something divine. By the *sublime* in Longinus, then, we must understand the extraordinary, the surprising, and, as I have translated it, the marvelous in discourse.

I have quoted these words of Genesis because they must fittingly illustrate my idea, and I have made use of them with all the more satisfaction in that they are cited with praise by Longinus himself, who in the darkness of paganism did not fail to recognize what was divine in these words of scripture.[22] But what are we to say of one of the most learned men of our century[23] who, enlightened with his knowledge of the Gospel, has been insensible to the beauty of this passage, and has gone so far—yes—as to assert, in a book he has written in proof of the Christian religion, that Longinus was mistaken in believing that these words were sublime? I have at least the satisfaction that some persons,[24] no less eminent for their piety than for their profound erudition, who have recently given us the translation of the book of Genesis, have not been of the opinion of that learned man, and in their Preface, among several excellent proofs they have brought forward that this book was dictated by the Holy Spirit, have cited the passage of Longinus, to show how strongly convinced Christians should be of a truth so clear—a truth that even a pagan has felt, and by the light of reason alone.

I should add that while we were working on this latest edition[25] of my book, Monsieur Dacier, who a short time ago gave us the *Odes* of Horace in French, passed on to me some very learned little notes he had made on Longinus, in which he sought new meanings unknown to interpreters up to now. I have been guided by some of them, but since I may be mistaken about those in which I do not agree with him, it is best to make my readers the judges. With this in mind I have put them after my Remarks,[26] Monsieur Dacier being not only a man of very great erudition, with a very fine critical sense, but of a courtesy all the more estimable in that it rarely accompanies great learning. He was the pupil of the celebrated Monsieur Lefebvre, father of that learned woman[27] to whom we owe the best translation yet to appear of Anacreon into French, and who is now working so that we may see Aristophanes, Sophocles, and Euripides in the same language.

In all my other editions, I have left this preface as it was when I had it printed for the first time, more than twenty years ago, and added nothing to it. But today, as I was going over the proofs[28] and was about to send them back to the printer, it seemed to me that it would not be a bad idea, in order to make more clear what Longinus understands by this word *sublime,* if I added here to the passage I have quoted from the Bible some other example, taken from a different source. Here is one that came to mind rather happily. It comes from the *Horace* of Monsieur Corneille. In this tragedy, whose first three acts are, in my opinion, the masterpiece of that illustrious writer, a woman who had been present at the combat of the Horatii and the Curiatii but had left a little too soon and had not seen the end of it, comes inopportunely to announce to old Horatius, the father, that two of his sons have been killed, and that the third, finding himself no longer in a position to resist, has fled. Then that old Roman, ruled by love of country, without giving himself the pleasure of weeping over the loss of his two sons, dead so gloriously, grieves only over the shameful flight of the third, who has, he declares, by so cowardly an action brought undying disgrace upon the name of Horatius; and when their sister, who is present, asks him, "What would you have him do against three?" he replies bluntly, "Die." That is very simple language. There is no one, however, who does not feel the heroic grandeur that is contained in that word "Die," which is all the more sublime because of its simplicity and naturalness, and because we are persuaded in this way that it is from the bottom of the heart this old hero speaks, and in the grip of a truly Roman anger. In fact, the thing would have lost a great deal of its force if instead of "Die" he had said, "Follow the example of his two brothers," or "Sacrifice his life for the good and the glory of his country." So it is the very simplicity of what he says that makes its grandeur. These are things Longinus calls sublime, things he would have admired in Corneille, if he had lived in Corneille's time, much more than he would those big words with which, at the beginning of *La Mort de Pompée,* Ptolemy fills his mouth in order to magnify the empty circumstances of a rout he never saw.

## Questions

1. What, if anything, strikes you as different or new in how Boileau writes about the sublime? Explain.

2. Consider Boileau's definition of the sublime in Reflection XII (quoted above, at the end of this chapter's headnote). In what ways does his view differ from that of Longinus? Explain. Is this a case of creative misreading, insightful interpretation, or something else?

3. To what extent is the sublime in Longinus and/or Boileau mostly a matter of rhetoric, style, or oratory? Explain. How might it have been possible for later theorists to extend the sublime to nature?

4. Do you see any seeds of the erosion of classical ideals of beauty in this Preface? Explain.

## Further reading

Brody, Jules. *Boileau and Longinus.* Geneva: Droz, 1958.
Doran, Robert. *The Theory of the Sublime from Longinus to Kant.* Cambridge: Cambridge University Press, 2015.
Gilby, Emma. *Sublime Worlds: Early Modern French Literature.* London: Legenda, 2006.
Hache, Sophie. *La Langue du Ciel: le Sublime en France au XVIIe Siècle.* Paris: H. Champion, 2000.
Litman, Théodore A. *Le Sublime en France, 1660–1714.* Paris: Nizet, 1971.
Porter, James I. *The Sublime in Antiquity.* Cambridge: Cambridge University Press, 2015.

# CHAPTER 7
# JOHN DENNIS, FROM *THE GROUNDS OF CRITICISM IN POETRY* (1704)

The Augustan dramatist and critic John Dennis (1657–1734) gave accounts of "enthusiasm" and the "sublime" toward the end of the seventeenth century. Citing examples from the poetry of Homer, Virgil, Milton, and Tasso, in *Remarks on a Book Entitled Prince Arthur, an Heroic Poem* (1696), Dennis argued that poetical genius is nothing but a "passion," or the ability to evoke and express enthusiasm. "The pride of Soul . . . is the cause of that Elevation, which Longinus so much extolls, and which, he says, is the image of the greatness of the mind." Elevation or "greatness of mind" is a kind of "pride well regulated." Dennis thus defends a self-admiration theory according to which the "transported" soul has a "conscious view of its own excellency."

One of the chapters in Dennis's important but relatively overlooked *The Advancement and Reformation of Modern Poetry* (1701) is called "The Passion is the chief thing in Poetry, and that all Passion is either ordinary Passion, or Enthusiasm." "Enthusiasm" refers to the intense transport of soul. Long before William Wordsworth and other Romantic poets, Dennis thus claimed that passion (the "pathetic") is the distinguishing mark of poetry. He distinguished ordinary from extraordinary passion (enthusiasm). "I call that ordinary Passion, whose cause is clearly comprehended by him who feels it, whether it be Admiration, Terror or Joy; and I call the very same Passions Enthusiasms, when their cause is not clearly comprehended by him who feels them."

Enthusiasm is the "elevation, and vehemence and fury proceeding from the Great and Terrible and Horrible Ideas." When a poet describes the statue of Laocoön, his imagination is "inflamed" and "participates" in the danger, Dennis wrote, thereby prefiguring theories of imagination that would be developed by Anna Aikin and Wordsworth. Dennis, who criticized Longinus for describing the sublime's effects while not telling us what the sublime is, offered his own definition: "The sublime is a great thought expressed with the Enthusiasm that belongs to it. . . . Now I have endeavoured to show what it is in Poetry that works these effects. So that take the Cause and the Effects together, and you have the Sublime." To evoke enthusiasm, Dennis also insisted, the poet needs to have "recourse to Religion" or to religious ideas.

In the following excerpt from his last major critical treatise, *The Grounds of Criticism in Poetry* (1704), Dennis extends and sometimes modifies his account of enthusiasm.

## Note on the text

Source: Excerpted from John Dennis, *The Grounds of Criticism in Poetry*, 15–93. London: Geo. Strahan and Bernard Lintott, 1704.

Some of the spelling, capitalization, format, and style has been reproduced in order to retain a flavor of the original text, though on occasion it has been necessary to modify these and related stylistic matters. The ellipsis in square brackets "[…]" indicates omissions made by the volume editor. Editorial additions or clarifications have been indicated as such using " – Ed."

## CHAP. IV

*What the greater Poetry is, what Enthusiasm is.*

The greater Poetry then, is an Art by which a Poet justly and reasonably excites great Passion, in order to please and instruct, and make Mankind better and happier; so that the first and grand Rule in the greater Poetry is, that a Poet must every where excite great Passion; but in some Branches of the greater Poetry, it is impossible for a Poet every where to excite in a very great degree, that which we vulgarly call Passion: As in the Ode for Example, and in the Narration of the Epic Poem. It follows then that there must be two sorts of Passion. *First*, That which we call Vulgar Passion; and *Secondly*, Enthusiasm.

*First*, Vulgar Passion or that which we commonly call Passion, is that which is moved by the Objects themselves, or by the Ideas in the ordinary Course of Life, I mean that common Society which we find in the World. As for Example, Anger is moved by an Affront that is offered us in our presence, or by the relation of one; Pity by the sight of a mournful Object, or the relation of one; Admiration or Wonder, (the common Passion I mean, for there is an Enthusiastic Admiration, as we shall find anon) by the sight of a strange Object, or the relation of one.

But *Secondly*, Enthusiastic Passion or Enthusiasm, is a Passion which is moved by the Ideas in Contemplation or the Meditation of Things, that belong not to common Life: Most of our Thoughts in Meditation, are naturally attended with some sort and some degree of Passion, and this Passion if it is strong I call Enthusiasm: Now, the Enthusiastic Passions are chiefly Six, Admiration, Terror, Horror, Joy, Sadness, Desire, caused by Ideas occurring to us in Meditation, and producing the same Passions that the Objects of those Ideas would raise in us, if they were set before us in the same Light that those Ideas give us of them. And here I desire the Reader to observe, that Ideas in Meditation, are often very different from what Ideas of the same Objects are, in the course of common Conversation. As for Example, the Sun mentioned in ordinary Conversation, gives the Idea of a round flat shining Body, of about Two Foot Diameter. But the Sun occurring to us in Meditation, gives the Idea of a vast and glorious Body, and the top of all the visible Creation, and the brightest material Image of the Divinity. I leave the Reader therefore to judge, if this Idea must not necessarily be attended with Admiration, and that Admiration I call Enthusiasm. So Thunder mentioned in common Conversation, gives an Idea of a black Cloud, and a great Noise, which makes no great Impression upon us. But the Idea of it occurring in Meditation, sets before us the most forcible, most resistless, and consequently the most dreadful Phaenomenon in Nature: So that this Idea must move a great deal of Terror in us, and 'tis this sort of Terror that I call Enthusiasm. And 'tis this sort of Terror, or Admiration, or Horror, and so of the rest, which expressed in Poetry, make that Spirit, that Passion, and that Fire which so wonderfully please. [...]

We shall at present treat of the Enthusiastic Passions, and how they are to be raised. We have taken notice above that they are to be moved by Ideas occurring in Contemplation, that they are to be moved in a great degree, and yet justly and reasonably. We shall now show that the strongest Enthusiastic Passions, that are justly and reasonably raised, must be raised by religious Ideas, that is, by Ideas which either show the attributes of the Divinity, or relate to his Worship. And this we shall endeavour to prove, 1*st*. by Reason; 2*ly*. by Authority; 3*ly*. by Examples.

*First*, We shall endeavour to prove it by Reason. Since the foresaid Passions are to be moved in a great Degree, and are to be moved by their Ideas, it follows, That to be justly and reasonably moved, they must be moved by great Ideas. And therefore the stronger the Enthusiasm is, the greater must the Ideas be. Now those Ideas are certainly the greatest, which are worthiest to move the greatest and the wisest Men: For there the Enthusiastic Passions in Poetry are truly admirable, when the greater and more violent they are, the more they show the largeness of Soul, and greatness of Capacity of the Writer. For Men are moved for Two Reasons, either because they have weak Minds and Souls, that are capable of being moved by little Objects, and consequently by little and ordinary Ideas; or because they have greatness of Soul and Capacity, to discern and feel the great ones; for the Enthusiastic Passions being caused by the Ideas, it follows, That the more the Soul is capable of receiving Ideas whose Objects are truly great and wonderful, the greater will the Enthusiasm be that is caused by those Ideas; From whence it follows, that the greater the Soul is, and the larger the Capacity, the more will it be moved by religious Ideas; which are not only great and wonderful, but which almost alone are great and wonderful to a great and wise Man; and which never fail to move very strongly, unless it is for want of due Reflection, or want of Capacity in the Subject.

Since therefore the Enthusiasm in the greater Poetry, is to hold Proportion with the Ideas; and those Ideas are certainly the greatest, which are worthiest to move the greatest and the wisest Men; and Divine Ideas, or Ideas which show the Attributes of God, or relate to his Worship, are worthiest to move the greatest and the wisest Men; because such Ideas belong to Objects which are only truly above them, and consequently truly Admirable, Desirable, Joyful, Terrible, &c. it follows, That the greatest and strongest Enthusiasm that can be employed in Poetry, is only justly and reasonably to be derived from Religious Ideas.

But here we desire the Reader's leave to make this Observation, That since Religious and Divine Ideas, or Ideas which show the Attributes, or relate to the Worship of the Divinity, are the worthiest to move the greatest and the wisest Men; and the greater and wiser the Men are, the more they must move and raise them: As for Example, The greater and more comprehensive the Soul is, which reflects upon the Idea of God, the more that Idea must fill that Soul with Admiration; it follows, That as great Passion, only is the adequate Language of the greater Poetry; so the greater Poetry, is only the adequate Language of Religion; and that therefore the greatest Passion, is the Language of that sort of Poetry; because that sort of Poetry is the worthiest Language of Religion.

But *Secondly*, We shall proceed to prove by Authority, That the strongest Enthusiastic Passions in Poetry, are only justly and reasonably to be raised by Religious Ideas: And this we shall show by the Authority of the greatest Critics among the Ancients, *Aristotle, Hermogenes,* and *Longinus.* […]

I could add an infinite number of Examples, if it were not altogether needless, for what has been said, may suffice to show that a Poet who intends: to give that Elevation, and that Gravity to his Poem; which Compose Majesty can fetch his Ideas from no Object so proper as from God. For as great Elevation must be produced by a great Admiration, as every Passion which the Poet excites, ought to be just and Reasonable, and Adapted to its Object, it is impossible that any one, who is not stupid, can seriously contemplate his Maker, but that his Soul must be exalted and lifted up towards its Primitive Objects, and be filled and inspired with the highest Admiration. For 'tis then that the Enthusiasm in Poetry is Wonderful and Divine, when it shows the Excellence of the Authors discernment, and the largeness of his Soul; now all the Ideas of God are such, that the more large and comprehensive the Soul of a Poet is; and the more it is capable of Receiving those Ideas the more is it sure to be raised and filled and lifted to the Skies with wonder; The Spirit or the Passion in Poetry ought to be proportioned to the Ideas, and the Ideas to the Object, and when it is not so it is utterly false. And therefore whenever in Poetry there is a great Spirit which is derived from Ideas, whose Objects are unworthy to move the Soul of a great and a wise Man, there that Spirit is either false or at least has nothing sublimely admirable in it. But nothing but God, and what relates to God, is worthy to move the Soul of a great and a wise Man. But let us proceed to consider the glorious works of the Creator, which next to Himself are worthy to move with Admiration, all who are worthy to be called wise, because these when they are reflected upon, by the Great and the Wise, never fail to declare his Eternal Power and Godhead. Our Religion tells us that the first, the Greatest, and most Glorious of His works are the Angels, who whether we consider their Power, their Swiftness, their Science, or their Sanctity, are fit Objects of our Admiration and Consequently of Lofty and Elevated Poetry. Let us see then how *Tasso* describes the Angel *Gabriel* and his descent, in the first Canto of the *Jerusalem.* […]

The next Ideas [after angels and immaterial substances – Ed.] that are most proper to produce the Enthusiasm of Admiration, are the great Phaenomena of the Material World; because they too lead the Soul to its Maker, and show, as the Apostle says, his Eternal Power and Godhead: As the Heavens and Heavenly Bodies, the Sun, the Moon, the Stars, and the immensity of the Universe, and the Motions of the Heaven and Earth.

[…]

I could here bring Examples of the same kind of Spirit, derived in due Proportion from Ideas of Sublunary Things, as of the Four Elements Water, Earth, Air, Fire, Winds and Meteors of all sorts, Seas, Rivers, Mountains, but I am afraid of running into Length, and heaping too many Citations one upon another. Besides it will be very convenient to make two or three Remarks here.

*First*, That the Wonders of the Universe, afford the more admirable Ideas and a more admirable Spirit, the more they show the attributes of the Creator or relate to his Worship. *Secondly*, That Natural Philosophy is absolutely necessary to a Poet, not only that he may adorn his Poem, with the useful knowledge it affords, but because the more he knows the immense Phaenomena of the Universe, the more he will be sure to admire them. For the more we know of Things that are never to be comprehended by us, the more that knowledge must make them appear wonderful. The *Third* Remark that I shall make is this, That they to whom Nature has given that happy Elevation of Thought, which alone can make a great Poet, will often be directed by that tendency to greatness, which they have within them to Ideas, from which they may derive a lofty Spirit […].

[…] Let us now pass to the next Enthusiastic Passion which is Terror; than which if it is rightly managed, none is more capable of giving a great Spirit to Poetry. This Passion scarce ever goes by itself, but is always more or less complicated with Admiration. For every thing that is Terrible is great at least to him to whom it is Terrible. 'Tis now our business to show two Things. First, what this Enthusiastic Terror is; and Secondly, from what Ideas it is chiefly to be derived.

First let us show what this sort of Enthusiasm is, and in order to do that, let us show as briefly as we can, what the Common Passion is which we call Terror. Fear then, or Terror, is a Disturbance of Mind proceeding from the apprehension of an approaching evil, Threatening Destruction or very great trouble either to us or ours. And when the disturbance comes suddenly with surprise, let us call it Terror; when gradually, Fear. Things then that are powerful, and likely to hurt, are the causes of Common Terror, and the more they are powerful and likely to hurt, the more they become the causes of Terror, which Terror, the greater it is, the more it is joined with wonder, and the nearer it comes to astonishment. Thus we have shown what Objects of the Mind are the causes of Common Terror, and the Ideas of those Objects are the causes of Enthusiastic Terror.

Let us now show from what Ideas this Enthusiastic Terror is chiefly to be derived. The greatest Enthusiastic Terror then must needs be derived from Religious Ideas, for since the more their Objects are Powerful, and likely to hurt, the greater Terror their Ideas produce: What can produce a greater Terror than the Idea of an Angry God? Which puts me in mind of that admirable Passage of *Homer*, about the Fight of the Gods, in the Twentieth of the Iliads, cited by *Longinus* in his Chapter of the Loftiness of the Conceptions. […]

To this [i.e., why Longinus did not plainly define the sublime. – Ed.] I answer, that tho' *Longinus* did by long Study, and habitude know the Sublime when he saw it, as well as any Man, yet he had not so clear a knowledge of the Nature of it as to explain it clearly to others. For if he had done that, as the Objector says, he would have defined it, but he has been so far from defining it, that in one place he has given an account of it that is contrary to the true nature of it. For he tells us in that Chapter which treats of the Fountains of Sublimity, that Loftiness is often without any Passion at all. Which is contrary to the true nature of it. The sublime is indeed often without Common Passion, as ordinary Passion is often without that. But then it is never without Enthusiastic Passion. For the Sublime is nothing else but a great Thought, or Great Thoughts moving the Soul from its Ordinary Situation by the Enthusiasm which naturally attends them. Now *Longinus* had a notion of Enthusiastic Passion; for he establishes it in that very Chapter for the second Source of Sublimity.

Now *Longinus* by affirming that the Sublime may be without not only that, but ordinary Passion, says a thing that is not only contrary to the true Nature of it, but contradictory of Himself. For he tells us in the beginning of the Treatise that the Sublime does not so properly persuade us, as it Ravishes and Transports us, and produces in us a certain Admiration mingled with astonishment and with surprise, which is quite another thing than the barely Pleasing or the barely persuading; that it gives a noble Vigour to a Discourse, an invincible force which commits a pleasing Rape upon the very Soul of the Reader; that whenever it breaks out where it ought to do, like the Artillery of *Jove*, it Thunders blazes and strikes at once, and shows all the united force of a Writer. Now I leave the Reader to Judge, whether *Longinus* has not been saying here all along that Sublimity is never without Passion. [...]

Thus the definition which we have laid down, being according to *Longinus* his own Doctrine, the true definition of the Sublime, and showing clearly the thing which he has not done, nor given any definition at all of it, it seems plain to me, that he had no clear and distinct Idea of it; and consequently Religion might be the thing from which it is chiefly to be derived and he but obscurely know it; but that Religion is that thing from which the Sublime is chiefly to be derived, let us show by the Marks which he has given of the latter; which will further strengthen our Definition. First, says he, that which is truly sublime has this peculiar to it, that it exalts the Soul and makes it conceive a greater Idea of itself; filling it with Joy, and with a certain noble Pride, as if [it – Ed.] itself had produced what it but barely Reads.

Now here it is plain, that the highest Ideas must most exalt the Soul, but Religious Ideas are the highest.

The more the Soul is moved by the greatest Ideas, the more it conceives them, but the more it conceives of the greatest Ideas, the greater Opinion it must have of its own Capacity. By consequence the more it is moved by the Wonders of Religion the more it values itself upon its own Excellences. Again, The more the Soul sees its Excellence the more it Rejoices. [...]

But to return to Terror, we may plainly see by the foregoing Precepts and Examples of *Longinus*, that this Enthusiastic Terror contributes extremely to the Sublime, and Secondly that it is most produced by Religious Ideas.

First, Ideas producing Terror contribute extremely to the Sublime. All the Examples that *Longinus* brings of the loftiness of the Thought, consist of terrible Ideas. And they are Principally such Ideas that work the effects, which he takes notice of, in the beginning of his Treatise, *viz.* that Ravish and Transport the Reader, and produce a certain Admiration mingled with Astonishment and with Surprise. For the Ideas which produce Terror are necessarily accompanied with Admiration, because every thing that is terrible is great to Him to whom it is Terrible; and with Surprise without which Terror cannot subsist; and with Astonishment, because every thing which is very Terrible is Wonderful and Astonishing; and as Terror is perhaps the violentest of all the Passions, it consequently makes an impression which we cannot resist, and which is hardly to be defaced, and no Passion is attended with greater Joy than Enthusiastic Terror; which proceeds from our reflecting that we are out of Danger at the very time that we see it before us. And as Terror is one of the violentest of all Passions if it is very great, and the hardest to be resisted, nothing gives more force, nor more vehemence to a Discourse. But Secondly, it is plain from the same *Longinus*, that this Enthusiastic Terror is chiefly to be derived from Religious Ideas. For all the Examples which he has brought of the Sublime, in his Chapter of the Sublimity of the Thoughts consists of most Terrible and most Religious Ideas, and at the same time every Man's Reason will inform him, that every thing that is Terrible in Religion is the most Terrible thing in the World.

But that we may set this in a clearer Light, let us lay before the Reader the several Ideas which are capable of producing this enthusiastic Terror, which seem to me to be those which follow, *viz.* Gods, Daemons, Hell, Spirits and Souls of Men, Miracles, Prodigies, Enchantments, Witchcrafts, Thunder, Tempests, raging Seas, Inundations, Torrents, Earthquakes, Volcanoes, Monsters, Serpents, Lions, Tigers, Fire, War, Pestilence, Famine, &c.

Now of all these Ideas none are so terrible as those which show the Wrath and Vengeance of an Angry God. For nothing is so wonderful in its effects, and consequently the Images or Ideas of those effects must carry a great deal of Terror with them, which we may see was *Longinus* his Opinion by the Examples which he brings in his Chapter of the Sublimity of the Thoughts. Now of things which are terrible those are the most terrible which are the most wonderful, because that seeing them both threatening and powerful, and not being able to fathom the greatness and extent of their Power, we know not how far and how soon they may hurt us. [...]

But here it will be convenient to Answer an Objection. For how come some of the forementioned Ideas which seem to have but little to do with Religion, [seem – Ed.] to be Terrible to great and to wise Men, as it is plain that such, when they read the Descriptions of them in *Homer* and *Virgil*, are terrified?

To which we Answer, that the care which Nature has inrooted in all of their own Preservation, is the Cause that Men are unavoidably terrified, with any thing that threatens approaching evil. 'Tis now our business to show how the Ideas of Serpents, Lions, Tigers, &c. were made by the art of those great Poets, to be terrible to their Readers at the same time that we are secure from their Objects.

'Tis very plain that it is the Apprehension of Danger which causes that emotion in us which we call Terror, and it signifies nothing at all to the purpose whether the Danger is real or imaginary; and 'tis as plain too, that the Soul never takes the Alarm from any thing so soon as it does from the Senses, especially those two noble ones of the Eye and the Ear, by reason of the strict affinity which they have with the Imagination; and the Evil always seems to be very near, when those two Senses give notice of it; and the nearer the Evil is the greater still is the Terror. But now let us see how those two Poets, did by Virtue of their Ideas, bring even absent, Terrible Objects, within the reach of those two noble Senses. First then to bring an absent Terrible Object before our Sight, they drew an Image or Picture of it; but to draw an Image or Picture of a Terrible Object, so as to surprise and astonish the Soul by the Eye, they never failed to draw it in violent Action or Motion; and in Order to that they made choice of Words and Numbers, which might best express the violence of that Action or Motion. For an absent Object can never be set before the Eye in a true Light, unless it is shown in violent Action or Motion. Because unless it is shown so, the Soul has leisure to reflect upon the Deceit. But violent Motion can never be conceived without a violent agitation of Spirit, and that sudden agitation surprises the Soul and gives it less time to Reflect; and at the same time causes the Impressions that the Objects make to be so Deep, and their traces to be so profound, that it makes them in a manner as present to us as if they were really before us. For the Spirits being set in a violent emotion, and the Imagination being fired by that agitation; and the Brain being deeply penetrated by those Impressions, the very Objects themselves are set as it were before us, and consequently we are sensible of the same Passion that we should feel from the things themselves. For the warmer the Imagination is, the less able we are to Reflect, and consequently the things are the more present to us of which we draw the Images; and therefore when the Imagination is so inflamed as to render the Soul utterly incapable of reflecting there is no difference between the Images and the things themselves; as we may see for example by Men in Raging Fevers. But those two great Poets [Homer, Virgil – Ed.] were not satisfied with setting absent Objects before our Eyes, by showing them in violent motion; but if their motion occasioned any Extraordinary Sounds that were terrifying; they so contrived their Numbers and Expressions, as that they might be sure to ring those sounds in the very Ears of their Readers. [...]

## Questions

1. How does Dennis's understanding of the causes, effects, and definition of the sublime differ from that of Longinus? How does Dennis characterize the relation between enthusiasm and the sublime?

2. Assess Dennis's argument for the claim that enthusiasm requires recourse to religion, "religious ideas," above all, the idea of God. Do you have to be "religious" to feel enthusiastic terror? Explain.

3. Dennis discusses the created "works" of God as potential elicitors of enthusiasm. In what ways is this like (or unlike) developments toward the natural or environmental sublime?

4. In your view, what is the conceptual relation between terror (fear) and the sublime?

## Further reading

Albrecht, William Price. *The Sublime Pleasures of Tragedy: A Study of Critical Theory from Dennis to Keats*. Lawrence: The University Press of Kansas, 1975.

Doran, Robert. *The Theory of the Sublime from Longinus to Kant*. Cambridge: Cambridge University Press, 2015.

Hooker, Edward Niles, ed. *The Critical Works of John Dennis*, 2 vols. Baltimore: The Johns Hopkins Press, 1939.

Morris, David Brown. *The Religious Sublime*. Lexington: University Press of Kentucky, 1972.

Paul, H. G. *John Dennis; His Life and Criticism*. New York: AMS Press, 1966.

Wood, Theodore E. B. *The Word 'Sublime' and Its Context, 1650–1760*, 169–88. The Hague: Mouton, 1972.

# CHAPTER 8
# GIAMBATTISTA VICO, "ON THE HEROIC MIND" (1732)

In "On the Heroic Mind," Giambattista (or Giovanni Battista) Vico (1668–1744), a Neapolitan professor of rhetoric and eloquence, addresses university students at the Royal Academy of Naples in 1732. Vico understands university education in a broad, pluralistic, and humanistic sense, and holds that it benefits the individual and society alike. He emphasizes the importance of studying languages and poetry, in addition to the social and natural sciences. What is the connection to the sublime? A "hero" is someone who "seeks the sublime." Such heroism can be achieved through education, especially one that aims at "Almighty God," who, Vico asserts, is sublime.

Vico implies that there is sublimity in nature ("this whole frame of marvels spread out before us"), and he considers "the sublime themes of nature." Nevertheless, he hardly offers a version of the natural or environmental sublime. The passage continues, "nothing exceeds man in greatness and nothing is of more worth than man's well-being."

## Note on the text

Source: Reprinted from Giambattista Vico, "On the Heroic Mind." *Social Research: An International Quarterly* 43 (4) (Winter 1976): 886–903. Translated by Elizabeth Sewell and Anthony C. Sirignano. Baltimore, MD: John Hopkins University Press.

Editorial insertions are from this translation, unless otherwise noted using " – Ed." The footnotes are taken from this translation, with occasional modifications. Spelling, style, and format have been reproduced, again with some modifications.

## *Translators' note*

We have used as our principal text G.B. *Vico: Opere,* edited by Fausto Nicolini, vol. 7, *Scritti Vari e Pagine Sparse* in Scrittori d'Italia, 174 (Bari, 1940), 3–20, with the emendations included in the Appendix to vol. 8 in the same series, Scrittori d'Italia, 183 (1941), 265–66: hereafter, *Nicolini.* A second text available to us for comparison was *Giambattista Vico: Opere,* edited by Francesco Saverio Pomodoro, vol. 1 (Naples: Stamperia de' classici latini, 1858), 260–69: hereafter, *Pomodoro.* We are indebted to Nicolini not merely for the above but for his translation into Italian of "De mente heroica" in *Giambattista Vico: Opere,* edited by Fausto Nicolini, in *La Letteratura Italiana: Storia e Testi,* vol. 43 (Milan-Naples, 1953), 909–26.

### "On the Heroic Mind: An Oration Given at the Royal Academy of Naples"

## October 20, 1732

To His Excellency, Count Aloys Thomas von Harrach, Viceroy of the Kingdom of Naples, a man most vigilant, virtuous and honorable, who instructed four nobly born sons in the illustrious arts of peace and war through the example of his ancestors and above all his own, this oration, which guides by precept the young, desirous of learning, to the acquisition of heroic wisdom, is dedicated by the Royal Academy of Naples in witness of its obedience and its gratitude for the many and great services he bestowed upon it.

My young listeners, you of such hopeful promise: for some considerable time now, this royal University has witnessed a lapse in that most profitable custom by which the academic year was annually inaugurated by a solemn oration delivered to you students with all due formality. And the appointed day having come round once more, our recently invested honorable Prefect of Studies, a man of very great learning in all fields and lavish in regard to the fullest possible provision of educational advantages for you, has seen fit to reinstate the old custom. As for myself—I who have carried out the duties of Professor of Eloquence in this very place for over thirty-three years and am almost wasted away by the rigors of intellectual work—I take it to be my task to bring before you a theme which is wholly new. That theme shall not be youthfully tricked out with lovelocks of apothegms and curled ringlets of speech; no, it must be replete to the fullest possible extent with the weight and gravity inherent in its own subject matter, with the greatest fruitfulness for yourselves. This theme by its own nature overflows with greatness, with splendor, with sublimity, and in speaking of it,

> I'd rather, I,
> Be like a whetstone, that an edge can put
> On steel, though itself be dull and cannot cut…[1]

Since you are roused by such promises and are ready to listen with attentive welcome to something which concerns yourselves, I will, in the very first exordium of this oration, declare it to you.

Noble students, you are to bend your best efforts toward your studies, not surely with such an end in view as the gaining of riches, in which the low money-grubbing crowd would easily beat you out: nor for high office and influence, in which would be far outdone by the military and by courtiers; and still less for that which leads philosophers on, namely, the love of learning itself, enthralled by which almost all of them pass their whole lives withdrawn from the public light in order to get the full enjoyment, from the tranquil working of their minds and nothing else. Something far more exalted than this is expected of you. "Well, but what is it?" one of you may say, marveling; "Are you asking of us something surpassing the human condition itself?" I do indeed so reckon it; but although surpassing, yet befitting that nature of yours.

I repeat: it is expected of you that you exert yourselves in your studies in order to manifest the heroic mind you possess and to lay foundations of learning and wisdom for the blessedness of the human race; by this course of action, not only will riches and wealth, even while you disdain them, accrue to you, but also honor and power will come looking for you, though you care for none of these things. When I speak of your manifesting the heroic mind through studies, I am not choosing those words lightly. If heroes are those who, as poets say or as they invent, were wont to boast of their divine lineage from "all-judging Jove," this much is certain: the human mind, independent of any fiction and fables, does have a divine origin which needs only schooling and breadth of knowledge to unfurl itself. So you see. I do ask of you things greatly surpassing the human: the near-divine nature of your minds—that is what I am challenging you to reveal.

"Hero" is defined by philosophers as one who seeks ever the sublime. Sublimity is, according to these same philosophers, the following, of the utmost greatness and worth: first, above nature, God Himself; next, within nature, this whole frame of marvels spread out before us, in which nothing exceeds man in greatness and nothing is of more worth than man's well-being, to which single goal each and every single hero presses on, in singleness of heart. By the report of just such good deeds spread far and wide amongst humankind—that voice crying abroad through all nations and people which Cicero elegantly calls by the name of "glory"—the hero generates for himself an immortal name. Therefore from the very start you must direct your studies toward

Almighty God; and next, for the sake of His glory Who commands us to care for the whole human race, toward the well-being of all mankind. To it then, my young auditors, born in your turn for the greatest and best! Heroic in mind, turn your heart and will, brimming over with God, to the pursuit of your studies, and then, purged and purified of all earthly desires, put to the test, by the giant strides you will make, that divine truth: "The fear of the Lord is the beginning of wisdom."

For the mind, which takes pleasure in the divine, the infinite, the eternal, cannot *not* tackle the sublime, not attempt the monumental, not accomplish the outstanding. This is in no way a rash point of view: witness men of piety (I think of Cardinal Caesar Baronius and many others) who, when they turned their minds to scholarship, burned the midnight oil to such good purpose, a certain divine grace aiding, that they produced works one may marvel at, for their solidity as much as for their originality and learning.

While with heroic mind you are making your bow to wisdom on this first threshold, survey with swelling hearts the scene exhibited here before your eyes. Seated on your right, these reverend senior members of the university, marked out by their titles and insignia of honor, represent that public education which His Imperial Majesty Charles VI of Austria, King of the Spains, has provided in this place for your instruction. Just as in the school of courage he has prepared for himself in field and battle line military leaders of utmost valor for the protection of the Holy Roman Empire and its appanages [granted lands and estates – Ed.], so too in the school of wisdom may he produce the like from among you in this sheltered spot to bless those same dominions. To this he invites you, both by the numerous privileges in law accorded you, and by the outstanding honors bestowed principally of your account upon the official ranks here before you—you the co-equal hope of the commonwealth, the second especial preoccupation of our supreme ruler. His imperial administrator, His Excellency Count Aloys Thomas von Harrach, who with supreme courage and wisdom auspiciously presides as Viceroy over this Kingdom of Naples, so zealously fosters this our seat of learning, and befriends it so generously that in the space of the three years (before this it would have taken a century) he has nominated to the Emperor no less than five professors from this assembly for investiture as royal bishops. Consider, and again I say consider, what models of learning they must be. Each and every one of them has stored up in his memory by the command of each over his own discipline the principal writers in every field of learning, so as to have them ready to hand for your benefit. Furthermore, where they see this to be needful and profitable, they present them to you with explanations, corrections, and commentary of their own. Each one had to pass the test of giving a formal lecture to the members of his own faculty which had to be prepared within very narrow limits of time, and only after that examination were they elected to this their present rank of professor. What honor, what reverence you ought to pay them, you can realize by this fact: look at the Ministers of State, so many and so noble, seated on their left. By occupying that exalted station they acknowledge that they have to thank this university for the wisdom by virtue of which they have been called to the highest honors in the state. Let such all-sufficing proofs of achievement here before you conjure up a largeness of spirit in yourselves. Show forth that loveliest mark of magnanimity: the being docile in the best sense, biddable, grateful to these truly erudite professors of yours as they chasten you, instruct you, set you to rights. Their desire is that your estate be a shining ornament to this city of ours, resplendent not only in Italy but, one may say, throughout Europe. From patriotism, then, they devote themselves to you so that they may indicate you into every form of learning, the general of encyclopedic, the esoteric or acroamatic. This in very truth is the promise contained in the phrase, "a university education."

It is absolutely clear that from these your preceptors you are to master all the branches of knowledge. Crippled and tottering—such is the education of those who throw all their weight into the study of just one particular and specialized discipline. The various disciplines are of the same nature as the virtues. Socrates used to maintain in his teachings that the virtues and the disciplines were one and the same, and totally denied that any one of them was ever genuine unless all the others were present also. So? A look of trouble on your faces?

By what I have just said have I dashed your spirits? If so, you are doing a grave injustice to the divine wellsprings of your minds. Do not breed within you any indolent wishes about learning dropping down from heaven into your bosoms while you slumber. Stir yourselves up with a productive desire for wisdom. By your unceasing and undaunted labors, make trial of what you can do, put to the test how much you are capable of. Ply your gifts and energies in all possible directions. Stir your minds up, enkindle the divinity that fills you. If you take this course of action (poets come to it by nature, as it happens) you too will engender God-inspired marvels of your own, and surprise yourselves in the doing of it. What I am saying is weightily and clearly confirmed by Italian literati who in a forceful phrase, pertinent to our present subject of discussion, call a university a *Sapientia*.

*Sapientia*… Wisdom… [translators' ellipses – Ed.] Plato defines it as purge, curative, completion of the inner man. The man within, however, consists of both mind and soul, each part depraved through and through by original sin; the mind, created for truth, seething with errors and false opinions, the soul, born for virtue, racked by vices and pernicious desires. For this very reason, your university education has the following purpose and it is right that you should keep it fully in view: you have come together here, ailing as you are in mind and soul, for the treatment, the healing, the perfecting of your better nature. I do not want any idle scoffer making silly faces behind his hand at what I am saying. In confirmation of this I can adduce all those learned authors who, by a term consciously transposed from bodies to minds, call universities by the name of "public gymnasia." Hospitals as such were unknown to the ancients, and just as the powers of the body were reinvigorated, strengthened, and multiplied by gymnastics carried on in the public baths, so too today the powers of the mind in universities. Once you have thought this over, you will perceive the immense benefit arising from your studies, namely, that you pay close attention to your university work in order that you may resolve not just to appear learned but truly to be so, because you will wish to be healed, restored, made perfect by wisdom. In all other gifts stemming from nature or good fortune, men are content with the semblance of their desires. Only in this one regard, namely, health, all cannot help desiring the very thing itself.

Once you have this goal in view—it is the true goal of wisdom—there follows a demand: those other far lesser things such as wealth and public renown must fall away from your minds. Even if you lay up riches and accumulate honors, you will not cease to push on—on and on—as you grow in learning. All dishonesty will be far removed from your minds, all puffery and play-acting, since your desire is set on true erudition, not on the mere semblance of it. Untouched by any feeling of jealousy directed at yourselves, that feeling which consumes and tortures those avid of gain, ambitious of high place. What in their case is envy will amongst you turn into honorable rivalry. Since this goal we spoke of is a blessing open to everyone, beyond envy as are all divine things because they are infinite, you will yearn for your own ὁμοιοθειότητα—that "image and likeness of god" in mind and equally in soul, immune from any contagious of the flesh.

To proceed: those who are content with an inadequate stock of learning make such accusations as "inappropriate" or "off the mark" against the whole system of teaching in this university, where not only do individuals teach different things (or if they teach the same things, they do so by different proofs and different methods) but also they seem to teach in flat contradiction to one another. It is an awkward system, we admit; the best and most desirable plan should be uniform throughout. But such an apparently good method is nullified by three noble requirements essential to education: new discoveries, new truths revealed, new efforts better focused. Consequently, our method, which they find fault with, proves to be the best and this for the three related advantages, by no means negligible ones, it brings with it:

First, no one of you will have to swear an oath of fealty to any professor, as happens so often in the sectarianisms of the schools.

Next, you will not get totally absorbed, as can happen in private institutions, by any single period of human knowledge, the study of which is so transient that it no sooner arises than collapses, no sooner comes to the full than it is already obsolete: whereas learned laboring, which produces immortal works, has its being in eternity.

Lastly—and this touches our discussion most nearly—you will fully realize what each discipline imparts to the others (for each has some good in it) and what all contribute to that sum total itself, wisdom in its entirety, toward the laying-hold of the insistence and seriousness I can muster.

For this reason above all, attend the lectures of professors in all disciplines, with that aim in view which we have already set down: that their teachings may cure, heal, perfect all your faculties both of mind and soul. Thus metaphysics will free the intellect from the prison of the senses; logic will free the reasoning power from false opinions; ethics the will from corrupt desires. Rhetoric exists to ensure that the tongue does not betray nor fail the mind, nor the mind its theme; poetics to calm the uncontrolled turbulence of the imagination; geometry to hold in check innate errors; physics, in truth, to rouse you from the blank amazement with which nature and her marvels has transfixed you.

And still we are not at the greatest degree of good with which wisdom is dowered. With high expectation set before yourselves far more glorious things.

By the study of the languages which our Christian religion cultivates as her own, hold converse with the best-known nations of universal history: with the Hebrews in the most ancient tongue of all; with the Greeks, in the most elegant; with the Romans, in the most majestic. Seeing that languages are the natural vehicle, so to speak, of customs, through the Oriental languages which are necessary for the comprehension of the sacred tongue—Chaldean above all—let the Assyrians inspire you with magnificence in Babylon, greatest city of all; the Greeks with Attic elegance of life at Athens; the Romans with loftiness of spirit at Rome. Be present in mind, by your reading of histories, in the greatest empires which ever flourished on the face of the earth. In order to strengthen your prudence as citizens by examples, ponder the origins of peoples and races, how they grow, reach their highest point, fall away, and perish; how outrageous Fortune in her arrogance lords it over human affairs, and how, beyond Fortune, Wisdom maintains her steadfast and unshakable kingdom. But, by heaven, for a delight inexpressible, since most proper to man's nature with its strong bent toward unity, read the poets! Observe their cast of characters, people from all walks of life, in the ethical, the domestic, the political realm, sharply delineated according to the pure ideal type, and by that very fact most real. Compared with these ideal types, men in everyday life will seem rather to be the unreal characters, for where men are not consistent their lives do not cohere. So consider, with a certain godlike mind, human nature as portrayed in the fables of great poets: even in its wickedness it is the most beautiful, because always consistent, always true to itself, harmonious in all its parts, even as the aberrant prodigies and malignant plagues of nature are perceived by Almighty God as good and beautiful in the eternal order of His Providence. Once you have read great poets and thrilled with delight, read now, to be caught up in an admiration every whit as great, the sublime orators, whose art is marvelous in its adaptation to our flawed human nature: appealing to the passions originating in the body, they twist men's minds around, no matter how settled, into wishing the direct opposite. In this, moreover, Almighty God excels and He alone, but by His own vastly different ways of triumphant grace, Who draws the minds of men to Himself by heavenly delight, no matter how pinned down they are by earthly passions.

From these matters we may proceed to the sublime themes of nature. With geography as guide on that long march, make the circle of the whole range of lands and seas with the sun. Trace out, with astronomy's observations, the swooping tracks of the comets, those sightless couriers of the air. Let cosmography set you down at that spot where "the final ramparts of the universe go up in flames."[2] Further yet, let metaphysics, outpassing nature, lead you forth into those blessed and infinite fields of eternity. Once there, insofar as this is permitted to our finite minds, behold among the Divine Ideas those countless forms already curated and those which could come to creation if (as is actually not the case) this world would endure forever.

Make your way in this fashion through all three worlds, of things human, things natural, things eternal, and by learning and scholarship cultivate the godhead, so to speak, inherent in your minds. For in truth these sublime cogitations assuredly enjoin a hope that you will fashion for yourselves souls so lofty and upstanding that you will hold as infinitely beneath you all delights of the senses, all riches and wealth, positions of power and honor, and spurn them all.

Concerning the choice of authors, the wise administrators of this royal Academy have amply provided for your welfare in their program. According to that maxim of Quintilian's: "When it comes to teaching, the best authors ought to be singled out," you may, by attending the lectures dealing with these, succeed in acquiring the whole body of knowledge. I cite as example, in theology, the sacred books of the Old and New Testament, of which the Catholic Church offers the authoritative and correct interpretation. Her unbroken tradition, going back all the way to the time of the Apostles, has with solemn fidelity preserved that text in enduring archives of ecclesiastical history. Turning to jurisprudence: the *Corpus juris* of Justinian, most trustworthy witness of Roman antiquities, storehouse of Latin eloquence, most carefully stocked and preserved, the inviolable treasury of human laws. In medicine: Hippocrates above all, who earned the undying praise: "Never deceiving, by none deceived." In philosophy: Aristotle for the main, and where he is found wanting, other philosophers for outstanding reputation. And in the rest of the disciplines, other authors of equally distinguished rank.

To further your reading of these authors, the most exalted in all recorded history, the eminently learned professors here will instruct you by their commentaries, pointing out with their finger, as it were, the reasons why those authors excelled, each in his own branch of learning. This type of commentary will beguile you, from the beginning of your studies, into thumbing and poring over the best authors day and night. Further, it will stimulate you to shape in your minds more perfectly that Idea to which in all fields of knowledge men of genius are conformed. Hence, from being examples for you to follow, they will become exemplifications of that Idea. Thus, in going back to their original archetypes, you could very well rival these men of genius and even outstrip them. In this way and in this alone are the arts and sciences refined, increased, brought to completion. And there is no excuse for those who wear out their entire scholarly careers in reading second-rate authors, not to mention those even worse—authors scarcely recommended to them in this university's program of studies.

All the while that you are under instruction, concentrate solely on collating everything you learn so that the whole may hang together and all be in accord within any one discipline. For this task your guide will be the very nature of the human mind which rejoices in the highest degree in that which forms a unity, comes together, falls into its proper place; as witness the Latin, which seems to have derived *scientia*—that pregnant noun—from the same root that *scitus* comes from, meaning the same thing as "beautiful." It follows that just as beauty is the due proportion of the members, first each to each and secondly as a whole, in any outstandingly lovely body, so the beauty of the human mind, and once men have been captivated by this, they assuredly do not heed bodily forms, how radiant soever. So far are they from being disturbed by such things!

Once that habit of comparison has been established, you will acquire the capacity to compare the sciences themselves each with each, which go to make up, as celestial members, the divine body, so to speak, of wisdom as a whole. According to Pythagoras, this is what human reason is: the bringing together and comparison of intellectual entities, a process which he either explained or obfuscated by using numbers as an example of it. In this way you will bring all of human reason to its perfection, after the likeness of a most pure and clear-shining light, its rays directed wherever you turn the mind's eye, so that what they call "the universe of knowledge" and all its parts are seen to come together, answer one another, and stand as one, in any single thought you may be having, and, as it were, in any one point. And there you have it: the crowning exemplar of the man of unalloyed wisdom!

To what particular discipline above all others will you apply yourselves (for in order to be useful to your country you must pursue one in particular)? Your innate ability will teach you what that discipline is by the delight you feel in learning it as over against others. Nature, which Almighty God gives you as your guardian for this purpose, uses that yardstick so that you may recognize where your willing and ready Minerva waits. Although nature is the safest guide, I who now urge you on to the greatest and best do not consider that to be the most illuminating way. For often a man has capacities for the highest and best hidden within him and so deep asleep as to be almost completely or indeed completely unperceived by their possessor. Cimon the Athenian (you all know the story), a dull inert man, was desperately in love with a young girl; when she announced in jest—as if this would be an impossibility for him—that she would love him if he became an officer in the army, the man enlisted, and ended up a very famous general in the field. Socrates was born with a marked propensity for wrongdoing, but, once converted to the pursuit of wisdom by a divine impulse, he came to be known as the one who first called down philosophy from heaven, and earned the title "father of all philosophers." Let us set recent examples alongside those of past ages, eminent men who in the doing of something discovered, through the discernment of others, astonishing capabilities hitherto unknown to themselves. Cardinal Jules Mazarin comes on the scene on his own account as a courtier of private means, a soldier in the ranks and a legal practitioner. However, on one occasion after another there arose matters of state which were assigned to him wholly unexpectedly by persons of the highest degree, and he became an extremely able statesman, privy to the secret counsels of Louis XIV, King of France, and dying only after a long term of power—a very rare instance of great good fortune. Francesco Guicciardini practiced law in the Roman courts, until the popes of his time, against any desire or wishes of his, made him governor over a number of cities in the papal jurisdiction. When Charles VIII in the French wars threw all Italy into turmoil, Guicciardini on the orders of the papacy negotiated a number of very crucial affairs arising out of the war. And this was the reason why he turned his energies to chronicling the Italy of his time, becoming easily the greatest of all historians writing in the Italian language. In view of all this, let the eyes of your mind rove widely, exercise your talents full circle, pry out your veiled and hidden capacities, that you may recognize your unknown and perhaps superior talents.

After you have traversed the whole circle of knowledge, you must pursue whatever discipline you have chosen with a more exalted spirit even than that shown by learned men themselves. (Let me set out my general meaning with a few examples.) Do not practice medicine merely in order to work successful cures: nor jurisprudence in order to offer sage legal opinion; nor theology simply in order to watch over correct doctrine on sacred matters. Rather, following the precedent given you in lectures and readings, you must employ in your homework the same grandeur of spirit, the same sublime mastery. And so this kind of reading and listening to those undying works of the chief authors will build up in you a nature accustomed to excellence, which will of its own accord lead you on to employ those very authors as ever-present judges in your private studies. Put this question over and over again to your innermost selves: Supposing you are in medicine (I am going back to the examples already given)—"What if Hippocrates himself were to hear what I am thinking and writing?" If in law—"What if Cujas heard this?" In theology—"What if Melchior Cano heard it?" For whoever sets up as his critics authors who have lasted throughout the ages cannot but produce works which will also be admired by subsequent generations. By these giant strides which you take along the main road to wisdom, you will easily make such progress that not one single one of you will say, "I wander along the byroads of the Muses,"[3] and you will bring to completion challenging tasks attempted but not carried through by men of great capabilities and learning, or else you will undertake things never yet attempted. You doctors (I am going to wind up my theme by using my previous examples) must lay down further aphorisms, using medical reports and case histories collected from every quarter—a distinction which up till now was vested for two thousand years and more in Hippocrates alone. You lawyers must embrace the whole of jurisprudence, working through inferences in case law, by rulings upon legal terms, in which branch of learning Aemilius Papinian was considered past master, and Jacques Cujas rose to preeminence above all others in an age teeming with learned interpreters of the law. (I might mention that on this task as a whole Antoine Favre made a beginning in his *Jurisprudentia papinianaea*, a man great not only in regard to his age but also in his knowledge of the law; he did not, however, live to complete it, whether discouraged by the difficulty as he went along, or surprised by death, who knows.) You theologians must establish a system of moral philosophy based on Christian doctrine—Cardinal Sforza Pallavicino put his hand to it in a courageous attempt. Pascal published his *Pensées* so full of insight but fragmentary, Malebranche failed in the very attempt. Read the great Verulam's [Francis Bacon's – Ed.] *De augmentis scientiarum*—a book worth its weight in gold and, apart from a few passages, ever to be looked up to and borne in mind—and ponder how much of the world of learning does remain to be set to rights, filled in, disclosed.

Whatever you do, do not be taken in unawares by that opinion, springing either from envy or cowardice, which says that for this most blessed century of ours everything that could ever have been achieved in the world of learning has already reached its conclusion, its culmination, and perfection, so that nothing remains therein to be desired. It is a false opinion, stemming from scholards [scholars – Ed.] with petty minds. For this world is still young. To go back no further than the last seven centuries, four of which were overrun by barbarism, how many new inventions there have been, how many new sciences and arts discovered! The mariner's compass, ships propelled by sail alone, the telescope, the barometer of Torricelli, Boyle's air pump, the circulation of the blood, the microscope, the alembic of the Arabs, Arabic numerals, indefinite classes of magnitudes, gunpowder, cannon, cupolas in churches, movable type, rag paper, clockwork—each one a striking achievement and all of them unknown to antiquity. Hence there have come novelties in ships and navigation (and thereby a new world discovered and geography how marvelously expanded!), new observations in astronomy, new methods of timekeeping, new cosmographical systems, innovations in mechanics, physics, medicine, a new anatomy, new chemical remedies (which Galen so greatly desired), a new method of geometry (and arithmetic markedly speeded up), new arts of war, a new architecture, such an availability of books that they are as common as dirt now, such abundance of them that they grow wearisome. How is it that the nature of human genius is so suddenly exhausted that we must give up hope of any other equally goodly inventions?

Do not be discouraged, noble hearers; countless possibilities still remain, perhaps even greater and more excellent than those we have just enumerated. In the teeming bosom of nature and the busy marketplace of the arts, great things are there, laid out for all to see, destined for the good of humanity and overlooked until now simply because the heroic mind had not turned its attention that way. Great Alexander when he came to Egypt took in with one magnificent glance the isthmus dividing the Red Sea from the Mediterranean, where the Nile runs into the Mediterranean and Africa and Asia meet. He thought it a worthy site where a city might be founded bearing his name, Alexandria, which straightway became the most frequented merchant city of Africa and Asia and Europe, of the Mediterranean Sea, of the Ocean and the Indies. The sublime Galileo first observed the planet Venus "distinct with its duplicate horn"[4] and discovered marvels in cosmology. The towering Descartes observed the trajectory of a stone thrown from a sling, and thought up a new physics. Christopher Columbus felt a wind from the Western Ocean blowing in his face, and in the light of Aristotle's hypothesis that winds arise from land masses, he guessed at other lands beyond the high seas and discovered the New World. The great Grotius paid serious attention to that one remark of Livy's: "Peace and war have each their own laws," and produced admirable volumes entitled *De jure belli et pacis* which, with certain passages excised, deserve to be called "peerless." With such shining instances, examples so distinguished, before you, apply yourselves, young men born to great and good things, to your studies, with heroic mind and coequal greatness of soul. Cultivate knowledge as a whole. Celebrate the near-divine nature of your minds.

Take fire from the god who fills you. Attend your lectures, read, study long hours, with lofty spirit. Undergo herculean trials, which, once passed, vindicate with perfect justice your divine descent from true Jove, Him the greatest and best. Prove yourselves to be heroes by enriching the human race with further giant benefits. Riches and wealth, honor and power in this your country will with little trouble follow upon those noblest of services rendered to the human race. And even if these rewards fail to materialize, you are not going to be deterred. Like Seneca you will receive them with equanimity, that is to say, without exaltation, should they come; and, without dejection, if they take their leave, you will ascribe your loss to Fortune's witless frenzy. And you will be satisfied with this divine and imperishable reward: that Almighty God Who as I said at the beginning enjoins upon us solicitude for the whole of humankind has chosen some of you in particular for the revelation of His glory upon this earth.

## Questions

1. Vico advises students to direct studies "toward Almighty God." Is it possible to separate "heroism" (and sublimity) from a concept of God? From religion?

2. Does Vico's account of the sublime mind seem Platonic? Aristotelian? Explain.

3. Compare and contrast Vico's theory to Longinus's discussion of lofty thoughts, and to Dennis's view of language (poetry) and religion.

4. Does technological progress constrain and limit the experience of the sublime, or instead make it more prominent? (Consider the powers and reach of the internet today.)

5. Is Vico's Christian humanist, anthropocentric theory compatible with an "environmental" sublime? Explain.

## Further reading

Fiore, Silvia Ruffo. *Giambattista Vico and the Pedagogy of 'Heroic Mind' in the Liberal Arts*. Boston University: Paideia, 1998.

Vico, Giambattista. *On Humanistic Education* (*Six Inaugural Orations*. 1699–1707), trans. Giorgio A. Pinton and Arthur W. Shippee. Ithaca: Cornell University Press, 1993.

# CHAPTER 9
## EDMUND BURKE, FROM *A PHILOSOPHICAL ENQUIRY INTO THE ORIGIN OF OUR IDEAS OF THE SUBLIME AND BEAUTIFUL* (1759)

Edmund Burke (1729–1797) has exerted an enormous influence on the history of the sublime, one matched—at least hitherto—perhaps only by Kant and Longinus. In the *Enquiry* (first edition, 1757), Burke distinguishes between the sublime and the beautiful. Beauty is grounded in the passion of love and society, consists in a calming relaxation of our "nerves," and is a response caused by an object's (or person's) qualities of being small, smooth, polished, light, delicate, or "feminine." Sublimity, by contrast, is rooted in the fear of death and desire for self-preservation and consists in tension in our nerves. It is caused by qualities such as an object's vastness, infinity, and power, and Burke associates it with masculinity. Burke adopts a physiological and psychological method, providing empirical descriptions of sublime effects on our bodies and minds. But far from dwelling exclusively on the subject and subjective responses, Burke characterizes the qualities of objects that paradigmatically elicit the sublime, such as vastness, power, and obscurity.

The *Enquiry* quickly became known in Germany, largely through a review that Moses Mendelssohn published in *Bibliothek der schönen Wissenschaften* in 1758. For instance, Burke's influence can be seen in the theories offered by Mendelssohn and Kant in the early 1760s. Decades later, in the General Remark following §29 in the *Critique of the Power of Judgment*, Kant called Burke the "foremost" author of this empirical approach.

Burke's theory has—unsurprisingly—drawn both dissent and praise. Critics have pointed out the explicitly gendered nature of the characterizations of beauty as "feminine" and sublimity as "masculine." Nevertheless, psychological and neuroscientific approaches adopt and update a version of his physiological-biological method, as revealed by a recent study whose title echoes Burke's: "A Neurobiological Enquiry into the Origins of Our Experience of the Sublime and Beautiful."[1] Burke's interest-based and physiological approach has also been influential on "pragmatist" aesthetics, too.[2]

Burke was not just an author of aesthetic treatises; he was also a political leader, orator, and statesman. Burke was later known for his conservative reaction to the French Revolution (*Reflections on the Revolution in France*, 1790), even if he was also a supporter of the American colonies as they became more independent of England. Burke's response to the French Revolution was quickly rebuked by Mary Wollstonecraft (*A Vindication of the Rights of Man*, 1790, reprinted in the present volume).

It is easy to connect politics and the sublime during this period. Burke and Kant, for instance, responded quite differently to the French Revolution while each making use of the concepts of spectacle and spectatorship (for Kant, "sublime" enthusiasm for the republican movements). Kant's view seems closer to the one expressed in this anonymous entry (written by an Englishman) in *The Morning Post* (July 21, 1789), commenting on the fall of the Bastille on July 14: "An Englishman not filled with esteem and admiration at the *sublime* manner in which one of the most important revolutions the world has ever seen is now effecting, must be dead to every sense of virtue and of freedom."[3]

In 1780, ten years before his *Reflections on the Revolution in France*, Burke acknowledged the capacity for bloody spectacle to elicit awe. "I have ever observed, that the execution of one man [rather than many] fixes the attention and excites awe."[4] Burke implies that the state can control the psychology of the masses through deliberate, focused spectacle. It remains disputed, however, whether such spectacle can count as "sublime" and can evoke aesthetic awe, or instead fails to do so because it violates moral conditions that must be met by aesthetic experiences.

## Note on the text

Source: Excerpted from Edmund Burke, *A Philosophical Enquiry into the Origin of Our Ideas of the Sublime and Beautiful. The Second Edition. With an Introductory Discourse concerning Taste, and Several Other Additions*, 58–60, 84–87, 95–124, 237–39, 334–42. London: R. and J. Dodsley, 1759.

Burke's footnotes indicating other sections of his book have been omitted. Punctuation, spelling, format and related stylistic matters have occasionally been modified. Textual omissions made by the volume editor are indicated using "[...]," and the editor has indicated page runs for each section.

## [Pages 58–60]

### *Part I*

#### Section VII. Of the sublime
Whatever is fitted in any sort to excite the ideas of pain, and danger, that is to say, whatever is in any sort terrible, or is conversant about terrible objects, or operates in a manner analogous to terror, is a source of the *sublime*; that is, it is productive of the strongest emotion which the mind is capable of feeling. I say the strongest emotion, because I am satisfied the ideas of pain are much more powerful than those which enter on the part of pleasure. Without all doubt, the torments which we may be made to suffer, are much greater in their effect on the body and mind, than any pleasures which the most learned voluptuary could suggest, or than the liveliest imagination, and the most sound and exquisitely sensible body could enjoy. Nay I am in great doubt, whether any man could be found who would earn a life of the most perfect satisfaction at the price of ending it in the torments, which justice inflicted in a few hours on the late unfortunate regicide in France. But as pain is stronger in its operation than pleasure, so death is in general a much more affecting idea than pain; because there are very few pains, however exquisite, which are not preferred to death; nay, what generally makes pain itself, if I may say so, more painful, is, that it is considered as an emissary of this king of terrors. When danger or pain press too nearly, they are incapable of giving any delight, and are simply terrible; but at certain distances, and with certain modifications, they may be, and they are delightful, as we every day experience. The cause of this I shall endeavor to investigate hereafter. [...]

## [Pages 84–87]

### *Part I*

#### Section XVIII. The recapitulation
To draw the whole of what has been said into a few distinct points. The passions which belong to self-preservation, turn on pain and danger; they are simply painful when their causes immediately affect us; they are delightful when we have an idea of pain and danger, without being actually in such circumstances; this

delight I have not called pleasure, because it turns on pain, and because it is different enough from any idea of positive pleasure. Whatever excites this delight, I call *sublime*. The passions belonging to self-preservation are the strongest of all the passions.

The second head to which the passions are referred with relation to their final cause, is society. There are two sorts of societies. The first is, the society of sex. The passion belonging to this is called love, and it contains a mixture of lust; its object is the beauty of women. The other is the great society with man and all other animals. The passion subservient to this is called likewise love, but it has no mixture of lust, and its object is beauty; which is a name I shall apply to all such qualities in things as induce in us a sense of affection and tenderness, or some other passion the most nearly resembling these. The passion of love has its rise in positive pleasure; it is, like all things which grow out of pleasure, capable of being mixed with a mode of uneasiness, that is, when an idea of its object is excited in the mind with an idea at the same time of having irretrievably lost it. This mixed sense of pleasure I have not called *pain*, because it turns upon actual pleasure, and because it is both in its cause and in most of its effects, of a nature altogether different.

Next to the general passion we have for society, to a choice in which we are directed by the pleasure we have in the object, the particular passion under this head called sympathy has the greatest extent. The nature of this passion is to put us in the place of another in whatever circumstance he is in, and to affect us in a like manner; so that this passion may, as the occasion requires, turn either on pain or pleasure; but with the modifications mentioned in some cases in Sect. II. As to imitation and preference, nothing more need be said. [...]

[Pages 95–124]

## Part II

### Section I. Of the passion caused by the sublime

The passion caused by the great and sublime in *nature*, when those causes operate most powerfully, is Astonishment; and astonishment is that state of the soul, in which all its motions are suspended, with some degree of horror. In this case the mind is so entirely filled with its object, that it cannot entertain any other, nor by consequence reason on that object which employs it. Hence arises the great power of the sublime, that, far from being produced by them, it anticipates our reasonings, and hurries us on by an irresistible force. Astonishment, as I have said, is the effect of the sublime in its highest degree; the inferior effects are admiration, reverence and respect.

## Part II

### Section II. Terror

No passion so effectually robs the mind of all its powers of acting and reasoning as fear. For fear being an apprehension of pain or death, it operates in a manner that resembles actual pain. Whatever therefore is terrible, with regard to sight, is sublime too, whether this cause of terror, be endued with greatness of dimensions or not; for it is impossible to look on anything as trifling, or contemptible, that may be dangerous. There are many animals, who though far from being large, are yet capable of raising ideas of the sublime, because they are considered as objects of terror. As serpents and poisonous animals of almost all kinds. And to things of great dimensions, if we annex an adventitious idea of terror, they become without comparison greater. A level plain of a vast extent on land, is certainly no mean idea; the prospect of such a plain may be as extensive as a prospect of the ocean; but can it ever fill the mind with anything so great as the ocean itself? This is owing to several causes, but it is owing to none more than this, that the ocean is an object of no small terror. Indeed terror is in all cases whatsoever, either more openly or latently the ruling principle of the sublime. Several languages bear a strong testimony to the affinity of these ideas. They frequently use the same word to signify indifferently the modes of astonishment or admiration and those of terror. Θάμβος is in Greek, either fear or wonder; δεινός is terrible or respectable; αἰδέω, to reverence or to fear. *Vereor* in Latin, is what αἰδέο is in Greek. The Romans used the verb *stupeo*, a term which strongly marks the state of an astonished mind, to express the effect either of simple fear, or of astonishment; the word *attonitus* (thunderstruck) is equally expressive of the alliance of these ideas; and do not the French *étonnement*, and the English *astonishment* and *amazement*, point out as clearly the kindred emotions which attend fear and wonder? They who have a more general knowledge of languages, could produce, I make no doubt, many other and equally striking examples.

## Part II

### Section III. Obscurity

To make anything very terrible, obscurity seems in general to be necessary. When we know the full extent of any danger, when we can accustom our eyes to it, a great deal of the apprehension vanishes. Every one will be sensible of this, who considers how greatly night adds to our dread, in all cases of danger, and how much the notions of ghosts and goblins, of which none can form clear ideas, affect minds, which give credit to the popular tales concerning such sorts of beings. Those despotic governments, which are founded on the passions of men, and principally upon the passion of fear, keep their chief as much as may be from the public eye. The policy has been the same in many cases of religion. Almost all the heathen temples were dark. Even in the barbarous temples of the Americans at this day, they keep their idol in a dark part of the hut, which is consecrated to his worship. For this purpose too the druids performed all their ceremonies in the bosom of the darkest woods, and in the shade of the oldest and most spreading oaks. No person seems better to have understood the secret of heightening, or of setting terrible things, if I may use the expression, in their strongest light by the force of a judicious obscurity, than Milton. His description of death in the second book is admirably studied; it is astonishing with what a gloomy pomp, with what a significant and expressive uncertainty of strokes and colouring, he has finished the portrait of the king of terrors.

> The other shape,
> If shape it might be called that shape had none
> Distinguishable, in member, joint, or limb;
> Or substance might be called that shadow seemed;
> For each seemed either; black he stood as night;
> Fierce as ten furies; terrible as hell;
> And shook a deadly dart. What seemed his head
> The likeness of a kingly crown had on.

In this description all is dark, uncertain, confused, terrible, and sublime to the last degree.

### Section IV. Of the difference between clearness and obscurity with regard to the passions

It is one thing to make an idea clear, and another to make it *affecting* to the imagination. If I make a drawing of a palace, or a temple, or a landscape, I present a very clear idea of those objects; but then (allowing for the effect of imitation which is something) my picture can at most affect only as the palace, temple, or landscape would have affected in the reality. On the other hand, the most lively and spirited verbal description I can give, raises a very obscure and imperfect *idea* of such objects; but then it is in my power to raise a stronger *emotion* by the description than I could do by the best painting. This experience constantly evinces. The proper manner of conveying the *affections* of the mind from one to another, is by words; there is a great insufficiency in all other methods of communication; and so far is a clearness of imagery from being absolutely necessary to an influence upon the passions, that they may be considerably operated upon without presenting any image at all, by certain sounds adapted to that purpose; of which we have a sufficient proof in the acknowledged and powerful effects of instrumental music. In reality, a great clearness helps but little towards affecting the passions, as it is in some sort an enemy to all enthusiasms whatsoever.

## Part II

### Section IV
The same subject continued.

There are two verses in Horace's art of poetry that seem to contradict this opinion, for which reason I shall take a little more pains in clearing it up. The verses are,

> *Segnius irritant animos demissa per aurem,*
> *Quam quae sunt oculis subjecta fidelibus.*

> [What we learn merely through hearing makes less impression on our minds than what is presented to the faithful eye. – Ed.]

On this the Abbé du Bos founds a criticism, wherein he gives painting the preference to poetry in the article of moving the passions; principally on account of the greater *clearness* of the ideas it represents. I believe this excellent judge was led into this mistake (if it be a mistake) by his system, to which he found it more conformable than I imagine it will be found to experience. I know several who admire and love painting, and yet who regard the objects of their admiration in that art, with coolness enough in comparison of that warmth with which they are animated by affecting pieces of poetry or rhetoric. Among the common sort of people, I never could perceive that painting had much influence on their passions. It is true that the best sorts of painting, as well as the best sorts of poetry, are not much understood in that sphere. But it is most certain, that their passions are very strongly roused by a fanatic preacher, or by the ballads of Chevy-Chase, or the children in the wood, and by other little popular poems and tales that are current in that rank of life. I do not know of any paintings, bad or good, that produce the same effect. So that poetry, with all its obscurity, has a more general as well as a more powerful dominion over the passions than the other art. And I think there are reasons in nature why the obscure idea, when properly conveyed, should be more affecting than the clear. It is our ignorance of things that causes all our admiration, and chiefly excites our passions. Knowledge and acquaintance make the most striking causes affect but little. It is thus with the vulgar, and all men are as the vulgar in what they do not understand. The ideas of eternity, and infinity, are among the most affecting we have, and yet perhaps there is nothing of which we really understand so little, as of infinity and eternity. We do not anywhere meet a more sublime description than this justly celebrated one of Milton, wherein he gives the portrait of Satan with a dignity so suitable to the subject:

> *He above the rest*
> *In shape and gesture proudly eminent*

*Stood like a tower; his form had yet not lost*
*All her original brightness, nor appeared*
*Less than archangel ruined, and th' excess*
*Of glory obscured: as when the sun new ris'n*
*Looks through the horizontal misty air*
*Shorn of his beams; or from behind the moon*
*In dim eclipse disastrous twilight sheds*
*On half the nations; and with fear of change*
*Perplexes monarchs.*

Here is a very noble picture; and in what does this poetical picture consist? In images of a tower, an archangel, the sun rising through mists, or in an eclipse, the ruin of monarchs, and the revolutions of kingdoms. The mind is hurried out of itself, by a crowd of great and confused images; which affect because they are crowded and confused. For separate them, and you lose much of the greatness, and join them, and you infallibly lose the clearness. The images raised by poetry are always of this obscure kind; though in general the effects of poetry, are by no means to be attributed to the images it raises; which point we shall examine more at large hereafter. But painting, when we have allowed for the pleasure of imitation, can only affect simply by the images it presents; and even in painting a judicious obscurity in some things contributes to the effect of the picture; because the images in painting are exactly similar to those in nature; and in nature dark, confused, uncertain images have a greater power on the fancy to form the grander passions than those have which are more clear and determinate. But where and when this observation may be applied to practice, and how far it shall be extended, will be better deduced from the nature of the subject, and from the occasion, than from any rules that can be given.

I am sensible that this idea has met with opposition, and is likely still to be rejected by several. But let it be considered that hardly anything can strike the mind with its greatness, which does not make some sort of approach towards infinity; which nothing can do whilst we are able to perceive its bounds; but to see an object distinctly, and to perceive its bounds, is one and the same thing. A clear idea is therefore another name for a little idea. There is a passage in the book of Job amazingly sublime, and this sublimity is principally due to the terrible uncertainty of the thing described. *In thoughts from the visions of the night, when deep sleep falleth upon men, fear came upon me and trembling, which made all my bones to shake. Then a spirit passed before my face. The hair of my flesh stood up. It stood still,* but I could not discern the form thereof; *an image was before mine eyes; there was silence; and I heard a voice,—Shall mortal man be more just than God?* We are first prepared with the utmost solemnity for the vision; we are first terrified, before we are let even into the obscure cause of our emotion; but when this grand cause of terror makes its appearance, what is it? Is it not wrapt up in the shades of its own incomprehensible darkness, more aweful, more striking, more terrible, than the liveliest description, than the clearest painting, could possibly represent it? When painters have attempted to give us clear representations of these very fanciful and terrible ideas, they have, I think almost always failed; insomuch that I have been at a loss, in all the pictures I have seen of hell, whether the painter did not intend something ludicrous. Several painters have handled a subject of this kind, with a view of assembling as many horrid phantoms as their imagination could suggest; but all the designs I have chanced to meet of the temptations of St. Anthony, were rather a sort of odd, wild grotesques, than any thing capable of producing a serious passion. In all these subjects poetry is very happy. Its apparitions, its chimeras, its harpies, its allegorical figures, are grand and affecting; and though Virgil's Fame, and Homer's Discord, are obscure, they are magnificent figures. These figures in painting would be clear enough, but I fear they might become ridiculous.

*Part II*

Section V. Power

Besides those things which *directly* suggest the idea of danger, and those which produce a similar effect from a mechanical cause, I know of nothing sublime which is not some modification of power. And this branch rises as naturally as the other two branches, from terror, the common stock of everything that is sublime. The idea of power at first view, seems of the class of those indifferent ones, which may equally belong to pain or to pleasure. But in reality, the affection arising from the idea of vast power, is extremely remote from that neutral character. For first, we must remember, that the idea of pain, in its highest degree, is much stronger than the highest degree of pleasure; and that it preserves the same superiority through all the subordinate gradations. From hence it is, that where the chances for equal degrees of suffering or enjoyment are in any sort equal, the idea of the suffering must always be prevalent. And indeed the ideas of pain, and above all of death, are so very affecting, that whilst we remain in the presence of whatever is supposed to have the power of inflicting either, it is impossible to be perfectly free from terror. Again, we know by experience, that for the enjoyment of pleasure, no great efforts of power are at all necessary; nay we know, that such efforts would go a great way towards destroying our satisfaction: for pleasure must be stolen, and not forced upon us; pleasure follows the will; and therefore we are generally affected with it by many things of a force greatly inferior to our own. But pain is always inflicted by a power in some way superior, because we never submit to pain willingly. So that strength, violence, pain and terror, are ideas that rush in upon the mind together. Look at a man, or any other animal of prodigious strength, and what is your idea before reflection? Is it that this strength will be subservient to you, to your ease, to your pleasure, to your interest in any sense? No; the emotion you feel is, lest this enormous strength should be employed to the purposes of rapine and destruction. That power derives all its sublimity from the terror with which it is generally accompanied, will appear evidently from its effect in the very few cases, in which it may be possible to strip a considerable degree of strength of its ability to hurt. When you do this, you spoil it of everything sublime, and it immediately becomes contemptible. An ox is a creature of vast strength; but he is an innocent creature, extremely serviceable, and not at all dangerous; for which reason the idea of an ox is by no means grand. A bull is strong too; but his strength is of another kind; often very destructive, seldom (at least amongst us) of any use in our business; the idea of a bull is therefore great, and it has frequently a place in sublime descriptions, and elevating comparisons. Let us look at another strong animal in the two distinct lights in which we may consider him. The horse in the light of an useful beast, fit for the plough, the road, the draft, in every social useful light the horse has nothing sublime; but is it thus that we are affected with him, *whose neck is clothed with thunder, the glory of whose nostrils is terrible, who swalloweth the ground with fierceness and rage, neither believeth that it is the sound of the trumpet?* In this description the useful character of the horse entirely disappears, and the terrible and sublime blaze out together. We have continually about us animals of a strength that is considerable, but not pernicious. Amongst these we never look for the sublime; it comes upon us in the gloomy forest, and in the howling wilderness, in the form of the lion, the tiger, the panther, or rhinoceros. Whenever strength is only useful, and employed for our benefit or our pleasure, then it is never sublime; for nothing can act agreeably to us, that does not act in conformity to our will; but to act agreeably to our will, it must be subject to us, and therefore can never be the cause of a grand and commanding conception. The description of the wild ass, in Job, is worked up into no small sublimity, merely by insisting on his freedom, and his setting mankind at defiance; otherwise the description of such an animal could have had nothing noble in it. *Who hath loosed* (says he) *the bands of the wild ass? whose house I have made the wilderness and the barren land his dwellings. He scorneth the multitude of the city, neither regardeth he the voice of the driver. The range of the mountains is his pasture.* The magnificent description of the unicorn and of leviathan in the same book, is full of the same heightening circumstances: *Will the unicorn be willing to serve thee? canst thou bind the unicorn with his band in the furrow? wilt thou trust him because his strength is great?—Canst thou draw out leviathan with an hook? will he make a covenant with thee? wilt thou take him for a servant forever? shall not one be cast down even at the sight of him?* In short, wheresoever we find strength, and in what light soever we look upon power, we shall all along observe the sublime the concomitant of terror, and contempt the attendant on a strength that is subservient and innoxious. The race of dogs in many of their kinds, have generally a competent degree of strength and swiftness; and they exert these, and other valuable qualities which they possess, greatly to our convenience and pleasure. Dogs are indeed the most social, affectionate, and amiable animals of the whole brute creation; but love approaches much nearer to contempt than is commonly imagined; and accordingly, though we caress dogs, we borrow from them an appellation of the most despicable kind, when we employ terms of reproach; and this appellation is the common mark of the last vileness and contempt in every language. Wolves have not more strength than several species of dogs; but on account of their unmanageable fierceness, the idea of a wolf is not despicable; it is not excluded from grand descriptions and similitudes. Thus we are affected by strength, which is *natural* power. The power which arises from institution in kings and commanders, has the same connection with terror. Sovereigns are frequently addressed with the title of *dread majesty*. And it may be observed, that young persons little acquainted with the world, and who have not been used to approach men in power, are commonly struck with an awe which takes away the free use of their faculties. *When I prepared my seat in the street,* (says Job,) *the young men saw me, and hid themselves.* Indeed so natural is this timidity with regard to power, and so strongly does it inhere in our constitution, that very few are able to conquer it, but by mixing much in the business of the great world, or by using no small violence to their natural dispositions. I know some people are of opinion, that no awe, no degree of terror, accompanies the idea of power, and have hazarded to affirm, that we can contemplate the idea of God himself without any such emotion. I purposely avoided when I first considered this subject, to introduce the idea of that great and tremendous Being, as an example in an argument so light as this; though it frequently occurred to me, not as an objection to, but as a strong confirmation of, my notions in this matter. I hope, in what I am going to say, I shall avoid presumption, where it is almost impossible for any mortal to speak with strict propriety. I say then, that whilst we consider the Godhead merely as he is an object of the understanding, which forms a complex idea of power, wisdom, justice, goodness, all stretched to a degree far exceeding the bounds of our comprehension, whilst we consider the divinity in this refined and abstracted light, the imagination and passions are little or nothing affected. But because we are bound by the condition of our nature to ascend to these pure and intellectual ideas, through the medium of sensible images, and to judge of these divine qualities by their evident acts and exertions, it becomes extremely hard to disentangle our idea of the cause from the effect by which we are led to know it. Thus when we contemplate the Deity, his attributes and their operation coming united on the mind, form a sort of sensible image, and as such are capable of affecting the imagination. Now, though in a just idea of the Deity, perhaps none of his attributes are predominant, yet, to our imagination, his power is by far the most striking. Some reflection, some comparing is necessary to satisfy us of his wisdom, his justice, and his goodness; to be struck with his power, it is only necessary that we should open our eyes. But whilst we contemplate so vast an object, under the arm, as it were, of almighty power, and invested upon every side with omnipresence, we shrink into the minuteness of our own nature, and are, in a manner, annihilated before him. And though a consideration of his other attributes may relieve in some measure our apprehensions; yet no conviction of the justice with which it is exercised, nor the mercy with which it is tempered, can wholly remove the terror that naturally arises from a force which nothing can withstand. If we rejoice, we rejoice with trembling; and even whilst we are receiving benefits, we cannot but shudder at a power which can confer benefits of such mighty importance. When the prophet David contemplated the wonders of wisdom and power, which are displayed in the economy of man, he seems to be struck with a sort of divine horror, and cries out, *fearfully and wonderfully am I made!* An heathen poet has a sentiment of a similar nature; Horace looks upon it as the last effort of philosophical fortitude, to behold without terror and amazement, this immense and glorious fabric of the universe:

> *Hunc solem, et stellas, et decedentia certis*
> *Tempora momentis, sunt qui formidine nulla*
> *Imbuti spectent.*

> [That sun, and stars and seasons that pass in fixed courses: some can gaze upon these with no strain of fear. – Ed.]

Lucretius is a poet not to be suspected of giving way to superstitious terrors; yet when he supposes the whole mechanism of nature laid open by the master of his philosophy, his transport on this magnificent view which he has represented in the colors of such bold and lively poetry, is overcast with a shade of secret dread and horror:

> *His ibi me rebus quaedam Divina voluptas*
> *Percipit, atque horror, quod sic Natura, tua vi*
> *Tam manifesta patens ex omni parte retecta est.*

> [From all these things a certain Divine delight gets hold of me, and awesome dread, because Nature thus by your power has been so clearly laid open and manifest in every part. – Ed.]

But the Scripture alone can supply ideas answerable to the majesty of this subject. In the Scripture, wherever God is represented as appearing or speaking, everything terrible in nature is called up to heighten the awe and solemnity of the Divine presence. The Psalms, and the prophetical books, are crowded with instances of this kind. *The earth shook,* (says the Psalmist,) *the heavens also dropped at the presence of the Lord.* And what is remarkable, the painting preserves the same character, not only when he is supposed descending to take vengeance upon the wicked, but even when he exerts the like plenitude of power in acts of beneficence to mankind. *Tremble, thou earth! at the presence of the Lord; at the presence of the God of Jacob; which turned the rock into standing water, the flint into a fountain of waters!* It were endless to enumerate all the passages both in the sacred and profane writers, which establish the general sentiment of mankind, concerning the inseparable union of a sacred and reverential awe, with our ideas of the divinity. Hence the common maxim, *primus in orbe deos fecit timor* [Fear first made gods in the world – Ed.]. This maxim may be, as I believe it is, false with regard to the origin of religion. The maker of the maxim saw how inseparable these ideas were, without considering that the notion of some great power must be always precedent to our dread of it. But this dread must necessarily follow the idea of such a power, when it is once excited in the mind. It is on this principle that true religion has, and must have, so large a mixture of salutary fear; and that false religions have generally nothing else but fear to support them. Before the Christian religion had, as it were, humanized the idea of the Divinity, and brought it somewhat nearer to us, there was very little said of the love of God. The followers of Plato have something of it, and only something. The other writers of pagan antiquity, whether poets or philosophers, nothing at all. And they who consider with what infinite attention, by what a disregard of every perishable object, through what long habits of piety and contemplation it is, any man is able to attain an entire love and devotion to the Deity, will easily perceive, that it is not the first, the most natural, and the most striking effect which proceeds from that idea. Thus we have traced power through its several gradations unto the highest of all, where our imagination is finally lost; and we find terror quite throughout the progress, its inseparable companion, and growing along with it, as far as we can possibly trace them. Now as power is undoubtedly a capital source of the sublime, this will point out evidently from whence its energy is derived, and to what class of ideas we ought to unite it. [...]

[Pages 237–39]

*Part III*

Section XXVII. The sublime and beautiful compared

On closing this general view of beauty, it naturally occurs that we should compare it with the sublime; and in this comparison there appears a remarkable contrast. For sublime objects are vast in their dimensions, beautiful ones comparatively small; beauty should be smooth, and polished; the great, rugged and negligent; beauty should shun the right line, yet deviate from it insensibly; the great in many cases loves the right line; and when it deviates, it often makes a strong deviation; beauty should not be obscure; the great ought to be dark and gloomy; beauty should be light and delicate; the great ought to be solid, and even massive. They are indeed ideas of a very different nature, one being founded on pain, the other on pleasure; and however they may vary afterwards from the direct nature of their causes, yet these causes keep up an eternal distinction between them, a distinction never to be forgotten by any whose business it is to affect the passions. In the infinite variety of natural combinations we must expect to find the qualities of things the most remote imaginable from each other united in the same object. We must expect also to find combinations of the same kind in the works of art. But when we consider the power of an object upon our passions, we must know that when anything is intended to affect the mind by the force of some predominant property, the affection produced is like to be the more uniform and perfect, if all the other properties or qualities of the object be of the same nature, and tending to the same design as the principal;

> *If black, and white blend, soften, and unite*
> *A thousand ways, are there no black and white?*

If the qualities of the sublime and beautiful are sometimes found united, does this prove that they are the same, does it prove, that they are any way allied, does it prove even that they are not opposite and contradictory? Black and white may soften, may blend, but they are not therefore the same. Nor when they are so softened and blended with each other, or with different colors, is the power of black as black, or of white as white, so strong as when each stands uniform and distinguished. […]

[Pages 334–42]

*Part V*

Section VII. How words influence the passions

Now, as words affect, not by any original power, but by representation, it might be supposed, that their influence over the passions should be but light; yet it is quite otherwise; for we find by experience that eloquence and poetry are as capable, nay indeed much more capable of making deep and lively impressions than any other arts, and even than nature itself in very many cases. And this arises chiefly from these three causes. First, that we take an extraordinary part in the passions of others, and that we are easily affected and brought into sympathy by any tokens which are shown of them; and there are no tokens which can express all the circumstances of most passions so fully as words; so that if a person speaks upon any subject, he can not only convey the subject to you, but likewise the manner in which he is himself affected by it. Certain it is, that the influence of most things on our passions is not so much from the things themselves, as from our opinions concerning them; and these again depend very much on the opinions of other men, conveyable for the most part by words only. Secondly, there are many things of a very affecting nature, which can seldom occur in the reality, but the words that represent them often do; and thus they have an opportunity of making a deep impression and taking root in the mind, whilst the idea of the reality was transient; and to some perhaps never really occurred in any shape, to whom it is notwithstanding very affecting, as war, death, famine, &c. Besides, many ideas have never been at all presented to the senses of any men but by words, as God, angels, devils, heaven and hell, all of which have however a great influence over the passions. Thirdly, by words we have it in our power to make such *combinations* as we cannot possibly do otherwise. By this power of combining we are able, by the addition of well-chosen circumstances, to give a new life and force to the simple object. In painting we may represent any fine figure we please; but we never can give it those enlivening touches which it may receive from words. To represent an angel in a picture, you can only draw a beautiful young man winged: but what painting can furnish out anything so grand as the addition of one word, "the angel of the *Lord*?" It is true, I have here no clear idea, but these words affect the mind more than the sensible image did, which is all I contend for. A picture of Priam dragged to the altar's foot, and there murdered, if it were well executed would undoubtedly be very moving; but there are very aggravating circumstances which it could never represent,

*Sanguine foedantem* quos ipse sacraverat *ignes.*

[befouling with his blood the fires which he himself had consecrated. – Ed.]

As a further instance, let us consider those lines of Milton, where he describes the travels of the fallen angels through their dismal habitation,

——*O'er many a dark and dreary vale*
*They passed, and many a region dolorous;*
*O'er many a frozen, many a fiery Alp;*
*Rocks, caves, lakes, fens, bogs, dens, and shades of death,*
*A universe of death.*

Here is displayed the force of union in

*Rocks, caves, lakes, dens, bogs, fens, and shades;*

which yet would lose the greatest part of their effect, if they were not the

*Rocks, caves, lakes, dens, bogs, fens, and shades—*
*—of* Death.

This idea or this affection caused by a word, which nothing but a word could annex to the others, raises a very great degree of the sublime; and this sublime is raised yet higher by what follows, a "*universe of Death.*" Here are again two ideas not presentable but by language; and an union of them great and amazing beyond conception; if they may properly be called ideas which present no distinct image to the mind; but still it will be difficult to conceive how words can move the passions which belong to real objects, without representing these objects clearly. This is difficult to us, because we do not sufficiently distinguish, in our observations upon language, between a clear expression, and a strong expression. These are frequently confounded with each other, though they are in reality extremely different. The former regards the understanding; the latter belongs to the passions. The one describes a thing as it is; the latter describes it as it is felt. Now, as there is a moving tone of voice, an impassioned countenance, an agitated gesture, which affect independently of the things about which they are exerted, so there are words, and certain dispositions of words, which being peculiarly devoted to passionate subjects, and always used by those who are under the influence of any passion; they touch and move us more than those which far more clearly and distinctly express the subject matter. We yield to sympathy, what we refuse to description. The truth is, all verbal description, merely as naked description, though never so exact, conveys so poor and insufficient an idea of the thing described, that it could scarcely have the smallest effect, if the speaker did not call in to his aid those modes of speech that mark a strong and lively feeling in himself. Then, by the contagion of our passions, we catch a fire already kindled in another, which probably might never have been struck out by the object described. Words, by strongly conveying the passions, by those means which we have already mentioned, fully compensate for their weakness in other respects. It may be observed that very polished languages, and such as are praised for their superior clearness and perspicuity, are generally deficient in strength. The French language has that perfection, and that defect. Whereas the Oriental tongues, and in general the languages of most unpolished people, have a great force and energy of expression; and this is but natural. Uncultivated people are but ordinary observers of things, and not critical in distinguishing them; but, for that reason, they admire more, and are more affected with what they see, and therefore express themselves in a warmer and more passionate manner. If the affection be well conveyed, it will work its effect without any clear idea; often without any idea at all of the thing which has originally given rise to it.

It might be expected, from the fertility of the subject, that I should consider poetry as it regards the sublime and beautiful more at large; but it must be observed that in this light it has been often and well handled already. It was not my design to enter into the criticism of the sublime and beautiful in any art, but to attempt to lay down such principles as may tend to ascertain, to distinguish, and to form a sort of standard for them; which purposes I thought might be best effected by an enquiry into the properties of such things in nature as raise love and astonishment in us; and by showing in what manner they operated to produce these passions. Words were only so far to be considered, as to show upon what principle they were capable of being the representatives of these natural things, and by what powers they were able to affect us often as strongly as the things they represent, and sometimes much more strongly.

The END.

## Questions

1. Compare and contrast Burke's view of the causes, effects, and definition of the sublime with that of Longinus and Dennis.

2. How does Burke relate "terror" to gods and religion? Explain.

3. In what ways do art (poetry) and nature elicit the sublime, according to Burke? Explain in terms of his examples.

4. Why does Burke think language is better able to create or reflect sublime experiences than any other representational form? Explain his claim: "In all these subjects [grotesques, apparitions, etc.] poetry is very happy." In your view, is the poet freer and "happier" than the painter?

5. Based on Burke's account, could acts of terrorism be considered sublime? Explain.

6. Is the fact that Burke provides an explicitly *gendered* account fatal to his theory? Explain.

## Further reading

Armstrong, Meg. "'The Effects of Blackness': Gender, Race, and the Sublime in Aesthetic Theories of Burke and Kant." *Journal of Aesthetics and Art Criticism* 54 (3) (1996): 213–36. [Excerpted in the present volume.]

Boulton, James T., ed. *A Philosophical Enquiry into the Origin of Our Ideas of the Sublime and Beautiful.* Notre Dame: University of Notre Dame Press, 1958, 645–61.

Ferguson, Frances. *Solitude and the Sublime: Romanticism and the Aesthetics of Individuation.* London: Routledge, 1992.

Furniss, Tom. *Edmund Burke's Aesthetic Ideology: Language, Gender and Political Economy in Revolution.* Cambridge: Cambridge University Press, 1993.

Hipple, Walter John. *The Beautiful, the Sublime and the Picturesque in Eighteenth-Century British Aesthetic Theory,* 83–98. Carbondale: Southern Illinois University Press, 1957.

Ryan, Vanessa L. "The Physiological Sublime: Burke's Critique of Reason." *Journal of the History of Ideas* 62, no. 2 (2001): 265–79.

# CHAPTER 10
## MOSES MENDELSSOHN, FROM "ON THE SUBLIME AND NAIVE IN THE FINE SCIENCES" (1761)

---

Moses Mendelssohn (1729–1786) is considered one of the most gifted and intriguing figures of the German Enlightenment and a foremost representative of the Jewish Enlightenment. His "On Evidence in Metaphysical Sciences" (1763) garnered first prize in a contest staged by the Royal Prussian Academy of Sciences on the question of whether metaphysical truths are able to have the same sort of evidence as mathematical truths. (An essay by Immanuel Kant came in a close second.)[1]

In "On the Sublime and Naive in the Fine Sciences," Mendelssohn takes up the problem of so-called mixed sentiments. We seem to experience the latter sometimes when we see what is otherwise painful, ghastly, terrifying (as when we view a tragic drama), or does not exhibit the harmony or order typical of beauty. Mendelssohn had raised the issue in "On Sentiments" (1755), his first publication on aesthetic matters (and the first essay in the 1761 *Philosophical Writings*). A perfection in the *object* (or quality of the person arousing our sympathy), he says, is the source of the pleasure we feel. In "Rhapsody, or additions to the Letter on sentiments" (also included in *Philosophical Writings*), he differentiates between a representation's being a determination of the soul (a subjective relation), which is pleasant, and its being a picture of the object (objective relation), which is repugnant. The mixed sentiment can involve "perfection," but only does so on the side of the subject.

"On the Sublime and Naive in the Fine Sciences" was published as the penultimate essay in the 1761 *Philosophical Writings*, but it had been published anonymously in 1758 in *Library of Fine Sciences and Fine Arts* under the title, "Considerations of the Sublime and the Naive in the Fine Sciences." The essay provided a partial basis for the theory of mixed sentiments in "Rhapsody." In the essay, Mendelssohn offers a more extended account of the definition and forms of sublimity.

He distinguishes beauty, or something bounded which can be taken in by the senses all at once, from immensity, which is unbounded. He then distinguishes two kinds of immensity: extended (or "extensive") and non-extended ("intensive"). These can be called the enormous and the strong, respectively. Intensive immensity can be discerned, for instance, in virtue or genius. The sea's unfathomableness would be an example of extended immensity in nature; uniform repetition of temporal intervals in music would be an example of an attempt to represent the experience of an extended immensity in art. Mendelssohn displays a preference for non-extended or intensive immensities, presumably because of their clearer link to "perfection" (on the objective side) and virtue, rather than to an imperfection on our part (a limited cognitive-perceptual faculty), and since they are less likely to lead to satiation and disgust. "Power, genius, virtue have their unextended immensity that likewise arouses a spine-tingling sentiment but has the advantage of not ending, through tedious uniformity, in satiation and even disgust, as generally happens in the case of the extended immensity." Mendelssohn thereby places moral qualities such as virtue alongside intensive magnitudes such as might or power. Presumably, they are both kinds of capacity or strength.

Mendelssohn reserves the concept of "sublimity" for the perfect (complete) representation of such intensive immensity, a representation that produces (as Dahlstrom sometimes translates it) "awe or admiration" (*Bewunderung*) because it passes beyond our ordinary, customary expectations. "The enormous is for the outer sense precisely what the sublime is for the inner sense." Something that is intensively immense is said to be "strong," and when that strength is a matter of a perfection, it is called "sublime." Awe is the soul's condition when it looks at the "unexpectedly good."

Mendelssohn defines the sublime in art more generally, namely, as a "sensuously perfect representation" of something immense, capable of inspiring awe. He views artistic creation in terms of genius. Awe is a debt that we owe to "the extraordinary gifts of spirit," which he calls "genius." He clarifies that the experience of sublimity is a mode of feeling, not of knowing: awe directed at the sublime object neither directly follows from, nor aims at, a particular concept or conception. Still, toward the end of this excerpt, Mendelssohn suggests a way to resolve certain disputes and disagreements when judging sublimity. He draws on a distinction between sublimity in the matter or object represented, on the one hand, and the intentions of the artist to represent it in a certain way, on the other.

In the essay's final pages—omitted here for the sake of space—Mendelssohn considers "naive" (that is, simple and uncontrived) expressions that are well-suited to represent a sublime content or object.

## Note on the text

Source: Excerpted from Moses Mendelssohn, "On the Sublime and Naive in the Fine Sciences," in *Philosophical Writings,* edited and translated by Daniel O. Dahlstrom, 192–200, 210–18. New York, NY: Cambridge University Press, 1997.

The numbered footnotes in the essay are Dahlstrom's (though occasionally modified, for instance, for the sake of citation style or format). Mendelssohn is the author of the footnotes marked by asterisks. Mendelssohn sometimes makes use of an ellipsis; thus, a stand-alone ellipsis does not indicate anything has been omitted. As occurs throughout this anthology, the editor's textual omissions (e.g., between pages 200 and 210 in *Philosophical Writings*) are indicated by an ellipsis in squared brackets: "[…]".

## "On the sublime and naive in the fine sciences"

If one reads through Longinus' treatment of the sublime, one can only regret that Caecilius' writings on the subject have been lost.[2] To be sure, Longinus said of him that "he merely took the trouble, through countless examples of the sublime, of making a concept of it for us as though no one were acquainted with it; on the other hand, he completely omitted the most essential feature, namely, the means by which we are able to accustom our spirit to genuine majesty."[3] However, Longinus concerned himself only with the latter, presupposing the former as something that either ought to be familiar to everyone in his view or at least was known to Terentian[4] from Caecilius' writings. As a result, a very necessary part of our acquaintance with the sublime is missing, namely, the distinct definition of it. Some translators and interpreters of Longinus have tried to make up for this lack, but they do not appear to have succeeded very well in doing so.

Given the principles that have been established in the previous essays, principles of the nature of sentiments and the sources of fine sciences generally, perhaps a somewhat more perspicuous analysis can be given of the concept of the sublime which, as Longinus says, constitutes the height of perfection in writings.

We have seen that what is genuinely beautiful has definite boundaries which it may not overstep. If the full dimensions of the object cannot be taken in by the senses all at once, then it ceases to be *sensuously beautiful* and becomes *gigantic* or *enormous in extension*. The sentiment that is then aroused is, to be sure, of a mixed nature. For well-educated minds, those used to order and symmetry, there is something repugnant about this, since the senses ultimately can perceive the boundaries, but cannot comprehend them and combine them into *one* idea without considerable difficulty. – If the boundaries of this extension are deferred further and further, then they ultimately disappear completely from the senses and, a result, something *sensuously immense* emerges. The senses, which perceive things insofar as they are homogeneous, begin to ramble in an effort to comprehend the boundaries and end up losing themselves in what is immense. The result, as was shown in the first essay,[5] is initially a *trembling* or shudder that comes over us and then something similar to dizziness that often forces us to divert our eyes from the object. The unfathomable world of the sea, a far-reaching plain, the innumerable legions of stars, every height and depth that is beyond the reach of the eye, eternity, and other such objects of nature which appear immeasurable to the senses, arouse the sort of sentiment which in several instances, as was elaborated in that passage, is quite alluring, but in many cases is upsetting.

Because of the pleasantness of these sentiments art also makes use of them, seeking to produce them through imitation. The imitation of the sensuously immense in art is named straightforwardly "the grand or the enormous" [*das Große*]. By this is meant not an unlimited magnitude [*Größe*], but one that appears boundless and is able to awaken a pleasant shudder. In art there is a particular means of arousing this sentiment where what is genuinely immense cannot be presented. At equal spatial or temporal intervals, a single impression is repeated without alteration, uniformly, and frequently. The senses then do not perceive any symmetrical movement or any rule of order in terms of which they could somehow suppose the end of this repetition, and, by this means, they fall into a kind of unrest that is similar to shuddering at something immeasurable. An example in architecture is a straight corridor of pillars where they are similar to one another and stand at equal distances from one another. There is something *grand* about such a corridor of pillars that disappears as soon as the uniformity of the repetition is interrupted and something sticks out at certain places. The monotone repetition of a single sound, at equal intervals, has the same effect in music and is employed for the purpose of expressing reverence, fright, horror. In the fine sciences there are oratorical embellishments with a similar effect. An accumulation of conjunctives sometimes accomplishes this:

*And* the screaming *and* the deadly rage *and* the thundering heavens.

thus, too:

… *and* still is *and* still thinks *and* curses …[6]

Sometimes, too, this is accomplished by accumulating nouns while omitting conjunctives. Longinus cites an example from Xenophon: "They slung their shields together, closed ranks, fought, killed, perished" and another from Demosthenes: "For when someone is on the offensive he can employ many things that the offended party cannot even recount; gestures, glances, and things he says, in part as a daredevil, in part as an enemy, in part with the fist, in part in the face."[7] Here the nouns accumulate, sometimes with conjunctives, sometimes without. The climax, increasing step-by-step by the same degrees, has a similar effect (although it also is pleasing for other reasons which this is not the place to elaborate).

Just as there is an immensity of extended magnitude, the effect of which we have just described, so there is an *immensity of strength* or unextended magnitude that has effects similar to the former. Power, genius, virtue have their unextended immensity that likewise arouses a spine-tingling sentiment but has the advantage of not ending, through tedious uniformity, in satiation and even disgust, as generally happens in the case of the extended immensity. The instances of the immensity of strength are as diverse as they are enormous, and, as has already been called to mind in the cited passage, the sentiment that they arouse is unmixed from the side of the object. This is why the soul indulges in them with such fervor. The term commonly applied to what is intensively enormous is "strength," and strength in perfection is designated "the sublime." In general, one could also say: each thing that is or appears immense as far as the degree of its perfection is concerned is called *sublime*. God is called "the most sublime being." A truth is said to be "sublime" if it concerns a quite perfect or complete entity such as God, the universe, the human soul and if it is of immense use to the human race or its discovery would require a great genius.

In the fine arts and sciences the sensuously perfect representation of something immense will be *enormous, strong,* or *sublime* depending upon whether the magnitude concerns an extension and number, a degree of power, or, in particular, a degree of perfection.

The sentiment produced by the sublime is a composite one. The *magnitude* captures our attention, and since it is the magnitude of a perfection, the soul enjoys latching on to this object so that all adjoining concepts in the soul are obscured. The *immensity* arouses a sweet shudder that rushes through every fiber of our being, and the *multiplicity* prevents all satiation, giving wings to the imagination to press further and further without stopping. All these sentiments blend together in the soul, flowing into one another, and become a single phenomenon which we call *awe*. Accordingly, if one wanted to describe the sublime in terms of its effect, then one could say: "It is something sensuously perfect in art, capable of inspiring awe."

Each perfection that goes beyond our customary conceptions because of its magnitude, surpassing the expectation that we have of a certain object or even transcending what we can think of as perfect, is an object of *awe*. Regulus' resolve to return to Carthage, while aware of the torture that awaited the likes of him, is sublime and awe-inspiring because we would not have believed that duty, the duty to keep a promise even to an enemy, could have had so much power over a human heart.[8] The startling reconciliation of Augustus with Cinna in Corneille's famous tragedy produces the same effect because we would have outfitted the prince's character with a completely different way of proceeding. In *Cannut* the grace which Ulfo experiences does not produce so sudden a sentiment since it was not unexpected from a character as kind as Cannut's.*[9]

Finally, the properties of the Supreme Being which we recognize in his works inspire the most ecstatic awe and admiration [*Bewunderung*] because they surpass everything that we can conceive as enormous, perfect, or sublime.

Since the enormous and the sublime have such a related nature, it is apparent why artists so often support the sublime by means of the enormous and prepare us, as it were, for the spiritual representation of the sublime through the sensuous impression of something enormous. They enlarge the measure or the proportions of things that they want to represent as sublime. Artists make use of a bright glow which blinds because of its *strength* or else of a *darkness* that allows the boundaries of the objects to recede; but they never use a moderate light. No picture of the sublime is clearly distinguished; some features are enlarged hyperbolically, and the rest are left indefinite so that the imagination may lose itself in their magnitude:

… I stretch my head up into the clouds
My arm out into eternity …

---

*Thus, if Cannut could be put in circumstances in which his grace would be unexpected and would not flow so immediately from his general kind character, the effect would be indisputably far stronger. See *Bibliothek der schönen Wissenschaften*, Erster Band, Erster Theil, page 56.[10]

The sublime in literary composition is accompanied by the enormous in music, by the artificially immense in the repetition, and so forth. Not that everything enormous is also sublime, as one would commonly believe, but rather because similar sentiments mutually reinforce one another and because the enormous is for the outer sense precisely what the sublime is for the inner sense. The impression on the inner sense must, therefore, be strengthened if the outer senses are harmoniously attuned to it by a similar impression.

In the works of fine arts and sciences, the awe, like the perfection which it presupposes, belongs to two different genera. Either the object to be represented possesses awesome properties in and for itself, in which case the awe at the object becomes the dominating idea in the soul; or the object in itself is not so extraordinary, but the artist possesses the skill of elevating its properties and showing them in an uncommon light. In this case the awe is directed more at the imitation than at the original, more at the merits of the art than at the merits of the object. Because of this and insofar as each work is also a copy of the perfection of its creator, the awe in this case is directed, above all, at the artist and his splendid qualities. One admires his great wit, his genius, his imagination, and his soul's capacities that harmonize for so worthy a final purpose, the hidden essence of which he knew how to reveal in his work. What especially pleases us in the case of art, considered as art, is the reference to the spiritual gifts of the artist which make themselves visibly known. If they bear the characteristics of an uncommon genius or some otherwise extraordinary talent, then they inspire awe on our part.

This division will provide us with the opportunity of deciding the extent to which the sublime is compatible with an embellished expression and in what case it refuses to assume such a form. We will begin with the type of sublimity where the awe and admiration [*Bewunderung*] spring from the object itself.

The value of perfections of the external condition are all too slight to be able to be held in awe by someone intelligent. Thus, riches, splendor, stature, and undeserved power are easily excluded from the sublime.

Longinus puts it quite ingeniously, "When things are of the sort that despising them is regarded as something great, they can never themselves contain anything actually lofty in itself."[11] In fact we do not admire those who possess great riches or superior positions of rank as much as those who can have them and reject them out of noble magnanimity. Thus, too, the representation of these things in architecture and the ornamental arts, where enhancements of the external condition come into play, can become illustrious, proud, and magnificent, to be sure. But the representation can reach the level of the sublime only by means of a *noble simplicity,* that is, through avoidance of anything that would appear to place great value on those enhancements. Not the disappearance of wealth and splendor but rather a wise indifference to them elevates our soul and teaches it its own dignity. They only remain important to the garish individual who wants to stake his pride on them.

Uncommon physical strength without courage, a beautiful shape in an insignificant place on the body, a beautifully formed face that betrays neither spirit nor sentiment, an uncommon agility without charm and bearing, and so forth are all bodily perfections that can to be sure, inspire a slight degree of awe and admiration.* But we will never be so enthralled by them as when we admire the perfections of spirit. An enormous intellect, enormous and uncommon sensibilities, a fortunate imagination joined with penetrating sagacity, noble and passionate emotions that elevate themselves above the conceptions of commoner souls (be their goal a true or apparent good), and generally all great qualities of a spirit that take us by surprise sweep our soul up with

---

*The Dutch translator must not have understood me correctly here since, in an added note, he cites against me the examples of Helen, Zeuxis, Venus, and Antinous[12] as well as Apollo and Laocoön, each of which arouses not a slight degree, but the highest degree of admiration. As if the masterpieces of ancient art did not please more through the fullness of soul that they express than through mere bodily beauties? Does Venus or Antinous de' Medici have merely a beautiful and rule-governed form that reveals neither spirit nor sentiment? If, moreover, the translator wanted to see the awe extended to the visible knowledge of each important and particular novelty, then he did not consider that in German we distinguish "amazement" [*Verwunderung*] and "awe" [*Bewunderung*]. Amazement is the condition of the soul looking at the novel and unexpected; but awe is its condition when it looks at the unexpectedly good.

them, elevating it, as it were, above itself. The immensely enormous character of those qualities (qualities that, given the absence of any expectation, must also appear *novel*) anchors the attentiveness of the spirit and so weakens all other adjoining conceptions that the soul can find no way of moving to another object. Instead, the soul is momentarily stopped in its tracks and gazes, *astounded,* at this immensity, if I am permitted to use this word in the sense in which it has already been used by good writers. If this inability to leave the object persists for some time, such a condition of the mind is called *astonishment.*

Meanwhile, the awe is almost comparable to a lightning bolt which blinds us in one moment and disappears in the next, provided that its flame is not sustained and nourished by the fire of a gentler sentiment. If we love the object of which we are in awe or if it deserves our sympathy because of an undeserved agony, the awe alternates with the more familiar sentiment in our mind. We wish, hope, and fear for the object of our love or our sympathy and admire his or her great soul that is beyond hope and fear. If an artist by his power of enchantment can put us into such a frame of mind, then he has reached the pinnacle of his art and satisfied the worthiest calling of the fine arts. It is a pleasant spectacle for the gods, an ancient philosopher says, to see a virtuous soul wrestle with fate, to see him surrender everything to it but his virtue. "Ecce spectaculum dignum, ad quod respiciat intentus operi suo Deus: ecce par Deo dignum, *vir fortis cum mala fortuna compositus!*"*

These, then, are the most distinguished sorts of awe which can spring from the object itself without its being necessary to draw the perfections of the artist into consideration as well. We want to see the extent to which an external embellishment in the expression is compatible with it.

As has been recalled in the foregoing discussion, the genuinely sublime occupies the powers of the soul in such a manner that all adjoining conceptions which are somehow attached to it have to disappear. It is like the sun that by itself illuminates and by its radiance obscures all weaker lights. Also, in the moment when we perceive the sublime, neither wit nor imagination administer their office in order to direct us somehow to other conceptions. For the sublime or the object of awe was never linked, by laws of the imagination, to some other conception in our soul upon which it could naturally follow. If someone doubts this, he need only reflect on the fact that the unexpected, the novel, is an essential determination of the sublime, according to our explanation. This is precisely the source of the strong impression that awe makes on our mind, which is not infrequently followed by an astonishment or even a type of stupor, an absence of consciousness.

It becomes clear from this that excessive embellishment in the expression of things is not compatible with something sublime of the first type. Expansion by means of adjoining conceptions is unnatural since the later must all, as it were, recede into the darkest of shadows. Because of the length of time it takes, the analysis of the central concept would weaken the awe since it would let us feel the sublime only little by little. Similes, just like other decorations of speech, can take place even less since the sources of them (wit and imagination) cease to act in the course of the perception of the sublime and instead allow the soul the appropriate leisure to give itself up to the concept of the sublime in order to consider it [in] all its magnitude. The central concept of the sublime is actually this:

*Judicis argutum quod non formidat acumen.*[14]

One can say of it, "it prefers to be seen under the light" (*volet haec sub luce videri*), in contrast to what is the case for the adjoining conception, "that loves the dark" (*haec amat obscurum*).[15] Thus, in representing something sublime of this type, the artist must devote himself to a naive, unaffected expression which allows

---

*Seneca, *De Providentia,* C.II.9.[13]

the reader or spectator to think more than is said to him. The artist's expression, meanwhile, must always remain intuitive and, where possible, be traced back to individual instances so that the mind of the reader is awakened and inspired to reflect.

We will clarify these ruminations with some examples. [...]

Enough has been said about the first type of the sublime in which the basis for awe is to be found in the very matter to be represented. Perhaps I have dwelled far too long on this type. But sublime sensibilities demanded a far more extensive elaboration since there is hardly a single one that is to be placed in this class among all the examples of the sublime cited by Longinus. I consider Ajax's silence an exception which actually belongs to this type, as does the famous plea of this hero (cited by Longinus in the ninth section): "Oh, father Zeus! Save the Greeks from the darkness, let it become light that our eyes might see again. If you have decided to do so, at least kill us on a bright day!"[16]

The second type of sublimity is that in which the awe and admiration redound more on the art of the representation than on what is represented and, thus, as was previously shown, mostly on the genius and the extraordinary capabilities of the artist. In itself the object often can contain nothing elevated in stature, nothing extraordinary. But we admire the enormous talents of the poet, his effective imagination, his capacity to compose, his profound insight into the nature of things, into characters and passions, and the noble manner in which he was able to express his splendid thoughts. A human being who dies wandering around the battlefield is in itself not an object deserving our awe or admiration. But there is no one who is not in awe of Klopstock's genius when he sketches this object. The first fortunate insight by means of which he opens up a field to great thoughts was his portrayal, not of an ordinary person, but of an atheist in this condition.

> ...The approaching victor
> And the prancing horse, the din of the clanging armor,
> And the screaming and the deadly rage and the thundering
>     heavens
> Storm around him. He lies and sinks with his head split in two
> Mute and without a thought among the dead, believing that he is
>     perishing.
> Then he lifts himself up one more time and still is and still thinks
>     and curses
> The fact that he still is, and with pallid, dying hands he spews
> Blood towards heaven. God he curses and still wants to deny.[17]

What painters call a "fracas," the wild tumult on a battlefield which is sketched here with such splendid strokes, sets the mind of the reader in motion, the most extreme motion. In the midst of this powerful din, the furious despair of the atheist who now feels that a God exists draws all our attention to it, filling us with disgust and dismay. The dreadfulness, the horror storms our soul from all sides; everywhere we find the *sensuous immensity* that arouses shudder after shudder and, as was shown above, undergirds the sentiment of the sublime. – What a thought! "...God he curses and still wants to deny."

How sublime the following depiction of someone about to die is:

> ...the eyes of the one dying grow dim and stare,
> Seeing no more. The countenance of the earth and sky vanish

> from him
> Deep into the night. He no longer hears a human voice
> Nor the tender laments of friends. He himself cannot talk,
> And with quivering tongue scarcely stammers out the anguished
>     departure.
> He exhales deeply; a cold, anxious sweat runs
> Over his forehead, the heart beats slowly, then stands still, and he
>     is dead.[18]

This description has, as far as its intrinsic value is concerned, a great similarity with the description of Sappho's jealous love, which Longinus has preserved for us.[19] This fragment of a poem, the English *Spectator* says, is for poets what the well-known ancient torso was for Michelangelo.[20] – Now all these sort of objects such as death, a battlefield, despair are not, in and for themselves, admirable, and they become so merely in the imitation of them by the genius of the artist. But by their very nature they are frightening and dreadful, and support the sentiment of the sublime because of the sensuous immensity inherent in them. For this reason artists also prefer to select them.

However, there are also objects of a completely indifferent nature that do not provide the artist with the slightest support. It is left completely up to the artist's powers as to how sublime these objects appear to us, that is to say, to what extent they would deserve our awe and admiration. An example of this type is the passage in Demosthenes praised by Longinus.[21]

> Tell me the truth, do you want to keep running around, asking one another: "Is there any news?" What more do you need to hear than the news that a man from Macedonia is waging war on all of Greece? "Has Philip died?" No, by God he has not; he is merely indisposed. But, oh, you Athenians, what does this matter to you? If we suppose that something human did befall him, you would surely create some other Philip.[22]

Where does the greatness lie here? What else arouses the idea of the immense here but the admirable spirit of the speaker who knows how to make use of the most trivial circumstances so successfully in order to impart life, emphasis, and spirit to his address?

No one is more successful than Shakespeare in knowing how to draw some advantage from the most ordinary circumstances and to make them sublime by some effective twist. The effect of this sort of sublimity must be all the more intense, the more unsuspectingly it surprises and the less people expect such important and tragic consequences from so insignificant a cause. I will cite a few examples of this from *Hamlet*. [Mendelssohn cites passages such as the "O, what a rogue and peasant slave am I" soliloquy. – Ed.] [...]

If in his work the artist wants to convince us in visible and sensuous fashion of the perfection that he possesses to a high degree, then he must direct his attention to the finest and greatest beauties capable of animating his imagination. Minute brushstrokes testify, to be sure, to the artist's finishing touch, the toil and the care he took to please us. But the sublimity that warrants our awe and admiration is certainly not to be sought in them. Awe is a debt that we owe the extraordinary gifts of spirit. These gifts are called, in the narrowest sense of the word, "genius." Accordingly, where sensuous marks of genius are to be found in a work of art, we are ready to give the artist the admiration he deserves. Yet the insignificant attendant circumstances including the final execution of a picture (which, of course, is part of the painting but not essential to it) show only all too clearly the toil and trouble that the work cost the artist, and we are accustomed to subtract from the genius as much as we attribute to the toil.

Thus, one sees that in this type of sublimity the artist is free to apply all the wealth of his art in order to place in their true light the beauties that his manner of thinking has been fortunate enough to produce. This type of sublimity is thus distinguished from the first since preference is necessarily given a naive and unaffected presentation. At the same time, however, one sees that there are small beauties here as well that could perhaps preoccupy a lesser spirit at length but that the artist should not consider worthy of his attention and toil and that he may indulge only if they present themselves, as it were, of themselves. It will suffice to cite a single example of this. The holy poet of the psalms says of the sun (Psalm 19.6):

The sun rises like a groom from his bedroom
And delights, like a hero, in running the race.

Both similes are uncommonly sublime, and Hogarth finds a thought similar to the latter in particular in the image of Apollo, so famous in antiquity, whom the artist characterized quite splendidly as the god of the day because of the speed with which he seems to appear and shoot his arrows (where the arrows signify sunbeams). [...]

Our definition makes clear that this second type of the sublime can consist as much in thoughts as in the expression of them. This type of sublimity, in other words, can consist (1) in the understanding as well as in the imagination, in the invention, the similes, sentences, sensibilities, sketches of characters, passions, and mores of human beings, and of objects in nature, and (2) in the use of embellishments, in the selection of the sort of adjectives that designate the most sensuous properties, in the order and combination of the words, and, finally, in the melody and in the harmony of the phrase. For the artist can make his extraordinary talents known by means of all these beauties.

It will not be necessary to recall that one very often meets with both types of the sublime in the works of art. With regard to the notion of imitation, the essay "On the main principles of the fine arts and sciences"[23] has already indicated that our pleasure in the similarity of an artistic imitation is far greater than our pleasure in that of a copy produced by nature itself. For in the former case, regard for the artist is part of the mix and elevates the pleasure. Now this obtains not only for imitation but for all beautiful things in general, as was also recalled in the essay mentioned. They are far more pleasing when they are regarded at the same time as imprints of the perfections of the artist who produced them. However little he may himself seek to appear and to shine, footsteps of his genius will always be left behind which from time to time betray him and allow us to know the giant who is responsible for them. Hence, subjective sublimity can in many cases be combined with objective sublimity. Depending, however, upon whether the awe and admiration redound more to the object itself or to the skill of the artist, the expression can be more or less embellished, something that must be judged in each case on the basis of the makeup of the subject treated or of the aim of the artist.

Longinus appears to concern himself solely with the second type of sublimity and, since his essays are in everybody's hands, it would be superfluous to clarify all these observations by examples as well. My intention was merely to make clearer the concept of the sublime which is treated so diversely in the works of the fine arts and sciences, and I am satisfied if I have not completely failed at this. I am content to add some additional remarks.

Longinus says (in the seventh major part of his work) "generally you can be sure that something is genuinely beautiful and sublime if it is pleasing to everybody everywhere."[24]

Dissatisfied with this proposition of Longinus, Perrault says the following in his reply to Boileau's eleventh remark[25] about Longinus: "If this precept is assumed, the sublime would be found very rarely, since people of different ages, education, and lifestyles imagine the very same thing in very different ways."[26] It seems to me that Perrault is not wrong if what is being discussed is the second type of sublimity. A profound insight into the secrets of art are frequently required to be able to admire the artist's talents, and how few noble souls there are who possess this profound insight! But the sublimeness of an object and especially the sublimeness of certain sensibilities must certainly touch people of every sort as soon as they understand the words through which that sublimity has been expressed. Indeed, as long as their feelings have not been completely spoiled, even people with a common way of thinking must find some sublime sensibilities all the more awesome, the more it elevates them above their common way of thinking and the less they would have trusted the human soul with such perfections.

Someone might raise the following objection: Have not the most sophisticated art critics debated about passages as to whether they are to be counted among the sublime? The passage, for example, from Holy Scripture, "God said, Let there be light, and so forth" belongs indisputably to the first type of sublimity, and yet its sublimity has been doubted by clever minds. Where, then, is there the agreement that we would look upon as a sign of the first type of sublimity?

Consider, however, the fact that Longinus' opponents have never doubted that the event, "God said, Let there be light, and there was light" is in itself sublime. They have merely not wanted to concede that it was the aim of the Lawgiver to say something sublime by this. In other words, they acknowledged that this passage is an instance of the first type of sublimity, and only the sublimity of the second type was doubted by them. When one looks at the polemical treatises that have been exchanged regarding this passage, it is amazing how little the art critics have been interested in finding agreement with one another. One party appeals to the sublimity of the action and the simplicity of the expression; another passes over this in silence and speaks only of the intention of the Lawgiver who, to put it in human terms, certainly had no intention of assiduously applying the powers of his soul to produce something sublime. If they had explained themselves, the debate would have been resolved.

Hence, Longinus is not only right about the fact that what everyone everywhere finds pleasing must actually be beautiful and sublime, but one can also invert the proposition if one is speaking of the first type of sublimity, and say that the sublime must be pleasing to everyone everywhere. The words of the Greek art critic [Longinus – Ed.] that immediately follow also make it apparent that he is really speaking of the first type of the sublime when he says that it is pleasing to everyone everywhere, even though he does not explicitly present this essential distinction. He says: "If people with many different leanings, with dissimilar lifestyles, who are different in their sciences and in years, are nevertheless at the same time moved by something, then the union, as it were, of so many disunities provides all the greater certainty that the very things that one thus admires must unmistakably contain something majestic."[27] [...]

## Questions

1. Compared with other authors in this volume, what strikes you as similar, or different, about Mendelssohn's ideas?

2. Mendelssohn distinguishes sublimity in an *object* from a sublime *manner* of artistic presentation. What role do beauty and embellishment play here? How is this like, or unlike, other accounts of the sublime in art?

3. What aspects of Mendelssohn's account strike you as theological? Metaphysical? Explain.

4. How does Mendelssohn conceive of the relation between the ethical and the aesthetic, between virtue and sublimity?

5. Awe is the condition of the soul, Mendelssohn claims, "when it looks at the unexpectedly good." Do you think he needs still another type of sublimity to account for remarkable, stirring displays of virtue? Is his notion of a perfect, strong, intensive immensity sufficient to account for this? Explain.

6. Summarize and evaluate Mendelssohn's proposal about how to resolve certain disputes and disagreements when judging sublimity. What are its strengths and weaknesses? How is it like/unlike other proposals?

## Further reading

Altmann, Alexander. *Moses Mendelssohn: A Biographical Study*. Alabama: University of Alabama Press, 1973.

Beiser, Frederick. *Diotima's Children: German Aesthetic Rationalism from Leibniz to Lessing*, 196–243. Oxford: Oxford University Press, 2009. [Chapter 7: "Mendelssohn's Defense of Reason."]

Cohen, Hermann. *Kants Begründung der Aesthetik*. Berlin: F. Dümmler, 1889.

Dahlstrom, Daniel. "Moses Mendelssohn." In *A Companion to Early Modern Philosophy*, ed. Steven Nadler, 618–32. Malden, MA: Blackwell, 2002.

Freudenthal, Gideon. *No Religion Without Idolatry: Mendelssohn's Jewish Enlightenment*. Notre Dame, IN: Notre Dame University Press, 2012.

Guyer, Paul. *Kant and the Experience of Freedom: Essays on Aesthetics and Morality*, 131–60. Cambridge: Cambridge University Press, 1993. [Chapter 4: "The Perfections of Art: Mendelssohn, Moritz, and Kant."]

Munk, Reinier. *Moses Mendelssohn's Metaphysics and Aesthetics*. New York: Springer, 2011.

# CHAPTER 11
## ELIZABETH CARTER, FROM *LETTERS FROM MRS. ELIZABETH CARTER TO MRS. MONTAGU* (1762)

Throughout its long history, the sublime has been characterized in many kinds of texts and genres of writing, from treatises to notes and correspondence. The following is a 1762 letter to Elizabeth Montagu from Elizabeth Carter (Deal, Kent in 1717, London, 1806). Carter was an English poet ("Ode to Wisdom"), educationalist, and translator of Crousaz (1739), Algarotti (1739), and Epictetus (1758), among other things. She was a close friend of Samuel Johnson, who admired her abilities as a translator and declared her to be the best Greek scholar in England. In *A Room of One's Own* (Chapter 4), Virginia Woolf urges "homage to the robust shade of Eliza Carter—the valiant old woman who tied a bell to her bedstead in order that she might wake early and learn Greek."

Among Carter's other friends and correspondents were Edmund Burke, Sir Joshua Reynolds, Horace Walpole, Hannah More, and most of the other literary personages of the day. Carter was a member of the female intellectual circle, the Blue Stockings Society, organized and hosted by Elizabeth Montagu (1718–1800). Montagu played a crucial role of interlocutor, as this letter reveals.

In the letter, Elizabeth Carter describes one of her experiences of the sublime. ("I took a walk the other morning, which I believe you would have admitted to be in the true sublime.") She describes a mixed sentiment, a mixture of a feeling of smallness and of exaltation. She reports not only a feeling of her own "littleness," but also a positive uplift stemming from the expansion of the "soul" caused by surveying the "stupendous objects" and "wonders of Omnipotence." The view of great and astonishing objects "gives a noble extension to the powers of the mind." She implies that in addition to this mental expansion in response to natural wonders there is a second source of the pleasure in the sublime: release from everyday affairs and concerns.

She observes that the experience can be tiring—she says she can dwell in it only as much as the "head will allow" her—after which a return to ordinary affairs and common business, and "enjoyments of a gentler kind," is welcome. In the letter, she does exactly that. After recounting her stirring experience, she mentions (or asks about) friends, travel plans, Montagu's health, and other news.

### Note on the text

Source: Letter XLIII, reprinted from *Letters from Mrs. Elizabeth Carter to Mrs. Montagu, Between the Years 1755 and 1800, Chiefly upon Literary and Moral Subjects*, edited by Montagu Pennington, 3 vols., vol. 1, 165–70. London: F.C. and J. Rivington, 1817.

Punctuation, style, format, and spelling have occasionally been modified or updated. The volume editor has inserted comments in square brackets. The first footnote is by Carter.

## Letter XLIII.

Deal, July 2, 1762.

It was with great pleasure, my dear friend, that I accompanied you in your travels to the venerable ruins of castles distinguished by such interesting events in the history of our own country, which, call me as much a Goth as you please, will always have a more striking effect on my mind than any antiquities of Greece or Rome; and I must have visited every remarkable spot on British ground before I feel any curiosity to see the Tarpeian Rock, or the Tusculan Villa. I have often heard my sister describe Warwick and Kenilworth castles, and make the same honorable mention of the ivy that you do. I should have been very happy to have retraced the English annals with you, on the venerable spots which present every memorable transaction to one's mind in colours more vivid than those which strike one from merely reading the history in a closet. We should certainly have agreed extremely well in general, but I know not whether I might have been quite so charitable in my lamentation of the treachery of Warwick's confederates: it would be profanation to call it friendship betwixt such characters. What title had one who had prostituted great valor and great talents, and sacrificed every duty to pride, revenge, and caprice, to expect fidelity in leagues of guilt!

Though I believe nothing can be juster than your observation, that great part of the English history is rather a tissue of personal adventures, and catastrophes, than a series of political events[1]: it seems strange that this should be a reason why it is so little known, as upon that very account it is the more generally interesting and instructive. A mere series of political events, seems a kind of automaton, and few eyes are perspicacious enough to discern the springs by which it is moved, and few understandings sufficiently extensive to comprehend how far individuals are concerned in what affects the whole. But personal adventures and catastrophes are all life and action; every reader is concerned in them, as every reader has either felt the passions and principles from whence they are produced in his own breast, or has been affected by their operations on others.

I am heartily sorry for the vexatious operation which you are obliged to undergo. It is, indeed, very grievous to be confined in London, and to be obliged to quarrel with the sun, with whom one is upon such friendly terms. The weather is extremely fine here, and I make as much use of it as my head will allow me. I took a walk the other morning, which I believe you would have admitted to be in the true sublime. I rambled till I got to the top of a hill, from whence I surveyed a vast extent of variegated country all round me, and the immense ocean beneath. I enjoyed this magnificent spectacle in all the freedom of absolute solitude. Not a house, or a human creature was within my view, nor a sound to be heard but the voice of the elements, the whistling winds, and rolling tide. I found myself deeply awed, and struck by this situation. The first impression it gave me, was a sense of my own littleness, and I seemed shrinking to nothing in the midst of the stupendous objects by which I was surrounded. But I soon grew more important by the recollection that nothing which my eyes could survey, was of equal dignity with the human mind, at once the theatre and spectator of the wonders of Omnipotence. How vast are the capacities of the soul,[2] and how little and contemptible its aims and pursuits? I continued my speculations on this elevation, till my thoughts grew overpowered and fatigued, and I was very well contented to descend to humbler exercises and employments. The view of great and astonishing objects is sometimes very useful, and gives a noble extension to the powers of the mind; but for wise ends, it is not formed to dwell long upon them, without a weariness that brings it back to its duties in the ordinary affairs of the world, and to common business and amusement. And so after all the elevation of the thoughts from a view of the sublime and stupendous objects of nature, one is very glad to return to enjoyments of a gentler kind, the song of linnets, and the bloom of roses.

Mrs. Chapone is at Kensington with Mr. and Mrs. Mulso, and if you stay in town long enough to call on her there, it will make them all very happy; I had a letter from her lately, in which, on behalf of herself and Miss Burrows, she most strictly enjoins me to take care of them for next winter. *Nimirum intelligit—quanti me facias, etc.*[3]

It is from no manner of cruelty to myself that I shall not be so happy to wait on you to Sandleford, but that it really is not in my power. I hope I shall soon hear that you are escaped thither from the fiery air of London. Do not forget that you have promised to send me my Lord Lyttelton's vision.[4]

We are just settled in our new abode, and now it is doubtful whether we may not very soon be obliged to quit it, which you will think no very amusing prospect to people who have but just recovered the fatigue and inconvenience of one removal. I think on this and some other perplexities as little as I can, but they will sometimes harass my spirits. I was obliged to you for mentioning that our friends at Lambeth are well, for Miss Talbot has not writ to me [since – Ed.] time immemorial. I hope your eyes continue well.

Yours, etc.

## Questions

1. Comment on Carter's recollection of her experience of the "sublime." ("I took a walk the other morning. . . . I found myself deeply awed.") Is it in agreement with your own experiences? Explain. What are her views of self-awareness and self-admiration in the experience?

2. Carter reports that she "enjoyed this magnificent spectacle in all the freedom of absolute solitude." Do you think it is necessary to be alone to experience the sublime? Explain.

3. Summarize and assess her explanation of the sources of the exaltation or uplift (the positive moment) in the sublime.

4. Do Carter's descriptions and explanations remind you of other readings? Explain to what extent the genre of writing (e.g., correspondence) is significant here.

5. Critics sometimes maintain that the concept of the sublime is irredeemably patriarchal or masculinist. Do Carter's descriptions and explanations provide a counterexample to this claim? Explain.

## Further reading

Carter, Elizabeth, et al. *A Series of Letters between Mrs. Elizabeth Carter and Miss Catherine Talbot, from the Year 1741 to 1770: To Which Are Added Letters from Mrs. Elizabeth Carter to Mrs. Vesey, between the Years 1763 and 1787; Published from the Original Manuscripts in the Possession of the Rev. Montagu Pennington.* London: Rivington, 1809, 4 vols.

Carter, Elizabeth, and Montagu Pennington. *Memoirs of the Life of Mrs. Elizabeth Carter.* Cambridge: Cambridge University Press, 2011 [1807].

Dorr, Priscilla. "Elizabeth Carter (1717–1806) UK." *Tulsa Studies in Women's Literature* 5, no. 1 (1986): 138–40.

Monk, Samuel H. *The Sublime: A Study of Critical Theories in XVIII-Century England: With a New Preface by the Author.* Ann Arbor, MI: The University of Michigan Press, 1960.

Myers, Sylvia Harcstark. *The Bluestocking Circle: Women, Friendship, and the Life of the Mind in Eighteenth-Century England.* Oxford: Claredon, 1990.

Rogers, Katharine M. *Feminism in Eighteenth-Century England.* Urbana: University of Illinois Press, 1982.

Rowton, Frederic. *The Female Poets of Great Britain: Chronologically Arranged with Copious Selections and Critical Remarks,* ed. Marilyn L. Williamson. Detroit: Wayne State University Press, 1981. [Reprint of the 1851 edition.]

# CHAPTER 12
# IMMANUEL KANT, FROM *OBSERVATIONS ON THE FEELING OF THE BEAUTIFUL AND SUBLIME* (1764)

The following excerpt is from a popular treatise from Kant's "precritical" period, that is, before the publication of the *Critique of Pure Reason* in 1781. (The present volume also includes selections from the critical period: *Critique of the Power of Judgment* and *Anthropology from a Pragmatic Point of View.*) In the following excerpt, Kant (1724–1804) distinguishes the sublime and the beautiful, identifies and gives examples of three kinds of sublimity, and discusses moral feeling and sublimity. Kant's reference to "the mathematical representation of the immeasurable magnitude of the universe" (2:215), albeit brief, may be an undeveloped precursor to his critical theory of the mathematical sublime.

## Note on the text

Source: Excerpted from Immanuel Kant, *Observations on the Feeling of the Beautiful and Sublime,* translated by Paul Guyer. In *Anthropology, History, Education,* edited by Günter Zöller and Robert Louden, 23–32, 39. Cambridge: Cambridge University Press, 2007.

Endnotes with numerals are based on Paul Guyer's notes, with occasional modifications. Footnotes with an asterisk were written by Kant. German words and editorial remarks within square brackets are supplied by Guyer unless noted otherwise (though he uses footnotes rather than square brackets), whereas foreign words given by Kant are placed within round brackets.

The pagination in the Academy Edition (*Akademie Ausgabe*) of Kant's collected writings has been placed within the body of the text and is cited in the text and notes by volume: page number. For instance, "[2:207]" indicates page 207 in volume two of Kant's collected writings.

## [2:207] FIRST SECTON, ON THE DISTINCT OBJECTS OF THE FEELING FOR THE SUBLIME AND THE BEAUTIFUL

The different sentiments of gratification or vexation rest not so much on the constitution of the external things that arouse them as on the feeling, intrinsic to every person, of being touched by them with pleasure or displeasure. Hence arise the joys for some people in what is disgusting to others, the passion of a lover that is often a mystery to everyone else, or even the lively repugnance that one person feels [*empfindet*] in that which is completely indifferent to another. The field for observations of these peculiarities of human nature is very extensive and still conceals a rich lode for discoveries that are as charming as they are instructive. For now, I will cast my glance only on several places that seem especially to stand out in this region, and even on these more with the eye of an observer than of the philosopher.

Since a human being finds himself happy only insofar as he satisfies an inclination, the feeling that makes him capable of enjoying a great gratification without requiring exceptional talents is certainly no small matter. Stout persons, whose most inspired author is their cook, and whose works of fine taste are to be found in their cellar, get just as lively a joy from vulgarities and a crude joke as that of which persons of nobler sentiment are so proud. A comfortable man, who likes having books read aloud to him [2:208] because that helps him fall asleep; the merchant to whom all gratifications seem ridiculous except for that which a clever man enjoys when he calculates his business profits; he who loves the opposite sex only insofar as he counts it among the things that are to be enjoyed; the lover of the hunt, whether he hunts fleas, like Domitian,[1] or wild beasts, like A- [abbreviated by Kant – Ed.]: all of these have a feeling which makes them capable of enjoying gratification after their fashion, without their having to envy others or even being able to form any concept of others; but for now I do not direct any attention to this. There is still a feeling of a finer sort, thus named either because one can enjoy it longer without surfeit and exhaustion, or because it presupposes, so to speak, a susceptibility of the soul which at the same time makes it fit for virtuous impulses, or because it is a sign of talents and excellences of the intellect; while by contrast the former can occur in complete thoughtlessness. I will consider one aspect of this feeling. Yet I exclude here the inclination which is attached to lofty intellectual insights, and the charm of which a **Kepler** was capable when, as **Bayle** reports, he would not have sold one of his discoveries for a princedom.[2] This sentiment is altogether too fine to belong in the present project, which will touch only upon the sensuous feeling of which more common souls are also capable.

The finer feeling that we will now consider is preeminently of two kinds: the feeling of the **sublime** and of the **beautiful**.[3] Being touched by either is agreeable, but in very different ways. The sight of a mountain whose snow-covered peaks arise above the clouds, the description of a raging storm, or the depiction of the kingdom of hell by **Milton** arouses satisfaction, but with dread;[4] by contrast, the prospect of meadows strewn with flowers, of valleys with winding brooks, covered with grazing herds, the description of Elysium,[5] or **Homer's** depiction of the girdle of Venus[6] also occasion an agreeable sentiment, but one that is joyful and smiling. For the former to make its impression on us in its proper strength, we must have a **feeling** of the **sublime,** and order properly to **enjoy** the latter we must have a **feeling** for the **beautiful**. Lofty oaks and lonely shadows in sacred groves are **sublime**, flower beds, low hedges, and trees trimmed into figures are **beautiful**. The night is **sublime**, the day [2:209] is **beautiful**. Casts of mind that possess a feeling for the sublime are gradually drawn into lofty sentiments, of friendship, of contempt for the world, of eternity, by the quiet calm of a summer evening, when the flickering light of the stars breaks through the umber shadows of the night and the lonely moon rises into view. The brilliant day inspires busy fervor and a feeling of [second and third editions read: *for*] gaiety. The sublime **touches**, the beautiful **charms**. The mien of the human being who finds himself in the full feeling of the sublime is serious, sometimes even rigid and astonished. By contrast, the lively sentiment of the beautiful announces itself through shining cheerfulness in the eyes, through traces of a smile, and often through audible mirth. The sublime is in turn of different sorts. The feeling of it is sometimes accompanied with some dread or even melancholy, in some cases merely with quiet admiration and in yet others with beauty spread over a sublime prospect. I will call the first the **terrifying sublime**, the second the **noble**, and the third the **magnificent**. Deep solitude is sublime, but in a terrifying way.*,[7] For this reason great and

---

*I will only provide an example of the noble dread which the description of a total solitude can inspire, and to this end I will extract several passages from **Carazan's dream** in the *Bremen Magazine*, Volume IV, page 539. The more his riches had grown, the more did this miserly rich man bar his heart to compassion and the love of others. Meanwhile, as the love of humankind grew cold in him, the diligence of his prayers and religious devotions increased. After this confession, he goes on to recount: One evening, as I did my sums by my lamp and calculated the profit of my business, I was overcome by sleep. In this condition I saw the angel of death come upon me like a whirlwind, and he struck me, before I could plead against the terrible blow. I was petrified as I became aware that my fate had been cast for

extensive [2:210] wastes, such as the immense deserts of Schamo in Tartary, have always given us occasion to people them with fearsome shades, goblins, and ghosts.

The sublime must always be large, the beautiful can also be small. The sublime must be simple, the beautiful can be decorated and ornamented. A great height is just as sublime as a great depth, but the latter is accompanied with the sensation [*Empfindung* ] of shuddering, the former with that of admiration; hence the latter **sentiment** can be terrifyingly sublime and the former noble. The sight of an Egyptian pyramid is far more moving, as **Hasselquist** reports,[8] than one can imagine from any description, but its construction is simple and noble. St. Peter's in Rome is magnificent. Since on its frame, which is grand and simple, beauty, e.g., gold, mosaics, etc., are spread in such a way that it is still the sentiment of the sublime which has the most effect, the object is called magnificent.[9] An arsenal must be noble and simple, a residential castle magnificent, and a pleasure palace beautiful and decorated.[10]

A long duration is sublime. If it is of time past, it is noble, if it is projected forth into an unforeseeable future, then there is something terrifying in it. An edifice from the most distant antiquity is worthy of honor. **Haller's** description of the future eternity inspires a mild horror, and of the past, a transfixed admiration.[11]

---

eternity, and that to all the good I had done, nothing could be added, and from all the evil that I had done, nothing could be subtracted. I was led before the throne of he who dwells in the third heaven. The brilliance that flamed before me spoke to me thus: Carazan, your divine service is rejected. You have closed your heart to the love of humankind, and held on to your treasures with an iron hand. You have lived only for yourself, and hence in the future you shall also live alone and excluded from all communion with the entirety of creation for all eternity. In this moment I was ripped away by an invisible force and driven through the shining edifice of creation. I quickly left innumerable worlds behind me. As I approached the most extreme limit of nature, I noticed that the shadows of the boundless void sank into the abyss before me. A fearful realm of eternal silence, solitude and darkness! Unspeakable dread overcame me at this sight. I gradually lost the last stars from view, and finally the last glimmer of light was extinguished in the most extreme darkness. The mortal terrors of despair increased with every moment, just as every moment my distance from the last inhabited world increased. I reflected with unbearable anguish in my heart that if ten thousand years were to carry me further beyond the boundaries of everything created, I would still see forward into the immeasurable abyss of darkness without help or hope of return. In this bewilderment I stretched my hands out to actual objects with such vehemence that I was thereby awakened. And now I have been instructed to esteem human beings; for even the least of them, whom in the pride of my good fortune I had turned from my door, would have been far more welcome to me in that terrifying desert than all the treasures of Golconda. [end of 2:209]

## [2:211] SECOND SECTION. ON THE QUALITIES OF THE SUBLIME
## AND THE BEAUTIFUL IN HUMAN BEINGS IN GENERAL

Understanding is sublime, wit is beautiful. Boldness is sublime and grand, cunning is petty, but beautiful. Caution, said **Cromwell**, is a virtue for mayors.[12] Truthfulness and honesty is simple and noble, jocularity and pleasing flattery is fine and beautiful. Civility is the beauty of virtue. An unselfish urge to serve is noble, refinement (*politesse*) and courtliness are beautiful. Sublime qualities inspire esteem, but beautiful ones inspire love. People whose feelings run primarily to the beautiful seek out their honest, steady and serious friends only in case of need; for ordinary company, however, they choose jocular, clever, and courtly companions. One esteems many a person too highly to be able to love him. He inspires admiration, but he is too far above us for us to dare to come close to him with the familiarity of love.

Those in whom both feelings are united will find that they are more powerfully moved by the sublime than by the beautiful, but that without variation or accompaniment by the latter the former is tiring and cannot be enjoyed as long.* The lofty sentiments to which conversation a well-chosen company is sometimes elevated must intermittently dissolve into a cheerful joke, and laughing joys should make a beautiful contrast with moved serious countenances, allowing for an unforced alternation between both sorts of sentiment. **Friendship** has primarily the character of the sublime, but **sexual love** that of the beautiful. Yet tenderness and [2:212] deep esteem give the latter a certain dignity and sublimity, while flighty jocularity and intimacy elevate the coloration of the beautiful in this sentiment. In my opinion, **tragedy** is distinguished from **comedy** primarily in the fact that in the former it is the feeling for the **sublime** while in the latter it is the feeling for the **beautiful** that is touched. In the former there is displayed magnanimous sacrifice for the well-being of another, bold resolve in the face of danger, and proven fidelity. There love is melancholic, tender, and full of esteem; the misfortune of others stirs sympathetic sentiments in the bosom of the onlooker and allows his magnanimous heart to beat for the need of others. He is gently moved and feels the dignity of his own nature. Comedy, in contrast, represents intrigues, marvelous entanglements and clever people who know how to wriggle out of them, fools who let themselves be deceived, jests and ridiculous characters. Here love is not so grave, it is merry and intimate. Yet as in other cases, here too the noble can be united with the beautiful to a certain **degree**.

Even the vices and moral failings often carry with them some of the traits of the sublime or the beautiful, at least as they appear to our sensory feeling, without having been examined by reason. The wrath of someone fearsome is sublime, like the wrath of Achilles in the *Iliad*.[13] In general, the hero of **Homer** is **terrifyingly sublime**, that of **Virgil**, by contrast, **noble**. Open, brazen revenge for a great offense has something grand in it, and however impermissible it might be, yet in the telling it nevertheless touches us with dread and satisfaction. When Shah Nadir was attacked at night in his tent by some conspirators, as Hanway reports, after he had already received several wounds and was defending himself in despair, he yelled: **Mercy! I will pardon you all**. One of the conspirators answered, as he raised his saber high: **You have shown no mercy and deserve none**.[14] Resolute audacity in a rogue is extremely dangerous, yet it touches us in the telling, and even when he is dragged to a shameful death yet he ennobles himself to a certain degree when he faces it spitefully and with contempt. On the other side, a cunningly conceived scheme, even when it amounts to a piece of knavery, has

---

*The sentiments of the sublime stretch the powers of the soul more forcefully and therefore tire more quickly. One will read a pastoral longer at one sitting than Milton's *Paradise Lost* and la Bruyère longer than Young. It even seems to me to be a failing of the latter as a moral poet that he holds forth too uniformly in a sublime tone; for the strength of the impressions can only be refreshed by interspersing gentler passages. In the case of the beautiful nothing is more tiring than laborious art that thereby betrays itself. The effort to charm becomes painful and is felt to be wearisome. [end of 2:211]

something about it that is fine and worth a laugh. A wanton inclination (*coquetterie*) in a refined sense, namely an effort to fascinate and to charm, is perhaps blameworthy in an otherwise decorous person, [2:213] yet it is still beautiful and is commonly preferred to the honorable, serious demeanor.

The figure [*Gestalt*] of persons who please through their outward appearance [*Ansehen*] touches now upon one sort of feeling, now upon the other. A grand stature earns regard [*Ansehen*] and respect, a small one more intimacy. Even brownish color and black eyes are more closely related to the sublime, blue eyes and blonde color to the beautiful. A somewhat greater age is associated more with the qualities of the sublime, youth, however with those of the beautiful. It is similar with difference in station, and in all of those relations mentioned here even the costumes must match this distinction in feeling. Grand, sizable persons must observe simplicity or at most splendor in their dress, while small ones can be decorated and adorned. Darker colors and uniformity in costume are fitting for age, while youth radiates through brighter clothing with lively contrasts. Among the stations of similar fortune and rank, the cleric must display the greatest simplicity, the statesman the greatest splendor. The paramour can adorn himself as he pleases.

Even in external circumstances of fortune there is something that, at least in the folly of humankind, matches these sentiments. People commonly find themselves inclined to respect birth and title. Wealth, even without merit, is honored even by the disinterested, presumably because they associate with the representation of it projects for great actions that could be carried out by its means. This respect is even sometimes extended to many a rich scoundrel, who will never undertake such actions and has no conception of the noble feeling that can alone make riches estimable. What magnifies the evil of poverty is contempt, which cannot be entirely overcome even by merits, at least not before common eyes, unless rank and title deceive this coarse feeling and to some extent work to its advantage.

In human nature there are never to be found praiseworthy qualities that do not at the same time degenerate through endless gradations into the most extreme imperfection. The quality of the **terrifying sublime**, if it becomes entirely unnatural, [2:214] is **adventurous.**\* Unnatural things, in so far as the sublime is thereby intended, even if little or none of it is actually found, are **grotesqueries.** He who loves and believes the adventurous is a **fantast**, while the inclination to grotesqueries makes for a **crank.** On the other side, the feeling of the beautiful degenerates if the noble is entirely lacking from it, and one calls it **ridiculous.** A male with this quality, if he is young, is called a **dandy**, and if he is middle-aged, a **fop.** Since the sublime is most necessary for the greater age, an **old fop** is the most contemptible creature in nature, just as a young crank is the most repulsive and insufferable. Jokes and cheerfulness go with the feeling of the beautiful. Nevertheless, a good deal of understanding can show through, and to this extent they can be more or less related to the sublime. He in whose cheerfulness this admixture cannot be noticed **babbles.** He who babbles constantly is **silly.** One readily notices that even clever people occasionally babble, and that it requires not a little intelligence [*Geist*] to call the understanding away from its post for a brief time without anything thereby going awry. He whose speeches or actions neither entertain nor move is **boring.** The bore who nevertheless tries to do both is **tasteless.** The tasteless person, if he is conceited, is a **fool.**\*\*

I will make this curious catalogue of human frailties somewhat more comprehensible through examples, for he who lacks Hogarth's burin must use description to make up for what the drawing lacks in expression.[15]

---

\*In so far as sublimity or beauty exceed the known average, one tends to call them **fictitious.**

\*\*One quickly notices that this honorable company divides itself into two compartments, the cranks and the fops. A learned crank is politely called a **pedant.** If he adopts the obstinate mien of wisdom, like the **dunces** of olden and recent times, then the cap with bells becomes him well. The class of fops is more often encountered in high society. It is perhaps better than the former. At their expense one has much to gain and much to laugh at. In this caricature one makes a wry face at the other and knocks his empty head on the head of his brother. [end of 2:214]

Boldly undertaking danger for our own rights, for those of the fatherland, or for those of our friends is sublime. The crusades and ancient knighthood were **adventurous**; duels, a miserable remnant [2:215] of the latter out of a perverted conception of honor, are **grotesqueries**. Melancholy withdrawal from the tumult of the world out of a legitimate weariness is **noble**. The solitary devotion of the ancient hermits was **adventurous**. Cloisters and graves of that sort for the entombment of living saints are **grotesqueries**. Subduing one's passions by means of principles is **sublime**. Castigation, vows, and other such monkish virtues are **grotesqueries**. Holy bones, holy wood, and all that sort of rubbish, the holy stools of the Great Lama of Tibet not excluded, are **grotesqueries**. Among the works of wit and fine feeling, the epic poems of Virgil and Klopstock are among the **noble**, those of Homer and Milton among the **adventurous**. The *Metamorphoses* of Ovid are **grotesqueries**; the fairy tales of French lunacy are the most wretched grotesqueries that have ever been hatched. Anacreontic poems commonly come very close to the **ridiculous**.

The works of the understanding and acuity, to the extent that their objects also contain something for feeling, likewise take some part in the differences under consideration. The mathematical representation of the immeasurable magnitude of the universe, metaphysical consideration of eternity, of providence, of the immortality of our soul contain a certain sublimity and dignity. Yet philosophy [*Weltweisheit*] is also distorted by many empty subtleties, and the semblance of thoroughness does not prevent the four syllogistic figures from deserving to be counted as scholastic grotesqueries.

Among moral [*moralischen*] qualities, true virtue alone is sublime. There are nevertheless good moral [*sittlichen*] qualities that are lovable and beautiful and, to the extent that they harmonize with virtue, may also be regarded as noble, even though they cannot genuinely be counted as part of the virtuous disposition. Judgment about this is delicate and involved. One certainly cannot call that frame of mind virtuous that is a source of actions of the sort to which virtue would also lead but on grounds that only contingently agree with it, and which thus given its nature can also often conflict with the universal rules of virtue. A certain tenderheartedness that is easily led into a warm feeling of **sympathy** is beautiful and lovable, for it indicates a kindly participation in the fate of other people, to which principles of virtue likewise lead. But this kindly passion is nevertheless weak and is [2:216] always blind. For suppose that this sentiment moves you to help someone in need with your expenditure, but you are indebted to someone else and by this means you make it impossible for yourself to fulfill the strict duty of justice; then obviously the action cannot arise from any virtuous resolution, for that could not possibly entice you into sacrificing a higher obligation to this blind enchantment. If, by contrast, general affection towards humankind has become your principle, to which you always subject your actions, then your love towards the one in need remains, but it is now, from a higher standpoint, placed in its proper relationship to your duty as a whole. The universal affection is a ground for participating in his ill-fortune, but at the same time it is also a ground of justice, in accordance with whose precept you must now forbear this action. Now as soon as this feeling is raised to its proper universality, it is sublime, but also colder. For it is not possible that our bosom should swell with tenderness on behalf of every human being and swim in melancholy for everyone else's need, otherwise the virtuous person, like Heraclitus constantly melting into sympathetic tears,[16] with all this goodheartedness would nevertheless become nothing more than a tenderhearted idler.*

---

*On closer consideration, one finds that however loveable the quality of sympathy may be, yet it does not have in itself the dignity of virtue. A suffering child, an unhappy though upright woman may fill our heart with this melancholy, while at the same time we may coldly receive the news of a great battle in which, as may readily be realized, a considerable part of humankind must innocently suffer dreadful evils. Many a prince who has averted his countenance from melancholy for a single unfortunate person has at the same time given the order for war, often from a vain motive. There is here no proportion in the effect at all, so how can one say that the general love of mankind is the cause? [end of 2:216]

The second sort of kindly feeling which is to be sure beautiful and lovable but still not the foundation of a genuine virtue is **complaisance**: an inclination to make ourselves agreeable to others through friendliness, through acquiescence to their demands, and through conformity our conduct to their dispositions. This ground for a charming complaisance is beautiful, and the malleability of such a heart is kindly. Yet it is so far from being a virtue that unless higher principles [2:217] set bounds for it and weaken it, all sorts of vices may spring from it. For without even considering that this complaisance towards those with whom we associate is often an injustice to those who find themselves outside of this little circle, such a man, if one takes this impulse alone, can have all sorts of vices, not because of immediate inclination but because he gladly lives to please. From affectionate complaisance he will be a liar, an idler, a drunkard, etc., for he does not act in accordance with the rules for good conduct in general, but rather in accordance with an inclination that is beautiful in itself but which insofar as it is without self-control and without principles becomes ridiculous.

Thus true virtue can only be grafted upon principles, and it will become the more sublime and noble the more general they are. These principles are not speculative rules, but the consciousness of a feeling that lives in every human breast and that extends much further than to the special grounds of sympathy and complaisance. I believe that I can bring all this together if I say that it is the **feeling of the beauty and the dignity of human nature**.[17] The first is a ground of universal affection, the second of universal respect, and if this feeling had the greatest perfection in any human heart then this human being would certainly love and value even himself, but only in so far as he is one among all to whom his widespread and noble feeling extends itself. Only when one subordinates one's own particular inclination to such an enlarged one can our kindly drives be proportionately applied and bring about the noble attitude that is the beauty of virtue.

In recognition of the weakness of human nature and the little power that the universal moral feeling exercises over most hearts, providence has placed such helpful drives in us as supplements for virtue, which move some to beautiful actions even without principles while at the same time being able to give others, who are ruled by these principles, a greater impetus and a stronger impulse thereto. Sympathy and complaisance are grounds for beautiful actions that would perhaps all be suffocated by the preponderance of a cruder self-interest, but as we have seen they are not immediate grounds of virtue, although since they are ennobled by their kinship with it they also bear its name. Hence I can call them **adopted virtues**, but that which [2:218] rest on principles **genuine virtue**. The former are beautiful and charming, the latter alone is sublime and worthy of honor. One calls a mind in which the former sentiments rule a **good heart** and people of that sort **good-hearted**; but one rightly ascribes a **noble heart** to one who is virtuous from principles, calling him alone a **righteous** person. These adopted virtues nevertheless have a great similarity to the true virtues, since they contain the feeling of an immediate pleasure in kindly and benevolent actions. The good-hearted person will without any ulterior aim and from immediate complaisance conduct himself peaceably and courteously with you and feel sincere compassion for the need of another.

Yet since this moral sympathy is nevertheless not enough to drive indolent human nature to actions for the common weal [*gemeinnützig*], providence has further placed in us a certain feeling which is fine and moves us, or which can also balance cruder self-interest and vulgar sensuality. This is the **feeling for honor** and its consequence, **shame**. The opinion that others may have of our value and their judgment of our actions is a motivation of great weight, which can coax us into many sacrifices, and what a good part of humanity would have done neither out of an immediately arising emotion of goodheartedness nor out of principles happens often enough merely for the sake of outer appearance, out of a delusion that is very useful although in itself very facile, as if the judgment of others determined the worth of ourselves and our actions. What happens from this impulse is not in the least virtuous, for which reason everyone who wants to be taken for virtuous takes good care to conceal the motivation of lust for honor. This inclination is also not nearly so closely related as goodheartedness is to genuine virtue, since it is not moved immediately by the beauty of actions, but by their demeanor in the eyes of others. Since the feeling for honor is nevertheless still fine, I can call the similarity to virtue that is thereby occasioned the **simulacrum of virtue**.

[…]

[2:226] If I observe alternately the noble and the weak sides of human beings, I reprove myself that I am not able to adopt that standpoint from which these contrasts can nevertheless exhibit the great portrait of human nature in its entirety in a moving form. For I gladly grant that so far as it belongs to the project of great nature as a whole, [2:227] these grotesque attitudes cannot lend it other than a noble expression, although one is far too shortsighted to see them in this connection. Nevertheless, to cast even a weak glance on this, I believe that I can note the following. There are very **few** people who conduct themselves in accordance with **principles**, which is on the whole good, since it is so easy to err with these principles, and then the ensuing disadvantage extends all the further, the more general the principle is and the more steadfast the person who has set it before himself is. Those who act out of **goodhearted drives** are far more **numerous**, which is most excellent, although it cannot be reckoned to individuals as a special personal merit; for these virtuous instincts are occasionally lacking, but on average they accomplish the great aim of nature just as well as the other instincts that so regularly move the animal world. Those always who have their dear self before them as the sole focal point of their efforts and who attempt to make everything turn on the great axis of **self-interest** are the **most common,** and nothing can be more advantageous than this, for these are the most industrious, orderly, and prudent people; they give demeanor and solidity to the whole, for even without aiming at it they serve the common good, supply the necessary requisites, and provide the foundations over which finer souls can spread beauty and harmony. Finally, the **love of honor** is distributed **among all** human hearts, although in unequal measure, which must give the whole a beauty that charms to the point of admiration. For although the lust for honor is a foolish delusion if it becomes the rule to which one subordinates the other inclinations, yet as an accompanying drive it is most excellent. For while on the great stage each prosecutes his actions in accordance with his dominant inclinations, at the same time he is moved by hidden incentive to adopt in his thoughts a standpoint outside himself in order to judge the propriety of his conduct, how it appears and strikes the eye of the observer. In this way the different groups unite themselves in a painting of magnificent expression, where in the midst of great variety unity shines forth, and the whole of moral nature displays beauty and dignity. [End of the second section – Ed.]

## Questions

1. Explain the three kinds of sublimity Kant identifies here. Can you think of contemporary examples of each kind? Do you agree that there are distinct kinds of sublimity? If so, how are they best distinguished?

2. Do you agree with Kant that beauty and sublimity, while distinct, can be joined, as in the magnificent sublime? (Consider the example at the end of section two.) Explain.

3. Do you consider this treatise more a text in aesthetics, anthropology, ethics, a combination, or something else? Based on your answer, does this improve or diminish Kant's account of sublimity and beauty? Explain.

4. How does Kant's conception of humanity or human beings influence his theory of the sublime and/or dignity? Is this a weakness? Explain.

5. Why do you think Kant makes a distinct category for the "noble" sublime? Do you think this is justified, or should the noble-moral sublime be subsumed under another kind (and if so, which one)? More generally, how would you characterize the relation between virtue and sublimity?

6. How does Kant make use of a concept of disinterestedness (in contrast to "self-interest") in characterizing refined, fine, or "finer" feeling? How does the moral "feeling of the beauty and the dignity of human nature" relate to the latter?

### Further reading

Armstrong, Meg. "'The Effects of Blackness': Gender, Race, and the Sublime in Aesthetic Theories of Burke and Kant." *The Journal of Aesthetics and Art Criticism* 54, no. 3 (1996): 213–36. [Excerpted in the present volume].
Battersby, Christine. *The Sublime, Terror and Human Difference.* London: Routledge, 2007.
Brady, Emily. *The Sublime in Modern Philosophy.* Cambridge: Cambridge University Press, 2013.
Clewis, Robert R. "Kant's Distinction between True and False Sublimity." In *Kant's Observations and Remarks: A Critical Guide*, ed. Susan Shell and Richard Velkley, 116–43. Cambridge: Cambridge University Press, 2012.
Klinger, Cornelia. "The Concepts of the Sublime and the Beautiful in Kant and Lyotard". In *Feminist Interpretations of Immanuel Kant*, ed. Robin Schott, 191–211. University Park: Pennsylvania State University Press, 1997.
Shell, Susan Meld. *The Embodiment of Reason: Kant on Spirit, Generation, and Community.* Chicago: University of Chicago Press, 1996.

# CHAPTER 13
# ANNA AIKIN, "ON THE PLEASURE DERIVED FROM OBJECTS OF TERROR" (1773)

Anna Laetitia Aikin (1743–1825), also known as "Anna Letitia Barbauld" after her marriage, was an English essayist, poet, editor, and literary critic. "On the Pleasure Derived from Objects of Terror" was one of the first theoretical explorations of the Gothic response, and had a powerful influence on that genre of writing during the fifty years following its publication. It appeared first in a volume of critical essays that Aikin published with her brother, the Unitarian John Aikin, and was republished at least ten times up to 1820.[1]

The paradox that the essay attempts to resolve, as its title reveals, concerns why we would feel pleasure in response to an object of terror, as we do when feeling sublimity. The structure of this puzzle has emerged in various forms over the years. A basic issue common to the so-called paradoxes of tragedy, of horror, and the sublime is: why do we knowingly and willingly watch or perceive horrifying, terrible objects and events? Why are we pleased to the extent that we are afflicted? Aikin's own delightful phrase for the problem is, "paradox of the heart."[2] She considers a number of strategies intended to resolve this paradox, or more generally, the problem of "negative" pleasures.[3]

She first places aside scenes of misery in which we feel "virtuous sympathy" (or, as we might say today, empathy) for those who are suffering. She concentrates instead on "objects of pure terror," such as those seen in a dramatic tragedy, a "Gothic romance," and the "Eastern tale." The first possible solution she offers, drawing on her own experiences, has to do with narrative suspense and curiosity. Readers, sometimes despite their better judgment, endure the terrible in order to satisfy a craving to know what lies beyond. The feeling to be overcome is not a kind of "enjoyment," but a "dislike" to be endured.

Aikin prefers a second explanation, however. What is surprising causes a pleasant expansion of the imagination or imaginative activity. "A strange and unexpected event awakens the mind, and keeps it on the stretch; . . . our imagination, darting forth, explores with rapture the new world which is laid open to its view, and rejoices in the expansion of its powers." The "pain of terror" is then "lost in amazement." She offers a kind of "conversion" theory: initial pain is converted into something else, or at least "lost." Her explanation is centered on the pleasurable imaginative activity stimulated by the object that evokes terror or horror.

## Note on the text

Source: Reprinted from Anna Laetitia Aikin, "On the Pleasure Derived from Objects of Terror; with Sir Bertrand, A Fragment," in J. [John] and A. L. Aikin, *Miscellaneous Pieces, In Prose*, 119–27. London: J. Johnson 1773.

Punctuation, style, and spelling have occasionally been modified or updated. Italics or quotation marks have been added to titles. In editorial notes, the volume editor has made extensive use of Duffy and Howell's footnotes to this text.

## "On the pleasure derived from objects of terror; with Sir Bertrand, a fragment"

That the exercise of our benevolent feelings, as called forth by the view of human afflictions, should be a source of pleasure, cannot appear wonderful to one who considers that relation between the moral and natural system of man, which has connected a degree of satisfaction with every action or emotion productive of the general welfare. The painful sensation immediately arising from a scene of misery, is so much softened and alleviated by the reflex sense of self-approbation attending virtuous sympathy, that we find, on the whole, a very exquisite and refined pleasure remaining, which makes us desirous of again being witnesses to such scenes, instead of flying from them with disgust and horror. It is obvious how greatly such a provision must conduce to the ends of mutual support and assistance. But the apparent delight with which we dwell upon objects of pure terror, where our moral feelings are not in the least concerned, and no passion seems to be excited but the depressing one of fear, is a paradox of the heart, much more difficult of solution.

The reality of this source of pleasure seems evident from daily observation. The greediness with which the tales of ghosts and goblins, of murders, earthquakes, fires, shipwrecks, and all the most terrible disasters attending human life, are devoured by every ear, must have been generally remarked. Tragedy, the most favourite work of fiction, has taken a full share of those scenes; "it has supt full with horrors"[4]—and has, perhaps, been more indebted to them for public admiration than to its tender and pathetic parts. The ghost of Hamlet, Macbeth descending into the witches' cave, and the tent scene in Richard, command as forcibly the attention of our souls as the parting Jaffeir and Belvidera,[5] the fall of Wolsey,[6] or the death of Shore.[7] The inspiration of *terror* was by the ancient critics assigned as the peculiar province of tragedy; and the Greek and Roman tragedians have introduced some extraordinary personages for this purpose: not only the shades of the dead, but the furies, and other fabulous inhabitants of the infernal regions. Collins, in his most poetical ode to Fear, has finely enforced this idea.

> Tho' gentle Pity claims her mingled part,
>     Yet all the thunders of the scene are thine.[8]

The old Gothic romance and the Eastern tale, with their genii, giants, enchantments, and transformations, however a refined critic may censure them as absurd and extravagant, will ever retain a most powerful influence on the mind, and interest the reader independently of all peculiarity of taste. Thus the great Milton, who had a strong bias to these wildnesses of the imagination, has with striking effect made the stories "of forests and enchantments drear," a favourite subject with his *Penseroso*; and had undoubtedly their awakening images strong upon his mind when he breaks out,

> Call up him that left half-told
> The story of Cambuscan bold; etc.[9]

How are we then to account for the pleasure derived from such objects? I have often been led to imagine that there is a deception in these cases; and that the avidity with which we attend is not a proof of our receiving real pleasure. The pain of suspense, and the irresistible desire of satisfying curiosity, when once raised, will account for our eagerness to go quite through an adventure, though we suffer actual pain during the whole course of it. We rather choose to suffer the smart pang of a violent emotion than the uneasy craving of an unsatisfied desire. That this principle, in many instances, may involuntarily carry us through what we dislike, I am convinced from experience. This is the impulse which renders the poorest and most insipid narrative interesting when once we get fairly into it; and I have frequently felt it with regard to our modern novels, which, if lying on my table, and taken up in an idle hour, have led me through the most tedious and disgusting pages, while, like Pistol eating his leek,[10] I have swallowed and execrated to the end. And it will not only force us through dullness, but through actual torture—through the relation of a Damien's execution,[11] or an inquisitor's act of faith. When children, therefore, listen with pale and mute attention to the frightful stories of apparitions, we are not, perhaps, to imagine that they are in a state of enjoyment, any more than the poor bird which is dropping into the mouth of the rattle snake—they are chained by the ears, and fascinated by curiosity. This solution, however, does not satisfy me with respect to the well-wrought scenes of artificial terror which are formed by a sublime and vigorous imagination. Here, though we know beforehand what to expect, we enter into them with eagerness, in quest of a pleasure already experienced. This is the pleasure constantly attached to the excitement of surprise from new and wonderful objects. A strange and unexpected event awakens the mind, and keeps it on the stretch; and where the agency of invisible beings is introduced, of "forms unseen, and mightier far than we,"[12] our imagination, darting forth, explores with rapture the new world which is laid open to its view, and rejoices in the expansion of its powers. Passion and fancy co-operating elevate the soul to its highest pitch; and the pain of terror is lost in amazement.

Hence the more wild, fanciful, and extraordinary are the circumstances of a scene of horror, the more pleasure we receive from it; and where they are too near common nature, though violently borne by curiosity through the adventure, we cannot repeat it or reflect on it, without an over-balance of pain. In the *Arabian Nights* are many most striking examples of the terrible joined with the marvellous: the story of Aladdin, and the travels of Sinbad, are particularly excellent. *The Castle of Otranto*[13] is a very spirited modern attempt upon the same plan of mixed terror, adapted to the model of Gothic romance. The best conceived, and most strongly worked-up scene of mere natural horror that I recollect, is in Smollett's *Ferdinand Count Fathom*;[14] where the hero, entertained in a lone house in a forest, finds a corpse just slaughtered in the room where he is sent to sleep, and the door of which is locked upon him. It may be amusing for the reader to compare his feelings upon these, and from thence form his opinion of the justness of my theory. The following fragment, in which both these manners are attempted to be in some degree united, is offered to entertain a solitary winter's evening.[15] [...]

## Questions

1. Summarize and assess Aikin's analyses of the "paradox of the heart," that is, why we would take pleasure in response to an object of "horror." Consider how she appeals to curiosity and then to an expansion of the imagination.

2. In what ways did Gothic criticism and literature (e.g., *Frankenstein*) develop the concept of the sublime? How might Aikin's ideas be relevant here?

3. How is Aikin's account like, or unlike, other accounts of our responses to objects that are terrifying (vast, powerful, menacing, hostile)? Compare with the accounts of Dennis and Burke.

## Further reading

Barbauld, Anna Letitia. *Anna Letitia Barbauld: Selected Poetry & Prose*, ed. William McCarthy and Elizabeth Kraft. Peterborough, Ontario: Broadview Press Ltd., 2002.

Carroll, Noël. *The Philosophy of Horror, or Paradoxes of the Heart*. New York: Routledge, 1990.

McCarthy, William. *Anna Letitia Barbauld: Voice of the Enlightenment*. Baltimore: Johns Hopkins University Press, 2009.

Rodgers, Betsy. *Georgian Chronicle: Mrs. Barbauld and Her Family*. London: Methuen, 1958.

White, Daniel E. "The 'Joineriana': Anna Barbauld, the Aikin Family Circle, and the Dissenting Public Sphere." *Eighteenth-Century Studies* 32, no. 4 (1999): 511–33.

# CHAPTER 14
## MARY WOLLSTONECRAFT, FROM *A VINDICATION OF THE RIGHTS OF MEN* (1790)

Mary Wollstonecraft's (1759–1797) *A Vindication of the Rights of Men* was the first published reply to Burke's *Reflections on the Revolution in France*. She wrote it quickly. Burke's work appeared on the first of November 1790, and Wollstonecraft's response, initially anonymous, was in print by the end of the month. In December appeared a second edition, bearing her name on the title page.

In the brief "Advertisement" affixed to *A Vindication of the Rights of Men*, Wollstonecraft explains how in reading Burke's *Reflections* she soon became indignant. Her book opens with these words: "Mr. Burke's Reflections on the French Revolution first engaged my attention as the transient topic of the day; and reading it more for amusement than information, my indignation was roused by the sophistical arguments, that every moment crossed me, in the questionable shape of natural feelings and common sense" (iii). Her first *Vindication* focuses on the core of Burke's argument, aiming to show that his vision of history depends on a particular understanding of the role played by the nobility and the church. Below, she questions Burke's assumptions concerning masculinity and femininity, his contrasts between respect and love, and his opposition of reason to emotion. Her critique of Burke also acted as a springboard for a foundational work of modern feminism, the second *Vindication*, or *A Vindication of the Rights of Woman* (1792).

### Note on the text

Source: Excerpted from *A Vindication of the Rights of Men, in a Letter to the Right Honourable Edmund Burke; Occasioned by His Reflections on the Revolution in France* [first edition], 58–62, 102–10. London: J. Johnson, 1790.

Punctuation, style, and spelling have occasionally been modified or updated. Titles have been italicized.

### *A Vindication of the Rights of Men*

[...] Had you been in a philosophizing mood, had your heart or your reason been at home, you might have been convinced, by ocular demonstration, that madness is only the absence of reason.—The ruling angel had left its feat, and wild anarchy ensued. You would have seen that the uncontrolled imagination often pursues the most regular course in its most daring flight; and that the eccentricities are boldly relieved when judgment no longer officiously arranges the sentiments, by bringing them to the test of principles. You would have seen every thing out of nature in that strange chaos of levity and ferocity, and of all sorts of follies jumbled together. You would have seen in that monstrous tragi-comic scene the most opposite passions necessarily succeed, and sometimes mix with each other in the mind; alternate contempt and indignation; alternate laughter and tears; alternate scorn and horror.[1] – This is a true picture of that chaotic state of mind, called madness; when reason gone, we know not where, the wild elements of passion clash, and all is horror and confusion. You might have heard the best turned conceits, flash following flash, and doubted whether the rhapsody was not eloquent, if it had not been delivered in an equivocal language, neither verse nor prose, if the sparkling periods had not stood alone, wanting force because they wanted concatenation.

It is a proverbial observation, that a very thin partition divides wit and madness. Poetry is properly addressed to the imagination, and the language of passion is with great felicity borrowed from the heightened picture which the imagination draws of sensible objects concentred by impassioned reflection. And, during this 'fine frenzy,' reason has no right to rein-in the imagination, unless to prevent the introduction of supernumerary images; if the passion is real, the head will not be ransacked for stale tropes and cold rodomontade [i.e., vain boasting – Ed.]. I now speak of the genuine enthusiasm of genius, which, perhaps, seldom appears, but in the infancy of civilization; for as this advances reason clips the wing of fancy—the youth becomes a man.

Whether the glory of Europe is set, I shall not now enquire; but probably the spirit of romance and chivalry is in the wane; and reason will gain by its extinction.

From observing several cold romantic characters I have been led to confine the term romantic to one definition—false, or rather artificial, feelings. Works of genius are read with a prepossession in their favour, and sentiments imitated, because they were fashionable and pretty, and not because they were forcibly felt.

In modern poetry the understanding and memory often fabricate the pretended effusions of the heart, and romance destroys all simplicity; which, in works of taste, is but a synonymous word for truth. This romantic spirit has extended to our prose, and scattered artificial flowers over the most barren heath; or a mixture of verse and prose producing the strangest incongruities. The turgid bombast of some of your periods fully proves these assertions; for when the heart speaks we are seldom shocked by hyperbole, or dry raptures. [...]

Reading your *Reflections* warily over, it has continually and forcibly struck me, that had you been a Frenchman, you would have been, in spite of your respect for rank and antiquity, a violent revolutionist; and deceived, as you now probably are, by the passions that cloud your reason, have termed your romantic enthusiasm an enlightened love of your country, a respect for the fights of men. Your imagination would have taken fire, and have found arguments, full as ingenious as those you now offer, to prove that the constitution, of which so few pillars remained, that constitution which time had almost obliterated, was not a model sufficiently noble to deserve close adherence. And, for the English constitution, you might not have had such a profound veneration as you have lately acquired; nay, it is not impossible but you might have entertained the same opinion of the English Parliament, that you professed to have during the American war.

Another observation which, by frequently occurring, has almost grown into a conviction, is simply this, that had the English in general reprobated the French revolution, you would have stood forth alone, and been the avowed Goliah of liberty. But, not liking to see so many brothers near the throne of fame, you have turned the current of your passions, and consequently of your reasoning, another way. Had Dr. Price's sermon not lighted some sparks very like envy in your bosom, I shrewdly suspect that he would have been treated with more candour; nor is it charitable to suppose that any thing but personal pique and hurt vanity could have dictated such bitter sarcasms and reiterated expressions of contempt.

But without fixed principles even goodness of heart is no security from inconsistency, and mild affectionate sensibility only renders a man more ingeniously cruel, when the pangs of hurt vanity are mistaken for virtuous indignation, and the gall of bitterness for the milk of Christian charity.

Where is the dignity, the infallibility of sensibility, in the fair ladies, whom, if the voice of rumour is to be credited, the captive negroes curse in all the agony of bodily pain, for the unheard of tortures they invent? It is probable that some of them, after a flagellation, compose their ruffled spirits and exercise their tender feelings by the perusal of the last new novel.—How true these tears are to nature, I leave you to determine. But these ladies may have read your *Enquiries concerning the origin of our ideas of the Sublime and Beautiful*, and, convinced by your arguments, have laboured to be pretty, by counterfeiting weakness.

You may have convinced them that *littleness* and weakness are the very essence of beauty; and that the Supreme Being, in giving women beauty in the most supereminent degree, seemed to command them, by the powerful voice of Nature, not to cultivate the moral virtues that might chance to excite respect, and interfere with the pleasing sensations they were created to inspire. Confining thus truth, fortitude, and humanity, within the rigid pale of manly morals, they might justly argue, that to be loved, woman's high end and great distinction! they should 'learn to lisp, to totter in their walk,' and nick-name God's creatures. Never, they might repeat after you, was any man, much less a woman, rendered amiable by the force of those exalted qualities, fortitude, justice, wisdom, and truth; and thus forewarned of the sacrifice they must make to those austere, unnatural virtues, they would be authorised to turn all their attention to their persons, systematically neglecting morals to secure beauty. – Some rational old woman might chance to stumble at this doctrine, and hint, that in avoiding atheism you had not steered clear of the mussulman's [i.e., Muslim's] creed; but you could readily exculpate yourself by turning the charge on Nature, who made our idea of beauty independent of reason. Nor would it be necessary for you to recollect, that if virtue has any other foundation than worldly utility, you have clearly proved that one half of the human species, at least, have not souls; and that Nature, by making women little, smooth, delicate, fair creatures, never designed that they should exercise their reason to acquire the virtues that produce opposite, if not contradictory, feelings. The affection produced by them, to be uniform and perfect, should not be tinctured with the respect moral virtues inspire, lest pain should be blended with pleasure, and admiration disturb the soft intimacy of love. This laxity of morals in the female world is certainly more captivating to a libertine imagination than the cold arguments of reason, that give no sex to virtue. If beautiful weakness was interwoven in a woman's frame, if the chief business of her life is to inspire love, and Nature has made an eternal distinction between the qualities that dignify a rational being and this animal perfection, her duty and happiness in this life must clash with any preparation for a more exalted state. So that Plato and Milton were grossly mistaken in asserting that human love led to heavenly, and was only an exaltation of the same affection; for the love of the Deity, which is mixed with the most profound reverence, must be love of perfection, and not compassion for weakness.

To say the truth, I not only tremble for the souls of women, but for the good natured man, whom every one loves. The *amiable* weakness of their minds is a strong argument against its immateriality, and seems to prove that beauty relaxes the *solids* of the soul as well as the body.

It follows then immediately, from your own reasoning, that respect and love are antagonist principles; and that, if we really wish to render men more virtuous, we must endeavour to banish all enervating modifications of beauty from civil society. We must, only to carry your argument a little further, return to the Spartan regulations, and settle the virtues of men on the stern foundation of mortification and self-denial; for any attempt to civilize the heart, to make it humane by implanting reasonable principles, is a mere philosophic dream. If refinement inevitably lessens respect for virtue, by rendering beauty, the grand tempter, more seductive; if these relaxing feelings are incompatible with the nervous exertions of morality, the fun of Europe is not set; it begins to dawn, when cold metaphysicians try to make the head give laws to the heart.

But should experience prove that there is a beauty in virtue, a charm in order, which necessarily implies exertion, a depraved sensual taste may give way to a more manly one—and *melting* feelings to rational satisfactions. Both may be equally natural to man; the test is their moral difference, and that point reason alone can decide.

Such a glorious change can only be produced by liberty. Inequality of rank must ever impede the growth of virtue, by vitiating the mind that submits or domineers; that is ever employed to procure nourishment for the body, or amusement for the mind. And if this grand example is set by an assembly of unlettered clowns, if they can produce a crisis that may involve the fate of Europe, and 'more than Europe,' you must allow us to respect unsophisticated common sense, and reverence the active exertions that were not relaxed by a fastidious respect for the beauty of rank, or the dread of the deformity produced by a void in the social structure. [...]

## Questions

1. Summarize and evaluate some of Wollstonecraft's criticisms of Burke. (For instance, her understanding of his views of the French Revolution, the emotions, reason, genius, common sense, or gender.)

2. In particular, how does Wollstonecraft react to Burke's account of the beautiful and the sublime? What problems does she identify? Explain.

3. Explain the meaning of her claim that cold arguments of reason "give no sex to virtue."

4. Do you agree that Burke's characterizations of beauty (and sublimity) have a detrimental effect? Is it fatal to his theory—does it render it untenable? Explain.

## Further reading

Myers, Mitzi. "Politics from the Outside: Mary Wollstonecraft's first *Vindication*." *Studies in Eighteenth-Century Culture* 6 (1977): 113–32.

O'Neill, Daniel I. *The Burke-Wollstonecraft Debate: Savagery, Civilization, and Democracy*. University Park: Pennsylvania State University Press, 2007.

Taylor, Barbara. *Mary Wollstonecraft and the Feminist Imagination*. Cambridge: Cambridge University Press, 2003.

Wollstonecraft, Mary. *The Works of Mary Wollstonecraft*, ed. Janet Todd and Marilyn Butler. 7 vols. London: William Pickering, 1989.

# CHAPTER 15

## IMMANUEL KANT, FROM *CRITIQUE OF THE POWER OF JUDGMENT* (1790) AND *ANTHROPOLOGY FROM A PRAGMATIC POINT OF VIEW* (1798)

An excerpt from a precritical text of Immanuel Kant (1724–1804) appeared earlier in this volume; below, we turn to his mature or critical account. The first reading below is the "Analytic of the Sublime" (and section §30) in the *Critique of the Power of Judgment* (1790), Kant's third and final *Critique*, which is then followed by a brief excerpt from a collection of Kant's lectures on anthropology, a handbook published in 1798 as *Anthropology from a Pragmatic Point of View*.

Although there is insufficient space to reproduce it here, one other passage in the Kantian corpus should be mentioned: Kant's characterization of the enthusiastic response to the French Revolution, that is, to the attempt to realize the idea of a republic in the natural order.* The text, found in a work written in the middle to late 1790s, *The Conflict of the Faculties*, uses the language of sublimity ("zeal and grandeur of soul") to characterize the enthusiasm felt by spectators of the events in France. Kant calls it an enthusiasm "for upholding justice for the human race" and describes enthusiasm as a feeling that moves only toward the "ideal" and "purely moral, such as the concept of right." Kant even attributes two of the conditions of aesthetic judgment (universality and disinterestedness) to the feeling of enthusiasm. At the same time, in the *Critique of the Power of Judgment* Kant had called the feeling of enthusiasm "aesthetically sublime." Given the historical relations between enthusiasm (discussed by Longinus and John Dennis and many others) and the sublime, there is clearly much to be explored here. Indeed, the passage from *The Conflict of the Faculties* has given rise to influential interpretations by writers such as Hannah Arendt and Jean-François Lyotard.**

### Note on the text

Source: Reprinted from Immanuel Kant, *Critique of the Power of Judgment*, translated by Paul Guyer and Eric Matthews, 128–161. Cambridge: Cambridge University Press, 2000.

Kant is the author of the footnotes marked by asterisks. The lettered footnotes (dealing with linguistic matters) and the numbered endnotes are based on those in the translation of Guyer and Matthews, with occasional

---

*Kant, *The Conflict of the Faculties*, 7:85–87n, in §6 in the *Conflict* essay called "An Old Question Raised Again: Is the Human Race Constantly Progressing?".

**Jean-François Lyotard, *Enthusiasm: The Kantian Critique of History*, trans. Georges Van den Abbeele. Stanford: Stanford University Press, 2009 (Chapter 3, "What Is Delivered in Enthusiasm," 21–41). Jean-François Lyotard, *Lessons on the Analytic of the Sublime: (Kant's "Critique of Judgment," §§23–29)*, trans. Elizabeth Rottenberg (Stanford: Stanford University Press, 1994). Hannah Arendt, *Lectures on Kant's Political Philosophy*, ed. Ronald Beiner (Chicago: University of Chicago Press, 1982).

modifications. The volumes and pages in the Academy Edition of Kant's collected works are referred to by volume: page number as follows: "5:272." The Academy Edition pagination is also placed throughout the body of the text.

[5:244]

*Second Book*<br>*Analytic of the Sublime*

§23.<br>Transition from the faculty for judging[a] the beautiful to that for judging the sublime

The beautiful coincides with the sublime in that both please for themselves.[1] And further in that both presuppose neither a judgment of sense nor a logically determining judgment, but a judgment of reflection: consequently the satisfaction does not depend on a sensation, like that in the agreeable, nor on a determinate concept, like the satisfaction in the good; but it is nevertheless still related to concepts, although it is indeterminate which, hence the satisfaction is connected to the mere presentation or to the faculty for that, through which the faculty of presentation or the imagination is considered, in the case of a given intuition, to be in accord with the **faculty of concepts** of the understanding or of reason, as promoting the latter. Hence both sorts of judgments are also **singular**, and yet judgments that profess to be universally valid in regard to every subject, although they lay claim merely to the feeling of pleasure and not to any cognition of the object.

But notable differences between the two also strike the eye. The beautiful in nature concerns the form of the object, which consists in limitation; the sublime, by contrast, is to be found in a formless object insofar as **limitlessness** is represented in it, or at its instance, and yet it is also thought as a totality: so that the beautiful seems to be taken as the presentation of an indeterminate concept of the understanding, but the sublime as that of a similar concept of reason. Thus the satisfaction is connected in the first case with the representation of **quality**, but in this case with that of **quantity**. Also the latter pleasure is very different in kind from the former, in that the former (the beautiful)[b] directly brings with it a feeling of the promotion of life,[2] and hence is [5:245] compatible with charms and an imagination at play, while the latter (the feeling of the sublime)[c] is a pleasure that arises only indirectly, being generated, namely, by the feeling of a momentary inhibition of the vital powers and the immediately following and all the more powerful outpouring of them; hence as an emotion it seems to be not play but something serious in the activity of the imagination. Hence it is also incompatible with charms, and, since the mind is not merely attracted by the object, but is also always reciprocally repelled by it, the satisfaction in the sublime does not so much contain[d] positive pleasure as it does admiration or respect, i.e., it deserves to be called negative pleasure.[3]

The most important and intrinsic difference between the sublime and the beautiful, however, is this: that if, as is appropriate, we here consider first only the sublime in objects of nature (that in art is, after all, always restricted to the conditions of agreement with nature),[4] natural beauty (the self-sufficient kind) carries with it

---

[a]*Beurtheilungsvermögen.*
[b]The parenthetical phrase was added in the second edition.
[c]The parenthetical phrase was added in the second edition.
[d]This verb was added in the second edition.

a purposiveness in its form, through which the object seems as it were to be predetermined for our power of judgment, and thus constitutes an object of satisfaction in itself, whereas that which, without any rationalizing, merely in apprehension, excites in us the feeling of the sublime, may to be sure[a] appear in its form to be contrapurposive for our power of judgment, unsuitable for our faculty of presentation, and as it were doing violence to our imagination, but[b] is nevertheless judged all the more sublime for that.

But from this one immediately sees that we express ourselves on the whole incorrectly if we call some **object of nature** sublime, although we can quite correctly call very many of them beautiful; for how can we designate with an expression of approval that which is apprehended[c] in itself as contrapurposive? We can say no more than that the object serves for the presentation of a sublimity that can be found in the mind; for what is properly sublime cannot be contained in any sensible form, but concerns only ideas of reason, which, though no presentation adequate to them is possible, are provoked and called to mind precisely by this inadequacy, which does allow of sensible presentation. Thus the wide ocean, enraged by storms, cannot be called sublime. Its visage is horrible; and one must already have filled the mind with all sorts of ideas if by means of such an intuition it is to be [5:246] put in the mood for a feeling which is itself sublime, in that the mind is incited to abandon sensibility and to occupy itself with ideas that contain a higher purposiveness.

The self-sufficient beauty of nature reveals to us a technique of nature, which makes it possible to represent it as a system in accordance with laws the principle of which we do not encounter anywhere in our entire faculty of understanding, namely that of a purposiveness with respect to the use of the power of judgment in regard to appearances, so that this must be judged[d] as belonging not merely to nature in its purposeless mechanism but rather also to the analogy with[e] art. Thus it actually expands not our cognition of natural objects, but our concept of nature, namely as a mere mechanism, into the concept of nature as art: which invites profound investigations into the possibility of such a form. But in that which we are accustomed to call sublime in nature there is so little[f] that leads to particular objective principles and forms of nature corresponding to these that it is mostly rather in its chaos or in its wildest and most unruly disorder and devastation, if only it allows a glimpse of magnitude and might, that it excites the ideas of the sublime. From this we see that the concept of the sublime in nature is far from being as important and rich in consequences as that of its beauty, and that in general it indicates nothing purposive in nature itself, but only in the possible **use** of its intuitions to make palpable in ourselves a purposiveness that is entirely independent of nature. For the beautiful in nature we must seek a ground outside ourselves, but for the sublime merely one in ourselves and in the way of thinking that introduces sublimity into the representation of the former – a very necessary introductory remark, which entirely separates the ideas of the sublime from that of a purposiveness of **nature**, and makes of the theory of the sublime a mere appendix to the aesthetic judging[g] of the purposiveness of nature, since by this means no particular form is represented in the latter, but only a purposive use that the imagination makes of its representation is developed.

[5:247]

---

[a]In the second edition, *zwar*; in the first edition, *gar* (even).
[b]Added in the second edition.
[c]*aufgefaßt*; in the first edition, *abgefaßt* (conceived).
[d]*beurtheilt*.
[e]The words "the analogy with" were added in the second edition.
[f]Following the first edition in reading *so gar nichts* instead of *sogar nichts* (even nothing).
[g]*Beurtheilung*.

§24.

On the division of an investigation of the feeling of the sublime.

As far as the division of the moments of the aesthetic judging[a] of objects in relation to the feeling of the sublime is concerned, the analytic will be able to proceed in accordance with the same principle that was used in the analysis of judgments of taste. For as a judgment of the aesthetic reflecting power of judgment, the satisfaction in the sublime, just like that in the beautiful, must be represented as universally valid in its **quantity**, as without interest in its **quality**, as subjective purposiveness in its **relation**, and the latter, as far as its **modality** is concerned, as necessary. Thus the method here will not depart from that in the preceding section,[b] though some account must be taken of the fact that there, where the aesthetic judgment concerned the form of the object, we began with the investigation of quality, but here, in view of the formlessness that can pertain to that which we call sublime, we will begin with quantity as the first moment of the aesthetic judgment on the sublime; the ground for which, however, is to be seen from the preceding §.

But one division is necessary in the analysis of the sublime which that of the beautiful did not require, namely that into the **mathematically** and the **dynamically sublime**.[5]

For since the feeling of the sublime brings with it as its characteristic mark a **movement** of the mind connected with the judging[c] of the object, whereas the taste for the beautiful presupposes and preserves the mind in **calm** contemplation, yet this movement is to be judged[d] as subjectively purposive (because the sublime pleases), thus this movement is related through the imagination either to the **faculty of cognition** or to the **faculty of desire**, but in both relations the purposiveness of the given representation is judged[e] only with regard to this **faculty** (without an end or interest): for then the first is attributed to the object as a **mathematical**, the second as a **dynamical** disposition of the imagination, and thus the object is represented as sublime in the twofold manner intended. [5:248]

A.

On the mathematically sublime

§25.

Nominal definition of the sublime.

We call **sublime** that which is **absolutely great**.[f] However, to be great[g] and to be a magnitude[h] are quite different concepts (*magnitude* and *quantitas*). Likewise, **simply**[i] (*simpliciter*) **to say** that something is great is

---

[a]*Beurtheilung.*
[b]That is, the "Analytic of the Beautiful."
[c]*Beurtheilung.*
[d]*beurtheilt.*
[e]*beurtheilt.*
[f]*schlechthin groß.*
[g]*Groß-sein.*
[h]*eine Größe sein*; since Kant equates *Größe* with *Quantitas* and contrasts that with *magnitudo*, it would seem natural to translate *Größe* as "quantity" rather than "magnitude." However, he also equates it with *quantum*; in §23 he has used *Quantität* as a distinct German word; and in many of the claims that follow, "magnitude" will be a more natural translation than "quantity." We will therefore follow the practice of all the previous English translators in using "magnitude."
[i]*schlechtweg.*

also something entirely different from saying that it is **absolutely**[a] great (*absolute, non comparative magnum*).[b] The latter is that **which is great beyond all comparison.** – So what does the expression that something is great or small or medium-sized say? It is not a pure concept of the understanding that is thereby designated,[c] still less an intuition of sense, and just as little a concept of reason, since it does not bring with it any principle of cognition at all. It must therefore be a concept of the power of judgment, or derive from such a concept, and be grounded in a subjective purposiveness of the representation in relation to the power of judgment. That something is a magnitude (*quantum*) may be cognized from the thing itself, without any comparison with another; if, that is, a multitude of homogeneous elements together constitute a unity. But **how great** it is always requires something else, which is also a magnitude, as its measure. However, since in the judging[d] of magnitude not merely the multitude (number) but also the magnitude of the unit (of the measure) is involved, and the magnitude of this latter in turn always needs something else as a measure with which it can be compared, we see that any determination of the magnitude of appearances is absolutely[e] incapable of affording an absolute[f] concept of a magnitude but can afford at best only a comparative concept.

Now if I simply say that something is great, it seems that I do not have in mind any comparison at all, at least not with any objective measure, since it is not thereby determined at all how great the object is. However, even though the standard for comparison is merely subjective, the judgment nonetheless lays claim to universal assent;[g] the judgments "The man is beautiful" and "He is great" do not restrict themselves merely to the judging subject, but, like theoretical judgments, demand everyone's assent. [5:249]

But because in a judgment by which something is described simply as great it is not merely said that the object has a magnitude, but rather this is attributed to it to a superior extent than to many others of the same kind, yet without this superiority being given determinately, this judgment is certainly grounded on a standard that one presupposes can be assumed to be the same for everyone, but which is not usable for any logical (mathematically determinate) judging[h] of magnitude, but only for an aesthetic one, since it is a merely subjective standard grounding the reflecting judgment on magnitude. It may be, by the way,[i] empirical, as in the case of the average magnitude of the people known to us, of animals of a certain species, of trees, houses, mountains, etc., or a standard given *a priori*, which because of the deficiencies of the judging[j] subject is restricted to subjective conditions of presentation *in concreto*: as in the practical sphere, the magnitude of a certain virtue, or of public freedom and justice in a country; or in the theoretical sphere, the magnitude of the accuracy or inaccuracy of an observation or measurement that has been made, and so on.

Now it is noteworthy here that even if we have no interest at all in the object, i.e., its existence is indifferent to us, still its mere magnitude, even if it is considered as formless, can bring with it a satisfaction that is universally communicable, hence it may contain a consciousness of a subjective purposiveness in the use of our cognitive faculties: but not a satisfaction in the object, as in the case of the beautiful (since it can be formless), where the reflecting power of judgment finds itself purposively disposed in relation to cognition in general; rather in the enlargement of the imagination in itself.

---

[a]*schlechthin.*
[b]absolutely, not comparatively great.
[c]The words "that is thereby designated" were added in the second edition.
[d]*Beurtheilung.*
[e]*schlechterdings.*
[f]*absoluten.*
[g]Reading *Beistimmung* with the second edition rather than *Bestimmung* (determination) with the first.
[h]*Beurtheilung.*
[i]The word *übrigens* in the second edition replaces *nun* (now) in the first.
[j]The word *beurtheilenden* was inserted here in the second edition.

If (under the above-mentioned restriction) we say of an object absolutely[a] that it is great, this is not a mathematically determining judgment but a mere judgment of reflection about its representation, which is subjectively purposive for a certain use of our cognitive powers in the estimation of magnitude, and in that case we always combine a kind of respect with the representation, just as we combine contempt with that which we call absolutely small. Moreover, the judging[b] of things as great or small applies to everything, even to all their properties; hence we call even beauty great or small; the reason for which is to be sought [5:250] in the fact that whatever we may present in intuition in accordance with the precept of the power of judgment (and hence represent aesthetically) is entirely appearance, and hence is also a quantum.

If, however, we call something not only great, but simply, absolutely[c] great, great in every respect (beyond all comparison), i.e., sublime, then one immediately sees that we do not allow a suitable standard for it to be sought outside of it, but merely within it. It is a magnitude that is equal only to itself. That the sublime is therefore not to be sought in the things of nature but only in our ideas follows from this; but in which of these it lies must be saved for the deduction.[6]

The above explanation can also be expressed thus: **That is sublime in comparison with which everything else is small.** Here one readily sees that nothing can be given in nature, however great it may be judged[d] to be by us, which could not, considered in another relation, be diminished down to the infinitely small; and conversely, there is nothing so small which could not, in comparison with even smaller standards, be amplified for our imagination up to the magnitude of a world. The telescope has given us rich material for making the former observation, the microscope rich material for the latter.[e] Thus nothing that can be an object of the senses is, considered on this footing, to be called sublime. But just because there is in our imagination a striving to advance to the infinite, while in our reason there lies a claim to absolute totality, as to a real idea, the very inadequacy of our faculty for estimating the magnitude of the things of the sensible world awakens the feeling of a supersensible faculty in us; and the use that the power of judgment naturally makes in behalf of the latter (feeling), though not the object of the senses, is absolutely great, while in contrast to it any other use is small.[f] Hence it is the disposition of the mind resulting from a certain representation occupying the reflective judgment, but not the object, which is to be called sublime.

Thus we can also add this to the foregoing formulation of the explanation of the sublime: **That is sublime which even to be able to think of demonstrates a faculty of the mind that surpasses every measure of the senses.** [5:251]

§26.
On the estimation of the magnitude of things of nature that is requisite for the idea of the sublime.

The estimation of magnitude by means of numerical concepts (or their signs in algebra) is mathematical, but that in mere intuition (measured by eye) is aesthetic. Now we can, to be sure, obtain determinate concepts of **how great** something is only by means of numbers (or at any rate through approximations by means of numerical series progressing to infinity), whose unit is the measure; and to this extent all logical estimation of magnitude is mathematical. But since the magnitude of the measure must still be assumed to be known, then,

---

[a]Here and at the end of the sentence, *schlechtweg*.
[b]*Beurtheilung*.
[c]*schlechthin-, absolut-*.
[d]*beurtheilt*.
[e]In the first edition, "telescope" and "microscope" were plural rather than singular.
[f]In the first edition there is a comma rather than a period here.

if this in turn is to be estimated only by means of numbers whose unit would have to be another measure, and so mathematically, we can never have a primary or basic fundamental measure, and hence we can never have a determinate concept of a given magnitude. Thus the estimation of the magnitude of the basic measure must consist simply in the fact that one can immediately grasp it in an intuition and use it by means of imagination for the presentation of numerical concepts – i.e., in the end all estimation of the magnitude of objects of nature is aesthetic (i.e., subjectively and not objectively determined).[7]

Now for the mathematical estimation of magnitude there is, to be sure, no greatest (for the power of numbers goes on to infinity);[8] but for the aesthetic estimation of magnitude there certainly is a greatest; and about this I say that if it is judged[a] as an absolute measure, beyond which no greater is subjectively (for the judging[b] subject) possible, it brings with it the idea of the sublime, and produces that emotion which no mathematical estimation of magnitudes by means of numbers can produce (except insofar as that aesthetic basic measure is vividly preserved in the imagination), since the latter always presents only relative magnitude through comparison with others of the same species, but the former presents magnitude absolutely, so far as the mind can grasp it in one intuition.

To take up a quantum in the imagination intuitively, in order to be able to use it as a measure or a unit for the estimation of magnitude by means of numbers, involves two actions of this faculty: **apprehension**[c] (*apprehensio*) and **comprehension**[d] (*comprehensio aesthetica*). There is no difficulty with apprehension, because it can go on to infinity; but [5:252] comprehension becomes ever more difficult the further apprehension advances, and soon reaches its maximum, namely the aesthetically greatest basic measure for the estimation of magnitude. For when apprehension has gone so far that the partial representations of the intuition of the senses that were apprehended first already begin to fade in the imagination as the latter proceeds on to the apprehension of further ones, then it loses on one side as much as it gains on the other, and there is in the comprehension a greatest point beyond which it cannot go.

This makes it possible to explain a point that Savary[9] notes in his report on Egypt: that in order to get the full emotional effect of the magnitude of the pyramids one must neither come too close to them nor be too far away. For in the latter case, the parts that are apprehended (the stones piled on top of one another) are represented only obscurely, and their representation has no effect on the aesthetic judgment of the subject. In the former case, however, the eye requires some time to complete its apprehension from the base level to the apex, but during this time the former always partly fades before the imagination has taken in the latter, and the comprehension is never complete. – The very same thing can also suffice to explain the bewilderment or sort of embarrassment that is said to seize the spectator on first entering St. Peter's in Rome. For here there is a feeling of the inadequacy of his imagination for presenting the ideas[e] of a whole, in which the imagination reaches its maximum and, in the effort to extend it, sinks back into itself, but is thereby transported into an emotionally moving satisfaction.

I shall not yet add anything about the basis for this satisfaction, which is associated with a representation from which one should least expect it, namely one that makes us notice the inadequacy, consequently also the subjective non-purposiveness of the representation for the power of judgment in the estimation of magnitude; rather I only note that if the aesthetic judgment is to be **pure (not mixed up with anything teleological** as judgments of reason) and if an example of that is to be given which is fully appropriate for the critique of the **aesthetic** power of judgment, then the sublime must not be shown in products of art (e.g., buildings, columns,

---

[a] *beurtheilt.*
[b] *beurtheilenden.*
[c] *Auffassung.*
[d] *Zusammenfassung.*
[e] Reading *Ideen* as in the second edition, rather than the singular *Idee* as in the first.

etc.), where a human end determines the form as well as the magnitude,[10] nor in natural things [5:253] **whose concept already brings with it a determinate end** (e.g., animals of a known natural determination), but rather in raw nature (and even in this only insofar as it by itself brings with it neither charm nor emotion from real danger), merely insofar as it contains magnitude. For in this sort of representation nature contains nothing that would be monstrous (or magnificent or terrible); the magnitude that is apprehended may grow as large as one wants as long as it can be comprehended in one whole by the imagination. An object is **monstrous** if by its magnitude it annihilates the end which its concept constitutes.[11] The mere presentation of a concept, however, which is almost too great for all presentation (which borders on the relatively monstrous) is called **colossal**, because the end of the presentation of a concept is made more difficult if the intuition of the object is almost too great for our faculty of apprehension. – A pure judgment on the sublime, however, must have no end of the object as its determining ground if it is to be aesthetic and not mixed up with any judgment of the understanding or of reason.

\* \* \*

Since everything that is to please the merely reflecting power of judgment without interest must involve in its representation subjective and as such universally valid purposiveness, though here no purposiveness of the **form** of the object (as in the case of the beautiful) is the basis for the judging,[a] the question arises: what is this subjective purposiveness? and how is it prescribed as a norm that provides a ground for universally valid satisfaction in the mere estimation of magnitude, and indeed where that has been pushed almost to the point of the inadequacy of our faculty of imagination in the presentation of the concept of a magnitude?

The imagination, by itself, without anything hindering it, advances to infinity in the composition that is requisite for the representation of magnitude; the understanding, however, guides this by numerical concepts, for which the former must provide the schema;[12] and in this procedure, belonging to the logical estimation of magnitude, there is certainly something objectively purposive[b] in accordance with the concept of an end (such as all measuring is), but nothing that is purposive and pleasing for the aesthetic power of judgment. There is also in this intentional purposiveness nothing that would necessitate pushing the magnitude of the measure and hence the **comprehension** of the many [5:254] in one intuition to the boundaries of the faculty of imagination and as far as the latter might reach in presentations. For in the understanding's estimation of magnitudes (in arithmetic) one gets equally far whether one pushes the composition of the units up to the number 10 (in the decadic system) or only to 4 (in the tetradic system);[13] the further generation of magnitude in composition, or, if the quantum is given in intuition, in apprehension, proceeds merely progressively (not comprehensively) in accordance with an assumed principle of progression. In this mathematical estimation of magnitude the understanding is equally well served and satisfied whether the imagination chooses for its unit a magnitude that can be grasped in a single glance, e.g., a foot or a rod, or whether it chooses a German mile or even a diameter of the earth, whose apprehension but not composition is possible in an intuition of the imagination (not through *comprehensio aesthetica* though certainly through *comprehensio logica* in a numerical concept). In both cases the logical estimation of magnitude proceeds unhindered to infinity.

But now the mind hears in itself the voice of reason, which requires totality for all given magnitudes, even for those that can never be entirely apprehended although they are (in the sensible representation) judged[c]

---

[a] *Beurtheilung.*
[b] In the first edition, this reads "there is something that is certainly objectively purposive."
[c] *beurtheilt.*

as entirely given, hence comprehension in **one** intuition, and it demands a **presentation** for all members of a progressively increasing numerical series, and does not exempt from this requirement even the infinite (space and past time), but rather makes it unavoidable for us to think of it (in the judgment of common reason) as **given entirely** (in its totality).

The infinite, however, is absolutely (not merely comparatively) great. Compared with this, everything else (of the same kind of magnitude) is small. But what is most important is that even being able to think of it as **a whole** indicates a faculty of the mind which surpasses every standard of sense. For this would require a comprehension that yielded as a measure a unit that has a determinate relation to the infinite, expressible in numbers, which is impossible. But **even to be able to think** the given[a] infinite without contradiction requires a faculty in the human mind that is itself supersensible. For it is only by [5:255] means of this and its idea of a noumenon, which itself admits of no intuition though it is presupposed as the substratum of the intuition of the world as mere appearance, that the infinite of the sensible world is **completely** comprehended in the pure intellectual estimation of magnitude **under** a concept, even though it can never be completely thought in the mathematical estimation of magnitude **through numerical concepts**. Even a faculty for being able to think the infinite of supersensible intuition as given (in its intelligible substratum) surpasses any standard of sensibility, and is great beyond all comparison even with the faculty of mathematical estimation, not, of course, from a theoretical point of view, in behalf of the faculty of cognition, but still as an enlargement of the mind which feels itself empowered[b] to overstep the limits of sensibility from another (practical) point of view.

Nature is thus sublime in those of its appearances the intuition of which brings with them the idea of its infinity. Now the latter cannot happen except through the inadequacy of even the greatest effort of our imagination in the estimation of the magnitude of an object. Now, however, the imagination is adequate for the mathematical estimation of every object, that is, for giving an adequate measure for it, because the numerical concepts of the understanding, by means of progression, can make any measure adequate for any given[c] magnitude. Thus it must be the **aesthetic** estimation of magnitude in which is felt the effort at comprehension which exceeds the capacity[d] of the imagination to comprehend the progressive apprehension in one whole of intuition, and in which is at the same time perceived the inadequacy of this faculty, which is unbounded in its progression, for grasping a basic measure that is suitable for the estimation of magnitude with the least effort of the understanding and for using it for the estimation of magnitude. Now the proper unalterable basic measure of nature is its absolute whole, which, in the case of nature as appearance, is infinity comprehended. But since this basic measure is a self-contradictory concept (on account of the impossibility of the absolute totality of an endless progression), that magnitude of a natural object on which the imagination fruitlessly expends its entire capacity[e] for comprehension must lead the concept of nature to a supersensible substratum (which grounds both it and at the same time our faculty for thinking), which is great beyond any standard of sense and hence allows not so much the [5:256] object as rather the disposition of the mind in estimating it to be judged[f] **sublime**.

Thus, just as the aesthetic power of judgment in judging[g] the beautiful relates the imagination in its free play to the **understanding**, in order to agree with its **concepts** in general (without determination of them),

---

[a]The word "given" was added in the second edition.
[b]*vermögend.*
[c]The word "given" was added in the second edition.
[d]*Vermögen.*
[e]*Vermögen.*
[f]*beurtheilen.*
[g]*Beurtheilung.*

so in judging[a] a thing to be sublime the same faculty is related to **reason**, in order to correspond subjectively with its **ideas** (though which is undetermined), i.e., in order to produce a disposition of the mind which is in conformity with them and compatible with that which the influence of determinate (practical) ideas on feeling would produce.

It is also evident from this that true sublimity must be sought only in the mind of the one who judges, not in the object in nature, the judging[b] of which occasions this disposition in it. And who would want to call sublime shapeless mountain masses towering above one another in wild disorder with their pyramids of ice, or the dark and raging sea, etc.? But the mind feels itself elevated in its own judging[c] if, in the consideration of such things, without regard to their form, abandoning itself to the imagination and to a reason which, although it is associated with it entirely without any determinate end, merely extends it, it nevertheless finds the entire power of the imagination inadequate to its ideas.

Examples of the mathematically sublime in nature in mere intuition are provided for us by all those cases where what is given to us is not so much a greater numerical concept as rather a great unity as measure (for shortening the numerical series) for the imagination. A tree that we estimate by the height of a man may serve as a standard for a mountain, and, if the latter were, say, a mile high, it could serve as the unit for the number that expresses the diameter of the earth, in order to make the latter intuitable; the diameter of the earth could serve as the unit for the planetary system so far as known to us, this for the Milky Way, and the immeasurable multitude of such Milky Way systems, called nebulae, which presumably constitute such a system among themselves in turn, does not allow us to expect any limits here.[14] Now in the aesthetic judging[d] of such an immeasurable whole, the sublime does not lie as much in the magnitude of the number as in the fact that as we progress we always arrive at ever greater units; the systematic [5:257] division of the structure of the world contributes to this, representing to us all that is great in nature as in its turn small, but actually representing our imagination in all its boundlessness, and with it nature, as paling into insignificance beside the ideas[e] of reason if it is supposed to provide a presentation adequate to them.

§27.
On the quality of the satisfaction in the judging[f] of the sublime.

The feeling of the inadequacy of our capacity[g] for the attainment of an idea **that is a law for us** is **respect**.[15] Now the idea of the comprehension of every appearance that may be given to us into the intuition of a whole is one enjoined on us by a law of reason, which recognizes no other determinate measure, valid for everyone and inalterable,[h] than the absolute whole. But our imagination, even in its greatest effort with regard to the comprehension of a given object in a whole of intuition (hence for the presentation of the idea of reason) that is demanded of it, demonstrates its limits and inadequacy, but at the same time its vocation[i] for adequately realizing that idea as a law. Thus the feeling of the sublime in nature is respect for our own vocation, which we

---

[a]*Beurtheilung.*
[b]*Beurtheilung.*
[c]*Beurtheilung.*
[d]*Beurtheilung.*
[e]In the first edition this was singular.
[f]*Beurtheilung.*
[g]*Vermögens.*
[h]In the first edition, this word was "alterable."
[i]*Bestimmung.* Some occurrences of this word in this and the following sections could be translated as "determination," but some can only be translated as "vocation," so for the sake of consistency all will be translated that way.

show to an object in nature through a certain subreption (substitution of a respect for the object instead of for the idea of humanity in our subject), which as it were makes intuitable the superiority of the rational vocation of our cognitive faculty over the greatest faculty of sensibility.

The feeling of the sublime is thus a feeling of displeasure from the inadequacy of the imagination in the aesthetic estimation of magnitude for the estimation[a] by means of reason, and a pleasure that is thereby aroused at the same time from the correspondence of this very judgment of the inadequacy of the greatest sensible faculty in comparison with ideas of reason, insofar as striving for them is nevertheless a law for us. That is, it is a law (of reason) for us and part of our vocation to estimate everything great that nature contains as an object of the senses for us as small in comparison with ideas of reason; and whatever arouses the feeling of this supersensible vocation in us is in agreement with that law. Now the greatest effort of the imagination in the [5:258] presentation of the unity for the estimation of magnitude is a relation to something **absolutely great**, and consequently also a relation to the law of reason to adopt this alone as the supreme measure of magnitude. Thus the inner perception of the inadequacy of any sensible standard for the estimation of magnitude by reason corresponds with reason's laws, and is a displeasure that arouses the feeling of our supersensible vocation in us, in accordance with which it is purposive and thus a pleasure to find every standard of sensibility inadequate for the ideas of the understanding.[b]

The mind feels itself **moved** in the representation of the sublime in nature, while in the aesthetic judgment on the beautiful in nature it is in **calm** contemplation. This movement (especially in its inception) may be compared to a vibration, i.e., to a rapidly alternating repulsion from and attraction to one and the same object. What is excessive for the imagination (to which it is driven in the apprehension of the intuition) is as it were an abyss, in which it fears to lose itself, yet for reason's idea of the supersensible to produce such an effort of the imagination is not excessive but lawful, hence it is precisely as attractive as it was repulsive for mere sensibility. Even in this case, however, the judgment itself remains only aesthetic because, without having a determinate concept of the object as its ground, it represents merely the subjective play of the powers of the mind (imagination and reason) as harmonious even in their contrast. For just as imagination and **understanding** produce subjective purposiveness of the powers of the mind in the judging of the beautiful through their unison, so do imagination and **reason** produce subjective purposiveness through their conflict: namely, a feeling that we have pure self-sufficient reason, or[c] a faculty for estimating magnitude, whose preeminence cannot be made intuitable through anything except the inadequacy of that faculty which is itself unbounded in the presentation of magnitudes (of sensible objects). The measurement of a space (as apprehension) is at the same time the description of it, thus an objective movement in the imagination and a progression; by contrast, the comprehension of multiplicity in the unity not of thought but of intuition, hence the comprehension in one moment of that which is successively apprehended, is a regression, [5:259] which in turn cancels the time-condition in the progression of the imagination and makes **simultaneity** intuitable. It is thus (since temporal succession is a condition of inner sense and of an intuition) a subjective movement of the imagination, by which it does violence to the inner sense, which must be all the more marked the greater the quantum is which the imagination comprehends in one intuition. Thus the effort to take up in a single intuition a measure for magnitudes, which requires an appreciable time for its apprehension, is a kind of apprehension which, subjectively considered, is contrapurposive, but which objectively, for the estimation of

---

[a]The second edition repeats the word "estimation" (*Schätzung*) instead of just using the pronoun "that" (*die*).
[b]Following the second edition, which prints "of understanding" (*des Verstandes*) instead of "of reason" (*der Vernunft*).
[c]The word "or" was added in the second edition.

magnitude, is necessary, hence purposive; in this way, however, the very same violence that is inflicted on the subject by the imagination is judged[a] as purposive **for the whole vocation** of the mind.

The **quality** of the feeling of the sublime is that it is a feeling of displeasure concerning the aesthetic faculty of judging[b] an object that is yet at the same time represented as purposive, which is possible because the subject's own incapacity[c] reveals the consciousness of an unlimited capacity[d] of the very same subject, and the mind can aesthetically judge[e] the latter only through the former.

In the logical estimation of magnitude, the impossibility of ever attaining to absolute totality through the progression of the measurement of the things of the sensible world in time and space was recognized as objective, i.e., as an impossibility of **thinking** the infinite as even given, and not as merely subjective, i.e., as an incapacity[f] for **grasping** it; for there nothing at all turns on the degree of comprehension in one intuition as a measure, but everything comes down to a numerical concept. But in an aesthetic estimation of magnitude the numerical concept must drop out or be altered, and the comprehension of the imagination in respect of the unity of measure (so that the concept of a law of the successive generation of concepts of magnitude is avoided) is alone purposive for it. – Now if a magnitude almost reaches the outermost limit of our faculty of comprehension in one intuition, and yet the imagination is by means of numerical concepts (our capacity[g] for which we are aware is unlimited) summoned to aesthetic comprehension in a greater unity, then we feel ourselves in our mind as aesthetically confined within borders; but with respect to the necessary enlargement of the imagination to the point of adequacy to that which is unlimited in our faculty of reason, namely the idea of [5:260] the absolute whole, the displeasure and thus the contrapurposiveness of the faculty of imagination is yet represented as purposive for the ideas of reason and their awakening. It is precisely in this way, however, that the aesthetic judgment itself becomes purposive for reason, as the source of ideas, i.e., for an intellectual comprehension for which all aesthetic comprehension is small; and the object is taken up as sublime with a pleasure that is possible only by means of a displeasure.

B.

On the Dynamically Sublime in Nature

§28.

On nature as a power.

**Power** is a capacity[h] that is superior to great obstacles. The same thing is called **dominion** if it is also superior to the resistance of something that itself possesses power. Nature considered in aesthetic judgment as a power that has no dominion over us is **dynamically sublime.**

If nature is to be judged[i] by us dynamically as sublime, it must be represented as arousing fear (although, conversely, not every object that arouses fear is found sublime in our aesthetic judgment). For in aesthetic

---

[a] *beurtheilt.*
[b] *Beurtheilungsvermögen.*
[c] *Unvermögen.*
[d] *Vermögens.*
[e] *beurtheilen.*
[f] *Unvermögen.*
[g] *Vermögens.*
[h] *Vermögen.*
[i] *beurtheilt.*

judging[a] (without a concept) the superiority over obstacles can only be judged[b] in accordance with the magnitude of the resistance. However, that which we strive to resist is an evil, and, if we find our capacity[c] to be no match for it, an object of fear. Thus, for the aesthetic power of judgment[d] nature can count as a power,[e] thus as dynamically sublime, only insofar as it is considered an object of fear.

We can, however, consider an object as **fearful** without being afraid **of** it, if, namely, we judge[f] it in such a way that we merely **think** of the case in which we might wish to resist it and think that in that case all resistance would be completely futile. Thus the virtuous man fears God without being afraid of him, because he does not think of the case of wishing to resist God and his commands as anything that is worrisome [5:261] for **him.** But since he does not think of such a case as impossible in itself, he recognizes God as fearful.

Someone who is afraid can no more judge about the sublime in nature than someone who is in the grip of inclination and appetite can judge about the beautiful. The former flees from the sight of an object that instills alarm in him, and it is impossible to find satisfaction in a terror that is seriously intended. Hence the agreeableness in the cessation of something troublesome is **joyfulness.** But this joyfulness on account of liberation from a danger is accompanied with the proviso that one never again be exposed to that danger; indeed one may well be reluctant to think back on that sensation, let alone seek out the opportunity for it.

Bold, overhanging, as it were threatening cliffs, thunder clouds towering up into the heavens, bringing with them flashes of lightning and crashes of thunder, volcanoes with their all-destroying violence, hurricanes with the devastation they leave behind, the boundless ocean set into a rage, a lofty waterfall on a mighty river, etc., make our capacity[g] to resist into an insignificant trifle in comparison with their power. But the sight of them only becomes all the more attractive the more fearful it is, as long as we find ourselves in safety, and we gladly call these objects sublime because they elevate the strength of our soul above its usual level, and allow us to discover within ourselves a capacity[h] for resistance of quite another kind, which gives us the courage to measure ourselves against the apparent all-powerfulness of nature.

For just as we found our own limitation in the immeasurability of nature and the insufficiency of our capacity[i] to adopt a standard proportionate to the aesthetic estimation of the magnitude of its **domain**, but nevertheless at the same time found in our own faculty of reason another, nonsensible standard, which has that very infinity under itself as a unit against which everything in nature is small, and thus found in our own mind a superiority over nature itself even in its immeasurability: likewise the irresistibility of its power certainly makes us, considered as natural beings, recognize our physical[j] powerlessness, but at the same time it reveals a capacity[k] for judging[l] ourselves as independent of it and a superiority over nature on which is grounded a self-preservation of quite another kind than that which can be threatened and endangered by nature outside us, whereby the humanity in our [5:262] person remains undemeaned even though the human being must submit to that dominion. In this way, in our aesthetic judgment nature is judged[m] as sublime not insofar as it arouses

---

[a] *Beurtheilung.*
[b] *beurtheilt.*
[c] *Vermögen.*
[d] *Urtheilskraft.*
[e] *Macht.*
[f] *beurtheilen.*
[g] *Vermögen.*
[h] *Vermögen.*
[i] *Vermögens.*
[j] The word "physical" was added in the second edition.
[k] *Vermögen.*
[l] *beurtheilen.*
[m] *beurtheilt.*

fear, but rather because it calls forth our power[a] (which is not part of nature) to regard those things about which we are concerned (goods, health and life) as trivial, and hence to regard its power[b] (to which we are, to be sure, subjected in regard to these things) as not the sort of dominion over ourselves and our authority to which we would have to bow if it came down to our highest principles and their affirmation or abandonment. Thus nature is here called sublime merely because it raises the imagination to the point of presenting those cases in which the mind can make palpable to itself the sublimity of its own vocation even over nature.

This self-esteem is not diminished by the fact that we must see ourselves as safe in order to be sensible of this inspiring satisfaction, in which case (it might seem), because the danger is not serious, the sublimity of our spiritual capacity[c] is also not to be taken seriously.[16] For the satisfaction here concerns only the **vocation** of our capacity[d] as it is revealed to us in such a case, just as the predisposition to it lies in our nature; while the development and exercise of it is left to us and remains our responsibility.[e] And there is truth here, however much the person, if he takes his reflection this far, may be conscious of his present actual powerlessness.

To be sure, this principle seems far-fetched and subtle, hence excessive for an aesthetic judgment; but the observation of human beings shows the opposite, that it can be the principle for the most common judgings[f] even though one is not always conscious of it. For what is it that is an object of the greatest admiration even to the savage? Someone who is not frightened, who has no fear, thus does not shrink before danger but energetically sets to work with full deliberation. And even in the most civilized[g] circumstances this exceptionally high esteem for the warrior remains, only now it is also demanded that he at the same time display all the virtues of peace, gentleness, compassion and even proper care for his own person, precisely because in this way the incoercibility of his mind by danger can be recognized. Hence however much debate there may be about whether it is the statesman or the [5:263] general who deserves the greater respect in comparison to the other, aesthetic judgment decides in favor of the latter. Even war, if it is conducted with order and reverence for the rights of civilians, has something sublime about it, and at the same time makes the mentality of the people who conduct it in this way all the more sublime, the more dangers it has been exposed to and before which it has been able to assert its courage; whereas a long peace causes the spirit of mere commerce to predominate, along with base selfishness, cowardice and weakness, and usually debases the mentality of the populace.

This analysis of the concept of the sublime, to the extent that it is ascribed to power, seems to run counter to the fact that we usually represent God as exhibiting himself in anger but at the same time in his sublimity in thunder, storm, earthquake etc., where to imagine that our minds have any superiority over the effects and as it seems even over the intentions of such a power would seem to be at once both foolishness and outrage. Here it seems to be not a feeling of the sublimity of our own nature but rather submission, dejection, and a feeling of complete powerlessness that is the appropriate disposition of the mind to the appearance of such an object, and which is also usually associated with the idea of it in the case of natural occurrences of this sort. In religion in general submission, adoration with bowed head, and remorseful and anxious gestures and voice, seem to be the only appropriate conduct in the presence of the Deity, and so to have been adopted and still observed by most people. But this disposition of the mind is far from being intrinsically and necessarily

---

[a] *Kraft.*
[b] *Macht.*
[c] *Geistesvermögen.*
[d] *Vermögens.*
[e] In the first edition, this period was a comma, and the sentence continued to the end of the paragraph.
[f] *Beurtheilungen.*
[g] *allergesittesten.*

connected with the idea of the **sublimity** of a religion and its object. Someone who is genuinely afraid because he finds cause for that within himself, because he is conscious of having offended with his contemptible disposition[a] a power whose will is irresistible and at the same time just, certainly does not find himself in the right frame of mind to marvel at the greatness of God, for which a mood of calm contemplation and an entirely free[b] judgment is requisite. Only when he is conscious of his upright, God-pleasing disposition do those effects of[c] power serve to awaken in him the idea of the sublimity of this being, insofar as he recognizes in himself a sublimity of disposition suitable to God's will, and is thereby raised above the fear of such effects of nature, which he does not regard as outbursts of God's wrath. Even humility, as the [5:264] pitiless judging[d] of one's own failings, which otherwise, given consciousness of good dispositions, could easily be covered with the mantle of the fragility of human nature, is a sublime state of mind, that of voluntarily subjecting oneself to the pain of self-reproach in order gradually to eliminate the causes of it. In this way alone does religion internally distinguish itself from superstition, the latter not providing a basis in the mind for reverence[e] for the sublime, but only for fear[f] and anxiety before the being of superior power, to whose will the terrified person sees himself as subjected without holding him in great esteem; from which of course nothing can arise but the attempt to curry favor and ingratiate oneself, instead of a religion of the good conduct of life.[17]

Thus sublimity is not contained in anything in nature, but only in our mind, insofar as we can become conscious of being superior to nature within us and thus also to nature outside us (insofar as it influences us). Everything that arouses this feeling in us, which includes the **power**[g] of nature that calls forth our own powers,[h] is thus (although improperly) called sublime; and only under the presupposition of this idea in us and in relation to it are we capable of arriving at the idea of the sublimity of that being who produces inner respect in us not merely through his power, which he displays in nature, but even more by the capacity[i] that is placed within us for judging[j] nature without fear and thinking of our vocation as sublime in comparison with it.

§29.
On the modality of the judgment on the sublime in nature.

There are innumerable things in beautiful nature concerning which we immediately require consensus with our own judgment from everyone else and can also, without being especially prone to error, expect it; but we cannot promise ourselves that our judgment concerning the sublime in nature will so readily find acceptance by others. For a far greater culture, not merely of the aesthetic power of judgment, but also of the cognitive faculties on which that is based, seems to be requisite in order to be able to make a judgment about this excellence of the objects of nature. [5:265]

---

[a] *Gesinnung.*
[b] In the second edition, *freyes*; in the first edition, *zwangfreyes* (uncoerced or free from coercion).
[c] *der*; in the first edition, *seiner*, that is, God's power.
[d] *Beurtheilung.*
[e] *Ehrfurcht.*
[f] *Furcht.*
[g] *Macht.*
[h] *Kräfte.*
[i] *Vermögen.*
[j] *beurtheilen.*

The disposition of the mind to the feeling of the sublime requires its receptivity to ideas; for it is precisely in the inadequacy of nature to the latter, thus only under the presupposition of them, and of the effort of the imagination to treat nature as a schema for them, that what is repellent for the sensibility, but which is at the same time attractive for it, consists, because it is a dominion that reason exercises over sensibility only in order to enlarge it in a way suitable for its own proper domain (the practical) and to allow it to look out upon the infinite, which for sensibility is an abyss. In fact, without the development of moral ideas, that which we, prepared by culture, call sublime will appear merely repellent to the unrefined person. He will see in the proofs of the dominion of nature given by its destructiveness and in the enormous measure of its power, against which his own vanishes away to nothing, only the distress, danger, and need that would surround the person who was banished thereto. Thus the good and otherwise sensible Savoyard peasant (as Herr de Saussure relates) had no hesitation in calling all devotees of the icy mountains fools.[18] And who knows whether that would have been entirely unjust if that observer had undertaken the dangers to which he there exposed himself, as most travelers usually do, merely as a hobby, or in order one day to be able to describe them with pathos? But his intention was the edification of mankind, and this excellent man experienced the elevating sentiment[a] that he gave to the readers of his travels as part of the bargain.

But just because the judgment on the sublime in nature requires culture (more so than that on the beautiful), it is not therefore first generated by culture and so to speak introduced into society merely as a matter of convention; rather it has its foundation in human nature, and indeed in that which can be required of everyone and demanded of him along with healthy understanding, namely in the predisposition to the feeling for (practical) ideas, i.e., to that which is moral.[b]

This is the ground for the necessity of the assent of the judgment of other people concerning the sublime to our own, which we at the same time include in the latter. For just as we reproach someone who is indifferent in judging[c] an object in nature that we find beautiful with lack of **taste**, so we say of someone who remains unmoved by that which we judge to be sublime that he has no **feeling.** We demand both, however, of every human being, and also presuppose it in everyone who has any culture – only with this difference, that we immediately [5:266] require the former of everyone because in it the power of judgment relates the imagination merely to the understanding, as the faculty of concepts, but because the latter relates the imagination to reason, as the faculty of ideas, we require it only under a subjective presupposition (which, however, we believe ourselves to be justified in demanding of everyone), namely that of the moral feeling in the human being,[d] and so we also[e] ascribe necessity to this aesthetic judgment.

In this modality of aesthetic judgments, namely their presumed necessity, lies a principal moment for the critique of the power of judgment. For it makes us cognizant of an *a priori* principle in them, and elevates them out of empirical psychology, in which they would otherwise remain buried among the feelings of enjoyment and pain (only with the meaningless epithet of a **more refined** feeling),[f,19] in order to place them and by their means the power of judgment in the class of those which have as their ground *a priori* principles, and as such to transpose them into transcendental philosophy.

---

[a] *seelenerhebende Empfindung.*
[b] *dem moralischen*; in the first edition, *den moralischen*, which would refer back to the previous clause and thus be translated as "to the moral ideas."
[c] *Beurtheilung.*
[d] The words "in the human being" were added in the second edition.
[e] The word "also" was added in the second edition.
[f] The parenthetical remark was added in the second edition.

## General remark on the exposition of aesthetic reflective judgments.[20]

In relation to the feeling of pleasure an object is to be counted either among the **agreeable** or the **beautiful** or the **sublime** or the (absolutely) **good** (*iucundum, pulchrum, sublime, honestum*).

The **agreeable**, as an incentive for the desires, is of the same kind throughout, no matter where it comes from and how specifically different the representation (of sense and of sensation, objectively considered) may be.[21] Hence in judging[a] of its influence on the mind it is only a matter of the number[b] of the charms (simultaneous and successive), and as it were only of the mass of the agreeable sensation; and thus this cannot be made intelligible except by **quantity**. It also does not contribute to culture, but is simply a matter of enjoyment. – The **beautiful**, by contrast, requires the representation of a certain **quality** of the object, which also makes itself intelligible, and can be brought to concepts (although in the aesthetic judgment it is not brought to that); and it does contribute to culture, in that it at the same time teaches us to attend to purposiveness in the feeling of pleasure. – The **sublime** consists merely in the [5:267] **relation** in which the sensible in the representation of nature is judged[c] as suitable for a possible supersensible use of it. – The **absolutely good**, judged[d] subjectively in terms of the feeling that it instills (the object of the moral feeling) as the determinability of the powers of the subject by means of the representation of an **absolutely necessitating** law, is distinguished chiefly by the **modality** of a necessity resting on concepts *a priori*, which contains in itself not merely a **claim** but also a **command** that everyone should assent, and belongs in itself not to the aesthetic but to the pure intellectual[e] power of judgment; it is also ascribed, not in a merely reflecting but in a determining judgment, not to **nature** but to **freedom**.[22] But the **determinability of the subject** by means of this idea, and indeed of a subject that can sense in itself **obstacles** in sensibility but at the same time superiority over them through overcoming them as a **modification of its condition**, i.e., the moral feeling, is nevertheless related to the aesthetic power of judgment and its **formal conditions** to the extent that it can serve to make the lawfulness of action out of duty representable at the same time as aesthetic, i.e., as sublime, or also as beautiful, without sacrificing any of its purity; which would not be the case if one would place it in natural combination with the feeling of the agreeable.

If one draws the result from the exposition thus far of the two kinds of aesthetic judgment, the outcome would be the following brief explanations:

That is **beautiful** which pleases in the mere judging[f] (thus not by means of the sensation of sense nor in accordance with a concept of the understanding). From this it follows of itself that it must please without any interest.

That is **sublime** which pleases immediately through its resistance to the interest of the senses.

Both, as explanations of aesthetically universally valid judging,[g] are related to subjective grounds, namely on the one hand to those of sensibility, as it is purposive in behalf of the contemplative understanding, on the other, **in opposition** to those, as purposive for the ends of practical reason; and yet both, united in the same subject, are purposive in relation to the moral feeling. The beautiful prepares us to love something, even nature, without interest; the sublime, to esteem it, even contrary to our (sensible) interest.[23]

---

[a] *Beurtheilung.*
[b] *Menge.*
[c] *beurtheilt.*
[d] *beurtheilt.*
[e] In the first edition, the words "but to the pure intellectual" were enclosed in parentheses.
[f] *Beurtheilung.*
[g] *Beurtheilung.*

One can describe the sublime thus: it is an object (of nature) the [5:268] **representation of which determines the mind to think of the unattainability of nature as a presentation of ideas.**

Taken literally, and considered logically, ideas cannot be presented. But if we extend our empirical faculty of representation (mathematically or dynamically) for the intuition of nature, then reason inevitably comes in as a faculty of the independence of the absolute totality, and produces the effort of the mind, though it is in vain, to make the representation of the senses adequate to that. This effort, and the feeling of the unattainability of the idea by means of the imagination, is itself a presentation of the subjective purposiveness of our mind in the use of the imagination for its supersensible vocation, and compels us to **think** nature itself in its totality, as the presentation of something supersensible, subjectively, without being able to produce this presentation **objectively**.

For we quickly realize that nature falls completely short of the unconditioned in space and time, and thus of absolute magnitude, even though this is demanded by the commonest reason. And precisely by this are we reminded that we have to do only with a nature as appearance, and that this itself must be regarded as the mere presentation of a nature in itself (which reason has in the idea). This idea of the supersensible, however, which of course we cannot further determine, so that we cannot **cognize** nature as a presentation of it but can only **think** it, is awakened in us by means of an object the aesthetic judging[a] of which stretches imagination to its limit, whether that of enlargement (mathematically) or of its power over the mind (dynamically), in that it is grounded in the feeling of a vocation of the mind that entirely oversteps the domain of the former (the moral feeling), in regard to which the representation of the object is judged[b] as subjectively purposive.

In fact a feeling for the sublime in nature cannot even be conceived without connecting it to a disposition of the mind that is similar to the moral disposition; and, although the beautiful in nature likewise presupposes and cultivates a certain **liberality** in the manner of thinking, i.e., independence of the satisfaction from mere sensory enjoyment, nevertheless by means of it freedom is represented more as in **play** than as subject to a lawful **business**, which is the [5:269] genuine property of human morality, where reason must exercise dominion over sensibility; it is just that in the aesthetic judgment on the sublime this dominion is represented as being exercised by the imagination itself, as an instrument of reason.

The satisfaction in the sublime in nature is thus also only **negative** (whereas that in the beautiful is **positive**), namely a feeling of the deprivation of the freedom of the imagination by itself, insofar as it is purposively determined in accordance with a law other than that of empirical use. It thereby acquires an enlargement and power which is greater than that which it sacrifices, but whose ground is hidden from it, whereas it **feels** the sacrifice or deprivation and at the same time the cause to which it is subjected. The **astonishment** bordering on terror, the horror and the awesome shudder, which grip the spectator in viewing mountain ranges towering to the heavens, deep ravines and the raging torrents in them, deeply shadowed wastelands inducing melancholy reflection, etc., is, in view of the safety in which he knows himself to be, not actual fear, but only an attempt to involve ourselves in it by means of the imagination, in order to feel the power of that very faculty, to combine the movement of the mind thereby aroused with its calmness, and so to be superior to nature within us, and thus also that outside us, insofar as it can have an influence on our feeling of well-being. For the imagination, in accordance with the law of association, makes our state of contentment physically dependent; but the very same imagination, in accordance with principles of the schematism of the power of judgment (consequently to the extent that it is subordinated to freedom), is an instrument of reason and its ideas, but as such a power to assert our independence in the face of the influences of nature, to diminish the

---

[a]*Beurtheilung.*
[b]*beurtheilt.*

value of what is great according to these,[a] and so to place what is absolutely great only in its (the subject's) own vocation. This reflection of the aesthetic power of judgment, elevating itself to adequacy to reason (yet without a determinate concept of the latter), represents the object, precisely by means of the objective inadequacy of the imagination in its greatest extension to reason (as a faculty of ideas), as subjectively purposive.

Here one must attend above all to what was already pointed out above, that [5:270] in the transcendental aesthetic of the power of judgment it is strictly pure aesthetic judgments that are at issue, consequently the examples must not be drawn from those beautiful or sublime objects of nature that presuppose the concept of an end; for in that case it would be either teleological or grounded in mere sensations of an object (gratification or pain), and thus in the first case would not be an aesthetic purposiveness and in the second case not a merely formal purposiveness. Thus, if someone calls the sight of the starry heavens **sublime**, he must not ground such a judging[b] of it on concepts of worlds inhabited by rational beings, taking the bright points with which we see the space above us to be filled as their suns, about which they move in their purposively appointed orbits, but must take it, as we see it, merely as a broad, all-embracing vault; and it must be merely under this representation that we posit the sublimity that a pure aesthetic judgment attributes to this object. In just the same way, we must not take the sight of the ocean as we **think** it, enriched with all sorts of knowledge (which are not, however, contained in the immediate intuition), for example as a wide realm of water creatures, as the great storehouse of water for the evaporation which impregnates the air with clouds for the benefit of the land, or as an element that separates parts of the world from one another but at the same time makes possible the greatest community among them, for this would yield merely teleological judgments; rather, one must consider the ocean merely as the poets do, in accordance with what its appearance shows, for instance, when it is considered in periods of calm, as a clear watery mirror bounded only by the heavens, but also when it is turbulent, an abyss threatening to devour everything, and yet still be able to find it sublime. The same is to be said about the sublime and the beautiful in the human figure, where we do not look to concepts of the ends **for which** all its members exist for determining grounds of our judgment and must not let agreement with them **influence** our aesthetic judgment (which in that case would no longer be pure), though that they do not conflict with those ends is of course a necessary condition even of aesthetic satisfaction.[24] Aesthetic purposiveness is the lawfulness of the power of judgment in its **freedom.** The satisfaction in the object depends on the relation in which we would place the imagination: namely, that it entertain the mind by itself in free activity. If, on the contrary, something else determines the judgment, whether it be a [5:271] sensation of the senses or a concept of the understanding, then it is certainly lawful but not the judgment of a **free** power of judgment.

Thus if one speaks of an intellectual beauty or sublimity, then, **first**, these expressions are not entirely correct, because they are kinds of aesthetic representation that would not be found in us at all if we were simply pure intelligences (or even if we were to transform ourselves into such in our thoughts); **second**, although both, as objects of an intellectual (moral) satisfaction, are certainly compatible with the aesthetic insofar as they do not **rest** on any interest, nevertheless they are still difficult to unite with the aesthetic because they are supposed to **produce** an interest which, if the presentation is to agree with the satisfaction in aesthetic judging,[c] would never occur except by means of an interest of the senses, which is combined with it in the presentation, through which, however, damage would be done to the intellectual purposiveness and it would become impure.

---

[a]The first and second editions have *der ersteren*, the third *der letzteren*; in either case, the reference is back to "the influences of nature."
[b]*Beurtheilung.*
[c]*Beurtheilung.*

The object of a pure and unconditioned intellectual satisfaction is the moral law in all its power, which it exercises in us over each and every incentive of the mind **antecedent to it**; and, since this power actually makes itself aesthetically knowable only through sacrifices (which is a deprivation, although in behalf of inner freedom, but also reveals in us an unfathomable depth of this supersensible faculty together with its consequences reaching beyond what can be seen),[a] the satisfaction on the aesthetic side (in relation to sensibility) is negative, i.e., contrary to this interest, but considered from the intellectual side it is positive, and combined with an interest. From this it follows that the intellectual, intrinsically purposive (moral) good, judged[b] aesthetically, must not be represented so much as beautiful but rather as sublime, so that it arouses more the feeling of respect (which scorns charm) than that of love and intimate affection, since human nature does not agree with that good of its own accord, but only through the dominion that reason exercises over sensibility. Conversely, even that which we call sublime in nature outside us or even within ourselves (e.g., certain affects) is represented only as a power of the mind to soar above **certain**[c] obstacles of sensibility by means of moral[d] principles, and thereby to become interesting. [5:272]

I should like to dwell a little on the last point. The idea of the good with affect is called **enthusiasm**.[e,25] This state of mind seems to be sublime, so much so that it is commonly maintained that without it nothing great can be accomplished. Now, however, every affect* is blind, either in the choice of its end, or, even if this is given by reason, in its implementation; for it is that movement of the mind that makes it incapable of engaging in free consideration of principles, in order to determine itself in accordance with them.[f] Thus it cannot in any way merit a satisfaction of reason. Nevertheless, enthusiasm is aesthetically sublime, because it is a stretching of the powers through ideas, which give the mind a momentum that acts far more powerfully and persistently than the impetus given by sensory representations. But (what seems strange) even **affectlessness** (*apatheia, phlegma in significactu bono*)[g] in a mind that emphatically pursues its own inalterable principles is sublime, and indeed in a far superior way, because it also has the satisfaction of pure reason on its side.[26] Only such a mentality is called **noble** – an expression subsequently also applied to things, e.g., buildings, costume, a literary style, a bodily posture, etc., if it arouses not so much **astonishment** (an affect in the representation of novelty that exceeds expectation)[27] as **admiration** (an astonishment that does not cease when the novelty is lost), which happens when ideas in their presentation unintentionally and without artifice agree with aesthetic satisfaction.[28]

Every affect of the **courageous sort** (that is, which arouses the consciousness of our powers to overcome any resistance (*animi strenui*)[h]) is **aesthetically sublime**, e.g., anger, even despair (that is, the **enraged**, not the **despondent** kind). Affect of the **yielding** kind, however (which makes the effort at resistance itself into an object

---

***Affects** are specifically different from **passions**. The former are related merely to feeling; the latter belong to the faculty of desire, and are inclinations that make all determinability of the faculty of choice by means of principles difficult or impossible. The former are tumultuous and unpremeditated, the latter sustained and considered; thus indignation, as anger, is an affect, but as hatred (vindictiveness), it is a passion. The latter can never, in any circumstances, be called sublime, because while in the case of an affect the freedom of the mind is certainly **hampered**, in the case of passion it is removed.

[a]The parentheses around this part of the sentence were added in the second edition.
[b]*beurtheilt.*
[c]The emphasized word "certain" (*gewisse*) in the second edition replaces "the" in the first.
[d]Reading *moralische* with the first edition rather than *menschliche* with the second.
[e]Here Kant uses the word "*Enthusiasm*," not "*Schwärmerei*" [fanaticism].
[f]In the first edition, "that makes it incapable of determining itself through principles in accordance with free consideration."
[g]apathy, being phlegmatic in a positive sense.
[h]vigorous spirits or mental powers.

of displeasure (*animum languidum*)ᵃ) has nothing **noble** in it, although it can be counted as belonging to beauty of the sensory [5:273] kind.[29] Hence the **emotions** that can reach the strength of an affect are also quite diverse. We have **brave** as well as **tender** emotions. The latter, if they reach the level of an affect, are good for nothing at all; the tendency toward them is called **oversensitivity**.[30] A sympathetic pain that will not let itself be consoled, or with which, when it concerns invented evils, we consciously become involved, to the point of being taken in by the fantasy, as if it were real, proves and constitutes a tenderhearted but at the same time weak soul, which reveals a beautiful side, and which can certainly be called fantastic but not even enthusiastic. Novels, sentimental plays, shallow moral precepts, which make play with (falsely) so-called noble dispositions, but in fact enervate the heart, and make it unreceptive to the rigorous precept of duty and incapable of all respect for the dignity of humanity in our own person and the right of human beings (which is something entirely different from their happiness), and in general incapable of all firm principles; even a religious sermon that preaches a groveling, base currying of favor and self-ingratiation, which abandons all confidence in our own capacityᵇ for resistance against evil, instead of the energetic determination to seek out the powers that still remain in us, despite all our frailty, for overcoming inclinations; the false humility that finds the only way to be pleasing to the supreme being in self-contempt, in whimpering, feigned remorse and a merely passive attitude of mind – none of these have anything to do with that which can be counted as the beauty, let alone the sublimity, of a mentality.[31]

But even tumultuous movements of the mind, whether they be associated with ideas of religion, under the name of edification, or, as belonging merely to culture, with ideas that contain a social interest, no matter how much they stretch the imagination, can in no way claim the honor of being a **sublime** presentation, if they do not leave behind a disposition of mind that, even if only indirectly, has influence on the consciousness of its strength and resolution in regard to that which brings with it intellectual purposiveness (the supersensible). For otherwise all these emotions belong only to the **motion**ᶜ that we are glad to have for the sake of health. The agreeable exhaustion that follows such an agitation by the play of affects is an enjoyment of the [5:274] well-being resulting from the equilibrium of the various vital forces that is thus produced in us, which in the end comes down to the same thing as that which the voluptuaries of the Orient find so comforting when they have their bodies as it were kneaded, and all their muscles and joints softly pressed and flexed; only in the first case the moving principle is for the most part in us, while in the latter it is entirely outside us. Now many a person does believe himself to be edified by a sermon in which, however, nothing (no system of good maxims) has been erected, or improved by a tragedy when he is merely glad about a lucky escape from boredom. Thus the sublime must always have a relation to the **manner of thinking,** i.e., to maxims for making the intellectual and the ideas of reason superior to sensibility.

There need be no anxiety that the feeling of the sublime will lose anything through such an abstract presentation, which becomes entirely negative in regard to the sensible; for the imagination, although it certainly finds nothing beyond the sensible to which it can attach itself, nevertheless feels itself to be unbounded precisely because of this elimination of the limits of sensibility; and that separation is thus a presentation of the infinite, which for that very reason can never be anything other than a merely negative presentation, which nevertheless expands the soul. Perhaps there is no more sublime passage in the Jewish Book of the Law than the commandment: Thou shalt not make unto thyself any graven image, nor any likeness either of that which is in heaven, or on the earth, or yet under the earth, etc.[32] This commandment alone can explain the enthusiasm that the Jewish people felt in its civilizedᵈ period for its religion when it compared itself with other

---

ᵃenfeebled spirit.

ᵇ*Vermögen.*

ᶜHere Kant uses the Latinate word *Motion* instead of *Bewegung* (movement).

ᵈ*gesitteten.*

peoples, or the pride that Mohammedanism inspired. The very same thing also holds of the representation of the moral law and the predisposition to morality in us. It is utterly mistaken to worry that if it were deprived of everything that the senses can recommend it would then bring with it nothing but cold, lifeless approval and no moving force or emotion. It is exactly the reverse: for where the senses no longer see anything before them, yet the unmistakable and inextinguishable idea of morality remains, there it would be more necessary to moderate the momentum of an unbounded imagination so as not to let it reach the point of enthusiasm,[a] [33] rather than, from fear of the powerlessness of these ideas, to look for assistance for them in images and childish devices. That is why even governments [5:275] have gladly allowed religion to be richly equipped with such supplements and thus sought to relieve the subject[b] of the bother but at the same time also of the capacity[c] to extend the powers of his soul beyond the limits that are arbitrarily set for him and by means of which, as merely passive, he can more easily be dealt with.

This pure, elevating,[d] merely negative presentation of morality, by contrast, carries with it no risk of **visionary rapture**,[e] which is **a delusion of being able to** *see*[f] **something beyond all bounds of sensibility**,[g] i.e., to dream in accordance with principles (to rave with reason), precisely because the presentation in this case is merely negative. For the **inscrutability of the idea of freedom** entirely precludes any positive presentation;[34] but the moral law is sufficient in itself in us and originally determining, so that it does not even allow us to look around for a determining ground outside it. If enthusiasm can be compared with the **delusion of sense**,[h] then visionary rapture is to be compared with the **delusion of mind**,[i] the latter of which is least of all compatible with the sublime, since it is brooding and absurd. In enthusiasm, as an affect, the imagination is unreined; in visionary rapture, as a deep-rooted, oppressive passion, it is unruled. The former is a passing accident, which occasionally affects the most healthy understanding; the latter is a disease that destroys it.

**Simplicity** (artless purposiveness) is as it were the style of nature in the sublime, and so also of morality, which is a second (supersensible) nature, of which we know only the laws, without being able by intuition to reach the supersensible faculty in ourselves that contains the ground of this legislation.

It should further be remarked that, although the satisfaction in the beautiful, as much as that in the sublime, is not only clearly distinguished among the other aesthetic judgings[j] by means of universal **communicability**, but also, by means of this property, acquires an interest in relation to society (in which it can be communicated), nevertheless the **separation from all society** is also regarded as something sublime if it rests on ideas that look beyond all sensible interest. To be self-sufficient, hence not to need society, yet without being unsociable, i.e., fleeing it, is something that comes close to the sublime, just like any superiority over needs. In contrast, to flee from human beings out of **misanthropy**, because one is hostile to them, or out of **anthropophobia** (fear of people), because one fears them as enemies, is in part hateful and in part [5:276] contemptible. Nevertheless there is a kind of misanthropy (very improperly so called), the predisposition to which is often found in the mind of many well-thinking people as they get older, which is certainly philanthropic enough as far as

---

[a]Here and in the next paragraph, *Enthusiasm.*

[b]*Unterthan.*

[c]*Vermögen.*

[d]*seelenerhebende*, literally "soul-elevating."

[e]*Schwärmerei* [sometimes translated as "fanaticism" or even "delirium"].

[f]This word is set in spaced *Fettdruck* in Kant's text.

[g]Following the second edition in reading *Sinnlichkeit* instead of *Sittlichkeit* (morality) as in the first.

[h]*Wahnsinn.*

[i]*Wahnwitz.*

[j]*Beurtheilungen.*

their **benevolence** is concerned, but is because of long, sad experience far removed from any **pleasure**[a] in human beings; evidence of this is to be found in the tendency to withdraw from society, the fantastic wish for an isolated country seat, or even (in young people) the dream of happiness in being able to pass their life on an island unknown to the rest of the world with a small family, which the novelists or poets who write Robinsonades[35] know so well how to exploit. Falsehood, ingratitude, injustice, the childishness in ends that we ourselves hold to be important and great, in the pursuit of which people do every conceivable evil to each other, so contradict the idea of what they could be if they wanted to, and are so opposed to the lively wish to take a better view of them that, in order not to hate them, since one cannot love them, doing without all social joys seems to be only a small sacrifice. This sadness, not about the evil that fate imposes on other human beings (which is caused by sympathy), but over that which they do to themselves (which is based on antipathy in fundamental principles) is, since it rests on ideas, sublime, whereas the former can at best only count as beautiful. – Saussure,[36] as inspired as he is thorough, in the description of his travels in the Alps says of Bonhomme, one of the mountains of Savoy: "There reigns there a certain **tedious sadness**." But he also knew of an **interesting** sadness, which is instilled by the view of a wasteland to which human beings would move in order to hear or experience nothing more of the world, but which nevertheless must not be so completely inhospitable that it would offer human beings only an extremely burdensome refuge. – I make this remark only with the intention of recalling that even sorrow (not dejected sadness) can be counted among the **vigorous** affects if it is grounded in moral ideas, but if it is grounded in sympathy, and, as such, is also lovable, it belongs merely to the **mellowing** affects, only in order to draw attention to the disposition of the mind that is **sublime** only in the former case.

\* \* \*

[5:277] The transcendental exposition of aesthetic judgments that has now been completed can be compared with the physiological[b] exposition, as it has been elaborated by a **Burke** and many acute men among us, in order to see whither a merely empirical exposition of the sublime and the beautiful would lead. **Burke**,\* who deserves to be named as the foremost author in this sort of approach, brings out in this manner (page 223 of his work) "that the feeling of the sublime is grounded on the drive to self-preservation and on **fear**, i.e., a pain, which, since it does not go as far as the actual destruction of bodily parts, produces movements which, since they cleanse the finer or cruder vessels of dangerous and burdensome stoppages, are capable of arousing agreeable sensations, not, to be sure, pleasure, but a kind of pleasing horror, a certain tranquility that is mixed with terror."[37]

The beautiful, which he grounds on love (which, however, he would have known as separate from desire), he traces (pages 251–52) "to the relaxation, loosening and slackening of the fibers of the body, hence to a softening, a dissolution, an enervation, a sinking away, a dying away, a melting away of gratification."[39] And now he confirms this sort of explanation through cases in which the imagination is able to arouse the feeling of the beautiful as well as the sublime not only in association with the understanding, but even in association with sensory sensations. – As psychological remarks, these analyses of the phenomena of our mind are extremely fine,[c] and provide rich materials for the favorite researches of empirical anthropology.

---

\*According to the German translation of his essay, *Philosophische Untersuchungen über dem Ursprung unserer Begriffe vom Schönen und Erhabenen* (Riga: Hartknoch, 1773).[38]

[a]Here *Wohlgefallen*, in contrast to *Wohlwollen* ("benevolence") in the previous clause.
[b]In the first edition, the word printed here was "psychological."
[c]*schön.*

Moreover, it cannot be denied that all representations in us, whether they are objectively merely sensible or else entirely intellectual, can nevertheless subjectively be associated with gratification or pain, however unnoticeable either might be (because they all affect the feeling of life, and none of them, insofar as it is a modification of the subject, can be indifferent), or even that, as Epicurus maintained, **gratification** and **pain** are always[a] ultimately corporeal,[40] whether they originate from the imagination or even from representations of the understanding: because life without the feeling of the corporeal organ is [5:278] merely consciousness of one's existence, but not a feeling of well- or ill-being, i.e., the promotion or inhibition of the powers of life; because the mind for itself is entirely life (the principle of life itself), and hindrances or promotions must be sought outside it, though in the human being himself, hence in combination with his body.

If, however, one locates the satisfaction in the object entirely in the fact that it gratifies by means of charm and emotion, then one must not expect of **others** that they will assent to the aesthetic judgments that **we** make; for about that everyone is justified in consulting only his own private sense. In that case, however, all criticism[b] of taste also ceases entirely; for one would then have to make the example that others give by means of the contingent correspondence among their judgments into a **command** for assent from us, in opposition to which principle, however, we would presumably struggle and appeal to the natural right to subject the judgment that rests on the immediate feeling of our own well-being to our own sense, and not to that of others.

If, therefore, the judgment of taste must not be counted as **egoistic**, but necessarily, in accordance with its inner nature, i.e., of itself, not for the sake of the examples that others give of their taste, as **pluralistic**, if one evaluates it as one that may at the same time demand that everyone should consent to it, then it must be grounded in some sort of *a priori* principle (whether objective or subjective), which one can never arrive at by scouting about among empirical laws of the alterations of the mind: for these allow us to cognize only how things are judged, but never to prescribe how they ought to be judged, particularly in such a way that the command is **unconditioned**; though it is something of this sort that the judgments of taste presuppose when they would have the satisfaction known to be **immediately** connected with a representation. Thus the empirical exposition of aesthetic judgments may always make a start at furnishing the material for a higher investigation, yet a transcendental discussion of this faculty is still possible and essential for the critique of taste.[c] For unless this has *a priori* principles, it could not possibly guide the judgments of others and make claims[d] to approve or reject them with even a semblance of right.

What belongs to the remainder of the analytic of the aesthetic power of judgment contains first of all the:[e]

[5:279] Deduction of pure aesthetic judgments[f,41]

§30.
The deduction of aesthetic judgments concerning the objects of nature may not be directed towards that which we call sublime among them, but only to the beautiful.

---

[a]In the first edition, "all."
[b]*Censur.*
[c]In the first edition, the next sentence followed after a comma rather than a period.
[d]In the first edition, "judgments."
[e]This lead-in to the next section was added in the second edition.
[f]In the first edition, the heading "Third Book" (*Drittes Buch*) preceded this title.

The claim of an aesthetic judgment to universal validity for every subject, as a judgment that must be based on some principle *a priori*, needs a deduction (i.e., a legitimation of its presumption), which must be added to its exposition, if, that is, it concerns a satisfaction or dissatisfaction in the **form of the object**. The judgments of taste concerning the beautiful in nature are of this sort. For in this case the purposiveness has its ground in the object and its shape,[a] even if it does not indicate the relation of the object to others in accordance with concepts (for judgments of cognition), but rather generally concerns merely the apprehension of this form insofar as it shows itself in the mind to be suitable to the **faculty** both of concepts and of the presentation of them (which is one and the same as that of apprehension). Hence one can also raise many questions in regard to the beautiful in nature, concerning the cause of this purposiveness of its forms: e.g., how is one to explain why nature has spread beauty so extravagantly everywhere, even at the bottom of the ocean, where it is only seldom that the human eye (for which alone, after all, it is purposive) penetrates? and so on.

Only the sublime in nature – if we make a pure aesthetic judgment about it, which is not mixed with concepts of perfection, as objective purposiveness, in which case it would be a teleological judgment – can be considered as entirely formless or shapeless, but nevertheless as the object of a pure satisfaction, and can demonstrate subjective purposiveness in the given representation; and the question now arises, whether in the case of this kind of aesthetic judgment, beyond the exposition of what is thought in it, a deduction of its claim to some sort of [5:280] (subjective) principle *a priori* could also be demanded.

It will serve as an answer to this that the sublime in nature is only improperly so called, and should properly be ascribed only to the manner of thinking, or rather to its foundation in human nature.[b] The apprehension of an otherwise formless and nonpurposive object merely provides the occasion for becoming conscious of this, which in this way is **used** in a subjectively purposive way, but is not judged to be such **for itself** and on account of its form (as it were *species finalis accepta, non data*).[c] Hence our exposition of the judgments on the sublime in nature was at the same time their deduction. For when we analyzed the reflection of the power of judgment in these, we found in them a purposive relation of the cognitive faculties, which must ground the faculty of ends (the will) *a priori*, and hence is itself purposive *a priori*, which then immediately contains[d] the deduction, i.e., the justification of the claim of such a judgment to universally necessary validity.

We shall thus have to seek only the deduction of judgments of taste, i.e., of the judgments about the beauty of things in nature, and by this means accomplish the task for the whole of the aesthetic power of judgment in its entirety.

[End of §30 – Ed.]

---

[a]*Gestalt.*
[b]In the first edition, there was a comma rather than a period here, and the sentence continued thus: "for which the apprehension . . . merely provides the occasion."
[c]The appearance of finality is assigned, not given.
[d]In the first edition, "is."

*Anthropology from a Pragmatic Point of View*

## Note on the text

Source: Kant, Immanuel, *Anthropology from a Pragmatic Point of View*. In *Anthropology, History, Education,* edited by Günter Zöller and Robert Louden. Cambridge: Cambridge University Press, 2007. Pages 345–47.

Foreign words in curved brackets are given by Kant. Citations to the Academy Edition of Kant's collected works continue to be (as explained above) to the volume: page number.

§67. [7:241] [...] Beauty alone belongs to taste; it is true that the sublime belongs to aesthetic judgment, but not to taste. However, the representation of the sublime can and should nevertheless be beautiful in itself; otherwise it is coarse, barbaric, and contrary to good taste." [...]

[7:243] §68. On taste in regard to the sublime.

The *sublime* is awe-inspiring *greatness* (*magnitudo reverenda*) in extent or degree which invites approach (in order to measure our powers against it); but the fear that in comparison with it we will disappear in our own estimation is at the same time a deterrent (for example, thunder over our heads, or a high, rugged mountain). And if we ourselves are in a safe place, the collecting of our powers to grasp the appearance, along with our anxiety that we are unable to measure up to its greatness, arouses *surprise* (a pleasant feeling owing to its continual overcoming of pain).

The *sublime* is the counterweight but not the opposite of the beautiful; because the effort and attempt to raise ourselves to a grasp (*apprehensio*) of the object awakens in us a feeling of our own greatness and power; but the representation in thought of the sublime by *description* or presentation can and must always be beautiful. For otherwise the astonishment becomes a *deterrent*, which is very different from *admiration*, a judgment in which we do not grow weary of being astonished.

The *monstrous* is greatness that is contrapurposive (*magnitude monstrosa*). Writers, therefore, who wanted to extol the vast extent of the Russian empire have missed badly in calling it monstrous; for herein lies a reproach, as if it were *too great* for a single ruler. – A human being is *adventurous* who has the propensity to become entangled with events whose true account resembles a novel.

The sublime is therefore not an object for taste, but rather an object for the feeling of emotion; however, the artistic presentation of the sublime in description and embellishment (in secondary works, *parerga*) can and should be beautiful, since otherwise it is wild, coarse, and repulsive, and, consequently, contrary to taste.

## Questions

1. What seems new, and what familiar, in Kant's theory of the mathematical and dynamical sublime? How does it compare to his earlier theories, and to that of his predecessors?

2. In what ways is Kant's account "transcendental"? What do you take this to mean? How does Kant's approach differ from Burke's?

3. Do you agree that Kant's exposition of the sublime suffices for its "deduction" of its claim to "universally necessary validity" (that it is valid for all)? Explain. If he needs to argue more, what would the deduction look like?

4. Do you think the awakened "feeling of our own greatness and power" (*Anthropology* §68) must be reflexive and self-conscious? Explain. Must we be aware of such a "feeling" in a reflexive, self-attentive act?

5. Do you read Kant's remarks as implying that sublimity in art is possible? How might his representational view of art be constraining his account? Explain, discussing some examples.

## Further reading

Brady, Emily. *The Sublime in Modern Philosophy: Aesthetics, Ethics, and Nature.* Cambridge: Cambridge University Press, 2013.

Clewis, Robert R. *The Kantian Sublime and the Revelation of Freedom.* Cambridge: Cambridge University Press, 2009.

Crowther, Paul. *The Kantian Sublime: From Morality to Art.* Oxford: Oxford University Press, 1989.

Deligiorgi, Katerina. "The Pleasures of Contra-purposiveness: Kant, the Sublime, and Being Human." *Journal of Aesthetics and Art Criticism* 72, no. 1 (2014): 25–35.

Gracyk, Theodore A. "Sublimity, Ugliness, and Formlessness in Kant's Aesthetic Theory." *Journal of Aesthetics and Art Criticism* 45, no. 1 (1986): 49–56.

Guyer, Paul. *Kant and the Experience of Freedom: Essays on Aesthetics and Morality.* Cambridge: Cambridge University Press, 1993.

# CHAPTER 16
# FRIEDRICH SCHILLER, "ON THE SUBLIME (TOWARD THE FURTHER DEVELOPMENT OF SOME KANTIAN IDEAS)" (1793)

Friedrich Schiller (1759–1805) was a prominent German poet, playwright, historian, and philosopher. He composed *On the Aesthetic Education of Man in a Series of Letters* and "On Grace and Dignity" as well as plays such as *The Robbers, William Tell,* and *Mary Stuart*. In his essays, tragedies, and poetry, the theme of freedom plays a prominent role. In the fourth movement of the Ninth symphony, Beethoven set to music Schiller's poem "Ode to Joy," resulting in a work that is sometimes cited as an example of the sublime in music. (Wagner discusses the latter in his essay, "Beethoven," in the present volume.)

As its subtitle suggests, this essay was heavily influenced by Kant's "Analytic of the Sublime" in the *Critique of the Power of Judgment* (1790). The piece ("Vom Erhabenen") is Schiller's first composition on the sublime and was initially published in the third volume of his periodical *Neue Thalia* in 1793. Schiller emphasizes the "practical" sublime over the "cognitive" sublime, and his account of the sublime also includes an account of tragedy. More than Kant, Schiller emphasizes sublimity in art. In the second half of the essay, Schiller introduces the concept of the pathetically-sublime and connects it to one of the "laws" of tragic art. This essay was published alongside "On the Pathetic" (1793) and gives insight into his reflections on tragedy and the pathetic during this fruitful period.

In 1801, Schiller published another, perhaps better known, essay on the same topic, "Concerning the Sublime" ("Über das Erhabene"), which he appears to have written between 1793 and 1796.[1] The 1793 essay has been selected for this anthology, however, since the 1801 essay, though briefer and less overtly Kantian, is arguably denser and harder to follow. Moreover, the connection between the sublime and tragedy is more oblique and indirect in the 1801 essay than in this one. Finally, the 1793 essay introduces the category of the pathetically-sublime, illustrating one of Schiller's departures from Kant.

## Note on the text

Source: Excerpted from "On the Sublime," in Friedrich Schiller, *Essays*, edited by Daniel Dahlstrom and Walter Hinderer and translated by Daniel Dahlstrom, 22–44. London: Continuum, 1998.

Punctuation, style, and spelling have occasionally been modified. Unless noted otherwise, English and German words in square brackets are given by Dahlstrom. Due to considerations of space, the volume editor has omitted some passages in which Schiller quotes from or summarizes Kant; the ellipsis in square brackets "[…]" indicates such omissions.

## "On the sublime (toward the further development of some Kantian ideas)"

We call an object *sublime* if, whenever the object is presented or represented, our sensuous nature feels its limits, but our rational nature feels its superiority, its freedom from limits. Thus, we come up short against a sublime object *physically*, but we elevate ourselves above it *morally*, namely, through ideas.

Only as sensuous beings are we dependent; as rational beings we are free.

A sublime subject matter gives us *in the first place* a feeling of our dependency as natural beings, because *in the second place* it makes us aware of the independence that, as rational beings, we assert over nature, as much *inside* as *outside* ourselves.

We are dependent insofar as something *outside* us contains the reason why something is possible *inside* us.

As long as nature outside us conforms to conditions under which something becomes possible inside us, we cannot feel our dependency. If we are to become conscious of that dependency, then nature must be represented as conflicting with what for us is a *need* and yet is *possible* only through nature's compliance. Or, in other words, nature must stand in contradiction to our instincts or drives [*Triebe*].

Now all instincts at work within us as sensuous beings may be reduced to two fundamental instincts. First, we possess an instinct to alter the condition we find ourselves in, to express our existence, to be effective, all of which amount to acquiring representations or notions for ourselves. This fundamental instinct can thus be called "the instinct to represent things to ourselves" or, in short, "the cognitive instinct" [*Vorstellungstrieb*]. Second, we possess an instinct to maintain the condition we find ourselves in, to continue our existence, an instinct called "the instinct for self-preservation" [*Trieb der Selbsterhaltung*].

The cognitive instinct concerns knowing; the instinct for self-preservation concerns feelings, in other words, inner perceptions of existence.

By virtue of these two sorts of instincts we are *dependent* upon nature in two ways. The first kind of dependence becomes evident to us if the natural conditions for arriving at various sorts of knowledge are missing. We experience the second kind of dependency when nature contradicts the conditions that make it possible for us to continue to exist. In a parallel way, with the help of reason, we maintain our *independence* from nature in two senses: *first*, because (in a theoretical sense) we pass beyond natural conditions and can think more than we know; *second*, because (in a practical sense) we set ourselves above natural conditions and, by means of our will, can contradict our *desires*. When perception of some subject matter allows us to experience the former, it is *theoretically-magnificent*, something cognitively sublime. A subject matter providing us with the feeling of the independence of our will is *practically-magnificent*, a sublimeness of character [*ein Erhabenes der Gesinnung*].

In the case of what is theoretically-sublime, the cognitive instinct is contradicted by nature as an *object of knowledge*. In the case of what is practically-sublime, the instinct to preserve ourselves is contradicted by nature as an *object of feeling*. In the former scenario nature is considered merely as an object that should have expanded our knowledge; in the latter case it is represented as a power that can determine our own condition. Kant accordingly names the practically-sublime "the sublimity of power" or "the dynamically-sublime" in contrast to the mathematically sublime. However, since it is in no way possible on the basis of the concepts *dynamic* and *mathematical* to make clear or not whether the sphere of the sublime is exhausted by this division, I have preferred the division into the *theoretically-sublime* and the *practically-sublime*.

In what way we are dependent upon natural conditions in our cognitions and become conscious of this dependency will be sufficiently elaborated in the development of the theoretically-sublime. That our existence as sensuous beings is dependent upon natural conditions outside us is scarcely in need of a proof of its own. As soon as nature outside us alters its specific relationship to us, on which our physical well-being is based, our existence in the world afforded by the senses and connected to this physical well-being is also immediately challenged and endangered. Nature thus has in its power the conditions under which we exist and, in order that we pay attention to this relationship to nature, so indispensable to our existence, a vigilant sentry has been given to our physical life in the form of the *self-preservation instinct* and a warning has been given to this instinct in the form of pain. Thus, the moment our physical condition undergoes a change that threatens to transform it into its opposite, pain calls attention to the danger and summons the instinct of self-preservation to resist.

If the danger is of *the sort* that any resistance on our part would be futile, then *fear* must arise. Hence, if the existence of an object conflicts with the conditions of our own existence and if we do not feel ourselves up to its power, it is an object of fear, something *frightening*.

But it is only frightening for us as sensuous beings, because only as such are we dependent upon nature. That inside us that is not nature and not subordinated to natural law has nothing to fear from nature outside us, considered as a force. Represented as a force capable of determining our physical condition but having no power over our will, nature is *dynamically-* or *practically*-sublime.

The practically-sublime thus is distinct from the theoretically-sublime in that the former conflicts with the conditions of our existence, while the theoretically-sublime conflicts only with the conditions of knowledge. An object is theoretically-sublime insofar as it brings with it the notion [*Vorstellung*] of infinity, something the imagination does not feel itself capable of depicting. An object is practically-sublime insofar as it brings with it the notion of a danger that we do not feel ourselves capable of overcoming with our physical powers. We succumb in the attempt to grasp the idea [*Vorstellung*] of the theoretically-sublime or to resist the force of the practically-sublime. A peaceful ocean is an example of the former, a stormy ocean an example of the latter. An enormously high tower or mountain can provide something sublime for cognition. If it looms down over us, it will turn into something sublime for our emotional state. Again, both have this much in common with one another: precisely by contradicting the conditions of our existing and acting respectively, they disclose the very power within us that does not feel itself bound to these conditions, that is to say, a power that, on the one hand, is able to think more than the senses can apprehend and, on the other hand, fears nothing as far as its independence is concerned and suffers no violence in expressing itself, even if the senses accompanying it should be overcome by the frightful power of nature.

Yet, although both sorts of sublimity have a similar relation to our power of reason, they stand in a completely different relation to the sensuous side of us, and this is the basis for an important difference between them, a difference in strength as well as interest.

The theoretically-sublime contradicts the cognitive instinct, the practically-sublime the preservation instinct. In the first case what is contested is only an individual expression of the cognitive power of the senses. In the second case, however, what is contested is the ultimate basis of any possible expression of this power, namely, its very existence.

Now, of course, there is some displeasure involved in every failed attempt to know, since by this means an active instinct is confounded. Yet this displeasure can never amount to pain as long as we know that our existence is not dependent on the success or failure of such knowing and our self-respect does not suffer in the process.

However, if an object clashes with the conditions of our existence and the immediate sensation of it would cause pain, the image of the object inspires *fright*. For, in order to preserve the power itself, nature would have had to make arrangements completely different from those that it found necessary to sustain the activity of that power. In the case of a *frightful* object, then, the sensuous side of our nature is engaged in a quite different way than it is in the case of something infinite, since the self-preservation instinct clamors much more loudly than the cognitive instinct does. It is altogether different whether we have to fear losing a single notion or the basis of any possible notion, namely, our existence in the world of the senses, in other words, whether we have to fear for existence itself or for a single expression of it.

However, precisely for this reason, namely, because the *frightful* object assails our sensuous nature more violently than something *infinite* does, the distance between capabilities of the senses and capabilities that go beyond the senses is felt all the more keenly. Reason's superiority and the mind's inner freedom become all the more conspicuous. Since, then, the entire essence of the sublime rests upon the consciousness of this rational freedom of ours, and all pleasure afforded by the sublime is grounded precisely in this consciousness alone, it follows of itself (as experience also teaches) that the aesthetic image of what is *frightful* must stir us more powerfully and more pleasantly than the representation of the *infinite* does, and that the practically-sublime has, accordingly, a very great advantage over the theoretically-sublime, as far as the strength of the feeling is concerned.

While what is theoretically-magnificent actually expands only our *scope*, what is practically-magnificent, the dynamically-sublime, expands our *power*. Only by means of the latter do we really experience our true and complete independence from nature. For feeling oneself to be independent of natural conditions in the mere act of knowing and in one's entire inward existence is completely different from feeling oneself to be transported and elevated to a point beyond fate, beyond all contingencies, and beyond all natural necessity. Nothing matters more to a human being as a sensuous being than his existence, and no dependency is more oppressive to him than this, to regard nature as the very power reigning over his existence. He feels himself free of this dependency when he is witness to the practically-sublime. [...]

This sublimity of our rational character—this, our practical independence from nature, must, indeed, be distinguished from the sort of superiority that we know how to assert over nature as a power in individual instances, owing to either our physical or our intellectual powers. There is, of course, also something magnificent, but not at all sublime about this latter sort of superiority in itself. For example, a human being who struggles with a wild animal and subdues it by the strength of his arm or even by cunning; a raging river like the Nile whose power is broken by dams, and which the human intellect, by gathering its overflow in canals, can even transform from a destructive object into a useful one; a ship at sea that by its ingenious design is in a position to defy all the violence of the furious elements; in short, all those cases where by means of his inventive intellect the human being has forced nature to obey him and to serve his aims, even where nature is superior to him as a power and equipped to bring about his demise. All these cases, I say, do not awaken a feeling of the sublime, although they have something analogous to it and for that reason, in the aesthetic evaluation, are also pleasing. Yet why are they not sublime, given the fact that they make evident the superiority of humans over nature?

To answer this question we must return to the concept of the sublime, where the reason may be easily uncovered. According to this concept, the only sublime object is the object that is superior to us as *natural beings*, but from which we feel ourselves absolutely independent as rational beings, as beings not belonging to nature. Thus, on the basis of this conception, all *natural means* employed by human beings to withstand the power of nature are *excluded* from the category of the sublime. For this concept demands unconditionally that as natural beings we be no match for the object, and yet feel ourselves to be independent of it, owing to what in us is not of nature (and this is nothing other than pure reason). However, all those means cited, through which the human being is superior to nature (skillfulness, cunning, and physical strength), are taken from nature and hence they belong to the human being as a natural being. Accordingly, it is not as an intelligent being but as a sensuous being that a human being withstands those natural objects, that is to say, not morally through his inner freedom, but physically through application of natural forces. Also, it is not because he is an intelligent being that he is not overcome by these objects, but rather because as a sensuous being he is already superior to them. Yet where his physical powers are sufficient, there is nothing that could force him to have recourse to his intellectual self, to the inner self-sufficiency of his rational powers.

Therefore, for the feeling of the sublime it is absolutely requisite that we see ourselves with absolutely no *physical means of resistance* and look to our nonphysical self for help. The sort of object involved must therefore be *frightening* to the sensuous side of us, and that is no longer the case, the moment we feel ourselves equal to it through natural powers.

This is also confirmed by experience. The mightiest natural force is less sublime precisely to the degree to which it appears to be tamed by human beings, and it rapidly becomes sublime again as soon as it confounds human artifice. As a natural force superior to us, a horse that still gallops around wild and unbridled in the forests can be *frightening* and can even provide a subject matter for a sublime portrayal. Once tamed and harnessed to the yoke or before the wagons, the very same horse loses that frightfulness and thereby everything sublime about it. But if this horse, after it has been broken in, tears loose of its reins and, bucking in anger under its rider, violently regains its freedom, it is once again frightening and becomes sublime once more.

A human being's physical superiority over natural forces is therefore so little a reason for something being sublime that almost everywhere that superiority is encountered it weakens or completely destroys the sublimity of the object. We can, of course, with considerable pleasure, dwell on the human skill that is capable of subduing the wildest forces of nature. Yet the source of this pleasure is *logical* and not *aesthetic*; it is a result of reflection and is not inspired by the immediate image of something.

Hence, nature is practically-sublime only where it is *frightening*. But then the question arises: is this also the case in reverse? Is it also practically-sublime wherever it is *frightening*?

Here we must return once again to the concept of the sublime. As essential as it is that we feel ourselves as sensuous beings to be dependent upon the object, it is just as essential, on the other hand, that we feel ourselves as rational beings to be independent of that very object. Where the former is missing, where there is nothing in the object that frightens our sensuous nature, no sublimity is possible. Where the latter is absent, that is to say, where the object is *merely* frightening and we do not feel ourselves as rational beings to be superior to it, then sublimity is just as remote a possibility.

In order to experience something frightening as sublime and take pleasure in it, inner freedom on the part of the mind is an absolute requisite. Indeed, something frightening can be sublime merely by the fact that it allows us to experience our independence, our mind's freedom. Actual and serious fear, however, overcomes all freedom of mind.

Therefore, the sublime object must, of course, be frightening, but it may not incite actual fear. Fear is a condition of *suffering* and *violence*; only in a detached consideration of something and through the feeling of the activity inside ourselves can we take pleasure in something sublime. Thus either the fearful object may not direct its power at us at all or, if this happens, then our spirit must remain free, while our sensuous nature is being overwhelmed. This latter case is, however, extremely rare, and demands an *elevation* of human nature that can scarcely be considered possible in an individual. For where we actually find ourselves in danger, where we ourselves are the object of an inimical natural power, aesthetic judgment is finished. As sublime as a storm at sea may be when viewed from the shore, those who find themselves on the ship devastated by the storm are just as little disposed to pass this aesthetic judgment on it.

Hence, we are concerned only with the first case where we are able, of course, to witness the might of the frightful object but without it being directed at us, in other words, where we *know* that we are *safe* from that very object. It is only in the imagination, then, that we put ourselves in a position where this power could affect us and all resistance would be in vain. What is terrifying thus exists solely in the representation [*Vorstellung*] of it; yet even the mere representation of danger, if it is vivid enough, sets the preservation instinct in motion and the result is something analogous to what the actual sensation would produce. A shudder grips us, a feeling of anxiety stirs, our sensuous nature is aroused. And without this onset of actual suffering, without this serious attack on our existence, we would merely be playing with the object. And it must be *serious*, at least in the sensation, if reason is supposed to have recourse to the idea of its freedom. Consciousness of the freedom within us can be valid and worthwhile only insofar as it is serious about this; but it cannot be serious if we are merely playing with the representation of the danger.

I have said that we must be safe and secure if we are to enjoy what is *frightening*. Now there are, however, instances of misfortune and danger from which a human being can never know that he is safe and yet the representation of these misfortunes and dangers can still be and even actually is sublime. The concept of safety thus cannot be restricted to the fact that someone knows that he is physically out of danger, as, for example, when someone peers down into an enormous depression from a high and well-secured parapet or looks down at a stormy lake from a height. In such cases the fearlessness is, of course, based upon the certainty that one cannot be affected. But on what would anyone be willing to base his security in the face of fate, the omnipresent power of the divinity, painful diseases, poignant losses, or death? Here there is no physical basis at hand at all for putting oneself at ease. If we reflect on fate in its frightfulness, then we must without hesitation admit to ourselves that we are anything but removed from it.

There is accordingly a twofold basis for security. In the face of such evils as it is in our physical power to elude, we can have external, physical security. However, when confronted by the sort of evils that we are in no position to resist or evade by any natural means, we can have merely inner or moral security. This distinction is important, especially in relation to the sublime.

*Physical security* provides an immediate reason for our sensuous nature to be at ease, completely unrelated to our inner or moral condition. Thus, too, nothing at all is required to be able to regard an object without fear if we find ourselves in this physical safety when confronted by the object. For just this reason, one finds a far greater uniformity to people's judgments about the sublimity of *such objects*, the sighting of which is bound up with this physical security, than about those objects in the face of which one has only moral security. The cause is obvious. Physical security is beneficial to everyone in the same way. Moral security, on the other hand, presupposes a state of mind not found in all individuals. Yet, because this physical security holds only for our sensuous nature, it possesses nothing of itself that could please our rational nature and its influence is merely negative, in that it simply keeps the self-preservation instinct from being frightened and the freedom of mind from being overwhelmed.

In the case of inner or *moral security* things are completely different. This security is, of course, also a basis for putting our *sensuous nature* at ease (otherwise it would itself be sublime), but it is so only indirectly, through ideas of reason. We look upon the fearful without fear because we feel ourselves to be beyond the reach of its power over us as natural beings, either through the consciousness of our *innocence* or through the thoughts of the *indestructibility of our being*. This moral security and certitude thus postulate, as we see, *ideas of religion*, since only *religion*, not *morality*, sets out grounds for putting our sensuous nature at ease. Morality inexorably follows the prescription of reason, without any regard for the interest of our sensuous nature. It is religion, however, that seeks to establish a reconciliation, an agreement between the demands of reason and the inclinations of our sensuous nature. Hence, for moral security it does not at all suffice that we possess a moral disposition. Rather, it is also necessary that we think of *nature* in accord with the *moral law* or, what in this case is one and the same, that we think of nature under the sway of a pure rational being. Death, for example, is one such object in the face of which we have *only* moral security. For most people (since most people by far are more sensuous than they are rational) the vivid representation of all the terrors of death, joined with the certainty of being unable to escape it, would make it quite impossible to combine this image with as much composure as an aesthetic judgment requires—if the rational belief in an immortality, even for our sensuous nature, did not provide a tolerable way out.

Yet this must not be understood as though the image of death, if combined with sublimity, sustains this sublimity through the idea of immortality.—Nothing could be further from the truth!—The idea of immortality, as I am taking it to be here, can put our instinct to survive, that is to say, our sensuous nature, at ease and I must note, once and for all, that as far as making a sublime impression is concerned, our sensuous nature with its demands must be completely set aside and every basis for reassuring us must be sought in reason alone. Thus, the very idea of immortality, in which our sensuous side to a certain extent is still given its due (as it is put forward in all positive religions), can contribute nothing at all to the representation of death as a sublime object. Rather this idea must simply stand, as it were, in the background in order to come to the aid of our sensuous nature alone, in case the latter feels desperate and defenseless, exposed to all the terror of being annihilated, and threatened by the prospect of succumbing to this violent assault. If this idea of immortality, however, becomes the prevailing idea in the mind, death loses it[s] *fearfulness* and the *sublime* disappears.

If the divinity is represented in its omniscience, holiness, and might—an omniscience that illuminates all the crevices and corners of the human heart, a holiness that permits no impure emotion, and a might that has our physical fate in its power—it is a fearful image and can thus become a *sublime* one. We can have no physical security against the effects of this might, since it is as impossible to *elude* it as it is to *resist* it. We are thus left with only moral security that we base upon the justice of this being, together with our innocence. Because we are conscious of our innocence and thus secure in the face of the godhead, we look without terror upon the terrifying phenomena by means of which it makes its power known. When this unbounded, irresistible, and all-present power is represented, that moral security makes it possible for us not to lose our freedom of mind completely, for when that is gone, the mind is in no mood to make an aesthetic judgment. Yet this feeling of security, even though it has a moral basis, cannot be the cause of the sublime, for in the end it only provides a basis for reassuring our sensuous nature. This sense of security satisfies the instinct for self-preservation, but the sublime is never based upon the satisfaction of our instincts. If the image of divinity is to be practically-(dynamically) sublime, then we have to tie the feeling of our security *not to our existence* but rather *to our principles*. It has to be irrelevant to us how we fare as natural beings in the process, if we feel that, simply as intellects, we are independent of the effects of its might. But we feel that as rational beings we are not dependent even on divine omnipotence since even that omnipotence cannot destroy our autonomy, cannot determine our will against our principles. Only insofar, therefore, as we deny the divinity all *natural influence* on *determinations of our will*, is the representation of its power dynamically-sublime. [...]

The object of the practically-sublime must be frightening to the sensuous side of human nature; an evil must threaten our physical condition and the representation of the danger must set our self-preservation instinct in motion.

As far as the emotion involved in the preservation-instinct is concerned, our intelligible self, namely, that within us that is not of nature, must distinguish itself from the sensuous side of our being and become aware of its self-sufficiency, of its independence from everything that can affect its physical nature. In short, it must become conscious of its freedom.

This freedom, however, is in an unqualified sense only moral, not physical. Not as sensuous beings and neither through our natural powers nor through our intellect may we feel superior to the fearful object. For then our security would always be a function merely of physical causes; in effect, it would be empirical and as a result there would always remain a dependency upon nature. Instead, it must be completely irrelevant to us how we fare as sensuous beings in the process, and our freedom must consist merely in the fact that we regard, our physical condition, determined as it can be by nature, as something external and alien, having no influence on our moral person, and as something we do not count as part of our self.

Someone who overcomes what is fearful is *magnificent* [*groß*]. Someone who, even while succumbing to the fearful, does not fear it, is *sublime* [*erhaben*].

Hannibal was magnificent from a theoretical point of view, since he forged a passage over the untrodden Alps to Italy. He was magnificent in a practical sense, or sublime, only in misfortune.

Hercules was magnificent because he undertook and completed his twelve tasks.

Prometheus was sublime because, fettered to the Caucasus, he did not regret his deed and did not acknowledge having done anything wrong.

An individual can display magnificence in *good fortune*, sublimity only in *misfortune*.

Hence, any object that shows us our impotence as natural beings is practically-sublime, as long as it also discloses a capacity within us to resist that is of a completely different order. This capacity does *not*, of course, remove the danger to our physical existence, but (what is infinitely more) separates our physical existence from our personhood. Hence, when something sublime is represented or entertained, we become conscious, not of *material* security in a single instance, but rather of an *ideal* security extending over all possible instances. This is accordingly based, not on overturning or overcoming in any sense a danger threatening us, but rather on removing the sole and ultimate condition for something to be a danger to us. The experience of the sublime removes this condition by teaching us to regard the sensuous part of our being, what alone is subject to the danger, as an external, natural thing that has no effect at all on what we genuinely are as persons, our moral selves.

Having established the concept of the practically-sublime, we are in a position to classify it in terms of both the variety of objects that arouse it and the variety of our relationships to these objects.

There are three sorts of things that we distinguish in the representation of the sublime: *first*, the power of some natural object; *second*, the relation of this power to our capacity to resist it physically; *third*, the relation of this power to the moral person within us. The sublime is thus the effect of three images following upon one another: (1) an objective, physical power, (2) our subjective, physical impotence, and (3) our subjective, moral superiority. Although essentially all three elements must be combined in every representation of the sublime, it is nevertheless a contingent matter how we arrive at a representation of them, and this fact is the basis for a central, twofold distinction with respect to the sublimity of power.

1. Either some subject matter [*Gegenstand*] simply as a power or, in other words, the objective cause of suffering but not the suffering itself may be presented for viewing, and it is left to the individual making the judgment to produce the image of the suffering in himself and transform that subject matter into an object [*Objekt*] of fear by virtue of its relation to the preservation instinct and into something sublime by virtue of its relation to the moral person within him.

2. Or, in addition to the subject matter as a power, its fearfulness for human beings, the suffering itself, may be objectively represented as well, leaving nothing else for the individual making the judgment to do but apply it to his moral condition and produce something sublime out of something fearful.

An object [*Objekt*] of the first class is contemplatively-sublime, an object of the second class is pathetically-sublime.

## I The contemplative-sublimity of power

The kinds of subject matter that show us nothing more than a power of nature far superior to our own, but otherwise leave it up to us to relate that power to our physical state or to our moral character as persons, are sublime solely in a contemplative sense. I characterize them in this way because they do not take hold of the mind with such ferocity that it is unable to continue calmly contemplating them. In the case of what is contemplatively-sublime it is mostly a matter of the mind's own activity, because only one of the conditions of sublimity is provided externally, while the other two must be realized by the individual himself. For this reason the effect of the contemplatively-sublime is neither as intense nor as widespread as the effect of the pathetically-sublime. The effect is *not as widespread* because not everyone has sufficient imagination to produce in themselves a vivid image of the danger, nor do they all have enough moral self-sufficiency and fortitude not to try to avoid such an image. The effect is *not as powerful*, because the image of the danger in this case, even if it is quite vividly awakened, is nonetheless always *voluntary*, and it is much easier for the mind to remain in control of an image that it produced of itself. Hence, the contemplatively-sublime produces a slighter, but also less mixed sort of enjoyment.

For the contemplatively-sublime, nature provides nothing but some power-laden subject matter. It is left to the imagination to make something out of this that is frightening to humanity. How the sublime precisely turns out depends upon whether the part played by the imagination in producing what is fearful is respectively great or small, and whether the imagination does its job openly or furtively.

An abyss appearing at our feet, a thunderstorm, a flaming volcano, a mass of rock looming over us as though it were about to plunge down on us, a storm at sea, a bitter winter in the polar regions, a summer in the tropics, ferocious or poisonous animals, a flood—all these and more are the sorts of natural forces in the face of which our capacity to resist counts for nothing, natural forces that contradict our physical existence. Even certain ideal objects such as, for example, *time* considered as a power working quietly but inexorably, *necessity* with its rigorous laws from which no natural being can escape, and even the moral idea of *duty* that behaves often enough like an inimical power toward our physical existence, become fearful objects as soon as the *imagination* relates them to the preservation instinct, and they become sublime as soon as *reason* applies them to its supreme laws. In all these cases, however, since the fantasy first adds the fearful character and it is completely up to us to suppress an idea that we have produced ourselves, these objects belong to the class of the contemplatively-sublime.

Yet the image of danger still has a *real* basis here, and what is required is merely the simple operation of connecting the existence of these things with our physical existence in a *single* image. If this is done, something frightful is then present. Fantasy need contribute nothing on its own; instead it simply clings to what is presented to it.

Quite often subject matters taken from nature and in themselves neutral, are subjectively transformed by the intervention of fantasy into frightful powers, and fantasy itself does not merely *discover* what is frightful through comparison, *but rather creates* it quite arbitrarily without an adequate, objective basis for it. This is the case for the *extraordinary* and the *indeterminate*.

[…]

This fear of everything extraordinary disappears, to be sure, with the rise of culture, but not so completely that no trace of it remains in the *aesthetic* contemplation of nature, where people deliberately give themselves up to the play of fantasy. Writers know this quite well and accordingly do not fail to make use of *extraordinary* things, at least as an ingredient in what is frightful. A profound quiet, an immense emptiness, a sudden light in the dark are in themselves quite neutral things, distinguished by nothing but their extraordinariness and unusualness. Nevertheless, they arouse a feeling of fright or, at least, intensify its impression, and for that reason are suited to be something sublime.

If Virgil wants to scare us about the realm of Hades, he draws our attention above all to its emptiness and stillness. He calls it *loca nocte late tacentia*, "that silent, expansive plain of night," *domos vacuas Ditis et inania regna*, "the empty dwellings and hollow realms of Pluto."

During the initiations into the mysteries of the ancients a fearful, solemn impression was especially preferred, and to this end people also made use of silence in particular. A profound quiet provides the imagination with a free space to play and intensifies the expectation of something frightful that is supposed to come. In devotional exercises the silence observed by an entire community gathered together is a very effective means of prodding their fantasies and putting their minds in a solemn mood. Even folk superstition makes use of silence in its delusions, for, as is well known, a profound quiet must be observed if someone has to dig for a treasure. In the enchanted palaces of fairy tales a deathly silence reigns, awakening horrors, and it is part of the natural history of enchanted forests that nothing living moves within them. Even loneliness is frightful as soon as it is neither voluntary nor passing, such as, for example, the banishment to an uninhabited island. A far-flung desert, a solitary forest several miles long, losing one's way around a seemingly boundless lake—these are the sort of simple images that can stir up fears and should be used in poetry to depict the sublime. However, here (in the case of loneliness) there is already an objective basis of the fear, since the idea of a great loneliness also brings with it the idea of *helplessness*.

Fantasy proves itself to be far more skilled at making something terrifying out of something *mysterious*, indeterminate, and *impenetrable*. Here it is in its genuine element with a wide range of possibilities open to it, given the fact that the actual world sets no boundaries to it and its operations are not limited to any particular case. Yet, that it is inclined precisely to what is *terrible* and that the unknown is a source of *fear* more than hope, lies in the nature of the preservation instinct that guides it. Revulsion works with incomparably greater speed and force than desire does, and for this reason we rather suppose something bad than expect something good lying behind what is unknown.

*Darkness* can be terrifying and precisely for that reason is suited to the sublime. Yet it is not terrifying in itself, but rather because it conceals objects from us and thus delivers us up to the full force of the imagination. As soon as the danger becomes clear, a considerable part of the fear disappears. The sense of sight, the primary sentry of our existence, fails us in the darkness and we feel ourselves defenselessly exposed to the hidden danger. For this reason superstition puts all appearances of spirits at the midnight hour, and the realm of death is represented as a realm of endless night. [...]

Even the *indeterminate* is an ingredient of the terrible, and for no other reason than because it gives the imagination freedom to paint the picture as it sees fit. What is determinate, on the other hand, leads to distinct knowledge and withdraws the object from the arbitrary play of fantasy, because it subjects the object to the intellect.

Homer's portrayal of the underworld is all the more frightful, precisely because it, as it were, swims in a fog and the shapes of the spirits in Ossian[2] are nothing but ethereal cloud formations, leaving it to fantasy to provide the contours at will.

Everything that is *hidden*, everything *full of mystery*, contributes to what is terrifying and is therefore capable of sublimity. Of this sort is the inscription on the temple of Isis at Sais, in Egypt. "I am all that is, that has been, and that will be. No mortal man has lifted my veil."[3] It is precisely this uncertainty and mysteriousness that lend the terrifying character to people's images of the future after death. These feelings are expressed quite successfully in Hamlet's well-known soliloquy.

[...]

All religions have their mysteries that support a holy fright and, just as the majesty of divinity dwells in the all-holy behind the curtain, so the majesty of kings surrounds itself with mystery in order, by means of this artificial invisibility, to keep the respect of their subjects in a state of constant trepidation.

These are the most distinguished subspecies of the power that is contemplatively-sublime, and since it is grounded in the moral vocation common to every human being, one is justified in presupposing a receptiveness to it on the part of all human subjects. The lack of this receptiveness cannot be excused by some contingency of nature, as in the case of merely sensuous feelings; rather it may be considered an imperfection in the subject. At times one finds cognitive sublimity combined with the sublimity of power and the effect is all the greater, if not only the sensuous capacity to resist, but even the capacity to portray finds its match in an object and the sensuous side of human nature with its twofold demand [of knowing and living] is scorned.

## II  The pathetically-sublime

If something is presented to us in an objective way, not merely as a power in general, but at the same time as a power having catastrophic consequences for people—in other words, if it does not merely *show,* but also actually *expresses* its power in a hostile manner—then the imagination is no longer free to refer it to the preservation-instinct or not; instead, the imagination now *must* do so, it is objectively required to do so. Yet actual suffering does not permit an aesthetic judgment, since such suffering overcomes the mind's freedom. Thus, the fearful object may not demonstrate its destructive power on the individual judging, that is, we may not *ourselves* suffer, or rather we may suffer only *sympathetically*. However, even if the suffering we sympathize with exists outside us, it is too violent for our sensuous nature. The empathizing pain overwhelms all aesthetic enjoyment. Suffering can become aesthetic and arouse a feeling of sublimity only when either it is a mere illusion and fabrication or (in case it had happened in reality) it is presented, not immediately to the senses, but to the imagination. The image of another's suffering, combined with emotion and the consciousness of the moral freedom within us, is *pathetically-sublime*.

The sympathy or the empathizing (shared) emotion is no free expression of our mind, that we would first have to produce spontaneously in ourselves. Rather it is an involuntary affection [*Affektion*] on the part of our capacity to have feelings, determined by natural law. It does not at all depend upon our will whether we want to share in the suffering of some creature. The moment we have an image of it, we *must* feel it. *Nature*, not our *freedom* acts, and the movement of the mind hurries ahead of the decision.

Therefore, as soon as we hold on to the image of some suffering objectively, then, by virtue of the unchanging natural law of sympathy, a feeling for this suffering must follow within ourselves. By this means we make it our own, as it were. We *suffer with. Empathy* or *compassion* means not merely the shared grief, the fact of being moved by another's misfortune, but rather every sorrowful emotion, without distinction, which we feel when we enter into someone else's feelings. Hence, there are as many sorts of empathy as there are diverse sorts of suffering originally: empathizing fear, empathizing fright, empathizing anxiety, empathizing anger, empathizing despair.

Yet, if what arouses the emotion (or what is pathetic) is supposed to provide a basis for the sublime, it may not be pressed to the point where one is actually *suffering oneself*. Even in the midst of the most violent emotion we must *distinguish* ourselves from the individual who himself suffers, for the freedom of spirit is gone as soon as the illusion is transformed into the complete truth.

If empathizing is elevated to such a pitch that we seriously confuse ourselves with the person suffering, then we no longer control the emotion, but rather it controls us. On the other hand, if the sympathy remains within its aesthetic boundaries, then it combines two chief conditions of the sublime: a sensuously vital image of the suffering together with the feeling of one's own security.

But this feeling of security when faced with the image of someone else's suffering is in no sense the *basis* of what is sublime, and is not at all the *source* of the pleasure we draw from this image. The pathetic becomes sublime only through the consciousness of our moral, not our physical, freedom. Not because we see ourselves removed from this suffering by our good fortune (for then we would still always have a very poor guarantee of our security), but rather because we feel our moral self to be removed from the causality of this suffering, namely, from its influence upon what determines our willing, it *elevates* [*erhebt*] our mind and becomes *pathetically*-sublime.

It is not absolutely necessary that one actually feel the strength of soul within oneself to assert one's moral freedom in the face of a seriously imminent danger. We are talking here, not about what *happens*, but rather about what *should* and *can* happen; in other words, we are talking about our *calling*, not about what we actually *do*; about our power, not about its use. Because we see a heavily loaded freighter go down in the storm, we are able to feel ourselves quite unhappily in the position of the merchant, whose entire estate is swallowed up by the water. Yet at the same time, we still feel as well that this loss only concerns contingent things and that we have a duty to rise above it. However, nothing can be a duty if it cannot be realized, and what *should* happen must *be able* to happen. That, however, we *can* regard a loss with indifference, a loss that is rightly so poignant for us as sensuous beings, proves that there is a capacity within us to act according to laws completely different from those of the sensuous faculties, a capacity having nothing in common with natural instinct. Everything that makes us conscious of this capacity within us is *sublime*.

One can quite rightly say, therefore, that one will endure the loss of goods with nothing less than composure. This does not hinder the feelings of the sublime at all—if one only feels that one *should* disregard the loss and that a duty exists to allow it no influence on the self-determining of reason. Of course, all the aesthetic power of the magnificent and the sublime is lost on someone who does not even have a sense *for that duty*.

Hence, at least a capacity of the mind to become conscious of its rational determination and a receptivity to the idea of duty are indispensable, even if at the same time one also recognizes the limits that the weakness of humanity may have set to their exercise. In general, it would be dangerous for the enjoyment of the good as well as of the sublime, if one could only have a sense for what one has oneself achieved or what one trusts oneself to achieve. But it is a basic feature of humanity, and one worthy of respect, that humanity acknowledges a good thing, at least in *aesthetic* judgments, even if it would have to speak *against* itself, and that it pays homage to the pure ideas of reason, at least in feeling, even if it does not always have sufficient strength actually to *act* on those ideas.

Consequently, two main conditions must be met for the *pathetically-sublime*: *first*, a vivid image of *suffering*, in order to awaken the emotion of compassion with the proper strength, and *second*, an image of the *resistance* to the suffering, in order to call into consciousness the mind's inner freedom. Only by virtue of the first condition does the object become *pathetic*, only by virtue of the second condition does the pathetic become at the same time something *sublime*.

From this basic principle flow the two fundamental laws of all tragic art. These are *first*: portrayal of the suffering nature; *second*, portrayal of moral independence in the suffering.

## Questions

1. Explain Schiller's uses of the concept of "nature" ("natural beings," "natural conditions," inner/outer nature, etc.). In each case, with what is nature contrasted? Discuss his examples.

2. Compare and contrast Schiller's account with Kant's. Why does Schiller prefer the terms *theoretically-sublime* and the *practically-sublime* to Kant's mathematical and dynamical sublime? Does the role of imagination (or fancy) differ? What role does the "consciousness of freedom" play in each account? Does Schiller's account remind you any other theories? Explain.

3. Explain Schiller's theory of the pathetically-sublime. How does it differ from the contemplatively-sublime? What do empathy and suffering have to do with the pathetically-sublime? How does tragic art make use of or evoke the pathetically-sublime?

4. How does Schiller treat the sublime in art, and tragedy in particular? Discuss his "two fundamental laws" of tragic art.

## Further reading

Beiser, Frederick C. *Schiller as Philosopher: A Re-Examination*, esp. 257–62. Oxford: Oxford University Press, 2005.

de Man, Paul. "Kant and Schiller." In *Aesthetic Ideology*, ed. Paul de Man, 129–62. Minneapolis: University of Minnesota Press, 1996.

Schiller, Friedrich. "Concerning the Sublime." In Friedrich Schiller, *Essays*, ed. Daniel Dahlstrom and Walter Hinderer, trans. Daniel Dahlstrom, 70–85. London: Continuum, 1998.

Schiller, Friedrich. "On the Pathetic." In Friedrich Schiller, *Essays*, ed. Daniel Dahlstrom and Walter Hinderer, trans. Daniel Dahlstrom, 45–69. London: Continuum, 1998.

Schiller, Friedrich, et al. *Du Sublime: (de Boileau à Schiller): Suivi de la Traduction de* Über Das Erhabene *de Friedrich Schiller*, ed. Pierre Hartmann. Strasbourg: Presses universitaires de Strasbourg, 1997. [On the Sublime, from Boileau to Schiller, Followed by a Translation of Friedrich Schiller's "Concerning the Sublime."]

# CHAPTER 17
## ANNA SEWARD, LETTER TO REV. DR. GREGORY (1792)

Anna Seward (1747–1809), sometimes known as the "Swan of Lichfield," was an English Romantic poet and writer. In addition to elegies and sonnets, she wrote *Louisa, A Poetical Novel* (1782) and *Memoirs of the Life of Dr. Darwin* (1804), on the physician and botanist (and grandfather of the naturalist Charles Darwin) Erasmus Darwin, who resided for some time in Lichfield. After her death, Sir Walter Scott edited her *Poetical Works* in three volumes (Edinburgh, 1810).

According to Scott, when Seward was young she "imbibed a strong and enthusiastic partiality for mountainous scenery, and in general for the pleasures of landscape."[1] In one of her letters, Seward reports having "enthusiasm for marine scenery. After a sixteen years inland residence, I approached, with awe-mixed delight, the mighty mass of animated water."[2] She felt "pleasing awe" before rivers as well:

> A flooded valley, beneath the cloudy lour of a wintry moon, is one of those terrible graces in scenery, which the survey of danger, and the consciousness of protection, always form to people of strong imagination. I gaze with pleasing awe on the swoln, the extravagant, and usurping waters, as they roll over the fields, and, white with turbid foam, beat against the bushes.[3]

Below, she uses the term "awe" to describe her experience. In art, she considered "sublime" the music of Handel, the paintings of Salvator, and the poetry of Homer, Milton, Young, Coleridge, and Ossian. She was familiar with Burke's account of the sublime ("obscurity, which Burke pronounces a source of the sublime").[4]

The following letter to the preacher and author George Gregory (1754–1808) was written on March 25, 1792. At the beginning of the letter, she comments on Thomas Chatterton, a young English poet who committed suicide at the age of seventeen, and comments on Gregory's recently completed book on Chatterton. Seward then describes the feeling of transport she feels from reading "Ossian." ("Never yet have I opened the . . . volumes without a poignant thrill of pensive transport.") Ossian was the narrator and purported author of a cycle of epic poems published by the Scottish poet James Macpherson beginning in 1760.[5] When he published it, Macpherson said that it was a translation of an ancient manuscript in Scottish Gaelic which had come into his possession, and which was a copy of an original work written by Ossian; today, however, there is a consensus that much of the work is Macpherson's own invention.

In another letter, Seward describes her first experience reading Ossian around 1763: "In my sixteenth year I first read Ossian. Infinite was the delight which it inspired. If I did not dance for joy, as Cowper says he did on first reading Homer, I wept for joy; yet I then found, as since I have uniformly found, that I could not proceed with it to a very long sitting. Our imagination, whatever be its poetic appetite, will not bear the protraction of unrelieved sublimity."[6] (Like Elizabeth Carter, Seward thought that the intense experience of the sublime could be endured only briefly.) So, was Ossian sublime or bombastic? Seward admitted there was indeed pretentious "bombast" in Macpherson's volumes, but added that the bombast was due to Macpherson, while the "sublime" was due to Ossian.[7]

## Note on the text

Source: Reprinted from Anna Seward, *Letters of Anna Seward: Written Between the Years 1784 and 1807*, edited by Archibald Constable, 6 vols., vol. 3, 124–30. Edinburgh: George Ramsay & Company, 1811.

Punctuation, style, format, and spelling have occasionally been modified or standardized. Italics have been added to titles. Insertions in square brackets and the footnotes are written by the volume editor.

### LETTER XXXIX

Rev. Dr. Gregory.

March 25, 1792.

You are wise, my dear Sir, in not sluicing off your golden leisure into the unprofitable, the fameless channel of private correspondence. While I want resolution to avoid doing so, it is in vain to inquire after my literary pursuits. Some epistolary duty or other is always stepping in between me and them.

Now let me thank you for two instances of kind attention, which enabled me to pass several hours very agreeably; the introduction of your ingenious friend, Mr. Rogers of Liverpool, and the reperusal of your ingenious book, the *Life of Chatterton* [1789 – Ed.]. I read it with much interest and pleasure on its first appearance; for it is an eloquent, spirited, and valuable memoir of the most extraordinary genius which perhaps ever existed. This ill-starred youth [Chatterton – Ed.][8] certainly found ancient and curious manuscripts, which furnished the hint of his design, and upon which he poured the splendours of his rich imagination, kindling and flowering as he proceeded. Very superficially, indeed, is the perfection of modern harmony, and the grace of modern imagery, veiled by obsolete verbalism. The involuntary imitations, and often entire plagiarisms from our late poets, too striking for the possibility of coincidence, are, of themselves, sufficient proof how largely at least these poems are modern. You have pointed out several instances, and I am struck with several more which you do not notice.

I generally agree with you as to the high degree of estimation in which you hold the particular passages you cite in the notes. The description of morning, from the second part of the Battle of Hastings, is eminently poetic; but that of Salisbury Plain might surely have been written by anybody. Except the words "drear array," it contains no poetry. "There stands a pile of rugged mountains placed upon each other, which could not be the work of human hands." Those very words have, questionless, been used in common conversation by many a commonly sensible traveller, describing Stonehenge.

I think also that there is not much fertility of genius in the ballad, cited page 157. The comparison to the doe seeking shelter in green trees, is the only uncommon thought it contains. The shepherd's assertion, that none but his sheep will come to interrupt them, is in a canzonet, set to music by Morley, in Queen Elizabeth's time, and beginning, "Haste my Nannette," etc. The whole fascinating first eclogue I got by heart years ago. Substituting modern for the obsolete words, the rhythm became as melodious as the ideas are beautiful. Collins's eclogues probably suggested to Chatterton the idea of these, which are, I doubt not, wholly his. There is a striking similarity between my favourite Raufe and Robert, and the fourth of Collins, Agib and Secander. Sweet as is the latter, I yet prefer the simpler tenderness and native scenery of the imitation, to the oriental descriptions and flowing numbers of the original.

I am as sorry for your moleism to Ossian as to Sterne. It induces you to do Macpherson [Ossian's alleged "translator" – Ed.] a great deal too much honour. Not that I believe he had ancient manuscripts, any more than I believe his imagination responsible for the original, the solemn, the sublime mythology; the Salvatorial landscapes, and the countless emanations of natural and beautiful sensibilities, scattered through those fragments, collected with infinite industry by their editor from oral traditions.

Catching a portion of their fire, he connected them, doubtless, with much of his own, weaving them together for the Fingal [Ossian's father – Ed.], into something like a regular epic. Probably the episodes are entirely Erse [i.e., "Irish" – Ed.]. Internal evidence lies here, with all its weight, for the originality of the Erse poetry, as it is totally against it in the Rowleyan.

I impute the fustian [i.e., bombastic – Ed.] passages, of which it must be allowed there are several, to Macpherson; and it is almost all I can allow him as to the images and ideas. Great praise, however, he merits, for the judicious adoption of the style of the Scripture poetry for their vehicle. It amazes me, that any one, admiring the poetry of the sacred pages, can be insensible to excellence so much on a level, and resembling it so strikingly, without servile imitation.

We find, from Mason's edition of his friend's letters, how dear the Ossian was to Gray. Though Chatterton could not obtain its beauty when he attempted to write in that style, yet that he felt its high claims, is, by that attempt, demonstrated. We always admire before we imitate. I am an enthusiast to the writings of Chatterton; yet, if I was reduced to the choice of no more looking at a line of them, or of eternal abstinence from the pages of Ossian, I would, of the two, resign the former.

Never yet have I opened the Erse volumes without a poignant thrill of pensive transport. The lonely scenery of a barren and mountainous country rises before me. By turns I see the blue waves of their seas, rolling in light; and then, by the dark storm, lashed into foam, and bursting upon their rocks. I view the majestic and melancholy graces, in the persons of the warriors and their mistresses, walking over the silent hills. The tender consecration of the memory of their lost friends, and of the vanished years, are in unison with all the feelings of my soul; and their machinery, sailing upon the blasts of the desert, at once awes and delights me.

Not Homer himself has given us a speech of sublimer spirit and fire than the following:

"Fly, thou chief of peace," said Calmor, "fly to thy silent hills, where the spear of battle never shone! Pursue the dark-brown deer of Cromla, or stop, with thine arrows, the bounding roes of Lena! But, blue-eyed son of Semo, Cuchullin, scatter thou the sons of Lochlin, and roar through the ranks of their pride! Let no vessel from the kingdom of snow bound on the waves of Inistore! Ye winds of Erin rise!—howl ye whirlwinds of the heath!—amid your tempest let Calmor die, if ever chace was sport to him so much as the battle of shields!"[9]

The description of Crugal's ghost, in the second book of Fingal, is one of the sublimest, as that of Margaret, in Mallet's celebrated ballad, is one of the most beautiful that poetry can show us.

"His face was as the beam of the setting moon; his robes were of the clouds of the hill; his voice as the gale of the reedy lake; his eyes two decaying flames; and dark was the wound on his breast. Dim, and in tears he stood, and stretched his pale hand to the hero."[10]

"Her face was like an April morn,
Clad in a wintry cloud."[11]

I meant to have observed, before I quitted the subject of your Chattertonian volume, that I think you have not given sufficient praise to the impersonization of winter in the elegy on T. Phillips. It appears to me so finely conceived, as that no poet, living or dead, has ever excelled it.

By this prolix letter, you would not think that I have been a long invalid, from disorders contracted by the sedentary employment of a correspondence oppressively extended. I repeat, how much wiser are you, and how much better do you employ your time!

Adieu. All health, happiness, all celebrity attend you;—yet you are now surely treading beaten ground, whose fruit and flowers have all been gathered. However, as I have no great appetite for politics, and am consequently uninterested in the minute history of a period so near our own time, and with whose events we are so familiar, I have but an incompetent guess concerning the degree of acceptability with the public which your present undertaking will meet;—but I remain always, with great esteem, dear Sir, yours, etc.

## Questions

1. Consider some of her examples of sublimity in literature, such as the passage that begins as follows: "Fly, thou chief of peace . . ." Do you agree with her assessment that writing or speech can evoke the sublime? Explain.

2. Why does she consider certain literary texts or landscape paintings (by Salvator Rosa) sublime? Is it more because of the matter and object represented, or the manner in which it is presented by the artist, or both equally?

3. Do her examples of what is "sublime" or awe-inducing strike you as dated? Why or why not? If so, what would sublimity in the arts (literature, painting, even film) look like today? Explain.

## Further reading

Ashmun, Margaret. *The Singing Swan: An Account of Anna Seward and Her Acquaintance with Dr. Johnson, Boswell and Others of Their Time.* New Haven: Yale University Press, 1931.

Barnard, Teresa. *Anna Seward: A Constructed Life: A Critical Biography.* New York: Routledge, 2016.

Clarke, Norma. *British Women's Writing in the Long Eighteenth Century,* ed. Jennie Batchelor and Cora Kaplan. London: Palgrave Macmillan, 2005.

Faderman, Lillian. *Surpassing the Love of Men: Romantic Friendship and Love Between Women from the Renaissance to the Present,* 132–38. New York: William Morrow, 1981.

Heiland, Donna. "Swan Songs: The Correspondence of Anna Seward and James Boswell." *Modern Philology* 90, no. 3 (1993): 381–91.

Seward, Anna. *Bluestocking Feminism: Writings of the Bluestocking Circle, 1738–1785: Anna Seward,* vol. 4, ed. Jennifer Kelly. London: Pickering & Chatto, 1999.

# CHAPTER 18

# ANN RADCLIFFE, *THE MYSTERIES OF UDOLPHO: A ROMANCE* (1794)

*The Mysteries of Udolpho: A Romance* is a work of Gothic fiction by English novelist and poet, Ann Radcliffe (1764–1823). The novel was her fourth and most popular. (Jane Austen satirized it in her novel, *Northanger Abbey*.) Set in 1584, *The Mysteries of Udolpho* tells the story of how Emily St. Aubert, a young French woman who is orphaned after the death of her father, is subjected to cruelties by her aunt's husband, the Italian aristocrat Montoni, and imprisoned in Udolpho castle in Italy. Strange and fearful events take place in Montoni's castle, set high in the dark but majestic Apennines, but Emily ultimately escapes and is united with her lover, Valancourt.

Radcliffe reveals how the sublime was conceived and employed in early Gothic literature. She describes the "sublime scene" as Emily approaches Montoni's castle, "vast, ancient and dreary." Emily feels "elevated" by the Apennine scenery, even if she "seldom felt those emotions of indescribable awe" which she experienced when passing over the Alps. Still, she gazes with "melancholy awe" when she sees Montoni's castle. The "gothic greatness of its features, and its mouldering walls of dark grey stone, rendered it a gloomy and sublime object." "Silent, lonely, and sublime, it seemed to stand the sovereign of the scene, and to frown defiance on all, who dared to invade its solitary reign."

In the experience of sublimity (or awe), the imagination is in tension with reason: "her imagination, ever awake to circumstance, suggested even more terrors, than her reason could justify."

## Note on the text

Source: Excerpted from Ann Radcliffe, *The Mysteries of Udolpho: A Romance; Interspersed with Some Pieces of Poetry* [second edition], 4 vols., vol. 2, chap. 5, 164–74. London: G. G. and J. Robinson, 1794.

Punctuation, style, and spelling have occasionally been modified or updated. The volume editor has made use of Duffy and Howell's comments and notes on this text.[1] Footnotes and insertions in square brackets are written by the volume editor.

## *The Mysteries of Udolpho*

[…] At length, the travellers began to ascend among the Apennines. The immense pine-forests, which, at that period, overhung these mountains, and between which the road wound, excluded all view but of the cliffs aspiring above, except, that, now and then, an opening through the dark woods allowed the eye a momentary glimpse of the country below. The gloom of these shades, their solitary silence, except when the breeze swept over their summits, the tremendous precipices of the mountains, that came partially to the eye, each assisted to raise the solemnity of Emily's feelings into awe; she saw only images of gloomy grandeur, or of dreadful sublimity, around her; other images, equally gloomy and equally terrible, gleamed on her imagination. She was going she scarcely knew whither, under the dominion of a person, from whose arbitrary disposition she had already suffered so much, to marry, perhaps, a man who possessed neither her affection, or esteem; or to endure, beyond the hope of succour, whatever punishment revenge, and that Italian revenge, might dictate.— The more she considered what might be the motive of the journey, the more she became convinced, that it was for the purpose of concluding her nuptials with Count Morano, with the secrecy, which her resolute resistance had made necessary to the honour, if not to the safety, of Montoni. From the deep solitudes, into which she was immerging, and from the gloomy castle, of which she had heard some mysterious hints, her sick heart recoiled in despair, and she experienced, that, though her mind was already occupied by peculiar distress, it was still alive to the influence of new and local circumstance; why else did she shudder at the idea of this desolate castle?

As the travellers still ascended among the pine forests, steep rose over steep, the mountains seemed to multiply, as they went, and what was the summit of one eminence proved to be only the base of another. At length, they reached a little plain, where the drivers stopped to rest the mules, whence a scene of such extent and magnificence opened below, as drew even from Madame Montoni[2] a note of admiration. Emily lost, for a moment, her sorrows, in the immensity of nature. Beyond the amphitheatre of mountains, that stretched below, whose tops appeared as numerous almost, as the waves of the sea, and whose feet were concealed by the forests—extended the *campagna*[3] of Italy, where cities and rivers, and woods and all the glow of cultivation were mingled in gay confusion. The Adriatic bounded the horizon, into which the Po and the Brenta,[4] after winding through the whole extent of the landscape, poured their fruitful waves. Emily gazed long on the splendours of the world she was quitting, of which the whole magnificence seemed thus given to her sight only to increase her regret on leaving it; for her, Valancourt[5] alone was in that world; to him alone her heart turned, and for him alone fell her bitter tears.

From this sublime scene the travellers continued to ascend among the pines, till they entered a narrow pass of the mountains, which shut out every feature of the distant country, and, in its stead, exhibited only tremendous crags, impending over the road, where no vestige of humanity, or even of vegetation, appeared, except here and there the trunk and scathed branches of an oak, that hung nearly headlong from the rock, into which its strong roots had fastened. This pass, which led into the heart of the Apennine, at length opened to day, and a scene of mountains stretched in long perspective, as wild as any the travellers had yet passed. Still vast pine-forests hung upon their base, and crowned the ridgy precipice, that rose perpendicularly from the vale, while, above, the rolling mists caught the sun-beams, and touched their cliffs with all the magical colouring of light and shade. The scene seemed perpetually changing, and its features to assume new forms, as the winding road brought them to the eye in different attitudes; while the shifting vapours, now partially concealing their minuter beauties and now illuminating them with splendid tints, assisted the illusions of the sight.

Though the deep valleys between these mountains were, for the most part, clothed with pines, sometimes an abrupt opening presented a perspective of only barren rocks, with a cataract [i.e., a large waterfall – Ed.] flashing from their summit among broken cliffs, till its waters, reaching the bottom, foamed along with unceasing fury; and sometimes pastoral scenes exhibited their "green delights" in the narrow vales, smiling amid surrounding horror. There herds and flocks of goats and sheep, browsing under the shade of hanging woods, and the shepherd's little cabin, reared on the margin of a clear stream, presented a sweet picture of repose.

Wild and romantic as were these scenes, their character had far less of the sublime, than had those of the Alps, which guard the entrance of Italy. Emily was often elevated, but seldom felt those emotions of indescribable awe which she had so continually experienced, in her passage over the Alps.

Towards the close of day, the road wound into a deep valley. Mountains, whose shaggy steeps appeared to be inaccessible, almost surrounded it. To the east, a vista opened, that exhibited the Apennines in their darkest horrors; and the long perspective of retiring summits, rising over each other, their ridges clothed with pines, exhibited a stronger image of grandeur, than any that Emily had yet seen. The sun had just sunk below the top of the mountains she was descending, whose long shadow stretched athwart the valley, but his sloping rays, shooting through an opening of the cliffs, touched with a yellow gleam the summits of the forest, that hung upon the opposite steeps, and streamed in full splendour upon the towers and battlements of a castle, that spread its extensive ramparts along the brow of a precipice above. The splendour of these illumined objects was heightened by the contrasted shade, which involved the valley below.

"There," said Montoni, speaking for the first time in several hours, "is Udolpho."

Emily gazed with melancholy awe upon the castle, which she understood to be Montoni's; for, though it was now lighted up by the setting sun, the gothic greatness of its features, and its mouldering walls of dark grey stone, rendered it a gloomy and sublime object. As she gazed, the light died away on its walls, leaving a melancholy purple tint, which spread deeper and deeper, as the thin vapour crept up the mountain, while the battlements above were still tipped with splendour. From those, too, the rays soon faded, and the whole edifice was invested with the solemn duskiness of evening. Silent, lonely, and sublime, it seemed to stand the sovereign of the scene, and to frown defiance on all, who dared to invade its solitary reign. As the twilight deepened, its features became more awful in obscurity, and Emily continued to gaze, till its clustering towers were alone seen, rising over the tops of the woods, beneath whose thick shade the carriages soon after began to ascend.

The extent and darkness of these tall woods awakened terrific images in her mind, and she almost expected to see banditti [i.e., robbers – Ed.] start up from under the trees. At length, the carriages emerged upon a heathy rock, and, soon after, reached the castle gates, where the deep tone of the portal bell, which was struck upon to give notice of their arrival, increased the fearful emotions, that had assailed Emily. While they waited till the servant within should come to open the gates, she anxiously surveyed the edifice: but the gloom, that overspread it, allowed her to distinguish little more than a part of its outline, with the massy walls of the ramparts, and to know, that it was vast, ancient and dreary. From the parts she saw, she judged of the heavy strength and extent of the whole. The gateway before her, leading into the courts, was of gigantic size, and was defended by two round towers, crowned by overhanging turrets, embattled, where, instead of banners, now waved long grass and wild plants, that had taken root among the mouldering stones, and which seemed to sigh, as the breeze rolled past, over the desolation around them. The towers were united by a curtain, pierced and embattled also, below which appeared the pointed arch of a huge portcullis [i.e., a heavy, sliding door or grating – Ed.], surmounting the gates: from these, the walls of the ramparts extended to other towers, overlooking the precipice, whose shattered outline, appearing on a gleam, that lingered in the west, told of the ravages of war.—Beyond these all was lost in the obscurity of evening.

While Emily gazed with awe upon the scene, footsteps were heard within the gates, and the undrawing of bolts; after which an ancient servant of the castle appeared, forcing back the huge folds of the portal, to admit his lord. As the carriage-wheels rolled heavily under the portcullis, Emily's heart sunk, and she seemed, as if she was going into her prison; the gloomy court, into which she passed, served to confirm the idea, and her imagination, ever awake to circumstance, suggested even more terrors, than her reason could justify.

Another gate delivered them into the second court, grass-grown, and more wild than the first, where, as she surveyed through the twilight its desolation—its lofty walls, overtopt with bryony, moss and nightshade, and the embattled towers that rose above,—long-suffering and murder came to her thoughts. One of those instantaneous and unaccountable convictions, which sometimes conquer even strong minds, impressed her with its horror. The sentiment was not diminished, when she entered an extensive gothic hall, obscured by the gloom of evening, which a light, glimmering at a distance through a long perspective of arches, only rendered more striking. As a servant brought the lamp nearer, partial gleams fell upon the pillars and the pointed arches, forming a strong contrast with their shadows, that stretched along the pavement and the walls. […]

## Questions

1. What about this reading makes it an example of the Gothic sublime? Compare and contrast Radcliffe's approach with that of Mary Shelley (*Frankenstein*, excerpted in the present volume).

2. Radcliffe writes that the castle's "features became more awful in obscurity" as darkness falls; she describes Emily as fearful and anxious. Meanwhile, Burke wrote: "To make anything very terrible, obscurity seems in general to be necessary." Does Radcliffe's *Mysteries of Udolpho* seem to be in agreement with any other texts on the sublime (e.g., by Burke, Mary Shelley, Aikin)? Explain.

3. Does Radcliffe's description of the scenery (and its sublimity) strike you as dated? Explain.

## Further reading

Norton, Rictor. *Mistress of Udolpho: The Life of Ann Radcliffe*, esp. 66–81. London: Leicester University Press, 1999.

Rogers, Deborah D. *The Critical Response to Ann Radcliffe*. Westport, CT: Greenwood Press, 1994.

Stoler, John A. *Ann Radcliffe, the Novel of Suspense and Terror*. New York: Arno Press, 1980.

Townshend, Dale, and Angela Wright. *Ann Radcliffe, Romanticism and the Gothic*. Cambridge: Cambridge University Press, 2014.

Ware, Malcolm. *Sublimity in the Novels of Ann Radcliffe: A Study of the Influence upon Her Craft of Edmund Burke's "Enquiry into the Origin of Our Ideas of the Sublime and Beautiful."* Uppsala: Uppsala University, 1963.

# CHAPTER 19
## HELEN MARIA WILLIAMS, FROM *A TOUR IN SWITZERLAND* (1798)

Helen Maria Williams (1759–1827) was a British novelist, translator, and poet. She was an avid supporter of the French Revolution, moving to Paris in 1792 and later composing *A Tour in Switzerland* (1798). Her continued interest in the Revolution is evident at the end of the 1798 work: "It is natural to conclude, that the principles of that mighty revolution, which have already diffused themselves over remote regions of the globe, cannot fail to expand in those countries which are placed immediately within their influence."[1]

Like Carter and Radcliffe, Williams offers insight into the feeling of the sublime, vividly describing her "enthusiastic awe." In addition, she identifies a freedom from "trivial occupations" as a source of the pleasure in the sublime. She contrasts a Swiss boatman unloading his merchandise with an observing spectator. In front of a powerful natural wonder, the boatman is "inattentive to those thundering sounds which seem calculated to suspend all human activity in solemn and awful astonishment." In contrast, the absorbed spectator's "imagination" is "struck with the comparative littleness of fleeting man, busy with his trivial occupations." Such vast or powerful objects like the falls "call the musing mind from all its little cares and vanities, to higher destinies, and regions more congenial than this world to the feelings they excite." Williams also identifies an expansion of the mind, "the expanded spirit," in the sublime. But she does not offer a self-aggrandizement theory of the sublime; rather, in the sublime there is "a sort of annihilation of self." The self of "private affairs" appears diminished, and the person is directed outward toward the natural wonder.

In the experience of the sublime, there seems to be a stoppage of time (subjectively), a freezing of the time progression or time-series: "What an effort does it require to leave, after a transient glimpse, a scene, on which, while we meditate, we can take no account of time!"

Throughout *A Tour in Switzerland*, Williams reveals her enthusiasm for "sublime scenery" (Preface; see also 273), and for the "sublime landscapes of Switzerland" (46).[2] She arrived in Switzerland with much forethought, having imagined the country beforehand; her expectations were fulfilled.

> The first view of Switzerland awakened my enthusiasm most powerfully—'At length,' thought I, 'I am going to contemplate that interesting country, of which I have never heard without emotion!—I am going to gaze upon images of nature; images of which the idea has so often swelled my imagination, but which my eyes have never yet beheld.—I am going to repose my wearied spirit on those sublime objects—to sooth my desponding heart with the hope that the moral disorder I have witnessed shall be rectified, while I gaze on nature in all her admirable perfections; and how delightful a transition shall I find in the picture of social happiness which Switzerland presents'! (4).

Thus, she raises many themes addressed in the present volume: the "swelling" of the imagination in response to "sublime objects," the "admirable perfection" of nature, and the sublime's connection to moral and political affairs.

## Note on the text

Source: Reprinted from Helen Maria Williams, *A Tour in Switzerland; A View of the Present State of the Governments and Manners of those Cantons: with Comparative Sketches of the Present State of Paris*, 2 vols., vol. 1, 56–63. London: G.G. and J. Robinson, 1798.

Format, style, and spelling have occasionally been modified or updated. Insertions in square brackets are written by the volume editor.

## A Tour in Switzerland

[…] This neat and cheerful town [i.e., Zurich – Ed.], is divided into two parts by the Limmat, and delightfully situated on the northern extremity of its noble lake, which spreads, far as the eye can reach, its mass of limpid waters, bounded by vine-covered hills, whose slopes are thick-studded with houses and villages, while beyond this scene of picturesque beauty, the Alps, covered with their eternal snows, rise in the distant perspective, stretching towards the south-west, and mingling their summits with the clouds. It was not without the most powerful emotion that, for the first time, I cast my eyes on that solemn, that majestic vision, the Alps!—How often had the idea of those stupendous mountains filled my heart with enthusiastic awe!—So long, so eagerly, had I desired to contemplate that scene of wonders, that I was unable to trace when first the wish was awakened in my bosom—it seemed from childhood to have made a part of my existence.—I longed to bid adieu to the gayly-peopled landscapes of Zurich, and wander amidst those regions of mysterious sublimity, the solitudes of nature, where her eternal laws seem at all seasons to forbid more than the temporary visits of man, and where, sometimes, the dangerous passes to her frozen summits are inflexibly barred against mortal footsteps. The pleasure arising from the varying forms of smiling beauty with which we were surrounded, became a cold sensation, while expectation hung upon those vast gigantic shapes—that half-seen chaos—which excited the stronger feelings of wonder, mingled with admiration. But I was obliged, with whatever regret, to relinquish for the present a nearer view of those tremendous objects, since private affairs left me only sufficient leisure to visit the cataract [i.e., a large waterfall – Ed.] of the Rhine before I returned to Basel; whence, however, I soothed myself with the hope of being soon able to depart in search of the terrific scenes of the Alps, and the rich luxuriant graces of the Italian valleys of Switzerland. In the mean time we passed hastily through Zurich, in our way to Schaffhausen, for although I had been assured that the cataract of the Rhine was "but a fall of water," it had excited so tormenting a curiosity, that I found I should be incapable of seeing any thing else with pleasure or advantage, till I had once gazed upon that object.

When we reached the summit of the hill which leads to the fall of the Rhine, we alighted from the carriage, and walked down the steep bank, whence I saw the river rolling turbulently over its bed of rocks, and heard the noise of the torrent, towards which we were descending, increasing as we drew near. My heart swelled with expectation—our path, as if formed to give the scene its full effect, concealed for some time the river from our view; till we reached a wooden balcony, projecting on the edge of the water, and whence, just sheltered from the torrent, it bursts in all its overwhelming wonders on the astonished sight. That stupendous cataract, rushing with wild impetuosity over those broken, unequal rocks, which, lifting up their sharp points amidst its sea of foam, disturb its headlong course, multiply its falls, and make the afflicted waters roar—that cadence of tumultuous sound, which had never till now struck upon my ear—those long feathery surges, giving the element a new aspect—that spray rising into clouds of vapour, and reflecting the prismatic colours, while it disperses itself over the hills—never, never can I forget the sensations of that moment! when with a sort of annihilation of self, with every past impression erased from my memory, I felt as if my heart were bursting with emotions too strong to be sustained.—Oh, majestic torrent! which hast conveyed a new image of nature to my soul, the moments I have passed in contemplating thy sublimity will form an epoch in my short span!—thy course is coeval with time, and thou wilt rush down thy rocky walls when this bosom, which throbs with admiration of thy greatness, shall beat no longer!

What an effort does it require to leave, after a transient glimpse, a scene, on which, while we meditate, we can take no account of time! Its narrow limits seem too confined for the expanded spirit; such objects appear to belong to immortality; they call the musing mind from all its little cares and vanities, to higher destinies, and regions more congenial than this world to the feelings they excite. I had been often summoned by my fellow travellers to depart, had often repeated "but one moment more," and many "moments more" had elapsed, before I could resolve to tear myself from the balcony.

We crossed the river, below the fall, in a boat, and had leisure to observe the surrounding scenery. The cataract, however, had for me a sort of fascinating power, which, if I withdrew my eyes for a moment, again fastened them on its impetuous waters. In the background of the torrent a bare mountain lifts its head encircled with its blue vapours; on the right rises a steep cliff of an enormous height, covered with wood, and upon its summit stands the castle of Laufen, with its frowning towers, and encircled with its crannied wall; on the left human industry has seized upon a slender thread of this mighty torrent in its fall, and made it subservient to the purposes of commerce. Founderies, mills, and wheels are erected on the edge of the river, and a portion of the vast basin into which the cataract falls is confined by a dyke, which preserves the warehouses and the neighbouring huts from its inundations. Sheltered within this little nook, and accustomed to the neighbourhood of the torrent, the boatman unloads his merchandize, and the artisan pursues his toil, regardless of the falling river, and inattentive to those thundering sounds which seem calculated to suspend all human activity in solemn and awful astonishment; while the imagination of the spectator is struck with the comparative littleness of fleeting man, busy with his trivial occupations, contrasted with the view of nature in all her vast, eternal, uncontrollable grandeur. […]

## Questions

1. What sources of the pleasure in "enthusiastic awe" does Williams identify? Do you agree that these can be sources of pleasure in the sublime (aesthetic awe)? Would you identify any other ones? Explain.

2. Can you discern any references (implicit or explicit) to political or moral ideas in this reading? Why do you think that is the case? Explain.

3. Williams suggests that in the experience of sublimity ("enthusiastic awe") the self feels annihilated. Do you agree? How would one go about discerning or assessing whether this is true?

4. Is it significant that Williams is an English traveller in Switzerland? How might this have changed her perspective on the natural scenery she viewed? Does this imply anything about the sublime? Explain.

## Further reading

Blakemore, Steven. *Crisis in Representation: Thomas Paine, Mary Wollstonecraft, Helen Maria Williams, and the Rewriting of the French Revolution*. Vancouver: Fairleigh Dickinson University Press, 1997.

Bray, Matthew. "Helen Maria Williams and Edmund Burke: Radical Critique and Complicity." *Eighteenth-Century Life* 16, no. 2 (1992): 1–24.

Ellison, Julie. "Redoubled Feeling: Politics, Sentiment, and the Sublime in Williams and Wollstonecraft." *Studies in Eighteenth-Century Culture* 20, no. 1 (1991): 197–215.

Kennedy, Deborah. *Helen Maria Williams and the Age of Revolution.* Lewisburg, PA: Bucknell University Press, 2002.

Williams, Helen Maria. *Letters Written in France, in the Summer 1790, to a Friend in England* […]. London: T. Cadell, 1790.

# PART IV
## LATE MODERN

# CHAPTER 20
# WILLIAM WORDSWORTH, "THE SUBLIME
# AND THE BEAUTIFUL" (CIRCA 1810)

Not long after Kant died in 1804, British Romantic poets and authors such as William Wordsworth (1770–1850) took up and partially absorbed ideas from German Idealism. The Romantics illustrate various positions concerning how best to engage with, or even promote, the legacy of Kantian philosophy. They did this not only in poetry such as "The Prelude" (Wordsworth) but also in prose works, essays, and letters.

Wordsworth elaborated a theory of the sublime in his unfinished appendix, "The Sublime and the Beautiful." The following piece was envisioned as appendix III in *Guide to the Lakes* (first published in 1810, anonymously), or as it is known according to its fifth edition title, *A Guide through the District of the Lakes in the North of England, with a Description of the Scenery, &c. for the Use of Tourists and Residents* (1835).[1]

In a discussion of Wordsworth's poetry, fellow Romantic poet John Keats referred to Wordsworth's sublime as the "egotistical sublime," in opposition to his own view. He distinguished "the poetical Character"—by which he meant "that sort of which, if I am any thing, I am a Member"—from the "wordsworthian or egotistical sublime; which is a thing per se and stands alone."[2] This characterization of Wordsworth's view of the sublime has been influential, but perhaps the following prose piece will cast some doubt on it.

The published version of the *Guide to the Lakes* contains elements of the theory Wordsworth elaborates here. Perhaps following Coleridge, Wordsworth locates the sublime in the play between variety or "multitude" and "intense unity." Wordsworth emphasizes the repetition of "individual form," and (unlike Kant) gives an important role to color in eliciting the experience of the sublime, especially if the color is single-toned or monotonous. "For sublimity will never be wanting, where the sense of innumerable multitude is lost in, and alternates with, that of intense unity; and to the ready perception of this effect, similarity and almost identity of individual form and monotony of colour contribute. But this feeling is confined to the native immeasurable forest; no artificial plantation can give it" (1835 edition, 87). Thus, the sublime feeling is found more in nature (landscape) than in artificial gardens. In addition, Wordsworth distinguishes beauty and sublimity: "Sublimity is the result of Nature's first great dealings with the superficies of the earth; but the general tendency of her subsequent operations is towards the production of beauty; by a multiplicity of symmetrical parts uniting in a consistent whole" (1835 edition, 35). In the notes to the 1835 edition of *Guide to the Lakes*, he again explains the sublime in terms of a feeling of intense unity. The sublime is a response of "true enjoyment of grand separate Forms composing a sublime Unity, austere but reconciled and rendered attractive to the affections by the deep serenity that is spread over everything" (168). He elaborates these ideas in the appendix below, speaking of a "sense of sublimity" and "awe" that can be felt even by "a Child or an unpracticed person." Such claims raise questions about the supposed link between rationality and the sublime, or call into question how we should understand rationality and reason.

## Note on the text

Source: Reprinted from William Wordsworth, "The Sublime and the Beautiful," in *The Prose Works of William Wordsworth*, edited by W. J. B. Owen and Jane Worthington Symser, 3 vols., vol. 2, 349–60. Oxford: Clarendon Press, 1974.

Editorial footnotes dealing with variant readings and related philological issues have been omitted. Spelling, style, and formatting have occasionally been modified.

## "The Sublime and the Beautiful"

... amongst them.[3] It is not likely that a person so situated, provided his imagination be exercised by other intercourse, as it ought to be, will become, by any continuance of familiarity, insensible to sublime impressions from the scenes around him. Nay, it is certain that his conceptions of the sublime, far from being dulled or narrowed by commonness or frequency, will be rendered more lively and comprehensive by more accurate observation and by increasing knowledge. Yet, though this effect will take place with respect to grandeur, it will be much more strikingly felt in the influences of beauty. Neither the immediate nor final cause of this need here be examined; yet we may observe that, though it is impossible that a mind can be in a healthy state that is not frequently and strongly moved both by sublimity and beauty, it is more dependent for its daily well-being upon the love and gentleness which accompany the one, than upon the exaltation or awe which are created by the other.—Hence, as we advance in life, we can escape upon the invitation of our more placid and gentle nature from those obtrusive qualities in an object sublime in its general character; which qualities, at an earlier age, precluded imperiously the perception of beauty which that object if contemplated under another relation would have been capable of imparting. I need not observe to persons at all conversant in these speculations that I take for granted that the same object may be both sublime and beautiful; or, speaking more accurately, that it may have the power of affecting us both with the sense of beauty and the sense of sublimity; though (as for such Readers I need not add) the mind cannot be affected by both these sensations at the same time, for they are not only different from, but opposite to, each other. Now a Person unfamiliar with the appearances of a Mountainous Country is, with respect to its more conspicuous sublime features, in a situation resembling that of a Man of mature years when he looked upon such objects with the eye of childhood or youth. There appears to be something ungracious in this observation; yet it is nevertheless true, and the fact is mentioned both for its connection with the present work and for the importance of the general truth. Sensations of beauty and sublimity impress us very early in life; nor is it easy to determine which have precedence in point of time, and to which the sensibility of the mind in its natural constitution is more alive. But it may be confidently affirmed that, where the beautiful and the sublime co-exist in the same object, if that object be new to us, the sublime always precedes the beautiful in making us conscious of its presence—but all this may be both tedious and uninstructive to the Reader, as I have not explained what I mean by either of the words *sublime* or *beautiful*; nor is this the place to enter into a general disquisition upon the subject, or to attempt to clear away the errors by which it has been clouded.—But as I am persuaded that it is of infinite importance to the noblest feelings of the Mind and to its very highest powers that the forms of Nature should be accurately contemplated, and, if described, described in language that shall prove that we understand the several grand constitutional laws under which it has been ordained that these objects should everlastingly affect the mind, I shall deem myself justified in calling the Reader, upon the present humble occasion, to attend to a few words which shall be said upon two of these principal laws: the law of sublimity and that of beauty. These shall be considered so far at least as they may be collected from the objects amongst which we are about to enter, viz., those of a mountainous region—and to begin with the sublime as it exists in such landscape.

Let me then invite the Reader to turn his eyes with me towards that cluster of Mountains at the Head of Windermere; it is probable that they will settle ere long upon the Pikes of Langdale and the black precipice contiguous to them.—If these objects be so distant that, while we look at them, they are only thought of as the crown of a comprehensive Landscape; if our minds be not perverted by false theories, unless those mountains be seen under some accidents of nature, we shall receive from them a grand impression, and nothing more. But if they be looked at from a point which has brought us so near that the mountain is almost the sole object before our eyes, yet not so near but that the whole of it is visible, we shall be impressed with a sensation of sublimity.—And if this is analyzed, the body of this sensation would be found to resolve itself into three component parts: a sense of individual form or forms; a sense of duration; and a sense of power. The whole complex impression is made up of these elementary parts, and the effect depends upon their co-existence. For, if any one of them were abstracted, the others would be deprived of their power to affect.

I first enumerated individuality of form; this individual form was then invested with qualities and powers, ending with duration. Duration is evidently an element of the sublime; but think of it without reference to individual form, and we shall perceive that it has no power to affect the mind. Cast your eye, for example, upon any commonplace ridge or eminence that cannot be separated, without some effort of the mind, from the general mass of the planet; you may be persuaded, nay, convinced, that it has borne that shape as long as or longer than Cader Idris, or Snowdon, or the Pikes of Langdale that are before us; and the mind is wholly unmoved by the thought; and the only way in which such an object can affect us, contemplated under the notion of duration, is when the faint sense which we have of its individuality is lost in the general sense of duration belonging to the Earth itself. Prominent individual form must, therefore, be conjoined with duration, in order that Objects of this kind may impress a sense of sublimity; and, in the works of Man, this conjunction is, for obvious reasons, of itself sufficient for the purpose. But in works of Nature it is not so: with these must be combined impressions of power, to a sympathy with and a participation of which the mind must be elevated—or to a dread and awe of which, as existing out of itself, it must be subdued. A mountain being a stationary object is enabled to effect this connection with duration and individual form, by the sense of motion which in the mind accompanies the lines by which the Mountain itself is shaped out. These lines may either be abrupt and precipitous, by which danger and sudden change is expressed; or they may flow into each other like the waves of the sea, and, by involving in such image a feeling of self-propagation infinitely continuous and without cognizable beginning, these lines may thus convey to the Mind sensations not less sublime than those which were excited by their opposites, the abrupt and the precipitous. And, to complete this sense of power expressed by these permanent objects, add the torrents which take their rise within its bosom, and roll foaming down its sides; the clouds which it attracts; the stature with which it appears to reach the sky; the storms with which it arms itself; the triumphant ostentation with which its snows defy the sun, etc.

Thus has been given an analysis of the attributes or qualities the co-existence of which gives to a Mountain the power of affecting the mind with a sensation of sublimity. The capability of perceiving these qualities, and the degree in which they are perceived, will of course depend upon the state or condition of the mind, with respect to habits, knowledge, and powers, which is brought within the reach of their influence. It is to be remembered that I have been speaking of a visible object; and it might seem that when I required duration to be combined with individual form, more was required than was necessary; for a native of a mountainous country, looking back upon his childhood, will remember how frequently he has been impressed by a sensation of sublimity from a precipice, in which awe of personal apprehension were the predominant feelings of his mind, and from which the milder influence of duration seemed to be excluded. And it is true that the relative proportions in which we are affected by the qualities of these objects are different at different periods of our lives; yet there cannot be a doubt that upon all ages they act conjointly. The precipitous form of an individual cloud which a Child has been taught by tales and pictures to think of as sufficiently solid to support a substantial body, and upon which he finds it easy to conceive himself as seated, in imagination, and thus to invest it with some portion of the terror which belongs to the precipice, would affect him very languidly, and, surely, much more from the knowledge which he has of its evanescence than from the less degree in which it excites in him feelings of dread. Familiarity with these objects tends very much to mitigate and to destroy the power which they have to produce the sensation of sublimity as dependent upon personal fear or upon wonder; a comprehensive awe takes the place of the one, and a religious admiration of the other, and the condition of the mind is exalted accordingly.—Yet it cannot be doubted that a Child or an unpracticed person whose mind is possessed by the sight of a lofty precipice, with its attire of hanging rocks and starting trees, etc., has been visited by a sense of sublimity, if personal fear and surprise or wonder have not been carried beyond certain bounds. For whatever suspends the comparing power of the mind and possesses it with a feeling or image of intense unity, without a conscious contemplation of parts, has produced that state of the mind which is the consummation of the sublime.—But if personal fear be strained beyond a certain point, this sensation is destroyed, for there are two ideas that divide and distract the attention of the Spectator with an accompanying repulsion or a wish in the soul [that] they should be divided: the object exciting the fear and the subject in which it is excited. And this leads me to a remark which will remove the main difficulties of this investigation. Power awakens the sublime either when it rouses us to a sympathetic energy and calls upon the mind to grasp at something towards which it can make approaches but which it is incapable of attaining—yet so that it participates force which is acting upon it; or, secondly, by producing a humiliation or prostration of the mind before some external agency which it presumes not to make an effort to participate, but is absorbed in the contemplation of the might in the external power, and, as far as it has any consciousness of itself, its grandeur subsists in the naked fact of being conscious of external Power at once awful and immeasurable; so that, in both cases, the head and the front of the sensation is intense unity. But if that Power which is exalted above our sympathy impresses the mind with personal fear, so as the sensation becomes more lively than the impression or thought of the exciting cause, then self-consideration and all its accompanying littleness takes place of the sublime, and wholly excludes it. Or if the object contemplated be of a spiritual nature, as that of the Supreme Being, for instance (though few minds, I will hope, are so far degraded that with reference to the Deity they can be affected by sensations of personal fear, such as a precipice, a conflagration, a torrent, or a shipwreck might excite), yet it may be confidently affirmed that no sublimity can be raised by the contemplation of such power when it presses upon us with pain and individual fear to a degree which takes precedence in our thoughts over the power itself. For connect with such sensations the notion of infinity, or any other ideas of a sublime nature which different religious sects have connected with it: the feeling of self being still predominant, the condition of the mind would be mean and abject.—Accordingly Belial, the most sensual spirit of the fallen Angels, though speaking of himself and his Companions as full of pain, yet adds:

> Who would lose those thoughts
Which wander thro' Eternity?

The thoughts are not chained down by anguish, but they are free, and tolerate neither limit nor circumscription. Though by the opinions of many religious sects, not less than by many other examples, it is lamentably shown how industrious Man is in perverting and degrading his mind, yet such is its inherent dignity that, like that of the fallen Spirit as exhibited by the Philosophic and religious Poet, he is perpetually thwarted and baffled and rescued in his own despite.

But to return: Whence comes it, then, that that external power, to a union or communion with which we feel that we can make no approximation while it produces humiliation and submission, reverence or adoration, and all those sensations which may be denominated passive, does nevertheless place the mind in a state that is truly sublime? As I have said before, this is done by the notion or image of intense unity, with which the Soul is occupied or possessed.—But how is this produced or supported, and, when it remits, and the mind is distinctly conscious of his own being and existence, whence comes it that it willingly and naturally relapses into the same state? The cause of this is either that our physical nature has only to a certain degree been endangered, or that our moral Nature has not in the least degree been violated.—The point beyond which apprehensions for our physical nature consistent with sublimity may be carried, has been ascertained; and, with respect to power acting upon our moral or spiritual nature, by awakening energy either that would resist or that [?hopes][4] to participate, the sublime is called forth. But if the Power contemplated be of that kind which neither admits of the notion of resistance or participation, then it may be confidently said that, unless the apprehensions which it excites terminate in repose, there can be no sublimity, and that this sense of repose is the result of reason and the moral law. Could this be abstracted and reliance upon it taken away, no species of Power that was absolute over the mind could beget a sublime sensation; but, on the contrary, it could never be thought of without fear and degradation.

I have been seduced to treat the subject more generally than I had at first proposed; if I have been so fortunate as to make myself understood, what has been said will be forgiven. Let us now contract the speculation, and confine it to the sublime as it exists in a mountainous Country, and to the manner in which it makes itself felt. I enumerated the qualities which must be perceived in a Mountain before a sense of sublimity can be received from it. Individuality of form is the primary requisite; and the form must be of that character that deeply impresses the sense of power. And power produces the sublime either as it is thought of as a thing to be dreaded, to be resisted, or that can be participated. To what degree consistent with sublimity power may be dreaded has been ascertained; but as power, contemplated as something to be opposed or resisted, implies a twofold agency of which the mind is conscious, this state seems to be irreconcilable to what has been said concerning the consummation of sublimity, which, as has been determined, exists in the extinction of the comparing power of the mind, and in intense unity. But the fact is, there is no sublimity excited by the contemplation of power thought of as a thing to be resisted and which the moral law enjoins us to resist, saving only as far as the mind, either by glances or continuously, conceives that that power may be overcome or rendered evanescent, and as far as it feels itself tending towards the unity that exists in security or absolute triumph.—(When power is thought of under a mode which we can and do participate, the sublime sensation consists in a manifest approximation towards absolute unity.) If the resistance contemplated be of a passive nature (such, for example, as the Rock in the middle of the fall of the Rhine at Schaffhausen,[5] as opposed for countless ages to that mighty mass of Waters), there are undoubtedly here before us two distinct images and thoughts; and there is a most complex instrumentality acting upon the senses, such as the roar of the Water, the fury of the foam, etc.; and an instrumentality still more comprehensive, furnished by the imagination, and drawn from the length of the River's course, the Mountains from which it rises, the various countries through which it flows, and the distant Seas in which its waters are lost. These images and thoughts will, in such a place, be present to the mind, either personally or by representative abstractions more or less vivid.—Yet to return to the rock and the Waterfall: these objects will be found to have exalted the mind to the highest state of sublimity when they are thought of in that state of opposition and yet reconcilement, analogous to parallel lines in mathematics, which, being infinitely prolonged, can never come nearer to each other; and hence, though the images and feelings above enumerated have exerted a preparative influence upon the mind, the absolute crown of the impression is infinity, which is a modification of unity.

Having had the image of a mighty River before us, I cannot but, in connection with it, observe that the main source of all the difficulties and errors which have attended these disquisitions is that the attention of those who have been engaged in them has been primarily and chiefly fixed upon external objects and their powers, qualities, and properties, and not upon the mind itself, and the laws by which it is acted upon. Hence the endless disputes about the characters of objects, and the absolute denial on the part of many that sublimity or beauty exists. To talk of an object as being sublime or beautiful in itself, without references to some subject by whom that sublimity or beauty is perceived, is absurd; nor is it of the slightest importance to mankind whether there be any object with which their minds are conversant that Men would universally agree (after having ascertained that the words were used in the same sense) to denominate sublime or beautiful. It is enough that there are, both in moral qualities and in the forms of the external universe, such qualities and powers as have affected Men, in different states of civilization and without communication with each other, with similar sensations either of the sublime or beautiful. The true province of the philosopher is not to grope about in the external world and, when he has perceived or detected in an object such or such a quality or power, to set himself to the task of persuading the world that such is a sublime or beautiful object, but to look into his own mind and determine the law by which he is affected.—He will then find that same object has power to affect him in various manners at different times; so that, ludicrous as it...[6] to power as governed some where by the intelligence of law and reasons, and lastly to the transcendent sympathies which have been vouchsafed to her with the calmness of eternity.

Thus, then, is apparent how various are the *means* by which we are conducted to the same end—the elevation of our being; and the practical influences to be drawn from this are most important, but I shall consider them only with reference to the forms of nature which have occasioned this disquisition.

I have already given a faint sketch of the manner in which a familiarity with these objects acts upon the minds of men of cultivated imagination. I will now suppose a person of mature age to be introduced amongst them for the first time. I will not imagine him to be a man particularly conversant with pictures, nor an enthusiast in poetry; but he shall be modest and unpresumptuous, one who has not been insensible to impressions of grandeur from the universal or less local appearances and forms of nature (such as the sky, the clouds, the heavenly bodies, rivers, trees, and perhaps the Ocean), and coming hither desirous to have his knowledge increased and the means of exalting himself in thought and feeling multiplied and extended. I can easily conceive that such a man, in his first intercourse with these objects, might be grievously disappointed, and, if that intercourse should be short, might depart without being raised from that depression which such disappointment might reasonably cause. Such would have been the condition of the most eminent of our English Painters if his visits to the sublime pictures in the Vatican and the Sistine Chapel had not been repeated till the sense of strangeness had worn off, till the twilight of novelty began to dispel, and he was made conscious of the mighty difference between seeing and perceiving. I have heard of a Lady, a native of the Orcades (which naked solitudes from their birth she had never quitted), whose imagination, endeavouring to complete whatever had been left imperfect in pictures and books, had feasted in representing to itself the forms of trees. With delight did she look forward to the day when it would be permitted to her to behold the reality, and to learn by experience how far its grandeur or beauty surpassed the conceptions which she had formed—but sad and heavy was her disappointment when this wish was satisfied. A journey to a fertile Vale in the South of Scotland gave her an opportunity of seeing some of the finest trees in the Island; but she beheld them without pleasure or emotion, and complained that, compared with the grandeur of the living and ever-varying ocean in all the changes and appearances and powers of which she was thoroughly versed—that a tree or a wood were objects insipid and lifeless.—Something of a like disappointment, or perhaps a kind of blank and stupid wonder (one of the most oppressive of sensations), might be felt by one who had passed his life in the plains of Lincolnshire and should be suddenly transported to the recesses of Borrowdale or Glencoe. And if this feeling should not burden his mind, innumerable are the impressions which may exclude him from a communication with the sublime in the midst of objects eminently capable of exciting that feeling: he may be depressed by the image of barrenness; or the chaotic appearance of crags heaped together, or seemingly ready to fall upon each other, may excite in him sensations as uncomfortable as those with which he would look upon an edifice that the Builder had left unfinished; and many of the forms before his eyes, by associations of outward likeness, merely may recall to his mind mean or undignified works of art; and every where might he be haunted or disturbed by a sense of incongruity, either light and trivial, or resembling in kind that intermixture of the terrible and the ludicrous which dramatists who understand the constitution of the human mind have not unfrequently represented when they introduce a character disturbed by an agency supernatural or horrible to a degree beyond what the mind is prepared to expect from the ordinary course of human calamities or afflictions. So that it appears that even those impressions that do most easily make their way to the human mind, such as I deem those of the sublime to be, cannot be received from an object however eminently qualified to impart them, without a preparatory intercourse with that object or with others of the same kind.

But impediments arising merely from novelty or inexperience in a well disposed mind disappear gradually and assuredly. Yet, though it will not be long before the Stranger will become conscious of the sublime where the power to raise it eminently exists, yet, if I may judge from my own experience, it is only very slowly that the mind is opened out to a perception of images of Beauty co-existing in the same object with those of sublimity. As I have explained at large what I mean by the world sublimity, I might with propriety here proceed to treat of beauty, and to explain in what manner I conceive the mind to be affected when it has a sense of the beautiful. But I cannot pass from the sublime without guarding the ingenuous reader against those caprices of vanity and presumption derived from false teachers in the philosophy of the fine arts and of taste, which Painters, connoisseurs, and amateurs are perpetually interposing between the light of nature and their own minds. Powerful indeed must be the spells by which such an eclipse is to be removed; but nothing is wanting, save humility, modesty, diffidence, and an habitual, kindly, and confident communion with Nature, to prevent such a darkness from ever being superinduced. 'Oh', says one of these tutored spectators, 'what a scene should we have before us here upon the shores of Windermere, if we could but strike out those pikes of Langdale by which it is terminated; they are so intensely *picturesque* that their presence excludes from the mind all sense of the sublime.' Extravagant as such an ejaculation is, it has been heard from the mouths of Persons who pass for intelligent men of cultivated mind.

## Questions

1. What is the role of the imagination in Wordsworth's account? How does he think the imagination can mediate between mind and world?

2. What does Wordsworth mean by "intense unity," and what is its role in producing the "sensation of sublimity?"

3. Explain the three components of sublime objects (concerning form, duration, and power).

4. Do you agree with Wordsworth's views of the kinds and qualities of objects that paradigmatically evoke the sublime? Explain.

## Further reading

Emily Brady, *The Sublime in Modern Philosophy*, esp. 100–06. Cambridge: Cambridge University Press, 2013.

Weiskel, Thomas. *The Romantic Sublime: Studies in the Structure and Psychology of Transcendence*, esp. 44–62. London: John Hopkins, 1986.

Wlecke, Albert O. *Wordsworth and the Sublime*. Berkeley: University of California Press, 1973.

# CHAPTER 21

## MARY SHELLEY, FROM *FRANKENSTEIN; OR, THE MODERN PROMETHEUS* (1818)

Mary Wollstonecraft Shelley (1797–1851) was the daughter of Mary Wollstonecraft, the author of *A Vindication of the Rights of Men* (1790) and *A Vindication of the Rights of Woman* (1792), who died due to complications of giving birth to Mary. Mary Shelley's father was the radical-anarchist philosopher William Godwin. At the age of sixteen, Mary Shelley eloped with the young poet Percy Bysshe Shelley, and they eventually married in 1816. The first edition of *Frankenstein* was published about two years later.

Much of the sublimity depicted in and elicited by *Frankenstein* is due to its plot, glacial and Arctic settings (Mont Blanc, the North Pole, and impassable frozen seas), and its themes of animation and creation, life and death, self-preservation and annihilation. Although it was written before the advent of genetic engineering and the digital revolution, *Frankenstein* at once presents (what has been called) the technological, feminist, Gothic, and natural sublimes.

It is an exemplary instance of the Gothic sublime, which draws from associated feelings of fear and terror. Shelley does not depict the sublime as an experience of reason's soaring over sensibility. Rather, as the following excerpt reveals, Shelley shows a keen interest in proto-Freudian themes, such as what dreams—and writing and reading about them—reveal about suppressed and hidden desires. More than a century before psychoanalytic vocabulary was in place, eighteenth-century Gothic (which is not limited to and indeed precedes Shelley's work) "can be seen as a mode of investigating the unconscious, those nameless and often prohibited urges on the edge of experience."[1]

The following extracts portray, first, Victor Frankenstein's passionate, laborious research into animation, leading to the creation of the monster (or "wretch"), and second, the confrontation between the Victor and the wretch on top of an icy glacier near Mont Blanc. (Curiously, in the popular imagination the name of the wretch's *creator*, Frankenstein, is now associated with the monster. The novel itself hints at the collapse of the distinction between creator and created. For instance, after giving life to the wretch, "I passed the night wretchedly," Victor reports. He also says to the wretch, "You have made me wretched beyond expression.")

In the first excerpt, Victor explains his enthusiastic and rapturous research into animation and how he imbued matter with life in "a kind of enthusiastic frenzy" (vol. 3, ch. 2, 38). The wretch is observed for the first time. The creation of the eight-foot-tall wretch constitutes a moment of the sublime.[2] Moreover, it should be recalled that one mode of the "feminist" sublime locates the origin of the human disposition to feel awe in the natural responses to childbirth (though obviously different from the animation of the monster). In this respect, it is perhaps worth mentioning that by the time she composed the work, Mary Shelley had lost a baby in infancy (1815, a girl). She would lose another (also a girl) in 1818, and in 1819 she lost a third child, the three-year-old, William, the name given to the little boy (Victor's youngest brother) murdered by the wretch.

The second excerpt contains Victor's ascent to a glacier and his confrontation with the wretch at noon. "Listen to my tale," the wretch implores.

## Note on the text

Excerpted from *Frankenstein; or, The Modern Prometheus*, 3 vols. [first edition], vol. 1, 81–92, 97–103, vol. 2, 12–31. London: Lackington, Hughes, Harding, Mavor, & Jones, 1818.
Format, spelling, and style have been reproduced, with occasional modifications.

The Preface of the 1818 edition was written by Percy Shelley. Revised editions were published in 1823 (supervised by Shelley's father, William Godwin, to whom the first edition was dedicated) and, with more substantial emendations, in 1831.

Recent editions of the 1818 and 1831 editions are the following. First edition of 1818: Mary Wollstonecraft Shelley, *Frankenstein*, edited by Susan Wolfson (New York: Pearson, 2007). Third edition of 1831: Mary Wollstonecraft Shelley, *Frankenstein*, edited by Johanna M. Smith (Boston: Bedford/St. Martin's, 2000).

## *Frankenstein; or, The Modern Prometheus*, Vol. 1, Ch. 3, 81–92

[…] One of the phaenomena which had peculiarly attracted my attention was the structure of the human frame, and, indeed, any animal endued with life. Whence, I often asked myself, did the principle of life proceed? It was a bold question, and one which has ever been considered as a mystery; yet with how many things are we upon the brink of becoming acquainted, if cowardice or carelessness did not restrain our inquiries. I revolved these circumstances in my mind, and determined thenceforth to apply myself more particularly to those branches of natural philosophy which relate to physiology. Unless I had been animated by an almost supernatural enthusiasm, my application to this study would have been irksome, and almost intolerable. To examine the causes of life, we must first have recourse to death. I became acquainted with the science of anatomy: but this was not sufficient; I must also observe the natural decay and corruption of the human body. In my education my father had taken the greatest precautions that my mind should be impressed with no supernatural horrors. I do not ever remember to have trembled at a tale of superstition, or to have feared the apparition of a spirit. Darkness had no effect upon my fancy; and a church-yard was to me merely the receptacle of bodies deprived of life, which, from being the seat of beauty and strength, had become food for the worm. Now I was led to examine the cause and progress of this decay, and forced to spend days and nights in vaults and charnel houses. My attention was fixed upon every object the most insupportable to the delicacy of the human feelings. I saw how the fine form of man was degraded and wasted; I beheld the corruption of death succeed to the blooming cheek of life; I saw how the worm inherited the wonders of the eye and brain. I paused, examining and analysing all the minutiae of causation, as exemplified in the change from life to death, and death to life, until from the midst of this darkness a sudden light broke in upon me—a light so brilliant and wondrous, yet so simple, that while I became dizzy with the immensity of the prospect which it illustrated, I was surprised that among so many men of genius, who had directed their inquiries towards the same science, that I alone should be reserved to discover so astonishing a secret.

Remember, I am not recording the vision of a madman. The sun does not more certainly shine in the heavens, than that which I now affirm is true. Some miracle might have produced it, yet the stages of the discovery were distinct and probable. After days and nights of incredible labour and fatigue, I succeeded in discovering the cause of generation and life; nay, more, I became myself capable of bestowing animation upon lifeless matter.

The astonishment which I had at first experienced on this discovery soon gave place to delight and rapture. After so much time spent in painful labour, to arrive at once at the summit of my desires, was the most gratifying consummation of my toils. But this discovery was so great and overwhelming, that all the steps by which I had been progressively led to it were obliterated, and I beheld only the result. What had been the study and desire of the wisest men since the creation of the world, was now within my grasp. Not that, like a magic scene, it all opened upon me at once: the information I had obtained was of a nature rather to direct my endeavours so soon as I should point them towards the object of my search, than to exhibit that object already accomplished. I was like the Arabian who had been buried with the dead, and found a passage to life aided only by one glimmering, and seemingly ineffectual light.

I see by your eagerness, and the wonder and hope which your eyes express, my friend, that you expect to be informed of the secret with which I am acquainted; that cannot be: listen patiently until the end of my story, and you will easily perceive why I am reserved upon that subject. I will not lead you on, unguarded and ardent as I then was, to your destruction and infallible misery. Learn from me, if not by my precepts, at least by my example, how dangerous is the acquirement of knowledge, and how much happier that man is who believes his native town to be the world, than he who aspires to become greater than his nature will allow.

When I found so astonishing a power placed within my hands, I hesitated a long time concerning the manner in which I should employ it. Although I possessed the capacity of bestowing animation, yet to prepare a frame for the reception of it, with all its intricacies of fibres, muscles, and veins, still remained a work of inconceivable difficulty and labour. I doubted at first whether I should attempt the creation of a being like myself or one of simpler organization; but my imagination was too much exalted by my first success to permit me to doubt of my ability to give life to an animal as complex and wonderful as man. The materials at present within my command hardly appeared adequate to so arduous an undertaking; but I doubted not that I should ultimately succeed. I prepared myself for a multitude of reverses; my operations might be incessantly baffled, and at last my work be imperfect: yet, when I considered the improvement which every day takes place in science and mechanics, I was encouraged to hope my present attempts would at least lay the foundations of future success. Nor could I consider the magnitude and complexity of my plan as any argument of its impracticability. It was with these feelings that I began the creation of a human being. As the minuteness of the parts formed a great hindrance to my speed, I resolved, contrary to my first intention, to make the being of a gigantic stature; that is to say, about eight feet in height, and proportionably large. After having formed this determination, and having spent some months in successfully collecting and arranging my materials, I began.

No one can conceive the variety of feelings which bore me onwards, like a hurricane, in the first enthusiasm of success. Life and death appeared to me ideal bounds, which I should first break through, and pour a torrent of light into our dark world. A new species would bless me as its creator and source; many happy and excellent natures would owe their being to me. No father could claim the gratitude of his child so completely as I should deserve theirs. Pursuing these reflections, I thought, that if I could bestow animation upon lifeless matter, I might in process of time (although I now found it impossible) renew life where death had apparently devoted the body to corruption.

These thoughts supported my spirits, while I pursued my undertaking with unremitting ardour. My cheek had grown pale with study, and my person had become emaciated with confinement. Sometimes, on the very brink of certainty, I failed; yet still I clung to the hope which the next day or the next hour might realize. One secret which I alone possessed was the hope to which I had dedicated myself; and the moon gazed on my midnight labours, while, with unrelaxed and breathless eagerness, I pursued nature to her hiding places. Who shall conceive the horrors of my secret toil, as I dabbled among the unhallowed damps of the grave, or tortured the living animal to animate the lifeless clay? My limbs now tremble, and my eyes swim with the remembrance; but then a resistless, and almost frantic impulse, urged me forward; I seemed to have lost all soul or sensation but for this one pursuit. It was indeed but a passing trance, that only made me feel with renewed acuteness so soon as, the unnatural stimulus ceasing to operate, I had returned to my old habits. I collected bones from charnel houses; and disturbed, with profane fingers, the tremendous secrets of the human frame. In a solitary chamber, or rather cell, at the top of the house, and separated from all the other apartments by a gallery and staircase, I kept my workshop of filthy creation; my eyeballs were starting from their sockets in attending to the details of my employment. The dissecting room and the slaughter-house furnished many of my materials; and often did my human nature turn with loathing from my occupation, whilst, still urged on by an eagerness which perpetually increased, I brought my work near to a conclusion. [...]

## Vol. 1, Ch. 4, 97–103

It was on a dreary night of November, that I beheld the accomplishment of my toils. With an anxiety that almost amounted to agony, I collected the instruments of life around me, that I might infuse a spark of being into the lifeless thing that lay at my feet. It was already one in the morning; the rain pattered dismally against the panes, and my candle was nearly burnt out, when, by the glimmer of the half-extinguished light, I saw the dull yellow eye of the creature open; it breathed hard, and a convulsive motion agitated its limbs.

How can I describe my emotions at this catastrophe, or how delineate the wretch whom with such infinite pains and care I had endeavoured to form? His limbs were in proportion, and I had selected his features as beautiful. Beautiful!—Great God! His yellow skin scarcely covered the work of muscles and arteries beneath; his hair was of a lustrous black, and flowing; his teeth of a pearly whiteness; but these luxuriances only formed a more horrid contrast with his watery eyes, that seemed almost of the same colour as the dun white sockets in which they were set, his shrivelled complexion, and straight black lips.

The different accidents of life are not so changeable as the feelings of human nature. I had worked hard for nearly two years, for the sole purpose of infusing life into an inanimate body. For this I had deprived myself of rest and health. I had desired it with an ardour that far exceeded moderation; but now that I had finished, the beauty of the dream vanished, and breathless horror and disgust filled my heart. Unable to endure the aspect of the being I had created, I rushed out of the room, and continued a long time traversing my bed-chamber, unable to compose my mind to sleep. At length lassitude succeeded to the tumult I had before endured; and I threw myself on the bed in my clothes, endeavouring to seek a few moments of forgetfulness. But it was in vain: I slept indeed, but I was disturbed by the wildest dreams. I thought I saw Elizabeth [Victor's fiancée – Ed.], in the bloom of health, walking in the streets of Ingolstadt. Delighted and surprised, I embraced her; but as I imprinted the first kiss on her lips, they became livid with the hue of death; her features appeared to change, and I thought that I held the corpse of my dead mother in my arms; a shroud enveloped her form, and I saw the grave-worms crawling in the folds of the flannel. I started from my sleep with horror; a cold dew covered my forehead, my teeth chattered, and every limb became convulsed; when, by the dim and yellow light of the moon, as it forced its way through the window-shutters, I beheld the wretch—the miserable monster whom I had created. He held up the curtain of the bed; and his eyes, if eyes they may be called, were fixed on me. His jaws opened, and he muttered some inarticulate sounds, while a grin wrinkled his cheeks.

He might have spoken, but I did not hear; one hand was stretched out, seemingly to detain me, but I escaped, and rushed down stairs. I took refuge in the court-yard belonging to the house which I inhabited; where I remained during the rest of the night, walking up and down in the greatest agitation, listening attentively, catching and fearing each sound as if it were to announce the approach of the demoniacal corpse to which I had so miserably given life.

Oh! no mortal could support the horror of that countenance. A mummy again endued with animation could not be so hideous as that wretch. I had gazed on him while unfinished; he was ugly then; but when those muscles and joints were rendered capable of motion, it became a thing such as even Dante could not have conceived.

I passed the night wretchedly. Sometimes my pulse beat so quickly and hardly, that I felt the palpitation of every artery; at others, I nearly sank to the ground through languor and extreme weakness. Mingled with this horror, I felt the bitterness of disappointment: dreams that had been my food and pleasant rest for so long a space, were now become a hell to me; and the change was so rapid, the overthrow so complete!

Morning, dismal and wet, at length dawned, and discovered to my sleepless and aching eyes the church of Ingolstadt, its white steeple and clock, which indicated the sixth hour. The porter opened the gates of the court, which had that night been my asylum, and I issued into the streets, pacing them with quick steps, as if I sought to avoid the wretch whom I feared every turning of the street would present to my view. I did not dare return to the apartment which I inhabited, but felt impelled to hurry on, although wetted by the rain, which poured from a black and comfortless sky.

I continued walking in this manner for some time, endeavouring, by bodily exercise, to ease the load that weighed upon my mind. I traversed the streets, without any clear conception of where I was, or what I was doing. My heart palpitated in the sickness of fear; and I hurried on with irregular steps, not daring to look about me:

> Like one who, on a lonely road,
> Doth walk in fear and dread,
> And, having once turn'd round, walks on,
> And turns no more his head;
> Because he knows a frightful fiend
> Doth close behind him tread*.

[...]

[In the next excerpt, Victor travels with his father and his fiancée Elizabeth to Mont Blanc, and finally confronts the creature—on a glacier at noon. – Ed.]

## Vol. 2, Ch. 1, 12–15

[...] The weather was uncommonly fine; and if mine had been a sorrow to be chased away by any fleeting circumstance, this excursion would certainly have had the effect intended by my father. As it was, I was somewhat interested in the scene; it sometimes lulled, although it could not extinguish my grief. During the

---

*Coleridge's "Ancient Mariner." [This footnote is found in the 1818 edition. – Ed.]

first day we travelled in a carriage. In the morning we had seen the mountains at a distance, towards which we gradually advanced. We perceived that the valley through which we wound, and which was formed by the river Arve, whose course we followed, closed in upon us by degrees; and when the sun had set, we beheld immense mountains and precipices overhanging us on every side, and heard the sound of the river raging among rocks, and the dashing of waterfalls around.

The next day we pursued our journey upon mules; and as we ascended still higher, the valley assumed a more magnificent and astonishing character. Ruined castles hanging on the precipices of piny mountains; the impetuous Arve, and cottages every here and there peeping forth from among the trees, formed a scene of singular beauty. But it was augmented and rendered sublime by the mighty Alps, whose white and shining pyramids and domes towered above all, as belonging to another earth, the habitations of another race of beings.

We passed the bridge of Pelissier, where the ravine, which the river forms, opened before us, and we began to ascend the mountain that overhangs it. Soon after we entered the valley of Chamounix. This valley is more wonderful and sublime, but not so beautiful and picturesque as that of Servox, through which we had just passed. The high and snowy mountains were its immediate boundaries; but we saw no more ruined castles and fertile fields. Immense glaciers approached the road; we heard the rumbling thunder of the falling avalanche, and marked the smoke of its passage. Mont Blanc, the supreme and magnificent Mont Blanc, raised itself from the surrounding *aiguilles*, and its tremendous *dome* overlooked the valley.

During this journey, I sometimes joined Elizabeth, and exerted myself to point out to her the various beauties of the scene. I often suffered my mule to lag behind, and indulged in the misery of reflection. At other times I spurred on the animal before my companions, that I might forget them, the world, and, more than all, myself. When at a distance, I alighted, and threw myself on the grass, weighed down by horror and despair. At eight in the evening I arrived at Chamounix. My father and Elizabeth were very much fatigued; Ernest, who accompanied us, was delighted, and in high spirits: the only circumstance that detracted from his pleasure was the south wind, and the rain it seemed to promise for the next day.

We retired early to our apartments, but not to sleep; at least I did not. I remained many hours at the window, watching the pallid lightning that played above Mont Blanc, and listening to the rushing of the Arve, which ran below my window.


## Vol. 2, Ch. 2, 16–31


The next day, contrary to the prognostications of our guides, was fine, although clouded. We visited the source of the Arveiron, and rode about the valley until evening. These sublime and magnificent scenes afforded me the greatest consolation that I was capable of receiving. They elevated me from all littleness of feeling; and although they did not remove my grief, they subdued and tranquillized it. In some degree, also, they diverted my mind from the thoughts over which it had brooded for the last month. I returned in the evening, fatigued, but less unhappy, and conversed with my family with more cheerfulness than had been my custom for some time. My father was pleased, and Elizabeth overjoyed. "My dear cousin," said she, "you see what happiness you diffuse when you are happy; do not relapse again!"

The following morning the rain poured down in torrents, and thick mists hid the summits of the mountains. I rose early, but felt unusually melancholy. The rain depressed me; my old feelings recurred, and I was miserable. I knew how disappointed my father would be at this sudden change, and I wished to avoid him until I had recovered myself so far as to be enabled to conceal those feelings that overpowered me. I knew that they would remain that day at the inn; and as I had ever inured myself to rain, moisture, and cold,

I resolved to go alone to the summit of Montanvert. I remembered the effect that the view of the tremendous and ever-moving glacier had produced upon my mind when I first saw it. It had then filled me with a sublime ecstasy that gave wings to the soul, and allowed it to soar from the obscure world to light and joy. The sight of the awful and majestic in nature had indeed always the effect of solemnizing my mind, and causing me to forget the passing cares of life. I determined to go alone, for I was well acquainted with the path, and the presence of another would destroy the solitary grandeur of the scene.

The ascent is precipitous, but the path is cut into continual and short windings, which enable you to surmount the perpendicularity of the mountain. It is a scene terrifically desolate. In a thousand spots the traces of the winter avalanche may be perceived, where trees lie broken and strewed on the ground; some entirely destroyed, others bent, leaning upon the jutting rocks of the mountain, or transversely upon other trees. The path, as you ascend higher, is intersected by ravines of snow, down which stones continually roll from above; one of them is particularly dangerous, as the slightest sound, such as even speaking in a loud voice, produces a concussion of air sufficient to draw destruction upon the head of the speaker. The pines are not tall or luxuriant, but they are sombre, and add an air of severity to the scene. I looked on the valley beneath; vast mists were rising from the rivers which ran through it, and curling in thick wreaths around the opposite mountains, whose summits were hid in the uniform clouds, while rain poured from the dark sky, and added to the melancholy impression I received from the objects around me. Alas! why does man boast of sensibilities superior to those apparent in the brute; it only renders them more necessary beings. If our impulses were confined to hunger, thirst, and desire, we might be nearly free; but now we are moved by every wind that blows, and a chance word or scene that that word may convey to us.

> We rest; a dream has power to poison sleep.
> > We rise; one wand'ring thought pollutes the day.
> We feel, conceive, or reason; laugh, or weep,
> > Embrace fond woe, or cast our cares away;
> It is the same: for, be it joy or sorrow,
> > The path of its departure still is free.
> Man's yesterday may ne'er be like his morrow;
> > Nought may endure but mutability!*

It was nearly noon when I arrived at the top of the ascent. For some time I sat upon the rock that overlooks the sea of ice. A mist covered both that and the surrounding mountains. Presently a breeze dissipated the cloud, and I descended upon the glacier. The surface is very uneven, rising like the waves of a troubled sea, descending low, and interspersed by rifts that sink deep. The field of ice is almost a league in width, but I spent nearly two hours in crossing it. The opposite mountain is a bare perpendicular rock. From the side where I now stood Montanvert was exactly opposite, at the distance of a league; and above it rose Mont Blanc, in awful majesty. I remained in a recess of the rock, gazing on this wonderful and stupendous scene. The sea, or rather the vast river of ice, wound among its dependent mountains, whose aerial summits hung over its recesses. Their icy and glittering peaks shone in the sunlight over the clouds. My heart, which was before sorrowful, now swelled with something like joy; I exclaimed—"Wandering spirits, if indeed ye wander, and do not rest in your narrow beds, allow me this faint happiness, or take me, as your companion, away from the joys of life."

---

*[Poem by P. B. Shelley – Ed.]

As I said this, I suddenly beheld the figure of a man, at some distance, advancing towards me with superhuman speed. He bounded over the crevices in the ice, among which I had walked with caution; his stature also, as he approached, seemed to exceed that of man. I was troubled: a mist came over my eyes, and I felt a faintness seize me; but I was quickly restored by the cold gale of the mountains. I perceived, as the shape came nearer, (sight tremendous and abhorred!) that it was the wretch whom I had created. I trembled with rage and horror, resolving to wait his approach, and then close with him in mortal combat. He approached; his countenance bespoke bitter anguish, combined with disdain and malignity, while its unearthly ugliness rendered it almost too horrible for human eyes. But I scarcely observed this; anger and hatred had at first deprived me of utterance, and I recovered only to overwhelm him with words expressive of furious detestation and contempt.

"Devil!" I exclaimed, "do you dare approach me? and do not you fear the fierce vengeance of my arm wreaked on your miserable head? Begone, vile insect! or rather stay, that I may trample you to dust! and, oh, that I could, with the extinction of your miserable existence, restore those victims whom you have so diabolically murdered!"

"I expected this reception," said the daemon. "All men hate the wretched; how then must I be hated, who am miserable beyond all living things! Yet you, my creator, detest and spurn me, thy creature, to whom thou art bound by ties only dissoluble by the annihilation of one of us. You purpose to kill me. How dare you sport thus with life? Do your duty towards me, and I will do mine towards you and the rest of mankind. If you will comply with my conditions, I will leave them and you at peace; but if you refuse, I will glut the maw of death, until it be satiated with the blood of your remaining friends."

"Abhorred monster! fiend that thou art! the tortures of hell are too mild a vengeance for thy crimes. Wretched devil! you reproach me with your creation; come on then, that I may extinguish the spark which I so negligently bestowed."

My rage was without bounds; I sprang on him, impelled by all the feelings which can arm one being against the existence of another.

He easily eluded me, and said,

"Be calm! I entreat you to hear me, before you give vent to your hatred on my devoted head. Have I not suffered enough, that you seek to increase my misery? Life, although it may only be an accumulation of anguish, is dear to me, and I will defend it. Remember, thou hast made me more powerful than thyself; my height is superior to thine; my joints more supple. But I will not be tempted to set myself in opposition to thee. I am thy creature, and I will be even mild and docile to my natural lord and king, if thou wilt also perform thy part, the which thou owest me. Oh, Frankenstein, be not equitable to every other, and trample upon me alone, to whom thy justice, and even thy clemency and affection, is most due. Remember, that I am thy creature: I ought to be thy Adam; but I am rather the fallen angel, whom thou drivest from joy for no misdeed. Everywhere I see bliss, from which I alone am irrevocably excluded. I was benevolent and good; misery made me a fiend. Make me happy, and I shall again be virtuous."

"Begone! I will not hear you. There can be no community between you and me; we are enemies. Begone, or let us try our strength in a fight, in which one must fall."

"How can I move thee? Will no entreaties cause thee to turn a favourable eye upon thy creature, who implores thy goodness and compassion? Believe me, Frankenstein: I was benevolent; my soul glowed with love and humanity: but am I not alone, miserably alone? You, my creator, abhor me; what hope can I gather from your fellow-creatures, who owe me nothing? they spurn and hate me. The desert mountains and dreary glaciers are my refuge. I have wandered here many days; the caves of ice, which I only do not fear, are a dwelling to me, and the only one which man does not grudge. These bleak skies I hail, for they are kinder to me than your fellow-beings. If the multitude of mankind knew of my existence, they would do as you do, and arm themselves for my destruction. Shall I not then hate them who abhor me? I will keep no terms with my enemies. I am miserable, and they shall share my wretchedness. Yet it is in your power to recompense me, and deliver them from an evil which it only remains for you to make so great, that not only you and your family, but thousands of others, shall be swallowed up in the whirlwinds of its rage. Let your compassion be moved, and do not disdain me. Listen to my tale: when you have heard that, abandon or commiserate me, as you shall judge that I deserve. But hear me. The guilty are allowed, by human laws, bloody as they may be, to speak in their own defence before they are condemned. Listen to me, Frankenstein. You accuse me of murder; and yet you would, with a satisfied conscience, destroy your own creature. Oh, praise the eternal justice of man! Yet I ask you not to spare me: listen to me; and then, if you can, and if you will, destroy the work of your hands."

"Why do you call to my remembrance circumstances of which I shudder to reflect, that I have been the miserable origin and author? Cursed be the day, abhorred devil, in which you first saw light! Cursed (although I curse myself) be the hands that formed you! You have made me wretched beyond expression. You have left me no power to consider whether I am just to you, or not. Begone! Relieve me from the sight of your detested form."

"Thus I relieve thee, my creator," he said, and placed his hated hands before my eyes, which I flung from me with violence; "thus I take from thee a sight which you abhor. Still thou canst listen to me, and grant me thy compassion. By the virtues that I once possessed, I demand this from you. Hear my tale; it is long and strange, and the temperature of this place is not fitting to your fine sensations; come to the hut upon the mountain. The sun is yet high in the heavens; before it descends to hide itself behind yon snowy precipices, and illuminate another world, you will have heard my story, and can decide. On you it rests, whether I quit forever the neighbourhood of man, and lead a harmless life, or become the scourge of your fellow-creatures, and the author of your own speedy ruin."

As he said this, he led the way across the ice: I followed. My heart was full, and I did not answer him; but, as I proceeded, I weighed the various arguments that he had used, and determined at least to listen to his tale. I was partly urged by curiosity, and compassion confirmed my resolution. I had hitherto supposed him to be the murderer of my brother, and I eagerly sought a confirmation or denial of this opinion. For the first time, also, I felt what the duties of a creator towards his creature were, and that I ought to render him happy before I complained of his wickedness. These motives urged me to comply with his demand. We crossed the ice, therefore, and ascended the opposite rock. The air was cold, and the rain again began to descend: we entered the hut, the fiend with an air of exultation, I with a heavy heart, and depressed spirits. But I consented to listen; and, seating myself by the fire which my odious companion had lighted, he thus began his tale.

## Questions

1. In what ways is Victor similar to the creature or wretch?

2. Analyze Victor's dream. What parallels exist between Elizabeth's corpse (in the dream) and the monster?

3. In the second excerpt, how does the "sublime" setting affect the encounter between Victor and the monster?

4. How does the sublimity evoked by, or described in, these excerpts differ from that of other writers and theorists?

## Further reading and viewing

*Blade Runner* (film), directed by Ridley Scott (1982). DVD Warner Home Video 1999.

Ferguson, Frances. *Solitude and the Sublime: Romanticism and the Aesthetics of Individuation*, 97–113. London: Routledge, 1992.

Freeman, Barbara Claire. *The Feminine Sublime: Gender and Excess in Women's Fiction*. California: University of California Press, 1995, esp. 79–90.

Kick, Linda Lee. *A Feminist Sublime and Grotesque: Dorothea Schlegel, Mary Shelley, George Sand, and their Twentieth-Century Daughters*. Santa Barbara: University of California, 2011.

Lintott, Sheila. "The Sublimity of Gestating and Giving Birth: Toward a Feminist Conception of the Sublime." In *Philosophical Inquiries Into Pregnancy, Childbirth, and Mothering: Maternal Subjects*, ed. Sheila Lintott and Maureen Sander-Staudt, 237–50. New York: Routledge, 2012.

Mishra, Vijay. *The Gothic Sublime*, 187–223. Albany: SUNY Press, 1994.

# CHAPTER 22
## ARTHUR SCHOPENHAUER, FROM *THE WORLD AS WILL AND REPRESENTATION* (1818)

Schopenhauer (1788–1860), one of the most important German philosophers in the nineteenth century, was influenced by Plato and Kant as well as by non-western and Indian philosophy. He is also renowned for his opposition to Hegelianism, which dominated European intellectual circles in the first part of the nineteenth century. He published the first edition of *The World as Will and Representation* when he was still relatively young (1818), and second and third editions appeared in 1844 and 1859, by which point he had become more celebrated.

According to Schopenhauer, the experience of the sublime lies on a continuum, extending from weaker or calmer experiences to the most moving and forceful. At the beginning of section §41, he appears to distinguish the beautiful and the sublime in terms of whether the object "invites and attracts" us or instead opposes the will. The difference between the two ultimately rests in the experiencing subject. "It is only a special modification of this subjective side which distinguishes the sublime from the beautiful."

Like Schiller and Schelling, Schopenhauer sees a connection between art (tragedy) and the sublime, that is, he understands dramatic tragedy in terms of the sublime. "Our pleasure in tragedy belongs not to the feeling of the beautiful, but to that of the sublime; it is, in fact, the highest degree of this feeling." The effect of tragedy is "analogous to that of the dynamically sublime, since, like this, it raises us above the will and its interest, and puts us in such a mood that we find pleasure in the sight of what directly opposes the will."[1] Schopenhauer thus provides the sketch of an answer to the so-called paradox of tragedy and the negative emotions, or why we would feel pleasure when we witness or observe something terrible or horrible.

### Note on the text

Source: Reprinted from Arthur Schopenhauer, *The World as Will and Representation*, translated by E. F. J. Payne, 2 vols., vol. 1, 200–07, 208–09 [section §39 and the beginning of section §41]. New York: Dover Publications, 1969.

Format and style have been reproduced, with occasional modifications.

### §39.

All these considerations are intended to stress the subjective part of aesthetic pleasure, namely, that pleasure in so far as it is delight in the mere knowledge of perception as such, in contrast to the will. Now directly connected with all this is the following explanation of that frame of mind which has been called the feeling of the *sublime*.

It has already been observed that transition into the state of pure perception occurs most easily when the objects accommodate themselves to it, in other words, when by their manifold and at the same time definite and distinct form they easily become representative of their Ideas, in which beauty, in the objective sense, consists.

Above all, natural beauty has this quality, and even the most stolid and apathetic person obtains therefrom at least a fleeting aesthetic pleasure. Indeed, it is remarkable how the plant world in particular invites one to aesthetic contemplation, and, as it were, obtrudes itself thereon. It might be said that such accommodation was connected with the fact that these organic beings themselves, unlike animal bodies, are not immediate object of knowledge. They therefore need the foreign intelligent individual in order to come from the world of blind willing into the world of the representation. Thus they yearn for this entrance, so to speak, in order to attain at any rate indirectly what directly is denied to them. For the rest, I leave entirely undecided this bold and venturesome idea that perhaps borders on the visionary, for only a very intimate and devoted contemplation of nature can excite or justify it.[2] Now so long as it is this accommodation of nature, the significance and distinctness of its forms, from which the Ideas individualized in them readily speak to us; so long as it is this which moves us from knowledge of mere relations serving the will into aesthetic contemplation, and thus raises us to the will-free subject of knowing, so long is it merely the *beautiful* that affects us, and the feeling to beauty that is excited. But these very objects, whose significant forms invite us to a pure contemplation of them, may have a hostile relation to the human will in general, as manifested in its objectivity, the human body. They may be opposed to it; they may threaten it by their might that eliminates all resistance, or their immeasurable greatness may reduce it to nought. Nevertheless, the beholder may not direct his attention to this relation to his will which is so pressing and hostile, but, although he perceives and acknowledges it, he may consciously turn away from it, forcibly tear himself from his will and its relations, and, giving himself up entirely to knowledge, may quietly contemplate, as pure, will-less subject of knowing, those very objects so terrible to the will. He may comprehend only their Idea that is foreign to all relation, gladly linger over its contemplation, and consequently be elevated precisely in this way above himself, his person, his willing, and all willing. In that case, he is then filled with the feeling of the *sublime*; he is in the state of exaltation, and therefore the object that causes such a state is called *sublime*. Thus what distinguishes the feeling of the sublime from that of the beautiful is that, with the beautiful, pure knowledge has gained the upper hand without a struggle, since the beauty of the object, in other words that quality of it which facilitates knowledge of its Idea, has removed from consciousness, without resistance and hence imperceptibly, the will and knowledge of relations that slavishly serve this will. What is then left is pure subject of knowing, and not even a recollection of the will remains. On the other hand, with the sublime, that state of pure knowing is obtained first of all by a conscious and violent tearing away from the relations of the same object to the will which are recognized as unfavorable, by a free exaltation, accompanied by consciousness, beyond the will and the knowledge related to it. This exaltation must not only be won with consciousness, but also be maintained, and it is therefore accompanied by a constant recollection of the will, yet not of a single individual willing, such as fear or desire, but of human willing in general, in so far as it is expressed universally through its objectivity, the human body. If a single, real act of will were to enter consciousness through actual personal affliction and danger from the object, the individual will, thus actually affected, would at once gain the upper hand. The peace of contemplation would become impossible, the impression of the sublime would be lost, because it had yielded to anxiety, in which the effort of the individual to save himself supplanted every other thought. A few examples will contribute a great deal to making clear this theory of the aesthetically sublime, and removing any doubt about it. At the same time, they will show the difference in the degrees of this feeling of the sublime. For in the main it is identical with the feeling of the beautiful, with pure will-less knowing, and with the knowledge, which necessarily appears therewith, of the Ideas out of all relation that is determined by the principle of sufficient reason. The feeling of the sublime is distinguished from that of the beautiful only by the addition, namely the exaltation beyond the known hostile relation of the contemplated object to the will in general. Thus there result several degrees of the sublime, in fact transitions from the beautiful to the sublime, according as this addition is strong, clamorous, urgent, and near, or only feeble, remote, and merely suggested. I regard it as more appropriate to the discussion to adduce first of all in examples these transitions, and generally the weaker degrees of the impression of the sublime, although those whose aesthetic susceptibility in general is not very great, and whose imagination is not vivid, will understand only the examples, given later, of the higher and more distinct degrees of that impression. They should therefore confine themselves to these, and should ignore the examples of the very weak degree of the above-mentioned impression, which are to be spoken of first.

Just as man is simultaneously impetuous and dark impulse of will (indicated by the pole of the genitals as its focal point), and eternal, free, serene subject of pure knowing (indicated by the pole of the brain), so, in keeping with this antithesis, the sun is simultaneously the source of *light*, the condition for the most perfect kind of knowledge, and therefore of the most delightful of things; and the source of *heat*, the first condition of all life, in other words, of every phenomenon of the will at its higher grades. Therefore, what heat is for the will, light is for knowledge. For this reason, light is the largest diamond in the crown of beauty, and has the most decided influence on the knowledge of every beautiful object. Its presence generally is an indispensable condition; its favorable arrangement enhances even the beauty of the beautiful. But above all else, the beautiful in architecture is enhanced by the favour of light, and through it even the most insignificant thing becomes a beautiful object. Now if in the depth of winter, when the whole of nature is frozen and stiff, we see the rays of the setting sun reflected by masses of stone, where they illuminate without warming, and are thus favorable only to the purest kind of knowledge, not to the will, then contemplation of the beautiful effect of light on these masses moves us into the state of pure knowing, as all beauty does. Yet here, through the faint recollection of the lack of warmth from those rays, in other words, of the absence of the principle of life, a certain transcending of the interest of the will is required. There is a slight challenge to abide in pure knowledge, to turn away from all willing, and precisely in this way we have a transition from the feeling of the beautiful to that of the sublime. It is the faintest trace of the sublime in the beautiful, and beauty itself appears here only in a slight degree. The following is an example almost as weak.

Let us transport ourselves to a very lonely region of boundless horizons, under a perfectly cloudless sky, trees and plants in the perfectly motionless air, no animals, no human beings, no moving masses of water, the profoundest silence. Such surroundings are as it were a summons to seriousness, to contemplation, with complete emancipation from all willing and its cravings; but it is just this that gives to such a scene of mere solitude and profound peace a touch of the sublime. For, since it affords no objects, either favourable or unfavorable, to the will that is always in need of strife and attainment, there is left only the state of pure contemplation, and whoever is incapable of this is abandoned with shameful ignominy to the emptiness of unoccupied will, to the torture and misery of boredom. To this extent it affords us a measure of our own intellectual worth, and for this generally the degree of our ability to endure solitude, or our love of it, is a good criterion. The surroundings just described, therefore, give us an instance of the sublime in a low degree, for in them with the state of pure knowing in its peace and all-sufficiency there is mingled, as a contrast, a recollection of the dependence and wretchedness of the will in need of constant activity. This is the species of the sublime for which the sight of the boundless prairies of the interior of North America is renowned.

Now let us imagine such a region denuded of plants and showing only bare rocks; the will is at once filled with alarm through the total absence of that which is organic and necessary for our sustenance. The desert takes on a fearful character; our mood becomes more tragic. The exaltation to pure knowledge comes about with a more decided emancipation from the interest of the will, and by our persisting in the state of pure knowledge, the feeling of the sublime distinctly appears.

The following environment can cause this in an even higher degree. Nature in turbulent and tempestuous motion; semi-darkness through threatening black thunder-clouds; immense, bare, overhanging cliffs shutting out the view by their interlacing; rushing, foaming masses of water; complete desert; the wail of the wind sweeping through the ravines. Our dependence, our struggle with hostile nature, our will that is broken in this, now appear clearly before our eyes. Yet as long as personal affliction does not gain the upper hand, but we remain in aesthetic contemplation, the pure subject of knowing gazes through this struggle of nature, through this picture of the broken will, and comprehends calmly, unshaken and unconcerned, the Ideas in those very objects that are threatening and terrible to the will. In this contrast is to be found the feeling of the sublime.

But the impression becomes even stronger, when we have before our eyes the struggle of the agitated forces of nature on a large scale, when in these surroundings the roaring of a falling stream deprives us of the possibility of hearing our own voices. Or when we are abroad in the storm of tempestuous seas; mountainous waves rise and fall, are dashed violently against steep cliffs, and shoot their spray high into the air. The storm howls, the sea roars, the lightning flashes from black clouds, and thunder-claps drown the noise of storm and sea. Then in the unmoved beholder of this scene the twofold nature of his consciousness reaches the highest distinctness. Simultaneously, he feels himself as individual, as the feeble phenomenon of will, which the slightest touch of these forces can annihilate, helpless against powerful nature, dependent, abandoned to chance, a vanishing nothing in face of stupendous forces; and he also feels himself as the eternal, serene subject of knowing, who as the condition of every object is the supporter of this whole world, the fearful struggle of nature being only his mental picture or representation; he himself is free from, and foreign to, all willing and all needs, in the quiet comprehension of the Ideas. This is the full impression of the sublime. Here it is caused by the sight of a power beyond all comparison superior to the individual, and threatening him with annihilation.

The impression of the sublime can arise in quite a different way by our imagining a mere magnitude in space and time, whose immensity reduces the individual to nought. By retaining Kant's terms and his correct division, we can call the first kind the dynamically sublime, and the second the mathematically sublime, although we differ from him entirely in the explanation of the inner nature of that impression, and can concede no share in this either to moral reflections or to hypostases from scholastic philosophy.

If we lose ourselves in contemplation of the infinite greatness of the universe in space and time, meditate on the past millennia and on those to come; or if the heavens at night actually bring innumerable worlds before our eyes, and so impress on our consciousness the immensity of the universe, we feel ourselves reduced to nothing; we feel ourselves as individuals, as living bodies, as transient phenomena of will, like drops in the ocean, dwindling and dissolving into nothing. But against such a ghost of our own nothingness, against such a lying impossibility, there arises the immediate consciousness that all these worlds exist only in our representation, only as modifications of the eternal subject of pure knowing. This we find ourselves to be, as soon as we forget individuality; it is the necessary, conditional supporter of all worlds and of all periods of time. The vastness of the world, which previously disturbed our peace of mind, now rests within us; our dependence on it is now annulled by its dependence on us. All this, however, does not come into reflection at once, but shows itself as a consciousness, merely felt, that in some sense or other (made clear only by philosophy) we are one with the world, and are therefore not oppressed but exalted by its immensity. It is the felt consciousness of what the Upanishads of the Vedas express repeatedly in so many different ways, but most admirably in the saying already quoted: *Hae omnes creaturae in totum ego sum, et praeter me aliud (ens) non est* (Oupnek'hat, vol. I, p. 122).[3] It is an exaltation beyond our own individuality, a feeling of the sublime.

We receive this impression of the mathematically sublime in quite a direct way through a space which is small indeed as compared with the universe, but which, by becoming directly and wholly perceptible to us, affects us with its whole magnitude in all three dimensions, and is sufficient to render the size of our own body almost infinitely small. This can never be done by a space that is empty for perception, and therefore never by an open space, but only by one that is directly perceivable in all its dimensions through delimitation, and so by a very high and large dome, like that of St. Peter's in Rome or of St. Paul's in London. The feeling of the sublime arises here through our being aware of the vanishing nothingness of our own body in the presence of a greatness which itself, on the other hand, resides only in our representation, and of which we, as knowing subject, are the supporter. Therefore, here as everywhere, it arises through the contrast between the insignificance and dependence of ourselves as individuals, as phenomena of will, and the consciousness of ourselves as pure subject of knowing. Even the vault of the starry heavens, if contemplated without reflection, has only the same effect as that vault of stone, and acts not with its true, but only with its apparent, greatness. Many objects of our perception excite the impression of the sublime; by virtue both of their spatial magnitude and of their great antiquity, and therefore of their duration in time, we feel ourselves reduced to nought in their presence, and yet revel in the pleasure of beholding them. Of this kind are very high mountains, the Egyptian pyramids, and colossal ruins of great antiquity.

Our explanation of the sublime can indeed be extended to cover the ethical, namely what is described as the sublime character. Such a character springs from the fact that the will is not excited here by objects certainly well calculated to excite it, but that knowledge retains the upper hand. Such a character will accordingly consider men in a purely objective way, and not according to the relations they might have to his will. For example, he will observe their faults, and even their hatred and injustice to himself, without being thereby stirred to hatred on his own part. He will contemplate their happiness without feeling envy, recognize their own good qualities without desiring closer association with them, perceive the beauty of women without hankering after them. His personal happiness or unhappiness will not violently affect him; he will be rather as Hamlet describes Horatio:

> for thou hast been
> As one, in suffering all, that suffers nothing;
> A man, that fortune's buffets and rewards
> Hast ta'en with equal thanks, *etc.* (Act III, Sc. 2.)

For, in the course of his own life and in its misfortunes, he will look less at his own individual lot than at the lot of mankind as a whole, and accordingly will conduct himself in this respect rather as a knower than as a sufferer. [End of §39 – Ed.]

## §41.

The course of our remarks has made it necessary to insert here a discussion of the sublime, when the treatment of the beautiful has been only half completed, merely from one side, the subjective. For it is only a special modification of this subjective side which distinguishes the sublime from the beautiful. The difference between the beautiful and the sublime depends on whether the state of pure, will-less knowing, presupposed and demanded by any aesthetic contemplation, appears of itself, without opposition, by the mere disappearance of the will from consciousness, since the object invites and attracts us to it; or whether this state is reached only by free, conscious exaltation above the will, to which the contemplated object itself has an unfavorable, hostile relation, a relation that would do away with contemplation if we gave ourselves up to it. This is the distinction between the beautiful and the sublime. In the object the two are not essentially different, for in every case the object of aesthetic contemplation is not the individual thing, but the Idea in it striving for revelation, in other words, the adequate objectivity of the will at a definite grade. Its necessary correlative, withdrawn like itself from the principle of sufficient reason, is the pure subject of knowing, just as the correlative of the particular thing is the knowing individual, both of which lie within the province of the principle of sufficient reason. [...]

## Questions

1. Characterize Schopenhauer's examples of the sublime. What makes them more (or less) sublime?

2. Explain and evaluate his distinction between the sublime and the beautiful.

3. Which elements in the sublime does Schopenhauer identify as subjective, and which objective? How are his "Platonism" and theory of "Ideas" evident there?

4. Explain how Schopenhauer's concept of "will-less" disinterestedness relates to his theory of the sublime. How could he use it to explain the diversity and variety of aesthetic experiences and responses to a given object or event?

5. Compare and contrast Schopenhauer's theory with other accounts of the sublime.

## Further reading

Shapshay, Sandra. "Schopenhauer's Transformation of the Kantian Sublime." *Kantian Review* 17, no. 3 (2012): 479–511.
Vandenabeele, Bart. "Schopenhauer on Aesthetic Understanding and the Values of Art." *European Journal of Philosophy* 16, no. 2 (2008): 194–210.
Vandenabeele, Bart. *The Sublime in Schopenhauer's Philosophy*. New York: Palgrave Macmillan, 2015.
Vasalou, Sophia. *Schopenhauer and the Aesthetic Standpoint: Philosophy as a Practice of the Sublime*. Cambridge: Cambridge University Press, 2013.
Young, Julian. "Death and Transfiguration: Kant, Schopenhauer, and Heidegger on the Sublime." *Inquiry* 48, no. 2 (2005): 131–44.

# CHAPTER 23
# GEORG WILHELM FRIEDRICH HEGEL,
# "SYMBOLISM OF THE SUBLIME" (1835)

Georg W. F. Hegel (1770–1831), one of the foremost German Idealists, is known for his version of dialectical thinking, according to which a "negation" is in turn "negated." Two words sharing a common a root (*heben*: to lift, raise) here deserve to be clarified: "sublation" (*Aufhebung*) and the "sublime" (*Erhabene*). Sublation can mean both cancellation and (somewhat paradoxically) preservation. It can refer at once to an overcoming ("clearing out of the way," for instance, "negating" a law) and a sustaining ("taking care of something").[1] It is in such sublations that the self-revealing "Absolute" (spirit) eventually comes to recognize and know itself. According to Hegel, this occurs in various stages of developing self-consciousness: art, religion, and philosophy. Art is subordinate to philosophy; philosophy is higher since, unlike art, it apprehends the Idea *as* Absolute, the Idea unqualified by embodiment in a sensible form. Meanwhile, inspired while at the same time disagreeing with Kant, Hegel defines the sublime in general as "the attempt to express the infinite, without finding in the sphere of phenomena an object which proves adequate for this representation."

In his *Lectures on Fine Art* (published posthumously in 1835), Hegel takes the discipline of aesthetics to be mainly a philosophy of fine art. He presents his account of the sublime in the section of *Lectures* called "Symbolism of the Sublime." "The symbol," as he uses the term,

> constitutes the beginning of art, alike in its essential nature and its historical appearance, and is therefore to be considered only, as it were, as the threshold of art. It belongs especially to the East and only after all sorts of transitions, metamorphoses, and intermediaries does it carry us over into the genuine actuality of the Ideal as the classical form of art.[2]

His theory of the sublime is thus found at the first of the three developmental stages of art (symbolic, classical, and romantic), which are distinguished by their degrees of sensuous embodiment of the Ideal or Spirit. "Symbolic" art represents the first stage of art consciousness whose spiritual content is still immersed in sensuousness; at this stage both the understanding of spirit and the spiritual character of reality are vague, and the selection of artistic means to represent spirit is only vaguely understood. Accordingly, Hegel's account of the sublime is not so much concerned with Romantic poetry, novels, and paintings as with Indian, Persian, Christian, and Hebrew poetry. While the biblical Psalms, used by Hegel to illustrate a "negative" or transcendent mode of apprehension of "substance" (the One, the Divine), may be familiar to many western readers, it is noteworthy that Hegel discusses the Indian and Persian traditions as well (to explain a "positive" or immanent mode of apprehension).

Like Burke, Hegel thinks poetry is "freer" than painting since poetry can use words, rather than visible images, to represent and describe its content. Poetry, for Hegel, is more able to express the infinite. Because poetry is the least embodied and sensuous of the art forms, it also is the highest. For Hegel, the infinite or unconditioned (idea) is supposed to be represented by the finite representation given in the poem. However, the infinite content *exceeds* this mode or form of representation. Hence the "sublime" leads to another mode of representation of the infinite, and the dialectical process continues, proceeding eventually to the other stages of art (and then to religion and, finally, philosophy). In this way, we can see that the sublime (*Erhabene*) can be understood in terms of the dialectical movement of sublation (*Aufhebung*). "This outward shaping which is itself annihilated in turn by what it reveals, so that the revelation of the content is at the same time a supersession of the revelation, is the sublime."

In the end, Hegel sees sublimity as a mode and stage of beauty, which he considers the more important aesthetic category. Although the sublime is one of the ways in which the relationship between the Ideal and the attempt at its configuration appears in art, Hegel does not give the sublime the esteemed status it had held in previous eighteenth-century accounts. Given Hegel's enormous influence on nineteenth-century thought, this view would have significant consequences for the sublime, diminishing the role of the sublime in subsequent aesthetic theory. Neo-Hegelian thinkers such as Benedetto Croce, for instance, consider sublimity to be a pseudo-aesthetic concept rather than a genuine aesthetic category.[3] Nonetheless, Carritt suggests using "the sublime" in the Hegelian sense according to which nothing is truly sublime but the Absolute (God).[4] By limiting sublimity to God as presented in Hebrew poetry, Carritt writes, Hegel provides the material for an adequate account of the sublime, which Carritt recommends extending to dramatic tragedy. He thinks Hegel accounts for the four main points that a theory needs to make sense of: (1) exceeding size or power (God's power is infinite), (2) which causes a negative state of being checked or repelled (the effect of the Absolute's power in crushing our sensuous individualities is naturally repulsive to us), (3) and then feelings of self-expansion or uplifting (we are uplifted by the spectacle of God's victory), (4) which are positive feelings of union with the object (we triumph spiritually in the Absolute's annihilation of the finite).

## Note on the text

Source: Reprinted from G.W.F. Hegel, *Aesthetics: Lectures on Fine Art*, translated by T. M. Knox, 2 vols., vol. 1, 362–77. Oxford: Oxford University Press, 1975.

Format, punctuation, italics, and spelling have been reproduced, with occasional modifications. Knox is the author of the footnotes and square brackets in the main body, unless otherwise noted. Footnotes written by the volume editor are indicated as such.

This text from Hegel's lectures on aesthetics is based on the student notes edited by H. G. Hotho, and scholars have long noted the deficiencies of this edition. Critics flag issues surrounding the student transcriptions of Hegel's lectures: possible additions and omissions by students, the accuracy of transcriptions (which are not verbatim reproductions), insufficiently indicated developments in the philosopher's position, and similar problems associated with lecture notes. While conceding these points, Knox's translation of the Hotho edition is here reprinted since the Hotho edition is the one scholars have traditionally studied, it has given rise to a history of reception, and it is widely available.

## Chapter II

## Symbolism of the sublime

The unenigmatic clarity of the spirit which shapes itself out of its own resources in a way adequate to itself is the aim of symbolic art, but it can only be reached if in the first place the meaning [*Bedeutung* – Ed.] comes into consciousness on its own account, separated from the entire world of appearance. For in the immediately intuited unity of the two [meaning and shape] lay the absence of art in the case of the ancient Parsis;[5] the contradiction between the separation of the two and what was nevertheless demanded, i.e. their immediate linkage, produced the fantastic symbolism of the Indians; while even in Egypt knowledge of the inner life and the absolute meaning was still not free, still not released from the world of appearance, and this provided the reason for the riddles and the obscurity of Egyptian symbolism.

Now the first decisive purification of the absolute [meaning] and its express separation from the sensuous present, i.e. from the empirical individuality of external things, is to be sought in the *sublime*. Sublimity lifts the Absolute above every immediate existent and therefore brings about the liberation which, though abstract at first, is at least the foundation of the spirit. For although the meaning thus elevated is not yet apprehended as concrete spirit, it is nevertheless regarded as the inner life, self-existent and reposing on itself, which by its very nature is incapable of finding its true expression in finite phenomena.

Kant has distinguished the sublime from the beautiful in a very interesting way, and his detailed discussion of this in the first part of the *Critique of Judgment* from §20 onwards[6] still always retains its interest despite all prolixity and the premised reduction of all categories to something subjective, to the powers of mind, imagination, reason, etc. In its general principle, this reduction must be recognized as correct to this extent, that sublimity – as Kant says himself – is not contained in anything in nature but only in our minds, in so far as we become conscious of our superiority to the nature within us and therefore to nature without. In this sense Kant's view is that 'the sublime, in the strict sense of the word, cannot be contained in any sensuous form but concerns only Ideas of Reason which, although no adequate representation of them is possible, may be aroused and called to our mind precisely by this inadequacy which does admit of sensuous representation' (*Critique of Judgment,* [third edition, Berlin – Ed.] 1799, p. 77 [§23]). The sublime in general is the attempt to express the infinite, without finding in the sphere of phenomena an object which proves adequate for this representation. Precisely because the infinite is set apart from the entire complex of objectivity as explicitly an invisible meaning devoid of shape and is made inner, it remains, in accordance with its infinity, unutterable and sublime above any expression through the finite.

Now the first content which the meaning gains here is this, that in contrast to the totality of appearance it is the inherently substantial *unity* which itself, as a pure thought, can be apprehended only by pure thought. Therefore this substance is now no longer able to have its configuration in something external, and thus far the strictly symbolical character vanishes. But if this inherent unity is to be brought before our vision, this is only possible if, as substance, it is also grasped as the creative power of all things, in which it therefore has its revelation and appearance and to which it thus has a positive relation. But at the same time this essentially expresses the fact of substance's elevation above individual phenomena as such, and above their totality, with the logical result that the positive relation is transposed into the negative one in which the substance is purified from everything apparent and particular and therefore from what fades away in it and is inadequate to it.

This outward shaping which is itself annihilated in turn by what it reveals, so that the revelation of the content is at the same time a supersession of the revelation, is the sublime. This, therefore, differing from Kant, we need not place in the pure subjectivity of the mind and its Ideas of Reason; on the contrary, we must grasp it as grounded in the one absolute substance *qua* the content which is to be represented.

The classification of the art-form of the sublime is likewise derived from the above-indicated double relationship of substance, as meaning, to the phenomenal world.

The character common to the two sides of this relation – i.e. the positive and the negative – lies in this, that the substance is raised above the single phenomenon in which it is to acquire representation, although it can be expressed only in relation to the phenomenal in general, because as substance and essentiality it is in itself without shape and inaccessible to concrete vision. As the first mode of apprehension, the affirmative one, we may cite pantheistic art as it occurs partly in India and partly in the later freedom and mysticism of the Mohammedan [i.e., Muslim – Ed.] Persian poets, and as we find it again also in the deeper inwardness of thought and sentiment in the Christian west.

In its general character at this stage substance is envisaged as immanent in all its created accidents, which thus are not yet degraded to serving, and merely adorning, the glorification of the Absolute, but are preserved affirmatively through the substance dwelling in them, although in every single thing it is only the One and the Divine which is to be imaged and exalted. Wherefore the poet, who in everything descries and marvels at this One and immerses himself, as well as things, in this contemplation, can preserve a positive relation to the substance to which he links everything.

The second [mode of] apprehension, namely the negative praise of the power and glory of the one God, we encounter as sublimity in the strict sense in Hebrew poetry. It cancels the positive immanence of the Absolute in its created phenomena and puts the *one* substance explicitly apart as the Lord of the world in contrast to whom there stands the entirety of his creatures, and these, in comparison with God, are posited as the inherently powerless and perishable. Now when the power and wisdom of the One is to be represented through the finitude of natural things and human fates, we no longer find here any Indian distortion into the shapelessness of the boundless; on the contrary, the sublimity of God is brought nearer to contemplation by reason of the fact that what exists in the world, with all its splendour, magnificence, and glory, is represented as only a serving accident and a transient show in comparison with God's being and stability.

## A  The pantheism of art

Nowadays the word 'pantheism' is at once liable to the crassest misunderstandings. This is because in one way 'everything' means in our modern sense 'all and everything in its purely empirical individuality', e.g., this mull with all its own qualities, with this colour, size so and so, shape, weight, etc., or that house, book, animal, table, chair, oven, cirrus clouds, etc. Now many contemporary theologians accuse philosophy of turning 'everything' into God, but when 'everything' is taken precisely in the sense just mentioned, what they allege about philosophy is as a matter of fact entirely false and their complaint against it is thus quite unjustified. Such an idea of Pantheism can only arise in crazy heads and is not found in any religion, not even amongst the Iroquois and the Eskimos, let alone in any philosophy. The 'everything' in what has been called 'Pantheism' is therefore not this or that individual thing, but rather is 'everything' in the sense of the *All*, i.e. of the one substance which indeed is immanent in individuals, but is abstracted from individuality and its empirical reality, so that what is emphasized and meant is not the individual as such but the universal soul, or, in more popular terms, truth and excellence which also have their presence in this individual being.

This constitutes the proper meaning of 'Pantheism' and under this meaning alone have we to talk of Pantheism here. It belongs primarily to the East which grasps the thought of an absolute unity of the Divine and the thought of all things as comprised in this unity. Now, as unity and All, the Divine can come into consciousness only through the vanishing of the particular individuals in which the Divine is expressed as present. On the one hand, that is to say, the Divine is envisaged here as immanent in the most various objects and indeed, more particularly, as the most excellent and most pre-eminent thing amongst and in the different existents; but, on the other hand, since the One is this thing and another and another again and rolls through all things, the individuals and particulars for this very reason appear as superseded and vanishing; for it is not any and every individual thing which is this One; on the contrary, the One is this totality of individuals which for contemplation coalesce into the totality. For if the One is life, for example, it is also death, and therefore precisely not only life; so that thus life or the sun or the sea do not, as life, sea, or sun, constitute the Divine and the One. Yet at the same time the accidental is not here posited expressly as negative and as a servant, as it is in sublimity proper, but, on the contrary, since the substance in everything particular is this One, the substance becomes *implicitly* something particular and accidental; yet, conversely, this individual thing changes all the same, and imagination does not restrict the substance to a specific existent but advances over each determinacy, abandoning it in order to proceed to another, and thus the individual existent becomes for its part something accidental, away and above which the one substance rises and therefore is sublime.

Such a way of looking at things can, on this account, be expressed artistically only in poetry, not in the visual arts which bring to our vision only as existent and static the determinate and individual thing which is to disappear in face of the substance present in such existents. Where Pantheism is pure, there is no visual art for its representation.

## 1 Indian poetry

As the first example of such pantheistic poetry we may once again cite the Indian which alongside its fantasticalness has brilliantly developed this aspect also.

The Indians, as we saw, have as their supreme Divinity the most abstract universality and unity, which does thereupon become specified in particular gods, Trimurti, Indra, etc.; but there is no holding fast to the specific; the subordinate gods revert all the same into the higher ones, and these into Brahma. Thus it is already clear that this universal constitutes the one permanent and self-identical foundation of everything. The Indians of course display in their poetry the double struggle (a) so to magnify the individual existent that in its sensuousness it may already appear adequate to the universal meaning, and (b) conversely, in face of the abstraction of the One, to waive all determinacy in a purely negative way. On the other hand, there appears even in the Indians the purer mode of representation of the above-mentioned Pantheism which emphasizes the immanence of the Divine in the individual who for the eye of contemplation is present and vanishing. In this mode of looking at things we could propose to find once more something of a resemblance to that immediate unity of pure thought and sense which we encountered in the Parsis; but in their case the One and the Excellent, considered on its own account, is itself something natural, i.e. light; whereas in the case of the Indians the One, Brahma, is merely the formless One which, only when transformed into the infinite multiplicity of terrestrial phenomena, provides an opportunity for the pantheistic mode of representation.

So it is said, e.g., of Krishna (*Bhagavad Gita*, 7. iv): 'Earth, water and wind, air and fire, spirit, understanding, and self-hood are the eight syllables of my essential power; yet recognise thou in me another and a higher being who vivifies the earth and carries the world: in him all beings have their origin; so know thou, I am the origin of this entire world and also its destruction; beyond me there is nothing higher, to me this All is linked as a chaplet of pearls on a thread; I am the taste in flowing water, the splendour in the sun and the moon, the mystical word in the holy scriptures, in man his manliness, the pure fragrance in the earth, the splendour in flames, in all beings the life, contemplation in the penitent, in living things the force of life, in the wise their wisdom, in the splendid their splendour; whatever natures are genuine, are shining or dark, they are from me, I am not in them, they are in me. Through the illusion of these three properties the whole world is bewitched and mistakes me the unalterable; but even the divine illusion, Maya, is my illusion, hard to transcend; but those who follow me go forth beyond illusion.'[7] Here such a substantial unity is expressed in the most striking way, in respect both of immanence in what is present and also transcendence over everything individual.

In a similar way, Krishna says of himself that amongst all different existents he is always the most excellent (10. xxi):[8] 'Among the stars I am the shining sun, amongst the lunary signs the moon, amongst the sacred books the book of hymns, amongst the senses the inward, Meru amongst the tops of the hills,[9] amongst animals the lion, amongst letters I am the vowel A, amongst seasons of the year the blossoming spring', etc.

But this recitation of the height of excellence, like the mere change of shapes in which what is to be brought before our eyes is always one and the same thing over again, despite the wealth of fancy which seems at first sight to be deployed there, still remains, precisely on account of this similarity of content, extremely monotonous and, on the whole, empty and wearisome.

## 2 Mohammedan poetry

Secondly, in a higher and more subjectively free way, oriental Pantheism has been developed in Mohammedanism, especially by the Persians.

Now here a characteristic relation appears, especially on the part of the individual poet:

a. Since the poet longs to descry the Divine in everything and does actually descry it, in face of it he now sacrifices his own personality, but he all the same apprehends the immanence of the Divine in his inner being thus enlarged and freed; and therefore there grows in him that serene inwardness, that free good fortune, that riotous bliss characteristic of the Oriental who, in renouncing his own particularity, immerses himself entirely in the Eternal and the Absolute, and feels and recognizes in everything the picture and presence of the Divine. Such a self-penetration by the Divine and a blissful intoxicated life in God borders on mysticism. In this connection Jalal-ed-Din Rumi [1207–73][10] is to be praised above all; Rückert[11] has given us most beautiful examples of his work; Rückert's marvellous power of expression enables him to play in the most ingenious and free way with words and rhymes, just as the Persians do. The love of God – with whom man identifies his personality by the most boundless surrender and whom, the One, he now glimpses in all spaces of the universe, to whom he relates each and everything, and to whom he brings everything back – constitutes here the centre which radiates in the widest way in every direction and region.

b. Furthermore, in sublimity, strictly so-called, as will be shown directly, the best objects and most splendid configurations are used only as a mere adornment of God and serve as a proclamation of the magnificence and glorification of the One, since they are set before our eyes only to celebrate him as the lord of all creation. In Pantheism, on the other hand, the immanence of the Divine in objects exalts mundane, natural, and human existence itself into a more independent glory of its own. The personal life of the spirit in natural phenomena and human affairs animates and spiritualizes them in themselves and founds anew a special relation between the subjective feeling, and soul, of the poet and the objects of his song. Filled by this soulful glory, the heart in itself is peaceful, independent, free, self-subsistent, wide, and great; and in this affirmative identity with itself the heart imagines and now makes its own the soul of things until it attains a like peaceful unity with it; it grows into the most blissful and cheerful intimacy with objects in nature and their splendour, with the beloved and the tavern, in short with everything worth praise and love. The western romantic deep feeling of the heart does display a similar absorption in nature's life, but on the whole, especially in the north, it is rather unhappy, unfree, and wistful, or it still remains subjective, shut in upon itself, and therefore becomes self-seeking and sentimental. Such oppressed and troubled deep feeling is expressed especially in the folksongs of barbarian peoples. On the other hand, a free, happy, depth of feeling is characteristic of Orientals, especially the Mohammedan Persians, who openly and cheerfully sacrifice their entire selves to God and to everything praiseworthy, yet in this sacrifice they do precisely retain the free substantiality which they can preserve even in relation to the surrounding world. So we see in the glow of passion the most widespread bliss and parrhesia [i.e., frankness – Ed.] of feeling through which, in the inexaustible wealth of brilliant and splendid images, there resounds the steady note of joy, beauty, and good fortune. If the Oriental suffers and is unhappy, he accepts this as the unalterable verdict of fate and he therefore remains secure in himself, without oppression, sentimentality, or discontented dejection. In the poems of Hafiz[12] we find complaints and outcries enough about the beloved, filling the glass, etc., but even in grief he remains just as carefree as he is in good fortune. So, e.g., he says once: 'Out of thanks that the presence of thy friend enlightens thee, in woe burn like the candle and be satisfied.'

The candle teaches us to laugh and cry; through the flame it laughs in cheerful splendour, while at the same time it melts away in hot tears; in its burning it spreads cheerful splendour. This is the general character of this whole poetry.

Just to mention a few more detailed pictures, the Persians have much to do with flowers and jewels, but above all with the rose and the nightingale. Especially common with them is the representation of the nightingale as the bridegroom of the rose. This gift of soul to the rose and the love of the nightingale is common, e.g., in Hafiz. 'Out of thanks, O rose, that thou art the queen of beauty', he says, 'beware that thou disdain not the nightingale's love.' He himself speaks of the nightingale of his own heart. Whereas if we speak in our poems of roses, nightingales, wine, this occurs in a quite different and more prosaic sense; the rose serves us as an adornment, 'garlanded with roses', etc., or we hear the nightingale and it just arouses our corresponding emotions; we drink wine and call it the banisher of care. But with the Persians the rose is no image or mere adornment, no symbol; on the contrary, it appears to the poet as ensouled, as an affianced beloved, and with his spirit he is engrossed in the soul of the rose.

The same character of brilliant Pantheism is still displayed in the most recent Persian poetry too. Von Hammer,[13] e.g., has informed us of a poem sent by the Shah with other gifts to the Emperor Francis in 1819. In 33,000 distichs it recounts the deeds of the Shah who has conferred his own name on the Court poet.

c. Goethe too, in contrast to his troubled youthful poems and their concentrated feeling, was gripped in his later years by this broad and carefree serenity, and, as an old man, inspired by the breath of the East, and with his soul filled with boundless bliss, turns in the poetic fervour of his heart to this freedom of feeling, a freedom that even in polemics keeps the most beautiful tranquillity. The songs in his *West-östliche Divan*[14] are neither *jeux d'esprit* nor insignificant social gallantries, but are the products of such a free feeling and abandon. He calls them himself in a song to Suleika: 'Poetic pearls, which the mighty surge of your passion cast up on my life's deserted shore, tenderly gathered with careful fingers, they are ranged on a necklace of jewels and gold.' 'Take', he calls to his beloved, 'Take them on thy neck, to thy bosom – raindrops of Allah, ripened in a modest shell.'[15]

For such poems there needed a sense self-confident in all storms and of the widest range, a depth and childlikeness of heart and 'a world of living buds which in their thrusting abundance presaged the nightingale's love and her soul-stirring song'.

## 3 Christian mysticism

Now the pantheistic unity, emphasized in relation to the subject who feels *himself* in this unity with God and senses God as this presence in subjective consciousness, is afforded in general by mysticism, developed as it has been in this more subjective way within Christianity too. As an example I will only cite Angelus Silesius, who, with the greatest audacity and depth of intuition and feeling, has expressed in a wonderfully mystical power of representation the substantial existence of God in things and the unification of the self with God and of God with human subjectivity.[16] The strictly Eastern Pantheism, on the other hand, emphasizes rather the contemplation of the one substance in all phenomena and their sacrifice by the subject who thereby acquires the supreme enlargement of consciousness as well as, through entire liberation from the finite, the bliss of absorption into everything that is best and most splendid.

## B The art of the sublime

But the one substance, grasped as the proper meaning of the entire universe, is in truth only established as substance when it is brought back into itself, as pure inwardness and substantial might, out of its presence and actuality in the vicissitudes of phenomena, and thereby is made *independent* itself over against finitude. Only through this intuition of the being of God as the purely spiritual and imageless, *contrasted* with the mundane and the natural, is spirit completely wrested from nature and sense and released from existence in the finite. Yet conversely the absolute substance remains in a *relation* to the phenomenal world, out of which it is reflected back into itself. This relation now acquires the abovementioned negative aspect, namely that the entire mundane sphere, despite the fullness, force, and splendour of its phenomena, is expressly established, in relation to the substance, as only the inherently negative, created by God, subjected to his power, and his servant. The world is therefore indeed regarded as a revelation of God, and he himself is the goodness which, although the created world has in itself no right to subsist and to relate itself to itself, yet permits it to thrive and gives it stability; still, the stability of the finite is without substance, and the creature, held over against God, is what is perishing and powerless, so that in the creator's goodness his *justice* has to be manifested at the same time; and this justice brings into actual appearance also, in the inherently negative, the powerlessness thereof and therefore the substance as that alone which has power.

This relation, when art asserts it as the fundamental one for both its content and its form, affords the art-form of sublimity, strictly so-called. Beauty of the Ideal must of course be distinguished from sublimity. For in the Ideal the inner life pervades external reality, whose inner being the inner life is, in the sense that both sides appear as adequate to one another and therefore precisely as pervading one another. In sublimity, on the contrary, external existence, in which the substance is brought before contemplation, is degraded in comparison with the substance, since this degradation and servitude is the one and only way whereby the *one* God can be illustrated in art; this is because the one God is explicitly without shape and is incapable of expression in his *positive* essence in anything finite and mundane. Sublimity presupposes the meaning in an independence in comparison with which the external must appear as merely subordinate, because the inner does not appear in it but so transcends it that nothing comes into the representation except as this transcendence and superiority.

In the symbol the shape was the chief thing. The shape was supposed to have a meaning, yet without being able to express it perfectly. In contrast to this symbol and its obscure content there is now the meaning as such and its clear intelligibility; and the work of art thus becomes the outpouring of the pure Being as the meaning of all things – but of the Being which establishes the incongruity of shape and meaning, *implicitly* present in the symbol, as the meaning of God himself, a meaning present in the mundane and yet transcending everything mundane [and this is incongruous]; and therefore the Being becomes sublime in the work of art which is to express nothing but this absolutely clear meaning. If therefore symbolic art in general may already be called *sacred* art because it adopts the Divine as the content of its productions, the art of sublimity is *the* sacred art as such which can be called exclusively sacred because it gives honour to God alone. Here on the whole the content, in its fundamental meaning, is still more restricted than it is in the symbol proper which does not get beyond striving after the spiritual, and in its reciprocal relations [between spirit and nature] affords a wide extension of spirit's transformation in natural productions and nature's transformation in echoes of the spirit.

This sort of sublimity in its first original character we find especially in the outlook of the Jews and in their sacred poetry. For visual art cannot appear here, where it is impossible to sketch any adequate picture of God; only the poetry of ideas, expressed in words, can. In handling this stage in more detail we may set out the following general points.

## 1 God as creator and Lord of the world

For its most general content this poetry has God, as Lord of the world that serves him, as not incarnate in the external world but withdrawn out of mundane existence into a solitary unity. What in symbolism proper was still bound into one, thus falls apart here into the two sides – the abstract independence of God and the concrete existence of the world.

    a. God himself, as this pure independence of the one substance, is necessarily without shape and, taken in this abstraction, cannot be brought nearer to our vision. What therefore imagination can grip at this stage is not what God is in his pure essentiality, since that inhibits representation by art in an appropriate shape. The sole divine topic which is left is therefore the *relation* of God to the world created by him.

    b. God is the creator of the universe. This is the purest expression of the sublime itself. For the first time, that is to say, ideas of procreation and the mere natural generation of things by God vanish and give place to the thought of *creation* by spiritual might and activity. 'God said: Let there be light; and there was light'; this Longinus[17] quoted long ago as in every way a striking example of the sublime. The Lord, the one substance, does proceed to manifestation, but the manner of creation is the purest, even bodiless, ethereal manifestation; it is the word, the manifestation of thought as the ideal power, and with its command that the existent shall be, the existent is immediately and actually brought into being in silent obedience.

    c. Yet God does not pass over, as may be supposed, into the created world as into his reality; he remains, on the contrary, withdrawn into himself, though with this opposition no fixed dualism is created. For what is brought forth is his work, which has no independence in contrast with him; on the contrary it is there only as the proof of *his* wisdom, goodness, and justice as such. The One is Lord over all, and natural things are not the presence of God but only powerless accidents which in themselves can only show him, not make him appear.[18] This constitutes the sublime so far as God is concerned.

## 2 The finite world bereft of God

Since the one God is separated in this way on the one hand from the concrete phenomena of the world and settled in his independence, while the externality of the existent is determined and disdained as the finite on the other hand, it follows that existence both natural and human now acquires the new position of being a representation of the Divine only because its finitude appears on its own surface.

    a. For the first time, therefore, nature and the human form confront us as prosaic and bereft of God. The Greeks tell us that when the heroes of the voyage of the Argonauts made ship through the narrows of the Hellespont, the rocks, which hitherto had clanged shut and then opened again like shears, suddenly stood there forever rooted to the ground.[19] This is similar to what we find in the sacred poetry of sublimity: in contrast with the infinite Being, the finite becomes fixed in its intelligible determinacy; whereas in the symbolic outlook nothing keeps its right place, since the finite collapses into the Divine, just as the Divine proceeds out of itself into finite existence.

If we turn from, e.g., the ancient Indian poems, to the Old Testament, we find ourselves at once on a totally different ground on which we can feel at home, no matter how strange and different from ours the situations, events, actions, and characters displayed there may be. Instead of a world of riot and confusion we come into situations and have figures before us which appear perfectly natural, and their firm patriarchal characters in their determinateness and truth are closely connected with us by being perfectly intelligible.

b. For this outlook which can grasp the natural course of events and assert the laws of nature, *miracle* gets its place for the first time. In India everything is miracle and therefore no longer miraculous. On a ground where an intelligible connection is continually interrupted, where everything is torn from its place and deranged, no miracle can tread. For the miraculous presupposes intelligible consequences and also the ordinary clear consciousness which alone calls a 'miracle' that interruption of this accustomed connection which is wrought by a higher power. Yet miracles in this sense are not a strictly specific expression of sublimity because the normal course of natural phenomena, as well as this interruption, is produced by the will of God and the obedience of nature.

c. The sublime in the strict sense we must look for, on the contrary, when the whole created world appears entirely as finite, restricted, not bearing or carrying itself, and for this reason can only be regarded as a glorifying accessory for the praise of God.

### 3 The human individual

At this stage the human individual seeks his own honour, consolation, and satisfaction in this recognition of the nullity of things and in the exaltation and praise of God.

a. In this connection the Psalms supply us with classic examples of genuine sublimity set forth for all time as a pattern in which what man has before himself in his religious idea of God is expressed brilliantly with the most powerful elevation of soul. Nothing in the world may lay claim to independence, for everything is and subsists only by God's might and is only there in order, in praise of this might, to serve him and to express its own unsubstantial nullity. While therefore we found in the imagination of substantiality and its pantheism an infinite *enlargement,* here we have to marvel at the force of the *elevation* of the mind which abandons everything in order to declare the exclusive power of God. In this connection Psalm 104 is of magnificent power. 'Who coverest thyself with light as with a garment; who stretchest out the heavens like a curtain' and so on. Light, heavens, clouds, the wings of the wind are here nothing in and by themselves but only an external vesture, the chariot or the messenger for the service of God. Then, further on, God's wisdom is extolled, which has put everything in order: the springs which burst forth in the depths, the waters that flow between the mountains, and the birds of heaven sitting by the waters and singing under the boughs; grass, wine which delights the heart of man, and the cedars of Lebanon which the Lord hath planted; the sea where creatures swarm, and there are whales which God hath made to play therein. – And what God has created, he also maintains, but [v. 29] 'thou hidest thy face and they are troubled; thou takest away their breath; they die and return to their dust'. The nullity of man is spoken of more expressly in Psalm 90, 'a prayer of Moses, the man of God', when it says [vv. 5–7]: 'Thou carriest men away as with a flood; they are as a sleep, even as grass which in the morning flourisheth and in the evening is cut down and withereth. This is thy wrath for our transgressions, and thine anger that we must so suddenly be carried away'.

b. Therefore, so far as man is concerned, there are bound up with sublimity at the same time the sense of man's finitude and the insurmountable aloofness of God.

($\alpha$) Therefore the idea of *immortality* does not arise originally in this sphere, for this idea involves the presupposition that the individual self, the soul, the human spirit, is something absolute. In sublimity, only the One is imperishable, and in contrast with him everything else is regarded as arising and perishing, but not as free and infinite in itself.

($\beta$) Therefore, further, man views himself in his *unworthiness* before God; his exaltation consists in fear of the Lord, in trembling before his wrath, and we find depicted in a penetrating and affecting way grief over nullity, and the cry of the soul to God in complaint, suffering, and lament from the depths of the heart.

($\gamma$) Whereas if the individual in his finitude holds to himself firmly over against God, then this willed and intended finitude becomes *wickedness,* which, as evil and sin, belongs only to the natural and human, but, like grief and the negative in general, can find no sort of place in the one inherently undifferentiated substance.

c. Yet, thirdly, within this nullity man nevertheless gains a freer and more independent position. For on the one hand, along with the substantial peace and constancy of God in respect of his will and its commands for men, there arises the *law;* on the other hand, in man's exaltation there lies at the same time the complete and clear distinction between the human and the Divine, the finite and the Absolute, and thereby the judgement of good and evil, and the decision for one or the other, is transferred to the subject himself. Relationship to the Absolute and the adequacy or inadequacy of man thereto has therefore also an aspect accruing to the individual and his own behaviour and action. Thereby in his righteousness and adherence to the law he finds at the same time an *affirmative* relation to God, and has in general to connect the external positive or negative situation of his existence – prosperity, pleasure, satisfaction, or grief, misfortune, oppression – with his inner obedience to or stubbornness against the law, and therein accept well-being and reward or trial and punishment.

## Questions

1. What does Hegel think the sublime has to do with the "finite" and "infinite" (substance, Being)? Why is the sublime associated with the developmental stage he calls "symbolic" art?
2. Explain the concept of God in his theory.
3. To what extent is Hegel's theory an *aesthetic* one? What should be the role of feeling or subjective states in aesthetics?
4. Summarize and evaluate Hegel's discussion of poetry and the sublime.
5. Should we consider the sublime to be a type of beauty? Explain.

## Further reading

Desmond, William. *Art and the Absolute: A Study of Hegel's Aesthetics*. Albany: State University of New York Press, 1986.

Guyer, Paul. "The Post-Kantian German Sublime." In *The Sublime: From Antiquity to the Present*, ed. Timothy M. Costelloe, 102–17, esp. 109–12. Cambridge: Cambridge University Press, 2012.

Hegel, Georg Wilhelm Friedrich. *The Philosophy of Fine Art*, trans. Francis Plumtre Beresford Osmaston, vol. 2, esp. 87–88. New York: Hacker Art Books, 1975.

Kirwan, James. *Sublimity: The Non-Rational and the Irrational in the History of Aesthetics*. London: Routledge, 2005.

Pillow, Kirk. *Sublime Understanding: Aesthetic Reflection in Kant and Hegel*. Cambridge, MA: MIT Press, 2000.

# CHAPTER 24
## RICHARD WAGNER, FROM "BEETHOVEN" (1870)

German composer, author, and artist Richard Wagner (1813–1883) published this essay in 1870, to commemorate the centenary of the birth of Ludwig van Beethoven on December 17, 1770. Wagner calls Beethoven "the true archetype of the Musician."

Like Schopenhauer, whom he first read in the mid-1850s, Wagner adopts a version of the Kantian claim that space and time are a priori forms of intuition. Wagner also accepts the distinction between the thing in itself and appearances, that is, between the noumenal and the phenomenal. Through space and time, we experience the phenomenal world ("appearances") in a lawful manner. Yet this does not imply that the noumenal world is completely inaccessible: music can show the world as it is itself—including its conflict, striving, or drama. According to what he calls his "philosophy of music," the "Idea of the whole World" reveals itself in music. Music is the "revelation of the inner vision of the Essence of the world." Meanwhile, the musician feels a kind of insightful, inspired "ecstasy."

The category most fitting for music, Wagner thinks, is not the beautiful—a theme taken up by Eduard Hanslick in his 1854 book, *On the Musically Beautiful*—but the sublime. Music can "be judged by nothing but the category of the *sublime*." Thus, it is not surprising that music composed by Wagner is frequently cited as an example of the musical sublime. (In the following, the translator's footnotes draw connections to some of Wagner's operas.) Wagner thinks Beethoven's orchestral music, too, is to be associated with the "sublime," since it is freed from the "hampering of traditional or conventional forms." Beethoven makes use of these forms in innovative and inspired ways that are characteristic of his "genius," revealing the "inner meaning" of the conventional musical forms. In addition, Wagner develops an original theory of the perfect art-form. Traces of his idea of the total work of art or collective artwork (*Gesamtkunstwerk*) can be discerned at the end of this excerpt.

Wagner's conception of the sublime thus reflects a kind of optimism for the future, though one based on the past (such as Greek art and Beethoven). At one point in this essay, Wagner writes, "Who could have the presumption to say he was able to form a true idea of the grandeur, the divine sublimity of the Plastic world of ancient Greece? Each glance at a single fragment of its ruins makes us feel with awe that we here are standing in presence of a Life for whose judgment we have not even the first beginning of a scale. That world had earned the right to teach us by its very ruins how the remainder of man's earthly life might yet be fashioned into something bearable." As an artist, composer, and writer, Wagner attempted to contribute to this fashioning.

To understand Wagner's remarks on "ecstasy," the words of a contemporary film and opera director, Werner Herzog, may be helpful. In one of his essays, Herzog examines "ecstatic" truth and the sublime: he claims that his film *Fitzcarraldo* is "about an opera being staged in the rainforest." In the film, native peoples believe that ordinary life is an illusion behind which lies the reality of dreams. Herzog comments: "As I did [produce opera], one maxim was crucial for me: an entire world must undergo a transformation into music, must *become* music; only then would we have produced opera." Feelings in opera, Herzog says, are like axioms in mathematics, and cannot be explained any further. "The axioms of feeling in the opera lead us . . . in the most secret ways, on a direct path to the sublime. . . . Its [opera's] sublimity has allowed opera to survive."[1] It is hard to resist the thought that these ideas were inspired by Wagner.

## Note on the text

Source: Excerpted from Richard Wagner, "Beethoven," in *Richard Wagner's Prose Works*, translated by William Ashton Ellis, 8 vols., vol. 5, 59–126. London: Kegan Paul, Trench, Trübner, & Co., 1896. A German version can be found in Richard Wagner, "Beethoven," in *Sämtliche Schriften und Dichtungen*, 12 vols., vol. 9, 61–126. Leipzig: Breitkopf and Härtel, 1912 [sixth edition].

First publication: Richard Wagner, *Beethoven*. Leipzig: E. W. Fritzsch, 1870 [73 pages].

Several of the translator's notes have been removed. Whether notes have been written by the volume editor, the translator, or by Wagner, is clarified within the notes. Notes have occasionally been modified. Square brackets with " – Ed." indicate insertions by the present volume editor. The translator occasionally used round brackets to indicate the German word used by Wagner; some of these have been silently omitted. Page numbers of the translation are given in square brackets, for instance, "[62]". Spelling, style, and format of the translation have been reproduced, with occasional modifications. Some of the German titles have been translated into English.

## "Beethoven"

### Preface

[59] As the author of the accompanying work felt a longing to contribute his quota to the celebration of the hundredth birthday of our great BEETHOVEN, and as no other opportunity worthy of that event was offered him, he has chosen a literary exposition of his thoughts, such as they are, on the import of Beethoven's music. The form of treatment came to him through the fiction that he had been called to deliver a speech at an ideal feast in honour of the great musician; as that speech, however, was not to be delivered in reality, he might give it the advantage of a greater compass than would have been permissible in the case of an address to an actual audience. Hereby it became possible for him to conduct the reader through a more searching inquiry into the nature of Music, and thus to submit to the consideration of men of serious culture a contribution to the Philosophy of Music; as which the following treatise may be regarded on the one hand, whilst the fiction that it is being read to a German audience upon a given day of this so uncommonly significant year, on the other, made natural a warm allusion to the stirring events of the time. [...]

### Beethoven

[...] [65] But it was *Schopenhauer* who first defined the position of Music among the fine arts with philosophic clearness, ascribing to it a totally different nature from that of either plastic or poetic art. He starts from wonder at Music's speaking a language immediately intelligible by everyone, since it needs no whit of intermediation through abstract concepts (*Begriffe*); which completely distinguishes it from Poetry, in the first place, whose sole material consists of concepts, employed by it to visualise [*Veranschaulichung* – Ed.] the *Idea*. For according to this philosopher's so luminous definition it is the Ideas of the world and of its essential phenomena, in the sense of Plato, that constitute the 'object' of the fine arts; whereas, however, the Poet interprets these Ideas to the visual consciousness (*dem anschauenden Bewusstsein*) through an employment of strictly rationalistic concepts in a manner quite peculiar to his art, Schopenhauer believes he must recognise *in Music itself an*

*Idea of the world*, since he who could entirely translate it into abstract concepts would have found withal a philosophy to explain the world itself. [66] Though Schopenhauer propounds this theory of Music as a paradox, since it cannot strictly be set forth in logical terms, he also furnishes us with the only serviceable material for a further demonstration of the justice of his profound hypothesis; a demonstration which he himself did not pursue more closely, perhaps for simple reason that as layman he was not conversant enough with music, and moreover was unable to base his knowledge thereof sufficiently definitely on an understanding of the very musician whose works have first laid open to the world that deepest mystery of Music; for *Beethoven*, of all others, is not to be judged exhaustively until that pregnant paradox of Schopenhauer's has been solved and made right clear to philosophic apprehension.—

In making use of this material supplied us by the philosopher I fancy I shall do best to begin with a remark in which Schopenhauer declines to accept the Idea derived from a knowledge of "relations" as the essence of the Thing-in-itself, but regards it merely as expressing the objective character of things, and therefore as still concerned with their phenomenal appearance. "And we should not understand this character itself"—so Schopenhauer goes on to say—"were not the inner essence of things confessed to us elsewhere, dimly at least and in our Feeling. For that essence cannot be gathered from the Ideas, nor understood through any mere *objective* knowledge; wherefore it would ever remain a mystery, had we not access to it from quite another side. Only inasmuch as every observer (*Erkenner*) is an Individual withal, and thereby part of Nature, stands there open to him in his own self-consciousness the adit [i.e., access – Ed.] to Nature's innermost; and there forthwith, and most immediately, it makes itself known to him as *Will*."[2]

If we couple with this what Schopenhauer postulates as the condition for entry of an Idea into our consciousness, namely "a temporary preponderance of intellect over will, or to put it physiologically, a strong excitation of the [67] sensory faculty of the brain (*der anschauenden Gehirnthätigkeit*) without the smallest excitation of the passions or desires," we have only further to pay close heed to the elucidation which directly follows it, namely that our consciousness has two sides: in part it is a consciousness of *one's own self* which is the will; in part a consciousness of *other things*, and chiefly then a *visual* [intuitive – Ed.] knowledge of the outer world, the apprehension of objects. "The more the one side of the aggregate consciousness comes to the front, the more does the other retreat."[3]

After well weighing these extracts from Schopenhauer's principal work it must be obvious to us that musical conception, as it has nothing in common with the seizure of an Idea (for the latter is absolutely bound to physical perception of the world), can have its origin nowhere but upon that side of consciousness which Schopenhauer defines as facing inwards. Though this side may temporarily retire completely, to make way for entry of the purely apprehending 'subject' on its function (i.e. the seizure of Ideas), on the other hand it transpires that only from this inward-facing side of consciousness can the intellect derive its ability to seize the Character of things. If this consciousness, however, is the consciousness of one's own self, i.e. of the Will, we must take it that its repression is indispensable indeed for purity of the outward-facing consciousness, but that the nature of the Thing-in-itself—inconceivable by that physical [or intuitive – Ed.] mode of knowledge—would only be revealed to this inward-facing consciousness when it had attained the faculty of seeing within as clearly as that other side of consciousness is able in its seizure of Ideas to see without.

For a further pursuit of this path Schopenhauer has also given us the best of guides, through his profound hypothesis[4] concerning the physiologic phenomenon of Clairvoyance, [68] and the Dream-theory he has based thereon. For as in that phenomenon the inward-facing consciousness attains the actual power of sight where our waking daylight consciousness feels nothing but a vague impression of the midnight background of our will's emotions, so from out this night *Tone* bursts upon the world of waking, a direct utterance of the Will. [...]

[69] [L]et us first recall our philosopher's profound remark adduced above, that we should never understand even the Ideas that by their very nature are only seizable through will-freed, i.e. objective contemplation, had we not another approach to the Essence-of-things which lies beneath them, namely our direct consciousness of our own self. By this consciousness alone are we enabled to understand withal the inner nature of things outside us, inasmuch as we recognise in them the selfsame basic essence that our self-consciousness declares to be our very own. Our each illusion hereanent [i.e., concerning this – Ed.] had sprung from the mere *sight* of a world around us, a world that in the show of daylight we took for something [70] quite apart from us[5] first through (intellectual) perception of the Ideas, and thus upon a circuitous path, do we reach an initial stage of undeception, in which we no longer see things parcelled off in time and space, but apprehend their generic character; and this character speaks out the plainest to us from the works of Plastic art, whose true province it therefore is to take the illusive surface (*Schein*) of the light-shown world and, in virtue of a most ingenious playing with that semblance, lay bare the Idea concealed beneath. In daily life the mere sight of an object leaves us cold and unconcerned, and only when we become aware of that object's bearings on our will, does it call forth an emotion; in harmony wherewith it very properly ranks as the first aesthetic principle of Plastic art, that its imagings shall entirely avoid such references to our individual will, and prepare for our sight that calm which alone makes possible a pure Beholding of the object according to its own character. Yet the effector of this aesthetic, will-freed contemplation, into which we momentarily plunge, here remains nothing but the *show* of things. And it is this principle of tranquillisation by sheer pleasure in the semblance, that has been extended from Plastic art to all the arts, and made a postulate for every manner of aesthetic pleasing. Whence, too, has come our term for *beauty* (*Schönheit*); the root of which word in our German language is plainly connected with Show (*Schein*) as object, with Seeing (*Schauen*) as subject.—

But that consciousness which alone enabled us to grasp the Idea transmitted by the Show we looked on, must feel compelled at last to cry with Faust: "A spectacle superb! But still, alas! a spectacle. Where seize I thee, o Nature infinite?"

This cry is answered in the most positive manner by *Music*. Here the world outside us speaks to us in terms intelligible beyond compare, since its sounding message to our ear is of the selfsame nature as the cry sent forth to it [71] from the depths of our own inner heart. The Object of the tone perceived is brought into immediate rapport with the Subject of the tone emitted: without any reasoning go-between we understand the cry for help, the wail, the shout of joy, and straightway answer it in its own tongue. If the scream, the moan, the murmured happiness in our own mouth is the most direct utterance of the will's emotion, so when brought us by our ear we understand it past denial as utterance of the same emotion; no illusion is possible here, as in the daylight Show, to make us deem the essence of the world outside us not wholly identical with our own; and thus that gulf which seems to sight is closed forthwith.

Now if we see an art arise from this immediate consciousness of the oneness of our inner essence with that of the outer world, our most obvious inference is that this art must be subject to aesthetic laws quite distinct from those of every other. All aesthetes hitherto have rebelled against the notion of deducing a veritable art from what appears to them a purely pathologic element, and have consequently refused to Music any recognition until its products show themselves in a light as cold as that peculiar to the fashionings of plastic art. Yet that its very rudiment (*ihr blosses Element*) is felt, not seen, by our deepest consciousness as a world's Idea, we have learned to recognise forthwith through Schopenhauer's eventful aid, and we understand that Idea as a direct revelation of the oneness of the Will; starting with the oneness of all human being, our consciousness is thereby shown beyond dispute our unity with Nature, whom equally we recognise through Sound.[6]

Difficult as is the task of eliciting Music's nature as an art, we believe we may best accomplish it by considering the inspired musician's modus operandi. In many respects this must radically differ from that of other artists. As to the latter we have had to acknowledge that it must be preceded by a will-freed, pure beholding of the object, an act [72] of like nature with the effect to be produced by the artwork itself in the mind of the spectator. Such an object, however, to be raised to an Idea by means of pure Beholding, does not present itself to the musician at all; for his music is itself a world's-Idea, an Idea in which the world immediately displays its essence, whereas in those other arts this essence has to pass through the medium of the understanding (*das Erkenntniss*) before it can *become* displayed. We can but take it that the *individual will*, silenced in the plastic artist through pure beholding, awakes in the musician as the *universal Will*, and—above and beyond all power of vision—now recognises itself as such in full self-consciousness. Hence the great difference in the mental state of the concipient musician and the designing artist; hence the radically diverse effects of music and of painting: here profoundest stilling, there utmost excitation of the will. In other words we here have the will in the Individual as such, the will imprisoned by the fancy (*Wahn*) of its difference from the essence of things outside, and unable to lift itself above its barriers save in the purely disinterested beholding of objects; whilst there, in the musician's case, the will feels *one* forthwith, above all bounds of individuality: for Hearing has opened it the gate through which the world thrusts home to it, it to the world. This prodigious breaking-down the floodgates of Appearance must necessarily call forth in the inspired musician a state of ecstasy wherewith no other can compare: in it the will perceives itself the almighty Will of all things: it has not mutely to yield place to contemplation, but proclaims itself aloud as conscious World-Idea. One state surpasses his, and one alone,—the Saint's, and chiefly through its permanence and imperturbability; whereas the clairvoyant ecstasy of the musician has to alternate with a perpetually recurrent state of individual consciousness, which we must account the more distressful the higher has his inspiration carried him above all bounds of individuality. And this suffering again, allotted him as penalty for the state of inspiration in which he so unutterably entrances us, might [73] make us hold the musician in higher reverence than other artists, ay, well-nigh give him claim to rank as holy. For his art, in truth, compares with the communion of all the other arts as *Religion* with the *Church*.

We have seen that in the other arts the Will is longing to become pure Knowledge, but that this is possible only in so far as it stays stock-still in its deepest inner chamber: it is as if it were awaiting tidings of redemption from there outside; content they it not, it sets itself in that state of clairvoyance; and here, beyond the bounds of time and space, it knows itself the world's both One and All. What it here has seen, no tongue can impart[7] as the dream of deepest sleep can only be conveyed to the waking consciousness through translation into the language of a second, an allegoric dream which immediately precedes our wakening, so for the direct vision of its self the Will creates a second organ of transmission,—an organ whose one side faces toward that inner vision, whilst the other thrusts into the reappearing outer world with the sole direct and sympathetic message, that of Tone. The Will cries out; and in the countercry it knows itself once more: thus cry and countercry become for it a comforting, at last an entrancing play with its own self.

Sleepless one night in Venice, I stepped upon the balcony of my window overlooking the Grand Canal: like a deep dream the fairy city of lagoons lay stretched in shade before me. From out the breathless silence rose the strident cry of a gondolier just woken on his barque; again and again his voice went forth into the night, till from remotest distance its fellow-cry came answering down the midnight length of the Canal: I recognised the drear melodic phrase to which the well-known lines of Tasso were also wedded in his day, but which in itself is certainly as old as Venice's canals and people. After many a solemn pause the ringing dialogue took quicker life, and seemed [74] at last to melt in unison; till finally the sounds from far and near died softly back to new-won slumber. Whatever could sun-steeped, colour-swarming Venice of the daylight tell me of itself, that that sounding dream of night had not brought infinitely deeper, closer, to my consciousness?—Another time I wandered through the lofty solitude of an upland vale in Uri. In broad daylight from a hanging pasture-land came shouting the shrill yodel of a cowherd, sent forth across the broadening valley; from the other side anon there answered it, athwart the monstrous silence, a like exultant herd-call: the echo of the towering mountain walls here mingled in; the brooding valley leapt into the merry lists of sound.—So wakes the child from the night of the mother-womb, and answer it the mother's crooning kisses; so understands the yearning youth the woodbird's mate-call, so speaks to the musing man the moan of beasts, the whistling wind, the howling hurricane, till over him there comes that dreamlike state in which the ear reveals to him the inmost essence of all his eye had held suspended in the cheat of scattered show, and tells him that his inmost being is one therewith, that only in *this* wise can the Essence of things without be learned in truth.

The dreamlike nature of the state into which we thus are plunged through sympathetic hearing—and wherein there dawns on us that other world, that world from whence the musician speaks to us—we recognise at once from an experience at the door of every man: namely that our eyesight is paralysed to such a degree by the effect of music upon us, that with eyes wide open we no longer intensively see. We experience this in every concert-room while listening to any tone-piece that really touches us, where the most hideous and distracting things are passing before our eye, things that assuredly would quite divert us from the music, and even move us to laughter, if we actively saw them; I mean, besides the highly trivial aspect of the audience itself, the mechanical movements of the band, the whole peculiar working [75] apparatus of an orchestral production. That this spectacle—which preoccupies the man untouched by the music—at last ceases to disturb the spellbound listener, plainly shows us that we no longer are really conscious of it, but, for all our open eyes, have fallen into a state essentially akin to that of hypnotic clairvoyance. And in truth it is in this state alone that we immediately belong to the musician's world. From out that world, which nothing else can picture, the musician casts the meshwork of his tones to net us, so to speak; or, with his wonder-drops of sound he dews our brain as if by magic, and robs it of the power of seeing aught save our own inner world.

[…]

[76] [W]e first must dwell on a crucial point in the aesthetic judgment (*Urtheil*) of Music as an art. For we find that from the forms wherein Music seems to join hands [77] with the outer world of Appearance there has been deduced an utterly preposterous demand upon the character of her utterances. As already mentioned, axioms founded simply on a scrutiny of Plastic art have been transferred to Music. That such a solecism could have been committed, we have at any rate to attribute to the aforesaid "nearest approach" of Music to the visual side of the world and its phenomena. In this direction indeed the art of Music has taken a development which has exposed her to so great a misapprehension of her veritable character that folk have claimed from her a function similar to that of plastic works of art, namely the susciting of our *pleasure in beautiful forms*. As this was synchronous with a progressive decline in the judgment of plastic art itself, it may easily be imagined how deeply Music was thus degraded; at bottom, she was asked to wholly repress her ownest nature for mere sake of turning her outmost side to our delectation.

Music, who speaks to us solely through quickening into articulate life the most universal concept of the inherently speechless Feeling, in all imaginable gradations, can once and for all be judged by nothing but the category of the *sublime*; for, as soon as she engrosses us, she transports us to the highest ecstasy of consciousness of our infinitude. [78] On the other hand what enters only *as a sequel* to our plunging into contemplation of a work of plastic art, namely the (temporary) liberation of the intellect from service to the individual will through our discarding all relations of the object contemplated to that will—the required effect of *beauty* on the mind,—is brought about by Music at her very *first entry*; inasmuch as she withdraws us at once from any concern with the relation of things outside us, and—as pure Form set free from Matter—shuts us off from the outer world, as it were, to let us gaze into the inmost Essence of ourselves and all things. Consequently our verdict on any piece of music should be based upon a knowledge of those laws whereby the effect of Beauty, the very first effect of Music's mere appearance, advances the most directly to a revelation of her truest character through the agency of the Sublime. It would be the stamp of an absolutely empty piece of music, on the contrary, that it never got beyond a mere prismatic toying with the effect of its first entry, and consequently kept us bound to the relations presented by Music's outermost side to the world of vision.

Upon this side alone, indeed, has Music been given any lasting development; and that by a systematising of her rhythmic structure (*Periodenbau*) which on the one hand has brought her into comparison with Architecture, on the other has made her so much a matter of superficies (*ihr eine Überschaulichkeit gegeben hat*) as to expose her to the said false judgment by analogy with Plastic art. Here, in her outermost restriction to banal forms and conventions, she seemed, e.g., to Goethe so admirably suited for a standard of poetical proportion (*zur Normirung dichterischer Konzeptionen*). To be able in these conventional forms so to toy with Music's stupendous powers that her own peculiar function, the making known the inner essence of all things, should be avoided like a deluge, for long was deemed by aesthetes the true and only acceptable issue of maturing the art of Tone. But to have pierced through these forms to the innermost essence of Music in such a [79] way that from that inner side he could cast the light of the Clairvoyant on the outer world, and show us these forms themselves again in nothing but their inner meaning,—this was the work of our great *Beethoven*, whom we therefore have to regard as the true archetype of the Musician.—

[…]

Let us turn from this to a piece of dance-music, to an orchestral symphonic movement modelled on the dance-motive, or finally to a downright operatic *pièce*: we find [80] our fancy chained forthwith by a regular order in the recurrence of rhythmic periods, the *plastic* element that forms the chief factor in Melody's insistence. Music developed along these lines has very properly been given the name of "secular," in opposition to that "spiritual." Elsewhere I have expressed myself plainly enough upon the principle of this development,[8] and here will merely touch upon its already-noted aspect of the allegoric dream; whence it would seem that the musician's "eye," now woken to the phenomena of the outer world, attaches itself to such of them whose inner essence it can understand forthwith. The outer laws which he thus derives from the gestures of life, and finally from its every element of motion, become the laws of Rhythm in virtue whereof he constructs his periods of contrast and return. The more these periods are instinct with the true spirit of Music, the less will they be architectonic emblems diverting our attention from the music's pure effect. On the contrary, wherever that aforesaid inner Spirit of Music—sufficiently described above— tones down its surest manifestation for sake of this columnar ordering of rhythmic parts, there nothing will arrest us but that outward symmetry, and we shall necessarily reduce our claims on Music herself to a prime demand for regularity.—Music here quits her state of lofty innocence; she loses her power of redeeming from the curse of Appearance: no longer is she the prophetess of the Essence of things, but herself becomes entangled in the illusive show of things outside us. For to *this* music one wants to *see* something as well, and that something to-be-seen becomes the chief concern: as "Opera" proves right plainly, where spectacle, ballet and so forth make out the [81] lure, the main attraction, and visibly enough proclaim the degeneracy of the music there employed.

————

We will now illustrate the above by an inquiry into the *evolution of Beethoven's genius*; and here, to abandon generalities, we have first to consider the practical maturing of the master's own peculiar style. […]

[93] Never has any art in the world created aught so radiant (*etwas so Heiteres*) as these Symphonies in A [seventh symphony – Ed.] and F [eighth symphony – Ed.], with all their so closely allied tone-works from this godlike period of the master's total deafness. The effect upon the hearer is precisely that deliverance from all earthly guilt, as the after-effect is the feeling of a forfeited paradise wherewith we return to the world of semblances. Thus do these glorious works preach penitence and a contrite heart with all the depth of a divine revelation.

Here the only aesthetic term to use, is the *Sublime*: for here the operation of the Radiant at once transcends all pleasure in the Beautiful, and leaves it far behind. Each challenge of self-vaunting Reason is hushed forthwith by the Magic mastering our whole nature; knowledge pleads confession of its error,[9] and the transport of that avowal bids our deepest soul to shout for joy, however earnestly the spellbound features of the listener betray his marvel at the impotence of all our seeing and our thinking to plumb this truest of all worlds. [...]

[100] [W]e undoubtedly [101] should make a grave mistake if we thought the Artist could ever conceive save in a state of profound cheerfulness of soul. The mood expressed in the conception must therefore belong to that world's-Idea itself which the artist seizes and interprets in his artwork. But, as we have taken for granted that in Music the Idea of the whole World reveals itself, the inspired musician must necessarily be included in that Idea, and what he utters is therefore not his personal opinion of the world, but the World itself with all its changing moods of grief and joy, of weal and woe. The conscious doubt of *Beethoven the man* was included in this World, as well; and thus his doubt is speaking for itself, in nowise as an object of his reflection, when he brings the world to such expression as in his Ninth Symphony, for instance, whose first movement certainly shows us the Idea of the world in its most terrible of lights. Elsewhere, however, this very work affords us unmistakable evidence of the purposely ordaining will of its creator; we are brought face to face with it when he stops the frenzy of despair that overwhelms each fresh appeasement, and, with the anguished cry of one awaking from a nightmare, he speaks that actual Word whose ideal sense is none other than: "Man, despite all, *is* good!" [...]

[102] Surveying the historical advance which the art of Music made through Beethoven, we may define it as the winning [103] of a faculty withheld from her before: in virtue of that acquisition she mounted far beyond the region of the aesthetically Beautiful, into the sphere of the absolutely Sublime; and here she is freed from all the hampering of traditional or conventional forms, through her filling their every nook and cranny with the life of her ownest spirit. And to the heart of every human being this gain reveals itself at once through the character conferred by Beethoven on music's chiefest Form, on *Melody*, which has now rewon the utmost natural simplicity, the fount whereat in every age, for every need, it may renew itself and thrive to richest, amplest multiplicity. And this we may sum in a single term, intelligible to everyone: Melody has been emancipated by Beethoven from all influence of the Mode, of shifting taste, and raised to an eternal purely-human type. Beethoven's music will be understood throughout all time, whereas the music of his predecessors will for the most part stay un-understandable save by aid of art-historical Reflection.—

But, on the path whereon Beethoven arrived at this memorable ennoblement of Melody, there is yet another advance to note: to wit, the new meaning gained by *Vocal music* in its relation to purely Instrumental music. [...]

[104] Moreover the experience that a piece of music loses nothing of its character even when the most diverse texts are laid beneath it, shows the relation of Music to *Poetry* to be a sheer illusion: for it transpires that in vocal music it is not the poetic thought one seizes—which in choral singing, in particular, one does not even get intelligibly articulated—but at most the mood that thought aroused in the musician when it moved him to music. The union of Music and Poetry must therefore always end in such a subordination of the latter that we can only wonder above all at our great German poets returning again and again to the problem, to say nothing of the attempt. They evidently were instigated by the effect of music in *Opera*: and here, at any rate, appeared to lie the only field whereon the problem might be solved at last. Now, whether our poets' hopes were directed more to music's formal symmetry of structure, or more to its profoundly stirring effect on the feelings, they obviously could have only proposed to use the mighty aids it seemed to offer to give their poetic aim alike a more precise expression and a [105] more searching operation. They may have thought that Music would gladly render them this service if, in lieu of the trivial operatic subject and opera-text, they brought her a poetic conception to be taken seriously. What continually held them back from serious attempts in this

direction may have been a vague, but legitimate doubt whether Poetry would be noticed at all, as such, in its co-operation with Music. Upon careful consideration it cannot have escaped them that in Opera, beyond the music, only the scenic goings-on, but not the explanatory poetic thought, engrossed attention; that Opera, in fact, merely arrested *hearing* and *sight* in turn. That a perfect aesthetic satisfaction was not to be gained for either the one receptive faculty or the other, is fully accounted for by the circumstance noted above, namely that opera-music did not attune us to that devotional state (*Andacht*)—the only one in keeping with Music— in which vision is so far reduced in power that the eye no longer sees objects with the wonted intensity; on the contrary, as found before, we here were but superficially affected, more excited than filled by the music, and consequently desired to *see* something too,—by no means to *think*, however, for our whole faculty of thought was stolen from us by just that shuttlecock desire for entertainment, thrown hither and thither in its distracting battle with tedium.

[...]

[106] But the feeling that here occurs to everyone can only be made a matter of clear knowledge by our returning to the philosopher's explanation of Music itself.

Seeing that Music does not portray the Ideas inherent in the world's phenomena, but is itself an Idea of the World, and a comprehensive one, it naturally includes the Drama in itself; as Drama, again, expresses the only world's-Idea proportionate (*adäquat*) to Music. Drama towers above the bounds of Poetry in exactly the same manner as Music above those of every other art, and especially of plastic art, through its effect residing solely in the Sublime. As a drama does not depict human characters, but lets them display their immediate selves, so a piece of music gives us in its motive. The character of all the world's appearances according to their inmost essence (*An-sich*). Not only are the movement, interchange and evolution of these motives analogous to nothing but the Drama, but a drama representing the Idea can be understood with perfect clearness through nothing but those moving, evolving and alternating motives of Music's. We consequently should not go far astray, if we defined Music as man's qualification *a priori* for fashioning the Drama. Just as we construct for ourselves the world of semblances through application of the laws of Time and Space existing *a priori* in our brain, so this conscious representment of the world's Idea in Drama would thus be foreordained by those inner laws of Music, operating in the dramatist equally unconsciously [107] with the laws of Causality we bring into employment for apperception of the phenomenal world. [...]

[108] We have called Music the revelation of the inner vision of the Essence of the world, and Shakespeare we might term a Beethoven who goes on dreaming though awake. What holds their spheres asunder, are the formal conditions of the laws of apperception obtaining in each. The perfect art-form would therefore have to take its rise from the point where those respective laws could meet. [...]

[111] This awaking out of deepest Want we witness in that redoubtable leap from instrumental into vocal music—so offensive to ordinary aesthetic criticism—which has led us from our discussion of Beethoven's Ninth Symphony to [112] the above prolonged digression. What we here experience is a certain overcharge, a vast compulsion to unload without, only to be compared with the stress to waken from an agonising dream; and the important issue for the Art-genius of mankind, is that this special stress called forth an artistic deed whereby that genius gained a novel power, the qualification for begetting the highest Artwork.

As to that Artwork itself; we can only conclude that it will be *the most perfect Drama*, and thus stand high above the work of Poetry. This we may conclude after having recognised the identity of the Shakespearian and the Beethovenian Drama, whilst we may assume, on the other hand, that it will bear the same relation to "Opera" as a play of Shakespeare's to a literature-drama, a Beethovenian symphony to an opera's music.

That Beethoven returns in the course of his Ninth Symphony to the 'choral cantata with orchestra,' must not mislead our judgment of that eventful leap from instrumental into vocal music; we have already gauged the import of this choral portion of the symphony, and found it pertaining to the strictest field of Music: beyond that said ennoblement of Melody, we have in it no formal innovation; it is a Cantata with words, to which the music bears no closer relation than to any other vocal text. For we know that it is not the verses of a text-writer, and were he a Goethe or Schiller, that can determine Music. *Drama* alone can do that; and not the dramatic poem, but the drama that moves before our very eyes, the visible counterpart of Music, where word and speech belong no more to the poet's thought, but solely to the action.

It is not the *work* of Beethoven, then, but the unparalleled artistic *deed* contained therein, that we must stamp on our minds as climax of the musician's genius, when we declare that an artwork founded and modelled throughout on this deed must afford withal the perfect *art-form*: that form wherein, for Drama as for Music in especial, each vestige of conventionality would be entirely upheaved. And this Form would also be the only one to thoroughly [113] fit the German Spirit, so powerfully individualised in our great Beethoven: the new, the Purely-human art-form made by it, and yet originally immanent in it; the form for which, when likened with the antique world, the new still goes a-lacking. [...]¹⁰

## Questions

1. In your opinion, can music be sublime? What kind of music? Explain.

2. Compare and contrast Wagner's theory of the musical sublime with the theories of the sublime offered by Schiller, Schopenhauer (§39), and/or Nietzsche (*The Birth of Tragedy*).

3. Explain what Wagner means by "drama" and the perfect "art-form." How does drama add to the latter?

4. What are the metaphysical commitments of Wagner's theory of the sublime art? Do they make his theory weaker or stronger, in your view? Explain.

## Further reading

Hanslick, Eduard. *On the Musically Beautiful*. Indianapolis: Hackett, 1986 [1854].

Seidl, Arthur. *Vom Musikalisch-Erhabenen. Prolegomena zur Aesthetik der Tonkunst* [On the Musically Sublime. Prolegomena to an Aesthetics of Music]. Regensburg: Wasner, 1887.

Wurth, Kiene Brillenburg. *Musically Sublime: Indeterminacy, Infinity, Irresolvability*. New York: Fordham University Press, 2012.

Young, Julian. "Richard Wagner and the Birth of *The Birth of Tragedy*." *International Journal of Philosophical Studies* 16, no. 2 (2008): 217–45.

Zöller, Günter. "The Musically Sublime. Richard Wagner's Post-Kantian Philosophy of Modern Music." In *Das Leben der Vernunft. Beiträge zur Philosophie Immanuel Kants,* ed. Dieter Hüning, Stefan Klingne, and Carsten Olk, 635–60. Berlin and Boston: Walter de Gruyter, 2013.

# CHAPTER 25
## FRIEDRICH NIETZSCHE, FROM *THE BIRTH OF TRAGEDY* (1872), *JOYFUL WISDOM* (1882), AND *THUS SPOKE ZARATHUSTRA* (1883–85)

Although Nietzsche (1844–1900) never offered a systematic theory of the sublime, versions of the sublime can be located in several places. For instance, it can be seen in *The Birth of Tragedy*'s remarks on ecstatic intoxication, feeling of primordial unity, and oneness with a larger whole. It can also be found in three *Joyful Wisdom* sections (124, 125, 343) on the "death of God," and finally, in section 35 of the second Part of *Thus Spoke Zarathustra*, called "The Sublime Ones." These passages are excerpted here.

It should also be mentioned that Nietzsche's use of the term *Sublimierung* (sublimation) in writings such as *Beyond Good and Evil* (1886) influenced the Freudian and psychoanalytic concept of sublimation, that is, the redirection of internal impulses and drives. (See also Julia Kristeva's contribution to this volume.) But whether or not such sublimation still counts as a version of the "sublime" is for readers to decide.

### Notes on the texts

Source: Excerpted from Friedrich Nietzsche, *The Birth of Tragedy: Out of the Spirit of Music*, translated by Ian Johnston, 2017, excerpted by permission of the translator. Endnotes clarifying terms or references were composed by Johnston.

Source: Excerpted from Friedrich Nietzsche, *Joyful Wisdom*, translated by Thomas Common, in *The Complete Works of Friedrich Nietzsche*, edited Oscar Levy, 18 vols., vol. 10, 167–69, 275–76. T.N. Foulis: Edinburgh and London, 1910. Archaic language (e.g., "thee, wilt") in *Joyful Wisdom* has been modernized and the punctuation and spelling (e.g., "to-day") have occasionally been modified and updated. The ellipsis "…" is placed by Nietzsche.

Source: Excerpted from Friedrich Nietzsche, *Thus Spake Zarathustra. A Book for All and None*, translated by Thomas Common, in *The Complete Works of Friedrich Nietzsche*, edited Oscar Levy, 18 vols., vol. 11, [Part II, Section 35] 138–41. T.N. Foulis: Edinburgh and London, 1911. Archaic language has been modernized.

### The Birth of Tragedy

*The Birth of Tragedy* (1872) makes claims in what is now called "aesthetics" yet at the same time is an original contribution to the field of classical philology, contextualizing tragedy and art historically while endorsing a therapeutic use of art. Nietzsche's *The Birth of Tragedy* contains twenty-five sections and a Preface to composer-author Richard Wagner, with whom Nietzsche once had a friendship but later broke. (For Wagner's ideas on sublimity in music, see his contribution to this volume.) *The Birth of Tragedy* analyzes the combination of the "Apollonian" and "Dionysian" in Greek (Attic) tragedy in the fifth century BCE. (In Greek mythology, Dionysus, son of Zeus and the mortal Semele, was the god of wine, associated with ecstatic and intoxicated group rituals.) Nietzsche examines the works of tragedians (such as Sophocles) who wrote before tragedy's "death-struggle" and the rise of Euripides and New Attic Comedy (section 11). Nietzsche criticizes Socrates for privileging reason and the "rational" over the aesthetic values, and he praises tragedy (art) as a healthy, life-affirming Dionysian response to suffering. "Tragedy sits in the midst of this superfluity of life, suffering, and joy, in sublime [*erhabener*] ecstasy; it listens to a distant melancholy song—which tells of the mothers of being, whose names are: delusion, will, woe. Yes, my friends, believe with me in the Dionysian life and in the re-birth of tragedy. The time of the Socratic man is up" (section 20; editor's translation). Art is a way to cope with suffering. "Art alone is able to turn those thoughts of disgust at the horror or absurdity of existence into imaginary representations, through which it is possible to go on living. These are the *sublime* as the artistic subjugation of the horrible and the *comic* as the artistic release from disgust of the absurd. The satyric chorus of the dithyramb is the saving deed of Greek art" (section 7, editor's translation). (A dithyramb was an inspired, wild, or enthused choral hymn.)

We can read the "Dionysian" as one of Nietzsche's versions of the sublime, with its ecstatic experiences of true reality and "primordial unity," its intoxication and loss of self. Nietzsche's concept of this true or real unity is influenced by Schopenhauer's ideas that the "world" in itself is one and can be described as "will" and striving. The illusory world, or the world represented to us according to a "principle of individuation," is Apollonian, and is exemplified in the poetry of Homer (section 5). But despite his being plainly influenced by Schopenhauer and quoting him widely in *Birth of Tragedy* (especially section 16), Nietzsche claimed that the book was thoroughly *Hegelian*. In 1888 he looked back on the work: "It smells offensively of Hegel; only in one or two formulae is it infected with the bitter odor of corpses which is peculiar to Schopenhauer. An 'Idea'[1]— the antagonism of the two concepts Dionysian and Apollonian—is translated into metaphysics; history itself is depicted as the development of this 'Idea'; in tragedy this antithesis is sublated [*aufgehoben*] into a unity; from this standpoint things which theretofore had never been face to face are suddenly confronted, and *comprehended* [*begriffen*] and illuminated by each other."[2]

The first excerpt comes from the beginning of *The Birth of Tragedy*. It appears after a preface to Wagner in which Nietzsche mentions Wagner's essay on Beethoven (which the composer wrote, Nietzsche says, amid the terrors and "sublimities" of the Franco-Prussian war) and in which he calls Wagner his "sublime" predecessor.

# 1

We will have achieved much for scientific study of aesthetics when we come, not merely to a logical understanding, but also to the certain and immediate apprehension of the fact that the further development of art is bound up with the duality of the *Apollonian* and the *Dionysian*, just as reproduction similarly depends upon the duality of the sexes, their continuing strife and only periodically occurring reconciliation. We take these names from the Greeks, who gave a clear voice to the profound secret teachings of their contemplative art, not in ideas, but in the powerfully clear forms of their divine world.

With those two gods of art, Apollo and Dionysus, we establish our recognition that in the Greek world there exists a huge contrast, in origin and purposes, between the visual arts, the Apollonian, and the non-visual art of music, the Dionysian.[4] These two very different drives go hand in hand, for the most part in open conflict with each other and simultaneously provoking each other all the time to new and more powerful offspring, in order to perpetuate in them the contest of that opposition, which the common word "Art" only seems to bridge, until at last, through a marvellous metaphysical act of the Greek "will," they appear paired up with each other and, as this pair, finally produce Attic tragedy, as much a Dionysian as an Apollonian work of art.

In order to bring those two drives closer to us, let us think of them first as the separate artistic worlds of *dream* and of *intoxication*, physiological phenomena between which we can observe an opposition corresponding to the one between the Apollonian and the Dionysian. According to the idea of Lucretius, the marvellous divine shapes first stepped out before the mind of man in a dream.[5] It was in a dream that the great artist saw the delightful anatomy of superhuman existence, and the Greek poet, questioned about the secrets of poetic creativity, would have also recalled his dreams and given an explanation similar to the one Hans Sachs provides in *Die Meistersinger*.[6]

> My friend, that is precisely the poet's work—
> To figure out his dreams, mark them down.
> Believe me, the truest illusion of mankind
> Is revealed to him in dreams:
> All poetic art and poeticizing
> Is nothing but interpreting true dreams.

The beautiful appearance of the world of dreams, in whose creation each man is a complete artist, is the precondition of all plastic art, and also, in fact, as we shall see, an important part of poetry. We enjoy the form with an immediate understanding; every shape speaks to us; nothing is indifferent and unnecessary. For all the most intense life of this dream reality, we nevertheless have the thoroughly unpleasant sense of their *illusory quality*: that, at least, is my experience. For the frequency, indeed normality, of this response, I could point to many witnesses and the utterances of poets. Even the philosophical man has the presentiment that under this reality in which we live and have our being lies hidden a second, totally different reality and that thus the former is an illusion. And Schopenhauer specifically designates as the trademark of philosophical talent the ability to recognize at certain times that human beings and all things are mere phantoms or dream pictures.

Now, just as the philosopher behaves in relation to the reality of existence, so the artistically excitable man behaves in relation to the reality of dreams: he looks at them precisely and with pleasure, for from these pictures he fashions his interpretation of life; from these events he rehearses his life for himself. This is not merely a case of the agreeable and friendly images which he experiences in himself with a complete understanding; they also include what is serious, cloudy, sad, dark, sudden scruples, teasing accidents, nervous expectations, in short, the entire "divine comedy" of life, including the Inferno—all this moves past him, not just like a shadow play—for he lives and suffers in the midst of these scenes—and yet also not without that fleeting sense of illusion. And perhaps several people remember, like me, amid the dangers and terrors of a dream, successfully cheering themselves up by shouting: "It is a dream! I want to dream it some more!" I have also heard accounts of some people who had the ability to set out the causality of one and the same dream over three or more consecutive nights. These facts are clear evidence showing that our innermost beings, the secret underground in all of us, experiences its dreams with deep enjoyment and a sense of delightful necessity.

In the same manner the Greeks expressed this joyful necessity of the dream experience in their Apollo; Apollo, as the god of all the plastic arts, is at the same time the god of prophecy. In accordance with the root meaning of his association with "brightness," he is the god of light; he also rules over the beautiful appearance of the inner fantasy world. The higher truth, the perfection of this condition in contrast to the sketchy understanding of our daily reality, as well as the deep consciousness of a healing and helping nature in sleep and dreaming, is at the same time the symbolic analogy to the capacity to prophesy the truth, as well as to art in general, through which life is made possible and worth living. But also that delicate line which the dream image may not cross so that it does not work its effect pathologically—otherwise the illusion would deceive us as crude reality—that line must not be absent from the image of Apollo, that boundary of moderation, that freedom from more ecstatic excitement, that fully wise calm of the god of images. His eye must be "sun-like," in keeping with his origin; even when he is angry and gazes with displeasure, the consecration of the beautiful illusion rests on him.

And so concerning Apollo one could endorse, in an eccentric way, what Schopenhauer says of the man trapped in the veil of Maja: "As on the stormy sea which extends without limit on all sides, howling mountainous waves rise up and sink and a sailor sits in a row boat, trusting the weak craft, so, in the midst of a world of torments, the solitary man sits peacefully, supported by and trusting in the *principium individuationis* [principle of individuation]" (*World as Will and Idea*, I.1.3).[7] In fact, we could say of Apollo that the imperturbable trust in that principle and the calm sitting still of the man caught up in it attained its loftiest expression in him, and we may even designate Apollo himself as the marvellous divine image of the *principium individuationis*, from whose gestures and gaze all the joy and wisdom of "illusion," together with its beauty, speak to us.

In the same place Schopenhauer also described for us the tremendous *awe* which seizes a man when he suddenly doubts his ways of comprehending illusion, when the principle of reason, in any one of its forms, appears to suffer from an exception. If we add to this awe the ecstatic rapture, which rises up out of the same collapse of the *principium individuationis* from the innermost depths of a human being, indeed, from the innermost depths of nature, then we have a glimpse into the essence of the *Dionysian*, which is presented to us most closely through the analogy to *intoxication*.

Either through the influence of narcotic drink, of which all primitive men and peoples speak in their hymns, or through the powerful coming on of spring, which drives joyfully through all of nature, that Dionysian excitement arises; as it intensifies, the subjective fades into complete forgetfulness of self. Even in the German Middle Ages, under the same power of Dionysus, constantly growing hordes thronged from place to place, singing and dancing; in these St. John's and St. Vitus's dances we recognize the Bacchic chorus of the Greeks once again, with its precursors in Asia Minor, right back to Babylon and the orgiastic *Sacaea*.[8]

There are people who, from a lack of experience or out of apathy, turn mockingly or pityingly away from such phenomena as from a "sickness of the people," with a sense of their own health. These poor people naturally do not have any sense of how deathly and ghost-like this very "health" of theirs sounds, when the glowing life of the Dionysian throng roars past them.

Under the magic of the Dionysian, not only does the bond between man and man lock itself in place once more, but also nature itself, no matter how alienated, hostile, or subjugated, rejoices again in her festival of reconciliation with her prodigal son, man. The earth freely offers up her gifts, and the beasts of prey from the rocks and the desert approach in peace. The wagon of Dionysus is covered with flowers and wreaths; under his yolk stride panthers and tigers.

If someone were to transform Beethoven's *Ode to Joy* into a painting and not restrain his imagination when millions of people sink dramatically into the dust, then we could come close to the Dionysian. Now the slave a free man; now all the stiff, hostile barriers break apart, those things which necessity and arbitrary power or "saucy fashion" have established between men. Now, with the gospel of world harmony, every man feels himself not only united with his neighbour, reconciled and fused together, but also as one with him, as if the veil of Maja had been ripped apart, with only scraps fluttering around in the face of the mysterious primordial unity. Singing and dancing, man expresses himself as a member of a higher community: he has forgotten how to walk and talk and is on the verge of flying up into the air as he dances. The enchantment speaks out in his gestures. Just as the animals now speak and the earth gives milk and honey, so something supernatural also echoes out of him: he feels himself a god; he himself now moves in as lofty and ecstatic a way as he saw the gods move in his dream. The man is no longer an artist; he has become a work of art: the artistic power of all of nature, to the highest rhapsodic satisfaction of the primordial unity, reveals itself here in the transports of intoxication. The finest clay, the most expensive marble—man—is here worked and chiselled, and the cry of the Eleusinian mysteries rings out to the chisel blows of the Dionysian world artist: "Do you fall down, you millions? World, do you have a sense of your creator?"[9]

## 2

Up to this point, we have considered the Apollonian and its opposite, the Dionysian, as artistic forces which break forth out of nature itself, *without the mediation of the human artist*, and in which the human artistic drives are for the time being satisfied directly—on the one hand, as a world of dream images, whose perfection has no connection with an individual's high level of intellect or artistic education, on the other hand, as the intoxicating reality, which once again does not respect the individual, but even seeks to abolish the individual and to redeem him through a mystical feeling of collective unity. In comparison to these unmediated artistic states of nature, every artist is an "imitator," and, in fact, is an artist either of Apollonian dream or Dionysian intoxication or, finally—as in Greek tragedy, for example—simultaneously an artist of intoxication and of dreams. As the last, it is possible for us to imagine how he sinks down in Dionysian drunkenness and mystical obliteration of the self, alone and apart from the rapturous choruses, and how, through the Apollonian effects of dream, his own state now reveals itself to him, that is, his unity with the innermost basis of the world, *in a metaphorical dream picture*.

Having set out these general assumptions and comparisons, let us now approach the *Greeks*, in order to recognize to what degree and to what heights those *artistic drives of nature* were developed in them: in that way we will be in a position to understand more deeply and to assess the relationship of the Greek artist to his primordial images or, to use Aristotle's expression, his "imitation of nature."

In spite of all their literature on dreams and numerous dream anecdotes, we can speak of the *dreams* of the Greeks only hypothetically, although with fair certainty. Given the incredibly clear and accurate plastic capability of their eyes, along with their intelligent and open love of colour, one cannot go wrong in assuming that, to the shame of all those born later, their dreams also had a logical causality of lines and circumferences, colours, and groupings, a sequence of scenes rather like their best bas reliefs, whose perfection would certainly entitle us, if such a comparison were possible, to describe the dreaming Greek man as Homer and Homer as a dreaming Greek man, in a deeper sense than when modern man, with respect to his dreams, has the temerity to compare himself with Shakespeare.

On the other hand, we do not need to speak merely hypothetically when we are to expose the immense gap which separates the *Dionysian Greeks* from the Dionysian barbarians. In all quarters of the old world—setting aside here the newer worlds—from Rome to Babylon, we can confirm the existence of Dionysian celebrations, of a type, at best, related to the Greek type in much the same way as the bearded satyr, whose name and attributes are taken from the goat, is related to Dionysus himself. Almost everywhere, the central point of these celebrations consisted of an exuberant sexual promiscuity, whose waves flooded over all established family practices and its traditional laws. The very wildest bestiality of nature was here unleashed, creating that abominable mixture of lust and cruelty, which has always seemed to me the real "witches' cauldron."

From the feverish excitement of those festivals, knowledge of which reached the Greeks from all directions by land and sea, they were, it seems, for a long time completely secure and protected through the figure of Apollo, drawn up here in all his pride. Apollo could counter by holding up the head of Medusa, for no power was more dangerous than this massive and grotesque Dionysian force.[10] Doric art has immortalized that majestic bearing of Apollo as he stands in opposition.[11] This resistance became more dubious and even impossible as similar impulses finally broke out from the deepest roots of Hellenic culture itself: now the effect of the Delphic god, in a timely final process of reconciliation, limited itself to taking the destructive weapon out of the hand of the powerful opponent.

This reconciliation is the most important moment in the history of Greek culture. Wherever we look, the revolutionary effects of this event manifest themselves. It was the reconciliation of two opponents, who from now on observed their differences with a sharp demarcation of the border line to be kept between them and with occasional gifts sent to honour each other, but basically the gap was not bridged over. However, if we see how, under the pressure of that peace agreement, the Dionysian power revealed itself, then we now understand the meaning of the festivals of world redemption and days of transfiguration in the Dionysian orgies of the Greeks, in comparison with that Babylonian Sacaea, which turned human beings back into tigers and apes.

In these Greek festivals, for the first time nature achieves its artistic jubilee. In them, for the first time, the tearing apart of the *principii individuationis* becomes an artistic phenomenon. Here that dreadful witches' cauldron of lust and cruelty was without power. The strange mixture and ambiguity in the emotions of the Dionysian celebrant only remind him—as healing potions remind one of deadly poison—of that phenomenon that pain awakens joy, that the jubilation in his chest rips out cries of agony. From the most sublime joy echoes the cry of horror or the longingly plaintive lament over an irreparable loss. In those Greek festivals it was as if a sentimental feature of nature is breaking out, as if nature has to sigh over her dismemberment into separate individuals.

The song and the language of gestures of such a doubly defined celebrant was for the Homeric Greek world something new and unheard of, and in it Dionysian *music*, in particular, awoke fear and terror. If music was apparently already known as an Apollonian art, this music, strictly speaking, was a rhythmic pattern like the sound of waves, whose artistic power had been developed for presenting Apollonian states. The music of Apollo was Doric architecture expressed in sound, but only in intimate tones characteristic of the cithara.[12] It kept at a careful distance, as something un-Apollonian, the particular element which constitutes the character of Dionysian music and, along with that, of music generally, the emotionally disturbing tonal power, the unified stream of melody, and the totally incomparable world of harmony.

In the Dionysian dithyramb man is aroused to the highest intensity of all his symbolic capabilities; something never felt forces itself into expression, the destruction of the veil of Maja, the sense of oneness as the presiding genius of form, in fact, of nature itself. Now the essence of nature is to express itself symbolically; a new world of symbols is necessary, the entire symbolism of the body, not just the symbolism of the mouth, of the face, and of the words, but the full gestures of the dance, all the limbs moving to the rhythm. And then the other symbolic powers grow, those of the music, in rhythm, dynamics, and harmony—with sudden violence.

To grasp this total unleashing of all symbolic powers, man must already have attained that high level of freedom from the self which desires to express itself symbolically in those forces. Because of this, the dithyrambic servant of Dionysus will be understood only by someone like himself! With what astonishment must the Apollonian Greek have gazed at him! With an amazement which was all the greater as he sensed with horror that all this might not be really so foreign to him, that, in fact, his Apollonian consciousness was, like a veil, merely covering the Dionysian world in front of him. […]

## Joyful Wisdom

The second excerpt is from *Joyful Wisdom* (1882). Nietzsche is famous, or perhaps notorious, for having a "madman" declare that "God is dead" (*Joyful Wisdom* 125). Nietzsche's remarks on the wiping away of horizons make innovative use of imagery and terms traditionally used in discourses on the sublime: infinity and freedom. The metaphor of being at sea in section 124 prepares readers for the parable of the madman. Section 343 further discusses the death of God.

## 124

*In the Horizon of the Infinite.*—We have left the land and have gone aboard ship! We have broken down the bridge behind us,—nay, more, the land behind us! Well, little ship! look out! Beside you is the ocean; it is true it does not always roar, and sometimes it spreads out like silk and gold and a gentle reverie. But times will come when you will feel that it is infinite, and that there is nothing more frightful than infinity. Oh, the poor bird that felt itself free, and now strikes against the walls of this cage! Alas, if homesickness for the land should attack you, as if there had been more *freedom* there,—and there is no "land" any longer!

## 125

*The Madman.*—Have you ever heard of the madman who on a bright morning lighted a lantern and ran to the market-place calling out unceasingly: "I seek God! I seek God!"—As there were many people standing about who did not believe in God, he caused a great deal of amusement. Why, is he lost? said one. Has he strayed away like a child? said another. Or does he keep himself hidden? Is he afraid of us? Has he taken a sea-voyage? Has he emigrated?—the people cried out laughingly, all in a hubbub. The insane man jumped into their midst and transfixed them with his glances. "Where is God gone?" he called out. "I mean to tell you! *We have killed him,*—you and I! We are all his murderers! But how have we done it? How were we able to drink up the sea? Who gave us the sponge to wipe away the whole horizon? What did we do when we loosened this earth from its sun? Whither does it now move? Whither do we move? Away from all suns? Do we not dash on unceasingly? Backwards, sideways, forwards, in all directions? Is there still an above and below? Do we not stray, as through infinite nothingness? Does not empty space breathe upon us? Has it not become colder? Does not night come on continually, darker and darker? Shall we not have to light lanterns in the morning? Do we not hear the noise of the grave-diggers who are burying God? Do we not smell the divine putrefaction?—for even Gods putrefy! God is dead! God remains dead! And we have killed him! How shall we console ourselves, the most murderous of all murderers? The holiest and the mightiest that the world has hitherto possessed, has bled to death under our knife,—who will wipe the blood from us? With what water could we cleanse ourselves? What lustrums [*Sühnfeiern*, i.e., sacrifices – Ed.], what sacred games shall we have to devise? Is not the magnitude of this deed too great for us? Shall we not ourselves have to become Gods, merely to seem worthy of it? There never was a greater event,—and on account of it, all who are born after us belong to a higher history than any history hitherto!"—Here the madman was silent and looked again at his hearers; they also were silent and looked at him in surprise. At last he threw his lantern on the ground, so that it broke in pieces and was extinguished. "I come too early," he then said, "I am not yet at the right time. This prodigious event is still on its way, and is travelling,—it has not yet reached men's ears. Lightning and thunder need time, the light of the stars needs time, deeds need time, even after they are done, to be seen and heard. This deed is as yet further from them than the furthest star,—*and yet they have done it!*"— It is further stated that the madman made his way into different churches on the same day, and there intoned his *Requiem aeternam deo.*[13] When led out and called to account, he always gave the reply: "What are these churches now, if they are not the tombs and monuments of God?"—

## 343

*What Our Cheerfulness Signifies.*—The most important of more recent events—that "God is dead," that the belief in the Christian God has become unworthy of belief—already begins to cast its first shadows over Europe. To the few at least whose eye, whose *suspecting* glance, is strong enough and subtle enough for this drama, some sun seems to have set, some old, profound confidence seems to have changed into doubt: our old world must seem to them daily more darksome, distrustful, strange, and "old." In the main, however, one may say that the event itself is far too great, too remote, too much beyond most people's power of apprehension, for one to suppose that so much as the report of it could have *reached* them; not to speak of many who already knew *what* had really taken place, and what must all collapse now that this belief had been undermined,—because so much was built upon it, so much rested on it, and had become one with it: for example, our entire European morality. This lengthy, vast, and uninterrupted process of crumbling, destruction, ruin, and overthrow which is now imminent: who has realised it sufficiently today to have to stand up as the teacher and herald of such a tremendous logic of terror, as the prophet of a period of gloom and eclipse, the like of which has probably never taken place on earth before? ... Even we, the born riddle-readers, who wait as it were on the mountains posted between today and tomorrow, and engirt [*hineingespannt*, i.e., surrounded – Ed.] by their contradiction, we, the firstlings and premature children of the coming century, into whose sight especially the shadows which must forthwith envelop Europe *should* already have come—how is it that even we, without genuine sympathy for this period of gloom, contemplate its advent without any *personal* solicitude or fear? Are we still, perhaps, too much under the *immediate effects* of the event—and are these effects, especially as regards *ourselves*, perhaps the reverse of what was to be expected—not at all sad and depressing, but rather like a new and indescribable variety of light, happiness, relief, enlivenment, encouragement, and dawning day? ... In fact, we philosophers and "free spirits" feel ourselves irradiated as by a new dawn by the report that the "old God is dead"; our hearts overflow with gratitude, astonishment, presentiment, and expectation. At last the horizon seems open once more, granting even that it is not bright; our ships can at last put out to sea in face of every danger; every hazard is again permitted to the discerner; the sea, *our* sea, again lies open before us; perhaps never before did such an "open sea" exist.

## Thus Spoke Zarathustra

The third and final excerpt comes from Nietzsche's *Thus Spoke Zarathustra* (1883–85). ("Zarathustra" is the name Nietzsche uses for his re-interpretation of Zoroaster, the ancient Persian prophet, in order to make him a spokesperson for his ideas.) In a section called "Before Sunrise" (Part 3, *Thus Spoke Zarathustra*), Nietzsche plays with, and inverts, the traditional sublime metaphor of height or loftiness. Zarathustra calls the heavens "the *abyss* of light." "Up to your height to toss myself—that is *my* depth! In your purity to hide myself—that is *my* innocence!" "Together did we learn everything; together did we learn to ascend beyond ourselves to ourselves, and to smile cloudlessly."[3] Like Petrarch (see his contribution to this volume), Zarathustra's sublime involves an ascent to a mountain peak: "And climbed I mountains, *whom* did I ever seek, if not you, upon mountains?" However, Zarathustra seeks not union with God, but to realize an act of self-overcoming, to rise beyond himself. Section 35 from Part 2 is excerpted below: "The Sublime Ones" [*Von den Erhabenen*].

It reveals Nietzsche's grappling with the will-centered sublime, which, we can assume, is for Nietzsche the legacy of the Kantian sublime. Nietzsche appears to prefer beauty and laughter to sublimity and solemnity. "Oh, how my soul laughed at his [a sublime person's] ugliness!" says Zarathustra. "To stand with relaxed muscles and with unharnessed will: that is the hardest for all of you, you sublime ones!" Nonetheless, Nietzsche appears to offer his own version of the sublime (*Erhabene*).

## XXXV. — The sublime ones

Calm is the bottom of my sea: who would guess that it hides droll monsters!

Unmoved is my depth: but it sparkles with swimming enigmas and laughters.

A sublime one saw I today, a solemn one, a penitent of the spirit: Oh, how my soul laughed at his ugliness!

With upraised breast, and like those who draw in their breath: thus did he stand, the sublime one, and in silence:

O'erhung with ugly truths, the spoil of his hunting, and rich in torn raiment [clothing – Ed.]; many thorns also hung on him—but I saw no rose.

Not yet had he learned laughing and beauty. Gloomy did this hunter return from the forest of knowledge.

From the fight with wild beasts returned he home: but even yet a wild beast gazes out of his seriousness—an unconquered wild beast!

As a tiger does he ever stand, on the point of springing; but I do not like those strained souls; ungracious is my taste towards all those self-engrossed ones.

And you tell me, friends, that there is to be no dispute about taste and tasting?[14] But all life is a dispute about taste and tasting!

Taste: that is weight at the same time, and scales and weigher; and alas for every living thing that would live without dispute about weight and scales and weigher!

Should he become weary of his sublimeness, this sublime one, then only will his beauty begin—and then only will I taste him and find him savoury.

And only when he turns away from himself will he o'erleap his own shadow—and verily! into *his* sun.

Far too long did he sit in the shade; the cheeks of the penitent of the spirit became pale; he almost starved on his expectations.

Contempt is still in his eye, and loathing hides in his mouth. To be sure, he now rests, but he has not yet taken rest in the sunshine.

As the ox ought he to do; and his happiness should smell of the earth, and not of contempt for the earth.

As a white ox would I like to see him, which, snorting and lowing [i.e., bellowing – Ed.], walks before the plough-share: and his lowing should also laud all that is earthly!

Dark is still his countenance; the shadow of his hand dances upon it. O'ershadowed is still the sense of his eye.

His deed itself is still the shadow upon him: his doing obscures the doer. Not yet has he overcome his deed.

To be sure, I love in him the shoulders of the ox: but now do I want to see also the eye of the angel.

Also his hero-will has he still to unlearn: an exalted one [*Gehobener*] shall he be, and not only a sublime one [*Erhabener*]:—the ether itself should raise him, the will-less one!

He has subdued monsters, he has solved enigmas. But he should also redeem his monsters and enigmas; into heavenly children should he transform them.

As yet has his knowledge not learned to smile, and to be without jealousy; as yet has his gushing passion not become calm in beauty.

Verily, not in satiety shall his longing cease and disappear, but in beauty! Gracefulness belongs to the munificence of the magnanimous.

His arm across his head: thus should the hero repose; thus should he also surmount his repose.

But precisely to the hero is *beauty* the hardest thing of all. Unattainable is beauty by all ardent wills.

A little more, a little less: precisely this is much here, it is the most here.

To stand with relaxed muscles and with unharnessed will: that is the hardest for all of you, you sublime ones!

When power becomes gracious and descends into the visible—I call such condescension [i.e., descent – Ed.], beauty.

And from no one do I want beauty so much as from you, you powerful one: let your goodness be your last self-conquest.

All evil do I accredit to you: therefore do I desire of you the good.

Verily, I have often laughed at the weaklings, who think themselves good because they have crippled paws!

The virtue of the pillar shall you strive after: more beautiful does it ever become, and more graceful—but internally harder and more sustaining—the higher it rises.

Yes, you sublime one, one day shall you also be beautiful, and hold up the mirror to your own beauty.

Then will your soul thrill with divine desires; and there will be adoration even in your vanity!

For this is the secret of the soul: when the hero has abandoned it [the soul – Ed.], then only approaches it in dreams—the superhero.—

Thus spoke Zarathustra.

## Questions

1. Explain the influence of Schopenhauer on *The Birth of Tragedy*'s claims about appearances and reality, or about music, tragedy, and art. (Consider section 16 of *The Birth of Tragedy*, where Nietzsche quotes and discusses Schopenhauer.)

2. Discuss and evaluate the ideals and ways of living proposed by Zarathustra. How are art, tragedy, or music responses to pessimism in life?

3. What would a life-affirming or redemptive art look like today? Could it be "successful" from a market-based perspective? Do you find Nietzsche's view of art compelling? Explain.

4. To what extent, and in what ways, are Nietzsche's versions of the "sublime" tied to his philosophy of religion and metaphysics? To his ethics?

## Further reading

Gasser, Reinhard. *Nietzsche und Freud*. Berlin: Walter de Gruyter, 1997.

Vandenabeele, Bart. "Schopenhauer, Nietzsche, and the Aesthetically Sublime." *Journal of Aesthetic Education* 37, no. 1, (2003): 90–106.

Young, Julian. *Friedrich Nietzsche: A Philosophical Biography*. Cambridge: Cambridge University Press, 2010.

Young, Julian. *Nietzsche's Philosophy of Art*. Cambridge: Cambridge University Press, 1992.

# CHAPTER 26
## RUDOLF OTTO, FROM *THE IDEA OF THE HOLY* (1917)

Otto (1869–1937) was a German Lutheran theologian and author of *Das Heilige* (*The Holy*) (1917), excerpted here. Writing in the tradition of German theologian Friedrich Schleiermacher but also an admirer of the American pragmatist William James, Otto attempted to characterize the "wholly other" or the "numinous": the objective source of the awesome and fascinating "mystery" evoking religious experiences that lie, he thought, at the heart of the world's religions. (Otto's term "numinous" is derived from the Latin *numen*, or "divine power," "spirit.") In the midst of a profound response to the numinous—the *mysterium tremendum et fascinans*—a person feels both fascinated and repelled. But to what exactly? In the presence of what or whom? The origin is the holy, the *numen*:

> The [i.e., Schleiermacher's] "creature-feeling" is itself a first subjective concomitant and effect of another feeling-element, which casts it like a shadow, but which in itself indubitably has immediate and primary reference to an object [*Objekt*] outside the self. Now this object is just what we have already spoken of as "the numinous."

In other words, Otto answers that people sometimes feel they are "in the presence of that which is a *mystery inexpressible and above all creatures*."[1]

Numinous experience, for Otto, is qualitatively quite unlike any other experience. It is a religious feeling providing a unique form of religious knowledge inaccessible to our ordinary rational understanding. Because it resists literal description, it must be approached, if at all, indirectly and through analogy.[2] In the first excerpt below, Otto uses the sublime to describe, by analogy, the feeling of the numinous. The sublime is the "schema" of the numinous. A *schema*, a term taken from Kant, is (loosely speaking) a translation from one sphere or domain into another one, made possible by an essential kinship between the two things. The sublime, as a schema, makes the numinous palpable in the aesthetic sphere.

> While the element of "dread" is gradually overborne, the connexion of "the sublime" and "the holy" becomes firmly established as a legitimate schematization and is carried on into the highest forms of religious consciousness—a proof that there exists a hidden kinship between the numinous and the sublime which is something more than a merely accidental analogy, and to which Kant's *Critique of Judgement* bears distant witness.[3]

In the second excerpt, Otto explains how the numinous can be represented in a variety of art forms traditionally considered sublime, including some works of architecture, Chinese painting, and music.

### Note on the text

Source: Excerpted from Rudolf Otto. *The Idea of the Holy, An Inquiry Into the Non-rational Factor in the Idea of the Divine and Its Relation to the Rational*, translated by John W. Harvey, 41–46, 65–71. London: Oxford University Press, 1972 [first edition, 1923].

Otto's footnotes have been reproduced.

Footnotes added by the volume editor have been indicated as such. Spelling, format, and style from the 1972 edition have been reproduced, with occasional modifications.

## Chapter VII: Analogies and associated feelings

In order to give an adequate account of this second aspect of the numinous, we were led to add to its original designation as *mysterium tremendum* that it at the same time exercises a supreme 'fascination'. And this its dual character, as at once an object of boundless awe and boundless wonder, quelling and yet entrancing the soul, constitutes the proper *positive* content of the *mysterium* as it manifests itself in conscious feeling. No attempt of ours to describe this harmony of contrasts in the import of the *mysterium* can really succeed; but it may perhaps be adumbrated, as it were from a distance, by taking an analogy from a region belonging not to religion but to aesthetics. In the category and feeling of the *sublime* we have a counterpart to it, though it is true it is but a pale reflection, and moreover involves difficulties of analysis all its own. The analogies between the consciousness of the sublime and of the numinous may be easily grasped.[4] To begin with, 'the sublime', like 'the numinous', is in Kantian language an idea or concept 'that cannot be unfolded' or explicated (*unauswickelbar*).[5] Certainly we can tabulate some general 'rational' signs that uniformly recur as soon as we call an object sublime; as, for instance, that it must approach, or threaten to overpass, the bounds of our understanding by some 'dynamical' or 'mathematical' greatness, by potent manifestations of force or magnitude in spatial extent. But these are obviously only conditions of, not the essence of, the impression of sublimity. A thing does not become sublime merely by being great. The concept itself remains unexplicated; it has in it something mysterious, and in this it is like that of 'the numinous'. A second point of resemblance is that the sublime exhibits the same peculiar dual character as the numinous; it is at once daunting, and yet again singularly attracting, in its impress upon the mind. It humbles and at the same time exalts us, circumscribes and extends us beyond ourselves, on the one hand releasing in us a feeling analogous to fear, and on the other rejoicing us. So the idea of the sublime is closely similar to that of the numinous, and is well adapted to excite it and to be excited by it, while each tends to pass over into the other.

### The law of the association of feelings

As these expressions 'excite' and 'pass over' will later assume importance, and as the latter in particular is hedged about with misconceptions which are prominent in the modern doctrines of Evolution and give rise to quite erroneous conclusions, we will enter at once upon a closer consideration of them.

It is a well-known and fundamental psychological law that ideas attract one another, and that one will excite another and call it into consciousness, if it resembles it. An entirely similar law holds good with regard to feelings. A feeling, no less than an idea, can arouse its like in the mind; and the presence of the one in my consciousness may be the occasion for my entertaining the other at the same time. Further, just as in the case of ideas the law of reproduction by similarity leads to a mistaken substitution of ideas, so that I come to entertain an idea $x$, when $y$ would have been the appropriate one, so we may be led to a corresponding substitution of feelings, and I may react with a feeling $x$ to an impression to which the feeling $y$ would normally correspond. Finally, $I$ can pass from one feeling to another by an imperceptibly gradual transition, the one feeling $x$ dying away little by little, while the other, $y$, excited together with it, increases and strengthens in a corresponding degree. But it is important here to recognize the true account of the phenomenon. What passes over undergoes transition is not the feeling itself. It is not that the actual feeling gradually changes in quality or 'evolves', i.e. transmutes itself into a quite different one, but rather that *I* pass over or make the transition from one feeling to another as my circumstances change, by the gradual decrease of the one and increase of the other. A transition of the actual feeling into another would be a real 'transmutation', and would be a psychological counterpart to the alchemist's production of gold by the transmutation of metals.

And yet it is this transmutation that is assumed by the modern 'Evolutionism'—more properly to be called 'Transmutationism'—by the introduction of the equivocal phrase, 'gradually evolve' (i.e. from a thing of a certain quality to something qualitatively different), or the no less equivocal words 'Epigenesis', 'Heterogony',[6] and their like. In this way, they would have us believe, the feeling, e.g., of moral obligation, 'evolves' or develops. At first, so it is said, all that exists is the simple constraint of uniform custom, as seen in the community of the clan. Then, out of that, it is said, arises the idea of a universally obligatory 'ought'. How the idea can do so is not disclosed. Now such a theory misses the fact that in moral obligation we have something *qualitatively* quite different from constraint by custom. The finer and more penetrating psychological analysis that can apprehend differences in quality is rudely ignored and in consequence the whole problem is misconceived. Or, if something of the essential difference is felt, it is covered up and glozed over by the phrase 'gradually evolve', and the one thing is made to turn into the other *par la durée* [lit., "by the duration" – Ed.], much as milk grows sour from standing. But 'ought' is a primary and unique meaning, as little derivable from another as blue from bitter, and there are not transmutations in the psychological any more than in the physical world. The idea 'ought' is only 'evolvable' out of the spirit of man itself, and then in the sense of being 'arousable', because it is already potentially implanted in him. Were it not so, no 'evolution' could effect an introduction for it.

The evolutionists may be quite correct in reconstructing the kind of historical process that took place, viz. the gradual and successive entry upon the scene of different 'moments' of feeling-consciousness in historical sequence, and the order of entry itself may have been correctly discovered. But the explanation of this process is quite different from that which they intend; it is, namely, the law of the excitation and arousing of feelings and ideas according to the measure of their resemblance. There is in point of fact a very strong analogy between constraint by custom and constraint by moral obligation, as both are constraints upon conduct. Consequently the former can *arouse* the latter in the mind if it—the latter—was already potentially planted there; the feeling of ought may start into consciousness at the presence of the other feeling, and the man may gradually effect a transition to it from that other. But what we are concerned with is the *replacement* of the one by the other, and not the *transmutation* of the one into the other.

Now it is just the same with the feeling of the numinous as with that of moral obligation. It too is not to be derived from any other feeling, and is in this sense 'unevolvable'. It is a content of feeling that is qualitatively *sui generis*, yet at the same time one that has numerous analogies with others, and therefore it and they may reciprocally excite or stimulate one another and cause one another to appear in the mind. Instead of framing 'epigenetic' and other fabrications of the course the evolution of religion has taken, it is our task to inquire into these 'stimuli' or 'excitations', these elements that cause the numinous feeling to appear in consciousness, to intimate by virtue of what analogies they came to be able to do so, and so to discover the series or chain of these stimuli by whose operation the numinous feeling was awakened in us.

Such a power of stimulation characterizes the feeling of the sublime, in accordance with the law we found, and through the analogies it bears to the numinous feeling. But this is indubitably a stimulus that only makes its appearance late in the excitation-series, and it is probable that the feeling of the sublime is itself first aroused and disengaged by the precedent religious feeling not from itself, but from the rational spirit of man and its *a priori* capacity.

## Schematization

The 'association of ideas' does not simply cause the idea *y* to reappear in consciousness with the given idea *x* occasionally only, it also sets up under certain circumstances lasting combinations and connexions between the two. And this is no less true of the association of feelings. Accordingly, we see religious feeling in permanent connexion with other feelings which are conjoined to it in accordance with this principle of association. It is, indeed, more accurate to say 'conjoined' than really 'connected', for such mere conjunctions or chance connexions according to laws of purely external analogy are to be distinguished from necessary connexions according to principles of true inward affinity and cohesion. An instance of a connexion of this latter kind—an example, indeed, of an inner *a priori* principle—is (following the theory of Kant) the connexion of the category of causality with its temporal 'schema', the temporal sequence of two successive events, which by being brought into connexion with the category of causality is *known* and recognized as a causal relation of the two. In this case analogy between the two—the category and the schema—has also a place, but it is not chance external resemblance but essential correspondence, and the fact that the two belong together is here a necessity of our reason. On the basis of such a necessity the temporal sequence 'schematizes' the category.

Now the relation of the rational to the non-rational element in the idea of the holy or sacred is just such a one of 'schematization', and the non-rational numinous fact, schematized by the rational concepts we have suggested above, yields us the complex category of 'holy' itself, richly charged and complete and in its fullest meaning. And that the schematism is a genuine one, and not a mere combination of analogies, may be distinctly seen from the fact that it does not fall to pieces, and cannot be cut out as the development of the consciousness of religious truth proceeds onwards and upwards, but is only recognized with greater definiteness and certainty. And it is for the same reason inherently probable that there is more, too, in the combination of 'the holy' with 'the sublime' than a mere association of feelings; and perhaps we may say that, while as a matter of historical genesis such an association was the means whereby this combination was awakened in the mind and the occasion for it, yet the inward and lasting character of the connexion in all the higher religions does prove that 'the sublime' too is an authentic 'schema' of 'the holy'. [...]

## Chapter IX: Means of expression of the numinous

[...]

### 3 *Means by which the numinous is expressed in art*

In the arts nearly everywhere the most effective means of representing the numinous is 'the sublime'. This is especially true of architecture, in which it would appear to have first been realized. One can hardly escape the idea that this feeling for expression must have begun to awaken far back in the remote Megalithic Age. The motive underlying the erection of those gigantic blocks of rock, hewn or unworked, single monoliths or titanic rings of stone, as at Stonehenge, may have well been originally to localize and preserve and, as it were, to store up the numen in solid presence by magic; but the change to the motive of *expression* must have been from the outset far too vividly stimulated not to occur at a very early date. In fact the bare feeling for solemn and imposing magnitude and for the pomp of sublime pose and gesture is a fairly elementary one, and we cannot doubt that this stage had been reached when the *mastabas*, obelisks, and pyramids were built in Egypt. It is indeed beyond question that the builders of these temples, and of the Sphinx of Gizeh, which set the feeling of the sublime, and together with and through it that of the numinous, throbbing in the soul almost like a mechanical reflex, must themselves have been conscious of this effect and have intended it.

Further, we often say of a building, or indeed of a song, a formula, a succession of gestures or musical notes, and in particular of certain manifestations of ornamental and decorative art, symbols, and emblems, that they make a 'downright magical' impression, and we feel we can detect the special characteristic of this 'magical' note in art with fair assurance even under the most varying conditions and in the most diverse relationships. The art of China, Japan, and Tibet, whose specific character has been determined by Taoism and Buddhism, surpasses all others in the unusual richness and depth of such impressions of the 'magical', and even an inexpert observer responds to them readily. The designation 'magical' is here correct even from the historical point of view, since the origin of this language of form was properly magical representations, emblems, formularies, and contrivances. But the actual impression of 'magic' is quite independent of this historical bond of connexion with magical practices. It occurs even when nothing is known of the latter; nay, in that case it comes out most strongly and unbrokenly. Beyond dispute art has here a means of creating a unique impression—that of the magical—apart from and independent of reflection. Now the magical is nothing but a suppressed and dimmed form of the numinous, a crude form of it which great art purifies and ennobles. In great art the point is reached at which we may no longer speak of the 'magical', but rather are confronted with the numinous itself, with all its impelling motive power, transcending reason, expressed in sweeping lines and rhythm.[7] In no art, perhaps, is this more fully realized than in the great landscape painting and religious painting of China in the classical period of the T'ang and Sung dynasties. It has been said of this great art:

> These works are to be classed with the profoundest and sublimest of the creations of human art. The spectator who, as it were, immerses himself in them feels behind these waters and clouds and mountains the mysterious breath of the primeval Tao, the pulse of innermost being. Many a mystery lies half-concealed and half-revealed in these pictures. They contain the knowledge of the 'nothingness' and the 'void', of the 'Tao' of heaven and earth, which is also the Tao of the human heart. And so, despite their perpetual agitation, they seem as remotely distant and as profoundly calm as though they drew secret breath at the bottom of a sea.[8]

To us of the West the Gothic appears as the most numinous of all types of art. This is due in the first place to its sublimity; but Worringer in his work *Probleme der Gothik*[9] has done a real service in showing that the peculiar impressiveness of Gothic does not consist in its sublimity alone, but draws upon a strain inherited from primitive magic, of which he tries to show the historical derivation. To Worringer, then, the impression Gothic makes is one of magic; and, whatever may be said of his historical account of the matter, it is certain that in this at least he is on the right track. Gothic *does* instill a spell that is more than the effect of sublimity. But 'magic' is too low a word: the tower of the Cathedral of Ulm is emphatically not 'magical', it is *numinous*. And the difference between the numinous and the merely magical can nowhere be felt more clearly than in the splendid plate Worringer gives in his book of this marvellous work of architecture. But when this is said, we may still keep the word magic in use to denote the style and means of artistic expression by which the impression of the numinous comes into being.

But in neither the sublime nor the magical, effective as they are, has art more than an indirect means of representing the numinous. Of directer methods our Western art has only two, and they are in a noteworthy way *negative*, viz. *darkness* and *silence*. The darkness must be such as is enhanced and made all the more perceptible by contrast with some last vestige of brightness, which it is, as it were, on the point of extinguishing; hence the 'mystical' effect begins with semi-darkness. Its impression is rendered complete if the factor of the sublime comes to unite with and supplement it. The semi-darkness that glimmers in vaulted halls, or beneath the branches of a lofty forest glade, strangely quickened and stirred by the mysterious play of half-lights, has always spoken eloquently to the soul, and the builders of temples, mosques, and churches have made full use of it.

*Silence* is what corresponds to this in the language of musical sounds. 'Yahweh is in His holy Temple, let all the earth keep silence before Him.' (Habakkuk, ii. 20.) Neither we nor (probably) the prophet any longer bear in mind that this 'keeping silence' (as εὐφημεῖν [euphēmein] in Greek), if regarded from the historical, 'genetic' standpoint, springs from the fear of using words of evil omen, which therefore prefers to be altogether speechless. It is the same with Tersteegen in his 'God is present, let all in us be silent'. With prophet and psalmist and poet we feel the necessity of silence from another and quite independent motive. It is a spontaneous reaction to the feeling of the actual *numen praesens*.[10] Once again, what is found coming upon the scene at a higher level of evolution cannot be explained by merely interpolating links in a 'historico-genetic' chain of development; and the Psalmist and Tersteegen and even we ourselves are at least as interesting subjects for the analysis of the psychologist of religion as are the 'primitives', with their habitual practice of εὐφημία [euphēmia], the silence that merely avoids words of ill augury.

Besides silence and darkness oriental art knows a third direct means for producing a strongly numinous impression, to wit, *emptiness* and *empty distances*. Empty distance, remote vacancy, is, as it were, the sublime in the horizontal. The wide-stretching desert, the boundless uniformity of the steppe, have real sublimity, and even in us Westerners they set vibrating chords of the numinous along with the note of the sublime, according to the principle of the association of feelings. Chinese architecture, which is essentially an art in the laying out and grouping of buildings, makes a wise and very striking use of this fact. It does not achieve the impression of solemnity by lofty vaulted halls or imposing altitudes, but nothing could well be more solemn than the silent amplitude of the enclosed spaces, courtyards, and vestibules which it employs. The imperial tombs of the Ming emperors at Nanking and Peking are, perhaps, the strongest example of this, including, as they do, in their plan the empty distances of an entire landscape. Still more interesting is the part played by the factor of void or emptiness in Chinese painting.[11] There it has almost become a special art to paint empty space, to make it palpable, and to develop variations upon this singular theme. Not only are there pictures upon which 'almost nothing' is painted, not only is it an essential feature of their style to make the strongest impression with the fewest strokes and the scantiest means, but there are very many pictures—especially such as are connected with contemplation—which impress the observer with the feeling that the void itself is depicted as a subject, is indeed the main subject of the picture. We can only understand this by recalling what was said above on the 'nothingness' and the 'void' of the mystics and on the enchantment and spell exercised by the 'negative hymns'. For 'void' is, like darkness and silence, a negation, but a negation that does away with every 'this' and 'here', in order that the 'wholly other' may become actual.[12]

Not even music, which else can give such manifold expression to all the feelings of the mind, has any positive way to express 'the holy'. Even the most consummate Mass-music can only give utterance to the holiest, most 'numinous' moment in the Mass—the moment of transubstantiation—by sinking into stillness: no mere momentary pause, but an absolute cessation of sound long enough for us to 'hear the silence' itself; and no devotional moment in the whole Mass approximates in impressiveness to this keeping silence before the Lord. It is instructive to submit Bach's Mass in B minor to the test in this matter. Its most mystical portion is the 'Incarnatus' in the 'Credo', and there the effect is due to the faint, whispering, lingering sequence in the fugue structure, dying away *pianissimo*. The held breath and hushed sound of the passage, its weird cadences, sinking away in lessened thirds, its pauses and syncopations, and its rise and fall in astonishing semitones, which render so well the sense of awe-struck wonder—all this serves to express the *mysterium* by way of intimation, rather than in forthright utterance. And by this means Bach attains his aim here far better than in the 'Sanctus'. This latter is indeed an incomparably successful expression of Him, whose is 'the power and the glory', an enraptured and triumphant choric hymn to perfect and absolute sovereignty. But it is very far distant from the mood of the text that accompanies the music, which is taken from Isaiah vi, and which the composer should have interpreted in accordance with that passage as a whole. No one would gather from this magnificent chorus that the Seraphim covered their faces with two of their wings.[13] In this point Mendelssohn[14] shows very fine sensibility in his musical setting of Psalm 2 at the words (v. 11): 'Serve the Lord with fear, and rejoice with trembling'. And here too the matter is expressed less in the music itself than in the way the music is restrained and repressed—one might almost say, abashed—as the Cathedral choir at Berlin so well knows how to render it. And, if a final example may be cited, the 'Popule meus' of Thomas Luiz gets as near to the heart of the matter as any music can. In this the first chorus sings the first words of the '*Trisagion*': 'Hagios, ho theos, hagios ischyros, hagios athanatos', and the second chorus sings in response the Latin rendering of the words: 'Sanctus deus, sanctus fortis, sanctus immortalis', each chorus thrilling with a sort of muffled tremor. But the *Trisagion* itself, sung *pianissimo* by singers kept out of sight far at the back, is like a whisper floating down through space, and is assuredly a consummate reproduction of the scene in the vision of Isaiah.[15]

## Questions

1. What is it about the numen (the holy) that requires description through the use of analogies? Do you see any problems with this approach?

2. Explain Otto's view that the sublime "schematizes" the numinous. How are they essentially kin—what features of the sublime and the numinous make such schematizing possible? Discuss concrete examples and experiences.

3. Otto claims that in music, the feeling of the sublime (and numinous) can come from the absence of sound, or silence. Do you agree? Explain. How about silence generally? Can the numinous (or sublime) be found in other, non-musical instances of silence? Explain.

4. Compare and contrast, with respect to the sublime, Otto on "darkness" with Burke on "obscurity."

5. Discuss what Otto says about "emptiness and empty distances" in Chinese architecture and painting. Consider his claims in light of Guo Xi's paintings and writings.

6. Compare Otto's claim that the sublime schematizes the *numinous*, with Kant's claim that the *morally good*, when judged aesthetically, is represented by the sublime (*Critique of the Power of Judgment* 5:271: the "good, judged aesthetically, must not be represented so much as beautiful but rather as sublime"). How are their motivations and arguments similar, and how are they different?

## Further reading

Almond, Philip C. *Rudolf Otto: An Introduction to His Philosophical Theology*. Chapel Hill: University of North Carolina Press, 1984.

Davidson, Robert F. *Rudolf Otto's Interpretation of Religion*. Princeton: Princeton University Press, 1947.

Melissa, Raphael. *Rudolf Otto and the Concept of Holiness*. Oxford: Clarendon Press, 1997.

Poland, Lynn. "The Idea of the Holy and the History of the Sublime." *The Journal of Religion* 72 (1992): 175–97.

Ware, Owen. "Rudolf Otto's Idea of the Holy: A Reappraisal." *Heythrop Journal* 48, no. 1 (2007): 48–60.

# PART V
## CONTEMPORARY

# CHAPTER 27
## BARNETT NEWMAN, "THE SUBLIME IS NOW" (1948)

Newman (1905–1970) was an American artist known for his abstract work making use of color fields. Some of his signature work included fields of solid color separated by thin vertical lines that Newman called "zips." These paintings were often very large, the largest being 20 feet wide.

In the following article, Newman uses the concepts of the sublime and the beautiful to discuss his vision for a new kind of painting, as American avant-garde painters strive to distinguish their work from European art.

### Note on the text

Source: Reprinted from Barnett B. Newman, "the sublime is now," *Tiger's Eye*, vol. 1, no. 6, December 1948, 51–53.

The orthography and style of the original publication have been reproduced.

### *the sublime is now*

The invention of beauty by the Greeks, that is, their postulate of beauty as an ideal, has been the bugbear of European art and European aesthetic philosophies. Man's natural desire in the arts to express his relation to the Absolute became identified and confused with the absolutisms of perfect creations—with the fetish of quality—so that the European artist has been continually involved in the moral struggle between notions of beauty and the desire for sublimity.

The confusion can be seen sharply in Longinus, who despite his knowledge of non-Grecian art, could not extricate himself from his platonic attitudes concerning beauty, from the problem of value, so that to him the feeling of exaltation became synonymous with the perfect statement—an objective rhetoric. But the confusion continued on in Kant, with his theory of transcendent perception, that the phenomenon is *more* than phenomenon; and with Hegel, who built a theory of beauty, in which the sublime is at the bottom of a structure of *kinds of beauty*, thus creating a range of hierarchies in a set of relationships to reality that is completely formal. (Only Edmund Burke insisted on a separation. Even though it is an unsophisticated and primitive one, it is a clear one and it would be interesting to know how closely the Surrealists were influenced by it. To me Burke reads like a Surrealist manual.)

The confusion in philosophy is but the reflection of the struggle that makes up the history of the plastic arts. To us today there is no doubt that Greek art is an insistence that the sense of exaltation is to be found in perfect form, that exaltation is the same as ideal sensibility, in contrast, for example, with the Gothic or Baroque, in which the sublime consists of a desire to destroy form; where form can be formless.

The climax in this struggle between beauty and the sublime can best be examined inside the Renaissance and the reaction later against the Renaissance that is known as modern art. In the Renaissance the revival of the ideals of Greek beauty set the artists the task of rephrasing an accepted Christ legend in terms of absolute beauty as against the original Gothic ecstacy [sic] over the legend's evocation of the Absolute. And the Renaissance artists dressed up the traditional ecstacy in an even older tradition—that of eloquent nudity or rich velvet. It was no idle quip that moved Michelangelo to call himself a sculptor rather than a painter, for he knew that only in his sculpture could the desire for the grand statement of Christian sublimity be reached. He could despise with good reason the beauty-cults who felt the Christ drama on a stage of rich velvets and brocades and beautifully textured flesh tints. Michelangelo knew that the meaning of the Greek humanities for his time involved making Christ—the man, into Christ—who is God; that his plastic problem was neither the medieval one, to make a cathedral, nor the Greek one, to make a man like a god, but to make a cathedral out of man. In doing so he set a standard for sublimity that the painting of his time could not reach. Instead, painting continued on its merry quest for a voluptuous art until in modern times, the Impressionists, disgusted with its inadequacy, began the movement to destroy the established rhetoric of beauty by the Impressionist insistence on a surface of ugly strokes.

The impulse of modern art was this desire to destroy beauty. However, in discarding Renaissance notions of beauty, and without an adequate substitute for a sublime message, the Impressionists were compelled to preoccupy themselves, in their struggle, with the culture values of their plastic history so that instead of evoking a new way of experiencing life they were able only to make a transfer of values. By glorifying their own way of living, they were caught in the problem of what is really beautiful and could only make a restatement of their position on the general question of beauty; just as later the Cubists, by their Dada gestures of substituting a sheet of newspaper and sandpaper for both the velvet surfaces of the Renaissance and the Impressionists, made a similar transfer of values instead of creating a new vision, and succeeded only in elevating the sheet of paper. So strong is the grip of the *rhetoric* of exaltation as an attitude in the large context of the European culture pattern that the elements of sublimity in the revolution we know as modern art, exist in its effort and energy to escape the pattern rather than in the realization of a new experience. Picasso's effort may be sublime but there is no doubt that his work is a preoccupation with the question of what is the nature of beauty. Even Mondrian, in his attempt to destroy the Renaissance picture by his insistence on pure subject matter, succeeded only in raising the white plane and the right angle into a realm of sublimity, where the sublime paradoxically becomes an absolute of perfect sensations. The geometry (perfection) swallowed up his metaphysics (his exaltation).

The failure of European art to achieve the sublime is due to this blind desire to exist inside the reality of sensation (the objective world, whether distorted or pure) and to build an art within a framework of pure plasticity (the Greek ideal of beauty, whether that plasticity be a romantic active surface, or a classic stable one.) In other words, modern art, caught without a sublime content, was incapable of creating a new sublime image, and unable to move away from the Renaissance imagery of figures and objects except by distortion or by denying it completely for an empty world of geometric formalisms—a *pure* rhetoric of abstract mathematical relationships, became enmeshed in a struggle over the nature of beauty; whether beauty was in nature or could be found without nature.

I believe that here in America, some of us, free from the weight of European culture, are finding the answer, by completely denying that art has any concern with the problem of beauty and where to find it. The question that now arises is how, if we are living in a time without a legend or mythos that can be called sublime, if we refuse to admit any exaltation in pure relations, if we refuse to live in the abstract, how can we be creating a sublime art?

We are reasserting man's natural desire for the exalted, for a concern with our relationship to the absolute emotions. We do not need the obsolete props of an outmoded and antiquated legend. We are creating images whose reality is self-evident and which are devoid of the props and crutches that evoke associations with outmoded images, both sublime and beautiful. We are freeing ourselves of the impediments of memory, association, nostalgia, legend, myth, or what have you, that have been the devices of Western European painting. Instead of making *cathedrals* out of Christ, man, or "life," we are making it out of ourselves, out of our own feelings. The image we produce is the self-evident one of revelation, real and concrete, that can be understood by anyone who will look at it without the nostalgic glasses of history.

## Questions

1. What does Newman consider to be characteristic of American painting in comparison to "Western European" painting? How might Newman's artworks relate to this? What other artworks come to mind?

2. How does Newman make use of the distinction between the sublime and the beautiful?

3. Do you think that viewing Newman's paintings can elicit feelings of the sublime? Explain.

## Further reading

Danto, Arthur. "The Abuse of Beauty," in the present volume.
Lyotard, Jean-François. "The Sublime and the Avant-Garde," in the present volume.
Ratcliff, Carter. "The Sublime Was Then: The Art of Barnett Newman." In *Sticky Sublime*, ed. Bill Beckley, 211–39. New York: Allworth Press, 2001.

# CHAPTER 28
## JULIA KRISTEVA, FROM *POWERS OF HORROR: AN ESSAY ON ABJECTION* (1980)

This excerpt from the opening pages of Kristeva's *Powers of Horror* discusses the "abject" and the sublime. In this influential book, Julia Kristeva draws on the theories of Sigmund Freud and Jacques Lacan to examine concepts such as horror, marginalization, and the Oedipal complex.

Central to Kristeva's analysis is the concept of the abject. Unlike an "object" opposed to me, "what is abject . . . is radically excluded and draws me toward the place where meaning collapses." Not limited to filth and waste, the abject is caused by "what disturbs identity, system, order. What does not respect borders, positions, rules. The in-between, the ambiguous, the composite." The abject's breaking of order, law, and limits is one a way in which it is "edged with" the sublime.

### Note on the text

Source: Excerpted from Julia Kristeva, *Powers of Horror: An Essay on Abjection*, translated by Leon S. Roudiez, 1–12. New York: Columbia University Press, 1982. Original title: *Pouvoirs de l'horreur. Essai sur l'abjection.* Paris: Éditions du Seuil, 1980.

The style and format of Roudiez's translation have been reproduced, with occasional modifications. Ellipsis, insertions in square brackets, and the footnote are found in Roudiez's translation. Some typographical errors in the translation have been silently corrected by the volume editor.

### I Approaching abjection

No Beast is there without glimmer of infinity,
No eye so vile nor abject that brushes not
Against lightning from on high, now tender, now fierce.

Victor Hugo, *La Légende des siècles*

### Neither subject nor object

There looms, within abjection, one of those violent, dark revolts of being, directed against a threat that seems to emanate from an exorbitant outside or inside, ejected beyond the scope of the possible, the tolerable, the thinkable. It lies there, quite close, but it cannot be assimilated. It beseeches, worries, and fascinates desire, which, nevertheless, does not let itself be seduced. Apprehensive, desire turns aside; sickened, it rejects. A certainty protects it from the shameful—a certainty of which it is proud holds on to it. But simultaneously, just the same, that impetus, that spasm, that leap is drawn toward an elsewhere as tempting as it is condemned. Unflaggingly, like an inescapable boomerang, a vortex of summons and repulsion places the one haunted by it literally beside himself.

When I am beset by abjection, the twisted braid of affects and thoughts I call by such a name does not have, properly speaking, a definable *object.* The abject is not an ob-ject facing me, which I name or imagine. Nor is it an ob-jest [*sic*], an otherness ceaselessly fleeing in a systematic quest of desire. What is abject is not my correlative, which, providing me with someone or something else as support, would allow me to be more or less detached and autonomous. The abject has only one quality of the object—that of being opposed to I. If the object, however, through its opposition, settles me within the fragile texture of a desire for meaning, which, as a matter of fact, makes me ceaselessly and infinitely homologous to it, what is *abject,* on the contrary, the jettisoned object, is radically excluded and draws me toward the place where meaning collapses. A certain "ego" that merged with its master, a superego, has flatly driven it away. It lies outside, beyond the set, and does not seem to agree to the latter's rules of the game. And yet, from its place of banishment, the abject does not cease challenging its master. Without a sign (for him), it beseeches a discharge, a convulsion, a crying out. To each ego its object, to each superego its abject. It is not the white expanse or slack boredom of repression, not the translations and transformations of desire that wrench bodies, nights, and discourse; rather it is a brutish suffering that "I" puts up with, sublime and devastated, for "I" deposits it to the father's account [*verse au père—père-version*]: I endure it, for I imagine that such is the desire of the other. A massive and sudden emergence of uncanniness, which, familiar as it might have been in an opaque and forgotten life, now harries me as radically separate, loathsome. Not me. Not that. But not nothing, either. A "something" that I do not recognize as a thing. A weight of meaninglessness, about which there is nothing insignificant, and which crushes me. On the edge of non-existence and hallucination, of a reality that, if I acknowledge it, annihilates me. There, abject and abjection are my safeguards. The primers of my culture.

## The improper/unclean

Loathing an item of food, a piece of filth, waste, or dung. The spasms and vomiting that protect me. The repugnance, the retching that thrusts me to the side and turns me away from defilement, sewage, and muck. The shame of compromise, of being in the middle of treachery. The fascinated start that leads me toward and separates me from them.

Food loathing is perhaps the most elementary and most archaic form of abjection. When the eyes see or the lips touch that skin on the surface of milk—harmless, thin as a sheet of cigarette paper, pitiful as a nail paring—I experience a gagging sensation and, still farther down, spasms in the stomach, the belly; and all the organs shrivel up the body, provoke tears and bile, increase heartbeat, cause forehead and hands to perspire. Along with sight-clouding dizziness, *nausea* makes me balk at that milk cream, separates me from the mother and father who proffer it. "I" want none of that element, sign of their desire; "I" do not want to listen, "I" do not assimilate it, "I" expel it. But since the food is not an "other" for "me," who am only in their desire, I expel *myself,* I spit *myself* out, I abject *myself* within the same motion through which "I" claim to establish *myself.* That detail, perhaps an insignificant one, but one that they ferret out, emphasize, evaluate, that trifle turns me inside out, guts sprawling; it is thus that *they* see that "I" am in the process of becoming another at the expense of my own death. During that course in which "I" become, I give birth to myself amid the violence of sobs, of vomit. Mute protest of the symptom, shattering violence of a convulsion that, to be sure, is inscribed in a symbolic system, but in which, without either wanting or being able to become integrated in order to answer to it, it reacts, it abreacts. It abjects.

The corpse (or cadaver: *cadere,* to fall), that which has irremediably come a cropper, is cesspool, and death; it upsets even more violently the one who confronts it as fragile and fallacious chance. A wound with blood and pus, or the sickly, acrid smell of sweat, of decay, does not *signify* death. In the presence of signified death—a flat encephalograph, for instance—I would understand, react, or accept. No, as in true theater, without makeup or masks, refuse and corpses *show me* what I permanently thrust aside in order to live. These body fluids, this defilement, this shit are what life withstands, hardly and with difficulty, on the part of death. There, I am at the border of my condition as a living being. My body extricates itself, as being alive, from that border. Such wastes drop so that I might live, until, from loss to loss, nothing remains in me and my entire body falls beyond the limit—*cadere,* cadaver. If dung signifies the other side of the border, the place where I am not and which permits me to be, the corpse, the most sickening of wastes, is a border that has encroached upon everything. It is no longer I who expel, "I" is expelled. The border has become an object. How can I be without border? That elsewhere that I imagine beyond the present, or that I hallucinate so that I might, in a present time, speak to you, conceive of you—it is now here, jetted, abjected, into "my" world. Deprived of world, therefore, I *fall in a faint.* In that compelling, raw, insolent thing in the morgue's full sunlight, in that thing that no longer matches and therefore no longer signifies anything, I behold the breaking down of a world that has erased its borders: fainting away. The corpse, seen without God and outside of science, is the utmost of abjection. It is death infecting life. Abject. It is something rejected from which one does not part, from which one does not protect oneself as from an object. Imaginary uncanniness and real threat, it beckons to us and ends up engulfing us.

It is thus not lack of cleanliness or health that causes abjection but what disturbs identity, system, order. What does not respect borders, positions, rules. The in-between, the ambiguous, the composite. The traitor, the liar, the criminal with a good conscience, the shameless rapist, the killer who claims he is a savior. . . . Any crime, because it draws attention to the fragility of the law, is abject, but premeditated crime, cunning murder, hypocritical revenge are even more so because they heighten the display of such fragility. He who denies morality is not abject; there can be grandeur in amorality and even in crime that flaunts its disrespect for the law—rebellious, liberating, and suicidal crime. Abjection, on the other hand, is immoral, sinister, scheming, and shady: a terror that dissembles, hatred that smiles, a passion that uses the body for barter instead of inflaming it, a debtor who sells you up, a friend who stabs you. . . .

In the dark halls of the museum that is now what remains of Auschwitz, I see a heap of children's shoes, or something like that, something I have already seen elsewhere, under a Christmas tree, for instance, dolls I believe. The abjection of Nazi crime reaches its apex when death, which, in any case, kills me, interferes with what, in my living universe, is supposed to save me from death: childhood, science, among other things.

## The abjection of self

If it be true that the abject simultaneously beseeches and pulverizes the subject, one can understand that it is experienced at the peak of its strength when that subject, weary of fruitless attempts to identify with something on the outside, finds the impossible within; when it finds that the impossible constitutes its very *being,* that it *is* none other than abject. The abjection of self would be the culminating form of that experience of the subject to which it is revealed that all its objects are based merely on the inaugural *loss* that laid the foundations of its own being. There is nothing like the abjection of self to show that all abjection is in fact recognition of the *want* on which any being, meaning, language, or desire is founded. One always passes too quickly over this word, "want," and today psychoanalysts are finally taking into account only its more or less fetishized product, the "object of want." But if one imagines (and imagine one must, for it is the working of imagination whose foundations are being laid here) the experience of *want* itself as logically preliminary to being and object—to the being of the object—then one understands that abjection, and even more so abjection of self, is its only signified. Its signifier, then, is none but literature. Mystical Christendom turned this abjection of self into the ultimate proof of humility before God, witness Elizabeth of Hungary who "though a great princess, delighted in nothing so much as in abasing herself."[1]

The question remains as to the ordeal, a secular one this time, that abjection can constitute for someone who, in what is termed knowledge of castration, turning away from perverse dodges, presents himself with his own body and ego as the most precious non-objects; they are no longer seen in their own right but forfeited, abject. The termination of analysis can lead us there, as we shall see. Such are the pangs and delights of masochism.

Essentially different from "uncanniness," more violent, too, abjection is elaborated through a failure to recognize its kin; nothing is familiar, not even the shadow of a memory. I imagine a child who has swallowed up his parents too soon, who frightens himself on that account, "all by himself," and, to save himself, rejects and throws up everything that is given to him—all gifts, all objects. He has, he could have, a sense of the abject. Even before things for him *are*—hence before they are signifiable—he drives them out, dominated by drive as he is, and constitutes his own territory, edged by the abject. A sacred configuration. Fear cements his compound, conjoined to another world, thrown up, driven out, forfeited. What he has swallowed up instead of maternal love is an emptiness, or rather a maternal hatred without a word for the words of the father; that is what he tries to cleanse himself of, tirelessly. What solace does he come upon within such loathing? Perhaps a father, existing but unsettled, loving but unsteady, merely an apparition but an apparition that remains. Without him the holy brat would probably have no sense of the sacred; a blank subject, he would remain, discomfited, at the dump for non-objects that are always forfeited, from which, on the contrary, fortified by abjection, he tries to extricate himself. For he is not mad, he through whom the abject exists. Out of the daze that has petrified him before the untouchable, impossible, absent body of the mother, a daze that has cut off his impulses from their objects, that is, from their representations, out of such daze he causes, along with loathing, one word to crop up—fear. The phobic has no other object than the abject. But that word, "fear"—a fluid haze, an elusive clamminess—no sooner has it cropped up than it shades off like a mirage and permeates all words of the language with nonexistence, with a hallucinatory, ghostly glimmer. Thus, fear having been bracketed, discourse will seem tenable only if it ceaselessly confronts that otherness, a burden both repellent and repelled, a deep well of memory that is unapproachable and intimate: the abject.

## Beyond the unconscious

Put another way, it means that there are lives not sustained by *desire,* as desire is always for objects. Such lives are based on *exclusion.* They are clearly distinguishable from those understood as neurotic or psychotic, articulated by *negation* and its modalities, *transgression, denial,* and *repudiation.* Their dynamics challenges the theory of the unconscious, seeing that the latter is dependent upon a dialectic of negativity.

The theory of the unconscious, as is well known, presupposes a repression of contents (affects and presentations) that, thereby, do not have access to consciousness but effect within the subject modifications, either of speech (parapraxes, etc.), or of the body (symptoms), or both (hallucinations, etc.). As correlative to the notion of *repression,* Freud put forward that of *denial* as a means of figuring out neurosis, that of *rejection* (*repudiation*) as a means of situating psychosis. The asymmetry of the two repressions becomes more marked owing to denial's bearing on the object whereas repudiation affects desire itself (Lacan, in perfect keeping with Freud's thought, interprets that as "repudiation of the Name of the Father").

Yet, facing the ab-ject and more specifically phobia and the splitting of the ego (a point I shall return to), one might ask if those articulations of negativity germane to the unconscious (inherited by Freud from philosophy and psychology) have not become inoperative. The "unconscious" contents remain here *excluded* but in strange fashion: not radically enough to allow for a secure differentiation between subject and object, and yet clearly enough for a defensive *position* to be established—one that implies a refusal but also a sublimating elaboration. As if the fundamental opposition were between I and Other or, in more archaic fashion, between Inside and Outside. As if such an opposition subsumed the one between Conscious and Unconscious, elaborated on the basis of neuroses.

Owing to the ambiguous opposition I/Other, Inside/Outside—an opposition that is vigorous but pervious, violent but uncertain—there are contents, "normally" unconscious in neurotics, that become explicit if not conscious in "borderline" patients' speeches and behavior. Such contents are often openly manifested through symbolic practices, without by the same token being integrated into the judging consciousness of those particular subjects. Since they make the conscious/unconscious distinction irrelevant, borderline subjects and their speech constitute propitious ground for a sublimating discourse ("aesthetic" or "mystical," etc.), rather than a scientific or rationalist one.

## An exile who asks, "Where?"

The one by whom the abject exists is thus a *deject* who places (himself), *separates* (himself), situates (himself), and therefore *strays* instead of getting his bearings, desiring, belonging, or refusing. Situationist in a sense, and not without laughter— since laughing is a way of placing or displacing abjection. Necessarily dichotomous, somewhat Manichaean, he divides, excludes, and without, properly speaking, wishing to know his abjections is not at all unaware of them. Often, moreover, he includes himself among them, thus casting within himself the scalpel that carries out his separations.

Instead of sounding himself as to his "being," he does so concerning his place: *"Where* am I?"* instead of *"Who* am I?"* For the space that engrosses the deject, the excluded, is never *one,* nor *homogeneous,* nor *totalizable,* but essentially divisible, foldable, and catastrophic. A deviser of territories, languages, works, the *deject* never stops demarcating his universe whose fluid confines—for they are constituted of a non-object, the abject—constantly question his solidity and impel him to start afresh. A tireless builder, the deject is in short a *stray.* He is on a journey, during the night, the end of which keeps receding. He has a sense of the danger, of the loss that the pseudo-object attracting him represents for him, but he cannot help taking the risk at the very moment he sets himself apart. And the more he strays, the more he is saved.

## Time: forgetfulness and thunder

For it is out of such straying on excluded ground that he draws his jouissance. The abject from which he does not cease separating is for him, in short, a *land of oblivion* that is constantly remembered. Once upon blotted-out time, the abject must have been a magnetized pole of covetousness. But the ashes of oblivion now serve as a screen and reflect aversion, repugnance. The clean and proper (in the sense of incorporated and incorporable) becomes filthy, the sought-after turns into the banished, fascination into shame. Then, forgotten time crops up suddenly and condenses into a flash of lightning an operation that, if it were thought out, would involve bringing together the two opposite terms but, on account of that flash, is discharged like thunder. The time of abjection is double: a time of oblivion and thunder, of veiled infinity and the moment when revelation bursts forth.

## Jouissance and affect

Jouissance, in short. For the stray considers himself as equivalent to a Third Party. He secures the latter's judgment, he acts on the strength of its power in order to condemn, he grounds himself on its law to tear the veil of oblivion but also to set up its object as inoperative. As jettisoned. Parachuted by the Other. A ternary structure, if you wish, held in keystone position by the Other, but a "structure" that is skewed, a topology of catastrophe. For, having provided itself with an *alter ego*, the Other no longer has a grip on the three apices of the triangle where subjective homogeneity resides; and so, it jettisons the object into an abominable real, inaccessible except through jouissance. It follows that jouissance alone causes the abject to exist as such. One does not know it, one does not desire it, one joys in it [*on en jouit*]. Violently and painfully. A passion. And, as in jouissance where the object of desire, known as object *a* [in Lacan's terminology], bursts with the shattered mirror where the ego gives up its image in order to contemplate itself in the Other, there is nothing either objective or objectal to the abject. It is simply a frontier, a repulsive gift that the Other, having become *alter ego*, drops so that "I" does not disappear in it but finds, in that sublime alienation, a forfeited existence. Hence a jouissance in which the subject is swallowed up but in which the Other, in return, keeps the subject from foundering by making it repugnant. One thus understands why so many victims of the abject are its fascinated victims—if not its submissive and willing ones.

We may call it a border; abjection is above all ambiguity. Because, while releasing a hold, it does not radically cut off the subject from what threatens it—on the contrary, abjection acknowledges it to be in perpetual danger. But also because abjection itself is a composite of judgment and affect, of condemnation and yearning, of signs and drives. Abjection preserves what existed in the archaism of pre-objectal relationship, in the immemorial violence with which a body becomes separated from another body in order to be—maintaining that night in which the outline of the signified thing vanishes and where only the imponderable affect is carried out. To be sure, if I am affected by what does not yet appear to me as a thing, it is because laws, connections, and even structures of meaning govern and condition me. That order, that glance, that voice, that gesture, which enact the law for my frightened body, constitute and bring about an effect and not yet a sign. I speak to it in vain in order to exclude it from what will no longer be, for myself, a world that can be assimilated. Obviously, I *am* only *like* someone else: mimetic logic of the advent of the ego, objects, and signs. But when I *seek* (myself), *lose* (myself), or experience *jouissance*—then "I" is *heterogeneous*. Discomfort, unease, dizziness stemming from an ambiguity that, through the violence of a revolt *against,* demarcates a space out of which signs and objects arise. Thus braided, woven, ambivalent, a heterogeneous flux marks out a territory that I can call my own because the Other, having dwelt in me as *alter ego*, points it out to me through loathing.

This means once more that the heterogeneous flow, which portions the abject and sends back abjection, already dwells in a human animal that has been highly altered. I experience abjection only if an Other has settled in place and stead of what will be "me." Not at all another with whom I identify and incorporate, but an Other who precedes and possesses me, and through such possession causes me to be. A possession previous to my advent: a being-there of the symbolic that a father might or might not embody. Significance is indeed inherent in the human body.

## At the limit of primal repression

If, on account of that Other, a space becomes demarcated, separating the abject from what will be a subject and its objects, it is because a repression that one might call "primal" has been effected prior to the springing forth of the ego, of its objects and representations. The latter, in turn, as they depend on another repression, the "secondary" one, arrive only *a posteriori* on an enigmatic foundation that has already been marked off; its return, in a phobic, obsessional, psychotic guise, or more generally and in more imaginary fashion in the shape of *abjection,* notifies us of the limits of the human universe.

On such limits and at the limit one could say that there is no unconscious, which is elaborated when representations and affects (whether or not tied to representations) shape a logic. Here, on the contrary, consciousness has not assumed its rights and transformed into signifiers those fluid demarcations of yet unstable territories where an "I" that is taking shape is ceaselessly straying. We are no longer within the sphere of the unconscious but at the limit of primal repression that, nevertheless, has discovered an intrinsically corporeal and already signifying brand, symptom, and sign: repugnance, disgust, abjection. There is an effervescence of object and sign—not of desire but of intolerable significance; they tumble over into non-sense or the impossible real, but they appear even so in spite of "myself' (which is not) as abjection.

## Premises of the sign, linings of the sublime

Let us pause a while at this juncture. If the abject is already a wellspring of sign for a non-object, on the edges of primal repression, one can understand its skirting the somatic symptom on the one hand and sublimation on the other. The *symptom:* a language that gives up, a structure within the body, a non-assimilable alien, a monster, a tumor, a cancer that the listening devices of the unconscious do not hear, for its strayed subject is huddled outside the paths of desire. *Sublimation,* on the contrary, is nothing else than the possibility of naming the pre-nominal, the pre-objectal, which are in fact only a trans-nominal, a trans-objectal. In the symptom, the abject permeates me, I become abject. Through sublimation, I keep it under control. The abject is edged with the sublime. It is not the same moment on the journey, but the same subject and speech bring them into being.

For the sublime has no object either. When the starry sky, a vista of open seas or a stained glass window shedding purple beams fascinate me, there is a cluster of meaning, of colors, of words, of caresses, there are light touches, scents, sighs, cadences that arise, shroud me, carry me away, and sweep me beyond the things that I see, hear, or think. The "sublime" object dissolves in the raptures of a bottomless memory. It is such a memory, which, from stopping point to stopping point, remembrance to remembrance, love to love, transfers that object to the refulgent point of the dazzlement in which I stray in order to be. As soon as I perceive it, as soon as I name it, the sublime triggers—it has always already triggered—a spree of perceptions and words that expands memory boundlessly. I then forget the point of departure and find myself removed to a secondary universe, set off from the one where "I" am—delight and loss. Not at all short of but always with and through perception and words, the sublime is a *something added* that expands us, overstrains us, and causes us to be both *here,* as dejects, and *there,* as others and sparkling. A divergence, an impossible bounding. Everything missed, joy—fascination. […]

## Questions

1. What does Kristeva mean by the abject and abjection? Explain, giving some examples.
2. In elaborating her views, how does Kristeva employ distinctions between subject and object, and inside and outside?
3. To what purpose does Kristeva put the concept of the "sublime"?

4. How are the abject and the sublime related? How does each relate to, and differ from, sublimation? (Sublimation is briefly explained in the Introduction to the present volume.)

## Further reading

Beardsworth, Sara. *Julia Kristeva, Psychoanalysis and Modernity*. Albany: SUNY Press, 2004.

Butler, Judith. *Bodies That Matter: On the Discursive Limits of "Sex."* New York: Routledge, 1993.

Freud, Sigmund. *Totem and Taboo*. London: W. W. Norton, 1989.

Oliver, Kelly. *Ethics, Politics, and Difference in Julia Kristeva's Writings*. New York: Routledge, 1993.

Radden, Jennifer. *The Nature of Melancholy: From Aristotle to Kristeva*. New York: Oxford University Press, 2008.

Žižek, Slavoj. *The Sublime Object of Ideology*. London: Verso, 1989.

# CHAPTER 29
## FREDRIC JAMESON, FROM "POSTMODERNISM, OR THE CULTURAL LOGIC OF LATE CAPITALISM" (1984)

Fredric Jameson is a Marxist theorist and American literary critic. Some of his best-known works are *Marxism and Form, The Political Unconsciousness,* and *Postmodernism, or The Cultural Logic of Late Capitalism,*[1] in which the following excerpt was reprinted.

Below, Jameson employs the notion of the *technological* sublime—or "postmodern" and "hysterical" sublime. In the experience of the hysterical sublime, the world "momentarily loses its depth and threatens to become a glossy skin, a stereoscopic illusion, a rush of filmic images without density." Like Jean-François Lyotard, Jameson understands the sublime to concern the limits of figuration and representation. "Our faulty representations of some immense communicational and computer network are themselves but a distorted figuration of something even deeper, namely the whole world system of present-day multinational capitalism."

Jameson divides up "cultural periodization" into three stages: realism, modernism, and postmodernism. Like writers such as David Nye and Mario Costa, Jameson examines a recent form of sublimity made possible by developments in technology in modernity and postmodernity.

Culturally, economically, and/or socially based approaches such as Jameson's Marxist account inevitably lead to the question of whether the sublime is a "social construct" or not—and what this means. One might expect some of these accounts to veer into incoherence: to claim to give a theory of something that the theory claims cannot be theorized since it is too varied and culturally dependent. One might wonder, after all, what one is giving a theory *of.* Thankfully, one instance of the cultural-social approach—represented by David Nye in the following quote on the American technological sublime—avoids incoherence. "The experience of sublimity is based on a universal capacity for a certain kind of emotion. But Americans nevertheless shaped this emotion to their situation and needs."[2] Thus, Nye implies that the capacity for the experience is grounded in human being's biological and psychological capacities, while the particular way in which that capacity is realized or instantiated is largely a product of particular, complex situations, histories, and cultural contingencies.

### Note on the text

Source: Excerpted from Fredric Jameson, "Postmodernism, or the Cultural Logic of Late Capitalism." *New Left Review* 1, 146 (1984): 76–80.
The format and style have been reproduced, with occasional modifications.

### IV The hysterical sublime

Now we need to complete this exploratory account of postmodernist space and time with a final analysis of that euphoria or those intensities which seem so often to characterize the newer cultural experience. Let us stress again the enormity of a transition which leaves behind it the desolation of Hopper's buildings or the stark Midwest syntax of Sheeler's forms, replacing them with the extraordinary surfaces of the photorealist cityscape, where even the automobile wrecks gleam with some new hallucinatory splendour. The exhilaration of these new surfaces is all the more paradoxical in that their essential content—the city itself—has deteriorated or disintegrated to a degree surely still inconceivable in the early years of the 20th century, let alone in the previous era. How urban squalor can be a delight to the eyes, when expressed in commodification, and how an unparalleled quantum leap in the alienation of daily life in the city can now be experienced in the form of a strange new hallucinatory exhilaration—these are some of the questions that confront us in this moment of our inquiry. Nor should the human figure be exempted from investigation, although it seems clear that for the newer aesthetic the representation of space itself has come to be felt as incompatible with the representation of the body: a kind of aesthetic division of labour far more pronounced than in any of the earlier generic conceptions of landscape, and a most ominous symptom indeed. The privileged space of the newer art is radically anti-anthropomorphic, as in the empty bathrooms of Doug Bond's work. The ultimate contemporary fetishization of the human body, however, takes a very different direction in the statues of Duane Hanson— what I have already called the simulacrum, whose peculiar function lies in what Sartre would have called the *derealization* of the whole surrounding world of everyday reality. Your moment of doubt and hesitation as to the breath and warmth of these polyester figures, in other words, tends to return upon the real human beings moving about you in the museum, and to transform them also for the briefest instant into so many dead and flesh-coloured simulacra in their own right. The world thereby momentarily loses its depth and threatens to become a glossy skin, a stereoscopic illusion, a rush of filmic images without density. But is this now a terrifying or an exhilarating experience?

It has proved fruitful to think such experience in terms of what Susan Sontag once, in an influential statement, isolated as 'camp'. I propose a somewhat different cross-light on it, drawing on the equally fashionable current theme of the 'sublime', as it has been rediscovered in the works of Edmund Burke and Kant; or perhaps, indeed, one might well want to yoke the two notions together in the form of something like a camp or 'hysterical' sublime. The sublime was for Burke, as you will recall, an experience bordering on terror, the fitful glimpse, in astonishment, stupor and awe, of what was so enormous as to crush human life altogether: a description then refined by Kant to include the question of representation itself—so that the object of the sublime is now not only a matter of sheer power and of the physical incommensurability of the human organism with Nature, but also of the limits of figuration and the incapacity of the human mind to give representation to such enormous forces. Such forces Burke, in his historical moment at the dawn of the modern bourgeois state, was only able to conceptualize in terms of the divine; while even Heidegger continues to entertain a fantasmatic relationship with some organic precapitalist peasant landscape and village society, which is the final form of the image of Nature in our own time.

Today, however, it may be possible to think all this in a different way, at the moment of a radical eclipse of Nature itself: Heidegger's 'field path' is after all irredeemably and irrevocably destroyed by late capital, by the green revolution, by neocolonialism and the megapopolis, which runs its superhighways over the older fields and vacant lots, and turns Heidegger's 'house of being' into condominiums, if not the most miserable unheated rat-infested tenement buildings. The *other* of our society is in that sense no longer Nature at all, as it was in precapitalist societies, but something else which we must now identify.

## The apotheosis of capitalism

I am anxious that this other thing should not overhastily be grasped as technology per se, since I will want to show that technology is here itself a figure for something else. Yet technology may well serve as adequate shorthand to designate that enormous properly human and anti-natural power of dead human labour stored up in our machinery, an alienated power, what Sartre calls the counterfinality of the practico-inert, which turns back on and against us in unrecognizable forms and seems to constitute the massive dystopian horizon of our collective as well as our individual praxis.

Technology is, however, on the Marxist view the result of the development of capital, rather than some primal cause in its own right. It will therefore be appropriate to distinguish several generations of machine power, several stages of technological revolution within capital itself. I here follow Ernest Mandel who outlines three such fundamental breaks or quantum leaps in the evolution of machinery under capital: "The fundamental revolutions in power technology—the technology of the production of motive machines by machines—thus appears as the determinant moment in revolutions of technology as a whole. Machine production of steam-driven motors since 1848; machine production of electric and combustion motors since the 90s of the 19th century; machine production of electronic and nuclear-powered apparatuses since the 40s of the 20th century—these are the three general revolutions in technology engendered by the capitalist mode of production since the 'original' industrial revolution of the later 18th century." (*Late Capitalism*, p. 18.)

The periodization underscores the general thesis of Mandel's book *Late Capitalism*, namely that there have been three fundamental moments in capitalism, each one marking a dialectical expansion over the previous stage: these are market capitalism, the monopoly stage or the stage of imperialism, and our own—wrongly called postindustrial, but what might better be termed multinational capital. I have already pointed out that Mandel's intervention in the postindustrial involves the proposition that late or multinational or consumer capitalism, far from being inconsistent with Marx's great 19th-century analysis, constitutes on the contrary the purest form of capital yet to have emerged, a prodigious expansion of capital into hitherto uncommodified areas. This purer capitalism of our own time thus eliminates the enclaves of precapitalist organization it had hitherto tolerated and exploited in a tributary way: one is tempted to speak in this connection of a new and historically original penetration and colonization of Nature and the Unconscious: that is, the destruction of precapitalist third world agriculture by the Green Revolution, and the rise of the media and the advertising industry. At any rate, it will also have been clear that my own cultural periodization of the stages of realism, modernism and postmodernism is both inspired and confirmed by Mandel's tripartite scheme.

We may speak therefore of our own age as the Third (or even Fourth) Machine Age; and it is at this point that we must reintroduce the problem of aesthetic representation already explicitly developed in Kant's earlier analysis of the sublime—since it would seem only logical that the relationship to, and representation of, the machine could be expected to shift dialectically with each of these qualitatively different stages of technological development.

It is appropriate therefore to recall the excitement of machinery in the preceding moment of capital, the exhilaration of futurism most notably, and of Marinetti's celebration of the machine gun and the motor car. These are still visible emblems, sculptural nodes of energy which give tangibility and figuration to the motive energies of that earlier moment of modernization. The prestige of these great streamlined shapes can be measured by their metaphorical presence in Le Corbusier's buildings, vast Utopian structures which ride like so many gigantic steamship liners upon the urban scenery of an older fallen earth. Machinery exerts another kind of fascination in artists like Picabia and Duchamp, whom we have no time to consider here; but let me mention, for the sake of completeness, the ways in which revolutionary or communist artists of the 1930s also sought to reappropriate this excitement of machine energy for a Promethean reconstruction of human society as a whole, as in Fernand Leger and Diego Rivera.

What must then immediately be observed is that the technology of our own moment no longer possesses this same capacity for representation: not the turbine, nor even Sheeler's grain elevators or smokestacks, not the baroque elaboration of pipes and conveyor belts nor even the streamlined profile of the railroad train—all vehicles of speed still concentrated at rest—but rather the computer, whose outer shell has no emblematic or visual power, or even the casings of the various media themselves, as with that home appliance called television which articulates nothing but rather implodes, carrying its flattened image surface within itself.

Such machines are indeed machines of reproduction rather than of production, and they make very different demands on our capacity for aesthetic representation than did the relatively mimetic idolatry of the older machinery of the futurist moment, of some older speed-and-energy sculpture. Here we have less to do with kinetic energy than with all kinds of new reproductive processes; and in the weaker productions of postmodernism the aesthetic embodiment of such processes often tends to slip back more comfortably into a mere thematic representation of content—into narratives which are *about* the processes of reproduction, and include movie cameras, video, tape recorders, the whole technology of the production and reproduction of the simulacrum. (The shift from Antonioni's modernist *Blowup* to DePalma's postmodernist *Blowout* is here paradigmatic.) When Japanese architects, for example, model a building on the decorative imitation of stacks of cassettes, then the solution is at best a thematic and allusive, although often humorous, one.

Yet something else does tend to emerge in the most energetic postmodernist texts, and it is the sense that beyond all thematics or content the work seems somehow to tap the networks of reproductive process and thereby to afford us some glimpse into a postmodern or technological sublime, whose power or authenticity is documented by the success of such works in evoking a whole new postmodern space in emergence around us. Architecture therefore remains in this sense the privileged aesthetic language; and the distorting and fragmenting reflections of one enormous glass surface to the other can be taken as paradigmatic of the central role of process and reproduction in postmodernist culture.

As I have said, however, I want to avoid the implication that technology is in any way the 'ultimately determining instance' either of our present-day social life or of our cultural production: such a thesis is of course ultimately at one with the post-Marxist notion of a 'postindustrialist' society. Rather, I want to suggest that our faulty representations of some immense communicational and computer network are themselves but a distorted figuration of something even deeper, namely the whole world system of present-day multinational capitalism. The technology of contemporary society is therefore mesmerizing and fascinating, not so much in its own right, but because it seems to offer some privileged representational shorthand for grasping a network of power and control even more difficult for our minds and imaginations to grasp—namely the whole new decentered global network of the third stage of capital itself. This is a figural process presently best observed in a whole mode of contemporary entertainment literature, which one is tempted to characterize as 'high tech paranoia', in which the circuits and networks of some putative global computer hook-up are narratively mobilized by labyrinthine conspiracies of autonomous but deadly interlocking and competing information agencies in a complexity often beyond the capacity of the normal reading mind. Yet conspiracy theory (and its garish narrative manifestations) must be seen as a degraded attempt—through the figuration of advanced technology—to think the impossible totality of the contemporary world system. It is therefore in terms of that enormous and threatening, yet only dimly perceivable, other reality of economic and social institutions that in my opinion the postmodern sublime can alone be adequately theorized.

## Questions

1. Compare and contrast Jameson's account of the "postmodern" sublime with that of Jean-François Lyotard (in the present volume). Where do they agree? Disagree?

2. *Has* the aesthetic representation of technology changed over the past three hundred years? If so, does this entail that that the sublime is a 'social construct'? Does it imply the sublime is too varied and culturally dependent to allow it to be theorized in a general manner? Explain.

3. Describe your experience of some of the kinds of technology mentioned by Jameson. Do certain forms of technology (but not others) tend to create the experience of the sublime? Explain. Characterize this kind of sublimity in your own terms.

## Further reading

Clemente, Marie-Christine. "The Sublime Dimension of 9/11." In *The Sublime Today: Contemporary Readings in the Aesthetic*, ed. Gillian Borland Pierce, 163–90. Newcastle upon Tyne: Cambridge Scholars, 2012.

Costa, Mario. *Il Sublime Tecnologico*. Salerno: Edisud, 1990. See also Mario Costa, *Le Sublime Technologique*. Lausanne: Iderive, 1994.

Gilbert-Rolfe, Jeremy. *Beauty and the Contemporary Sublime*, 125–44. New York: Allworth Press, 1999.

Helmling, Steven. *The Success and Failure of Fredric Jameson: Writing, the Sublime, and the Dialectic of Critique*. Albany: SUNY Press, 2001.

Lyotard, Jean-François. "The Sublime and the Avant-Garde," in the present volume.

Marx, Leo. *The Machine in the Garden: Technology and the Pastoral Ideal in America*. New York: Oxford University Press, 1964.

Mosco, Vincent. *The Digital Sublime: Myth, Power and Cyberspace*. Cambridge, MA: MIT Press, 2004.

# CHAPTER 30
## JEAN-FRANÇOIS LYOTARD, "THE SUBLIME AND THE AVANT-GARDE" (1985)

Jean-François Lyotard (1924–1998) was a French philosopher, art critic, and literary theorist, influenced by Augustine, Kant, Marx, Freud, Heidegger, Adorno, and Wittgenstein. In addition to composing works such as *The Differend*, Lyotard wrote frequently on late twentieth-century art. As "The Sublime and the Avant-Garde" reveals, he was interested in how avant-garde art can evoke or represent the sublime and how it raised philosophical questions about the nature of painting.

Lyotard's central concept of the differend (*différend*) springs from a combination of diverse intellectual sources: Kant's separation of the theoretical/practical/aesthetic spheres and the concept of an inexhaustible "idea" of reason; Wittgenstein's descriptions of language games and rule-following; and Heidegger's concern with temporality and the historical event (*Ereignis*)—or, as Lyotard puts it, the fact "that it happens." Like a Kantian idea, Lyotard's indeterminable differend (or "the indeterminate") is not a phenomenon that can be exhibited by or given in experience.

Like other francophone writers, Lyotard uses the concept of the sublime to make sense of the unpresentable.[1] Like the differend, the experience of the sublime forces the mind to go beyond what can be understood or even represented. At the same time, the stretching or effort in the sublime is "gratifying."[2] It is the joy of discovering an affinity within the disagreement between nature and reason, namely, of discovering that even if presented as vast or great, nature (including human nature, the natural history of man, the French Revolution) always will be "small in comparison with" the Ideas of reason.[3] In this way, Lyotard connects the sublime to the political sphere.

In *Enthusiasm*, an historically-politically oriented work, Lyotard distinguishes various kinds of "phrases" or language games: the cognitive, historico-political, ethical, and aesthetic. Most "phrase families" have unique rules of presentation: the ethical has its rules, the cognitive other ones, and so on. For instance, the cognitive phrase remains governed by the rule of "intuitional" or direct presentation. Unlike the cognitive phrase, however, the "sublime phrase" judges in the absence of any rules. In the aesthetic phrase—that of sublimity and beauty—there is no determinable presentation of the referent or object. It is not a matter of finding an intuition for a given concept, or of subsuming a direct presentation under a concept. In addition, there can be no direct translation among these heterogeneous phrases; Lyotard here offers the metaphor of different islands in an archipelago. Nevertheless, passage between the islands or phrase families is possible. The phrases can be connected to each other through analogies or bridges. The sublime provides one such passage between the aesthetic and the political-historical (and the ethical).

In *Lessons on the Analytic of the Sublime*, Lyotard interprets enthusiasm as a kind of sublimity. In *Enthusiasm*, Lyotard makes three observations about spectators' enthusiasm for the French Revolution (more precisely: the idea of a republic). Lyotard's interpretation of Kant is worth summarizing here to illustrate his use of phrase families and the sublime as a bridge or analog. First, the enthusiasm experienced by the spectators, according to Kant, is an "extreme" mode of the sublime feeling. This instance of historico-political enthusiasm "sees nothingness" and relates it back to "the unpresentable." Second, the "event" that Kant sought within the historical experience in order to validate the claim that humanity is constantly "progressing" toward the better is the spectators' shared enthusiasm. The spectators' collective enthusiasm is an "aesthetic analog of pure, republican fervor." Third, the agreement or consensus invoked by the sublime feeling puts us in the middle of the archipelago: it acts as a kind of bridge, providing passage between the aesthetic and the ethical and the political.

In general, Lyotard does not shy away from paradoxical formulations. This is also true of what he says about sublimity: it presents the unpresentable, or at least that there is the unpresentable (or, that the absolute exists). The sublime is the "sentimental paradox," the paradox of experiencing publicly and *de jure*, as a group, that something "formless" (the revolutionary upheavals) alludes to a beyond of experience (the unpresentable idea of reason, in Kant's terminology). Yet even in the politically oriented work, *Enthusiasm*, Lyotard makes a remark that he elaborates more fully in the following essay, which lies closer to art criticism and history, cultural studies, and aesthetics.

> What is required for this abstract presentation [in the sublime], which presents nothingness, is that the imagination be 'unbounded'. . . . This would be a good point of departure for a philosophy of abstract art. If the aesthetics of Romanticism is certainly linked to the philosophy of the sublime, so-called abstract art would be its most radical emanation and perhaps its exit route.[4]

This claim is dealt with more fully in this 1985 essay, one of Lyotard's most influential discussions on the sublime. Lyotard comments on Kant and the sublime, "Even before romantic art had freed itself from classical and baroque figuration, the door had thus been opened to inquiries pointing towards abstract and Minimal art. Avant-gardism is thus present in germ in the Kantian aesthetic of the sublime." While the essay is in part a defense of avant-garde art, it is also a commentary on capitalism. "There is something of the sublime in capitalist economy," Lyotard writes, bringing to mind what Frederic Jameson calls the postmodern or hysterical sublime. In turn, Lyotard notes the effects of art markets on the artworld. "Sublimity is no longer in art, but in speculation on art."

In the end, Lyotard does not defend a "theory" of the sublime in the empirical or transcendental psychological traditions of Burke and Kant, but instead employs the sublime to make sense of being—the unfolding of the "There is." Lyotard calls on the sublime in order to respond to the event, the occurrence that takes place before thought and conceptualization and hence is indeterminate—the "It happens" that makes up human history.

## Note on the text

Source: Lyotard, Jean-François. "The Sublime and the Avant-Garde." *Paragraph* (1985), 6: 1-18, trans. Lisa Liebmann, Geoff Bennington, and Marian Hobson. This text was first published In *Art Forum* 22 (8) (1984): 36-43, trans. Lisa Liebmann. Alterations were made to the French text by Jean-François Lyotard when he gave the paper in Cambridge in March 1984, and these have been translated by Geoff Bennington and Marian Hobson and incorporated into this translation.

Lyotard sometimes makes use of an ellipsis; thus, a stand-alone ellipsis does not indicate that anything has been omitted: the essay is reprinted in its entirety. Punctuation, style, format, and spelling have occasionally been modified or standardized. Foreign words and some quotes (e.g., *Is it happening?*) have been italicized. Insertions in square brackets are found in the 1985 translation, unless otherwise indicated by " – Ed." All footnotes are written by the volume editor.

## "The sublime and the avant-garde"

### 1.

In 1950-1951, Barnett Baruch Newman painted a canvas measuring 2.42 m by 5.42 m which he called *Vir Heroicus Sublimis*. In the mid-sixties he entitled his first three sculptures *Here I*, *Here II*, *Here III*. Another painting was called *Not Over There, Here*, two paintings were called *Now*, and two others were entitled *Be*. In December 1948, Newman wrote an essay entitled *The Sublime is Now*.

How is one to understand the sublime, or, let us say provisionally, the object of a sublime experience, as a 'here and now'? Quite to the contrary, isn't it essential to this feeling that it alludes to something which can't be shown or presented (as Kant said *dargestellt*)? In a short unfinished text dating from late 1949, *Prologue for a New Aesthetic*, Newman wrote that in his painting, he was not concerned with a 'manipulation of space nor with the image, but with a sensation of time'. He added that by this he did not mean time laden with feelings of nostalgia, or drama, or reference and history, the usual subjects of painting. After this denial [*dénégation*] the text stops short.

So, what kind of time was Newman concerned with, what 'now' did he have in mind? Thomas B. Hess, his friend and commentator, felt justified in writing that Newman's time was the *Makom* or the *Hamakom* of Hebraic tradition—the *there*, the site, the place, which is one of the names given by the Torah to the Lord, the Unnameable. I do not know enough about *Makom* to know whether this was what Newman had in mind. But then again, who does know enough about *now*? Newman can certainly not have been thinking of the 'present instant', the one that tries to hold itself between the future and the past, and gets devoured by them. This *now* is one of the temporal 'ecstasies' that has been analyzed since Augustine's day and particularly since Edmund Husserl, according to a line of thought that has attempted to constitute time on the basis of consciousness. Newman's *now* which is no more than *now* is a stranger to consciousness and cannot be constituted by it. Rather it is what dismantles consciousness, what deposes consciousness, it is what consciousness cannot formulate, and even what consciousness forgets in order to constitute itself. What we do not manage to formulate is that something happens, *dass etwas geschieht*. Or rather, and more simply, that it happens . . . *dass es geschieht*. Not a major event in the media sense, not even a small event. Just an occurrence.

This isn't a matter of sense or reality bearing upon *what* happens or *what* this might mean. Before asking questions about what it is and about its significance, before the *quid*, it must 'first' so to speak 'happen', *quod*. That it happens 'precedes', so to speak the question pertaining to what happens. Or rather, the question precedes itself, because 'that it happens' is the question relevant as event, and it 'then' pertains to the event that has just happened. The event happens as a question mark 'before' happening as a question. *It happens* is rather 'in the first place' *is it happening, is this it, is it possible?* Only 'then' is any mark determined by the questioning: is this or that happening, is it this or something else, is it possible that this or that?

An event, an occurrence—what Martin Heidegger called *ein Ereignis*—is infinitely simple, but this simplicity can only be approached through a state of privation. That which we call thought must be disarmed. There is a tradition and an institution of philosophy, of painting, of politics, of literature. These 'disciplines' also have a future in the form of Schools, of programmes, projects, and 'trends'. Thought works over what is received, it seeks to reflect on it and overcome it. It seeks to determine what has already been thought, written, painted or socialized in order to determine what hasn't been. We know this process well, it is our daily bread. It is the bread of war, soldiers' biscuit. But this agitation, in the most noble sense of the word (agitation is the word Kant gives to the activity of the mind that has judgement and exercises it), this agitation is only possible if something remains to be determined, something that hasn't yet been determined. One can strive to determine this something by setting up a system, a theory, a programme or a project—and indeed one has to, all the while anticipating that something. One can also inquire about the remainder, and allow the indeterminate to appear as a question mark.

What all intellectual disciplines and institutions presuppose is that not everything has been said, written down or recorded, that words already heard or pronounced are not the last words. 'After' a sentence, 'after' a colour, comes another sentence, another colour. One doesn't know which, but one thinks one knows if one relies on the rules that permit one sentence to link up with another, one colour with another, rules preserved in precisely those institutions of the past and future that I mentioned. The School, the programme, the project—all proclaim that after this sentence comes that sentence, or at least that one kind of sentence is mandatory, that one kind of sentence is permitted, while another is forbidden. This holds true for painting as much as for the other activities of thought. After one pictorial work, another is necessary, permitted or forbidden. After one colour, this other colour; after this line, that one. There isn't an enormous difference between an avant-garde manifesto and a curriculum at the École des Beaux Arts, if one considers them in the light of this relationship to time. Both are options with respect to what they feel is a good thing to happen subsequently. But both also forget the possibility of nothing happening, of words, colours, forms or sounds not coming; of this sentence being the last, of bread not coming daily. This is the misery that the painter faces with a plastic surface, of the musician with the acoustic surface, the misery the thinker faces with a desert of thought, and so on. Not only faced with the empty canvas or the empty page, at the 'beginning' of the work, but every time something has to be waited for, and thus forms a question at every point of questioning [*point d'interrogation*], at every 'and what now?'

The possibility of nothing happening is often associated with a feeling of anxiety, a term with strong connotations in modern philosophies of existence and of the unconscious. It gives to waiting, if we really mean waiting, a predominantly negative value. But suspense can also be accompanied by pleasure, for instance pleasure in welcoming the unknown, and even by joy, to speak like Baruch Spinoza, the joy obtained by the intensification of being that the event brings with it. This is probably a contradictory feeling. It is at the very least a sign the question mark itself, the way in which *it happens* is withheld and announced: *Is it happening?* The question can be modulated in any tone. But the mark of the question is 'now', *now* like the feeling that nothing might happen: the nothingness now.

Between the seventeenth and eighteenth centuries in Europe this contradictory feeling—pleasure and pain, joy and anxiety, exaltation and depression—was christened or re-christened by the name of the *sublime*. It is around this name that the destiny of classical poetics was hazarded and lost; it is in this name that aesthetics asserted its critical rights over art, and that romanticism, in other words, modernity, triumphed.

It remains to the art historian to explain how the word sublime reappeared in the language of a Jewish painter from New York during the forties. The word *sublime* is common currency today to colloquial French to suggest surprise and admiration, somewhat like America's 'great' but the idea connoted by it has belonged (for at least two centuries) to the most rigorous kind of reflection on art. Newman is not unaware of the aesthetic and philosophical stakes with which the word *sublime* is involved. He read Edmund Burke's *Enquiry* and criticized what he saw as Burke's over 'surrealist' description of the sublime work. Which is as much as to say that, conversely, Newman judged surrealism to be over-reliant on a pre-romantic or romantic approach to indeterminacy. Thus, when he seeks sublimity in the here-and-now he breaks with the eloquence of romantic art but he does not reject its fundamental task, that of bearing pictorial or otherwise expressive witness to the inexpressible. The inexpressible does not reside in an over there, in another word, or another time, but in this: in that (something) happens. In the determination of pictorial art, the indeterminate, the 'it happens' is the paint, the picture. The paint, the picture as occurrence or event is not expressible, and it is to this that it has to witness.

To be true to this displacement in which consists perhaps the whole of the difference between romanticism and the 'modern' avant-garde, one would have to read *The Sublime is Now* not as *The Sublime is Now* but as

*Now the Sublime is Like This.* Not elsewhere, not up there or over there, not earlier or later, not once upon a time. But as here, now, it happens that, . . . and it's this painting. Here and now there is this painting, rather than nothing, and that's what is sublime. Letting go of all grasping intelligence and of its power, disarming it, recognizing that this occurrence of painting was not necessary and is scarcely foreseeable, a privation in the face of *Is it happening?* guarding the occurrence 'before' any defense, any illustration, and any commentary, guarding before being on one's guard, before 'looking' [*regarder*] under the aegis of *now,* this is the rigour of the avant-garde. In the determination of literary art this requirement with respect to the *Is it happening?* found one of its most rigorous realizations in Gertrude Stein's *How to Write.* It's still the sublime in the sense that Burke and Kant described and yet it isn't their sublime any more.

# 2.

I have said that the contradictory feeling with which indeterminacy is both announced and missed was what was at stake in reflection on art from the end of the seventeenth to the end of the eighteenth centuries. The sublime is perhaps the only mode of artistic sensibility to characterize the modern. Paradoxically, it was introduced to literary discussion and vigorously defended by the French writer who has been classified in literary history as one of the most dogged advocates of ancient classicism. In 1674 Boileau published his *Art Poétique* but he also published *Du Sublime,* his translation or transcription from the *Peri tou hupsou.* It is a treatise, or rather an essay, attributed to a certain Longinus about whose identity there has long been confusion and whose life we now estimate as having begun towards the end of the first century of our era. The author was a rhetorician. Basically, he taught those oratorical devices with which a speaker can persuade or move (depending on the genre) his audience. The didactics of rhetoric had been traditional since Aristotle, Cicero, and Quintilian. They were linked to the republican institution; one had to know how to speak before assemblies and tribunals.

One might expect that Longinus' text would invoke the maxims and advice transmitted by this tradition by perpetuating the didactic form of *technē rhetorikē.* But surprisingly, the sublime, the indeterminate, were destabilizing the text's didactic intention. I cannot analyze this uncertainty here. Boileau himself and numerous other commentators, especially Fénélon, were aware of it and concluded that the sublime could only be discussed in sublime style. Longinus certainly tried to define sublimity in discourse, writing that it was unforgettable, irresistible, and most important, thought-provoking—'*il y a à partir d'elle beaucoup de réflexion*' (*hou polle anatheoresis*) (from the sublime springs a lot of reflection). He also tried to locate sources for the sublime in the ethos of rhetoric in its pathos, in its techniques: figures of speech, diction, enunciation, composition. He sought in this way to bend himself to the rules of the genre of the 'treatise' (whether of rhetoric or poetics, or politics) destined to be a model for practitioners.

However, when it comes to the sublime, major obstacles get in the way of a regular exposition of rhetorical or poetic principles. There is, for example, wrote Longinus, a sublimity of thought sometimes recognizable in speech by its extreme simplicity of turn of phrase at the precise point where the high character of the speaker makes one expect greater solemnity. It sometimes even takes the form of outright silence. I don't mind if this simplicity, this silence, is taken to be yet another rhetorical figure. But it must be granted that it constitutes the most indeterminate of figures. What can remain of rhetoric (or of poetics) when the rhetorician in Boileau's translation announces that to attain the sublime effect 'there is no better figure of speech than one which is completely hidden, that which we do not even recognize as a figure of speech?' Must we admit that there are techniques for hiding figures, that there are figures for the erasure of figures? How do we distinguish between a hidden figure and what is not a figure? And what is it, if it isn't a figure? And what about this, which seems to be a major blow to didactics: when it is sublime, discourse accommodates defects, lack of taste, and formal imperfections. Plato's style for example, is full of bombast and bloated strained comparisons. Plato, in short, is a mannerist, or a baroque writer compared to a Lysias, and so is Sophocles compared to an Ion, or Pindar compared to a Bacchylides. The fact remains that, like those first named, he is sublime whereas the second ones are merely perfect. Shortcomings in technique are therefore trifling matters if they are the price to be paid for 'true grandeur'. Grandeur in speech is true when it bears witness to the incommensurability between thought and the real world.

Is it Boileau's transcription that suggests this analogy, or is it the influence of early Christianity on Longinus? The fact that grandeur of spirit it not of this world cannot but suggest Pascal's hierarchy of orders. The kind of perfection that can be demanded in the domain of *technē* isn't necessarily a desirable attribute when it comes to sublime feeling. Longinus even goes so far as to propose inversions of reputedly natural and rational syntax as examples of sublime effect. As for Boileau, in the preface he wrote in 1674 for Longinus' text, in still further addenda made in 1683 and 1701 and also in the *Tenth Réflexion* published in 1710 after his death [*sic* – Ed.] he makes final the previous tentative break with the classical institution of *technē*. The sublime, he says, cannot be taught, and didactics are thus powerless in this respect; the sublime is not linked to rules that can be determined through poetics; the sublime only requires that the reader or listener have conceptual range, taste, and the ability 'to sense what everyone senses first'. Boileau therefore takes the same stand as Père Bouhours, when in 1671 the latter declared that beauty demands more than just a respect for rules, that it requires a further 'je ne sais quoi', also called *genius* or something 'incomprehensible and inexplicable', a 'gift from God', a fundamentally 'hidden' phenomenon that can be recognized only by its effects on the addressee. And in the polemic that set him against Pierre-Daniel Huet, over the issue of whether the Bible's *Fiat Lux, et Lux fuit* is sublime, as Longinus thought it was, Boileau refers to the opinion of the Messieurs de Port Royal and in particular to Silvestre de Saci: the Jansenists are masters when it comes to matters of hidden meaning, of eloquent silence, of feeling that transcends all reason and finally of openness to the *Is it happening?*

At stake in these poetic-theological debates is the status of works of art. Are they copies of some ideal model? Can reflection on the more 'perfect' examples yield rules of formation that determine their success in achieving what they want, that is persuasiveness and pleasure? Can understanding suffice for this kind of reflection? By meditating on the theme of sublimity and of indeterminacy, meditation about works of art imposes a major change on *technē* and the institutions linked to it—Academies, Schools, masters and disciples, taste, the enlightened public made up of princes and courtiers. It is the very destination or destiny of works which is being questioned. The predominance of the idea of *technē* placed works under a multiple regulation, that of the model taught in the studios, Schools and Academies, that of the taste shared by the aristocratic public, that of a purposiveness of art, which was to illustrate the glory of a name, divine or human, to which was linked the perfection of some cardinal virtue or other. The idea of the sublime disrupts this harmony. Let us magnify the features of this disruption. Under Diderot's pen, *technē* becomes '*le petit technique*' (mere trivial technique). The artist ceases to be guided by a culture which made of him the sender and master of a message of glory: he becomes, in so far as he is a genius, the involuntary addressee of an inspiration come to him from an 'I know not what.' The public no longer judges according to the criteria of a taste ruled by the tradition of shared pleasure: individuals unknown to the artist (the 'people') read books, go through the galleries of the Salons, crowd into the theatres and the public concerts, they are prey to unforeseeable feelings: they are shocked, admiring, scornful, indifferent. The question is not that of pleasing them by leading them to identify with a name and to participate in the glorification of its virtue, but that of surprising them. 'The sublime', writes Boileau, 'is not strictly speaking something which is proven or demonstrated, but a marvel, which seizes one, strikes one, and makes one feel'. The very imperfections, the distortions of taste, even ugliness, have their share in the shock-effect. Art does not imitate nature, it creates a world apart, *eine Zwischenwelt* [a between world – Ed.] as Paul Klee will say; *eine Nebenwelt* [a side world – Ed.], one might say in which the monstrous and the formless have their rights because they can be sublime.

You will (I hope) excuse such simplification of the transformation which takes place with the modern development of the idea of the sublime. The trace of it could be found before modern times, in medieval aesthetics—that of the Victorines for example. In any case, it explains why reflection on art should no longer bear essentially on the 'sender' instance/agency of works, but on the 'addressee' instance. And under the name 'genius' the latter instance is situated, not only on the side of the public, but also on the side of the artist, a feeling which he does not master. Henceforth it seems right to analyze the ways in which the subject is affected, its way of receiving and experiencing feelings, its ways of judging works. This is how aesthetics, the analysis of the addressee's feelings, comes to supplant poetics and rhetoric, which are didactic forms, of and by the understanding, intended for the artist as sender. No longer 'How does one make a work of art?', but 'What is it to experience an affect proper to art?'. And indeterminacy returns, even within the analysis of this last question.

## 3.

Baumgarten published his *Aesthetica,* the first aesthetics, in 1750. Kant would say of this work simply that it was based on an error. Baumgarten confuses judgement, in its determinant usage, when the understanding organizes phenomena according to categories, with judgement in its reflexive usage when, in the form of feeling, it relates to the indeterminate relationship between the faculties of the judging subject. Baumgarten's aesthetics remains dependent on a conceptually determined relationship to the work of art. The sense of beauty is for Kant, on the contrary, kindled by a free harmony between the function of images and the function of concepts occasioned by an object of art or nature. The aesthetics of the sublime is still more indeterminate: a pleasure mixed with pain, a pleasure that comes from pain. In the event of an absolutely large object—the desert, a mountain, a pyramid—or one that is absolutely powerful—a storm at sea, an erupting volcano—which like all absolutes can only be thought, without any sensible/sensory intuition, as an Idea of reason, the faculty of presentation, the imagination, fails to provide a representation corresponding to this Idea. This failure of expression gives rise to a pain, a kind of cleavage within the subject between what can be conceived and what can be imagined or presented. But this pain in turn engenders a pleasure, in fact a double pleasure: the impotence of the imagination attests *a contrario* to an imagination striving to figure even that which cannot be figured, and that imagination thus aims to harmonize its object with that of reason— and that furthermore the inadequacy of the images is a negative sign of the immense power of ideas. This dislocation of the faculties among themselves gives rise to the extreme tension (Kant calls it agitation) that characterizes the pathos of the sublime, as opposed to the calm feeling of beauty. At the edge of the break, infinity, or the absoluteness of the Idea can be revealed in what Kant calls a negative presentation, or even a non-presentation. He cites the Jewish law banning images as an eminent example of negative presentation: optical pleasure when reduced to near nothingness promotes an infinite contemplation of infinity. Even before romantic art had freed itself from classical and baroque figuration, the door had thus been opened to inquiries pointing towards abstract and Minimal art. Avant-gardism is thus present in germ in the Kantian aesthetic of the sublime. However, the art whose effects are analyzed in that aesthetics is, of course, essentially made up of attempts to represent sublime objects. And the question of time, of the *Is it happening?*, does not form part—at least not explicitly—of Kant's problematic.

I do, however, believe that question to be at the centre of Edmund Burke's *Philosophical Enquiry into the Origin of our Ideas of the Sublime and Beautiful,* published in 1757. Kant may well reject Burke's thesis as empiricism and physiologism, he may well borrow from Burke the analysis of the characterizing contradiction of the feeling of the sublime, but he strips Burke's aesthetic of what I consider to be its major stake—to show that the sublime is kindled by the threat of nothing further happening. Beauty gives a positive pleasure. But there is another kind of pleasure that is bound to a passion stronger than satisfaction, and that is pain and impending death. In pain the body affects the soul. But the soul can also affect the body as though it were experiencing some externally induced pain, by the sole means of representations that are unconsciously associated with painful situations. This entirely spiritual passion, in Burke's lexicon, is called terror. Terrors are linked to privation: privation of light, terror of darkness; privation of others, terror of solitude; privation of language, terror of silence; privation of objects, terror of emptiness; privation of life, terror of death. What is terrifying is that the *It happens that* does not happen, that it stops happening.

Burke wrote that for this terror to mingle with pleasure and with it to produce the feeling of the sublime, it is also necessary that the terror-causing threat be suspended, kept at bay, held back. This suspense, this lessening of a threat or a danger, provokes a kind of pleasure that is certainly not that of a positive satisfaction, but is, rather, that of relief. This is still a privation, but it is privation at one remove; the soul is deprived of the threat of being deprived of light, language, life. Burke distinguishes this pleasure of secondary privation from positive pleasures, and he baptizes it with the name *delight*.

Here then is an account of the sublime feeling: a very big, very powerful object threatens to deprive the soul of any 'it happens', strikes it with 'astonishment' (at lower intensities the soul is seized with admiration, veneration, respect). The soul is thus dumb, immobilized, as good as dead. Art, by distancing this menace, procures a pleasure of relief, of delight. Thanks to art, the soul is returned to the agitated zone between life and death, and this agitation is its health and its life. For Burke, the sublime was no longer a matter of elevation (the category by which Aristotle defined tragedy), but a matter of intensification.

Another of Burke's observations merits attention because it heralds the possibility of emancipating works of art from the classical rule of imitation. In the long debate over the relative merits of painting and poetry, Burke sides with poetry. Painting is doomed to imitate models, and to figurative representations of them. But if the object of art is to create intense feelings in the addressee of works, figuration by means of images is a limiting constraint on the power of emotive expression since it works by recognition. In the arts or language, particularly in poetry, which Burke considered to be not a genre with rules, but the field where certain researches into language have free rein, the power to move is free from the verisimilitudes of figuration. 'What does one do when one wants to represent an angel in a painting? One paints a beautiful young man with wings: but will painting ever provide anything as great as the addition of this one word—the Angel of the *Lord*? and how does one go about painting, with equal strength of feeling, the words "A universe of death" where ends the journey of the fallen angels in Milton's *Paradise Lost*?'

Words enjoy several privileges when it comes to expressing feelings: they are themselves charged with passionate connotations; they can evoke matters of the soul without having to consider whether they are visible; finally, Burke adds, 'It is in our power to effect with words combinations that would be impossible by any other means.' The arts, whatever their materials, pressed forward by the aesthetics of the sublime in search of intense effects, can and must give up the imitation of models that are merely beautiful, and try out surprising, strange, shocking combinations. Shock is, *par excellence,* the evidence of (something) *happening,* rather than nothing, suspended privation.

Burke's analyses can easily, as you will have guessed, be resumed and elaborated in a Freudian-Lacanian problematic (as Pierre Kaufman and Baldine Saint Girons have done). But I recall them in a different spirit, the one my subject—the avant-garde—demands. I have tried to suggest that at the dawn of romanticism, Burke's elaboration of the aesthetics of the sublime, and to a lesser degree Kant's, outlined a world of possibilities for artistic experiments in which the avant-gardes would later trace out their paths. There are in general no direct influences, no empirically observable connections. Manet, Cézanne, Braque, and Picasso probably did not read Kant or Burke. It is more a matter of an irreversible deviation in the destination of art, a deviation affecting all the valencies of the artistic condition. The artist attempts combinations allowing the event. The art-lover does not experience a simple pleasure; or derive some ethical benefit from his contact with art, but expects an intensification of his conceptual and emotional capacity, an ambivalent enjoyment. Intensity is associated with an ontological dislocation. The art-object no longer bends itself to models, but tries to present the fact that there is an unpresentable; it no longer imitates nature, but is, in Burke, the actualization of a figure potentially there in language. The social community no longer recognizes itself in art-objects, but ignores them, rejects them as incomprehensible and only later allows the intellectual avant-garde to preserve them in museums as the traces of offensives that bear witness to the power, and the privation, of the spirit.

## 4.

With the advent of the aesthetics of the sublime, the stake of art in the nineteenth and twentieth centuries was to be the witness to the fact that there is indeterminacy. For painting, the paradox that Burke signalled in his observations on the power of words is, that such testimony can only be achieved in a determined fashion. Support, frame, line, colour, space, the figure—were to remain, in romantic art, subject to the constraint of representation. But this contradiction of end and means had, as early as Manet and Cézanne, the effect of casting doubt on certain rules that had determined, since the Quattrocento, the representation of the figure in space and the organization of colours and values. Reading Cézanne's correspondence, one understands that his oeuvre was not that of a talented painter finding his 'style', but that of an artist attempting to respond to the question: what is a painting? His work had at stake to inscribe on the supporting canvas only those 'colouristic sensations', those 'little sensations' that of themselves according to Cézanne's hypothesis, constitute the entire pictorial existence of objects, fruit, mountain, face, flower, without consideration of either history or 'subject', or line, or space, or even light. These elementary sensations are hidden in ordinary perception which remains under the hegemony of habitual or classical ways of looking. They are only accessible to the painter and can therefore only be re-established by him at the expense of an interior ascesis [i.e., self-discipline – Ed.] that rids perceptual and mental fields of prejudices inscribed even in vision itself. If the viewer does not submit to a complementary ascesis, the painting will remain senseless and impenetrable to him. The painter must not hesitate to run the risk of being taken to be a mere dauber. 'One paints for very few people', writes Cézanne. Recognition from the regulatory institutions of painting—Academy, salons, criticism, taste—is of little importance compared to the judgement made by the painter-researcher and his peers on the success obtained by the work of art in relation to what is really at stake: to make seen what makes one see, and not what is visible.

Maurice Merleau-Ponty elaborated on what he rightly called 'Cézanne's doubt' as though what was at stake for the painter was indeed to grasp and render perception at its birth—perception 'before' perception. I would say: colour in its occurrence, the wonder that 'it happens' ('it', something: colour), at least to the eye. There is some credulity on the part of the phenomenologist in this trust he places in the 'originary' value of Cézanne's 'little sensations'. The painter himself, who often complained of their inadequacy, wrote that they were 'abstractions', that 'they did not suffice for covering the canvas'. But why should it be necessary to cover the canvas? Is it forbidden to be abstract?

The doubt which gnaws at the avant-gardes did not stop with Cézanne's 'colouristic sensations' as though they were indubitable, and for that matter, no more did it stop with the abstractions they heralded. The task of having to bear witness to the indeterminate carries away, one after another the barriers set up by the writings of theorists and by the manifestos of the painters themselves. A formalist definition of the pictorial object, such as that proposed in 1961 by Clement Greenberg when confronted with American 'post plastic' abstraction, was soon overturned by the current of Minimalism. Do we have to have stretchers so that the canvas is taut? No. What about colours? Malevitch's black square on white had already answered this question in 1915. Is an object necessary? Body art and happenings went about proving that it is not. A space, at least, a space in which to display, as Duchamp's 'fountain' still suggested? Daniel Buren's work testifies to the fact that even this is subject to doubt.[5]

Whether or not they belong to the current that art history calls Minimalism or *arte povera*, the investigations of the avant-gardes question one by one the constituents one might have thought 'elementary' or at the 'origin' of the art of painting. They operate *ex minimis*. One would have to confront the demand for rigour that animates them with the principle sketched out by Adorno at the end of *Negative Dialectics*, and that controls the writing of his *Aesthetic Theory*: the thought that 'accompanies metaphysics in its fall', he said, can only proceed in terms of 'micrologies'.

Micrology is not just metaphysics in crumbs, any more than Newman's painting is Delacroix in scraps. Micrology inscribes the occurrence of a thought as the unthought that remains to be thought in the decline of 'great' philosophical thought. The avant-gardist attempt inscribes the occurrence of a sensory *now* as what cannot be presented and which remains to be presented in the decline of great representational painting. Like micrology, the avant-garde is not concerned with what happens to the 'subject', but with: 'Does it happen?', with privation. This is the sense in which it still belongs to the aesthetics of the sublime.

In asking questions of the *It happens* that the work of art is, avant-garde art abandons the role of identification that the work previously played in relation to the community of addressees. Even when conceived, as it was by Kant, as a *de jure* horizon or presumption rather than a *de facto* reality, a *sensus communis* (which, moreover, Kant refers to only when writing about beauty, not the sublime) does not manage to achieve stability when it comes to interrogative works of art. It barely coalesces, too late, when these works, deposited in museums, are considered part of the community heritage and are made available for its culture and pleasure. And even here, they must be objects or they must tolerate objectification, for example through photography.[6]

In this situation of isolation and misunderstanding, avant-garde art is vulnerable and subject to repression. It seems only to aggravate the identity-crisis that communities went through during the long 'depression' that lasted from the thirties until the end of 'reconstruction' in the mid-fifties. It is impossible here even to suggest how the Party-states born of fear faced with the 'Who are we?', and the anxiety of the void, tried to convert this fear or anxiety into hatred of the avant-gardes. Hildegarde Brenner's study of artistic policy under Nazism, or the films of Hans-Jürgen Sylberberg, do not merely analyze these repressive manoeuvres. They also explain how neo-romantic, neo-classical, and symbolic forms imposed by the cultural commissars and collaborationist artists—painters and musicians especially—had to block the negative dialectic or the *Is it happening?* by translating and betraying the question as a waiting for some fabulous subject or identity: 'Is the pure people coming?', 'Is the Führer coming?', 'Is Siegfried coming?'. The aesthetics of the sublime, thus neutralized and converted into a politics of myth, was able to come and build its architectures of human 'formations' on the Zeppelin Feld in Nürnberg.

Thanks to the 'crisis of overcapitalization' that most of today's so-called highly developed societies are going through, another attack on the avant-gardes is coming to light. The threat exerted against the avant-garde search for the artwork event, against attempts to welcome the *now* no longer requires Party-states to be effective. It proceeds 'directly' out of market economics. The correlation between this and the aesthetics of the sublime is ambiguous, even perverse. The latter, no doubt, has been and continues to be a reaction against the matter-of-fact positivism and the calculated realism that governs the former, as writers on art such as Stendhal, Baudelaire, Mallarmé, Apollinaire, and Breton all emphasize.

Yet there is a kind of collusion between capital and the avant-garde. The force of scepticism and even of destruction that capitalism has brought into play, and that Marx never ceased analyzing and identifying, in some way encourages among artists a mistrust of established rules and a willingness to experiment with means of expression, with styles, with ever-new materials. There is something of the sublime in capitalist economy. It is not academic, it is not physiocratic, it admits of no nature. It is, in a sense, an economy regulated by an Idea—infinite wealth or power. It does not manage to present any example from reality to verify this Idea. In making science subordinate to itself through technologies, especially those of language, it only succeeds, on the contrary, in making reality increasingly ungraspable, subject to doubt, unsteady.

The experience of the human subject—individual and collective—and the aura that surrounds this experience, are being dissolved into the calculation of profitability, the satisfaction of needs, self-affirmation through success. Even the virtually theological depth of the worker's condition, and of work, that marked the socialist and union movements for over a century, is becoming devalorized, as work becomes a control and manipulation of information. These observations are banal, but what merits attention is the disappearance of the temporal continuum through which the experience of generations used to be transmitted. The availability of information is becoming the only criterion of social importance. Now information is by definition a short-lived element. As soon as it is transmitted and shared, it ceases to be information, it becomes an environmental given, and 'all is said', we 'know'. It is put into the machine memory. The length of time it occupies is, so to speak, instantaneous. Between two pieces of information, 'nothing happens', by definition. A confusion thereby becomes possible, between what is of interest to information and the director, and what is the question of the avant-gardes, between what happens—the new—and the *Is it happening?*, the *now*.

It is understandable that the art-market, subject like all markets to the rule of the new, can exert a kind of seduction on artists. This attraction is not due to corruption alone. It exerts itself thanks to a confusion between innovation and the *Ereignis*, a confusion maintained by the temporality specific to contemporary capitalism. 'Strong' information, if one can call it that, exists in inverse proportion to the meaning that can be attributed to it in the code available to its receiver. It is like 'noise'. It is easy for the public and for artists, advised by intermediaries—the diffusers of cultural merchandise—to draw from this observation the principle that a work of art is avant-garde in direct proportion to the extent that it is stripped of meaning. Is it not then like an event?

It is still necessary that its absurdity does not discourage buyers, just as the innovation introduced into a commodity must allow itself to be approached, appreciated and purchased by the consumers. The secret of an artistic success, like that of a commercial success, resides in the balance between what is surprising and what is 'well-known', between information and code. This is how innovation in art operates: one re-uses formulae confirmed by previous success, one throws them off-balance by combining them with other, in principle incompatible, formulae, by amalgamations, quotations, ornamentations, pastiche. One can go as far as kitsch or the grotesque. One flatters the 'taste' of a public that can have no taste, and the eclecticism or a sensibility enfeebled by the multiplication of available forms and objects. In this way one thinks that one is expressing the spirit of the time, whereas one is merely reflecting the spirit of the market. Sublimity is no longer in art, but in speculation on art.

The enigma of the *Is it happening?* is not dissolved for all this, nor is the task of painting that there is something which is not determinable, the *There is* [*Il y a*] itself, out of date. The occurrence, the *Ereignis*, has nothing to do with the *petit frisson*, the cheap thrill, the profitable pathos, that accompanies an innovation. Hidden in the cynicism of innovation is certainly the despair that nothing further will happen. But innovating means to behave as though lots of things happened, and to make them happen. Through innovation the will affirms its hegemony over time. It thus conforms to the metaphysics of capital, which is a technology of time. The innovation 'works'. The question mark of the *Is it happening?* stops. With the occurrence, the will is defeated. The avant-gardist task remains that of undoing the presumption of the mind with respect to time. The sublime feeling is the name of this privation.

## Questions

1. How does Lyotard think the sublime is connected to avant-garde art? What does this have to do with the limits of representation? Discuss his examples.

2. How does Lyotard interpret the claim that the sublime is "now"? Is that still true today, or only with respect to particular (avant-garde) movements in art history?

3. Is it possible to represent the unrepresentable—an apparent paradox? Or, the *fact* that there is something unpresentable? How would one do so? Explain.

4. More generally, how much paradox is acceptable in an account (theory) of the sublime?

5. Lyotard writes, "There is something of the sublime in capitalist economy." Do you agree? Is there anything sublime about capitalist markets? Explain.

6. Lyotard writes, "Sublimity is no longer in art, but in speculation on art." How do capitalist markets affect the possibility of the sublime, and of avant-garde art? Do you think the artworld has turned away from avant-garde art and conceded to globalized capitalism? Explain.

## Further reading

Lyotard, Jean-François. *The Differend: Phrases in Dispute.* Minneapolis: University of Minnesota Press, 1988.

Lyotard, Jean-François. *Enthusiasm: The Kantian Critique of History,* trans. Georges Van den Abbeele. Stanford: Stanford University Press, 2009.

Lyotard, Jean-François. *Lessons on the Analytic of the Sublime: (Kant's "Critique of Judgment," §§23-29),* trans. Elizabeth Rottenberg. Stanford: Stanford University Press, 1994.

Rancière, Jacques. *The Future of the Image.* London: Verso, 2009.

Richir, Marc. *Du Sublime en Politique.* Paris: Payot, 1991.

Silverman, Hugh J. *Lyotard: Philosophy, Politics, and the Sublime.* New York: Routledge, 2002.

# CHAPTER 31
## MEG ARMSTRONG, FROM "'THE EFFECTS OF BLACKNESS': GENDER, RACE, AND THE SUBLIME IN AESTHETIC THEORIES OF BURKE AND KANT" (1996)

In the following excerpt, Meg Armstrong examines the sublime in terms of gender, sexuality, and race and racism, analyzing two of the most prominent modern theorists of the sublime. Focusing on Burke (1757) and the "precritical" Kant (1764), she considers the "ideology" of the aesthetic and the sublime. She examines "the complex relationships between aesthetics and the politics of gender and race," and offers "possible strategies for countering dominant Euroaesthetic visions of beauty and sublimity" (229).

Armstrong analyzes the concept of "bodies" in Burke and Kant's writings, as they attempt to establish the (alleged) sublimity expressed in racial and gendered differences. She calls into doubt Burke's naturalistic approach, and, perhaps in the tradition of Wollstonecraft, she questions the political and social assumptions underlying his discourse. In particular, she puts pressure on Burke's premise that the "effects of blackness" are natural, rather than constructed through association and cultivated by culture and history.

### Note on the text

Source: Excerpted from Meg Armstrong, "'The Effects of Blackness': Gender, Race, and the Sublime in Aesthetic Theories of Burke and Kant." *The Journal of Aesthetics and Art Criticism* 54, no. 3 (1996): 213–36.

The format, spelling, and style of the article have been reproduced, with occasional modifications. Ellipses in square brackets indicate deletions by the volume editor, whereas ellipses without brackets are by Armstrong.

### "'The effects of blackness': gender, race, and the sublime in aesthetic theories of Burke and Kant"

> Stereotypes, however inaccurate, are one form of representation. Like fictions, they are created to serve as substitutions, standing in for what is real. They are there not to tell it like it is but to invite and encourage pretense. They are a fantasy, a projection onto the Other that makes them less threatening. Stereotypes abound when there is distance. They are an invention, a pretense that one knows when the steps that would make real knowing possible cannot be taken—are not allowed.
>
> — bell hooks[1]

Of course, to have a phenomenal knowledge of others may in fact be enough for using them to our own advantage. But it may not be felt sufficient for constructing the kind of universal subjectivity which a ruling class requires for its ideological solidarity. For this purpose, it might be possible to attain to something which, while not strictly knowledge, is nonetheless very like it. This pseudo-knowledge is known as the aesthetic.

— Terry Eagleton[2]

Black bodies, reflecting none, or but a few rays, with regard to sight are but as so many vacant spaces dispersed among the objects we view.

— Edmund Burke[3]

In the eighteenth century, largely through the influence of an aesthetic treatise by Edmund Burke and the *precritical* aesthetics of Immanuel Kant, the sublime became both an effect of an *object* which inspired terror *and* the disposition of a subject capable of aesthetic judgment. What has not often been recognized in subsequent analyses of these texts is that in each the sublime is described not only through analogies to the differences between the sexes (Burke and Kant), but also as a product of an aesthetic disposition inherent in sexual, national, and historical characteristics (Kant), and is sometimes provoked by images of racial difference (Burke and Kant). The description of the sublime in terms of culture, race, nation, or gender ought now to be a highly remarkable feature of discussions of aesthetics, particularly to the extent that it suggests that aesthetic discourse was not only integral to the construction of a "self-determining" bourgeois subject, but also that this subject was positioned within growing discourses of difference in the eighteenth and nineteenth centuries.[4] There is, however, a provocative silence on the relation between the sublime and the exotic, and even the most insightful commentaries on the romantic sublime spawned by recent interests in deconstruction have neglected to mention the prevalent association between the sublime and various, embodied, forms of difference.[5] The reason for this is, perhaps, that the philosophical discourses of sublimity turn away from such embodied (and often "exotic") forms at the same time that they abjure the relevance of historical and cultural contingencies which have thrown them into the line of vision.[6] The repetitive motions with which the national, cultural, racial, or gendered bodies of the sublime are erased in order to assert the "naturalness" of aesthetic vision indicates a persistent anxiety and ambivalence surrounding the relationship between subjectivity, aesthetics, and the production of images—one could even say stereotypes—of difference.

Prior to Kant's third *Critique* [published in 1790 – Ed.], natural objects or "majestic scenes in nature" (mountains, oceans, vast spaces), sublime objects or phenomena which are suggestive of things not readily encompassed, conceptualized, or represented, are joined by "culturally unintelligible" *bodies* and *others*. It is a cliché of criticism that romantic poets reformulated theologically transcendent ideas in natural symbolism, and that natural objects and phenomena familiar in European countries became emblems of sublimity in the secular imagination of lyric poets. What is not often observed in discussions of this reformulation is not simply that the *naturalization* also applies to its attachment to specific bodies but also that these bodies are often imported from foreign domains, "other" by virtue of racial or cultural differences, often from regions important to imperialistic designs of European empires.[7] Yet, even if such bodies are initially "abject"—neither subject nor object—they quickly become *subjected to* an aesthetic discourse. By positioning the subject within a constellation of images of foreign bodies which compel sublime vision, the aesthetic uses these "abject" or "black bodies" to organize desires for difference while compelling the disavowal of the transgressive passions with which they are associated. The "ideology of the aesthetic"[8] is, then, not limited to the construction of a subject which must position itself within the coercive demands of the state. Rather, aesthetic discourse at least since Burke and Kant locates this subject within a global network of "bodies" (sensual signs of the sublime) whose gendered, national, and racial markings are integral to that subject's self-identification (if not also its unspoken or illegitimate desires). […]

And here another, far less transcendent but perhaps more troubling, possibility emerges. The sublime is not simply a moment of terror and privation on the way to a recovery of self-possession and mastery (or recognition of oneself within a transcendent symbolic order); rather, the sublime exceeds this drama of identification and marks the sheer ecstasy of the image of foreign bodies. Making the sublime less terrifying or obscure is the business of aesthetic discourse; in Burke's *Enquiry*, the aesthetic works to contain passions, direct desire, and steady what is already an unsteady and passionate eye for excess. In this work, there is not only no end, but by definition, no satisfaction.

## I No satisfaction: deceptive passions of the "unsteady eye"

Edmund Burke's *A Philosophical Enquiry into the Origin of our Ideas of the Sublime and Beautiful*[9] stimulated eighteenth-century psychological interests in the sublime, and contributed to their popularity in the 1780s and 1790s.[10] Burke's *Enquiry* provides a detailed account of properties (vastness, darkness, etc.) generally understood to be sublime. His argument and interpretation also, however, offer an initial instance of how aesthetic categories are used to create or replicate racial and gender-based distinctions. Burke builds his interpretation of the difference between the beautiful and the sublime from a "primary" distinction between the sexes. To this opposition (beauty: feminine :: sublime: masculine), Burke, schooled as he is in gothic horror stories, ascribes sublimity to "dark" or "black" things. Not surprisingly, the heterosexual opposition between genders is matched with another between light and dark (beauty: feminine: light :: sublime: masculine: dark).

It is significant that one of Burke's primary examples of the terrifying natural "effects of blackness" complicates his associational matrix. Here, it is precisely a *black female* which is sublime, suggesting that the feminine can be *both* (safely) beautiful and, as in the case of a body which is both black *and* female, sublime and threatening. The contradictions in Burke's text sometimes make his argument less coherent while at the same time indicating a limit to his claim that distinctions between the beautiful and the sublime are founded in "natural" effects. In short, these contradictions suggest the work of an ideological process of making what is contingent and local, perhaps even idiosyncratic, in matters of taste appear to be natural, and thus beyond dispute.

The terror and ambivalence which surrounds the image of the black female may be symptomatic of the pressure exerted by culturally marked categories of race and gender upon aesthetic discourse, of an excess which troubles (where it also thrills?) aesthetic vision. If the *Enquiry* is Burke's attempt to provide the "invariable and certain laws" of taste outlined in the introduction, the associational matrixes he sketches—and in the process of illustrating, often confounds—are also *exclusionary*: they mark not only the contours of beauty and sublimity but also cast some bodies "outside" the boundaries Burke has set for each category of aesthetic experience. The black female is one such abject being, a product of the ideological contradictions produced by Burke's (gendered) distinctions between beauty and sublimity.[11] At the same time, Burke's fascination with passion and desire is part of an attempt to contain the thrill provoked by sublime images, to turn the gaze away from this excess and to channel vision into socially acceptable or "satisfactory" appropriations of terror and ecstasy—which, ironically, gives "no satisfaction," ensuring a continual need for terrifying novelties.

[...]

Creating a preference, hoping to fix an object, Burke aligns beauty with the feminine and the sublime with the masculine, addresses the male subject, and gives him his object: "the beautiful feminine." Now it is not only that the sublime has to do with pain and danger, and beauty with the pleasures of love, but also that the dangers of the sublime relate to the active and "the masculine," and the pleasures of beauty to the passive tenderness of "the feminine." Burke's rhetoric elicits the reader's appreciation of the "naturalness" of such associations, and directs attention away from any already-constructed cultural base.[12] [...]

What all of this indicates is, first of all, a need demonstrated throughout the *Enquiry* (and particularly in passages relating to the beautiful or sublime qualities of the feminine or masculine, or the horrors of "darkness"), to treat the character of aesthetic traits as *natural* or pure—separate from secondary considerations (desire, possession) or the interference of cultural prejudice. [...] It is not accidental that Burke's desire to distinguish between the sublime and the beautiful also forces a separation of the power and greatness of male authority from the small, feminine thing which is beautiful, primarily because "we love what submits to us." The submission of the unsteady eye, like that of the feminine, is the desired accomplishment of the aesthetic.

## II "The effects of *blackness*" and "the cries of *animals*"

Throughout the *Enquiry*, Burke is clearly interested in the psychological reaction to beautiful or sublime objects, but the emphasis is placed on the properties of *objects themselves* in aesthetic experience as they affect the eye, the primary organ of sensibility, rather than on the function of particular faculties. The objects and bodies which interest Burke are those which are capable of producing a strong reaction in the subject, and the highly physiological nature of this response is assumed to strengthen his argument that such effects are natural rather than constructed merely through association.[13] The imagined subject of aesthetic experience necessarily remains a *reactionary* agent, not one who actively constructs categories of aesthetic judgment. This subject is, then, split from Burke himself who is capable of educating us to respond fully to objects which naturally provoke (potentially universal) feelings of pleasure and pain proper to experiences of beauty or sublimity. While he describes the psychology of *feelings* (pleasure, pain, and delight) in detail in part I, they are in fact preparatory to a classification of *objects*[14] which produce these feelings, rather than the basis of a reflective psychological analysis of the importance of aesthetic experience in the construction of subjectivity as such. [...]

Darkness is terrible before all association with particular things. To support his point, Burke recounts the story of Mr. Cheselden, a surgeon who removes a young boy's cataracts and restores his sight. Given that the boy has been blind since birth, Burke argues that his reactions to darkness, or to blackness, can be taken as entirely "natural." The boy had seen a black object and felt "great uneasiness" which was succeeded by horror a few months later "upon accidentally seeing a negro woman" (*E*, p. 144). Burke feels that this horror stems from a natural inclination to be frightened by anything dark or, rather, anything *black*, as it is the purpose of this and the subsequent section to extend Burke's aesthetic judgments of darkness to blackness in general (e.g., see part IV, sec. XVII, "The effects of BLACKNESS"). The passage is very important, and I will quote from it at length:

> I must observe, that the ideas of darkness and blackness are much the same; and they differ only in this, that blackness is a more confined idea. Mr. Cheselden has given us a very curious story of a boy, who had been born blind, and continued so until he was thirteen or fourteen years old; he was then couched for a cataract, by which operation he received his sight. Among many remarkable particulars that attended his first perceptions, and judgments on visual objects, Cheselden tells us, that the first time the boy saw a black object, it gave him great uneasiness; and that some time after, upon accidentally seeing a negro woman, he was struck with great horror at the sight. The horror, in this case, can scarcely be supposed to arise from any association. The boy appears by the account to have been particularly observing, and sensible for one of his age: and therefore, it is probable, if the great uneasiness he felt at the first sight of black had arisen from its connexion with any other disagreeable ideas, he would have

observed and mentioned it. For an idea, disagreeable only by association, has the cause of its ill effect on the passions evident enough at the first impression; in ordinary cases, it is indeed frequently lost; but this is, because the original association was made very early, and the consequent impression repeated often. In our instance, there was no time for such an habit; and there is no reason to think, that the ill effects of black on his imagination were more owing to its connexion with any disagreeable ideas, than that the good effects of more cheerful colours were derived from their connexion with pleasing ones. *They had both probably their effect from their natural operation.* (*E*, pp. 144–145; my emphasis)

According to Burke, the boy's horror at the sight of a black woman is purely owing to his extreme fear of "darkness." After considering various corporeal and mental causes of the discomfort Burke claims is associated with blackness, he explains that the pains originally felt in the effects of black do subside—particularly as we become accustomed to them. It then seems that our horror or pain in the experience of blackness is simply because we are not *used* to black: "Custom reconciles us to every thing. After we have been used to the sight of black objects, the terror abates ... yet the nature of the original impression still continues." Black "will always have something melancholy in it" because we will always find the change from black to other colors "too violent" (*E*, pp. 148–149). Only when the thing ceases to be new, when its shock value has diminished, will the horror evoked by its (natural?!) associations subside.

Burke's discussion of the Cheselden example provides an excellent allegory for the politics of vision and power, and raises again the difficult issue of race and gender in discussions of aesthetic experience. If we return to the issue of the "unsteady gaze," what might the boy's horror signify within Burke's account of sublime vision; what does it mean for the steady eye which has, until the rupture signified by the black female, struggled to govern the *Enquiry*? It may be worth speculating that in Burke's account the threat to the boy centers upon the provocation of a *reactive* (and not controlling) stance in him, aligning him with the passivity of the feminine, here given the added iconic valence of subordination through slavery. Burke's categorization of black as terrible *in itself* (by *nature*) may be interpreted, in this example, as an attempt to control the signification of the black and the feminine for the masculine gaze, by asserting that this reaction is natural and unavoidable and would not put the (ultimate) agency or power of the boy into question. The boy may be in the process of mastering—or becoming accustomed to—his physiological reactions, but he is clearly not (yet) able to contain the "effects of blackness" (blackness as a mark of race, but also as a mark of the feminine which is abject if it is not "beautiful").

[...] Nineteenth-century images of the black female produced in Europe and Britain emphasized her (the black female was often equated with the Hottentot) grotesque nature as well as her (pathological) lasciviousness; the black female is represented, in both physical form and alleged desire, as a monstrous creature.[15] As such, she becomes the site for another form of the sublime, one which draws upon the lure of her abjection, and the thrill which is not contained within the polite society of the sexes imagined by Burke. True to his wish to classify the effects of objects as beautiful or sublime, however, she also serves as a stereotype of difference, a collecting pool for all that is imagined as excessive to the ideology of Burke's aesthetic.

## III  "The paramour may adorn himself as he pleases": Kant and the bearded lady[16]

Immanuel Kant's *Critique of Judgment* attempts to thoroughly isolate "pure" judgments of beauty and sublimity from all of the secondary considerations (now called "interests") which had troubled Burke. In order to do this, Kant isolates the sublime within the fortress of the faculties ("bodies" in the mind) themselves; this seclusion only comes, however, after an extended exploration of the dispositions toward aesthetic experience consequent to gender and national affiliation. Before the *Critique of Judgment* is the less well-known precritical aesthetic philosophy, *Observations on the Feeling of the Beautiful and Sublime* (1763) [published in 1764 – Ed.], first published only six years after Burke's *Enquiry*. Kant's discussion of forms of difference between the beautiful and the sublime in *Observations* bear striking resemblance to the tone of Burke's own, especially in the attention Kant gives to the analogical relationships between these aesthetic "feelings" and gender. Kant, however, extends Burke's inchoate references to the "effects of blackness" and peoples of "duskier complexions" to an elaborate typing of national characteristics according to the propensity of different national subjects for beautiful or sublime feelings. The difference between Kant and Burke is also apparent, however, in Kant's emphasis on the importance of the *disposition,* rather than in the "nature of external things."[17] Of course, since the beautiful and the sublime are, in fact, dispositions of "external things" or bodies which themselves are judged to partake of beauty or sublimity to various degrees and kinds (i.e., the sublime American Indian or Arab), the distinction is somewhat blurred.

This difference between his own aesthetic philosophy and that of Burke's has the odd effect of allowing Kant to later sort through the capacities of different personalities, sexes, and national characters on the basis of the relative abilities of each to experience the beautiful and the sublime. Thus, while in the third *Critique* the ability to make pure aesthetic judgments serves as a basis upon which to separate philistines from civilized subjects, here it aids more blatant classificatory purposes. Kant will, from these amazingly homogeneous dispositions for aesthetic experience (one would think there were more varieties of feeling than the pleasure and pain associated only with the beautiful and three kinds of sublime), sort through melancholics, phlegmatics, cholerics, females, males, Italians, Germans, Englishmen, and Indians. One might regard the *Observations* as a classificatory chart of all the impure aesthetic judgments, those tainted with material or other interests as well as the perceptual and corporeal matrices provided by cultural constructions of gender, race, and nation.

[...]

Having divided the sublime into the terrifying, noble, and splendid, Kant then simply names what is associated with beauty (e.g., things delicate or pleasing) and the sublime (things strong, often tragic). In the course of one such list, Kant says, "[i]n fact, dark coloring and black eyes are more closely related to the sublime, blue eyes and blonde coloring to the beautiful" (*O*, p. 54). [...]

Most interesting of all is the fourth section of *Observations*, "Of National Characteristics." [...]

Section four is still, however, reminiscent of other contemporary interests in typologies of national character and racial difference, and the expression of national character in the arts and sciences.[18] [...] Kant's conception of "national" aesthetic feeling may be compared as well to discussions of "national literatures" which would only increase in the nineteenth century. [...] His erasure of the nationalistic or cultural bases of aesthetic judgment in his later work [i.e., *Critique of Judgment* – Ed.], and the effort to distinguish pure and impure judgments, prefigures the hiddenness of aesthetic and metaphorical ("non-scientific") constructions of difference in dominant discourses of race and gender in the nineteenth century. [...]

"National character" expresses the sublime as either terrifying, noble, or splendid. Tastes for each kind of sublimity, as well as for the beautiful, are "not original by nature" (*O*, p. 98). Although he does not tell us how he knows, Kant believes that he has "reason to be able to ascribe" the feeling of the terrifying to "the Spaniard," the splendid to "the Englishman," and the noble to "the German." From these initial observations, a calculus of tastes is elaborated, comparing the European nations to each other. [...]

The remaining passages of section four elaborate the tastes for beauty and sublimity in the European countries of Spain, Italy, France, England, Germany, and Holland. At the end of the section, a "fleeting glance" is cast "over the other parts of the world." It is here that we find generalizations about the tastes of Arabs, Japanese, Chinese, "Negroes of Africa," and North American "savages." What had previously been said of the

Spanish and French is here applied to Arabs and Persians, in whose national character the European traits are magnified and excessive. Thus, the Arabs : Spanish :: Persians : French :: Japanese : Englishmen, with the Indians and Chinese so enchanted by the grotesque as to elude European classificatory categories altogether, and the African having "by nature no feeling that rises above the trifling" (O, p. 110).[19] [...]

Kant's ensuing description of the tastes of Indians and Chinese as "grotesque" anticipates, however ironically, Victor Hugo's redefinition, in the "Preface to Cromwell,"[20] of the sublime as participating in the grotesque.[21] Hugo's illustration of this grotesque sublimity is evident not only in his novels but in various poems in *Les Orientales* which equate the sublimity of the Orient with its monstrous idols and other grotesques. Kant's complete dismissal of "Negroes" as lacking any finer feeling, and thus retaining perhaps the lowest spot in this hierarchy of racially or nationally based tastes, is often repeated in later aesthetic comments comparing various nations, for instance at European and American fairs and expositions in the nineteenth century.[22] American Indians rate second only to the African Negro, it appears, in their capacity for "finer feelings." While Kant feels the Cherokee Attakullaculla is equal to the finest Greek in his sense of honor, he judges American Indians on the whole to be lacking in "feeling for the beautiful in moral understanding," and generally apathetic (O, p. 112).

[...] Despite the many idle, armchair traveler observations Kant himself has offered, often in bad taste, of such apparently homogeneous cultural groups as "Persians," "Indians," "Chinese," and "Canadian savages," Kant retreats from his own comparative historical and cultural aesthetic to offer a master-narrative which had governed the *Observations* all along. The "old illusions" of false and grotesque art—in which some Asian tastes participate—must be cast off, in favor of what will, in the third *Critique,* struggle to become universal bases for aesthetic judgment. The "exotics" (which begin with the sublime southern Europeans, and proceed to Asians and North Americans) are grotesque aberrations of beauty and sublimity to be subordinated, and perhaps eliminated, in the hearts of new "world-citizens." And in order to do this, the exotic bodies which had populated Kant's precritical aesthetic philosophy must now be made to disappear.

In the *Critique of Judgment*, these bodies are stripped of their national characteristics and feelings, and made to play in the gendered roles of reason and imagination. The sublime becomes a moment in which reason attempts, with the aid of the imagination, to represent the unpresentable—to give expression to the noumena. For Kant, obviously, the unpresentable is not quite the same opportunity for celebration it has become among postmodern critics. For Lyotard, the "unpresentable" is a mark of the "postmodern sublime"; fascination with it defines the postmodern condition as one of perpetual play or of an infinite language game in which the "object" never "appears" or can never be part of a vision of totality so what is now imagined as a "transnational" network of objects and imagined worlds,[23] or a collage of cultural artifacts, has become part of the stock and trade of postmodern sublimity. For Kant, however, it appears that the confusion of national characteristics and aesthetic feeling must be repressed in favor of an abstract aesthetic mechanism for calculating *universal* experiences of the beautiful and the sublime. [...]

[...] Rather, sublimity typically occurs in the *Critique* when the imagination experiences extreme terror and awe at the power and magnitude of "natural" phenomena. These moments are most likely to arise when the mind contemplates scenes of nature's majesty—great oceans, mountains, storms—though they may also be provoked by more properly "cultural" phenomena such as pyramids,[24] the bravery of soldiers, or even war itself. Such images, however, are "too big" and also "not big enough": they terrify at the same time that it is impossible for them to match the idea of infinity, might, or totality which they stir in the subject. They are inadequate images, although they refer (negatively) to that which is more powerful than the imaginative presentation of an object. At the same time, after reading *Observations,* we see that they are also symptomatic of an erasure of cultural, national, and gender-based differences which had previously been a more prominent part of Kant's discussion of the sublime.

The sublime in the third *Critique* becomes distinct from that of precursors such as Burke to the extent that, in pure judgments of beauty and sublimity, Kant emphasizes the subject's response to the object rather than any quality of the object itself *and* because he has ceased to "nationalize" the various imaginations and tastes of the subject he describes. Instead, he creates "the subject of aesthetic experience" whose disposition is not spoken of as part of a particular national or racial group, and whose experience (presumably based upon a collage of experiences to be had in German, French, and English art and literature at the end of the eighteenth century) is put forth as universal.

Kant's emphasis on the aesthetic response joins the sublime to an element of the supersensible in the subject, providing a legitimate basis for aesthetic and moral judgments. Somewhat fortuitously, this inward turning also takes him away from the difficult matters of sublimity provoked by cultural difference, and the sense that beauty and sublimity are produced by "national" traits or sentiments. Likewise, he is able to ignore the implication that "tastes" in transcendent beings, as referred to in his remarks on the grotesque and idolatrous religions of Asia in *Observations,* may be created in particular cultural milieus. [...]

It might seem that a distinctive feature of the sublime of the third *Critique* is that it inevitably rationalizes *away* the threat (or the subversive promise!) of the vision of foreign bodies confronted in the *Observations.* Just as the imagination attempts to surpass nature at the very moment it most fears materiality, the third *Critique* erases the earlier imagination of nationality in terms of the sublime in order to envision a totality which is not dependent upon the hazardous contingencies embodied by Spaniards, paramours, and bearded ladies. The imagination's impasse in the third *Critique* might then be read as indicative of a larger failure to articulate the ideological processes by which an aesthetic totality emerges to repair the ruptures created within an increasingly fragmented, inchoate, and global network of cultures, images, and signs.

## IV "An amputation, an excision, a hemorrhage"[25]

Burke's *Enquiry* mobilizes a fascination with the physiological effects of images, colors, and light upon vision, and with the relationship between the events or experiences of the body and states of mind. Throughout, and especially in part IV, Burke describes an education of the mind through bodily experiences of various passions; working sometimes from very simple physiological observations, the training of the eye becomes an ordering of passion and the subordination of crude reactions to the discipline of proper aesthetic appreciation. Inevitably, given the "obvious" primacy of observations of the human body and the landscapes in which it moves, his discussion of "natural" physiological reactions becomes closely linked to the production of particular kinds of (embodied) responses to images of sex and race. Experiences and expressions of love, like those of terror, reflect the perpetual education of vision necessary to the orders of beauty and sublimity. Similarly, Kant's *Observations* is preoccupied with the classification of national types according to their dispositions, these in turn contributing not only to their capacities for aesthetic experience but to their own performance as noble, terrifying, and splendid emblems of the sublime. The pedagogy contained in these aesthetic treatises becomes especially striking when compared to later discussions of the effects of racial stereotyping upon the "black bodies" which "are but as so many vacant spaces dispersed among the objects we view" (*E*, p. 147). In other words, these bodies are those which remain (alternatively, are repressed as) unintelligible and sublime not only according to the rhetoric of Burke's *Enquiry,* but as they are also translated (in however indirect a manner) into discussions of race in other media. Aesthetic ideology has, then, an oppressive political force which is inscribed on the flesh it marks as other, and it is in resistance to this force that the aesthetic might be subverted from within. [...]

My analysis suggests agreement with W. J. T. Mitchell's view that Burke's attribution of liveliness to "oriental languages" or horror to "blackness" and "darkness" is not so much indicative of the mechanics of hearing and vision but is part of the political rhetoric that is embedded in Burke's aesthetic theory.[26] [...][27]

## Questions

1. Discuss the examples of the black female and Cheselden's newly seeing boy. How, according to Armstrong, do they put into question Burke's account of beauty and sublimity?

2. How does Armstrong see the relation between Kant's precritical account and his critical account in *Critique of Judgment* (1790)? Explain.

3. Do you agree with Armstrong's summary and assessment of Burke? The precritical Kant? The critical Kant? Explain.

4. How does Armstrong employ the concept of a "body" in her argument? Does her argument contain an equivocation between two different senses of "body" (physical object absorbing light rays; the flesh of a person)? Explain.

5. Should (must?) a theory of the sublime account for, or be connected to, racial, ethnic, national, gendered, and/or sexual differences? If so, would that still be an *aesthetic* theory, or some other kind (political, cultural, social)? Or is it impossible to make such demarcations? Explain.

6. If Armstrong's arguments are sound, is the concept of the sublime worth saving? Can it be saved? Explain.

## Further reading

Battersby, Christine. *The Sublime, Terror and Human Difference*. London: Routledge, 2007.

Battersby, Christine. "Stages on Kant's Way: Aesthetics, Morality and the Gendered Sublime." In *Feminism and Tradition in Aesthetics*, ed. Peggy Zeglin Brand and Carolyn Korsmeyer, 88–114. University Park: The Pennsylvania University Press, 1995.

Freeman, Barbara Claire. *The Feminine Sublime: Gender and Excess in Women's Fiction*. Berkeley: University of California Press, 1995.

Gould, Timothy. "Intensity and Its Audiences: Toward a Feminist Perspective on the Kantian Sublime." In *Feminism and Tradition in Aesthetics*, ed. Peggy Zeglin Brand and Carolyn Korsmeyer, 66–87. University Park: Pennsylvania State University Press, 1995.

James, Robin. "Oppression, Privilege, & Aesthetics: The Use of the Aesthetic in Theories of Race, Gender, and Sexuality, and the Role of Race, Gender, and Sexuality in Philosophical Aesthetics." *Philosophy Compass* 8, no. 2 (2013): 101–16.

Klinger, Cornelia. "The Concepts of the Sublime and the Beautiful in Kant and Lyotard." In *Feminist Interpretations of Immanuel Kant*, ed. Robin Schott, 191–211. University Park: Pennsylvania State University Press, 1997.

Lintott, Sheila. "The Sublimity of Gestating and Giving Birth: Toward a Feminist Conception of the Sublime." In *Philosophical Inquiry into Pregnancy, Childbirth, and Mothering: Maternal Subjects*, ed. Sheila Lintott and Maureen Sander-Staudt, 237–49. London: Routledge, 2011.

Mann, Bonnie. *Women's Liberation and the Sublime: Feminism, Postmodernism, Environment*. Oxford: Oxford University Press, 2006.

Yaeger, Patricia. "'The Language of Blood': Toward a Maternal Sublime." *Genre: Forms of Discourse and Culture* 25, no. 1 (1992): 5–24.

Yaeger, Patricia. "Toward a Female Sublime." In *Gender and Theory: Dialogues on Feminist Criticism*, ed. Linda Kauffman, 191–212. Oxford: Blackwell, 1989.

Zylinska, Joanna. *On Spiders, Cyborgs, and Being Scared: The Feminine and the Sublime*. Manchester: Manchester University Press, 2001.

# CHAPTER 32
# CYNTHIA A. FREELAND, "THE SUBLIME IN CINEMA" (1999)

Freeland has published extensively on ancient philosophy, feminist theory, aesthetics, philosophy of art, and philosophy of film. Below, Freeland analyzes the capacity of film to evoke the sublime. She holds that certain films can be fruitfully described as sublime and that the concept of the sublime can facilitate more diverse descriptions of films as artworks. She describes four basic features of the sublime and explains how her account is inspired by Kant (and Burke) yet differs from Kant's theory. She shows how psychological and neuroscientific approaches might contribute to a theory of the sublime in film, but raises two challenges to cognitive approaches.

Freeland gives numerous examples of films that evoke the sublime but focuses on *The Passion of Joan of Arc* (*La Passion de Jeanne d'Arc*) (1928), *Aguirre: The Wrath of God* (*Aguirre, der Zorn Gottes*) (1972), and *Children of Paradise* (*Les Enfants du Paradis*) (1945).

## Note on the text

Source: Freeland, Cynthia A. "The Sublime in Cinema." In *Passionate Views: Film, Cognition, and Emotion*, edited by Carl R. Plantinga and Greg M. Smith, 65–83 (endnotes: 262–65). Baltimore: Johns Hopkins University Press, 1999.

The format, style, and endnotes of the original chapter have been reproduced, with occasional modifications. Due to considerations of space, some endnotes as well as passages on Kant and on cognitive science, and three reproductions (a frame enlargement from each of the three films Freeland discusses), have been omitted. Textual omissions made by the volume editor are indicated using "[…]".

## "The sublime in cinema"

### Reviving the sublime

The sublime has been held to be a grand object, often a natural one, that produces in us a characteristic combination of painful and pleasurable feelings of terror plus awe and elevation. Immanuel Kant gives as examples "shapeless mountain masses towering one above the other in wild disorder, with their pyramids of ice, or ... the dark tempestuous ocean."[1] The term *sublime* has also been used to describe certain artworks and emotional experiences they evoke in audiences. As an aesthetic term it was elaborated by Longinus, refined by Edmund Burke and Immanuel Kant, and applied to the analysis of works by landscape painters, romantic poets, Gothic novelists, and composers like Beethoven.

Are some films sublime? The concept of the sublime had lost its prevalence by the time cinema arose, and it has been little used to describe films.[2] Though the sublime has seen renewed attention lately from continental authors,[3] for those interested in cognitive studies of the arts it may seem to denote only an antique or even a "debased" aesthetic concept.[4] What have we to do with this notion unearthed from the creaky architectonic of the *Critique of Judgment*?

In this chapter I argue that there are certain films best described as sublime and that this concept may facilitate more diverse descriptions of films as artworks. I believe it is plausible to view figures like Burke and Kant as antecedents of the current enterprise of cognitive science. Burke tried, in true empiricist spirit, to locate sources of emotions in the human nervous system and perceptual apparatus.[5] And Kant identified mental capacities relevant to our responses to art—capacities that function to relate humans to the natural world. We have advanced beyond Kant and Burke, but contemporary cognitive studies can still learn certain lessons from them.

My account of the sublime identifies it in terms of four basic features derived from the Kantian analysis. To begin, I outline these basic features, illustrating them with a film example. I then review Kant's account of the psychology of the sublime, before moving on to consider how the sublime might be described in two frameworks of contemporary cognitivism: the recent work of psychologist Ed S. Tan on film emotions, and studies of emotions by various neuroscientists.[6] Both kinds of analysis, I argue, confront challenges in accounting for our experiences of sublime films as works of art.

## Four features of the sublime

People will cite their own candidates for the cinematic sublime: perhaps the face of Garbo in *Queen Christina* (1933),[7] the burning of Atlanta in *Gone with the Wind* (1939), or the spaceship ballets of *2001: A Space Odyssey* (1968).[8] I am inclined to call a few entire films sublime, and I discuss three of them here: *The Passion of Joan of Arc* (Carl Dreyer, 1928), *Aguirre: The Wrath of God* (Werner Herzog, 1972), and *Children of Paradise* (Marcel Carné, 1945). All are particularly powerful and warrant this special aesthetic characterization.

To call an object "sublime" means, first and most centrally, that it calls forth a characteristic conflict between certain feelings of pain and pleasure—it evokes what Burke labeled "rapturous terror." On the one hand, the sublime prompts a painful feeling sometimes designated as terror, fear, or dread. But the sublime object does not cause merely pain or terror, but also "rapture": we find it exhilarating and exciting. Kant and Burke emphasized that so long as we are safe, the ineffable, great element before us in the awesome object evokes a certain intellectual pleasure of astonishment or elevation. Kant thought that this pleasure was tied to an awareness of features of our moral selves; Burke instead linked it to the power of the artist's creative mind. My account will fall somewhere in between these alternatives.

To illustrate this first feature of emotional conflict, let us consider *The Passion of Joan of Arc,* a uniquely powerful film that offers viewers a sustained experience of heightened feelings. On the one hand the film is very painful and disturbing. Joan's (Maria Falconetti) accusers glare at her with cruel and horrible faces; her funeral pyre is prepared and ultimately consumes her. *The Passion of Joan of Arc* offers a visual depiction of painful feelings that are so extreme they almost pass beyond representation. Joan's intense anguish is matched only by her profound religious faith. This character's penetrating sorrow and deep mysterious conviction are simply there on the screen for us to see, in Falconetti's astonishing and ravishing face. When I say "ravishing," I mean to indicate that another emotion is involved in our experience of this movie, a feeling of awed pleasure. There is something exalting about the film's power and beauty. Dreyer keeps Falconetti's marvelous face under constant and intense scrutiny; it remains luminous even under torture.

This leads me to the second characteristic feature of the sublime object. Something about it is "great" and astonishing. It is bold and grand, to use Longinus's language. Or, as Kant puts it, "*Sublime* is the name given to what is *absolutely great*" (94/248; Kant's emphasis). The sublime object is vast, powerful, and overwhelming. Used about an artwork, "sublime" is a term of aesthetic praise, signifying that the work has a grandeur or a superlative kind of greatness. This is why accounts of the sublime were so often linked to theories of artistic genius. Kant also makes the interesting observation that in the case of something sublime, "it is not permissible to seek an appropriate standard outside itself, but merely in itself. It is a greatness comparable to itself alone" (97/250).

Dreyer's film and the others I shall discuss are great in this sense, highly distinctive and original achievements, so powerful that they merit a special kind of descriptive label surpassing "beauty." To be sure, the film *Joan* is beautiful: it strikingly juxtaposes close-ups of faces with the blank white cells of the monastery. But it moves beyond beauty to the kind of grandeur we associate with the label "sublime." This is partly due to its subject matter, but also to the film's treatment of this grand subject matter. Joan of Arc is represented in the film as great and extreme—even somehow unfathomable in her faith and ability to withstand her tormentors. The film effectively depicts a woman who inspires reverence. It is a superlatively great film.

A third feature of the sublime is that it evokes ineffable and painful feelings, through which a transformation occurs into pleasure and cognition. The ineffable feelings are related to the second feature, greatness: something about the sublime object is so powerful or vast that it is hard to grasp or take in, and painful. Kant says that the sublime involves an experience of something "almost too great" to be presented or represented (100/253).[9] In Kant's view, the ineffability of the sublime object is tied to the overload on imagination or senses that it presents to us, hence to its painfulness. But, still, this gets translated into something we can conceptualize and feel pleasure at. Kant puts this point by saying that the sublime is defined as "an object (of nature) the representation of which determines the mind to regard the elevation of nature *beyond our reach* as *equivalent to* a presentation of ideas" (119/268; my emphasis). In more modern terms, we might say that the sublime object presents us with a sensory and emotional experience of some sort that is so extreme, unsettling, or intense that it would be disturbing on its own. But in its context it forces us to shift into another mental mode, cognition, or thought. We become more able to handle the deep feelings evoked by the work, and we put a label on them and on the work. Within this new reflective mode, we categorize the object in some way, and through its painfulness we find it pleasurable, exhilarating, or elevating.

In the film *Joan*, the ineffable element is its unusually great emotional intensity. Feeling is expressed by the film itself (and by its actors) on such a grand level as to be overwhelming. Here I begin to depart from Kant, though, as I shall redescribe the shift he spoke of from the ineffable to the cognized, and from pain to pleasure. I suggest that the shift occurs when we regard the deep and painful feelings evoked by a work as crucial for its success as powerful and uplifting art. We are disturbed by the nearly inexpressible pain and emotional intensity of *Joan,* and yet enraptured by its artistic production of painfulness. This paradox of emotions arises when we conceptualize the film's deep emotional intensity as part of an artistic rendering of a viewpoint on its subject.[10]

A fourth and final feature of the sublime is that it prompts moral reflection. Here again I follow Kant in outline, but disagree on the details. For Kant, the describable aspect of the sublime involves a sense of our own moral capacities and duties. The ineffability is both "out there" in the great natural object and "in us," in our depth of feeling about the object. He regarded our awareness of the sublimity of an object outside ourselves as an awareness of the moral law and of certain of our own moral duties. Hence Kant describes this feature of the sublime as part of a universal teleology of nature (a central topic of the third *Critique*).

Kant held quite subtle and sophisticated views about the relations between aesthetics and ethics. I depart from him because I reject his account of the nature of morality and the sorts of cognition it requires; I simply do not accept his view of how natural (or perhaps aesthetic) objects support our recognition of a supposed universal moral law. So I suggest reconceiving this feature of the sublime as follows. Certain aesthetic objects give rise to the central emotional conflicts of the sublime. The ineffably dreadful and painful experience grounds the pleasure of elevation, because it stimulates our human capacities to value powerful artworks. In particular, we are elevated in engaging through the work in reflection that is somehow about the pain or terror it evokes.

Morality is clearly a concern of *The Passion of Joan of Arc*. Let me review how we shift from the deep emotional experience of this film to an elevated cognition about its power as an artwork. What sustains the viewer through an experience of this film's painful emotions and disturbing visions is our respectful and awed recognition of its power and aesthetic qualities. Shot after shot, in their framing, juxtapositions, and intensity, work together to express a moral vision—the critique of this woman's—Joan's—agonizing pain, isolation, and oppression. The film could be said to underscore Joan's conviction and faith by the very way it presents her, this woman with an exalted face, as someone saintly who rises above the fear, of death and the laws of the men who try to condemn her. The representation of so much suffering is indeed painful, but it is justified and made enjoyable within the film's expert construction and through its attitude about such suffering. A range of responses to Joan is depicted within the movie: she bewilders or angers some of the judges, prompts others to ridicule and spit at her, and inspires the peasants to revolt. In the end, I suggest, our aesthetic response to the film (and to the work within it of Falconetti and Dreyer) is like that of the monk who falls at Joan's feet in a kind of awe, terror, and reverence. There is something deeply pleasurable about this film that we can feel even while also being pained at what it depicts.

My brief sketch and illustration of four features of the sublime began with the emotional conflict describable as "rapturous terror." This is closely intertwined with the three other features I have mentioned: greatness, cognition of the ineffable, and moral reflection. These features make the sublime distinctive. I shall next review in more detail Kant's account of how these features were linked, so as to explain further both why I disagree with Kant and how I would locate the four features in films. This will pave the way for my consideration of revisions and updates in our theorizing about emotions of the sublime.

## Kant on the sublime

Kant's "Analytic of the Sublime" occupies an extensive portion of *The Critique of Judgement* (1790).[11] The aesthetic is analyzed here within the framework of Kant's faculty psychology. He describes the beautiful as involving interactions between the faculties of *imagination* and *understanding*; these get activated pleasurably by the beautiful in the rather notorious "free play" he discusses earlier in the third *Critique*. There is a kind of restful contemplation in the beautiful, as opposed to a "mental movement" or even a "vibration" in the sublime (107/258). The sublime prompts "a pleasure that only arises indirectly, being brought about by the feeling of a momentary check to the vital forces followed at once by a discharge all the more powerful" (91/245).

The sublime crucially depends upon a tension between our highest sensible faculty, imagination, and our highest human faculty, reason. Kant speaks of the sublime as involving a kind of "outrage on the imagination" (91/245), because the object is so massive, powerful, or extended that it is beyond our capacity to imagine, that is, supersensible. Such an object might be the "starry skies above" mentioned in a famous passage at the conclusion of the *Second Critique*.[12] [...]

Let me now move from Kant's account back to my topic of films. I would like to provide an illustration of the details of the Kantian analysis of the sublime as it might apply to films, while at the same time explaining my departures from his view. Let us consider, then, how Kant's framework might be applied to my second film example, Herzog's *Aguirre: The Wrath of God*. *Aguirre* is interesting to take up here because it is in some sense a film or artwork *about* the sublime in nature. Through its particular representation of sublime landscapes, the film itself becomes sublime.

*Aguirre* begins with an extraordinary sequence offering a distant, soaring view of the Andes Mountains. It is not simply the scenery here that is sublime, but also the representation of it. Herzog's camera is literally elevated in the opening scene. Viewers seem to float down eerily through cloud-topped peaks and jagged ravines. The sensation of floating, a kind of disturbing yet exciting dislocation, is enhanced by the film's repetitive, high-pitched musical score. From a great distance, the camera reveals a line of miniature humans who can barely be seen. It reinforces feelings of the sublime by making the scenery vast and overwhelming in proportion to the ant-like human enterprise within it. The column turns out to be a long line of conquistadors in armor, women in velvet dresses and starched white ruffs, Indian and black slaves, horses, cannons, pigs, and so on. The magnitude of their endeavor is extraordinary yet still minuscule within nature's overwhelming vastness.

A second sublime landscape in the film is the river that the conquistadors encounter upon their descent from the jagged mountain peaks. They find themselves amid an overwhelming trackless jungle, and ride rafts in danger from rapids and whirlpools. The camera places us there, like the adventurers, on the river and in danger of being sucked under and destroyed. (In one scene, a horse forced off their raft simply disappears into the watery jungle without a sound or a trace.) This film visually displays its sublime landscape, just as Dreyer's film displayed Falconetti's face. Though this landscape is depicted as threatening, strange, and ominous, it also has a terrible serene beauty. It is huge and impressively indifferent to the humans it dwarfs.

Consider, then, how *Aguirre* presents the first two features I mentioned above, the characteristic emotional conflict of the sublime and its related grandeur or scope. The mountains, river, and jungle are grand not just in themselves as natural objects but in the way they function as *Aguirre's* subject matter. The film depicts these natural objects in ways so as to represent their power, extension, and grandeur, arousing a conflict in emotions of the viewer. Just as *Joan* evokes in viewers pain over the visual display of her suffering, here too the viewers feel great dread. We become almost tortured in waiting for each new disaster to unfold for the characters, watching their snail-paced progress through the vast landscapes. And yet while these aspects of the representation of the landscape and figures within it are overwhelming and painful, other aspects of the film are elevating and pleasurable. So we can speak as Kant did of a "movement" or "vibration" in our perception of this object. It is crucial that we, unlike the depicted conquistadors, are safe as we encounter the jungle. We can enjoy seeing the film's awesome depiction of power, space, and beauty—and perhaps we enjoy even Aguirre's depths of insanity (since of course we are not subject to his murderous tantrums). Watching this jungle as Herzog shows it in the film, we can appreciate intellectually his representation of how it crushes the humans within it, and this can move us to a feeling of loftiness and respect. Their enterprise is shown to be mad and is defeated accordingly.

This is, however, where I part ways with Kant. For him, the respect the sublime object awakens in us is really "about" ourselves, about our human capacities and our recognition of duty and obligation to the moral law. The third and fourth features of the sublime are crucially connected for Kant, since the switch from painful ineffability to pleasurable cognition is also a shift from sensibility into a moral framework where we feel respect for the moral law. I agree that one aspect of an experience of a sublime film like *The Passion of Joan of Arc* or *Aguirre* involves painful and ineffable feelings. *Aguirre* is very slow-paced; Herzog allows the camera to observe the unfolding of this astonishing natural landscape, so as to express its vastness and convey its magnitude, evoking dread and terror at its power. I suggest that we switch from our somewhat overloaded sensory and emotional experiences of things seen and depicted in the film to a more cognitive, intellectual appreciation of *how* the film depicts its great subject, including moral reflection on its point of view. We are prompted by certain extreme features of the depiction to become aware of and to enjoy our experience on another level. This does not involve "the Moral Law," but rather cognition of the film as a powerful artwork prompting moral reflection. My suggested emendation of Kant is that in describing the shift from the sensory to the cognitive, we should consider the experience of "elevation" as occurring when we shift from the perspective *within* the film to a perspective *about* the film. This shift accompanies the shift from a predominantly emotional or imaginative experience on the sensory level to a more intellectual or cognitive experience including pleasurable reflection on the film's moral point of view.[13]

I now offer a further proposal about how sublime cinema prompts such shifts from the ineffably painful to pleasurable cognition, from dread to elevation. This happens most notably at various moments in the film where we cannot avoid becoming aware of the movie *as* a movie. Although I am happy to describe certain films as a whole as sublime, I also say that certain scenes in these films are particularly sublime or particularly effective. That is, certain cognitive shifts occur at moments of the rupture of representation, when films draw our attention to themselves and to their perspective on what is depicted. These ruptures prompt our recognition of the filmmaker's desire and ability to show us something about a person or landscape.

There are many such moments of rupture prompting such recognition in *Aguirre*. I have already mentioned the effectiveness of the film's opening scenes, where devices of framing and dislocation announce the film's point of view on the characters it is about to show. Another rupture is prompted by the deliberate framing devices in the beautifully composed scene of Aguirre's daughter's death. The filmmaker hides our view of the arrow that has pierced her breast, so that her death is at the same time horrible, painful, yet a mysterious graceful swooning into her father's arms. Again at the film's conclusion, we are shown an extraordinary vision of the mad Aguirre, clad in armor and helmet astride his rickety raft, which has suddenly become awash with skittering small monkeys. The camera reinforces the "viewedness" of this scene when it makes an uncharacteristic move from the slow pace of historical realism into a more modern mode: apparently mounted on a helicopter, it drops far back, jolting us, and then swoops in with frightening speed to circle the mad warrior. Finally it retreats, and restores us to the earlier realist mode of calm detached observation. These shifts remind us we are seeing a depiction and reinforce a particular point of view on the mad conquistador.

The most extraordinary moment of rupture in this film occurs when we witness a deliberately hallucinatory sequence showing a fully rigged sailing ship lofted high into a treetop. The few survivors in the raft, mad from poison arrows, thirst, hunger, and fever, see this vision and say, "That is not a ship." As film viewers, we too cannot be sure whether we see the ship or a hallucination. The scene could be said to "vibrate" as Kant put it. The boat looks real, but the thought of a sailing ship in a treetop goes beyond what seems possible or cognizable.

These ruptures in *Aguirre* prompt a shift from emotions felt primarily within the film narrative to reflection about the film. Such devices are also present in *Joan of Arc*, a film that similarly draws attention to itself with its careful framing of scenes—with, for example, compositions of frames depicting a small head in relation to a large white space, or the use of unusual angles of view, from well below a face or far above a scene. *Joan* further prompts an awareness of our presence as "audience" through its frequent depiction of carnival entertainers waiting for the trial to lead to its predestined conclusion. These emphasize the fact that for us, just as for the peasants in the film, Joan's trial and execution provide an entertainment or spectacle.

Kant held that the experience of the sublime occupied a border space between the aesthetic and the moral. I have rejected his insistence that the shift from ineffable to cognized is precisely the transition from imagination to reason's recognition of the moral law. Rather, the sublime art object prompts a shift from sensory, emotional involvement in the object to aesthetic enjoyment and cognitive appreciation. Such appreciation involves awareness of artistry and reflection upon moral matters. Here I am also following Burke: we are prompted by the sublime to feel respect for something human—not for the moral law and our obligations, but for the ability to construct powerful art with a moral vision.

I have also suggested that we are prompted to shift to this recognition when we have a cognitive appreciation of the film as a film, not as mere entertainment or as sensory and emotional spectacle. Recognizing the film's artistry takes us to a level of reflection upon it as a whole, including an appreciation of what it aims to *say* about the painful things it depicts. In *Joan of Arc,* Dreyer provides a fierce critique of Joan's oppression and torture, and *Aguirre* links the painful emotions involved in its visions to a moral assessment of colonizers dominated by greed and the lust for gold.[14] Appreciating the work requires recognizing the moral vision it offers, though not necessarily accepting that vision.

## Cognitivism revisits the sublime

Kant's faculty psychology frames his account of the sublime. How might a more contemporary psychological theory describe the emotional conflicts of the sublime? Let us consider two broad types of contemporary cognitive approaches to the emotions, first that of a psychologist, and second that of a neuroscientist.

Psychologist Ed S. Tan presents a cognitive analysis of emotions in film in his recent book, *Emotion and the Structure of Narrative Film: Film as an Emotion Machine.*[15] Tan explores cinema-watching as an active, conscious experience combining thought and motions. Like other cognitivists, Tan sees emotions as adaptive forms of behavior that facilitate organismic response to the environment (232). He seeks to identify images, narrative devices, and so on that will trigger specific kinds of emotional responses in viewers—responses that scientists can study empirically.

Tan treats films as constructed artefacts or "machines" designed with a specific function: they simulate our natural environment in ways to which we respond with appropriate emotions.

[...]

To consider how one might generate an account of the sublime within this sort of psychological framework, we need to examine Tan's distinction between "fiction emotions" and "artefact emotions" (65, 82). Fiction emotions are tied to the "diegetic effect," the illusion of being present in the fictional world (52–56). Fiction emotions would include immediate empathetic responses of ineffable pain evoked by films, such as our empathy for the tortured Joan or dread about the conquistadors' fate in *Aguirre.* By comparison, artefact emotions involve recognition of a film's construction or of its artistry (65); this latter category encompasses aesthetic emotions such as awe at great acting, wonder at cinematography, and so on. Thus artefact emotions might include the pleasurable cognition of greatness I have described as our response to the sublimity of both *Joan* and *Aguirre.*

Tan says that when features of film as artefact come to the fore, they are often regulated by the film to sustain certain narrative effects, that is, to foster the production of fictions (192, 82, 238). He also hints that an experience of the sublime might be available only to certain viewers, since he hypothesizes that artefact emotions are linked to the factor of "cinephilia" (34–35). That is, some artefact emotions are tied to the competences of certain viewers who enjoy the cognitive games of cinema (49); they are less recognized by "most natural viewers." For example, I have suggested that in the sublime we take pleasure in something painful, signaled by moments of rupture in the film's fictive surface, but Tan says that the main reason for most viewers to "direct their attention toward the artificiality of the fiction" is "because the essence of what is being depicted on the screen is not to their liking" (81). I confess to feeling suspicion about this distinction between cinephiles and natural viewers, but I cannot argue with Tan's comment that "more research on the viewer is clearly needed" (65). I believe there are further challenges for a psychological theory like Tan's, so let us now consider how he might describe the effectiveness of a specific scene from my final example of a sublime film, *Children of Paradise.*

This movie can be praised at many levels: cinematic spectacle, dialogue, characterization, narrative complexity, and acting. One thing that makes it stand out as "incomparable" is the presence of the mime Jean-Louis Barrault. Certain scenes he is in are especially effective at prompting emotions of the sublime, and I shall consider one in detail here. In this scene, Barrault plays the character Baptiste, a mime acting in a play he has written. Dressed in Pierrot costume [i.e., the white clothes of the clownish character from the *Commedia dell'arte* – Ed.], he enacts despair over the loss of the goddess-statue he worships. Our point of view is that of the represented audience at the theater, but we know more than they: the statue-goddess is Garance (Arletty), the woman Baptiste loves but whom he has lost because he lacked faith in her love. The film is about the nature of art, emotions, acting, and authenticity. It supports the view that emotions like love are "really very simple," deep, and permanent. Baptiste has lost his chance to be with Garance through testing her love too much.

On stage, the Pierrot finds a rope and plans to hang himself, but is diverted when a laundry-maid wants the rope to hang her clothes. We also know that this, laundry-maid is really Nathalie (Maria Cesarès), who helplessly loves Baptiste. Distracted, the Pierrot gazes off to the horizon in search of his lost goddess. The camera, which until now has depicted the entire scene from the audience's perspective in the theater, suddenly shifts—and Tan would point to this as a controlling device that directs and produces our emotions. We first see a point-of-view shot depicting Baptiste's view of Garance in the wings flirting with her new lover, Frédérik (Pierre Brasseur). A reverse shot shows the pain, shock, and anger on Baptiste's face. His pain is very intense and strange, and our view of him is suspended for an unusually long time. Tan would say that the extended close-up cues particular fiction emotions of pity and empathy.

To go this far only would ignore aspects of this scene and of our response to it that are relevant to what makes it sublime. We do not simply feel certain emotions in empathy with Baptiste. We also have an emotional conflict, because there is something intensely pleasurable and uplifting about the scene and the way it fits into the film as a whole. That is, we have another emotion that is perhaps broader in scope and different from the first emotion, one linked to an appreciation of the film as a work of art. Tan would say that this is a kind of artefact emotion.

Artefact emotions may be most strongly felt during moments of "rupture" like those I described in *Aguirre*. It is possible to identify such moments here as well. *Children of Paradise* prompts recognition of its status as artefact by a doubling of the audience, contrasting us as its viewing audience with the represented audience in the mime theater. Lacking our knowledge and point-of-view shots, that audience may think that Baptiste is still in character when he is suspended in his long moment of anguish. What they see as simply Baptiste's good acting is for us an almost delicious ambiguity or tension. Is Baptiste miming or expressing pain? Does he enact the Pierrot's despair, or his own? And doesn't Barrault play this scene marvelously![16] This tension in this scene is pleasurable because we recognize that the film is using reflexive elements of artistic self-representation to create a powerful emotional effect. Baptiste's expression is so strange it becomes frightening (indeed, his despair boils over in later mimes where he enacts murderous desires). His suspended stare is so excruciating that it prompts the frightened Nathalie to drop her character in the mime and cry out "Baptiste!" in shock and horror. Her cry startles the theater audience, which does not comprehend what has occurred as we do. Nathalie, too, is forced into a kind of rupture of representation, paralleling the rupture or vacillation in the shift between Baptiste and the Pierrot, and in our own appreciation of the film as both a story in progress and a reflexive artwork.

Tan might say that the sublimity here involves this shift between fiction and artefact emotions. The film works as a machine due to the effective way in which this scene, and others in it, are crafted. Through its careful structure of narrative, music, dialogue, and point-of-view shots, such as close-ups of Baptiste and Nathalie, the film prompts our own conflicting emotional responses: fiction emotions of sadness, horror, pity, dread, and shock, combined with aesthetic emotions of awe and admiration. Tan's contemporary cognitivist account tries to describe some psychological laws that film exemplifies. These laws would explain how emotions are produced and what role they play in our human behavioral economy.

On my own revised Kantian-Burkean account, the sublime involves a shift from overwhelmingly painful emotions to pleasurable reflection about a work's moral viewpoint. This point raises a certain challenge for an account like Tan's. The psychologist studying viewers' artefact emotions may need to develop tools to study both their concepts of art (which Tan proposes to do by studying "cinephiles") and their concepts of morality. Like *Joan* and *Aguirre, Children of Paradise* is a sublime artwork not just because it prompts deep emotions but because those emotions are linked to moral reflection. The subject of this movie as a whole concerns the values involved in art, acting, and feeling emotion. The power to create art and beauty is associated with the power to feel deep, sincere, and "simple" emotions like love. Thus Baptiste and Garance are contrasted as "good" with all the other weaker characters in the film. Baptiste is a dedicated master artist whose performances are gripping and gorgeous, and the interruptions of his art (here and later in the film) are horrifying and painful. In this scene there is a unique reflexivity, as the film meditates about art and about moral values through a number of representations, juxtaposing the art of the director Carné with that of the actor Barrault and the mime Baptiste. This artistry and depth are what exalts the film audience.[17]

## Cognitive neuroscience

I turn now to consider a more biologically oriented approach from cognitive neuroscientists who differentiate mental functions according to human evolutionary history. They locate and explain emotions in terms of the development and operation of various systems in the brain and nervous system. Cognitive science replaces Kant's talk about "faculties" with talk of various "emotion systems" that interact with "information-processing systems."[18] The emotions currently studied are often rather primitive, such as a rat's fear of a cat. Still, some of the results are fascinating, and they suggest new ways of accounting for more subtle and complex emotional phenomena, including conflicts between the sublime emotions of fear or terror versus exaltation.

Cognitive neuroscientists challenge aspects of the folk psychologies we inherit from Western thinkers. First, they challenge certain philosophical notions of *rationality* in the tradition, as they break down distinctions between reason and emotion. For example, they maintain that some emotions can bypass cognition and the brain's cortical tissues (although other information processing is still necessary). Or they note the role played by emotions in making rational decisions.[19] This is interesting because it suggests that both of the key emotions involved in the sublime—fear and elevation—might involve dimensions of feeling as well as of cognition.

Cognitive neuroscientists also challenge the philosophical presumption that emotions are *conscious*. Joseph LeDoux argues that "the conscious feelings that we know and love (and hate) our emotions by are just red herrings, detours, in the scientific study of emotions" (18).[20] Again, I find this suggestive because it might indicate why we cannot always describe or pinpoint our emotions, including perhaps the "ineffable" emotions evoked by a powerful artwork. Nevertheless, some kind of experiencing or processing is going on in response to the work, and it might lead, as, Kant thought—though not by the paths Kant thought—to yet other emotions and cognitions.

LeDoux and others also challenge a *voluntaristic* account of emotions. LeDoux writes,

> Emotions are things that happen to us rather than things we will to occur. …We have little direct control over our emotional reactions. While conscious control over emotions is weak, emotions can flood consciousness. This is so because the wiring of the brain at this point in our evolutionary history is such

that connections from the emotional systems to the cognitive systems are stronger than connections from the cognitive systems to the emotional systems.[21]

Once again this is important because it means that emotions arise in response to things and can "overcome" us, much as the painfulness of what is great in something sublime can "overwhelm" us or "flood" our receptive system. The question next arises whether, if one kind of flooding occurs, a shift to another system can take place?

In other words, how many conflicting basic emotion systems are there, and how do they interact and possibly conflict when we experience complex stimuli? Currently these seem to be open questions. [...]

And what of the emotions of the sublime—the characteristic combination of exaltation and fear? Recall that "respect" for Kant was a complex, rarefied emotion ("delight") involving our awareness of inadequacy before the moral law. Neuroscientists may not currently study such a complex emotion (nor may they ever wish to), but presumably they believe that even such a lofty phenomenon as the sublime must have roots within our basic, brain-based emotional systems. Interestingly, Antonio Damasio comes close to saying just this, while fending off incipient charges of reductivism: "Realizing that there are biological mechanisms behind the most sublime human behavior does not imply a simplistic reduction to the nuts and bolts of neurobiology. In any case, the partial explanation of complexity by something less complex does not signify debasement."[22]

Somehow the brain is capable of self-awareness of its own kinds of capacities, and it has the ability to organize inputs from various systems into an integrated conscious experience. This is true both for the inputs from different emotion systems and inputs from the emotion and information-processing or cognitive systems. LeDoux suggests that the "pure" states of the three basic emotion systems he describes may be described as *anxiety, panic or rage,* and *hope or elation.* It is interesting to note that fear, one of the sublime emotions, seems to occur within a separate system from elation. And these systems may operate in distinct ways through different kinds of conjunctions with cognitive processes (or neocortical pathways). This suggests a new approach to discussing conflicts of the sublime experience: such conflicts reflect the simultaneous operation of multiple emotion systems, which themselves might have distinctive kinds of links (and even multiple links each) to our cognitive systems.

Thus it could turn out that the sublime object is being processed in different ways simultaneously by different mental systems. Perhaps after a certain point of perceptual processing of, say, a fearful stimulus, the limits of the more primitive system are reached and so we shift to another emotional system working with another kind of input and another layer of cognitive or categorical analysis. Perhaps within our complexly evolved human brain we are then able to reintegrate the overwhelmingly enormous input into our normal functioning—as a rat or cat cannot—by changing it into an abstraction that we can handle better. Fear arises in one system when our perceptual system begins to break down or be overwhelmed. Elation comes when we gain mastery over the perceived object by integrating it into our rational framework. This rational framework would need to be complex, so as to include the socially constructed notions used in our discourse about art and morality. Here also would have to be located the reflexiveness of our emotions that refer to other emotions. So in experiences of the sublime we combine pain and pleasure that is felt somehow at or about that pain. This is admittedly a very speculative account of how future scientists might redescribe the kind of conflict of the sublime that Kant located between the mental faculties of reason and imagination. But it suggests that there may well be a successor cognitive account for the phenomenon Kant observed.[23]

Kant used the subdivision of mind to ground his theory of moral value. Reason, the "highest" faculty, was also the most valued. Talk of "higher" brain functions in cognitive science tends instead to indicate stages of evolutionary development.[24] Although such language is not typically linked to any framework of moral theory, it can be. There are interesting efforts to draw connections both between recent studies of brain function and behavior and ethical theory. These proposals suggest that there will be a number of new and distinctive approaches to grounding ethics on this new sort of psychology.[25]

## Conclusion

The sublime, as I have described it, is an experience involving four key features. At its heart is the emotional conflict between terror or dread and elevation. Second, the sublime involves something great or vast. In speaking of this second feature, I amended Kant's account in two important ways, focusing on artworks, not natural objects, and claiming that the grandeur belongs not only to the world in the work but to the work itself, to the way that world is depicted or shown.

Third, the greatness of the sublime is linked to an overwhelming, painful, ineffable effect the object has on the perceiver. I have described this feature of ineffability by mentioning representations in each film of certain feelings or landscapes that disturb us and strain our capacity for experience (such as Joan's faith and suffering, Baptiste's desperate love, or the conquistadors' dread in the Amazonian jungle). But this ineffable pain turns into pleasure as the object also prompts a shift into cognition. Unique and sublime films prompt our appreciative, awed reflection on how they use the film medium to disturb us in artful ways.

The fourth feature of the sublime is that such reflection is elevating because it includes a powerful moral perspective. I revised Kant by describing this as cognition of how human artists can offer powerful moral reflections in their works. To illustrate our switch or vacillation between the sublime emotions (the rapturous terror), I focused on scenes of rupture, and described how our awareness of the self-referential aspects of filmic art mediate between emotional involvement and more distanced aesthetic and moral appraisal.

I have also outlined challenges that cognitivist accounts face in capturing these four features of the sublime. There are two primary challenges. The first centers on the reflexivity of the emotions of the sublime. It is crucial to the sublime that one somehow feels exaltation, elevation or pleasure *about* what one is overwhelmed by or fears. Empirically based approaches to the study and explanation of the emotions need to capture this reflexive element. The second, deeper challenge concerns the ways in which values enter into our experience of the sublime. When we find a film sublime, we both evaluate it as an excellent, superlatively great artwork and also are elevated by reflection on the moral issues it raises and its perspective on those issues.

Tan's psychological approach provides a certain basis for discussing the reflexivity of emotions, in describing how artefact and fiction emotions might ramify and interact. I expressed concerns above, however, about whether his "machine" account of films can explain how our aesthetic emotions are tied to active and complex cognitions of moral value. Similarly, neuroscience research indicates that there may be brain-based grounds for emotional conflicts like those of the sublime, even though the details will obviously be different from what Kant envisaged with his primitive theory of mental faculties. Still, neuroscientists may capture what I call the reflexivity of emotions by emphasizing complexity of communication between cognitive and emotion systems and the presence of feedback loops in the brain. Again, like Tan, the neuroscientists, too, face the second challenge, because the meta-emotions of film viewers involve not just our wiring and physiology, but our higher-level cognitions of value. We have these because we are humans using complex concepts that reflect our social organization as beings who make artworks, interpret them, and can understand their moral visions. When we see and react to Joan's suffering we need to have thoughts about patriarchy, nationalism, and religion, just as *Aguirre* requires conceptualizations of colonialism, incest, and madness, and *Children of Paradise* meditates on the values of artistic originality and emotional authenticity. I do not wish to suggest that it is impossible to account for these thoughts about values and their role in prompting our emotions. My goal has been, rather, to say that it will be a complex task to explain what makes certain films sublime.[26]

## Questions

1. Are there any films (or film scenes) that you consider sublime? Why or why not? If so, explain in what sense they are "sublime."

2. If you were a director, what cinematic techniques might you use to elicit the sublime? How might you evoke the complex feeling of delightful terror, vastness or grandeur, the (partial) comprehension of an ineffable feeling, and moral reflection?

3. How is Freeland's account inspired by Kant (or Burke), and in what ways does it depart from that theory? Explain the significance of Freeland's notion of "rupture."

4. What two challenges does Freeland's account raise for the psychological and neuroscientific approaches? Do you agree? Explain.

5. Discuss and evaluate Freeland's account of the sublime. How might her ideas be used in future research in psychology or neuroscience?

## Further reading

Freeland, Cynthia A. *But Is It Art?* Oxford: Oxford University Press, 2001.
Freeland, Cynthia A. "Bill Viola and the Video Sublime." *Film-Philosophy* 3, no. 28 (1999): 1–7.
Freeland, Cynthia A., and Thomas E. Wartenberg. *Philosophy and Film.* New York: Routledge, 1994.
Herzog, Werner. "On the Absolute, the Sublime, and Ecstatic Truth." *Arion* 17, no. 3 (2010): 1–12.
Ishizu, Tomohiro, and Semir Zeki, "A Neurobiological Enquiry into the Origins of Our Experience of the Sublime and Beautiful." *Frontiers in Human Neuroscience* 8, no. 891 (2014): 1–10.
Pence, Jeffrey. "Cinema of the Sublime: Theorizing the Ineffable." *Poetics Today* 25, no. 1, (2004): 29–66.
Pezzotta, Elisa. *Stanley Kubrick: Adapting the Sublime.* Jackson: University Press of Mississippi, 2013.

# CHAPTER 33
# ARTHUR DANTO, "BEAUTY AND SUBLIMITY" (2003)

Arthur Danto (1924–2013) was one of the foremost American art critics and philosophers of art. He is widely known for his (Hegel-inspired) proclamation of the "end of art" and his discussion of its significance. In *The Abuse of Beauty*, which is based on his Paul Carus lectures, Danto traces the evolution of the concept of beauty over the past century and explores how beauty was removed from the definition of art. In previous times it was widely agreed that the main purpose of art was to make something beautiful, but beauty eventually came to be regarded as nonessential and even an artistic shortcoming. Danto argues that even if beauty is not, and should not be, the fundamental or essential purpose of art, it does have an important role to play and is not something critics and artists should avoid. Beauty is an "option" for art, but "not a necessary condition." He shows with numerous examples that most art is not, in fact, beautiful. At the same time, Danto argues for the partial rehabilitation of beauty.

In the following chapter, Danto gives a brief history of the sublime. He mentions some differences between the beautiful and the sublime: "The mark of the sublime by contrast was ecstasy or *enthusiasmos*." Discussing artists ranging from Michelangelo and Leonardo to Barnett Newman (who has a chapter in the present volume), Danto examines the relevance of sublimity to the creation and appreciation of certain artworks. Finally, Danto adheres to a common but disputable reading of Kant according to which any appeal to concepts of the object or artwork would render a potential judgment of the sublime "cognitive," and thus prevent one from judging the object to be sublime. This reading raises the question of which concepts (if any), on Danto's view, are to be taken into consideration in the experience and appreciation of artworks (and how concepts could be relevant at all if concepts necessarily render a judgment cognitive)—as his interpretation of artworks such as Newman's *Onement I* seems to require.

## Note on the text

Source: Reprinted from Arthur Danto, "Beauty and Sublimity," in *The Abuse of Beauty: Aesthetics and the Concept of Art*, 143–160. Peru, IL: Open Court Publishing Company, 2003.

Insertions in square brackets were written by Danto; comments by the volume editor are indicated by " – Ed." The numbers assigned to Figures have been reordered so as to begin with "1." Format and style have occasionally been modified, and some minor errors in Danto's text have been silently corrected. References to Kant's three *Critiques* have been capitalized and italicized.

## "Beauty and sublimity"

In 1948, *The Tiger's Eye* – an influential magazine devoted to literature and the arts – published a symposium titled "Six Opinions on What Is Sublime in Art?" There had been little of note written on this topic since Hegel's lectures on aesthetics in the 1820s but it must have seemed to the editors of the magazine, who were very close to the Abstract Expressionist movement, that something was beginning to happen in painting that put it in candidacy for sublimity. Two of the movement's more intellectual figures – Robert Motherwell and Barnett Newman – were among the symposiasts, but it was Newman who wrote with an excitement and conviction that the title of his contribution perfectly conveys: "The Sublime is Now." Early that year, allegedly on his forty-third birthday – January 29th, 1948 – Newman had made what he regarded as a major breakthrough, not only in his own painting, but in painting as such, with a work he was to call *Onement I*. There can be little question, I think, that Newman connected this work with the tremendousness conveyed by the idea of the sublime. It was somehow too momentous an achievement, in his mind at least, to think of as merely beautiful, or beautiful, really, at all. Some decades later, the post-modernist thinker, Jean-François Lyotard, was to write that in the "aesthetic of the sublime … the logic of the avant-gardes finds its axioms."[1] And it is clear from the way in which Newman polarizes the two concepts, that he saw no possibility of finding the axioms of his art in the aesthetic of the beautiful. If there was to be an aesthetic for *Onement I*, nothing less than the sublime would suffice. There are, as I have pointed out, a great many aesthetic qualities other than beauty. But none of them poses quite the challenge to beauty that sublimity does, and I shall close my discussion of the abuse of beauty with this last chapter in its history.

**Figure 1** Barnett Newman, *Onement I*, 1948. "Beyond mere beauty." Digital Image © the Museum of Modern Art / Licensed by SCALA / Art Resource, NY.

Avant-garde intellectuals, in mid-twentieth century America, and especially in New York, inevitably saw the world in terms of polar opposition. This was doubtless a consequence of having been brought up on the *Communist Manifesto*, in which society is dramatically portrayed as now split into "two great hostile classes facing each other: Bourgeoisie and Proletariat." The subtext of Greenberg's[2] "Avant-Garde and Kitsch," for example, was the struggle between two incompatible philosophies of culture which he respectively identified with Fascism (= Kitsch) and Socialism (= Avant-Garde). Philip Rahv, an editor of the influential *Partisan Review*, in which Greenberg's essay had been published, spoke of American writers as grouped into two polar types: "Paleface and Redskin," exemplified respectively by Henry James and Walt Whitman. Newman could not resist placing the sublime with the beautiful in polar contrast with one another:

> The invention of beauty by the Greeks, that is, their postulate of beauty as an ideal, has been the bugbear of European art and European aesthetic philosophies. Man's natural desire in the arts to express his relation to the Absolute became identified and confused with the absolutisms of perfect creations – with the fetish of quality – so that the European artist has been continually involved in the moral struggle between notions of beauty and the desire for sublimity.[3]

With equal inevitability, Newman sees the history of art as an aesthetic struggle, between "the [...] exaltation [...] to be found in perfect form"[4] on one side, and, on the other, "a desire to destroy form, where form can be formless." It is, he argues, "the impulse of modern art [...] to destroy beauty," which has precisely been the argument of this book.

## American sublime

Newman framed the polarity between beauty and sublimity within another polarity, that between Europe and America. "The failure of European art to achieve the sublime is due to this blind desire ... to build an art within a framework of [...] the Greek ideal of beauty." This is because European art was "unable to move away from the Renaissance imagery of figures and objects except by distortion or by denying it completely for an empty world of geometrical formalisms." But – "I believe that here in America, some of us, free from the weight of European culture, are finding the answer, by completely denying that art has any concern with the problem of beauty and where to find it." This opposition between Europe and America is echoed by Robert Motherwell, the only American in the movement in fact to have visited Europe, and whose sensibility among masters of New York School owed most to a kind of European culture. It was Motherwell who invented the term "The New York School" to distinguish what he and his peers were doing from "The School of Paris." And in an important interview of 1968, Motherwell said: "I think that one of the major American contributions to modern art is sheer size. There are lots of arguments as to whether it should be credited to Pollock, Still, Rothko, even Newman ... The surrealist tone and literary qualities were dropped, and [it was] transformed into something plastic, mysterious, and sublime. No Parisian is a sublime painter, nor a monumental one."

Let me round off my little catalog of polarities by reverting to Rahv. "While the redskin glories in his Americanism, to the paleface it is a source of endless ambiguities." James may have been a paleface, but he tirelessly pursued the moral allegory of the culturally and morally innocent American among the sophisticated (and corrupt) Europeans. He could not resist giving the hero of his 1877 novel, *The American*, the allegorical name "Newman." The New Man has come to the Old World on a cultural pilgrimage in 1868, having made his fortune manufacturing wash tubs; and James has a bit of fun at his hero's expense by inflicting him with an "aesthetic headache" in the Louvre, where his story begins. "I know very little about pictures or how they are painted," Newman concedes; and as evidence, James has him ordering, as if buying shirts, half a dozen copies of assorted old masters from a pretty young copyist who thinks he is crazy, since, as she puts its, "I paint like a cat."

By a delicious historical coincidence, Barnett Newman – another New Man – visits the Louvre for the first time in 1968, exactly a century later. By contrast with James's hero, this Newman has had the benefit of having read Clement Greenberg and had himself gone through a Surrealist phase. So he is able to tell his somewhat patronizing guide – the French critic Pierre Schneider – to see Uccello's *The Battle of San Romano* as "a modern painting, a flat painting," and to explain why Mantegna's Saint Sebastian bleeds no more than a piece of wood despite being pierced with arrows. He sees Géricault's *Raft of the Medusa* as 'tipped up' like one of Cézanne's tables – "It has the kind of modern space you wouldn't expect with that kind of rhetoric." And in general the new New Man is able to show European aesthetes a thing or two about how to talk about the Old Masters – and incidentally how to look at his own work, which so many even of his New York School contemporaries found intractable. In Rembrandt, for example, Newman sees "All that brown, with a streak of light coming down the middle of them – as in my own painting." His guide, the critic Pierre Schneider, European to the core, pretends to see Newman as a redskin – "a noble savage with a protective disguise, just as the Huron, to be left in peace, pretends to be an oilman."

## Surpassing every standard of sense

Beauty had been put on the defensive as early as the eighteenth century, when the concept of the sublime first entered Enlightenment consciousness through the translation by Boileau of a text on the subject by a somewhat obscure rhetorician, traditionally known as Longinus; and *A Philosophical Enquiry into the Origin of Our Ideas of the Sublime and Beautiful*, by the Irish statesman, Edmund Burke. Beauty, in the Enlightenment had become inextricably connected with taste, and refined taste was the defining mark of aesthetic cultivation. Aesthetic education implies that there are rules that one can learn, as in moral education, though it would be expected that in both, the pupil will in time be on his or her own, and know when something is beautiful or right respectively through having acquired good taste in each. It was entirely correct of Newman to connect the idea of beauty with perfection. The mark of the sublime by contrast was ecstasy or *enthusiasmos*. These terms or, better, their equivalents, continue to play a role in the vocabulary of aesthetic appraisal. We speak of ourselves as "blown away" or as "knocked out" or "bowled over" or "shattered" by a work of art, and this goes well beyond finding ourselves enough pleased to judge it perfect. Reading Longinus caused the cultivated audiences of the eighteenth century to wonder why their art never lifted them out of themselves, which is what "ecstasy" means, and thus the idea of the sublime collided with the sphere of the tasteful as a disruptive force, much in the way the god Dionysus invaded Thebes in Euripides's unsettling play, *The Bacchae*. Grace and beauty all at once seemed paltry and insufficient. A recent commentator compared the impact of *On the Sublime* to that of Freud's writings on our own times. In proposing sex as the main drive in human conduct, Freud made everyone restless and emotionally uncertain, and feeling that in terms of orgasmic promise, something was missing from our civilized little lives. Think of Thomas Mann's character in *Death in Venice*. Beauty was a source of pleasure – but sublimity, in art and especially in nature, produced what Burke spoke of as "the strongest emotion which the mind is capable of feeling."

But what exactly was that feeling? In a review devoted to some pictures by the German Romantic painter, Caspar David Friedrich, in which one or more personages is shown from behind and gazing at the Moon, the *New Yorker* art critic, Peter Schjeldahl, expressed reservations on the critical usefulness of the term. The sublime, he writes, is a "hopelessly jumbled philosophical notion that has had more than two centuries to start meaning something cogent and hasn't succeeded yet." And he goes on, affecting a sublime historical cluelessness: "As an adjective in common use, the word is correctly employed not by Immanuel Kant but by Frank Loesser: 'The compartment is air-conditioned, and the mood sublime.'" Nothing that rocked an entire and largely self-congratulatory culture like the Enlightenment could have meant something so innocuously gushy. Here is a good example of how the term was actually employed in common eighteenth-century usage. Abigail Adams, in 1775, describes in a letter to her husband, the noise of cannons, which she observed from the top of Penn's Hill in Boston. "The sound I think is one of the Grandest in Nature and is of the true Species of the Sublime. 'Tis now an incessant roar. But O the fatal ideas that are connected with the sound. How many of our dear country men must fall?" The Sublime was in fact associated with fear in Burke's writing, and in some degree in Kant's, but mostly Kant treated it with reference to such feelings as wonderment and awe – words he uses in the Conclusion of his *Critique of Practical Reason,* in one of his most famous passages:

> Two things flood the mind with ever increasing wonder and awe [*Bewunderung und Ehrfurcht*],[5] the more often and the more intensely it concerns itself with them: the starry heavens above me and the moral law within me.

So a piece of art would be sublime that elicits in a subject this complex mixture of wonder and awe. The German word is compounded of two morphemes, connoting deference and fear, though the latter is scarcely implied by its English equivalent. More than a feeling for beauty, the responsiveness to sublimity, Kant realized, is a product of culture. But it "has its root in human nature." It is part of what we are. Longinus too says something to this effect:

> We are (heaven knows) somehow driven by nature to wonder not at small streams, even if they are clear and useful, but at the Nile and the Danube and the Rhine, and still more at the Ocean; nor, of course, are we more astonished by that little flame which we kindle ... than by the gleam of the heavenly bodies, though they are often gloomed over, nor do we generally consider it [i.e., the little flame] more worthy of wonder than the craters of Aetna, whose eruptions carry up rocks and whole mounds from the abyss and sometimes pour forth rivers. ...[6]

Kant cites such examples in his discussion of the Sublime:

> Bold overhanging, and as it were threatening rocks; clouds piled up in the sky, moving with lightning flashes and thunder peals; volcanoes in all the violence of destructive hurricanes with their track of devastation; the boundless ocean in the state of tumult; the lofty waterfall of a mighty river, and such like.

My "native informant" from the eighteenth century, Abigail Adams again, used a precisely Kantian vocabulary when she embarked on her first ocean voyage to join her husband in Europe. Finally able to go up on deck after suffering sea-sickness, she noted in her diary, that she "beheld the vast and boundless ocean before us with astonishment, and wonder."

What is fascinating in Kant is that we are in the same way "driven by nature" to have a comparable attitude toward morality, which he explicitly characterizes in terms of the power or might "which it exercises in us," whatever our personal interests. Abigail Adams, in whom duty almost always trumped personal interest and inclination, would have accepted this totally. But where would we find a comparable power in art? Here Kant's experience was severely limited by what Newman speaks of as "the Renaissance imagery of individuals and objects." The art Kant knew was entirely representational, and though sublime things can be represented, they cannot be represented as sublime. This is one major difference between the beautiful and the sublime: the beautiful *can* be represented as beautiful. "The sublime of art is always limited by the conditions of agreement with nature," he writes, which restates the mimetic theory of art Kant takes as given. The mimetic theory rests on a congruity of boundaries, which is the condition of drawing. Kant specifies that "the beautiful in nature is connected with the form of the object, which consists in having definite boundaries." The sublime, by contrast, "is to be found in a formless [what Adams speaks of as "boundless"] object, so far as in it or by occasion of it boundlessness is represented, and yet its totality is also present to thought."

Consider the paintings of the artist, Vija Celmans, who does pictures of the starry heavens or of the ocean. These are paradigms of the sublime, since we know that what they depict are "boundless totalities." Yet we could not easily think of her paintings themselves as sublime, mainly because they do not elicit in us any special feeling of wonder on the scale that sublimity seems to require. And that in part is because of the scale of the pictures themselves, which one could hold in one's hands, as at a picture dealer's. Somewhat closer might be the seascapes or landscapes exhibited recently at the Pennsylvania Academy as examples of "The American Sublime" – the paintings whose makers subscribed to the theory that God expresses himself in nature and does so with particular vehemence in those aspects of nature which have a certain grandeur. I refer to the so-called Hudson River School, which flourished in the mid-nineteenth century, and whose archetypically large-scale paintings featured nature itself at its largest – the Andes, or Niagara Falls, or the Grand Canyon. Such paintings perfectly illustrate Longinus's descriptions of the natural sublime, though I am uncertain whether there would have been paintings in his age which could have done so. There can be little question that the Hudson River artists reverted to large size in order to instill the awe and wonderment their depicted scenes aroused.

Kant, who of course never visited Rome, does speak of

> The bewilderment or, as it were, perplexity which it is said seizes the spectator on his first entrance into St. Peter in Rome. For there is here a feeling of the inadequacy of his imagination for presenting the ideas of a whole, wherein the imagination reaches its maximum and, in striving to surpass it, sinks back into itself, by which, however, a kind of emotional satisfaction is produced.

I have often been struck by the fact that the original decorative program for the Sistine Chapel had the vault painted as the starry heavens above – which would in anticipation of Kant have had what went on in the chapel itself as "the moral law within," inner and outer reference giving an architectural embodiment to the two sublimities. Julius II wanted something more "modern" when he commissioned Michelangelo to decorate the vault – and the Sistine ceiling itself, I believe, is a good example of at least part of how the sublime works in art. It is so if we consider that the sublime belongs, if we may borrow Wittgenstein's expression, to "the world as we find it," without any prior or special knowledge. Let me explain by returning to the starry heavens for just a moment.

Neither of the great wonder-eliciting things that Kant writes about in the second *Critique*'s[7] Conclusion is "shrouded in obscurity beyond my own horizon." Rather, Kant says, "I see them before me and connect them immediately with my own existence." I stress the fact of immediacy in connection with the starry heavens, because Kant wants to say that if we are to speak of it as sublime, "we must regard it, just as we see it, as a distant, all embracing vault."[8] *Just as we see it* means that we would see it as sublime no matter in what relationship we stand to the history of astronomical science. That is part of the reason that it belongs to aesthetics. In respect to its sublimity, we are on the same footing as what Kant would refer to as savages. So we must see the starry heaven the way anyone anywhere would see it, whatever their cultural condition. Kant of course had written on the nebular hypothesis, and even seems to have entertained a thesis about life on other planets. Thus he writes that if we regard the starry heavens as sublime, "We must not place at the basis of our judgments concepts of worlds inhabited by rational beings and regard the bright points, with which we see the space above us as filled, as their suns moving in circles, purposively fixed with reference to them." But sublimity has nothing to do with scientific thought.

To round the point off, this is what he says about the ocean as well:

> If we are to call the sight of the ocean sublime, we must not *think* of it as we ordinarily do, as implying all sorts of knowledge (that are not contained in immediate intuition). For example, we sometimes think of the ocean as a vast kingdom of aquatic creatures, or as the great source of those vapours that fill the air with clouds for the benefit of the land. ... To call the ocean sublime we must regard it as the poets do, merely by what strikes the eye.

Whatever, then, Kant may have meant by "the oftener and more steadily we reflect on *der bestirnte Himmel*,"[9] he cannot have meant: "The more astronomical knowledge we acquire." The wonderment remains that of the poet and not of the scientist. The scientist, if anything, destroys the sublimity, the way Newton, to Keats's despair, unraveled the rainbow. "Science murders to dissect" was Wordsworth's putdown. The more we know, one might say, the less we feel. The mark of being in the presence of sublimity is, as with Stendhal, the swoon. If I remember rightly, there were female swooners at Gauguin's exhibition in 1888 in Paris. One gets a whiff of what the sublime must have meant in the eighteenth century when one reads Gauguin on the academic painters of his own time, who lived by the rules. "How safe they are on dry land, those academic painters, with their *trompe l'oeil* of nature. We alone are sailing free on our ghost-ship, with all our fantastical imperfections."

This is just how we feel when we first visit the Chapel to see the great work. Who understands what is happening up there? More important, one might say, who needs to understand it as far as the *sublimity* of the experience is concerned? The ceiling's restorer prided himself on getting as close as possible to "Michelangelo as artist and as man" by proceeding brushstroke by brushstroke across the vast expanse. But that is like the nightbird winging beneath the starry heavens. It gives it no sense of the circumambient sublimity. Neither, in fairness, does an image-by-image analysis of the ceiling, from the Creation to the Drunkenness of Noah. One does not need to know that program, tremendous as it is, to feel the sublimity of the painting. That feeling is importantly at odds with that kind of art historical knowledge which is on the same level as the theory of infinite worlds alluded to in the *Critique of Judgment*. So I take it then that this is what Kant has in mind with reference to "connecting [it] immediately with my own existence." And this in turn refers to his point about sublimity having to do with human nature and not merely with culture. The sublimity of things has nothing to do with special knowledge. Interestingly enough, this is analogous with something Kant says about the experience of beauty having nothing to do with bringing what we experience as beautiful under a concept. We find it beautiful before we know anything about it, as happened, in my own case, when I first saw one of Motherwell's *Spanish Elegies*.

In any case, Kant would not have known any example of sublimity in Königsberg, nor, given the Renaissance model with which he worked, could he have, though this requires a distinction. There is a sense in which he ought to have been able to imagine something that at least would be in candidacy for the sublime, and a sense in which he could not. He could not have imagined as art the kind of paintings Newman and Motherwell did. His position in the history of art limited his imagination severely. But he ought to have been able to think about artistic wonders, since the idea of wonders was certainly part of his culture. Let me discuss this briefly.

It is told of Michelangelo that he was seized with a remarkable vision in the course of several trying months spent in the marble quarries of Carrara, where he had gone in 1503 to select stones for the tomb of Pope Julius II. One day, his biographer Condivi tells us,

He saw a crag that overlooked the sea, which made him wish to carve a colossus that would be a landmark for sailors from a long way off, incited thereto principally by the suitable shape of the rock from which it could have been conveniently carved, and by emulation of the ancients … and of a surety he would have done it if he had had time enough.

Michelangelo's inspiration was presumably the Colossus of Rhodes, one of the Seven Wonders of the ancient world – an immense sculpture, estimated to have stood more than 110 feet high, that according to legend straddled the mouth of a busy harbor. It was a wonder even when seen lying on the ground. "Few people can make their arms meet round the thumb," according to Pliny.

One tends to think of grace and balance, beauty and *disegno* [drawing – Ed.] as the paramount aesthetic virtues of Renaissance art, and indeed as marks of good taste in the fine arts well into modern times. But the idea of the colossus seems to belong to another aesthetic altogether, in which wonder and astonishment play the defining role. This other aesthetic was certainly embodied in the Seven Wonders themselves, and it inflected the great artistic figures of the sixteenth century, Leonardo and Michelangelo pre-eminently, who radiated, like some figure of ancient mythology, the aura of wizards. The colossus somehow emblematizes Michelangelo's visionary imagination, embodied in many of his signature works – the gigantic *David*, the immense decorative program enacted single-handedly over the course of fifteen years across the Sistine ceiling, the tremendous vision of the Julian tomb itself, which, as perhaps the greatest sculptural commission of modern times, was to have incorporated more than forty large-scale figures. Leonardo's projected equestrian monument to Francesco Sforza was described by a contemporary as "the most gigantic, stupendous, and glorious work ever made by the hands of man." Leonardo worked on it over the course of fifteen years, and it stood twelve *braccia* high.[10]

I have selected these colossi as paradigms only in part for the immensity of their scale, but mainly because, like the Seven Wonders – had the Julian Tomb been realized it would have been an eighth – they were meant to elicit feelings of wonder and awe, to which their scale contributes. Something is a colossus, for example, only because it underscores the limitations of those who experience it. It is perhaps in order to make visible the difference between themselves and their subjects that rulers have themselves represented as colossal, as in a seated portrait of Constantine the Great, thirty-odd feet tall, remnants of which still astonish when we see them in Rome.

But the idea of sublimity must entail something more than great size: "I attach little importance to physical size," the logician Frank Ramsey once wrote. "I take no credit for weighing nearly seventeen stone." So it is easy to understand why Kant – or Burke – felt that he had to add the sense of terror as the further condition. But Longinus's literary paradigms were the *Iliad* and a great poem of Sappho's, neither of which are terrifying. What they may do is remind us of our own limitations if we have artistic ambitions, and I think the feeling of wonder is connected with limitations in this way. "And still they gazed, and still their wonder grew, that one small head could carry all he knew," Edward Arlington Robinson wrote about a village prodigy. Kant brings these considerations into play in one of his formulations: "The sublime is that, the mere ability to think which shows a faculty of mind surpassing every standard of sense." I think the beauty of Helen of Troy was sublime in this sense. There is a very moving passage in Book III, where Helen leaves her weaving behind, and walks to the gates of Troy, to watch the warriors, who have paused for a moment before Menaleos, her husband, and Alexandros, her lover, fight over her. The elders of Troy were just then sitting in council – "And these, as they saw Helen along the tower approaching, murmuring softly to each other uttered their winged words: 'Surely there is no blame upon Trojans and strong-greaved Achaians if for long time they suffer hardship for a woman like this one. Terrible is the likeness of her face to immortal goddesses.'"

We can imagine that someone was as beautiful as Helen, but we cannot imagine her beauty. That is one of the deep differences between words and pictures. In a related way, we can possess pictures of the Colossus of Rhodes, but no picture can show us its size. It can at best show us its scale, by showing a lot of tiny humans at its base, the way Piranesi[11] did when he wanted to show the monuments of Rome as wondrous. But this brings us back to the limits of art as Kant understood it. Since sublimity is internally related to size; indeed to vastness, it cannot be pictured. That is one of the problems with Newman. The reproductions in a catalog of his characteristic paintings are incapable of showing their size, nor hence their sublimity. You have to be in front of and in fact rather close to them, in order to experience it. But again, terror is no part of the experience. My own sense, for what it is worth, is that the sort of vicarious terror Kant, and especially Burke had in mind, does play a role in human enjoyment – in ghost stories, horror movies, scary rides in amusement parks, in "cheap thrills," as it were. There may be cases where the experience of the sublime has terror as a component feeling, but it is not integral to the concept, in the way wonder itself is. After all, neither the starry heavens above nor the moral law within induce terror when we contemplate them. Parenthetically, fear continues to play its role in, of all things, the postmodern theory of the sublime developed by Lyotard, who speaks of the feeling in questions as "an admixture of fear and exaltation." One cannot but wonder – I at least cannot – how often Lyotard can have had this feeling in front of works of art. If it is like ecstasy, it cannot be something we can be overcome by several times in a single visit to a gallery of art. My sense is that Lyotard was overcome by the literature on the subject rather than by actual aesthetic experiences he had had on the rue de Seine in Paris.

It is difficult not to wonder, on the other hand, whether Kant would have written the lyrical and romantic conclusion to the 1788 *Critique of Practical Reason,* in which he has recourse to an aesthetic vocabulary and a set of relationships for which there is really no place in the critical system as he had so far developed it, had it not been for the concept of the sublime. The starry heavens above and the moral law within can in effect be consigned to the domains respectively covered by Kant's first two *Critiques* – the realm of nature, one might say, and the realm of freedom. And these in turn are referred to the two great powers of the human mind – to represent the world as a rational system, as covered by universal laws; and to prescribe the laws which universally define moral conduct. The philosophical portrait drawn by the first two *Critiques* is of a being at once cognitive and legislative. But it is not an entirely adequate portrait if the concluding passage represents part of our reality as human. Wonder and awe are feelings that do not seem to belong to the somewhat austere, even severe personage the first two *Critiques* would lead us to believe ourselves to be. So we learn something fundamental about ourselves in contemplating our portrait that the portrait itself does not show. We learn that we are not "pure intelligences" but creatures of feelings, and not simply of feelings, but of powerful feelings, such as astonishment and awe. Small wonder, as we say, that a third *Critique* had to be written to connect us to the other two aspects of our being. And since the capacity for wonder is disclosed to us in this striking passage, the sublime – which is wonder's content – can hardly be an afterthought in the *Critique of Judgment*. And the world as an aesthetic presence is inseparable from what we are.

## The rediscovery of man

Let us now return to Newman. There is a remarkable passage in Kant that does bear on Abstract Expressionist aesthetics:

> Perhaps the most sublime passage in Jewish Law is the commandment "Thou shalt not make unto thee any graven image, or any likeness of anything that is in heaven or on earth, or under the earth," etc. This commandment alone can explain the enthusiasm that the Jewish people in its civilized era felt for its religion when it compared itself with other peoples, or can explain the pride that Islam inspires.

This in effect prohibited Jews or Muslims from being artists since, though of course, like all the Commandments, it was and is violated in both religions. But until Modernism, there was no way of being a painter without making pictures. One could at best engage in decoration, which is the only alternative to picturing that Kant acknowledges. Paintings that are not pictures would have been a contradiction in terms. This in effect ruled out the possibility of making paintings that were *sublime*. But modernism opened up the possibility of aniconic[12] painting, and this somehow brought with it the possibility of sublimity as an attainable aesthetic. As Newman said, "The Sublime is Now."

Newman regarded his breakthrough work, *Onement I*, as a painting and not a picture. The catalog text to a major exhibition of Newman's work says that *Onement I* "represents nothing but itself" – that it is about itself as a painting. I can't believe that. I can't believe that what Newman regarded in terms momentous enough to merit this title, was simply a painting about painting. It is about something that can be said but cannot be shown, at least not pictorially. In general, the suffix "-ment" is attached to a verb – like "atone" or "endow" or "command" – where it designates a state – the state of atoning, for example – or a product. So what does "Onement" mean? My own sense is that it means the conditions of being one, as in the incantation "God is one." It refers, one might say, to the oneness of God. And this might help us better understand the difference between a picture and a painting. Consider again the Sistine Ceiling, where Michelangelo produces a number of pictures of God. Great as these are, they are constrained by the limitation that pictures can only show what is visible, and decisions have to be made regarding what God looks like. How would one *picture* the fact that God is one? Since *Onement I* is not a picture, it does not inherit the limitations inherent in picturing. Abstract painting is not without content. Rather, it enables the presentation of content without pictorial limits. That is why, from the beginning, abstraction was believed by its inventors to be invested with a spiritual reality. It was as though Newman had hit upon a way of being a painter without violating the Second Commandment, which only prohibits images. Lyotard, incidentally, attempts to build the unpresentability of its content into his analysis of the sublime – but I think he had to mean that the sublime was *unpicturable*. Boldly post-modern as Lyotard took his aesthetic to be, it was curiously limited to painting.

Newman himself gave to one of his paintings the title *Vir Heroicus Sublimis,* which meant, as he explained to David Sylvester, "that man can be or is sublime in his relation to his sense of being aware." And it was his view, so far as I understand it, that he used scale to awaken this sense of self-awareness in relationship to his paintings: they imply, one might say, the scale of the viewer:

> One thing that I am involved in about painting is that the painting should give a man a sense of place: that he knows he's there, so he's aware of himself. In that sense he related to me when I made the painting because in that sense I was there. … Standing in front of my paintings you had a sense of your own scale. The onlooker in front of my painting knows that he's there. To me, the sense of place not only has a mystery but has that sense of metaphysical fact.

It is this "mystery," this "metaphysical fact," that scale and wonder evoke when we speak of the sublime. Scholars speak of the Renaissance discovery of man. We can, I think, accordingly speak of the rediscovery of man in Abstract Expressionism. But it is important that we recognize that we whose existence is implied by such paintings are not diminished, as we are by the starry heavens above. The scale of the painting is intended to induce a certain self-awareness, and this is what brings the status of sublimity with it. It implies the body of the viewer, without making us small because the painting is large. What Newman aspired to instill through such paintings as *Vir Heroicus Sublimis* is wonder and awe at ourselves as here. I cannot help but think that the concept Newman required was that of Heidegger's central notion, namely that of *Dasein* – of being there and aware of being there.[13]

**Figure 2** Barnett Newman, *Vir Heroicus Sublimis*, 1950–51. "A sense of your own scale." Digital Image © the Museum of Modern Art / Licensed by SCALA / Art Resource, NY.

But there is another way of thinking about this that I find magnificently expressed in an answer given by the great Russian novelist, Vladimir Nabokov, when an interviewer asked him if he was surprised by anything in life. Nabokov responded:

The marvel of consciousness – that sudden window swinging open on a sunlit landscape amid the night of non-being.

I find this passage sublime, and it is a matter of chagrin to me that until fairly recent times, no philosopher has spoken of consciousness with this kind of wonder and awe. Certainly Kant did not. He finds the starry heavens and the moral law within as matters of wonder and awe without noticing that they pale in comparison with the fact that he is aware of them, that the universe, inner and outer, is open to something that is in itself unpicturable and perhaps even unintelligible, given the internal limits of human understanding. Small wonder philosophers took it for it granted – it never became an object that had to be reckoned with in drawing up the inventory of wonders.

Meanwhile, I note that Nabokov cannot forebear speaking of something beautiful as the object of consciousness – a landscape, sunny, and seen through a window frame. If consciousness disclosed only unrelieved disgustingness, we would wonder why we had such an endowment. But this brings us back to the two worlds of G. E. Moore that we considered early in our study.[14] The world of sheer disgustingness would not be one we could wish to be conscious of for very long, nor for the matter live a life that would lose its point without sunlight. If I point to a painting of a sunlit landscape and pronounce it sublime, someone might correct me and say I am confusing the beautiful and the sublime. I would cite Nabokov and reply that the beautiful *is* the sublime "amid the night of non-being." Kant brings these considerations into play in the formulation we noted above: "The sublime is that, the mere ability to think which shows a faculty of mind surpassing every standard of sense." I might even, if feeling impish, add: It is sublime because it is in the mind of the beholder. Beauty is an option for art and not a necessary condition. But it is not an option for life. It is a necessary condition for life as we would want to live it. That is why beauty, unlike the other aesthetic qualities, the sublime included, is a value.[15]

## Questions

1. Danto writes above, "The scientist . . . destroys the sublimity, the way Newton . . . unraveled the rainbow." Do you think acquisition of knowledge (of nature) runs counter to the sublime, or instead that it helps a person experience it? Explain in terms of your experiences or by giving concrete examples.

2. How does Danto make use of artworks and artists in his discussion of the sublime? Evaluate their effectiveness. What does this imply about the possibility of the sublime in art (i.e., artistic sublimity)? What does representational or mimetic art (the "Renaissance model"), as opposed to nonrepresentational or abstract art, have to do with this issue?

3. How does this chapter support Danto's larger philosophical project (see introductory headnote on Danto, above)? How does Danto seem to understand the "aesthetic" qualities of art in this reading? Does he pay sufficient (or instead too much) attention to an artwork's *cognitive* elements? Explain.

4. Do you see any gaps in Danto's brief history of the sublime? Explain. How would your version go?

## Further reading

Carrier, David, Noël Carroll, et al. *Danto and His Critics: Art History, Historiography, and After the End of Art. History and Theory* 37, no. 4 (1998): 1–143. [David Carrier, Frank Ankersmit, Noël Carroll, Michael Kelly, Brigitte Hilmer, Robert Kudielka, Martin Seeland, and Jacob Steinbrenner address Danto's work, with a final response by Danto].

Costello, Diarmuid. "On Late Style: Arthur Danto's *The Abuse of Beauty*." *British Journal of Aesthetics* 44, no. 4 (2004): 424–39.

Danto, Arthur. *The Transfiguration of the Commonplace: A Philosophy of Art.* Cambridge, MA: Harvard University Press, 1981.

Danto, Arthur, et al. "Symposium: Arthur Danto, *The Abuse of Beauty*." *Inquiry* 48, no. 2 (2005): 145–200. [This issue on *The Abuse of Beauty* includes discussion by critics and Danto's replies.]

# CHAPTER 34
# VLADIMIR J. KONEČNI, "THE AESTHETIC TRINITY: AWE, BEING MOVED, THRILLS" (2005)

Vladimir J. Konečni was born in 1944 in Belgrade, where he received degrees in clinical psychology and philosophy, followed by a PhD in experimental and social psychology in 1973 at the University of Toronto. He taught for thirty-five years in the Department of Psychology of the University of California, San Diego, where he has been Emeritus Professor since 2008. In addition to having several specialties within mainstream experimental psychology (including emotion and decision-making), Konečni has contributed to various areas of empirical aesthetics (visual arts, architecture, theater, research methodology), as well as the psychology and philosophy of music.

In the following essay, Konečni introduces the notion of an "aesthetic trinity" in order to account for peak aesthetic responses lying on a spectrum—from thrills or chills, to being moved or touched, to the "aesthetic awe" that is typically induced by a sublime "stimulus-in-context." Aesthetic awe is conceived as a primordial mixture of joy and fear, which, like joy, requires existential safety. It is virtually indistinguishable from the fundamental emotions, yet one that can be more easily "switched off," because the sublime is nonsocial and noninteractive. Aesthetic awe is always accompanied by the responses of being touched and (physiological) chills, but the latter two can also occur in awe's absence.

Konečni characterizes aesthetic awe as the ultimate humanistic moment, the prototypical aesthetic response to a sublime stimulus. He maintains that the sublime is pan-cultural and encompasses great beauty, rarity, and physical grandeur, and holds that for music to become sublime, it requires a "colossal" performance setting. The essay concludes by discussing the possibilities of changing current trends in the artworld and of converting the elitist guilt that often accompanies aesthetic awe into aesthetic altruism.

In May 2004, a longer version of this paper was presented as a plenary lecture at the Wuhan University Aesthetics Conference on "Beauty and the Way of Modern Life" in Wuhan, China. It has led to subsequent developments and elaborations, including an article in *Philosophy Today* in 2011 (listed in the Further reading).

## Note on the text

Source: Reprinted from Vladimir J. Konečni, "The Aesthetic Trinity: Awe, Being Moved, Thrills." *Bulletin of Psychology and the Arts* 5 (2) (2005): 27–44.

The format of the original publication has been largely reproduced, with some modifications to spelling, punctuation, citation style, and similar stylistic matters.

## "The Aesthetic Trinity: Awe, Being Moved, Thrills"

There is little doubt that human beings can respond powerfully and profoundly to great works of art, to extraordinary man-made objects, and to rare wonders of nature. Such "stimuli" (to use a technical, if rather pale, term), as well as the various components of the occasions of one's exposure to them (including, especially, one's resulting subjective state), leave deep impressions and are highly memorable: People include them in lists of their peak life experiences (cf. Gabrielsson, 2001; Maslow, 1964, 1968; Panzarella, 1980).

It would seem that such an aesthetic phenomenon, perhaps the ultimate humanistic moment (Konečni, 2003b, p. 339), deserves serious inquiry, if not a central place, in a mature psychological aesthetics. The purpose of this paper is to identify some key conceptual relations in this domain of extreme aesthetic experience and to propose heuristically useful definitions and nomenclature. Specifically, the paper discusses (a) aesthetic awe, (b) being moved or touched, and (c) thrills or chills, as the primordial and prototypic human responses to the sublime.

Among other benefits of this nomenclature, it is hoped that the use of the imprecise and misleading references to "aesthetic emotions" and "musical emotions" will hitherto be minimized. A section of the paper is devoted to a justification of this plea.

## The sublime

### Stimulus-in-context

The sublime has been discussed as a partner to the beautiful since at least a (now lost) first-century treatise by Caecilius of Calacta (referred to by the third-century Longinus or else a later pseudo-Longinus; cf. Berlyne, 1971). However, it can be documented that almost all the major commentators on the sublime in the tradition of philosophical aesthetics—from Burke (1757/1990) to Tarozzi Goldsmith (1999), by way of Kant (1790/1986) and Lyotard (1991/1994), have in their various statements confused the concept of the sublime by alternately (and sometimes simultaneously) treating it as both an object (or its attributes) external to the experiencing person and as the subjective, internally felt consequence of one's exposure to a relevant stimulus array. In this paper, the sublime is considered to be external to the subject, as the ultimate aesthetic *stimulus-in-context*—a term which emphasizes that (especially its spatial) context is often an essential feature of a sublime stimulus. The Great Wall of China needs rolling hills to be sublime, and so did, ephemerally, the Running Fence (in Marin, Napa, and Sonoma Counties, California) by Christo (Javacheff).

### Rarity and beauty

According to all major commentators from Burke to Tarozzi Goldsmith, the sublime always includes, but is not limited to, exceptional, universally acknowledged, beauty, which is also a strongly held position of this paper. However, the beautiful (as defined in numerous one- and two-factor models—cf. Berlyne, 1971) comparatively rarely includes or contains the sublime. Without wishing to enter a laborious and mostly—for the purpose of this paper—irrelevant discussion about the definition, universality, and relativity of beauty, the merely beautiful is here assumed to be far more common than the sublime, but also to be one of its obligatory components.

The beautiful will be treated as the extreme high end of the dimension of aesthetic pleasingness, as an attribute that is located in nature, in human artifacts, and, especially, in the synergy of an artifact and its natural milieu. It can be, at least in some contexts, objectively defined and empirically measured, for example, in the case of the "golden section" that has been studied from antiquity (Green, 1995; Konečni, 1997, 2001, 2003a, 2005b; Konečni & Cline, 2001).

## Physical grandeur

The rarity of the sublime is presumably a statistical concomitant of its often being immense in size—a relationship that is understandable from the standpoint of logistical baserates and evolutionary adaptation—and Derrida (1978), along with many others, has described the sublime as "colossal" (and also as "erect" and "petrified"—a reference presumably to the Pyramids of El Gizeh, especially the Cheops, or Khufu).

An object may be sublime despite an absence of physical grandeur, because of the unique or extraordinary context in which it is encountered. It is here assumed that the *Mona Lisa* is more sublime in the Louvre than if exhibited in another grand museum (that is, if it ever went "on tour"). But the contextual contrast can be expected to play a part, so that its sublime quality would be restored if the painting were placed in, say, the Angkor Wat in Cambodia or in a tiny Lutheran church in the remote fishing village of Kulusuk on Greenland. Note that it is here hypothesized that the multifaceted contrast with *Mona Lisa*'s customary home, rather than the physical size of the new one, would be operative.

Music, to be a sublime stimulus and induce aesthetic awe, may also require physical grandeur—of the space in which it is performed—in addition to having certain structural features and a significant personal associative context. This issue is addressed in a later section of the paper.

## Existential security

In contrast to Tarozzi Goldsmith's critical standpoint (1999, p. 96), the position of this essay is in agreement with Burke's and Kant's claims that the sublime can be "apprehended" only when the subject (experiencer) is "not in danger"—though one should add here "apprehended as aesthetically relevant." In this view, whether or not there is an objective degree of danger in a stimulus and its context, the subject will respond to it as a sublime object (that is, *aesthetically*, which would include finding it beautiful), only if there is no subjectively judged physical threat [cf. "accommodation" in Keltner and Haidt, 2003]. Berlyne (1971, p. 93) offers a brief, but lucid, analysis of this crucial characteristic of the sublime and the aesthetically-relevant physiological response to it, to the effect that "in stimulus situations classifiable as art, there are cues that inhibit the aversion system [in the brain] at least partially."

The notion of the sublime that involves an absence of physical threat is here extended to include a reasonable degree of existential comfort and security in the life of the potential experiencer: Existential well-being is considered a *sine qua non* for experiencing a potentially sublime stimulus as indeed sublime (rather than as simply a source of income or even as a nuisance). For example, the Cheops and the Great Sphinx may not be sublime to the desperately poor living at the feet of these wonders.

## God's dwelling is sublime

It is little wonder that sublime objects—immense, beautiful, rare, and often inaccessible or difficult to reach even if one lives in relative proximity—have been regarded as the dwellings of the deities or as their creations from the dawn of time in literally every part of the world and in every conceivable "pagan" and monotheistic religion. Admittedly, this is far more likely in the case of natural objects, especially mountain peaks and formations (from Denali to Ayer's Rock, and from Kilimanjaro to Olympus to Tai Shan to Fuji-san), than of man-made ones, but there are many exceptions. Antiquity may be necessary. There is no Sydney Opera House or Golden Gate Bridge cult (although the San Francisco Bay Area-based Grateful Dead "deadheads" may beg to differ), but there is the Parthenon, the Stonehenge, the Wailing Wall, St. Sophia, Machu Pichu, the Ka'ba, St. Peter's—in addition to the Cheops Pyramid.

One may venture to speculate that the naturally sublime objects first had an aesthetic impact and only subsequently acquired the legends and the religious mythology, whereas many of the man-made sublime structures—*all* of which were built, until the industrial revolution, at least ostensibly as religious objects (except perhaps for the Great Wall of China)—incorporated the aesthetic sublime from the start, presumably, in part, by intuitively imitating the key attributes of the sublime in nature.

The aesthetic and the religious are therefore often blurred in the sublime, in both the conception and the "consumption"—an idea that would not surprise art historians. Berlyne (1971) may have had similar notions when he formulated "ecological" stimulus variables, the impact of which arises from the classically-conditioned associations.

## Commonalities in the sublime across cultures

"The [aesthetic] wisdom in many cultures has some common features…" (Chen, 2004, p. 1). The position of this paper with regard to pan-cultural aesthetic wisdom is that the commonalities across cultures are due to the fact that all living humans are products of the fundamentally similar selective evolutionary pressures and the same broad laws of supply and demand in the context of finite resources, which has shaped the neuro-mental (brain-mind) apparatus of the *homo sapiens* (including his aesthetic responsiveness). These pressures continue in our time and it is therefore not surprising that there are common elements across time and cultures in both the intuitive definition of the sublime and the authentic responses to it—the primordial responses of aesthetic awe, of being deeply moved, and of experiencing thrills/chills.

It is sometimes uncritically assumed that "the modernization of ancient [aesthetic] wisdom may offer a solution [to present-day problems]" (Chen, 2004, p. 1). The hope that the ancient or classical aesthetic ideas (these two terms are used interchangeably in the present essay), especially if "modernized," can alleviate some of the blight of contemporary life—"a neo-Chan (neo-Zen) solution to pollution," to coin a mildly plausible, aesthetics-based, environmental clean-up campaign slogan for China and Japan—is probably unrealistic. The problem is that such solutions are in all respects subject to the same laws of supply and demand that were mentioned above and therefore are often superficial at best and of limited and ephemeral usefulness.

Therefore, the position of this essay is that rather than modernizing the features of the ancient approach that have led to awe-inspiring and moving aesthetic solutions, one should explore their *core attributes*—while obviously despising the brutal economics involved in the creation of the ancient sublime structures. These issues are further pursued in the final, *Implications*, section of the paper.

## Awe and aesthetic awe

### Awe

In their far-reaching, systematic paper, Keltner and Haidt (2003, p. 308) analyze the etymology of awe and usefully point out that according to the *Oxford English Dictionary* the meaning changed from fear of a divine being to " 'dread mingled with veneration…'" and, significantly, to " '…the attitude of a mind subdued to profound reverence in the presence of supreme authority, moral greatness, or sublimity, or mysterious sacredness.'" Keltner and Haidt (2003) do not pursue the notion of sublimity or of the sublime; they consider awe to be a "family" of emotions (e.g., Keltner, 2004) and in the very title of their paper mention awe as an "aesthetic" emotion (as well as a "moral" and "spiritual" one).

Keltner and Haidt (2003, p. 306) think of "primordial awe [as] center[ing] upon the emotional reaction of a subordinate to a powerful leader," which would presumably make it closely related to one of the fundamental emotions, fear. The point of disagreement arises when Keltner and Haidt regard aesthetic awe as a culturally-elaborated extension of the primordial version (p. 310). The present view is that aesthetic awe is a response to the sublime that is as primordial as fear—and joy; in fact, it is assumed in this paper that it is composed of some elements experienced in both of these fundamental emotions. Whether the fact that it is a mixture makes aesthetic awe less fundamental than fear and joy is an open question.

## Aesthetic awe

*Origin.* Aesthetic awe has presumably occurred from primeval times as a response, initially, to the unexpectedly encountered natural wonders, and, later, to human artifacts also. As has already been implied, it involves a sense of suspense and of a controllable, interesting (as opposed to pleasing, in standard psycho-aesthetic terms) degree of risk. However, existential security cannot be in doubt—as it is not in joy. One is overwhelmed, but safely so: Niagara is fantastic, powerful, astounding, and extraordinarily beautiful, but I am safe (and not the one tumbling down the falls in a barrel)!

*Aesthetic awe and the fundamental emotions.* The centrality of the concept of the fundamental emotions in biopsychology is justified by their enormous evolutionary significance. They are psychologically and metabolically costly and usually reserved for emergencies. When they occur, they are major existential events in human phenomenology. Among many other characteristics, they flood consciousness and are pan-cultural in terms of experience and expression; they usually have an unambiguous cause as well as object toward, or regarding which, to act (Konečni, 2003b, p. 332).

Aesthetic awe is here proposed as the prototypical subjective reaction to a sublime stimulus. It is the most pronounced, the ultimate, aesthetic response, in all ways similar to the fundamental emotions. One possible difference needs to be mentioned. The experiencing person can cognitively "switch off" aesthetic awe at will by altering the focus of attention to other external and internal domains. This is because the sublime stimulus, a non-sentient, non-interacting, object—unlike the customary human causes of fear, anger, joy, and grief—does not press, from existential and evolutionary points of view, to be attended to urgently. In the language of legal psychology, aesthetic awe does not have a "knife focus."

Aesthetic awe shares with both joy and grief the state of being moved, and, with the former, thrills also. Its requirement of existential safety differentiates it from—but places on the same continuum as—fear. With joy it shares the experience of thrills, which in fear is felt as chills. With all the fundamental emotions it shares a truly dramatic fluctuation in physiological arousal.

There are two moot reasons and a bad one for the fact that aesthetic awe had not been hitherto included among the fundamental emotions. The first debatable reason is the above-mentioned ease with which aesthetic awe can presumably be switched off—because the sublime does not react to the experiencer. The second moot reason is a statistical one, involving baserates [Berlyne's (1971) "collative variables"]: The sublime is extremely rare—and therefore a response to it has not been deemed important enough in folk tales and scientific nomenclature to deserve the status of the fundamental.

The bad reason is a challenge to aesthetic awe on adaptationist grounds. Music itself has been thus challenged (cf. Huron, 2001; Pinker, 1997). However, in the case of music, Miller (2000; cf. Gurney,

1880) provides a logically defensible explanation in terms of sexual selection (although music's role in primeval dance, with its providing opportunities for display of health and endurance, is not sufficiently emphasized).

Aesthetic awe (with the accompaniment of being moved and thrills) is assumed in this paper also to have been sexually selected. The experiencer's attributes and behaviors of (a) reverence (i.e., the presumed private access to the supernatural), (b) the apparent emotional and intellectual sensitivity (useful in child-rearing), and (c) elite-membership, demonstrated by the possession of the economic and physical means that enable the encounter with the sublime stimulus, make the experiencer of aesthetic awe a highly desirable sexual mate.

*Recall and the physiological response.* Like the sublime in stimulus sampling, aesthetic awe is, by definition, exceedingly rare in response sampling. It is of limited duration in terms of its acute physiological concomitants, but its immense original phenomenological impact (the flooding of consciousness at the time of the initial occurrence) insures that it can be easily recalled and remembered forever.

The ease and vividness of recall of the aesthetic-awe-inspiring occasions may well mean that the intensively recalled aesthetic awe can produce a physiological reaction (specifically, thrills or chills)—just as the recollections of fear-, anger-, joy-, and grief-inducing situations produce various autonomic (differential) physiological responses (e.g., Ekman, Levenson, & Friesen, 1983). An important assumption of the present paper, however, is that whereas the intensive recall of the sublime and aesthetic-awe can reproduce a state of being moved, the Wow! of the original aesthetic awe is irreproducible.

*Aesthetic awe, elitism, and (pseudo-?)altruism.* One is overwhelmed by the sublime stimulus, but is safe—and *special*, one should add—a member of the chosen survivors, of the *electi*, of an elite—to have managed to be safely, and often exclusively, viewing the sublime stimulus. Importantly, to know how to "apprehend" it and generalize from it, while being joyous: "[F]eeling privileged to regard Mozart as a brother,...[sense] the larger truth hidden in the pinnacles of human achievement, and yet [realize], with some resignation, [one's] miniscule [place] in the universe" (Konečni, 2003b, p. 339).

Suggesting that a sense of elitism may be an aspect of "lofty sentiments" (Konečni, 2003b, p. 339) may seem cynical, but is realistic from an adaptationist perspective. Instead, Haidt's (2000) idea of "elevation," of "rising up, including openness to altruism" (Haidt, 2004), implies a belief in the existence of "true altruism" that has been challenged by contemporary biologists on both theoretical and empirical grounds (Hamilton, 1964; Konečni, 1976; Trivers, 1971; Wilson, 1975). Thinking of oneself as being among the deep and sensitive *electi* may move one to some semblance of philanthropic behavior perhaps in part because one may feel guilty, rightly or wrongly, that one has not arrived at that status by chance or through a "democratic process" (Konečni, 2004c).

*Aesthetic awe and hallucinations.* By being defined as a response to a sublime stimulus, the future potential research on aesthetic awe should conceptually exclude drug-induced hallucinations and trance states that have been counted by various authors, especially Maslow (1964, 1968), as being among "peak experiences." This is not meant to doubt the importance of such experiences or the great value of studying them. In fact, if one is truly open-minded, one must admit that one person's Cheops is another's LSD tablet.

*Seeking aesthetic awe.* The sublime is often an object that has been famous since antiquity and people who do not live near it may spend a lifetime hoping and planning to experience it. To do so, they often travel far and experience great inconvenience, expense, and even danger. When the sublime object has a religious significance, this travel is sometimes formalized as pilgrimage (including, for example, the compulsory Muslim hajj to the $10.5 \times 12 \times 15$-meter Ka'ba in Mecca), but the religious ones are far from being the only occasions for exhausting, expensive, and dangerous travel to the sublime [cf. Loewenstein's (1999) discussion of extreme mountaineering and polar attempts, typically by pairs of people or small teams; solo attempts on the mountains, the Poles, and the oceans are in an even more exclusive league].

The approach to the sublime object may involve a gradual buildup of expectations that is akin to development in 19th-century musical compositions, except that it may be spread over hours, days, or much longer periods. There is typically also an increase in thoughts and activities that contribute to the eventual state of aesthetic awe. In the final stage of the approach, even though one may factually know that the sublime is "just around the corner," there is the shock, the "Wow!," when it is suddenly revealed, or revealed in full.

## Being moved or touched

### Being moved: A genuine subjective state

In the present approach, aesthetic awe is considered to be always accompanied by the state of being moved or touched (these terms are used interchangeably). However, it is hypothesized that there are many instances of being moved by aesthetic stimuli that do not encompass, or reach, the ethereal, but powerful, aesthetic awe experience. In addition, one can be moved by non-aesthetic, usually social, stimuli that are of marginal relevance for this paper.

*Aesthetic stimuli.* Scherer and Zentner (2001, p. 384–85) have provided some interesting, albeit very brief and somewhat self-contradictory, comments on the state of being touched. As they point out, the German noun *Rührung* has no substantive counterparts in English and French (although there are nouns for both the stimulus and the response sides, for example, in Serbian: *dirljivost* and *dirnutost*). They think of being moved both as a good descriptor of an intense response to music and as a feeling that is "rather vaguely described." They point to the absence of a "concrete action tendency" and bring up the accompanying (though not conceptually essential for the Scherer-Zentner position) "…moist eyes, chills, thrills, or gooseflesh…" They view the state of being touched as one that should be regarded as a genuine emotion—while also saying that it is really not one (by their own Table 16.1, p. 363).

Even without a substantive, and contrary to the Scherer-Zentner characterization of it as a vague descriptor, "being moved" is actually a very distinctive subjective state that, like aesthetic awe, can be readily, reliably, and accurately reported. However, it is assumed in this paper that being touched is a response to a far greater range of stimuli than is the case with aesthetic awe. Moreover, the personal associative context plays a greater role in being moved than it does in aesthetic awe (Konečni, 1995–2004). For these reasons, being touched is considered to be more removed from the fundamental emotions both conceptually and phenomenologically than is the case with aesthetic awe.

In the present view, the examples of being moved, with the accompaniment of chills, can come from poetry, theatre (cf. Konečni, 1991; Shweder & Haidt, 2000; Stanislavky, 1936), film, opera (Stanislavski & Rumyantsev, 1975), and music. When the music-listening situation is physically ordinary, but a significant personal associative context exists, music with certain structural elements (Brown & Konečni, 2004; Sloboda, 1991) can induce a state of being moved and thrills. A later section addresses this issue in more detail.

*Non-aesthetic stimuli.* The fact that one can undoubtedly be moved by events other than those clearly delineated as aesthetic or artistic does not diminish the usefulness of the concept. Witnessing, in the real world, certain acts of forgiveness, sacrifice, and generosity is a frequent cause of being touched, although it would seem, from the present viewpoint, doubtful that one needs to invoke a new emotion – "elevation"—as Haidt (2000) does, to deal with the resulting state.

In summary, in the present account, the category of events that can induce a state of being moved includes both aesthetic and non-aesthetic members. Among the aesthetic events, very few, the sublime, can produce aesthetic awe in addition to the state of being moved. Analogously, among the non-aesthetic ones, witnessing certain acts, for example, of extreme (apparent) selflessness may produce awe in the Keltner and Haidt (2003) moral or spiritual sense, in addition to being moving. (Witnessing such acts may involve sympathy and empathy that are usually missing in one's being moved by aesthetic stimuli.) The term "elevation" (Haidt, 2000) may become useful if it can be shown that being moved either by aesthetic stimuli (e.g., music), or by acts of selflessness, has similar behavioral consequences, such as an increase in the probability of prosocial acts. Research that addresses these questions is currently being pursued (Brown & Konečni, 2004; Haidt 2004).

## Epiphany and love

In the present view, merely witnessing a beautiful natural spectacle—a sunset, a starry night, a chain of snow-capped mountains—is not sufficient to induce a state of being moved without the involvement of additional factors. Such, non-aesthetic, factors, a few of which are mentioned below, may predispose the experiencer to be moved by sights that are indeed objectively beautiful, but are encountered too frequently and regularly to have (or maintain) the power, on their own, to move.

*Victory over mortality fears.* One may be moved by the starry sky that one has frequently encountered on that special occasion when one teaches a young child, one's genetic heir, for the first time, about the infinity of cosmos and the relativity and continuity of life. Or one may, on another occasion, finally manage to relate one's moral core to infinite space-time, which one perhaps finds in Kant's sentence (1788/1996) that is etched on his tombstone: "A starry sky above me and a moral law within." Such a personal victory over mortality fears should perhaps be considered an epiphany.

*Solution of a complicated problem.* A fairly common natural sight may move one when it coincides or follows closely in time one's finding the solution to an important and elusive intellectual problem or one's reaching the decision concerning a major issue in one's life. The beauty of the sight "harmonizes" with the post-solution or post-decision inner peace.

*Boundless love and falling in love.* It is not important whether an average starry night is genuinely perceived as magnificent by a person falling in love or whether one craftily embellishes it (and then perhaps begins to believe it), in order to prod one's partner into responding romantically: A starry-night-cum-love idyll is likely to have played a part in the personal history of every reader of this paper.

## Being moved by reading about being moved

Until this point, the experiencer's states of aesthetic awe and of being moved were discussed as responses to real events—to the real-world sublime and aesthetic stimuli. However, especially in an article on aesthetic issues, it would not do to neglect people's highly relevant responses to the described and acted-out events in the worlds within legends, novels, plays, operas.

Whereas books and reading them are obviously real, the events in them are either real, but described or depicted, or entirely fictional. The experiencer as the direct witness is replaced by the reader who is presented with the results of the author's interpretive lens. Even more interestingly, the story may describe a character experiencing aesthetic awe and being moved: What does the reader feel (other than admiration for the great writing)? The implications of the reader's one- or even two-step removal from the aesthetic stimulus (such as, for example, when characters are described as responding to film scenes within novels or actors emotionally respond to plays within plays) are instructive in the light of this essay's position. A few illustrative examples follow.

*Saul/St. Paul; Arjuna.* A rather detailed account of awe, epiphany, and conversion that was experienced by Saul on the road to Damascus (The Acts 9.3–7), and the mythical Arjuna in the Bhagavadgita section of the Hindu epic the Mahabarata, is provided by Keltner and Haidt (2003, pp. 298–99). Both Saul/Paul and Arjuna are described in the original texts as experiencing a great deal of fear, and therefore, from the present viewpoint—although some of Arjuna's visions could be considered aesthetic—portraying these personages' *aesthetic* awe was certainly not the primary intent of the two sources' anonymous authors.

It is an empirical question, but it would seem that most present-day readers of the two accounts would experience neither awe not aesthetic awe. They might, however, be moved and experience chills.

*Natasha Rostova*. In Lyov Tolstoy's (1869/1931, pp. 387–88) *War and Peace*, there is a famous moonlight-cum-love scene involving the teenage Countess Natasha Rostova and Prince Andrey Bolkonsky, which is instructive from the standpoints of both the author's various intentions and the reader's likely reactions.

Natasha is falling in love with Andrey. Late at night, she gazes at the moon and says to Sonya, her teenage companion, "…almost with tears in her voice…'Do you know such an exquisite night has never, never been before.'" Sonya is unimpressed by the moonlit garden scene and wants to sleep. Andrey, nearby, can "hear the rustle of her garments and even her breathing" but "dare[s] not stir for fear of betraying his unintentional presence." Natasha continues to Sonya: "'…do look, what a moon!… One has only to squat on one heels like this—see—and to hold to one's knees—as tight, as tight as one can—give a great spring and one would fly away.'"

So, Tolstoy apparently thinks, via Sonya's fictional behavior, that the beauty of the moonlight and starry night in the real world is not sufficient by itself to induce aesthetic awe or being moved or thrills—the states which Natasha is unequivocally described as experiencing, but only with the big help from her headlong falling in love. Nor does empathy with her friend in the throes of aesthetic awe move sleepy Sonya. Nor does Tolstoy say anything about Andrey's being moved—for Andrey, an impeccable gentleman, is too embarrassed and too scared of being discovered to have the mental luxury of being moved.

On the other hand, the reader (perhaps like Tolstoy himself while writing this short scene) is moved and gets thrills and a lump in the throat from "listening" to Natasha as she creates aesthetic awe out of average moonlight and true love. However, the reader, in the terminology of this paper, does not experience aesthetic awe.

*The sublime, aesthetic awe, and fate*. In his short story *Fate* (1991/2001) the contemporary Chinese writer Jin Shui intuitively, and without mentioning any aesthetic issues, explores the nature of the sublime, of aesthetic awe, and of being moved. There are three key sequential elements in the story: (a) a mention of magnificent man-made and natural wonders that are located worldwide; (b) the narrator's intense anticipation of seeing them; and (c) a fateful event that forever precludes the narrator from fulfilling his dream.

The story is explicitly autobiographical and written in the first person. Because cruel fate affects a real person, and moreover one who speaks to the reader directly from the world of the story, the reader's empathy is more likely.

A young mainland-Chinese man is riding on his bicycle in his hometown, happy because he would soon realize his dream of going abroad to study (he is one of "the chosen").

"An ordinary summer night. I whistled a tune. The world is very large. I think I'll go to visit the Grand Canyon in Arizona on one of my vacations and Niagara Falls on another. If I live very frugally, maybe I can also visit the Great Pyramid of Cheops, St. Mark's Cathedral, Mount Fuji" (p. 24).

The narrator/protagonist is listing sublime objects and experiencing anticipatory aesthetic awe. The reader does not himself feel aesthetic awe, especially because the objects are not even described. He is, however, being inexorably drawn into the story by the familiarity of the sublime objects and by rooting for the narrator in his quest; this development (as in music) increases the likelihood of subsequently being moved.[1] There is also an element of suspense, of a certain unease that something untoward might soon happen in the story: The reader is safe, but the protagonist—and the author!—are not.

Indeed the protagonist has a bicycle accident, for which there is no one and nothing to blame (except for an aubergine lying in the street), and in a split of a second, his life is changed forever, for he is left paralyzed below the waist.

To this the adequately primed reader responds with being deeply moved and with chills. It is clear that the reader's reaction is caused largely by the magnitude of the protagonist's loss, the reader's identification with the narrator, and the consequent empathy. But even though the primary stimulus for the reader is not aesthetic, her empathy with the protagonist is enabled, in large part, by the latter's response of anticipated awe to the sublime objects the reader knows about, has herself experienced, or would very much want to experience.

*The sublime, aesthetic awe, and guilt.* Sigmund Freud saw the Acropolis for the first time when he was a mature man, at 48 years of age, in 1904, but never forgot the aesthetic awe he experienced on the occasion. In a letter to Romain Rolland in 1936, when Freud was 80 and Rolland 70, Freud described a complex state that one can describe as being deeply moved by finally reaching something that had been so grandiose as to appear out of reach.

Writing about this letter, Zbigniew Herbert (2003), a Polish critic, comments that in reading it he experienced the state of being moved in part because, in his own case, when he was confronted by the sublime works of man or nature, he always felt guilt concerning the people dear to him who could not be present to share his aesthetic awe. The guilt, sense of loss, separation from friends, and an evocation of past grieving to which Herbert alludes, may be important for the chills/thrills response.

The writer of the present paper recalls his first glimpse of the Acropolis and the Parthenon at eleven years of age: Aesthetic awe at this magnificent object, within reach, but so high, splendid, and mighty—and the sense of wonder and being moved, accompanied by the thrills—all to be remembered forever; and, unlike Freud and Herbert, no sense of regret or guilt—the blessing of childhood and immaturity.

## Thrills or chills

These terms[2] refer to the archaic physiological response of short duration to aesthetic (and other) stimuli: Piloerection on the back of the neck; shivers down the spine that can spread to arms and other parts of the body; sometimes a lump in the throat or even tears. The state can be reported by the experiencing person with a high degree of reliability; also, chills can be objectively measured in terms of skin conductivity (Blood and Zatorre, 2001; Panksepp, 1998). Since Goldstein's (1980) pioneering study, there has been a considerable amount of controlled laboratory work on this phenomenon, especially in response to music (e.g., Brown & Konečni, 2004; Konečni, 1995–2004; Panksepp, 1995; Sloboda, 1991; Waterman, 1996).

Goldstein (1980) has shown that the incidence of thrills in response to music can be reduced by drugs that are opiate receptor antagonists, such as naloxone. In addition, sophisticated scanning techniques, such as positron emission tomography have been used to monitor the cerebral blood flow, during the experience of thrills, in the ventral striatum, the midbrain, and the amygdala that are also involved in the fundamental emotions (Blood & Zatorre, 2001). However, it is important to stress that just because the stimulus situations that produce the fundamental emotions, and those that produce chills, both cause blood-flow changes in the same general areas of the brain, does not necessarily mean that the respective phenomenological experiences and evolutionary implications are the same in the two cases. Thrills sometimes accompany the fundamental emotions, but far more frequently occur in their absence.

In the present approach, thrills are considered to be the most frequent response to aesthetic stimuli. In response to the sublime, thrills always occur together with aesthetic awe and being moved. Additionally, it is assumed that most occurrences of being moved are also accompanied by chills; the exceptions consist of the relatively rare people who have a lower threshold for experiencing (or admitting to) being moved than for experiencing (or admitting to) thrills (Konečni, 1995–2004). Music with certain structural elements (Brown & Konečni, 2004; Sloboda, 1991), but devoid of personal associations and heard in an ordinary space, is a frequent cause of chills—without the deeper aesthetic responses being present. Finally, there are the horror and tear-jerker movies, in which a person also does not experience either aesthetic awe or being moved, but only chills or tears. The superficiality of these responses from an aesthetic point of view, despite their appeal to some, is demonstrated by the ease with which the experiencer can terminate the response.

It should be noted that all the aesthetic responses, especially being moved and thrills, require that the experiencer attends closely to the relevant stimuli. The paper does not deal with "background music" (in the broad sense).

## Music as a special case

Certain psychophysical attributes of spatial stimulus arrays (cf. Berlyne, 1971), including vast size and appealing proportions, contribute to their sublime quality and capacity to induce aesthetic awe. The question, from the standpoint of the present approach, is whether music can be sublime and which of its features make it able to move and touch the listeners.

Research participants have reported (e.g., Konečni, 1995–2004; Panksepp, 1995; Sloboda, 1991) that various structural features of music, including crescendos, unusual harmonies, dissonant chords, high-pitched solo vocals, guitar "riffs," sudden changes in dynamics, and fast tempo on percussion instruments, among others, can cause them to experience thrills. Surprise and incongruity (Berlyne, 1971), a violation of expectations (Meyer, 1956), and traditional melodies that are typically described as "beautiful" (cf. Gurney, 1880) may also cause chills.

However, these structural-temporal (harmonic, melodic, modal, dynamic, and timbre-based), and lower-level cognitive, effects are not, in the present view, sufficient to make music touching. One often experiences thrills while listening to music without being moved. In addition, one can analytically, without being moved, in the tradition of Eduard Hanslick's dictum "the beautiful is and remains beautiful though it arouse[s] no emotion whatever" (1854/1986; cf. Stravinsky, 1936), admire the score or the gift and skill of the composer and performers—as if the sonic stimulus were a chess or mathematical problem.

Furthermore, the possibility that music and emotional experience have similar temporal patterns (Gurney, 1880; Langer, 1942), and that a listener of (even non-"program") music can therefore decipher that it is attempting to evoke or depict an emotional state, does not necessarily move the listener. Being moved is a serious matter and it cannot be cheaply induced.

Buttressed by research (Konečni, 1995–2004) that has demonstrated enormous individual differences, the present contention is that what makes a piece of music moving for a particular listener is her personal associative context. The phenomenological experience of being moved may be similar, but the associative web that is interposed between the sound and the state of being touched is unique to each person (cf. Budd, 1985, p. 53; Gurney, 1880). And even though this personal associative web can also be activated by non-musical aesthetic and non-aesthetic stimuli, chills are here regarded as far more frequent and predictable—archaic, but shallow—than the state of being moved.

Finally, can music be sublime? Can it induce aesthetic awe—a state that is more profound, exhilarating, and elevating than are those of being moved and experiencing thrills, but includes them? In the present view, to be sublime, music must be "colossal," and this status it can achieve only by being performed in vast architectural spaces that have not only excellent acoustic qualities, but are also of extraordinary beauty. Perhaps the prototypical examples of this, and, not surprisingly also the ones with the longest tradition of performance of music of the highest caliber, are European mediaeval cathedrals and churches. In them one can encounter a truly sublime combination of vast space and soaring music, in addition to various stimuli that can produce a wealth of personal associations (including those classically conditioned since childhood), so that the result can be the "aesthetic trinity" of awe, being moved, and experiencing thrills.[3]

## Implications

### *Aesthetic and musical "emotions"*

The nomenclature that has been proposed in this paper can perhaps replace the unsystematic, imprecise, and sometimes casual references to the aesthetic and musical "emotions," with which the literature is replete, and lead to a conceptual re-orientation and methodological improvements.

In the belief system and parlance of many a Sue Doe and music and art teacher, music and art induce fundamental emotions in the listener and viewer. Such folk views are often echoed by the musicological position that music directly causes emotions (e.g., most chapters in the Juslin and Sloboda, 2001, edited volume; Budd, 1985, p. 31) and the call for "aesthetic emotions" and "musical emotions" that is returned by the titles of articles published in major journals (e.g., Keltner and Haidt, 2003; Krumhansl, 1997).

The conceptual, methodological, and terminological problems in the literature, as seen from the present position, fall in several related categories (these issues are further pursued in papers by Brown & Konečni, 2004, and Konečni 2004a, b):

1. A confusion is introduced by many investigators, both conceptually and methodologically, and for both research subjects and readers of articles, between the "emotions" in the music (which is non-sentient and can only depict or evoke emotions) and the induced subjective state of the listener (e.g., Krumhansl, 1998; Sloboda & Lehmann, 2001).

2. The casual use of the plural in "aesthetic or musical emotions" suggests that authors frequently ignore the biological significance of the emotions (cf. Budd, 1985). After all, every language possesses, for multiple extraneous reasons, literally hundreds of labels for things "emotional"—and these labels some authors misapply to internal states.

3. The terms for the emotions that are produced by interacting with human beings in major life situations are too readily used for the effects of music. Debatable theoretical assumptions about emotions translate into debatable methods. Research participants may, for example (Krumhansl, 1997), be asked to rate continuously the "amount of sadness [or happiness or fear] they experience" (p. 340) in response to six three-minute musical excerpts that are "chosen to represent" sadness, happiness, and fear (two each). In 18 minutes, the subjects are thus implicitly—and highly unrealistically—expected to experience two episodes each of the fundamental emotions of sadness, happiness, and fear (in a mixed order) and respond during these episodes continuously on a "sadness" (or "happiness" or "fear") scale.

4. The few experiments that claim to have demonstrated a causal effect of music on emotion (Krumhansl, 1997; Nykliček, Thayer, & Van Doornen, 1997; Witvliet & Vrana, 1996) have actually produced rather ambiguous results, yet are readily overinterpreted in secondary sources. In general, music has been too uncritically regarded as a link between cognition and emotion (e.g., Gaver & Mandler, 1987; Krumhansl, 2002).

5.  With the notable exception of the research by Vaitl, Vehrs, and Sternagel (1993) on 27 listeners' responses to Wagner's operas at Bayreuth, the special situations in which music can become sublime are not considered by the papers that claim a causal effect of music on emotion. In fact, most research studies are set up in such a way—in terms of the choice of musical materials, research locations, duration of listening, and other methodological details—that even being moved is most unlikely to be experienced by the participants. What one gets in most studies, at best, are thrills—and verbal ratings of the music.

It would seem that most researchers are keen listeners to music and that they have repeatedly experienced aesthetic awe, the state of being moved, and chills in their private lives. However, these profound personal responses to music, and presumably to other arts, have generally not inspired research that could adequately explore them. It is hoped that this essay is a useful step toward rectifying the current research and theoretical trends.

## The aesthetic trinity and the artworld

*The classical and the modern: A discontinuity.* From a musical segment to Iguaçú Falls, and from the droplets on a cobweb below a leaf in the lower reaches of Mt. Fuji to a Rothko manifold or the Great Wall of China— crumbling and reduced to a third of its original size (Xinhua/Reuters, 2004)—aesthetic stimuli, man-made and natural, have been analyzed and thought about by generations of artists, critics, and both philosophical and empirical aestheticians.

When the evidence is examined, a sharp discontinuity with the ancient and the classical is observed in the art of the 20th-century, especially in Europe and America (areas of massive and influential art production), such that many approaches in many art forms—serial and aleatory music, DADA, postmodern dance, conceptual, "bluff," and "decay" art, "anti-illusionist" theatre, visual and "nonsense" poetry, to mention just a few without regard to chronology—have systematically severed the link with the ancient and classical approaches. In so doing, they have eliminated the sublime: Aesthetic awe and being moved have become unacceptable responses to which public art must not cater.[4]

The rejection of the sublime and the moving can be labeled "destructive deconstruction." This art-political agenda has had considerable economic and social costs and detrimental implications for how public art is done and financed worldwide.

*Aesthetics and politics.* In large part, especially in the last third of the 20th century, destructive deconstruction has been vigorously promoted by the new art hyper-elite, the highly politicized museum curators and international festival directors, with the connivance of governmental art bureaucrats. All have striven to eliminate classical art, treating it as a weapon of oppression that had been wielded by the dead (and half-dead), white (and off-white), (mostly) heterosexual, exploitative males.

The present position is that these curators and the postmodern artists shaped by them have not attacked the exploitative, wasteful, and militaristic oppressors, but rather the primordial core of the human aesthetic-emotional response—that is, the perceptual, cognitive, and, especially, emotional apparatus that our species uses to deal with the sublime and the deeply moving.

For this reason, the prediction of this essay is that postmodernism (broadly defined) will fail and that it would have failed even if its political objectives were just and equitable.

Although it is true that magnificent art inspires aesthetic awe and moves deeply regardless of its stated deconstructive intentions, the layers of nonsense that are introduced for selfish or political reasons do not come cheap. The political pretense in 20th-century art has had quite real human and economic costs.

To give a pre-postmodern example, Bertolt Brecht proved to be too masterful a dramatist to be able to prevent the audiences at his "epic" (presumably anti-Stanislavskian and anti-bourgeois) Berlin stagings of *Mother Courage* from Aristotelian cathartic sobbing (Konečni, 1991), but another way of viewing his approach is that the entire "distancing" (*Verfremdung*) idea and the associated removal of empathy (*Einfühlung*) were simply politically expedient. Note that this disingenuousness of Brecht's (perhaps itself insincere—which adds another twist, one that was used also by Picasso, and rather common in 20th-century art) had an immeasurable social cost incurred by the explicit support of the world-famous Berliner Ensemble for the highly repressive German Democratic Republic (DDR).

As an apparent counter-example, it could be claimed that Christo's running fences, wrapped islands and coastlines, curtained-off canyons, thousands of blue and yellow umbrellas dispersed simultaneously on hillsides in two countries, and wrapped classical bridges, genuinely inspire aesthetic awe and move—yet seem to be the crystallization of postmodernism. However, the point is that they induce aesthetic awe despite their tongue-in-cheek ephemerality and, especially, despite the equally tongue-in-cheek process of (pseudo-) democratic and ecologically-conscious negotiation with the local authorities (among whom have been the Paris *clochards* and the Marin County, California, farmers) that is supposedly a crucial part of Christo's works. One's response to them is aesthetic awe in part because the emphatically ephemeral attribute of the works is so stunningly juxtaposed with their sublime quality.

It remains an open question whether the politically-correct blather that surrounds Christo's works analogously contributes to their impact by its triviality being juxtaposed with the works' monumentality: Is it necessary to be oblivious to hype in order to experience aesthetic awe?

It is instructive to contrast Christo's sublime ephemera with those that can be thought of as the hallmark of recent postmodernism, namely, the rapidly reproducing examples of "decay art." In them one observes an economically, aesthetically, and olphactorily foul paradox of the obscenely expensive, cutting-edge scientific procedures being used by museums to preserve and restore what, in its original state, shrilly (though disingenuously) insisted on being sticky, messy, and rotting—ephemeral (cf. Barnes, 2003).

This is a joke in the Duchamp tradition, but one that would offend the grand bluff-master's sense of clarity and order (observed in his excellent chess-playing), as well as his purity (the urinal and bicycle wheel were reputedly spotless). One has here a pseudo-progression of the "new"—but it is a costly exercise that is radically dissociated from the tradition that leads back to the ancient sublime.

*Art consumption and altruism.* One might wonder about the broader layers of sensitive art consumers and their private and genuine, as opposed to the public and scared, reaction to the new curatorial dogma. Such people are likely to be over-represented among those who, when experiencing aesthetic awe, guiltily regard themselves as privileged and "chosen."

To convert into *aesthetic altruism* the guilty component of the elitism that has been here hypothesized as an ingredient of aesthetic awe—perhaps experienced precisely by those who most genuinely seek the sublime in art and nature—seems to be a socially responsible alternative to destructive deconstruction. One should strive for a serious philanthropy with global ambitions that would be devoted to financing the contemporary creation of the "new old" sublime art—in parallel with the conservation of the existing natural and man-made wonders—as a post-postmodern, enlightened, version of *noblesse oblige*.

It might be argued that the project of destructive deconstruction seeks social justice by dismantling the sublime. The contention here, however, is that the goal of making the sublime widely accessible is eminently more just and altruistic than is the metaphorical and literal cultivation of termites for the purpose of demonstrating how allegedly rotten the ancient sublime house is.

This is not the occasion to discuss the bread part of *panem et circenses* [bread and circus games – Ed.], nor is it possible here to suggest how decency and equity should be brought into the cynical Roman formula; but the sublime is the deadly enemy of the circus as a crass and violent entertainment. Education that encourages the quest for aesthetic awe would be a welcome part of a political agenda that is devoted to a constructive role of aesthetics in contemporary life.

## Questions

1. Summarize and evaluate Konečni's theory of the "aesthetic trinity." For what reasons does he criticize theories that refer to the "aesthetic emotions" or "musical emotions"?

2. How might Konečni's theory be used in future philosophical and empirical studies of the sublime or aesthetic awe?

3. Explain, in your own words, Konečni's views on elitist guilt as well as the political, social, and artistic implications of his account of the sublime in art. What do you consider to be the strengths and weaknesses of his views?

## Further reading

Chirico, Alice, et al. "The Potential of Virtual Reality for the Investigation of Awe." *Frontiers in Psychology* 7, no. 26 (2016), article 1766: 1–6.

Konečni, Vladimir J., Rebekah A. Wanic, and Amber Brown. "Emotional and Aesthetic Antecedents and Consequences of Music-Induced Thrills." *The American Journal of Psychology* 120, no. 4 (2007): 619–43.

Konečni, Vladimir J. "Aesthetic Trinity Theory and the Sublime." *Philosophy Today* 55, no. 1 (2011): 64–73.

Prade, Claire, and Vassilis Saroglou. "Awe's Effects on Generosity and Helping." *The Journal of Positive Psychology* 11, no. 5 (2016): 522–30.

Yaden, David B., Jonathan Haidt, Ralph W. Hood, David Vago, and Andrew Newberg. "The Varieties of Self-Transcendent Experience." *Review of General Psychology* 21, no. 2 (2017): 143–60.

# CHAPTER 35
# JANE FORSEY, "IS A THEORY OF THE SUBLIME POSSIBLE?" (2007)

Jane Forsey is the author of numerous articles and studies in philosophical aesthetics, including a book on the aesthetic aspects of everyday life, in particular, the aesthetics of design. Below, Forsey asks challenging questions about the possibility of a theory of the sublime, raising concerns about a theory's claims regarding ontological and epistemological transcendence. In 2005, Forsey presented an early version of the paper in a panel called "Knowing the Sublime."

Her article was reprinted in *The Possibility of the Sublime* (2017), followed by comments by six authors, and a response by Forsey (see Further reading).

## Note on the text

Source: Reprinted from Jane Forsey, "Is a Theory of the Sublime Possible?" *Journal of Aesthetics and Art Criticism* (2007) 65 (4): 381–89.

The format and style of the original publication have been reproduced, with occasional modifications. The volume editor has made comments using square brackets in the main body text, in order to preserve the footnote numbering found in Forsey's original article.

## "Is a theory of the sublime possible?"

The aesthetic notion of the sublime has had a great deal of attention in the last decade or so, engendering monographs by Paul Crowther, Jean-François Lyotard, and Kirk Pillow, critical anthologies from Dabney Townsend and from Andrew Ashfield and Peter de Bolla, and numerous journal articles, conference panels, and symposia.[1] This renewal of interest is perhaps timely: a notion that conjures up the inexplicable, the overwhelming, and the horrendous may be well suited to the current age. It is perhaps also timely that we take a step back from this respectable and growing body of research to attend to a single voice that once asked a very important question: "How is a theory of the sublime possible?"[2] Guy Sircello was concerned that our efforts to capture and explain the sublime have in fact resulted in claims that are either contradictory or incoherent, due to tensions between (often unarticulated) epistemological and ontological commitments. He also sought to remedy the very problem he posed, with suggestions as to how a coherent theory of the sublime should proceed.

The present article takes up the problem as Sircello first voiced it, but without his final optimism. What I offer amounts to an error theory: our current theorizing about the sublime rests on a mistake. I will claim that if we accept the problem as Sircello had described it, his own proposed solution is bound to fail. But if we reject his general methodological assumptions, what we will be left with is so limited that a general theory of the sublime will remain out of our reach. Additionally, I will expand on the evidence Sircello garnered for his case by attending in some detail to the most sophisticated treatment of the sublime we have: that of Immanuel Kant's work in the third *Critique*.

## I The problem of the sublime

But first, the problem itself. Sircello took as his starting point the generally accepted notion that sublime experience "professes to 'see' beyond human powers of knowledge and description" and that because of this it is inaccessible to rational thought (p. 541). Further, in the descriptions of the sublime he canvassed, Sircello found the operation of a general assumption that our cognitive powers are revealed, in the moment, to have what he called "radically limited access" to some broadly construed notion of "reality" (p. 543). There is a great deal of *prima facie* evidence for this general claim. Sircello mined such sources as the Tao, Zen Buddhism, and the poetry of Wordsworth and the Romantics, but philosophers writing on the sublime provide similar evidence, and it is with philosophical theory that I am most concerned. Consider the following:

1. Joseph Addison wrote in the *Spectator* of 1712 that "our imagination loves to be filled with an object, or to grasp at anything that is too big for its capacity."[3]

2. The Earl of Shaftsbury rhapsodized about the sublimity of nature in this way: "Thy being is boundless, unsearchable; impenetrable. In thy immensity all thought is lost; fancy gives over its flight: and wearied imagination spends itself in vain."[4]

3. Edmund Burke claimed that the passion caused by the sublime is astonishment, "and astonishment is that state of the soul, in which all its motions are suspended.... The mind is so entirely filled with its object that it cannot entertain any other nor by consequence reason on that object which employs it."[5]

4. In the twentieth century, Jean-François Lyotard famously wrote of the postmodern as truly sublime, that which "puts forward the unpresentable in presentation itself ... that which searches for new presentations, not in order to enjoy them but in order to impart a stronger sense of the unpresentable."[6]

In each of these cases, as with others, we grasp at and fail to achieve an understanding of some notion of "reality." This is Sircello's main premise: that sublime experience embodies a certain kind of cognitive failure. In these moments we become aware of our limitations; whatever we construe this broad notion of reality to be, it remains tantalizingly out of reach. This experience generates, for Sircello, the first of two themes he identified as running through the majority of sublime discourse, the theme of "epistemological transcendence" (p. 542), which he articulated in the following proposition.

An experience of the sublime presents the object of the experience, i.e., the sublime, as epistemologically inaccessible. (p. 545)

At first glance, this is not a contentious thesis: much writing about sublime experience seems to suggest that what is unique *is just* this moment of being overwhelmed by a sense of something incomprehensible, or incommensurable, or more powerful than we are. And, of course, to be made aware of the limitations of our cognitive capacities is at the same time to transcend them, insofar as we reflect on them. This is another powerful motif in writing on the sublime that I will return to below.

Sircello's concern was that this initial theme of epistemological transcendence tends to embody a second theme that leads us into difficulty. The first theme interprets "the experience of the sublime" as denoting an experience of an *object,* although it leaves open the question of what this object might be, or whether it indeed exists (p. 545), referring instead to "reality" at large. The second theme, what Sircello called "ontological transcendence," addresses this object directly and suggests that sublime experience represents something *as existing* that is inaccessible to our cognitive powers, something "on a level of being ... which transcends that of humankind and all of humankind's possible environments" (p. 545). After all, he went on to say, it is implausible to assert that we have an experience, called sublime, that is without any object, or that the sublime is both an object of experience and one that does not exist (p. 545). However, to imply that an epistemologically in accessible object *does* exist, Sircello claimed, is to end in either incoherence or contradiction, and cause any attempts at a theory to fail. Let me take each of these charges in tum.

Regarding the charge of incoherence, we must ask how we can have an experience—and describe that experience—which presents an object that is *in no way* epistemologically accessible. This would be tantamount, Sircello noted, to having a visual experience of an invisible object: impossible (p. 546). Consider James Usher, a contemporary of Burke's, who wrote:

> Because the philosophers of our days can assign no form, nor size, nor color, to the object of their sublime awe, they conclude it to be vain and superstitious. ... The truth is, the impression of this obscure presence ... is beyond the verge of the philosophy of the ideas of sense. The disciples of this philosophy ... are not able to conceive that an object has been there which was not represented by a sensible idea, and which makes itself felt only by its influence.[7]

For Usher, we have an experience of an existent object that is inaccessible to our very modes of experiencing, as with Shaftsbury's earlier allusion to boundlessness and impenetrability. This is the incoherence with which Sircello was concerned.

However, sublime discourse that does not make incoherent claims falls into contradiction instead. Let me return to Addison for a moment: he lists among the objects of sublime experience "a vast uncultivated desert," "huge heaps of mountains, high rocks and precipices, or a wide expanse of waters."[8] Burke widens this list to include "serpents and poisonous animals of all kinds,"[9] and many in the Longinian tradition count poetry, architecture, and painting as candidates for the sublime, just as Lyotard included in his scope works of art and literature. For the most part, a long tradition of writing on the sublime has clearly described the objects of our experiences. Sircello reminds us that to do so, however, is consistently *not* to treat these objects as if they were epistemologically inaccessible (p. 546). Rocks and mountains are not things we do not comprehend or cannot comprehend; we would not describe them if we did not have access to them. When we do identify them as sublime objects, we are not treating them as, at the same time, inaccessible to rational thought. So we fall into contradiction: the sublime object is both transcendent and familiar.

On Sircello's diagnosis, we seem forced to concede that sublime discourse, so long as it embodies both these theses, is either incoherent or contradictory. This is a pressing problem if we seek to find in the sublime anything of philosophical interest. Theorists who wish to emphasize the transcendence of the sublime object are faced with the problem of explaining how we can actually have and describe an experience of it, as in the case of Usher. But theorists who wish to emphasize the experience itself as transcendent must somehow tell us what it is an experience *of,* if it is not to be a mere fantasy or hallucination. Telling us that it is an unusual experience of a usual object—a rock, a cliff, a storm, and soon—contradicts the first thesis with the second. The heart of the problem, then, is this: if we focus on the metaphysical status of the sublime object, our epistemology becomes problematic, but if we address instead the epistemological transcendence of a certain experience, we still seem forced to make *some* metaphysical claim about the object of that experience. The theme of epistemological transcendence, as Sircello interpreted it, provides indirect evidence for the second theme of ontological transcendence, with which it appears to be inextricably bound, and this seems to imply that, in fact, *nothing* can be sublime.

Can we overcome this problem and speak coherently about sublimity in some way? Sircello left a hint that we perhaps could if we can find a way to reinterpret the first theme so that it does not embody the second. For it is the first—that general notion that sublime experience somehow overwhelms our cognitive faculties—that has generated such interest in the topic. And it is the second—the ontological claim—that has been at the heart of the conceptual problems I have out lined. Sircello proposed that we attempt a weaker reading of the thesis of epistemological transcendence to exclude any metaphysical postulation. He argued that "epistemological transcendence may not presuppose *any* ontology and may not directly concern 'the real' at all, but only the limitations of our attempts to grasp it, whatever it is or is taken to be" (p. 540). Our mistake lay in assuming we were talking about some kind of object of experience and in attaching the quality of sublimity to that. Sircello concluded his paper with a proposed rearticulation of the thesis of epistemological transcendence, as follows: "for any possible given set of routes of epistemological access to reality, that set is insufficient to grasp the real and that in the moment of sublime experience we are perhaps made aware of this" (p. 540 [*sic* – Ed.]). [Forsey (383) slightly misquotes, and adds to, the original passage. Sircello, whose paper starts on 541, writes on 549: "[...] access to 'reality', that set is insufficient to provide a *complete* understanding or grasp of 'the real.'" – Ed.] It is this revised proposition I will turn to now.

## II The Kantian sublime

Kant becomes an interesting thinker in this regard, for he was notoriously coy about making any kind of metaphysical claim about the nature of the real. His most striking innovation on earlier thinkers was to move the locus of the sublime from a property of an object (whether natural or supernatural) to a feeling experienced by the knowing subject. This seems to indicate a focus on the epistemology of the experience, as Sircello had proposed. At first glance, Kant's work appears most likely to lead us out of the problems as presented, and therefore merits a more thorough consideration.

Kant states at the beginning of the "Analytic of the Sublime" that "we express ourselves incorrectly if we call any object of nature sublime ... All that we can say is that the object is fit for the presentation of a sublimity which can be found in the mind, for no sensible form can contain the sublime properly so-called"(§ 23, pp. 83–84).[10] And, more strongly, that *"Nichts* also, was Gegenstand der Sinnen sein kann, ist, auf diesen Fuß betrachtet, erhaben zu nennen; [*nothing*, therefore, which can be an object of the senses is, considered on this basis, to be called sublime]"(§ 24, p. 88).[11]

For all that Kant remains within the tradition in his mention of such familiar natural examples as "shapeless mountains piled in wild despair," "the gloomy, raging sea," and "crude nature" in general, he explicitly departs from earlier thinkers in denying that any of these things themselves are sublime *objects* of our experiences (§ 26, pp. 95, 91). Similarly, while in his discussion of the mathematical sublime he refers to seemingly inaccessible objects that are "boundless," "formless," and "absolutely great," or that bring with them "the idea of infinity," he again denies that these are sublime, for all that they occasion the feeling of sublimity in us when we confront them (§ 23, p. 82; § 25, p. 86; § 26, p. 94). His starting point thus seems to reject Sircello's first interpretation of epistemological transcendence in favor of something approaching the second. What is sublime for Kant is not something in the world—some portion of the "real" that we directly experience—but a feeling we have that is occasioned by certain sensory experiences.

Let us look at this feeling of sublimity more closely. Kant, in these sections, is not merely providing a phenomenology of certain kinds of experiences and the emotional charge we get from them. His interest is very much in epistemological transcendence: the mechanism by which we realize our cognitive limitations and the positive (moral) implications of this realization. With the mathematical sublime, for instance, which we experience when faced with vast and formless objects, the faculty of imagination cannot apprehend them as a whole in a single intuition as reason demands. This incommensurability of our imagination with the totalizing demands of reason produces at first a displeasure in our experience of failure and then a subsequent pleasure that is aroused by "the feeling of a supersensible faculty"—our awareness of the superiority of our powers of reason. It is this "state of mind [*Geistesstimmung*]," he notes, "and not the object, that is to be called sublime [*nicht aber das Objeckt erhaben zu nennen*]" (§ 25, pp. 88–89).[12]

Kant seems to suggest in these passages that, in the moment, we become aware of a part of us that transcends the natural world. As Malcolm Budd has put it, our ability to *think*, for example, the infinite as a whole "is possible only because we possess a supersensible faculty ... Accordingly, sublimity attaches only to the supersensible basis of human nature."[13] Kant writes that the failures of imagination in these moments nevertheless "carry our concept of nature to a supersensible substrate" that lies both at its basis and "*also* at the basis of our faculty of thought" (§ 26, p. 94). The sublime, then, is more than a feeling; it is an awareness of a part of ourselves that surpasses understanding: "*Erhaben ist, was auch nur denken zu konnen ein Vermogen des Gemüts beweiset, das jeden Maßstab der Sinne übertrifft* [the sublime is that, the mere ability to think which shows a faculty of the mind surpassing every standard of sense]" (§ 25, p. 89).[14]

This is equally clear in the sections on the dynamical sublime, in which we experience the force of nature without ourselves being in physical danger. The sight of storms, hurricanes, volcanoes, and other natural forces "exhibit our faculty of resistance as insignificantly small in comparison with their might" (§ 28, p. 100). Nevertheless, this sense of powerlessness leads us to discover in ourselves "a faculty of resistance of a quite different kind": that of our moral superiority (§ 28, p. 101). The sublime, Kant notes, "calls up a power in us (which is not nature)" but allows us to see that nature has no dominion over us, for all that it can overwhelm our physical strength (§ 28, p. 101). We become aware in that moment that while we may physically perish in a raging sea, there is a part of us that cannot be touched, even by the most violent of natural forces. That part of us—our moral being is "disclosed," or "emerges," or "is found" in our sensory experience of certain natural phenomena. What is truly sublime, then, is not an object of experience: it is an object of thought.

In his General Remark at the end of the "Analytic of the Sublime," Kant recapitulates his position. Ideas of reason, he reminds us, cannot be presented to the senses, and the failure of the imagination in the face of the sublime is due to its efforts to "make the representation of the senses adequate to these [ideas]" (§ 29, p. 108). But this failure, this effort on the part of the imagination "forces us ... to *think* nature itself in its totality as a presentation of something supersensible." We become aware, thereby, of something that surpasses nature and all our attempts at capturing it. "It is by this that we are reminded," Kant writes, "that we only have to do with nature as a phenomenon and that it must be regarded as the mere presentation of a nature in itself (of which reason has the idea) ... [T]his idea of the supersensible ... is awakened in us" by the experience of the sublime and "this judgment is based upon a feeling of the mind's destination, which entirely surpasses the realm of [the natural world]" (§ 29, pp. 108–109).

The dual movement of the mind—from a sense of our cognitive limitations to the transcendence of them—has little direct application, for Kant, to shapeless mountains and violent storms. These phenomena may provide the catalyst for epistemological transcendence but they are not the direct objects of sublime experience. The real point of these experiences is the realization of our own supersensible nature, a realization that occurs, as Malcolm Budd has noted, "only by conceiving of the sensible world of experience as being dependent on its intelligible basis, the world as it is in itself, thus making manifest ... our status as a *causa noumenon.*"[15] These myriad natural phenomena provide the occasions for our experiences but the real object of the sublime is us.[16]

The innovative aspect of Kant's discussion has been in moving the locus of the sublime from objects of the natural world to the subject of experience, but in doing so, Kant has not avoided metaphysical postulation, as Sircello had hoped, for he has resituated the transcendent object as well: what unfolds as truly sublime is our moral being, that part of us that is inaccessible to sensory experience but that we nevertheless become aware of in (certain) moments of cognitive failure. In the *Foundations of the Metaphysics of Morals,* Kant makes this ontological commitment clear: we "ascribe a certain sublimity and dignity to the person who fulfills all his [moral] duties. For though there is no sublimity in him in so far as he is subject to the moral law, yet *he is sublime* in so far as he is a giver of the law and subject to it for this reason only."[17] Again, in the *Critique of Practical Reason* Kant refers to the "sublimity of our own super sensuous existence [*die Erhabenheit unserer eigenen iibersinnlichen Existenz*]"; it is an awareness of the transcendent self as moral legislator that sublime experience was getting at all along.[18]

To be sure, Kant's account does not suffer from the incoherence in Sircello's first formulation of epistemological transcendence because Kant is not claiming that we have direct sensory experience of a transcendent object. But, while not incoherent, Kant's account shows us that the theme of ontological transcendence persists through Sircello's second articulation of the epistemological thesis. This formulation suggested that for any given set of routes of epistemological access to reality, that set is insufficient to grasp the real. We can see that this articulation still embodies an ontological claim: it represents something as existing that is inaccessible to our cognitive faculties but to which our experience of sublimity is directed. For all that Sircello sought to escape the problem by focusing on the epistemology of sublime experience, it seems that we cannot do this without bringing along some notion of the real, however this notion is construed. Kant's conception of sublimity, for all that it, too, focuses on the epistemological aspects of our experience, still carries with it an ontological claim about (transcendent) reality. With Sircello's second formulation, we escape incoherence only to find ourselves facing some ineffable or mysterious reality that we do not experience directly, that we cannot know, but that nevertheless we must posit as existing, of which the sublime gives us a glimmer. This revision of the original thesis does not succeed in omitting the theme of ontological transcendence: instead, as we see with the case of Kant, it renders the ontology all the more mysterious and all the more tantalizingly out of reach.

## III The impossibility of a theory of the sublime

Where does this discussion leave us regarding the possibility of a theory of the sublime? I will use this final section to canvas our options, and to make the negative argument that a theory of the sublime as it has been historically formulated is simply not possible. There are three immediate directions open before us in light of the forgoing.

First, we can simply accept Kant's account as the only way to generate a coherent theory of the sublime. Sircello, we can say, aptly revised his epistemological thesis to meet earlier problems of contradiction and incoherence, even if he was mistaken in his optimism that this revision would omit any metaphysics (Sircello, curiously, did not mention Kant in his paper). [In fact, Sircello mentions Kant three times: on pages 541, 542, and 544. – Ed.] But to accept Kant's account is possible only if we accept the entire Kantian system; the particular kind of cognitive failure we see with the mathematical sublime, for instance, rests on the Kantian theory of what constitutes cognitive success: that of the imagination being able to synthesize sensory experience for the purposes of determinant judgment. The true sublime object can only be a Kantian postulate about our moral being. If we go this route, the sublime becomes nothing more than evidence for—or a symptom of—Kant's whole architectonic. It may be the result of an (aesthetic) reflective judgment, but it is no longer a truly aesthetic concept and has peripheral use in aesthetic theory (although it may become of interest for ethics). This means that any account of the sublime we may seek to provide will be part of an interpretation of the Kantian system only; at best, we may be forced to admit that a theory of the sublime will be incoherent without at minimum a commitment to Kantian terminology. This conclusion may not be dire: a focus on judgments of sublimity may help illuminate Kant's moral theory. But I suggest that such an outcome would be unsatisfying for the many aesthetic theorists who have sought to rejuvenate the notion and claim it as their purview.

A second option is to further investigate Sircello's revised thesis in the hope that a wholly epistemological account of the sublime is possible. Kant, we can say, was wrong to link the requisite cognitive failure to moral transcendence. Instead, we can perhaps retain the notion of sublimity as a pleasure that results from cognitive failure without his moral conclusions. This is the route Malcolm Budd seems to have taken. He is critical of Kant's formulation of the sublime, claiming that it "appears to be no more than a product of his inveterate tendency to evaluate everything by reference to moral value ... a tendency that led him to moralize, in one way or another, any experience he valued."[19] If we reject the moralizing aspect of the Kantian account, a much more modest picture of the sublime emerges. The initial negative aspect of the experience remains an awareness of the inadequacy of our imagination or physical strength in the face of certain natural phenomena, but the final movement of the mind, rather than reaching toward some transcendent truth about our natures that we feel but cannot know, emerges directly from this experience of inadequacy. Budd has described it this way:

> With the sudden dropping away ... of our everyday sense of the importance of our self and its numerous concerns and projects, or the normal sense of the security of our body from external natural forces, the heightened awareness of our manifest vulnerability and insignificance ... is, after the initial shock, experienced with pleasure.[20]

This more modest interpretation of cognitive failure ends with an awareness of our vulnerability and humility; we are humbled in the face of natural phenomena that are either so vast as to preclude measure, or so powerful that we cannot withstand them. We realize our limitations at these times of cognitive failure, and this realization brings with it a certain pleasure (what Burke and Kant have both termed a "negative" pleasure).

Such an account seems more in keeping with the generally accepted notion of the sublime as a moment of being overwhelmed by a sense of things as incomprehensible, or more powerful than we are, but it stops short of claiming any transcendence attendant upon this moment (or at best a very thin notion of transcendence as the result of our realization of our own limitations). But we can ask of Budd's account why these moments of cognitive failure must be restricted to experiences that follow the general outlines of the Kantian mathematical and dynamical sublime. We have already given up the idea that sublimity resides in *objects* of experience as being contradictory if they are natural objects and incoherent if they are not. If we now reject the moment of moral transcendence that the sublime is meant to engender, as we reject the Kantian conception altogether, is the field not left wide open for any encounters that likewise humble us or draw attention to our vulnerability? Is this not what Lyotard had in mind for powerful works of art, for instance? Or, more prosaically, what of the cognitive failure I have occasionally experienced in the face of the *New York Times* crossword puzzle, or complex mathematical problems that truly humble me? What of the rush athletes experience from dangerous sports such as ice climbing or heli-skiing? What of the vulnerability I feel when riding my bicycle in rush-hour traffic and making it—just—home safely? Why are these sorts of experiences not also sublime or, at any rate, equal candidates for the kind of pleasure that a subjective account would properly call sublime? Budd's rejection of Kant's moral goals causes us to lose the initial reasons for focusing on the vast, formless, and threatening aspects of nature alone.

Indeed, if we seek a purely epistemological account of the sublime, must we not dismiss any reference to Kant's so-called dynamical experiences altogether? For these were not moments of cognitive failure *per se* but instead experiences of our physical vulnerability in the face of (natural) forces we *can* cognize but cannot withstand. On Budd's reading, it seems that *anything at all* could engender an experience of the sublime, provided that it overwhelms our cognitive capacities. This is why I have called his account "subjective," for it seems that the relevant experiences will be unique to the particular cognitive abilities of a given individual (*you* may have no difficulty with the crossword puzzle, for instance). But again, even this minimal reading will not work, for there remains an object of experience that causes cognitive failure, and any attempt to describe or delimit this object will lead to by now familiar problems.

This second option is also unsatisfying for a further reason. Why, we can ask, does the awareness of our cognitive limitations lead to *pleasure* in particular, even of a negative kind? Why does it not instead lead to frustration, humiliation, or determination to overcome our failures? Budd's revision of Kant does not explain why the realization of our failings should be met with such equanimity, absent the transcendence to an awareness of moral superiority. His account is not alone in this, if we reconsider the theorists I canvassed at the outset. Lyotard, for instance, does not explain why my incomprehension in the face of certain works of art leads me to awe or a deeper respect for them instead of a dismissal that they have "nothing to say to me." Again, the onus remains on a purely epistemological account to show how cognitive failure brings pleasure— of a certain kind—with it. This is something that Sircello's revised formulation equally lacks.

Let me turn now to our third option. I have rejected a theory of the sublime that attends to the object of experience because of its troubling ontology. I have also cast doubt on a purely epistemological account of cognitive failure because such an account will require *some* delineation of the object of experience if it seeks to circumscribe the notion of the sublime in any way. Sircello's attempted revision of the epistemological thesis thus will not succeed: he had hoped we could theorize about the sublime by attending to the experience itself but we cannot, finally, exclude the experiential object from our account if we begin with the methodological assumptions that initially drove Sircello's paper. I have said nothing so far about an *intersubjective* account of the sublime because there is almost no mention in the literature of this experience being culturally shared or even communicable. The sublime has been described as a wholly personal, even intimate experience without reference to others. If one wanted to attempt this line of inquiry, it will not be immune to the problems noted above: even an intersubjective epistemology must have reference to an object of (shared) experience, however that is conceived. What we now might consider, then, is a rejection of the delineation of the problem as Sircello first articulated it: the solution does not lie in a strictly epistemological account of the sublime, we may say, and sublime experience is not best construed as a species of cognitive failure. In fact, we may hazard that traditional theorizing about the sublime has been mistaken all along.

But what then is sublime experience? Experience as we normally understand the term is largely held to be intentional, with at least a perceived phenomenal content (whatever that content may turn out to be). If this experience is not conceptual, leading to the above-noted problems with epistemology, then we can suggest that it is perhaps emotional, a kind of feeling that we have when faced with some (or any) phenomena. That is, not only may we say that the sublime is not a species of cognitive failure, but also that it has nothing to do with cognition at all. Consider Budd's account again: his interest lies in our feelings of humility and vulnerability, in a pleasurable realization of human limitations. What he has offered here, we can claim, is an (incomplete) account of a type of feeling that is a response to the world. But if we seek to describe the sublime as a feeling (of pleasure) of a certain kind, we face a paradox: either feelings are intentional and object-regarding (and so are theorizable in the above problematic ways), or feelings are nonintentional and cannot be theorized at all.[21] Let me develop this a little further. On the one hand, feelings can be seen as intentional—like the feelings of love we have for somebody, or the feelings of resentment we have toward particular political decisions, or feelings of fear toward certain things, and so on. If feelings *are* intentional they can also be theorized, but if they are intentional we also return to the same objections: Why does the sublime capture feelings in response to some objects/situations and not others? Why *these* feelings (awe, incomprehension, and so forth) and not others?

If, however, we interpret feelings as nonconceptual and nonintentional, we are left with some thing that cannot readily be theorized at all: How do we provide a theory of this sort of thing beyond some kind of literary capturing of the feelings as they occur? They take no object and have naught to do with cognition. With this option we come full circle to the sources Sircello initially mined for his discussion of the sublime in literary and mystical texts. What he called "sublime discourse," as "language that is or purports to be ... expressive of sublime experience" (and which I take this side of the paradox to intend), he held in opposition to "talk about the sublime" that is reflective and analytic (and which includes the works of Burke and Kant) (p. 541). Sircello quoted, as examples of sublime discourse, Wordsworth:

> For I would walk alone / In storm and tempest or in starlight nights / Beneath the quiet heavens, and at that time / Have felt whate'er there is of power in sound / To breathe an elevated mood, by form / Or image unprofaned; and I would stand / Beneath some rock, listening to sounds that are / The ghostly language of the ancient earth, / Or make their dim abode in distant winds.[22]

And the *Tao te Ching*:

> The name that can be named / is not the eternal Name. // The un-nameable is the eternally real. / Naming is the origin / of all things. // Free from desire, you realize the mystery. / Caught in desire, you see only the manifestations. // Yet mystery and manifestations / arise from the same source. / This source is called darkness. // Darkness within darkness. / The gateway to all understanding.[23]

In both cases we have expressions of sublime experience that do not attempt to analyze or theorize that experience, that do not attempt to "talk about" the sublime at all, but instead use poetic language to communicate a feeling the author has or has had. While such descriptions or expressions may be evocative, they do nothing for a purported theory of the sublime. If this is what we are left with, it is so philosophically limited as to amount to nothing in the way of a theory of the sublime.

What may be most unsatisfying about this third option—the sublime as a feeling whether intentional or nonintentional—is that it rejects the history of talk about the sublime to date. The fundamental questions of a tradition—What kinds of objects are sublime? What does the sublime tell us about ourselves as subjects? and, centrally, What does sublime experience illuminate about the limitations of our access to the world? —have no purchase in a purely phenomenological or emotional account. This is deeply unsatisfying because if we accept this option, we must conclude that a theory of the sublime such as we have historically striven for is simply out of reach.

Let me briefly review my claims in closing. I have argued that if we accept Sircello's articulation of the problem with theories of the sublime, we are tasked with the difficulties attendant upon the notion of epistemological transcendence, the major theme that runs through historical attempts to theorize the sublime. This theme seems to incorporate a second theme of ontological transcendence that binds us to problematic ontological commitments even when these are unarticulated. Even the sophisticated treatment to which Kant subjected the sublime is not immune to this problem. The sublime, we have seen, cannot be an object of experience, but neither can it be a description of the cognitive failure of a given subject. If it is to deal only with some feeling or emotive state, it devolves to no theory whatsoever. In the one interpretation, the sublime can be nothing; in the second, anything; and in the third, it cannot be theorized at all.[24]

## Questions

1. Does Forsey's interpretation of authors from the history of aesthetics (Kant, Addison, Burke, et al.) seem accurate? Explain.

2. Do you agree with Forsey that it is inconsistent to claim that an object can be both transcendent and familiar? Explain.

3. Is there a tension between Forsey's dismissal of feeling-based theories toward the end of the article, on the one hand, and, on the other, her interpretation of the Kantian sublime as a "feeling" ("this feeling of sublimity")? Explain.

4. If you wanted to argue that a theory of the sublime were possible, how might you do that? Responding to the trilemma she presents at the end of her article, provide such an argument.

5. What does "theory" mean in Forsey's article, and in what way does she offer an "error theory"? What should a plausible or viable theory of the sublime provide or be able to do?

## Further reading

Brady, Emily. "The Environmental Sublime," in the present volume.
Clewis, Robert R. "Towards A Theory of the Sublime and Aesthetic Awe," in the present volume.
Deligiorgi, Katerina. "The Pleasures of Contra-purposiveness: Kant, the Sublime, and Being Human." *Journal of Aesthetics and Art Criticism* 72, no. 1 (2014): 25–35.
Forsey, Jane. *The Aesthetics of Design*. New York: Oxford University Press, 2013.
Forsey, Jane, Joseph Margolis, Rachel Zuckert, Tom Hanauer, Robert R. Clewis, Sandra Shapshay, and Jennifer A. McMahon. *The Possibility of the Sublime: Aesthetic Exchanges*, ed. Lars Aagaard-Mogensen. Newcastle upon Tyne: Cambridge Scholars Publishing, 2017.
Pillow, Kirk. *Sublime Understanding: Aesthetic Reflection in Kant and Hegel*. Cambridge, MA: MIT Press, 2000.
Shapshay, Sandra. "A Theory of Sublime Responses, the Thin and the Thick," in the present volume.

# CHAPTER 36
# SANDRA SHAPSHAY, "A THEORY OF SUBLIME RESPONSES, THE THIN AND THE THICK" (2017)

Sandra Shapshay works primarily on the history of aesthetics and ethics in the nineteenth century, with a particular focus on Schopenhauer and Kant, aiming to bring the insights of this history to bear on contemporary debates. In the following chapter, Shapshay responds to Jane Forsey's 2007 article and develops her own ideas on the sublime, in particular, the claim that there are at least two kinds of sublime responses: the thick and the thin.

## Note on the text

The following is a revised version of Sandra Shapshay, "Commentary on Jane Forsey's 'Is a Theory of the Sublime Possible?'," in *The Possibility of the Sublime: Aesthetic Exchanges*, edited by Lars Aagaard-Mogensen, 69–80. Newcastle upon Tyne: Cambridge Scholars Publishing, 2017. All changes have been made with the permission of the author.

In "The Sublime, Redux," in *The Possibility of the Sublime*, 92–106, Forsey replied to her commentators, including Shapshay.

## "A Theory of Sublime Responses, the Thin and the Thick"

Nearly ten years ago, Jane Forsey published a provocative article in the *Journal of Aesthetics and Art Criticism* titled "Is a Theory of the Sublime Possible?"[1] Against the prevailing tide of postmodern and Kantian enthusiasm for the sublime, she offered a negative answer to this question, arguing that historical and contemporary theorizing about the sublime faces a kind of irresolvable dilemma. The dilemma is essentially this: A theory of the sublime can either explain the sense of epistemological transcendence by making use of "problematic ontological commitments" (388), such as the claim to a transcendent reality or supersensible noumenal self as moral law-giver (Kant); or such a theory can shed these problematic ontological commitments (Sircello, Budd), but then will have tremendous difficulty in explaining the elevated pleasure—as opposed to mere cognitive frustration or existential anxiety—that seems to characterize genuinely sublime experience.[2]

For the past several years, I have been working on reconstructing historical theories of sublime experience for use in contemporary aesthetics, and I appreciate Forsey's challenge to aestheticians like myself to become more methodologically self-conscious. In what follows, I aim to show that such theoretical work in aesthetics can survive the above dilemma.[3]

## I Preliminary remarks on theorizing sublime responses

Before attempting to resolve the dilemma, however, one needs to clarify what a "theory of the sublime" is supposed to do. Forsey provides some guidance here: Such a theory should answer fundamental questions to the tradition like "What kinds of objects are sublime? What does the sublime tell us about ourselves as subjects? And, centrally, What does sublime experience illuminate about the limits of our access to the world?" (388). Indeed, a theory of the sublime should answer such questions, but they are actually secondary to the first order of business: To illuminate what I see as a *family of aesthetic responses* that share a common core—namely, an experience of feeling at once overwhelmed and humbled, but also exalted by an object, an environment, or a work of art—that many people have had and some have explicitly proclaimed to have had, especially in the European tradition and especially since the eighteenth-century to the present.[4]

Further, it is important to be clear on the nature of the object of theorizing. Unlike objects of study such as $H_2O$, the laws of thermodynamics, or the geological phenomenon of the Grand Canyon, sublime responses are *subjective human phenomena*. By 'subjective' I do not mean to say that there is no objectivity to judgments of the sublime—in fact I think they can be intersubjectively valid[5]—rather what I mean is that the sublime consists in a *subject's* affective and cognitive response to perceptual experience of an object like a work of art or, more paradigmatically, an environment.[6]

Unfortunately, some of the discussion of "The Sublime" to date has suffered from seeing the response as a univocal response that human beings have to such vast/overwhelming things in the world. In what follows I shall argue that aestheticians should *not* conceive of "the sublime" as a univocal phenomenon and should instead conceive of it as *a family of aesthetic responses*, paradigmatically but not exclusively to vast and overwhelming natural objects and environments. And where there is certainly family resemblance there are also important differences in the phenomenal character and cognitive richness of experiences properly called "sublime."

It should be noted at the outset, however, that there are limitations on any theory that aims to bring some clarity to *subjective* human responses, and accordingly a theory of sublime responses is not going to admit of a great deal of precision. Thus, to quote Aristotle concerning ethics, "our discussion will be adequate if it has as much clearness as the subject-matter admits of …. We must be content, then, in speaking of such subjects and with such premises to indicate the truth roughly and in outline."[7] In this Aristotelian spirit, then, I would like to offer a theory that lays out a spectrum of sublime responses—ranging from the thin to the thick—that share some core characteristic features, but I shall not be offering a Platonic list of necessary and sufficient conditions for having a sublime response.

What is more, I believe sublime responses are highly *historical and cultural*, unlike, say, the response of disgust. The disgust response has also been socially elaborated and is responsive to changing worldviews (e.g., shifting views on homosexuality), but it seems to have a more hard-wired, primordial core to it, for instance, in regard to rotting things, perforations of bodily integrity, and the like.[8] The disgust response also has a pan-cultural facial expression associated with it (a kind of slightly open-mouthed frown), which seems to play an important socio-biological function, warning others about unhealthful food.

But one might think the response of awe is a close cousin to or perhaps even synonymous with the sublime, and psychologists have theorized awe as having a primordial core, namely, "an emotional reaction of a subordinate to a powerful leader."[9] But I think awe, even culturally-elaborated awe, while bearing some resemblance to the sublime, is a distinct response. For psychologists Keltner and Haidt, awe consists in "emotional experiences that involve perceived vastness and a need for accommodation, whether in response to a charismatic leader, a grand vista, or a symphony…"[10] And while some of these experiences—to the grand vista or symphony—may be genuinely aesthetic, that is, involving distributed attention to the perceptual features of an object or environment, the feeling of being humbled by a charismatic leader, be it Hitler or Gandhi, need not involve actual aesthetic attention. So one main difference I see is that the sublime is an *aesthetic* response, involving aesthetic attention, but awe is a more general response and need not be aesthetic.

Another difference has to do with the phenomenology of awe and the sublime. The former seems an entirely humbling sort of experience. Martha Nussbaum writes, for instance that in "awe I want to kneel."[11] The emphasis here as well as in Keltner and Haidt's analysis seems to be on accommodation, submission, and on one's own humility with respect to the vast object/environment/person, whereas the paradigmatic phenomenology of the sublime involves a feeling of humility but also a feeling of *exaltation* of the self.

Consider, for example, one of the archetypical (though by now almost Kitsch) German Romantic paintings meant to capture and evoke a sublime response, Caspar David Friedrich's *Wanderer above a Sea of Fog*.

Note that the solitary wanderer in this painting, whose back faces us so that we are invited to take his perspective, is in the dead center of this painting, on a craggy, mountain pedestal, as it were. And note also

**Figure 3** *Wanderer über dem Nebelmeer*, Caspar David Friedrich, circa 1818, Hamburger Kunsthalle / bpk Bildagentur / Photo: Elke Walford / Art Resource, NY.

that while he is likely overwhelmed by the vastness and mysteriousness of the landscape, he is distinctly not kneeling. If he were kneeling, that would certainly express an emotion of awe. But by contrast, he stands proudly atop the peak, one knee jutting forward, one elbow jutting out, his jaunty walking stick completing the tripod on which he is balanced. It is an image that depicts and evokes simultaneously feelings of humility and exaltation (the sublime) rather than humility and accommodation (awe).

Speaking of sublime mountain vistas, some positive evidence for the claim that sublime responses have a cultural history can be found in Marjorie Hope Nicolson's classic study of discourse on the aesthetic experience of mountains. She argues that a profound shift in aesthetic attitudes occurred in the West between 1660 and 1800, noting that in the period from classical antiquity to the Renaissance, while there was a notion of the 'rhetorical sublime' dating to a treatise by Longinus, there was no corresponding 'natural sublime' response in recorded poetry and literature, at least with respect to mountainous landscapes. When mountains figured in literature they were described as "'Nature's Shames and Ills' and 'Warts, Wens, Blisters, Imposthumes' upon the otherwise fair face of Nature." But by the eighteenth-century mountains were regarded as "temples of Nature built by the Almighty" and "natural cathedrals."[12]

Although Nicolson's study does not treat recorded attitudes to other paradigmatically sublime phenomena, and it alone does not show that sublime response does not have a primordial core, the shift in attitudes toward mountains does provide some evidence to suggest that the 'natural sublime' may not be a perennial human response to vast or powerful nature, but is rather, a category of human aesthetic experience that developed when *beliefs and attitudes* about nature changed and helped to enable a response of 'delightful horror' rather than simply horror or repulsion. Additional support for the notion that there are decided shifts in the dynamics of taste in the history of nature appreciation, e.g., with respect to the aesthetic category of the picturesque, has been provided by the work of American cultural historian and critic, John Conron.[13]

Finally, another reason to think that sublime responses have a cultural history, is that they often rely largely on visual perception (of typically vast or powerful phenomena), and visual perception (meaning, the *interpretation* of what our retinal systems actually detect) seems itself to have a history. Although I cannot wade seriously into the longstanding debate whether 'vision has a history' that has raged among art historians and philosophers of perception, I would like to follow Bence Nanay here in siding with the pro-history-side of this debate. Nanay argues from art-historical evidence as well as from Renaissance art-critical discourse, that Western Europeans developed a kind of two-fold attention some time in the sixteenth-century. That is to say, before the sixteenth-century, it seems that Western Europeans only attended to what was represented in pictures rather than to the surface design of the picture (e.g., the brushstrokes themselves). Nanay concludes that there was likely "a shift, sometime in the sixteenth century, in the way we exercised our attention when looking at pictures."[14]

Given Nicolson's view that background metaphysical/theological *beliefs* can importantly affect aesthetic responses, and given Nanay's view that habits of visual attention seem to have changed in the course of history, and given that the sublime, unlike awe, is a specifically *aesthetic* response, I believe we have good reason to reckon with the likely historical situatedness of sublime responses.

Additionally, there is reason to believe that sublime response may not be universal among cultures. In a comparative study of everyday aesthetics in the Western and Japanese traditions, Yuriko Saito has pointed to the conspicuous absence of the category of the sublime in Japanese aesthetics and the conspicuous absence of paradigmatically sublime themes in works of art. She notes that in depictions and poetic descriptions of what would be paradigmatically sublime phenomena in the West (typhoons, for instance), Japanese artists tend to appreciate, depict or describe the beautiful calm *after* the typhoon.[15]

Further evidence for the cultural-situatedness of sublime responses can be garnered from work on cross-cultural visual attention. Recent empirical studies suggest that "while Westerners attend more to focal objects, East Asians are more likely to attend to the background context. For example, when looking at a short footage of an aquarium, Westerners tend to attend to the moving fish, whereas East Asians tend to attend to features such as the bubbles and the seaweed."[16] If visual attention itself varies across cultures, it is likely that sublime responses—many of which depend on visual perception—would also vary across cultures.

Given this evidence for the historical and cultural-situatedness of aesthetic responses like the sublime, and the intertwined nature of such responses with ideas about the human place in the cosmos, I believe that a theory of the sublime had better acknowledge that such responses may come and go in time and be present in certain cultures and not others. In this way, my treatment of the concept of the sublime here is very much in the spirit of Lydia Goehr's work in offering an historical understanding of the concept of the "musical work." Rather than seeing the "musical work" as a kind of Platonic essence, as analytic philosophers of music are wont to do, Goehr has argued that the concept has a distinctive origin and history within the European classical music tradition.[17] I believe the concept of "the sublime" as well as sublime responses themselves have an origin and a history that is intertwined with the self-understanding of human beings especially as concerns their relationship with nature.

Given these limitations on a theory of sublime aesthetic response, what productive theoretical work might still be done?

## II  Is there a contemporary sublime response?

Although I do not think sublime responses are perennial, hard-wired human responses to certain natural environments and works of art, nonetheless, experiences of being both overwhelmed and exalted, terrified and exhilarated, and humbled and elevated in the presence of certain natural environments and works of art seems still to be with us in European and Anglo-American descriptions of encounters with nature and art. Thus, this kind of aesthetic response is worth recognition by and theoretical attention from contemporary aestheticians.

Consider, for instance, John Muir's description of his experience of a windstorm in the forest of the Yuba River Valley:

> There is always something deeply exciting, not only in the sounds of winds in the woods, which exert more or less influence over every mind, but in their varied waterlike flow as manifested by the movements of the trees, especially those of the conifers…. The waving of a forest of the giant Sequoias is indescribably impressive and sublime…. Most people like to look at mountain rivers, and bear them in mind; but few care to look at the winds, though far more beautiful and sublime, and though they become at times about as visible as flowing water…. We all travel the milky way together, trees and men; but it never occurred to me until this storm-day, while swinging in the wind [atop a Douglas Spruce], that trees are travelers, in the ordinary sense. They make many journeys, not extensive ones, it is true; but our own little journeys, away and back again, are only little more than tree-wavings—many of them not so much.[18]

Not only does Muir use the term 'sublime' to describe his experience of this forest whipped up by a powerful wind storm, his description includes many of the hallmarks of the aesthetic category as theorized by Burke, Kant, and Schopenhauer: the environment is experienced as 'deeply exciting', 'indescribably impressive', and leads Muir to entertain thoughts, by his report *for the first time*, concerning the existential similarities between trees and human beings, namely, that the lives of trees also involve journeys, and that human journeys "away and back again, are only little more than tree-wavings." Here we have Muir describing a sense of being humbled by the sequoia journeys: they bring to mind the puniness of "our own little [human] journeys" which had formerly seemed quite grand and extensive, but now seemed "little more than tree-wavings—many of them not so much." But we also get a sense of Muir as being exalted by the thought that these giant, old, majestic trees and human beings all "travel the milky way together."

More recently, in an article for National Geographic, nature writer Donovan Webster recounts this experience of exploring a volcanic environment on the South Pacific island of Vanuatu:

> I lower myself into the volcano. Acidic gas bites my nose and eyes….The breathing of Benbow's pit is deafening … each new breath from the volcano heaves the air so violently my ears pop in the changing pressure—the temperature momentarily soars. Somewhere not too far below, red-hot, pumpkin-size globs of ejected lava are flying through the air….Yet suspended hundreds of feet above lava up to 2,200 degrees Fahrenheit that reaches toward the center of the Earth, I'm also discovering there's more. It is stupefyingly beautiful. The enormous noise. The deep, orangey red light from spattering lava….It is like nowhere else on Earth.[19]

Although the author never uses the term "sublime," the phrase "stupefyingly beautiful" seems synonymous. Webster experiences the volcanic environment as fearsome and recognizes that one significant slip of the rope would annihilate him, but in his relative safety he is able simultaneously to acknowledge the fearsomeness and to bracket the personal anxiety to appreciate the environment aesthetically. His experience is a mixed painful/pleasurable one, painful from the threatening nature of the lava, the "acidic gas" that irritates his nose and eyes, and from the strain on his ears caused by the "enormous noise" and atmospheric pressure, but also exhilaratingly pleasurable due to the display of "deep, orangey red light", the play of "pumpkin-size globs of ejected lava," and the environment's other-worldly appearance. Arguably, Webster is here describing a sublime response without explicitly utilizing the term.

Finally, take a description of being "emotionally moved by nature" given by aesthetician, Noël Carroll:

> Earlier I conjured up a scene where standing near a towering cascade, our ears reverberating with the roar of falling water, we are overwhelmed and excited by its grandeur. People quite standardly seek out such experiences. They are, pretheoretically, a form of appreciating nature. Moreover, when caught up in such experiences our attention is fixed on certain aspects of the natural expanse rather than others— the palpable force of the cascade, its height, the volume of water, the way it alters the surrounding atmosphere, etc. This does not require any special scientific knowledge. Perhaps it only requires being human, equipped with the senses we have, being small, and able to intuit the immense force, relative to creatures like us, of the roaring tons of water….That is, we may be aroused emotionally by nature, and our arousal may be a function of our human nature in response to a natural expanse.[20]

Carroll is making a point here against Allen Carlson's "scientific cognitivist" theory of proper environmental appreciation, but in the process he characterizes a version of the Burkean sublime response of being emotionally "overwhelmed and excited" by the grandeur of the cascade, while attending to its "palpable force" which makes us feel small and vulnerable, but which we behold excitedly at a safe distance.

## III  Two types of sublime response, the 'thin' and the 'thick'

Much of the theorizing of sublime experience in the eighteenth and nineteenth centuries aimed at explicating the source of the pleasure in these kinds of experiences. Of the three central aesthetic categories of the day—

the beautiful, the picturesque and the sublime—only the *sublime* threatened to seem paradoxical. While the "idea of beauty," for Burke, was "founded on pleasure," that of the sublime was founded "on pain";[21] thus he describes sublime pleasure in oxymoronic terms as a "delightful horror" and a "sort of tranquility tinged with terror."[22] More mildly, Addison characterizes sublime response as "a pleasing astonishment,"[23] and Kant describes it as a "negative" rather than a "positive pleasure," in which "the mind is not merely attracted by the object, but is also always reciprocally repelled by it."[24]

Philosophers took up the following questions: Why do people feel pleasure with respect to objects that do not conform to the conditions of beauty (e.g., harmony, proportion, delicacy) and are instead experienced as vast, overwhelming, or terrifying? (Burke); whence the pleasure with objects recognized as contrapurposive for our cognitive faculties, or which make us feel powerless or existentially insignificant? (Kant and Schopenhauer). Deepening the sense of paradoxicality is the view that the experience of the sublime is actually more profound and satisfying than that of the beautiful, Burke calling it the "strongest emotion which the mind is capable of feeling,"[25] even though, for its mixture with pain, the sublime seems less promising for aesthetic pleasure.

From this tradition we may derive a distinction between two phenomenological descriptions of sublime response that I call the 'thin' and the 'thick' sublime. Burke's physiological account understands the sublime as an immediate emotional but not highly intellectual aesthetic response (call this the 'thin sublime'), whereas Kant (and later Schopenhauer's) transcendental accounts understand the sublime as an emotional response in which the cognitive faculties play a significant role (call this the 'thick sublime').

Due to the differences in the phenomenological descriptions of sublime response, these accounts also offer differing explanations of the source of sublime pain and pleasure. While the 'thin' sublime accounts for the pain as resulting from a perceived threat to the organism and the pleasure as a physiologically generated sense of relief; the transcendental explanations of sublime response understand the pain as deriving from a more reflective recognition of human existential or cognitive limitation, and the pleasure from an equally reflective sense of human transcendence of those limitations. Thus, 'thick' sublime response involves reflection on the complexities of the relationship between human beings and the world in which we find ourselves, whereas 'thin' sublime response does not, and consists rather in a bare cognitive appraisal of the object and immediate affective arousal.[26]

In the foregoing quotes which describe sublime experiences, the passage from Muir describes, in my terms, a thick sublime experience since he describes it as including reflection on the frailty and insignificance of human journeys as well as the exalted way in which humans and giant sequoias alike travel the Milky Way together. By contrast, the passages from Webster and Carroll, which lack any account of reflection on the human place in nature, and focus rather on the formal, perceptual features of the environment which overwhelm, frighten, excite and exalt the spectator, seem to describe 'thin' sublime responses.

A similar distinction can be found in the work of Robert Clewis. In a recent essay review on Emily Brady's 2013 book, *The Sublime in Modern Philosophy: Aesthetics, Ethics, and Nature*, Clewis offers a helpful Kant-inspired distinction between 'adherent' and 'free' sublimity in the service of resolving a debate between Brady and "scientific cognitivists" concerning the appropriate aesthetic appreciation of nature.[27] An adherent judgment of the sublime, for Clewis, whether it be of nature or of art, would involve crucially "the incorporation of a concept of the object," that is, the incorporation of relevant scientific background knowledge of nature, or of the relevant art-historical context of the work being appreciated.[28] Whereas a 'free' judgment of the sublime would be a judgment that would not involve much in the way of background knowledge of the object of appreciation, but would rather be grounded on a response to the formal, perceptual features of the object or work.

While this distinction bears some similarity to the one I am making between thick and thin sublime response, however, they come apart in two ways. First, the adherent/free distinction tracks the cognitive stock (or lack thereof) concerning the object of appreciation that one *brings to* the encounter, whereas the thick/thin distinction tracks predominantly the cognitive reflection (or lack thereof) that *issues from* the encounter.

Thus, while there could certainly be a psychological link between bringing a good deal of background knowledge to an experience of the sublime and having a thick experience of the sublime—and in the case of Muir cited above, I think we might have a case of this sort—still the two distinctions are conceptually distinct, for one could bring a lot of background knowledge to the experience and still have a thin sublime experience. In the case of Webster in the volcano, for instance, while it seems he brought a great deal of scientific understanding to the experience, e.g., he knows that the lava gets up to "2,200 degrees Fahrenheit" and that it "reaches toward the center of the Earth," this background knowledge does not feature prominently in his aesthetic experience with the volcano. His response seems to be of a 'thin sublime' kind, that is, it is a response largely to the formal, perceptual features of the environment, e.g., "the enormous noise" and "the deep, orangey red light from spattering lava." In short, his background knowledge does not issue in any significant reflection on the self or the place of human beings generally in nature, and so while his experience may be adherent, it is not thick.

Another difference between Clewis's distinction and mine is that in adherent judgments of the sublime, the knowledge brought to bear concerns "facts known or believed about the object of contemplation" rather than "facts about the subject (its power, freedom)."[29] The 'thick sublime,' by contrast, involves facts known or believed about objects as well as facts known or believed about the subject(s) of aesthetic contemplation, for this kind of sublime experience has to do centrally with *the relationship* between the subject and the overwhelming object or environment.

Ultimately, then, while these two sets of distinctions overlap on the axis of 'how much or little cognition' is present in the judgment or experience of the sublime, they differ on (a) whether that cognition is *brought to* the encounter, or *issues from* the encounter, and (b) whether the cognition is solely *object* focused or is *both subject and object* focused.

## IV Addressing Forsey's dilemma

In order to utilize the Kantian 'thick' or Burkean 'thin' accounts of the sublime for contemporary aesthetics, however, one should answer a critic like Forsey, who sees both the thick and the thin sublime as problematic from a theoretical standpoint. With respect to the thick sublime (Kant's theory), she holds that while the theory can account for the source of pleasurable exaltation (i.e., in a felt recognition of the supersensible part of us, either rational-cognitive or rational-moral), it gets caught on the first horn of the dilemma in being ineluctably and egregiously tied to ungrounded, speculative-metaphysical ideas incompatible with a secular, scientific worldview. Thus the Kantian theory of the sublime seems to involve outmoded transcendent-metaphysical notions that should have no place in a contemporary aesthetic theory.

The thin sublime experience would seem to fare better by the lights of Forsey's criticisms, as it sheds such Kantian metaphysical underpinnings, but it gets caught on the second horn of the dilemma, that is, it is unclear without those moral-metaphysical underpinnings how the pleasure from the experience is to be generated at all. The source of pleasure is chalked up to the feeling of *relief* from cognitive frustration or existential threat, but this seems to open the floodgates to all manner of not-exactly-sublime-sounding experiences (giving up on difficult crossword puzzles and ice-climbing) to be classified erroneously as sublime.

In particular, Forsey cites the safe arrival home from riding one's bike in traffic as having all the hallmarks of this kind of non-metaphysically laden sublime response according to Budd's Burkean theory of the sublime, but she holds that this hardly seems to get at what sublime experience consists in (386). Let me try to respond to the difficulties Forsey has raised for both thick and thin accounts of sublime response in turn.

With respect to the thick variety of sublime experience, recall Marjorie Hope Nicolson's documentation of the change that took place between 1600 and 1800 with respect to recorded European aesthetic attitudes toward mountains. When people were in the grip of a theological view that saw mountains as God's punishment on humankind, as a result of the Fall, it makes sense that mountains would be viewed as ugly and scary. But when people later came to see mountains not as punishment but rather as evidence of God's supreme power and providence, mountains could be experienced, in light of this revised religious background, as sublime. But to answer Forsey's worry, can a sublime response to mountains, the starry night sky, or a raging storm at sea be understood nowadays in modern, secular, non-egregiously metaphysical terms?

I believe that the metaphysical commitments in a theory of "thick sublime" experience need not be understood as egregious, for one does not need not follow Kant in the positing of an actual "noumenal self" in order to cash out the sense of elevation felt in these experiences. In fact, the "ontological commitments" of the thick sublime may be understood as modest and reasonable, for instance, as a commitment to an experience of human freedom and moral responsibility that is very unlikely to be satisfactorily explained in naturalistic terms; or the experience of the simultaneous limitations on human knowledge but also the persistent and noble desire of human beings to push all cognitive boundaries. Muir's sense of elevation derives, it seems, from the fact that human beings and giant sequoia trees are all travelers in the same Milky Way. Understood in these ways, an explication of the source of the elevating pleasure need only be committed to a modest degree of mysterianism, i.e., the view that there are certain really persistent mysteries of the human condition relating to, for example, the nature of consciousness, the relationship between mind and brain, the feeling of free will and moral responsibility, and whether or not there is a purpose for human beings, or trees, or anything in the universe!

A modern scientific worldview might rule out certain "ontological commitments" as extravagantly speculative, but it remains consistent with scientific understanding to hold that certain facets of the human condition are likely to remain forever mysterious, such as the oddness of the human being's feeling of free will; the apparent ability to act in a non-egoistic fashion, say, even in the face of an existentially threatening storm; or the strangeness of a human being's desire to fathom nature in its totality, or to fathom the purpose of human beings in the universe, as well as the recognition of the difficulty (and perhaps impossibility) of ever attaining these cognitive goals. In short, such reflection in the course of an aesthetic encounter seems perfectly consistent with what our best science tells us about the relationship between human beings and nature. Science does not explain many of the oddities of the human condition nor does it rule out as irrational a train of aesthetic reflection on these and other very old, philosophical questions that tend to be sparked by vast and overwhelming environments or works of art.

Take for example the experience of overwhelming finitude but also exalting reflection on the place of humanity in the environment in an encounter with the starry night sky. Such response will likely persist no matter how much scientific, modern understanding one brings to the encounter. Given the vastness of the phenomenon, the long duration of the stars, and the mind-boggling scale of the universe, it seems likely for a subject's experience of the thick sublime to be only deepened by scientific understanding, by prompting more-informed reflection on how infinitesimally small she is in the universe, how short a human lifespan is, and even how briefly the human species has walked this planet, in comparison with the spatial and temporal vastness of the night sky.

In sum, feelings of humility and exaltation at various facets of the universe, reflection on human cognitive and existential limitations, as well as reflection on human powers and our strangely exceptional status within nature, have been and can be for many people, awakened through aesthetic experience with vast or threatening natural environments, and similar works of art, and it seems perfectly appropriate—by the lights of our best science—that this should be the case. In short, the "problematic ontological commitments" that

Forsey believes are ineluctably linked to such experience are not so ontological and not so problematic after all.

With respect to the 'thin sublime,' we need to take up Forsey's challenge for a theory to distinguish between a bona fide sublime response rather than an experience of mere relief. To help think through this, recall Carroll's description of being immediately emotionally moved by a perceptual encounter with a cascade:

> [Imagine] a scene where standing near a towering cascade, our ears reverberating with the roar of falling water, we are overwhelmed and excited by its grandeur....When caught up in such experiences our attention is fixed on certain aspects of the natural expanse rather than others—the palpable force of the cascade, its height, the volume of water, the way it alters the surrounding atmosphere, etc. This does not require any special scientific knowledge. Perhaps it only requires being human, equipped with the senses we have, being small, and able to intuit the immense force, relative to creatures like us, of the roaring tons of water....That is, we may be aroused emotionally by nature, and our arousal may be a function of our human nature in response to a natural expanse.[30]

In contrast with Carroll's description, here are some experiences Forsey thinks might be erroneously caught in the expansive net of a Burkean 'relief' theory of the sublime (Budd):

> [W]hat of the cognitive failure I have occasionally experienced in the face of the *New York Times* crossword puzzle, or complex mathematical problems that truly humble me? What of the rush athletes experience from dangerous sports such as ice-climbing or heli-skiing? What of the vulnerability I feel when riding my bicycle in rush-hour traffic and making it—just—home safely? Why are these sorts of experiences not also sublime or, at any rate, equal candidates for the kind of pleasure that a subjective account would properly call sublime? (386)

It seems the key to responding to Forsey's worries about a non-metaphysical theory promiscuously casting too wide a net onto non-sublime experiences is to ensure that the phenomenology laid out by such a theory is genuinely *aesthetic* (i.e., involves a special, pleasurable, sustained, distributed attention to the perceptual features of an object/environment). And to make it, further, sublime, it must include some feeling of being overwhelmed or humbled (cognitively or existentially) and a feeling of exaltation, not just mere relief.[31]

With this additional stipulation on the theory of the thin sublime, the experiences Forsey describes above could be candidates for sublime response but only provided that they involve some genuine *aesthetic* attention to the object/environment, as well as an emotional response that involves a feeling of being overwhelmed (limitation) and excited (exaltation). As described in bare form above, the experience of crossword puzzles, ice-climbing and bike-riding through traffic do not sound sublime, but they could very well be if they involved actual aesthetic attention and excited/exalted emotional arousal in response to a fearsome or overwhelming work or environment.

Thus, to sum up, I think the key to overcoming Forsey's dilemma for a theory of the thick sublime is to show that the metaphysical commitments really amount to no more than a modest mysterianism about certain aspects of the human condition, and is, accordingly, not egregiously speculative. And the key to resolving the promiscuity problem for a theory of the thin sublime is to spell out to a greater extent in the theory that the phenomenology must involve aesthetic attention and emotional arousal of an exalted nature.

In closing, I should add that Paul Crowther has offered what I believe is an excellent and underappreciated start at articulating a theory of the contemporary, *artistic* sublime. He gives a three-fold account of an artistic sublime that is loosely based on the framework of Kant's theory, an elaboration of what I have been calling the thick sublime. Crowther jettisons, however, Kant's faculty psychology and the pivotal role played by the recognition of one's rational vocation, proffering the following definition:

> the sublime is an item or set of items which, through the possession or suggestion of perceptually, imaginatively, or emotionally overwhelming properties, succeeds in rendering the scope of some human capacity vivid to the senses.[32]

He holds that this (thick) artistic sublime response to art may arise in three main ways:

1. "through the overwhelming perceptual scale of a work making vivid the scope of human artifice"
2. "through a work's overwhelming personal significance making vivid the scope of artistic creation"
3. "through the imaginatively overwhelming character of some general truth embodied in a work, making vivid the scope of artistic expression."[33]

Much more needs to be said to put flesh on the bones of this theory, obviously, but I wanted to offer one valuable attempt to theorize specifically artistic sublime responses in a manner that does not involve "problematic ontological commitments." Notwithstanding the looseness with which the term 'sublime' is often used in the academy and in the artworld today, I believe that two coherent accounts of sublime response—thin and thick sublime responses, constituting a spectrum of aesthetic responses with a shared phenomenological core—have emerged from the tradition of aesthetic theorizing that can withstand Forsey's criticisms. Such theories of the sublime are not just possible, but, updated as I have endeavored to do in this paper, I believe they can even be quite helpful in mapping the contemporary aesthetic landscape.

## Questions

1. Do you think the experience of the sublime is pan-cultural, culturally situated, or both? Explain.
2. How does what you have experienced or learned (say, background knowledge) affect your responses to the sublime?
3. Can you discern what Shapshay calls the "thin" and "thick" responses in any other accounts of the sublime (besides those of Burke and Kant/Schopenhauer)? Explain.
4. Does Shapshay imply that a person needs to be religiously oriented in order to have an experience of the "thick" sublime? Explain.

## Further reading

Forsey, Jane, Joseph Margolis, Rachel Zuckert, Tom Hanauer, Robert R. Clewis, Sandra Shapshay, and Jennifer A. McMahon. *The Possibility of the Sublime: Aesthetic Exchanges*, ed. Lars Aagaard-Mogensen. Newcastle upon Tyne: Cambridge Scholars Publishing, 2017.

# CHAPTER 37
## ROBERT R. CLEWIS, "TOWARDS A THEORY OF THE SUBLIME AND AESTHETIC AWE"

In *The Possibility of the Sublime*, Clewis commented on Jane Forsey's 2007 article on the sublime, and Forsey replied to commentators (see Note on the text).

Below, Clewis recasts his ideas in light of the broader aims of the present volume. He describes features of the objects that paradigmatically incite sublime experiences, characterizes the experience's phenomenology (what it feels like) and intersubjectivity, and identifies five distinct sources of the pleasures in the sublime.

He uses the terms "aesthetic awe" and the "sublime" interchangeably. This is not too far a departure from traditional use of the terms. Contemporary researchers and psychologists use the term "awe" (or sometimes "aesthetic awe") to refer to what writers from the history of aesthetics typically discussed under the terms "the sublime" and "sublimity" (and relatives thereof). Although we may wish to depart from tradition *if* we have compelling reasons to do so, it should be noted that there is a long tradition in the English language of using "awe" and the "sublime" in similar ways and contexts, as demonstrated by writings from Elizabeth Carter and William Wordsworth and contemporary authors such as Carolyn Korsmeyer (among many others). Aesthetic awe, in the proposed view, is a subset of awe. The word "aesthetic" is added, in order to distinguish the topic from the kind of awe felt in a religious experience (described, for instance, by Rudolf Otto) or the awe before a prominent or powerful leader (sociopolitical awe), as in the theory proposed by Dacher Keltner and Jonathan Haidt.[1] Due to its status as an "aesthetic" experience, aesthetic awe can be more easily switched off than can other fundamental emotions,[2] which differentiates aesthetic awe from uncontrollable fear before a great power or threat.

### Note on the text

Some of the following ideas appeared in Robert R. Clewis, "A Theory of the Sublime Is Possible," in *The Possibility of the Sublime: Aesthetic Exchanges*, edited by Lars Aagaard-Mogensen, 45–68. Newcastle upon Tyne: Cambridge Scholars Publishing, 2017. The present chapter is here published for the first time.

### "Towards a theory of the sublime and aesthetic awe"

Of late the sublime has been treated in two strikingly different ways. On the one hand, countless analyses in literary studies, criticism, film studies, and art history make use of the term to convey an object's or artwork's power to evoke an intense, striking, uplifting response, implicitly assuming that a theory of the sublime is possible, without much further discussion. Likewise, some psychologists study "awe" without digging too deeply into the conceptual difficulties.[3] Some film directors are guided by the concept—and, by their own admission, do so with a kind of trusting simplicity. In one of his essays, director Werner Herzog reflects, "The Absolute, the Sublime, the Truth. . . . What do these words mean? This is, I must confess, the first time in my life that I have sought to settle such questions outside of my work, which I understand, first and foremost, in practical terms."[4] On the other hand, some philosophers are skeptical that a viable theory is possible. In presenting her arguments for this conclusion, Jane Forsey claims that, "Our current theorizing about the sublime rests on a mistake."[5] Other scholars have agreed that there appears to be a conceptual problem with the notion of sublimity. "The underlying concern about untheorizability, dispensability, and mere fabrication (i.e., that there's really no *there* there with respect to the sublime) needs to be more directly confronted by aestheticians . . . who propose to retain the concept."[6] Well over a century ago, E. F. Carritt raised worries about the sublime, at least, about the version proposed by Oxford poetry professor A. C. Bradley, who maintained that sublimity was a species of beauty with the added quality of greatness or power. "We may ask if it [the sublime] is a real class at all or only an unessential concept under which almost any divergences from the central type of beauty . . . are arbitrarily put together."[7]

Although the state of scholarship has certainly been improved by responses to such skeptical inquiring, in particular to Forsey's pressing analysis, I do not think that such probing entails that a coherent and consistent theory of the sublime is beyond our reach. I propose that it is possible to come up with a coherent, even fruitful, theory of the sublime. I do not claim that my proposal resolves most of the theoretical issues, or answers nearly all of the conceptual questions, but I hope it is at least a start—an outline of a compelling theory.

In the following, therefore, I sketch a theory of the sublime that is intended to address the problems raised by Forsey and other writers. Drawing from both historical and contemporary sources, I outline a philosophical account of the sublime response and conceive of it as an "aesthetic" experience, which for the purposes of this chapter, I think of as primarily as a response to something perceived rather than thought or conceived. In focusing on perception, I do not intend to deny that experiences of the sublime might be induced by "great thoughts" (as Longinus put it), mathematical proofs, or the like—in short, intellectual content that is not readily perceived. It is just that it is easier to sketch an aesthetic theory with the perceptual cases in mind.

But, what should we expect from a theory of the sublime? Among other things, a convincing account of the sublime should give an explanation of the kinds of *objects* that elicit the experience, the *structure* of the various kinds of sublime responses, and the *sources* of the pleasures in the sublime. (A useful theory should perhaps also show how the sublime differs from negative emotions like disgust and fear, as well as from allied or related states like wonder and the feeling of beauty, but space allows for only passing mention of such differences.) While recognizing the historical and cultural contingency, and the situatedness, of experiences of the sublime (or "sublimes"), my proposal thus addresses the object, structure, and sources of the pleasure.

My account draws from a theory of imagination grounded in the biological and psychological features shared by human beings, and finds some support in—but is certainly not solely based on—recent empirical research. Readers of the present volume will likely be coming from a diverse set of disciplines, and discussions of empirical research can sometimes strike fellow scholars in the humanities as controversial, so perhaps I should say a word about my discussion of empirical research. To put it as briefly as possible, I think it is desirable if a philosophical theory is at least compatible with the latest scientific findings relevant to the topic in question. I take it as evident that philosophy (theory) and science should, where possible, be aligned, and that a philosophical account of a topic should be consistent with, and not contradict, what scientific findings suggest about that topic. I do not claim science is the only source for developing a philosophical theory and do not base my (provisional) theory of the sublime on science alone, but also have independent philosophical and phenomenological grounds for my views, which are also rooted in the contributions by writers from the history of aesthetics, many of them long forgotten or simply passed over. In other words, I look to empirical research for possible additional confirmation of my views and aim to modify the latter if scientific findings suggest that they should be revised.

## The object

As I mentioned in the Introduction to the present volume, there seems to be an unavoidable ambiguity confronting theories of the sublime. The "sublime" can refer to a person's feelings and experiences, and the term can be applied to the object that elicits those responses. I cannot at present see how the sublime can be adequately theorized without acknowledging and paying careful attention to both of these poles, the subjective and the objective. Reflection on the sublime over the course of the centuries (especially the modern period) recognizes both poles, referring, for instance, to feelings, experiences, and mental states as well as to sublime objects. Accordingly, I will deal with both poles.

No object, technically speaking, is inherently sublime. The sublimity of an object requires someone who experiences sublimity. Yet, the sublime is far from being an idiosyncratic response. In other words, we can speak about qualities or characteristics of objects that paradigmatically elicit the experience. Thus, I propose an approach according to which objects typically possessing certain properties or attributes, and perceived in the right contexts, are paradigmatically disposed to evoke the aesthetic experience of the sublime.[8]

Jane Forsey presented arguments against the proposal offered by Guy Sircello, who attempted to respond to questions he raised about the sublime.[9] Sircello wanted to find a way to reinterpret what can be called "epistemological transcendence" (i.e., the claim that one has limited epistemological access to a sublime object) in a way that did not entail "ontological transcendence" (i.e., the claim that an inaccessible sublime entity *exists*). Forsey argued—I think convincingly—that Sircello could not avoid this entailment. She identified the heart of the problem as this: "If we focus on the metaphysical status of the sublime object, our epistemology becomes problematic, but if we address instead the epistemological transcendence of a certain experience, we still seem forced to make *some* metaphysical claim about the object of that experience."[10] In other words, how can we have a fruitful, plausible theory about an object that is inaccessible?[11]

I need not rehearse her carefully crafted arguments here, for her analysis is clear and can stand on its own. However, I think she is wrong about one point; thankfully, this oversight provides a way out of the various dilemmas she puts forward. She holds that the claim that the sublime is familiar and transcendent is inconsistent or contains a contradiction. This strikes me as incorrect. This is the horn of the dilemma that can be grasped and shown to be false.

Taking a cue from Aristotle, we can say the sublime is familiar and transcendent, just not at the same time or in the same way. An object or event can be familiar at one time (or to some people), yet appear transcendent at another time. In experiences of the sublime, a possibly familiar object (say, the Alps for the alpine mountain inhabitants) can be perceived or imagined in a new light, in a rare moment. This move does not entail positing a metaphysically transcendent object—at least not anything beyond the object created by one's imagination (as will be discussed in the penultimate section).

Sircello's claim or thesis that the object is epistemologically inaccessible—a claim that presupposes what I call the "transcendent" or ineffable strand of the sublime—can be questioned for several reasons. First, it leads to the paradoxes Forsey identified; we can avoid the paradoxes if we drop the thesis that the object is epistemologically inaccessible. Second, the thesis fails to describe adequately or capture the phenomenology of the experience. The necessary emotional element of the experience—how the sublime feels—is noticeably absent from accounts emphasizing that the sublime is epistemologically inaccessible.[12] This point about phenomenology leads to a third reason we should give up the notion that this thesis is an essential part of a theory of the sublime: it seems to be based on a category mistake. The thesis that the sublime is epistemologically inaccessible characterizes the sublime as a failed mode of understanding. It turns the problem of the sublime into an epistemological issue, a matter of truth. Tellingly, throughout his paper, Sircello characterizes the problem in terms of adequation to "reality." It is likewise revealing that the conference panel at which Forsey presented an early version of her article in 2005 was called "Knowing the Sublime." The experience of the sublime should be conceived more in terms of play and emotion than in terms of a concern for truth or conformity to reality.

The experience of the sublime should not be conceived as being *of* an inaccessible sublime object. (The grammar of "of" may be misleading us here.) If we want to speak this way (focusing on the object pole), we should claim that an extraordinary experience is of an otherwise ordinary and accessible object: the mountain, volcano, falls, ravine, dam, dome, pyramid, and so on. To put it in psychologically oriented terms, in the sublime the object acts as a stimulus or elicitor of a (rare) mental state and subjective experience.

In contrast to such epistemologically oriented approaches and concerns with adequation, the sublime is better understood in terms of its phenomenological structure, intense emotions and responses (what Sandra Shapshay calls "thick and thin" responses),[13] and in terms of a play of imagination, as I explain below.[14] I propose that the sublime should be conceived as an intense, *affective* response involving our sensory, perceptual, and imaginative powers.[15] I see this as a genuinely aesthetic account—in a sense of "aesthetic" that is faithful to the origin of the word, *aesthēsis*, in which modes of pleasure (or pain) play a crucial and essential role.[16] As David Hume put it when discussing the aesthetic concepts of beauty and deformity: "Pleasure and pain, therefore, are not only necessary attendants of beauty and deformity, but constitute their very essence."[17]

If the sublime is an aesthetic response to an (epistemologically accessible) object, the aesthetic judgment of the sublime, considered as a statement, can take the propositional form "$x$ is sublime," as in the actual propositions, "This mountain is sublime" and "This pyramid is awe-inducing." (Silence, too, is a possible response to the sublime object or event, but in that case one utters no statement.) Poets from various traditions (east and west, north and south), from Li Po to Wordsworth, write about and describe their aesthetic responses to paradigmatic elicitors of the sublime such as mountains and waterfalls.[18]

The storms, rocks, and crags—the kinds of objects to which the predicate "sublime" typically is applied—are epistemologically accessible. Taking this approach removes the need to resolve the paradoxes generated by phrases such as "painting the unpaintable," "presenting the unpresentable," or "giving a finite representation of the infinite."[19] Such formulas were favored not just by German Idealists but also iterated in various francophone theories of the sublime in the late 1980s and 1990s. They are also traceable back to certain passages in Kant (from whom Lyotard and Derrida drew inspiration), Schopenhauer (for whom the sublime reveals the world "in itself"), Schelling, and Hegel. Such approaches give rise to the noted problems associated with how we can have epistemological access to a transcendent object or event.

The sublime object or event (concept, thought)[20] is experienced as, or perceived in that particular moment of attention, as novel, striking, or rare. The concept of novelty enjoyed a rich and detailed treatment by eighteenth-century writers such as Joseph Addison and Edmund Burke and even twentieth-century American pragmatists like Stephen Pepper.[21] The point here is not to fetishize the new or novel, but to emphasize that the object or event is experienced in an extraordinary and striking way, almost as if for the first time. Novelty—and related aesthetic qualities such as being striking—can be characterized as contextualized responses produced by an engagement or encounter between the perceiver and the object, including even old or antiquated artifacts. This explains part of the fascination with ancient ruins, and why they sometimes appear sublime. Novelty disrupts habit, which makes things look familiar and renders us indifferent.[22]

When the object is perceived as familiar, it is not usually part of a stirring and moving experience, nor is it typically accompanied by an intense feeling of satisfaction. As Joseph Priestley put it: "Whenever any object, how great so ever, becomes familiar to the mind . . . the sublime vanishes."[23] Wordsworth's poetry is likewise instructive: "No familiar shapes / Remained [. . .]; / But huge and mighty forms, that do not live / Like living men."[24] As mentioned, no object is inherently sublime. When an object is perceived to be sublime, it is because that same object is experienced in a different way (at a different time) and seen in a new light. The Alps are obviously familiar to the alpine farmers; nevertheless, I see no good reason to deny that the mountains could sometimes elicit sublime responses in the alpine farmers—just as it can in visitors, tourists, and climbers who are likely to perceive the mountainous forms as novel and striking. The fact that the farmers and inhabitants are already present in the natural environment and attuned to their surroundings may even imply that they are sensitive to new aesthetic experiences beyond the ordinary. As Wordsworth writes,

> It is not likely that a person so situated, provided his imagination be exercised by other intercourse, as it ought to be, will become, by any continuance of familiarity, insensible to sublime impressions from the scenes around him. Nay, it is certain that his conceptions of the sublime, far from being dulled or narrowed by commonness or frequency, will be rendered more lively and comprehensive by more accurate observation and by increasing knowledge.[25]

There may be moments of the sublime when the weather is just right, or when the moon appears in a particular way in the landscape. Likewise, some scenes from Kubrick's film *2001: A Space Odyssey* can be considered to be sublime, but they are likely to be viewed with familiarity to any movie house employees who screen the film regularly. While the employees may sometimes feel the sublime in response to such scenes, they need not do so, and they are unlikely do so when they are going about their work, stepping into an auditorium to check the fire exits, or helping late arrivals find their seats. In those moments, they have turned off their focus and are not giving the scene the absorbed attention required for the sublime response. Finally, the massive, magnificent dome or cathedral (pick your favorite example) may be well known to the people who work in the tourist industry that capitalizes on its sublime qualities. Once again, the workers (or nearby inhabitants) may have a sublime response every now and then; the point is simply that, insofar as they experience the object as familiar, the familiarity of the object makes the sublime response very unlikely.

Let us turn to vastness and other qualities associated with the sublime. The "sublime," I suggest, is paradigmatically predicated of objects or events perceived to be vast, grand, colossal, and/or powerful. Due to its size or might, such an object poses a risk or potential threat to the perceiver. It is thus seen (to use Kant's term) as "contra-purposive," that is, apparently unsuited for us, or running counter to our interests, be they cognitive or practical. On the one hand, it seems evident that a thing's size or power is an objective property. An object is $x$ many meters tall or wide, or is rated at $y$ gigawatts. On the other hand, size and power can be perceived in different ways, depending on one's perspective—just as with novelty and familiarity. One can be too close or too far to the object or event for the sublime to occur. It is an obvious fact that the distance from which a mountain, storm, or skyscraper is viewed changes one's experience of it.

As an aesthetic attribute, "vast" is a response-dependent term. The circumstances are crucial. Priestley made a similar point: "The ideas of *great* and *little* are confessedly relative."[26] Kant likewise writes that one should be neither too close nor too far to the Egyptian pyramids (having read reports of it by Savary), so that the object strikes one as being the right size to incite the sublime experience.[27] The Chinese art theoretician Guo Xi (ca. 1000–1090) made a similar observation while offering instruction to landscape painters. Guo Xi (Kuo Hsi) claimed: "A mountain looks this way close by, another way a few miles away, and yet another way from a distance of a dozen miles. Its shape changes at every step."[28] Thus, the perceiver must find the right distance, the sweet spot, and attend properly to the object if the effect is to be achieved. Not all paradigmatically "sublime" objects will always be experienced as sublime. This is one reason why the sublime is an aesthetic quality or property, rather than either a mathematical or merely physical attribute.

Although Burke certainly focuses on physiological and corporeal responses, some elements of his account plainly attend to the features of the object. Burke lists features of objects that in general evoke the sublime: being vast, rugged, massive, and/or powerful. To put it another way, there is a range of multi-sensory qualities or properties paradigmatically involved in the sublime. As Brady puts it in a list that is inspired by Burke's account, "Sublimity involves a range of qualities linked to vastness, enormous size, and power, such as the mysterious, dark, obscure, great, huge, powerful, towering, dizzying, blasting, raging, disordered, dynamic, tumultuous, shapeless, formless, boundless, frameless, and so on."[29] (Note that these are not intended to count as sufficient conditions for stimulating an experience of the sublime.) These challenging qualities contrast with the harmony, symmetry, or order that is typically thought to evoke a sense of beauty or to elicit a calm feeling of grandeur.

Before we turn to the subjective dimension of the sublime, it is worth assessing another potential candidate for the paradigmatically sublime object: ourselves. Some theorists claim (or read eighteenth-century theorists such as Kant or Baillie as claiming) that the sublime is, in the end, an experience of ourselves (as sublime, as great). Are we—or some quality deemed essential to us, such as our moral vocation, humanity, minds, or freedom—the sublime objects? This strikes me as implausible, not least for phenomenological reasons. Such a view would seem to entail that reflexivity is an essential part of the experience. However, it is dubitable that reflexivity is essential to the experience of the sublime. I think that the experience *can* sometimes give rise to a self-conscious reflection on the relation between the experiencing self and the object (what Shapshay calls a "thick" response), but it is not necessary. A "thin" response, in which we do not reflect on ourselves, is also possible.[30]

Empirical and experimental studies give further reasons to doubt that reflexivity is part of the experience of the sublime, and thus to doubt that in the experience we find ourselves to be sublime.[31] If this is correct, a sublime experience can be *reflective* (a matter of aesthetic contemplation), without being *reflexive* (about oneself), and even if the two can occur together in an experience of the sublime, it is useful to distinguish them conceptually. If so, an observer can apprehend or contemplate aesthetically, without explicitly thinking about herself—that is, without reflecting on her own greatness, rational powers, or agency (Shapshay's "thick" response), or even without thinking of herself in comparison to the vast object or natural environs (as Brady describes).[32]

## The structure of sublime responses

Above, I claimed that the vast or powerful object is experienced in a particular context, in a setting that allows the object to be experienced as remarkable, striking, novel, and/or rare. I now turn to the elements having to do with the experiencing subject.

In referring to the "structure" of an experience, one could arguably mean at least two things: the *phenomenology* of the sublime, and the *scope* of the experience—the sublime's being shared or intersubjective. Regarding the former, I hold that the object is responded to with intense, agreeable affect or emotion possessing a dual, that is, negative–positive, phenomenology. Related to the latter is the issue of whether the sublime is relative to certain times and places, or instead pan-cultural (or at least cross-cultural), that is, shared by different cultures. I turn to each of these.

First, let me acknowledge two commitments. As can be seen from the foregoing remarks, I follow Shapshay in speaking of sublime responses rather than of a single homogenous response. Yet the various kinds of responses do have something in common: they share a "phenomenological structure." Second, I do not think it is possible to come up with strict principles or laws for evoking the sublime or to give cases such that somebody *must* find some particular object to be sublime.[33]

I conceive of the subjective pole of the sublime as an intense, mixed, negative–positive experience. The feeling of being overwhelmed is combined with intense satisfaction. Moreover, certain conditions must be met by the experiencing subject. For instance, the person must be in a safe, secure position. So far, I take these claims about the structure of the experience to be rather uncontroversial, widely recognized by theorists over the centuries, from Kant and Schopenhauer to Brady and Freeland.

Since we are speaking of "phenomenology," let me explain some jargon. The phenomenological approach holds that in every act of consciousness there is an "intentional object," which means that there is an object of consciousness (or one might say, *for* consciousness). Forsey raised important questions about whether the feeling of the sublime can be intentional in this sense. If a feeling does not have an intentional object, it cannot be theorized coherently, she reasoned—and quite plausibly. For the feeling would be too undirected and idiosyncratic to be intelligibly generalizable. At most we might be able to report it or, if we were inclined, to write poetry about it. Thus, if we are to theorize a feeling or experience of the sublime, it needs to be demonstrated that the feeling or experience of the sublime has an object of consciousness, in other words, that it is "intentional." Fortunately, I take myself to have done just that in the previous section. There is an object of consciousness in the sublime: a person is conscious of the physical entity or mental object (e.g., a representation of the mountain, film scene, etc.), which is not epistemologically inaccessible.

The experience of the sublime contains a *negative* moment, in response to the object's contra-purposive qualities such as vastness or its menacing, dominating power. Theories have expressed this negative component in various ways, as feelings of vulnerability, uneasiness, and discomfort. Yet, unlike these feelings, and unlike loathing and disgust, the sublime has an uplifting and pleasurable side. This is what attracts us to such experiences, and leads us to remain in and prolong them if possible.

Theorists across the centuries, from Shaftesbury and Kant to Brady and Shapshay, generally describe the sublime as having a two-fold phenomenological structure. The possibility that the structure is actually *three*-fold, recently proposed by Chignell and Haltman, deserves to be mentioned. I am not convinced the third moment or step is necessary, but here is how that account goes. The three moments of the experience, according to their view, are initial bedazzlement, an outstripping of the cognitive faculties, and an epiphany (i.e., a life-affecting change of perspective).[34] But, aren't these really two moments in the end? Bedazzlement in front of the object, and cognitive outstripping, can be reduced to one (negative) moment. As for the positive moment, the lasting change of perspective: I agree that there is a positive moment, but am not sure that it should be conceived in terms of lasting impact. While the notion of a change of outlook may capture an element sometimes associated with the sublime or aesthetic awe, it seems better to leave it aside (at least for the moment, in a provisional outline), since it introduces complex, longitudinal elements into the experience. It may very well be true that the sublime experience can "change" us and that we can retain vivid memories of it that live on in us for days if not years, but it is not necessary that it do so. For the sake of parsimony, I will continue to focus on the original (non-longitudinal) experience as paradigmatic. And to account for this, it is sufficient to identify and describe a positive, pleasant element in the experience, above all caused by an expanded imaginative activity accompanying the perception of an object.

One other element of the phenomenology of the sublime I wish to mention, before turning to its intersubjectivity, is the altered perception of time. In the experience of sublimity, time appears to slow down. An altered sense of time perception in the sublime is something that has been studied empirically, and merits further study, but it is interesting to note that writers such as Helen Maria Williams,[35] Burke, and Kant independently made the same point.[36] Kant seems to have noticed that the sublime involves the sense that time has slowed down or even does not flow (which is perhaps one reason why he thinks that during the experience of the sublime one has a feeling or sensory hint of one's freedom). He claims that the "subjective movement of the imagination" "does violence" to "inner sense" and thus, by implication, to one's sense of time.[37] Likewise, Burke maintains that all the "motions" of the soul "are suspended" while experiencing "astonishment" (the passion caused by the sublime).[38]

I now turn to intersubjectivity. Is the feeling of aesthetic awe a shared and shareable experience? Is its pleasure intersubjectively communicable? Can it be felt in response to the same objects and events—together? And is it pan-cultural? These are important but difficult questions, and I can only begin to delve into them here.

Here it seems useful first to distinguish the *setting* of a subject or experiencer, who may be alone, from the *content* of the experience, which can be one of connectedness, a feeling of interconnection with other human beings.[39] Furthermore, we should distinguish both the setting and content of the experience from the implicit claim that others should agree with our judgment. The latter claim—that the judgment that *x* is sublime or awe-inducing has intersubjective validity—is not part of the content of the experience. Rather, it is attributed to the judgment: it is *about* the judgment. I take this to be what is meant by the claim that the experience is "shareable." Under similar conditions, others should agree with us that *x* is sublime and be able to have similar experiences. In Kant's jargon, the pleasure in the sublime has "subjective universality."[40] In other words, the judgment of the sublime makes a claim to be intersubjective.[41]

If the sublime were wholly personal and not communicable, we would be faced with the problems identified by Forsey. (But, as proposed in the previous section, there *is* an object of shared experience.) Although I depart from the over-moralized and reflexive elements in (one reading of) Kant's theory (such as the claim that the sublime must involve reflexive awareness of a moral calling), I follow Kant in asserting that a person making a judgment of sublimity, if asked about it, would think that she intends her judgment to be valid not just for her, but for others as well.

The stereotype that the sublime is felt by a solitary individual is widespread, but, if taken to imply that the sublime experience or satisfaction is not intersubjective, it is also mistaken. The (by now cliché) replications of Caspar David Friedrich paintings such as *Wanderer above the Sea of Fog* (1818) on covers of books about the sublime unfortunately seem to promote this misconception. Richard Rorty, like Forsey, adopts this understanding of the sublime, though he has in mind Lyotard's version. Rorty calls the sublime "wildly irrelevant to the attempt at communicative consensus which is the vital force" of common culture.[42] But such claims about the sublime are surprising for two reasons. First, they seem at times simply to be false, since we do sometimes experience the sublime with others, with friends and family, or in crowds, and discuss and debate what we see or hear. And even when we experience the sublime while alone, we still treat the sublime experience as if it were intersubjectively valid, desire others to agree with us, and so on. ("If you had been there, you would have felt the same thing," we might say to our friends.) Second, such claims are also surprising since the Kantian paradigm of the sublime is prominent and widely discussed, and Kant clearly states that the judgment of the sublime makes a claim to intersubjective validity. On his very influential account, we can be expected to be able to give reasons for our judgments, in other words, to communicate.

One phenomenon in particular brings out the intersubjective aspects of the sublime: a crowd. A crowd of spectators observing a sublime event provides a counterexample to Rorty's claim that the sublime is "wildly irrelevant" to the attempt at communicative consensus. Consider the collective admiration of an extraordinary athletic feat, or musical performance. Hans Ulrich Gumbrecht examines sports and athletic competitions admired by fans, who are "in communion with other enthusiastic fans."[43] The fans may even be from many different nations, yet feel a similar response. Gumbrecht's reference to being in "communion" is suggestive. Here is not a violent, frenzied, riotous, or fanatical crowd, but a collection of people who could potentially give reasons and grounds for their feelings of admiration and pleasure in response to the displayed events and outstanding feats. The achievements, movements, athletic plays, or events can evoke aesthetic responses bordering on the sublime. "Following an athletic event and feeling united with athletes and the crowd can yield some of the more addictively uplifting moments of our lives." Gumbrecht characterizes the sublime in response to "breath-taking . . . events and achievements" as a shared, collective experience, in "people's memory" as moments "never to be equaled."[44] In a crowd, as Elias Canetti observes, the individual feels that she is transcending the limits of her own person.[45] The loss of identity can be belittling for an individual, who feels lost in the masses. But it can also be uplifting, since the individual feels that she has become part of a greater whole. This negative–positive movement is precisely the structure of the sublime.

I now turn (briefly) to another difficult issue: pan-culturalism. There is some debate about whether the sublime is pan-cultural or not, that is, if it is found across all times and cultures.[46] The capacity for the sublime would appear to be pan-cultural in that it is grounded in basic biological and psychological features of human beings. At the same time, which particular objects or events elicit them would vary across time and place. Thus, in light of development, habitation, industrialization, encroachment, and the like, Kant may very well have been wrong to suggest that the sublime will be located primarily in natural wonders and landscape (though I myself think we can still feel such sublimity even today). Yet, even if he were wrong about which kinds of things evoke the sublime at any given moment in history, we could still find the sublime elsewhere, stimulated by other objects. The elicitors of the sublime responses change as our experiences and technologies vary. As noted in my remarks on novelty, familiarity is a main antagonist to the sublime in this respect. In short, while recognizing the historical situatedness of particular responses to objects (e.g., mountains), we should be skeptical of claims, made by writers such as James Elkins, that the concept of the sublime is useless since it is *irredeemably* bound by its particular history, its rootedness in eighteenth-century and nineteenth-century thought, and in particular, Romanticism.[47]

This is not to say that the *concept* of the sublime does not have a history. It clearly does. We should be keenly aware of the historical situatedness of the sublime and our responses to the objects deemed "sublime." Different objects will elicit aesthetic awe at different times. In her widely cited monograph, Marjorie Hope Nicolson documented the development of aesthetic responses to mountains during the modern period.[48] But this does not entail that the capacity for aesthetic awe is not a basic human ability. Likewise, it seems doubtful that we need to have formulated an explicit concept of the "aesthetic" (or of "aesthetic awe" and "sublimity") in order to have experiences that we now consider sublime.

In addition, we should be wary of thinking that the western versions of the sublime as presented above all in the writings of Burke, Kant, and Schopenhauer are the paradigms by which to judge the experience. As noted by both Brady and Shapshay, Yuriko Saito maintains that Japanese aesthetic theorists do not make use of the category of the sublime. Allegedly, Japanese writers or artists are interested in the beautiful calm after the typhoon, but not so much in the typhoon. Saito's claim has been taken to be evidence that the capacity for the sublime is not a basic human one.

This conclusion may be too hasty. First, it is possible that the Japanese response is broader, or more large-scale, than the western one, and that it includes both the typhoon *and* the calm. In other words, this may very well be the Japanese version of the sublime. Second, even if one insists that they are describing beauty alone rather than a combination of beauty and sublimity, Saito's claim seems to apply more to the sublime configured in paintings and poetry, than to Japanese aesthetic theory. Indeed, the Japanese actor and theorist Zeami Motokiyo (1363–1443) articulates a distinct aesthetic response to Mount Fuji and to nō theater that arguably concerns the experience of the sublime (see his contribution to this volume).

Finally, consider an analogous basic emotion: fear. The capacity for fear appears to be pan-cultural. Yet, like the sublime, fear has a history. People feel fear today, yet the objects that elicit it are not the ones that paradigmatically elicited it in the past (ghoblins, spirits, etc.). Fear has a history, but it is also a basic emotion. For these reasons, it strikes me as plausible to hold that the capacity for the sublime is pan-cultural, while the objects or events typically found to be sublime have varied over time and space, that is, with history and geography.

## Stretch of the imagination: Pleasures in the sublime

Why do we feel pleasure in the sublime at all, rather than frustration or just a feeling of smallness and insignificance? Several sources can be described. Below, I identify five distinct sources of the pleasure.

1. The stretching, expansion, or intense exercise of the mental faculties, above all the imagination (Aikin, Addison, Priestley).

2. The rising above or release from everyday affairs and concerns (Kant, Schopenhauer).

3. A sense of oneness with the world or finding a home or place in the universe (Schopenhauer), including a moral place or calling (Kant).

4. Engagement of the "fight, flight, or freeze" system, from a safe distance (hence, not inciting actual fear). This promotes a sense of vitality and elicits associated physiological responses (Kant, Burke).

5. Participation in the power or vastness, not of the world or universe as a whole, but of the object (Mendelssohn, Wordsworth).

Each source has some plausibility. Some of these sources may obtain at the same time; they can work conjointly. It seems unnecessary to insist that just one of these is the single, true source of the pleasure in sublime.

Source 1 is partly Aristotelian (or Leibnizian) in spirit. Aristotle claimed that the exercise of an ability or faculty brings pleasure. Accordingly, engaging and stretching the capacity for imagination brings pleasure. (Note that the imagination is here broadly construed and not limited to visualization.) The point is also made by modern writers from both the German scholastic (Leibnizian-Wolffian) and British traditions. In *Spectator* paper No. 412, Addison presents a version of this exercise theory: "Our imagination loves to be filled with an Object, or to grasp at any thing that is too big for its Capacity. We are flung into a pleasing Astonishment at such unbounded Views, and feel a delightful Stilness and Amazement in the Soul at the Apprehension of them."[49] Sometimes it is not the imagination per se that is said to be expanded or filled, but the mind or mental capacities in general. For instance, Burke writes that in the passion of the sublime (astonishment) the mind is "entirely filled" with the object.[50] But I think such claims can still be placed under source 1.

As Addison notes, the immense or powerful object is apprehended, even if with difficulty (in fact, such difficulty seems to add to the experience). The object, as we have seen, plays a crucial role in inciting the experience. Mendelssohn gives a version of this exercise theory, too. "The immensity arouses a sweet shudder that rushes through every fiber of our being, and the *multiplicity* prevents all satiation, giving wings to the imagination to press further and further without stopping."[51] While not entailing that the object is epistemologically inaccessible, this appeal to imagination still retains an aspect of the transcendent or metaphysical element that many theorists discern in the sublime. For instance Brady, like Shapshay, identifies in the sublime experience a (metaphysically modest) sense of mystery. She emphasizes the role of an expanded imagination: "If we want to keep hold of the transcendental thread in the sublime, we might speak of a type of aesthetic transcendence occurring through metaphysical imagination."[52]

According to source 1, a ground of the pleasure in the sublime is the striving and stretching of the mental faculties, in particular the imagination. The play of pushing, stretching, and expanding of our capacity for image-making (broadly construed) is a source of the pleasure. As Brady puts it: "The imagination is invigorated in trying to take in a desert landscape, with its never-ending reaches of sand and undulating forms. The emotional response is complex, perhaps a mix of feelings and thoughts related to death . . . and a more exhilarating feeling from the open and endless expanse."[53] The imagination is active in generating such thoughts and in taking in the undulating forms and vast expanse.[54] For all of his talk about the superiority of reason, even Kant clearly states that "the enlargement of the imagination in itself" leads to "satisfaction" in the sublime.[55]

Source 2 trades on the fact that it is pleasant to be relieved from everyday affairs and concerns. Kant at one point gives a version of this, too. "In our aesthetic judgment nature is judged as sublime not insofar as it arouses fear, but rather because it calls forth our power . . . to regard those things about which we are concerned (goods, health and life) as trivial."[56] This approach is even more prominent in Schopenhauer. He claims that the person experiencing the sublime rises above ordinary interests in a "will-less" contemplation of objects that are "terrible" or opposed to the will—objects called "sublime." The person thereby becomes "elevated precisely in this way above himself, his person, his willing," indeed even "all willing."[57] Likewise, the naturalist John Muir writes that "our own little journeys, away and back again, are only little more than tree-wavings— many of them not so much."[58] Muir is suggesting that our ordinary endeavors are usually unimportant and inconsequential, when looked at from a distance or in the greater scheme of things. It is agreeable to be free of cares, and we are free from cares when (just for a moment) we feel their relative unimportance. The removal of this burden—a release—is pleasant.

But, one might object, isn't it downright frightening? Doesn't the feeling of the relative superfluity of our everyday concerns lead to the chilling idea of our utter insignificance, the notion that we are just "dust in the wind?" Kant seems to have been aware of this risk. This leads to source 3.

Perhaps drawing from Stoic sources such as Seneca, Kant quickly added that the awareness of our capacity to set and act on goals (specifically moral ones) ultimately redeems us. Practical reason saves us from what existentialists later called nihilistic despair. Kant's claim that the sublime involves a recognition of the powers of reason—a claim emphasized in standard interpretations of Kant—can be understood in terms of this third source of the pleasure. It is a kind of homecoming for reason. According to Kant, such recognition of reason counts as an acknowledgment of the rational being's place in the teleological order of reason.

When it comes to source 3, Schopenhauer diverges from Kant and claims that our contemplation ("pure knowing") of the world brings us peace. "There arises the immediate consciousness that all these worlds exists only in our representation, only as modifications of the eternal subject of pure knowing" and we see that we are the "necessary, conditional supporter of all worlds and of all periods of time."[59]

The idea of "oneness" or unity with the world in source 3 may have too much idealistic baggage for some readers. But Schopenhauer (who cites the *Upanishads*) does not back down. "All this . . . shows itself as a consciousness, merely felt, that in some sense or other (made clear by philosophy) we are one with the world, and are therefore not oppressed but exalted by its immensity." If we are not willing to accept Schopenhauer's metaphysics and epistemology, we might be consoled by the fact that source 3 does not necessarily require these commitments. The source of the pleasure could be understood, more modestly, as the feeling of the dissolving of boundaries in general, or the feeling of unity or oneness, including harmony with morality and finding one's moral calling. Such sentiment appears to be felt during the "overview effect" reported by astronauts who observe our planet, the "pale blue dot" (as Carl Sagan calls it), from outer space.[60] According to one study,[61] viewing the earth from space has often prompted astronauts to report overwhelming emotion (aesthetic awe) and feelings of identification with humankind and the planet as a whole. They report intense satisfaction or contentment.[62]

The "world" with which one is in harmony can be understood in a metaphysically modest way, that is, in terms of environments, surroundings, or the earth. We can discern a relatively modest version of the "natural order" in Rousseau's writings. Or, one can locate a version of the notion in the explicitly post-metaphysical writings of Martin Heidegger, especially the later Heidegger. Drawing on the notion of "metaphysical imagination" inspired by Ronald Hepburn, Brady argues that in the sublime we realize we are part of nature and see ourselves as part of that greater whole, or something much greater than ourselves. "The sublime involves an appreciation of natural qualities that precipitate a new, felt awareness of our place in the world."[63]

But perhaps one might object not so much to the notion of a world per se, but more specifically, to teleology. One might object that source 3 presupposes a teleology that does not exist, and that there is no allotted, fixed place for human beings in the natural order. Joseph Margolis, a pragmatist, conveniently illustrates that it is possible to affirm source 3 while not accepting a fixed, unchanging (objective) teleology. Discussing landscape and landscape art, he writes, "landscape is a sign of our participating in a society's life, belonging, being at home. Hence, the beautiful and the sublime are perfectly valid." But he adds "but their validity . . . is settled internally, so to say, prior to an objective critique."[64] Those skeptical of a given or fixed teleology may be right. But thankfully, it might not matter much. The source of the pleasure only needs to appeal to the idea that we *think* there is a natural place for us. It does not require there actually to be one above and beyond the one we constitute and create. This leaves open the possibility that such pleasure, unless it is grounded in a meaning that is constituted in the way Margolis suggests, is illusory. And, even if it is illusory, it would not be the first time that a type of pleasure was based on an illusion.

Source 4 requires certain conditions of the viewer, namely, safety and security. The pleasure in the sublime is rooted in our instincts to self-preservation and is related to our natural capacity for fear. We are not so frightened that we no longer feel aesthetic awe, of course—as many theorists (including Kant) have noted.[65] We are drawn to the vast and powerful (contra-purposive) objects precisely because they elicit the noted stimulating effects. Seen from a biological perspective, the experience is pleasant since the object engages our self-preservation instincts, as Burke noticed. In Kant's terms, the pleasure in the sublime is generated "by the feeling of a momentary inhibition of the vital powers and the immediately following and all the more powerful outpouring of them."[66] In more contemporary words, the experience involves the release of certain neurotransmitters (e.g., norepinephrine) and is associated with bodily changes (e.g., increased heart rate, higher glucose levels, muscle readiness). John Onians writes, "Several of these reactions . . . make us feel more alert and engaged and so make us feel good. This is why the experience of the sublime may be one we seek and, when we obtain it, that we see to prolong."[67]

According to source 5, the subject "participates" in (to use a Platonic term) or "sympathizes" with (to use an eighteenth-century one) the object or its admirable qualities. For Wordsworth, one puts oneself in a position to share in the object's power or vastness.[68] As Mendelssohn puts it, "The magnitude of the object affords us gratification."[69] In another essay, he claims, "The *magnitude* captures our attention, and since it is the magnitude of a perfection, the soul enjoys latching on to this object." The pleasure in the sublime comes from sharing in the "perfections" of the object, such as its magnitude or power. In so doing, we become part of something larger or grander than ourselves. Carritt identifies "positive feelings of union with the object" in A.C. Bradley's account of the sublime, and Carritt himself claims that in the case of a storm or hurricane we "sympathise with the sublime object."[70] I would add that the pleasures of the sublime generated by one's being a part of and belonging to a large, enthusiastic, non-riotous crowd (in which one at the same time feels a loss of self) can be understood in terms of participation along these lines.

All five explanations of the source of the pleasure have something to offer, but I think the first one (expansion of imagination) is the most fundamental and far-reaching. It also has deep roots in the history of aesthetics.[71]

To see that it is the most far-reaching, let us ask: What exactly are we reflecting on? There are several answers, and listing them reveals that the imagination actively contributes to the other sources of pleasure. We may reflect on, or imagine, our freedom from everyday concerns, as in source 2. Or, we may imaginatively reflect on our unity with nature or our sense of purpose, as in source 3. The imagination is active in source 4, too. As Kant suggests, the imagination is expanded when we have the thought that even if an overpowering force of nature could destroy us, we can nonetheless view even life itself as trivial. "Thus nature is here called sublime merely because it raises the imagination to the point of presenting those cases in which the mind can make palpable to itself the sublimity of its own vocation even over nature." "The astonishment bordering on terror. . . etc., is, in view of the safety in which he knows himself to be, not actual fear, but only an attempt to involve ourselves in it by means of the imagination, in order to feel the power of that very faculty."[72] Finally, we can imaginatively participate in the object's vastness or power, as in source 5. We imagine what it is like to be that many light years away, or that many billions of years old: we feel a boost in the process. The imagination, in other words, seems to be active in the other sources of the pleasure, and deserves its place at the top of the list. In addition to the foregoing philosophical reasons, there seems to be some (initial and revisable) empirical evidence for the view that the imagination plays a crucial role in the sublime.[73]

I close this section with a passage that synthesizes many of my foregoing points. In his *Course of Lectures*, Priestley ties together the aforementioned themes of novelty, greatness, and imaginative activity:

> Great objects please us for the same reason that *new* objects do, *viz.*, by the exercise they give to our faculties. The mind, as was observed before, conforming and adapting itself to the objects to which its attention is engaged, must, as it were, enlarge itself, to conceive a great object. This requires a considerable effort of the imagination, which is also attended with a pleasing, though perhaps not a distinct and explicit consciousness of the strength and extent of our powers.[74]

Priestley explains the source of the pleasure, giving a version of the "exercise" theory, but he does much more than this. He lists properties such as greatness that render an object disposed to elicit sublimity. He emphasizes the effort and expansion of the imagination. He even conjectures that one need not be reflexively conscious of the source of the pleasure while feeling it ("not a distinct and explicit consciousness"). This conjecture seems quite plausible, and in making it, Priestley employs the tools of philosophical analysis to defend a claim which experimental studies of the sublime (or awe) appear to confirm.

## Concluding remarks

Conceiving of the sublime in the foregoing way allows theorists and researchers to sort through, filter out, or simplify the numerous—and often conflicting—theories of the "sublime" (sometimes preceded by an adjective such as "pre-oedipal," "oedipal," "urban," "melancholic," "performative," "angelic," "botanical," even "excremental"). Many of these accounts are ultimately not about the sublime at all, at least not in any agreed upon and serviceable sense.

At the beginning of this essay, I asserted that a philosophical theory of the sublime should be compatible, if possible, with scientific findings. (I certainly hope this assumption is not read as being "reductionistic"— reductionism and related concepts such as eliminativism deserve proper discussion of their own, and I have not taken a position on such issues here.) In addition, I hope that the foregoing outline or sketch paves the way not only for a coherent theory of the sublime, but also one that is potentially conducive to empirical and experimental studies, if feasible and useful. One does not have to be a proponent of positivism, scientism, eliminativism, or reductionism to recognize this as an additional benefit. In a similar vein, Konečni holds that it is advantageous for the sublime to be conceptualized so as to become amenable to experimental manipulation and measurement of its effects, if possible.[75] Anjan Chatterjee, a neuroscientist, writes: "What do neuroscientists make of notions such as 'the sublime'? The sublime is an emotional experience mentioned frequently in aesthetics . . . but one that has, so far, had little traction in affective neuroscience."[76] This is an exciting time for empirical research on the sublime. It is also an exciting time for theorists.

Not only might the sublime be fruitfully theorized, but some of this account's main claims or implications about the sublime as an object with certain general qualities could even be tested, or at least used in experimental settings. The following themes await further exploration: the feeling of community and belongingness during the experience; the sense of connection to humanity and to nature; attitudes toward the universe; the relation between the positive experience in the sublime and prosocial effects; empathy and the sublime; perceptions of space and time; the sublime's distinctness from other emotions and feelings such as beauty, fear, and wonder; the frequency and lasting impact (or not) of the experience; the demographics, habits, and dispositions of those who are inclined (or not) to feel the sublime; the effects of being with others (including crowds) rather than being isolated; moral constraints on the experience; the (negative-positive) valence of the feeling and phenomenology; physiological responses; the degree of self-awareness and reflexivity in the experience; feelings of significance or insignificance and smallness; the roles played by imagination and perception; the ideal distance from the perceived stimulus (when the latter is a physical object); and the properties or qualities of the elicitors of the sublime.

Since I suggested in this volume's Preface and Introduction that some feminist theorists have been critical of the sublime, let me say a brief word about how my proposal might be relevant here. Feminist approaches have understandably tended to be wary of the sublime. For instance, Judy Lochhead warns against letting "such terms as the sublime, the ineffable, the unpresentable . . . mask sedimented gender binaries that will keep the feminine in the ground."[77] However, if the sublime is no longer conceived as a response to the ineffable or unpresentable, then such criticisms might be avoided. Moreover, it is worth pointing out that several seventeenth- and eighteenth-century women authors contributed to theories of the sublime along the lines I have proposed. For instance, Anna Aikin gave a version of the exercise theory and explained the pleasure in sublime-like emotions in terms of an increased imaginative activity.

If feeling the sublime is a basic and shared human experience, even one that might contribute to human happiness and flourishing, it would be desirable to come up with an adequate theory of it. But perhaps there is something at stake beyond the satisfaction of our desire to understand ourselves and our surroundings, or to promote human wellbeing. Although I have not elaborated on this here, a viable theory could perhaps also be used in arguments supporting the conservation and protection of the natural environment.[78] A coherent theory could put us in better position to justify the recognition, preservation, and restoration of those cultural artifacts and natural wonders that induce sublime experiences.

Of course, I do not pretend to have answered all, nor even most of the pressing, theoretical questions surrounding the sublime, but I do hope to have addressed at least three of the main conceptual issues (concerning the object, structure, and pleasure), thereby outlining a coherent and viable proposal.[79]

## Questions

1. Summarize and assess the author's explanation of the kinds of objects that are disposed to elicit the sublime, the phenomenology and shareability of the experience, and the sources of the pleasures in the sublime.

2. Can you think of other sources of the pleasures in the sublime, in addition to the five sources proposed by the author? Explain. Assess whether he could respond that your proposed source could be subsumed under one of the sources he identifies.

3. In your view, what should be the relation between a theory of the sublime and empirical research? What counts as "scientism," and how, and to what extent, should it be avoided?

4. Do you think a theory of the sublime should be about the "ineffable" and unrepresentable? Should we be willing to accept that there are paradoxes raised by such a theory? Should we try to resolve them? Explain the advantages and disadvantages of both sides of this issue.

5. Do you think the experience of the sublime is pan-cultural, culturally situated, or both? Can it be both? Explain.

6. Evaluate the following claim (which the author makes in footnote 30): "When we learn the age of an ancient redwood, that information often plays a role in shaping our aesthetic experience and brings about what I have called an experience of adherent sublimity." How does knowledge—say, awareness of an object's background, context, history, or role—shape your experiences of the sublime?

## Further reading

Cochrane, Tom. "The Emotional Experience of the Sublime." *Canadian Journal of Philosophy* 42, no. 2 (2012): 125–48.

Deligiorgi, Katerina. "The Pleasures of Contra-purposiveness: Kant, the Sublime, and Being Human." *Journal of Aesthetics and Art Criticism* 72, no. 1 (2014): 25–35.

Forsey, Jane, Joseph Margolis, Rachel Zuckert, Tom Hanauer, Robert R. Clewis, Sandra Shapshay, and Jennifer A. McMahon. *The Possibility of the Sublime: Aesthetic Exchanges*, ed. Lars Aagaard-Mogensen. Newcastle upon Tyne: Cambridge Scholars Publishing, 2017. [This volume contains Forsey's 2007 article, six essays commenting on it, and Forsey's replies.]

Hanauer, Tom. "Sublimity and the Ends of Reason: Questions for Deligiorgi." *Journal of Aesthetics and Art Criticism* 74, no. 2 (2016): 195–99.

Yaden, David B., Jonathan Haidt, Ralph W. Hood, David Vago, and Andrew Newberg. "The Varieties of Self-Transcendent Experience." *Review of General Psychology* 21, no. 2 (2017): 143–60.

# CHAPTER 38
## EMILY BRADY, "THE ENVIRONMENTAL SUBLIME" (2012)

Emily Brady has published widely on aesthetics and the philosophy of art, eighteenth-century philosophy, environmental humanities and ethics, and animal studies. Below, she responds to three kinds of objections to the sublime: the historical, metaphysical, and anthropocentric. Following Ronald Hepburn, she emphasizes the activity of the "metaphysical imagination" in the experience of the sublime and parses "transcendence" in terms of an expanded imagination. "If we want to keep hold of the transcendental thread in the sublime, we might speak of a type of aesthetic transcendence occurring through metaphysical imagination."

Her interpretation of the sublime is enriched by a profound understanding of the complex history of the sublime, in particular eighteenth-century theories of the environmental sublime. At the same time, Brady touches on themes of interest to contemporary aesthetics and environmental philosophy, including the disputed notions of the "wilderness" and the "otherness" of nature, "transcendence" and alleged anthropocentrism in the sublime, ethical duties regarding nature, and the role of science in the proper appreciation of nature.

She expanded and published a version of this chapter in *The Sublime in Modern Philosophy* (pages 183–206)—see Further reading.

## Note on the text

Source: Reprinted from Emily Brady, "The Environmental Sublime," in *The Sublime: From Antiquity to the Present*, edited by Timothy Costelloe, 171–82. Cambridge: Cambridge University Press, 2012.

The format and style of the original publication have been reproduced, with occasional modifications. In order to preserve the footnote numbering found in the original publication, the volume editor has inserted comments in square brackets in the main body text.

## "The environmental sublime"

### Why the sublime, now?

Academic study of the sublime has been broad, crossing disciplines such as philosophy, literary theory, critical and cultural theory, art theory, landscape studies, and architecture. However, sublimity has been neglected in contemporary aesthetics, where one might expect it to be discussed; any attention it has received is mainly confined to Immanuel Kant's aesthetic theory or to discussions in the history of philosophy.[1] More generally, analytic philosophy has largely ignored the topic, and although continental philosophy has shown an interest, the focus tends to be on the artistic sublime, rather than the natural sublime, despite the legacy of the natural sublime bequeathed by the eighteenth century. This collection [*The Sublime: From Antiquity to the*

*Present* – Ed.] will certainly help to fill these gaps in the literature, and a key aim of this essay is to carve out a contemporary home for the sublime.

Why is discussion of the sublime neglected in these ways? It could be that the concept is considered of little relevance to current debates. Mary Mothersill's *Beauty Restored* is usually credited with reviving discussions of another concept, beauty, which, historically, was central to aesthetic theory and was usually set in contrast to the sublime.[2] Beauty is now very much back on the philosophical agenda – and on other agendas too. Is such a future possible for the sublime? Here I shall argue that the sublime is indeed relevant and that its relevance is tied to environmental thought and, in particular, to debates in environmental aesthetics. Making progress toward an environmental sublime begins by trying to understand various arguments for why the concept has been neglected. To this end, I examine and reply to three different arguments for its neglect, which I describe as follows: (1) the historical argument; (2) the metaphysical argument; and (3) the anthropocentric argument.

## The historical argument

The historical argument draws on historical reasons for why the sublime has been neglected, using these to argue that it is essentially an outmoded concept. Before addressing some of these reasons, let me first provide a very brief history of the concept to establish some context. The first treatise on the sublime, *On the Sublime,* is now generally attributed to Longinus, the first-century Greek critic. Influenced by classical discussions of rhetoric, including Aristotle's, Longinus articulated the sublime as a literary style. The treatise was apparently rediscovered in the sixteenth century, and its translation into English and French in the seventeenth century was pivotal to its reception by eighteenth-century literary criticism and aesthetic theory.

Philosophical discussion of the sublime reached a pinnacle in eighteenth-century aesthetic theory, when it was unusual not to include it within discussions of taste. Contemporary debates engage mainly with Edmund Burke's and Kant's theories of the sublime, but (as the chapters in the current volume [*The Sublime: From Antiquity to the Present* – Ed.] show) there is significant work on the topic by other writers during that period.

In Burke's empirical approach, the sublime is attributed to objects that are great, powerful, vast, infinite, massive, rugged, dark, and gloomy, as well as to loud sounds, bitter tastes, and stenches. The sublime involves an immediate feeling of delight mixed with terror in response to something distant enough not to be painful in a strong sense. We are completely overwhelmed by sublime objects: "The mind is so entirely filled with its object, that it cannot entertain any other, nor by consequence reason on that object which employs it."[3] Burke and, later, Kant argue that the sublime response occurs only if the spectator experiences the sublime object firsthand, and when situated in a safe position relative to it.

Although Kant's mature theory of the sublime, as it appears in the *Critique of the Power of Judgment* (1790), was influenced by Burke and earlier theories, he develops the concept through his own critical and transcendental philosophy.[4] Kant's approach is also distinctive for its almost exclusive focus on nature. Following other writers, he distinguishes between the "mathematically sublime," in which the senses and imagination are overwhelmed when confronted by the seemingly infinite magnitude of nature – such as a vast ocean – and the "dynamically sublime," in which the awesome power of nature – such as a raging sea – evokes anxious pleasure and calls forth an awareness of our distinctive capacities as moral beings, namely, freedom and the power of reason. We feel insignificant and powerless in comparison to the mightiness of nature, yet ultimately we judge ourselves, rather than objects, sublime as we discover a capacity to measure ourselves in relation to nature.

Although the sublime was then taken up in Romantic poetry and literature and in some later philosophical discussions, it has since not featured as a major category of aesthetic value. The historical reasons for this are no doubt myriad and complex, and I shall address only a few of them here. These reasons are tied to shifts in both the empirical and theoretical bases of the sublime. Empirical considerations are certainly relevant, because shifts in aesthetic taste and in theoretical discussion of aesthetic judgments can influence each other. On this point, it is useful to make a distinction between (1) experience of the sublime or sublime experiences, that is, the phenomenological experience of the sublime: for example, William Wordsworth's actual experience of Mt. Snowdon; (2) sublime discourse, or language that is immediately descriptive or expressive of such experiences and proceeds directly from them, for example, Wordsworth's poetic expression of this experience in *The Prelude;* and (3) talk about the sublime, that is, the "reflective or analytic discourse" on the topic, as we find in Burke, Kant, and other theories.[5] These three categories tend to run together in practice and are often difficult to separate, which in itself speaks to the strong relationship between them. Still, it is worth trying to keep the distinction in mind for clarity's sake and when teasing out some of the reasons behind the neglect of the sublime.

The early development of the sublime from its literary to natural treatment, and subsequent celebration by the Romantics, meant that it became deeply associated with natural objects and phenomena. In art history and theory, moves away from representational art and toward the expressive and avant-garde are responsible to some extent for diminishing philosophical interest in aesthetics of nature until very recently. Apart from eighteenth- and nineteenth-century Romantic conceptions of the sublime in painting and music, the sublime has also been of less interest in art until recently, when it has enjoyed resurgence among artists and postmodern theorists such as Barnett Newman and Jean-François Lyotard. Although these accounts have their own merits, I am not persuaded that the sublime, as it is originally and best understood, applies in important ways to art. We can find support for this claim in a range of eighteenth-century writers who argue that nature is the original sublime, and that art can only express sublimity through representation, and therefore only indirectly. Paintings, for example, do not possess the key qualities of vastness and overwhelming power required to evoke sublime feeling. Indeed, on many interpretations of Kant, artifacts are simply not candidates for the sublime response.[6] There may be cases of artifacts – art as well as technology – that we would want to call sublime, in which sublimity is being expressed metaphorically.[7] The limits of space do not allow me to provide a more thorough defense of this view, but it is a question worth pursuing in any new reflections on the sublime.

Alongside shifts in aesthetic theory and the arts lie significant changes in landscape tastes. Much has been written about how changes in European and North American landscape tastes made appreciation of the sublime possible in the first place, where fear and hatred of mountains, deserts, and other wild places became tempered by admiration and reverence.[8] This new landscape taste was made possible by a number of economic, social, religious, and technological factors that enabled many people to have direct, relatively safe access to such places. Theories of the sublime emerged in line with these changes, as more people – typically the elite, but also the middle classes – were in a position to appreciate sublime nature rather than simply fear it.[9]

Does the current neglect in *discourse* on the sublime reflect changes in taste and experience away from sublime objects? Has there been a decline in "taste" for the sublime? It could be argued that opportunities to appreciate the natural sublime have declined, presumably because many cultures and societies are now even less awed by nature. We appear to be less fearful, having developed technological means to control and exercise power over much of nature. For many people, great mountains and the vast sea may no longer evoke that edgy feeling of the sublime, and the anxious pleasure it involves. In other words, the relationship for many societies has become much less troubled. There may still be room for neighboring categories of response, such as awe, majesty, and wonder, but not really (it might be claimed) for the complex experience of the sublime, at least if we rely on an understanding of the concept as it was put forward in the eighteenth century. So, the main conclusion of the historical argument is that the sublime is no longer relevant theoretically because those very experiences so prevalent in the past just no longer exist, or if they exist they are, in fact, uncommon.

This conclusion is too quick, however. Our access to natural environments makes many of our experiences, thankfully, safe, and technology has also allowed us to access places that are still wild to a great extent – huge waterfalls, raging rivers, volcanic eruptions, the vast sea, space, deserts, and the like – in ways that still leave room for the sublime response. Although the concept of wilderness is highly contested, we still have experiences of more or less extreme wild places that offer possibilities for the sublime. In his essay "The Unhandselled Globe," Nick Entrikin's reflections suggest the possibility of a contemporary sublime: "As places on the margin, high places are invested with varied and often contradictory meanings, from landscapes of fear to morally valued 'pure' and natural landscapes. They have offered people sites of escape, reverence, physical challenge, discovery and learning, but at the same time have been sources of evil, human failure and death."[10] The emergence of extreme sports provides another example of ways people find risk where it may no longer exist, and some small degree of risk (if only fear "incurred in imagination," as Kant put it) is crucial to any experience of the sublime. Extreme sports are not in themselves experiences of the sublime, but they offer opportunities for aesthetic experiences of this kind because of the ways in which they situate people in the environment. There are cases, though, in which technology itself cannot match nature's power, even if it can deliver us to sublime places. Consider the eruption of Iceland's Eyjajallajoekull volcano in 2010, which caused severe disruption to flight travel across the United Kingdom and several other European countries. We also face catastrophic changes to the earth and its landscapes from climate change taking place now and predicted for the future, changes that are unmanageable through technological fixes. Models predicting changes on a huge scale provide a kind of indirect, representational picture of a great, sublime event on a huge temporal and spatial scale.

Present-day experiences of the sublime need not be limited to extreme or remote situations. On a clear night, away from light pollution, we can gaze at that very expanse celebrated in Kant's theory: "The starry heavens above." Granted, the vast earth can now be examined at our fingertips through Google Earth and the like, but there are many opportunities for direct experience of the natural sublime. It is also possible to argue that less technologically developed societies retain a greater sense of the sublime, although this is speculative, and proof would need to be found in empirical studies. In general, however, these points support the view that opportunities remain for experiencing phenomena commonly associated with the sublime, thus making our use of the concept still relevant today. But the problem doesn't end there. The concept itself is not without its problems, and a better grasp may help us to understand whether it can indeed be legitimately associated with actual experiences of the sublime in nature.

### The metaphysical argument

A major obstacle for the relevance of the sublime in contemporary thought, generally, has been its association with issues of a transcendental and metaphysical sort, stemming in large part from the influence of Kant's theory and its development in Romantic thought and literature.[11] The metaphysical argument gathers together objections to the metaphysical dimension of the sublime, whether understood in theological or nontheological terms. Such an argument might be characterized as a type of aesthetic eliminativism, an attempt, that is, to theorize away the metaphysical dimension of aesthetic responses. I am not convinced that we need to shy away from the metaphysical aspect of the sublime experience, however, even when an obvious alternative would be to favor an empirical account over a metaphysical one, such as those offered by Burke or Johann Gottfried Herder.[12] My worry is that such a choice would throw the baby out with the bathwater. Although I have not worked this out fully, what seems to distinguish the sublime from awe, wonder, and other neighboring concepts is (at least) its very metaphysical quality. To help support my views here, I turn to the late philosopher Ronald Hepburn, whose writings on the aesthetics of nature support the role of more speculative, metaphysical components of aesthetic experience, in addition to more particular or concrete ones.[13]

Hepburn offers careful reflections on what he calls "metaphysical imagination" in the aesthetic appreciation of nature:

> Why should metaphysical imagination be under-acknowledged today? I suspect that some of the undervaluers may wish to keep their own account of aesthetic engagement with nature well free of the embarrassment of what they see as the paradigm case of metaphysics in landscape. I mean Wordsworthian romanticism. … Embarrassment, because this is taken to express a religious experience whose object is very indeterminate, whose description virtually fails of distinct reference, and which may lack adequate rational support. … But my response to that is not to urge an aesthetic experience of nature *free* of metaphysics, for that would be grossly self-impoverishing, but rather, to encourage its endless variety. What comes to replace a theistic or pantheist vision of nature may well itself have the status of metaphysics – naturalistic, materialistic, or whatever: and may have its own metaphysical imaginative correlatives.[14]

Hepburn makes a substantive point that the metaphysical dimension of aesthetic experience of nature – especially as he ties it to metaphysical imagination – cannot be ignored. The problem is the abstract quality of the experience, the actual content of which can be difficult to pin down. But this is not in itself a reason to set the metaphysical aspect aside, for the claim does not entail that the experience cannot be analyzed or critically treated. It is not the metaphysical or transcendental aspect of the sublime that is the problem but rather the way this aspect has been associated with religious or mystical experiences and discourse on nature. Some eighteenth-century theories of the sublime associate it with God's power as symbolized in nature, but in Kant we find a more secular sublime, one better suited to understanding aesthetic appreciation of nature in contemporary times. I am not marginalizing spiritual, mystical, or religious experiences, for these can provide a significant basis for valuing nature; however, it is important to understand distinctions between aesthetic and religious modes of experience.

What role might the metaphysical imagination have in aesthetic valuing of nature, and how is this relevant to my defense of the sublime? Let me begin with the first part of the question, which will lead to the second. Appreciation may be metaphysically thin or thick (my terminology) for Hepburn: "Aesthetic experience of nature can include great diversity of constituents: from the most particular … rocks, stones, leaves, clouds, shadows – to the most abstract and general ways we apprehend the world – the world as a whole."[15] He defines metaphysical imagination as

> an element of interpretation that helps to determine the overall experience of a scene in nature. It will be construed as "seeing as…" or "interpreting as…" that has metaphysical character, in the sense of relevance to the whole of experience and not only to what is experienced at the present moment. Metaphysical imagination connects with, looks to, the "spelled out" systematic metaphysical theorizing which is its support and ultimate justification. But also it is no less an element of the concrete present landscape experience: it is fused with the sensory components, not a meditation aroused by these.[16]

This last point is especially important, because it clearly links the metaphysical aspect to perceptual qualities of environment, where the stimulus for aesthetic experience begins. This is a key point for environmental aesthetics, which in recent debates has wholeheartedly embraced the importance of developing theories that value nature on its own terms, or "nature as it really is" – as far as we can understand it.[17] We ought not confuse metaphysical imagination with mere fancy or reverie. Functioning in a nonfanciful mode, in response to natural objects and phenomena, metaphysical imagination, Hepburn says, "interprets nature as revealing metaphysical insights: insights about things such as the meaning of life, the human condition, or our place in the cosmos."[18]

The metaphysical dimension of aesthetic appreciation of nature is captured by Hepburn in the contemporary context of environmental aesthetics, in which it is contrasted with models that emphasize the role of science. He argues against a "one-sidedly science-dominated appreciation of nature" on various grounds, the discussion of which is beyond the scope of this chapter. But let me at least point out by way of emphasis that Hepburn again, in this context, defends metaphysical experience: "Science does not oust metaphysics: the questions of metaphysics arise on and beyond the boundary of science."[19] Essentially, we see here a celebration of a dimension of aesthetic experience that is ineliminable.

Hepburn's metaphysical imagination provides a reply to the skepticism of aesthetic eliminativism, but how might we more precisely apply this to the sublime? It helps us to explain a puzzling, difficult, yet crucial component of the sublime response, at least as characterized by Kant. In Kant's theory, the sublime involves an essential mix of negative and positive feeling. Negative feeling is associated with our capacities being overwhelmed by vast or powerful natural phenomena, whereas positive feeling is associated with an apprehension or felt awareness of freedom and our power of reason, through which we transcend awareness of the phenomenal realm and find ourselves able to measure up to nature.[20] The sublime involves an appreciation of natural qualities that precipitate a new, felt awareness of our place in the world. Metaphysical imagination helps to articulate that apprehension – an opening out of the felt experience that the anxious exhilaration of the sublime affords. If we want to keep hold of the transcendental thread in the sublime, we might speak of a type of aesthetic transcendence occurring through metaphysical imagination.

This type of metaphysical imaginative expansion complements the very distinctive role played by imagination in the Kantian sublime.[21] Imagination is, on Kant's account, "outraged" by nature.[22] Although it makes a great effort, imagination ultimately fails to present the aesthetic object to the mind. Most commentators simply leave the role of imagination at that: it fails. But we ought to recognize that imagination functions in vital ways in that very experience of failure. Briefly, in the mathematically sublime, imagination is expanded through the attempt to take in the apparently infinite, yet that activity in itself reveals a distinctive way imagination operates in the aesthetic response. The power of the imagination is opened out in relation to seemingly boundless objects – a vast glacier spread before us. In the dynamically sublime, imagination functions to present an imagined, distanced fear that is essential to the negative feeling associated with sublime qualities.[23] These crucial functions relate to an expansion of the mind and suggest an intensity absent in other types of aesthetic experience.

### The anthropocentric argument

So far, I have argued that the natural sublime, even in its metaphysical expression, is relevant for contemporary debates. It is not an outmoded concept tied to eighteenth-century experience or taste, and even its metaphysical aspect should not be a reason for suspicion. There is, however, another obstacle that must be overcome if the sublime is to be revalued in environmental thought and beyond, namely, the anthropocentric argument. This argument holds that the sublime is inherently anthropocentric, especially given the hierarchical relationship, it is claimed, that sublime aesthetic experience sets up between humans and nature.

The first thread of this argument claims that it is humanity that is valued rather than nature, such that the sublime becomes both *self-regarding* and *human regarding*. Many accounts of the sublime in poetry – going as far back as Longinus – point to how the human mind is elevated in its response. John Dennis, for example, wrote in 1696 that the "soul is transported upon it, by the consciousness of its own excellence, and it is exalted, there being nothing so proper to work on its vanity; … if the hint be very extraordinary, the soul is amazed by the unexpected view of its own surpassing power."[24] This elevation of the mind is brought into the context of responses to the natural sublime, in which we see in many eighteenth-century writers the idea that it is the human mind that is found to be sublime, as well as nature, in its capacity to find itself a measure to nature's might. In Kant's influential account, it is humanity (as moral personhood), reason, and freedom that is sublime and not, strictly speaking, nature itself. Kant writes that this is at least because sublimity is formless and so cannot be contained:

> We express ourselves on the whole incorrectly if we call some object of nature sublime, although we can quite correctly call very many of them beautiful; for how can we designate with an expression of approval that which is apprehended in itself as contrapurposive? We can say no more than that the object serves for the presentation of a sublimity that can be found in the mind; for what is properly sublime cannot be contained in any sensible form, but concerns only ideas of reason.[25]

Kant's view is carried into the humanist sublime of Romanticism, and it was John Keats who described Wordsworth's *Prelude* as the "egotistical sublime."[26] These ideas suggest that nature becomes the means to our own self-discovery, a way through which we realize our place in the world – a place that is viewed as greater than nature in many ways. Hepburn writes that Kant's theory downgrades "*nature*'s contribution in favor of the one-sided exalting of the rational subject-self"[27] and that "the natural, external world may come to be seen as of value in the sublime experience, *only* because it can make a person feel the capaciousness of his soul. Intensity of experience may become the solely prized value."[28] The sublime could be seen as a type of aesthetic experience that both distorts and humanizes nature, "degrading nature to our measure."[29]

Leading from this, a second thread of the argument is that the experience of and discourse about the sublime posits nature as an "other," different and separate from ourselves, and over which we have power. In William Cronon's well-known critique of the concept of wilderness, he argues that the sublime only serves to deepen the separation of humans and nature.[30] There are other objections that relate to the anthropocentric argument, but they lie beyond the scope of this chapter. Suffice to say they emerge from a range of positions including feminist, postcolonial, Marxist, and sociological thought.[31]

Confronting the sublime's historical legacy is a first step in replying to the anthropocentric argument. We can retain some of the most interesting features of the concept of the sublime, especially its strong association with appreciation of nature, while at the same time decoupling it from problematic connections to elitist notions of taste. Some of my earlier remarks against the historical argument have shown that there is something we can call a contemporary experience of the sublime, in which we are confronted not with some social construction but with a material experience of a natural world that "surprises and resists human desires and ambitions."[32] That is, there is something vital about the sublime that outruns criticisms of its theoretical and cultural underpinnings in eighteenth-century discussion of taste. It is worth remembering, too, that those discussions were not just about identifying appropriate categories of aesthetic taste for a particular kind of subject but were also concerned with investigating a distinctive kind of experience of the world, expressed as beauty, novelty, tragedy, sublimity, ugliness, and so on. Many eighteenth-century accounts speak to the centrality of nature as the original material of the sublime. James Beattie, a student of Alexander Gerard, sums up this point:

> The most perfect models of sublimity are seen in the works of nature. Pyramids, palaces, fireworks, temples, artificial lakes and canals, ships of war, fortification, hills leveled and caves hollowed by human industry, are mighty efforts, no doubt, and awaken in every beholder a pleasing admiration but appear

as nothing, when we compare them, in respect of magnificence, with mountains, volcanoes, rivers, cataracts, oceans, the expanse of heaven, clouds and storms, thunder and lightning, the sun, moon, and stars. So that, without the study of nature, a true taste in the sublime is absolutely unattainable.[33]

Kant's theory of the sublime was influenced by theories in this tradition and thus reflects an emphasis on nature, although, as we have seen, his ideas are expressed through the contours of his own philosophical system.[34]

I have argued elsewhere that the Kantian sublime is not anthropocentric in the ways various criticisms suggest, and although that argument is too complex to repeat here, a brief sketch will give some indication of its main claims.[35] Rather than reducing sublime appreciation to awareness of our moral vocation, I argue that we cannot overlook Kant's insistence that judgments of the sublime fall squarely within the aesthetic domain, and as such, natural objects, on his own disinterested notion of aesthetic judgment, cannot serve as mere triggers to grasping human sublimity. High mountains, thunderclouds and lightning, vast deserts, and starry skies are also valued for themselves. This is shown through an understanding of imagination's functioning and the direct attention given to nature in sublime appreciation. Furthermore, Kant's theory characterizes a form of aesthetic appreciation, which provides the outline of a distinctive aesthetic-moral relationship between humans and nature.[36] Various commentators on Kant have tried to draw out a connection between aesthetic appreciation of nature and a duty not to harm nature.[37] Specifically, Robert Clewis's interpretation of the sublime as a type of disinterested aesthetic judgment reveals sublime experience as preparing us for an attitude of respect for nature, even if that respect takes the form of an indirect duty.[38]

I have not shown conclusively (here, at least) how Kant's account escapes the objections of the anthropocentric argument, but I have pointed to how it is possible to recognize the element of humility running through reflections on the sublime in nature, through which we feel insignificant in the face of powers that exceed us. My aim has been to defend the more difficult, metaphysical Kantian concept of the natural sublime because it is truer to the concept in terms of its development and influence. In any case, and for the sake of moving my overall aims forward, let me show why we ought to be interested in sublime, non-anthropocentric valuing of nature.

How might we characterize appreciation of the natural sublime? I address this question by articulating how a distinctive aesthetic-moral relationship between humans and nature develops. This relationship can be seen as involving elements of both humility and self-reflection,[39] and rather than being cozy or easy it is characterized by agitation. Many contemporary theories in environmental aesthetics stress the deep engagement afforded by environmental appreciation as contrasted with scenic or picturesque appreciation, and with some forms of artistic appreciation.[40] I agree with these views, and I do think the sublime offers a type of environmental – environing – aesthetic experience, but it is not one of the intimate kind. The sublime is typified by feeling overwhelmed, anxious, and insignificant amid crashing waves, towering cliffs, great storms, and the like. This is not a delightful or contemplative experience of nature, as we might find in varieties of the beautiful. In this respect, the sublime does not define a relationship of loving nature, or even a friendly relationship with nature.[41] Rather, it is uncomfortable, even difficult – an imposition of environmental events. Returning to Entrikin, his reflections echo these ideas of humility: "extreme latitudes and elevations of the globe, vividly illuminate natural resistance to human projects … Some aspects of nature remain external to the weave of place-making and often function as barriers to such efforts."[42]

What sense can be made of the overwhelming quality of the sublime, and the sense of "otherness" often associated with it? It is an aesthetic response to nature as something much greater than ourselves, and as we have seen, this gives way to metaphysical imagination. But how are we to articulate this sense of otherness without falling foul of criticisms that otherness is simply an empty term?[43] One way around this is to adopt the concept of *mystery*, and to argue that it is the quality of mystery that characterizes this puzzling aspect of sublime experience, that is, some feature of a particular natural environment of phenomenon that cannot be known. This strategy is promising as a reply to the anthropocentric objection because it suggests that although we may appreciate a set of qualities associated with the sublime, some natural phenomena are certainly not completely within our grasps. Appreciating nature as having the quality of mystery underpins a kind of regard for nature where nature cannot be fully known or appropriated, which supports an attitude of humility.

Lyotard's philosophy enhances our understanding of how the self relates to environment in sublime experience. Although mainly directed at the sublime and art, Lyotard shows us how the subject of sublime feeling is decentered through encounters with the "inexpressible," "unpresentable," and "indeterminate." Discussing the sublime in Barnett Newman's artworks and ideas, Lyotard writes that "with the occurrence, the will is defeated."[44] In the context of nature, we might synthesize Lyotard's ideas to interpret the sublime as an overwhelming of the subject, in which the self is dislocated through a sense of nature as mysterious, and neither fully known nor appreciated by human reason. Lyotard interprets Kant to show this movement beyond a subject who "feels in the object the presence of something that transcends the object. The mountain peak is a phenomenon that indicates that it is also more than a phenomenon."[45] Against the anthropocentric argument, then, Lyotard shows how the sublime signifies a "dehumanizing" of aesthetic experience, and how it also renders a complex relationship between humans and nature arising out of an experience of great affect.

In a 2003 manuscript, "Mystery in an Aesthetic Context," Hepburn offers some interesting ways to understand mystery in aesthetic appreciation of both art and nature.[46] Although he does not align it explicitly with the sublime, some of his remarks on mystery in Romanticism are helpful here. Hepburn adopts the category of "indeterminate mystery" to describe that feature of Romanticism, which Isaiah Berlin described as "the absence of a structure of the world to which one must adjust oneself."[47] The sublime overwhelms through its qualities, but depending on the specific nature of those qualities, they express the infinite, the unknowable, or the nonsensual.[48]

Stan Godlovitch has adopted the idea of mystery to characterize his "acentric theory" of aesthetic appreciation of environment, which commentators have dubbed the "aloofness" or "mystery model."[49] The acentric perspective places the aesthetic subject in a position of radical desubjectivity, in which all cultural and even scientific interpretation is removed. In a position of being acutely aware of both nature's independence from us and that nature lies beyond our knowledge, our only appropriate aesthetic response is a sense of mystery.[50] Although Godlovitch in fact distinguishes mystery from the sublime because he views the latter concept as too culturally laden, his line of thought does help to express a quality associated with the sublime response. He pins down why the quality of mystery relates to the unknowable in nature, and how this may be connected to, or may even aesthetically ground, a moral attitude toward nature. I should add here, though, that I do not agree with Godlovitch's acentric aesthetic as such. A major objection is the apparent emptiness of the aesthetic subject it involves: what is left of aesthetic appreciation if it becomes *only* a sense of mystery, shorn of any layers or elements commonly associated with the aesthetic response? Mystery, as I see it, may helpfully characterize one aspect of sublime experience rather than aesthetic appreciation of nature more generally.

Turning back to the self, what sense can we make of the self-reflective component in the sublime? Hepburn indicates another useful direction by pointing to how aesthetic appreciation of nature offers opportunities for reflexivity that artistic experience (often) does not. That is, we are "involved in the natural situation itself… both actor and spectator, ingredient in the landscape … playing actively with nature, and letting nature, as it were, play with me and my sense of self." This type of involvement means that we may be able to experience ourselves in "an unusual and vivid way; and this difference is not merely noted, but dwelt upon aesthetically …

We are in nature and a part of nature; we do not stand over against it as over against a painting on a wall."[51] Applied to the sublime, we become a mere ingredient in the landscape, but we are at the same time aware of ourselves as overwhelmed, humbled by particular qualities in nature. This is a kind of self-reflection that need not be understood as anthropocentric, given its context.[52]

These aspects of appreciation function to fill out or in some sense articulate – at least in theoretical terms, but perhaps phenomenologically too – the metaphysical dimension of the sublime. First, mystery helps to articulate the aesthetic terms on which the sublime is overwhelming: what is literally supersensible, beyond our ken, profound, and ineliminable. Second, mystery can express a dimension of the aesthetic response that feeds into an ethical attitude, at least in terms of articulating the sublime in terms of that which cannot be overhumanized and overpowered. To this, add self-reflection understood in terms of reflexivity, and we have, arguably, a clearer understanding of the sublime as a distinctive aesthetic experience.[53] We also arrive at a kind of aesthetic interaction with nature. As we are affected by sublime qualities, we are forced into a position of admiration for nature, feeling both insignificant *and* aware of ourselves in relation to the power and magnitude of elements of the natural environment. Sublime experience could thus be said to constitute a type of meaningful relationship between humans and other parts of nature.

### The sublime and negative qualities

To conclude, I would like to make a final point about the relevance of the natural sublime. Quite apart from its metaphysical tone, it is important not to overlook the concrete phenomena and qualities that generate the sublime response in the first place. This feature of the sublime should be of great interest to aesthetics and beyond, especially given recent discussions concerning more difficult forms of aesthetic appreciation. Sublimity involves a range of qualities linked to vastness, enormous size, and power, such as the mysterious, dark, obscure, great, huge, powerful, towering, dizzying, blasting, raging, disordered, dynamic, tumultuous, shapeless, formless, boundless, frameless, and so on. These qualities are commonly contrasted with beauty, in which natural beauty is associated with harmony, for example, or smoothness, order, tranquility, and gracefulness. In an effort to support appreciation of nature on its own terms, some philosophers in environmental aesthetics have argued for the importance of recognizing the "unscenic."[54] The sublime is not the same as the unscenic, although there is overlap between some varieties of the sublime and unscenic landscapes. The sublime is closer, although not equivalent, to what has been described as "terrible beauty." Just as the sublime operated when it was first applied to so-called raw nature some three hundred years ago, it now contributes to understanding aesthetic qualities that can be characterized as more negative.

The natural sublime enables us to consider forms of appreciation in relation to more threatening or overwhelming natural qualities in nature and articulates, I believe, the unsentimental and complex side of environmental experience. The sublime potentially affords aesthetic responses that throw up epistemic value too, in which we grasp nature as something that cannot be appropriated and something that, after all, deserves respect. If the sublime is to have a place in current environmental thought, its value will lie in the relatively neglected qualities it identifies, the way it characterizes a distinctive type of aesthetic engagement with environment, and the particular aesthetic-moral relationship that emerges through that engagement.

### Questions

1. Restate in your own words Brady's arguments against the three main objections to the sublime (historical, metaphysical, and anthropocentric). Assess her arguments.

2. Can Brady's comments on the metaphysical objection be seen as a response to the challenges articulated by Jane Forsey (in the present volume)? Explain.

3. What role does the notion of "metaphysical imagination" play in Brady's account? Why does she appeal to imagination? What does "aesthetic eliminativism" have to do with this?

4. What does Brady mean by "mystery": how does she use this concept? Do you find it convincing? Explain.

5. Do you think that our scientific knowledge of nature generally enhances, or hinders, the mystery of (or in) nature? Explain.

6. In what ways is Brady's account inspired by Kant? Does her interpretation differ from your understanding of Kant? Explain.

## Further reading

Brady, Emily. *The Sublime in Modern Philosophy: Aesthetics, Ethics, and Nature*. Cambridge: Cambridge University Press, 2013.

Carlson, Allen. *Aesthetics and the Environment*. New York: Routledge, 2000.

Carroll, Noël. "On Being Moved By Nature: Between Religion and Natural History." In *Landscape, Natural Beauty and the Arts*, ed. Salim Kemal and Ivan Gaskell, 244–65. Cambridge: Cambridge University Press, 1993.

Clewis, Robert, R. "What's the Big Idea? On Emily Brady's Sublime." *The Journal of Aesthetic Education* 50 (2016): 104–18.

# CHAPTER SUMMARIES

Longinus
The topic of the ancient Greek text attributed to Longinus is lofty or excellent writing or discourse. The author combines ideas drawn from the rhetorical tradition of literary criticism with ideas from philosophers such as Plato. Longinus locates five sources of sublimity: great thoughts, strong and inspired emotion, lofty figures, noble diction, and elevated word-arrangement.

Bharata-Muni
The ancient Sanskrit treatise *Nāṭyaśāstra* (attributed to Bharata-Muni) focuses on how we experience what is represented on a theatrical stage, describing responses that bear similarities to the sublime. The handbook offers advice to actors on how to represent a *rasa* (emotional flavor) and elicit it in the audience. The remarks on the terrible, marvelous, and the heroic sentiments, as well as terror and astonishment, can be related or connected to the sublime.

Guo Xi
The Chinese painter and theorist discusses the high, deep, and level perspectives of mountains. The experience can be attained through positioning oneself at a particular level or distance with respect to the large objects, as well as through using painting techniques to convey these distances on a flat surface. His painting, *Early Spring* (see cover image), also takes up the "transcendent" strand of the sublime—represented in this painting by blank spots or mists.

Zeami Motokiyo
Zeami characterizes the levels of learning and mastering the Japanese theatrical art of nō. The first level emphasizes unknowability, describing a feeling that transcends cognition. Zeami's description of the second level appeals to the perception of a vast and striking object: Mount Fuji.

Francesco Petrarca
The author (Petrarch) describes his ascent of Mount Ventoux, using the description of the trek as an opportunity to confess his shortcomings. At the summit of the mountain, he reads a passage from Augustine's *Confessions*. He reflects on the triviality of ordinary affairs and admires the greatness of the mind drawing closer to God.

Nicolas Boileau Despréaux
In his Preface, the French poet and literary critic comments on his translation of Longinus's *Peri Hypsous*, which played a crucial role in the modern revival of the sublime.

John Dennis
According to Dennis, the sublime is found in great thoughts which move the soul via a passion (enthusiasm). Departing from Longinus, Dennis maintains that ideas producing terror are excellent elicitors of sublimity. God is the exemplary source of the sublime: to evoke the latter, the poet should have recourse to religious ideas.

## Chapter Summaries

### Giambattista Vico
The professor of rhetoric addresses university students at the Royal Academy of Naples. Philosophers, he says, define a "hero" as someone who seeks the sublime. Such heroism can be achieved through education, specifically, one that is directed at God.

### Edmund Burke
Burke adopts a physio-psychological method, providing empirical descriptions of sublime effects on human bodies and minds. Far from dwelling exclusively on the subjective responses, however, Burke characterizes the qualities of objects that paradigmatically elicit the sublime.

### Moses Mendelssohn
The author distinguishes beauty from immensity, which is unbounded. He then distinguishes extended from non-extended (intensive) immensity, that is, the enormous from the strong. Something that is intensively immense is said to be strong, and when that strength is a matter of "perfection," it is said to be sublime. He defines the sublime in art as a "sensuously perfect representation" of something immense, capable of inspiring awe. He defines awe as a debt that we owe to genius.

### Elizabeth Carter
Carter recounts one of her experiences of the sublime. She describes a mixed sentiment, a feeling of smallness combined with exaltation. In addition to a mental expansion in response to natural wonders, there is a second source of the pleasure in the sublime: release from everyday concerns.

### Immanuel Kant (*Observations on the Feeling of the Beautiful and Sublime*)
In this popular, "precritical" treatise, Kant distinguishes the sublime and the beautiful in terms of their phenomenology and qualities. He identifies and gives examples of three kinds of sublimity (noble, terrifying, magnificent). He discusses moral feeling in terms of sublimity.

### Anna Aikin
Aikin addresses the paradox surrounding why we feel pleasure in response to an object of terror—as in feeling sublimity or viewing a dramatic tragedy. Her explanation hinges on the pleasurable activity of the imagination, stimulated by the object evoking the terror.

### Mary Wollstonecraft
Wollstonecraft criticizes Edmund Burke's views of the sublime and beautiful. She maintains that his ideas rest on questionable views of gender, class, and religion.

### Immanuel Kant (*Critique of the Power of Judgment* and *Anthropology from a Pragmatic Point of View*)
In his influential "critical" account, Kant describes the feeling and judgment of the sublime as an interaction between the imagination and the powers of reason. The passage from the *Anthropology* summarizes his position.

### Friedrich Schiller
The German poet and playwright emphasizes the practical sublime over the theoretical and underscores the potential of dramatic tragedy to evoke the experience. Schiller therefore maintains that there can be sublimity

in art. He introduces the "pathetically-sublime" and, in one of his significant departures from Kant, connects it to one of the "laws" of tragic art.

## Anna Seward

In her letter to George Gregory, the "Swan of Lichfield" describes the feeling of transport she feels when reading "Ossian," the purported author of a cycle of Scottish Gaelic epic poems.

## Ann Radcliffe

An excerpt from her English Gothic novel reveals how the concept of the sublime was conceived and employed in early Gothic literature. In the sublime, Radcliffe suggests, the imagination is stimulated yet at the same time in tension with reason.

## Helen Maria Williams

Williams vividly describes her experience of "enthusiastic awe." The sublime contains an "annihilation" of the self; the self of private affairs feels diminished. One is directed outward, toward external surroundings. Time seems to slow down. She identifies a freedom from "trivial occupations" as a source of the pleasure in the experience.

## William Wordsworth

The English Romantic poet explains the sublime in terms of an intense unity and repetition of forms, above all, natural forms. He describes the sense of sublimity and "awe" that can be felt even by a child or "unpracticed" person.

## Mary Shelley

In the first of two excerpts from *Frankenstein*, the creator (Victor Frankenstein) explains his enthusiastic and rapturous research into animation and how he imbued matter with life in "a kind of enthusiastic frenzy." The wretch (the creature) is observed for the first time. In the second excerpt, Victor ascends a glacier and confronts the creature at noon.

## Arthur Schopenhauer

The sublime lies on a continuum, extending from weaker or calmer experiences to the most moving and exemplary experiences of sublimity. The difference between the sublime and the beautiful, the author holds, ultimately rests not so much in the objects as in the experiencing subject.

## Georg W. F. Hegel

The German Idealist philosopher discusses Indian, Persian, Christian, and Hebrew poetry and writings. Hegel defines the sublime as an external shaping which is itself annihilated in turn by what it reveals (the "infinite"). The (finite) revelation of the content (the infinite) is at the same time a supersession or overcoming of that revelation.

## Richard Wagner

The German composer thinks that music should be judged more by the category of the sublime than the beautiful. Wagner's conception of the artistic sublime reflects a kind of optimism for the future, albeit one that is based on Greek art and Beethoven.

## Chapter Summaries

Friedrich Nietzsche
The classical philologist and philosopher characterizes the sublime as a form of inspired enthusiasm: the sublime can be identified in the shared experience of Dionysian ecstasy. Second, Nietzsche's famous "madman" passage employs the rhetoric of the sublime. In a third excerpt, Nietzsche offers a non-Kantian version of the sublime.

Rudolf Otto
The German Lutheran theologian uses the sublime to describe the feeling of the numinous, or the religious feeling before the holy. The sublime is the "schema" of the numinous, rendering the numinous palpable in the aesthetic sphere. Otto explains how the numinous can be represented in a variety of art forms traditionally considered sublime, including some works of architecture, Chinese painting, and music.

Barnett Newman
The American abstract expressionist painter uses the categories of the sublime and the beautiful to discuss new directions for art. His essay reveals a desire among some American avant-garde painters to distinguish their work from European art.

Julia Kristeva
The author discusses the sublime and what she calls the "abject." Not limited to filth and waste, the abject is caused by what disturbs identity, order, law, and limits. Unlike an ordinary object, the abject draws us toward the place where meaning collapses. The breaking of limits reveals a way in which the abject is "edged with" the sublime.

Fredric Jameson
Jameson describes the sublime that is found in new technological forms—which he calls the "postmodern" or "hysterical" sublime. Like Lyotard, he understands the sublime to concern the limits of figuration and representation.

Jean-François Lyotard
Taking into account the sublime's history, Lyotard discusses the Kantian sublime and abstract art, especially the paintings of Barnett Newman. In addition to defending avant-garde art, Lyotard comments on capitalism and the market's effects on art.

Meg Armstrong
Discussing Burke and Kant, Armstrong examines the complex relationships between aesthetics and the politics of gender and race. She analyzes the use of the concept of "bodies" in Burke and Kant. She offers possible strategies for countering dominant Euro-aesthetic visions of beauty and sublimity.

Cynthia Freeland
Freeland holds that some films or film scenes can be fruitfully described as sublime, offering several examples. She describes four basic features of the sublime and clarifies how her account is inspired by Kant yet differs from his theory. She thinks psychological and neuroscientific approaches can contribute to a theory of the sublime in film, but raises two challenges for these approaches.

Arthur Danto

In giving an historical overview of the sublime, the art critic and philosopher identifies crucial differences between the beautiful and the sublime. Discussing artists ranging from Michelangelo and Leonardo to Newman, Danto examines the relevance of sublimity to the creation and appreciation of a variety of artworks.

Vladimir J. Konečni

Konečni introduces the notion of an "aesthetic trinity" in order to account for peak aesthetic responses lying on a spectrum—from thrills and chills, to being moved or touched, to aesthetic awe. The latter, a subjective state, is typically induced by an (objective) "stimulus-in-context" that properly deserves the term "sublime."

Jane Forsey

Forsey asks challenging questions about the very possibility of a theory of the sublime. She raises concerns about a theory's claims regarding ontological and epistemological transcendence, which she thinks any theory is forced to address.

Sandra Shapshay

Shapshay comments on Forsey's article and develops her own ideas on the sublime. Specifically, she defends the idea that there are at least two kinds of sublime responses: the thick and the thin.

Robert R. Clewis

The volume editor outlines general features of the objects that paradigmatically incite sublime experiences. He characterizes the experience's phenomenology and emphasizes its intersubjectivity or sharedness. Why should the sublime be pleasing and satisfying rather than unpleasant, frustrating, or upsetting? He identifies five sources of the pleasures in the sublime.

Emily Brady

In her account of the natural or environmental sublime, Brady responds to three kinds of objections to the sublime: historical, metaphysical, and anthropocentric. In so doing, she emphasizes the activity of the "metaphysical imagination" in the experience of the sublime.

# NOTES

## Editor's Introduction

1. Some anthologies on the sublime or (more broadly) aesthetics include texts from certain periods in the sublime's long history, especially the eighteenth century. For instance, Cian Duffy and Peter Howell, *Cultures of the Sublime: Selected Readings, 1750–1830* (Houndmills, Basingstoke and Hampshire: Palgrave Macmillan, 2011); *The Sublime: A Reader in British Eighteenth-century Aesthetic Theory*, ed. Andrew Ashfield and Peter de Bolla (Cambridge: Cambridge university Press, 1996); and *Eighteenth-Century British Aesthetics*, ed. Dabney Townsend (Amityville: Baywood Publishing, 1999). See also the French anthology, Friedrich Schiller, et al., *Du Sublime: (de Boileau à Schiller): Suivi de la Traduction de* Über das Erhabene *de Friedrich Schiller*, ed. Pierre Hartmann (Strasbourg: Presses universitaires de Strasbourg, 1997). Although there are several contributed volumes with chapters on the sublime, most studies are either written by contemporary authors (hence not constituting an historical anthology), or the contributed volumes focus on narrower topics such as contemporary art, rhetoric or literature, art history, and the arts. See, for instance, *Translations of the Sublime: The Early Modern Reception and Dissemination of Longinus'* Peri Hupsous *in Rhetoric, the Visual Arts, Architecture and the Theatre*, ed. Caroline van Eck, et al. (Leiden: Brill, 2012). *Beyond the Finite: The Sublime in Art and Science*, ed. Roald Hoffmann and Iain Boyd Whyte (New York: Oxford University Press, 2011). Simon Morley, *The Sublime* (London: Whitechapel Gallery, 2010). *The Sublime Now*, ed. Luke White and Claire Pajaczkowska (Newcastle upon Tyne: Cambridge Scholars Publishing, 2009). *Sticky Sublime*, ed. Bill Beckley (New York: Allworth Press, 2001). *The Most Sublime Act: Essays on the Sublime*, ed. Tadeusz Rachwal and Tadeusz Slawek (Katowice: Wydawnictwo Universytetu Śląskiego, 1994). *Of the Sublime: Presence in Question*, ed. Jean-François Courtine and trans. Jeffrey Librett (Albany: State University of New York Press, 1993). *The Textual Sublime: Deconstruction and Its Differences*, ed. Hugh J. Silverman and Gary E. Aylesworth (Albany: State University of New York Press, 1989).

2. Michelle Shiota, Belinda Campos, and Dacher Keltner, "The Faces of Positive Emotion: Prototype Displays of Awe, Amusement, and Pride," *Annals of the New York Academy of Sciences* 1000, no. 1 (2003): 296–99. An important early paper on awe (which also discusses the sublime) is Dacher Keltner and Jonathan Haidt, "Approaching Awe, a Moral, Spiritual, and Aesthetic emotion," *Cognition & Emotion* 17, no. 2 (2003): 297–314. That the experience of awe draws attention *away* from the self and toward the environment is maintained in Michelle Shiota, Dacher Keltner, and Amanda Mossman, "The Nature of Awe: Elicitors, Appraisals, and Effects on Self-Concept." *Cognition and Emotion* 21, no. 5 (2007): 944–63. Psychologists have studied awe as a kind of self-transcendent experience. David B. Yaden, Jonathan Haidt, Ralph Hood, Jr., David Vago, and Andrew Newberg, "The Varieties of Self-Transcendent Experience," *Review of General Psychology* 21, no. 2 (2017): 143–60. Empirical studies of awe continue to employ new technologies—perhaps with clinical payoffs. Alice Chirico, David Yaden, Giuseppe Riva, and Andrea Gaggioli, "The Potential of Virtual Reality for the Investigation of Awe," *Frontiers in Psychology* (2016) vol. 7, article 1766: 1–6. See also Vladimi Konečni's contribution to the present volume.

3. There are many instructive introductions and overviews of the sublime, which I will not attempt here to duplicate or supersede. James Porter analyzes the sublime in antiquity before and after Longinus, that is, in Greek and Roman poetry, philosophy, sciences, rhetoric, and literary criticism; James I. Porter, *The Sublime in Antiquity* (Cambridge: Cambridge University Press, 2015). For an overview to a volume containing many instructive chapters on the history of the sublime, see Costelloe's Introduction, in *The Sublime: From Antiquity to the Present*, ed. Timothy M. Costelloe (Cambridge: Cambridge University Press, 2012). Philip Shaw's concise introductory book is useful and adopts a cultural and literary perspective; Philip Shaw, *The Sublime* (London: Routledge, 2017 [2006]). James Kirwan traces the history of the sublime from its emergence in the eighteenth century to its resurgence in contemporary aesthetics; James Kirwan, *Sublimity: The Non-Rational and the Irrational in the History of Aesthetics* (London: Routledge, 2005). Baldine Saint Girons offers a helpful history of the sublime; Baldine Saint Girons, *Le*

*Sublime, de l'Antiquité à Nos Jours* (Paris: Desjonquères, 2005). An overview emphasizing linguistic and rhetorical themes, with an extensive bibliography, can be found in Kenneth Holmqvist and Jaroslaw Pluciennik, "A Short Guide to the Theory of the Sublime." *Style* 36, no. 4 (2002): 718–37. Their semantic project is developed in Kenneth Holmqvist and Jaroslaw Pluciennik, *Infinity in Language: Conceptualization of the Experience of the Sublime* (Newcastle upon Tyne: Cambridge Scholars Publishers, 2008). Sanford Budick traces the "cultural" sublime in the western tradition; Sanford Budick, *The Western Theory of Tradition: Terms and Paradigms of the Cultural Sublime* (New Haven: Yale University Press, 2000). The 1935 classic study by Monk is still very informative; Samuel H. Monk, *The Sublime: A Study of Critical Theories in XVIII-Century England: With a New Preface by the Author* (Ann Arbor: The University of Michigan Press, 1960); as are both Walter John Hipple, Jr., *The Beautiful, the Sublime, and the Picturesque in Eighteenth Century Aesthetic Theory* (Carbondale: The Southern Illinois University Press, 1957); and Meyer H. Abrams, *The Mirror and the Lamp* (New York: Norton, 1953). Two recommended bibliographies are Giovanni Lombardo and Francesco Finocchiaro, *Sublime Antico e Moderno: una Bibliografia* (Palermo: Università di Palermo, 1993); and Demetrio Marin, *Bibliography of the "Essay on the Sublime" (Peri Hypsous)* (Bari: Leiden, 1967). These are only a few of many studies and resources. Furthermore, background information about selections in the present volume can be found in brief headnotes preceding each reading.

4. Saint Augustine, *Confessions*, trans. R. S. Pine-Coffin (London: Penguin, 1961), 147 (*Confessions* 7.10.16). On oratory, rhetoric, and style, see Augustine, *On Christian Doctrine,* trans. D. W. Robertson, Jr. (Indianapolis: Bobbs-Merrill, 1958), book 4, chapters 12–27.

5. William James, *The Varieties of Religious Experience: A Study in Human Nature* (New York: Longmans Green, 1903).

6. Rudolf Otto, *The Idea of the Holy,* trans. John W. Harvey (London: Oxford University Press, 1972).

7. For a theology of the sublime responding to the theories of Kant, Heidegger, and Jean-Luc Nancy, see John Betz, "Beyond the Sublime: The Aesthetics of the Analogy of Being (Part One)," *Modern Theology* 21 (2005): 367–411; and John Betz, "Beyond the Sublime: The Aesthetics of the Analogy of Being (Part Two)," *Modern Theology* 22 (2006): 1–50. For a Kant-inspired theological perspective, see Clayton Crockett, *A Theology of the Sublime* (London: Routledge, 2001).

8. For a history of the word "sublime," see Theodore E. B. Wood, *The Word "Sublime" and Its Context 1650–1760* (The Hague: Mouton, 1972). On the etymology and transformations of the word "sublime," see Jan Cohn and Thomas N. Miles. "The Sublime in Alchemy, Aesthetics, Psychoanalysis," *Modern Philology* 74 (1977): 289–304.

9. It seems impossible to give a viable, comprehensive, lasting, once-and-for-all definition of the term. In my own chapter in this volume, I offer not a definition, but a sketch of a theory of the sublime. The sublime eludes a non-stipulative, final definition not so much because the sublime is "ineffable" as because it is an aesthetic term with a long and complicated history.

10. Ludwig Wittgenstein, *Tractatus Logico-Philosophicus*, trans. C. K. Ogden (London: Routledge & Kegan Paul, 1922), proposition 7. I think of this strand of the sublime as the "transcendent" strand.

11. I have sympathy for the idea that there are some parallels across texts and times—even in the absence of direct scholarly or literary influence. For instance, the discussions of fear or terror by Bharata and Burke, or the views of painting offered by Guo Xi and Barnett Newman, make for interesting comparisons, even if there was no influence of the former on the latter.

12. Monk, *The Sublime*, 213, n. 27.

13. Porter makes this argument throughout *The Sublime in Antiquity*.

14. Applying this principle (and employing a distinction between literary responses to the sublime and theories about the latter), I did not include selections from Percy Shelley's "Mont Blanc" or Milton's *Paradise Lost*, but did include a prose text by Wordsworth. Some selections (e.g., the excerpt from Mary Shelley's *Frankenstein*) remain in a gray area but were still included, whereas other borderline texts such as Melville's *Moby Dick* (on the whiteness of the whale) simply could not be included. See selection criterion 2.

15. Examples of recognizable authors not here reprinted include: Plato, Aristotle, Lucretius, Augustine, Plotinus, Bonaventure, Aquinas, John Baillie, Joseph Addison, Frances Hutcheson, Henry Home (Lord Kames), Alexander Gerard, David Hume, Archibald Alison, Shaftesbury, Johann Gottfried Herder, Thomas Reid, Friedrich Wilhelm Joseph Schelling, Friedrich Theodor Vischer, Henry David Thoreau, Victor Hugo, John Muir, George Santayana, Sigmund Freud, Martin Heidegger, Emmanuel Levinas, Slavoj Žižek, Jacques Lacan, Thomas Weiskel, Neil Hertz,

Jacques Derrida, Jean-Luc Nancy, Jacques Rancière, Marc Richir, Jean Baudrillard, Gilles Deleuze, Theodor Adorno, David Nye, Mario Costa, Christine Battersby, and Barbara Freeman. In some cases, a writer or tradition included in this volume is well studied—for example, Petrarch, Vico, Mendelssohn, Wordsworth—even if that tradition or writer's theory of the *sublime* is not sufficiently recognized. (Hume's philosophy in general has had enormous influence, but not his theory of the sublime. One could make the case that Hume's theory of the sublime deserves a place in this anthology even though he is so well studied—but the modern period was already so crowded.) The list of philosophers and writers omitted from this anthology but whose theories deserve consideration and attention is surely longer than the above list.

16. *Of the Sublime*, ed. Courtine.

17. Judy Lochhead, "The Sublime, the Ineffable, and Other Dangerous Aesthetics," *Women and Music: A Journal of Gender and Culture* 12, no. 1 (2008): 63–74, 72.

18. Freeman proposes a feminine sublime that confounds such constructions. Barbara Claire Freeman, *The Feminine Sublime: Gender and Excess in Women's Fiction* (Berkeley: University of California Press, 1995).

19. Bonnie Mann, *Women's Liberation and the Sublime: Feminism, Postmodernism, Environment* (New York: Oxford University Press, 2006), 31 (exclamation point in the original).

20. See James Colin McQuillan, *Early Modern Aesthetics* (London: Rowman & Littlefield International, 2016); and Townsend, *Eighteenth-Century British Aesthetics*, preface, iii–iv.

21. Li Bai or Li Po (701–762): Chinese poet and author of "Viewing the Waterfall at Mount Lu."

22. Lao-tzu, *Tao Te Ching*, trans. Stephen Mitchell (New York: HarperCollins, 1988), 14. This text could be classified under the ineffable or transcendent strand of the sublime.

23. *The Writings of Kwang-dze* [*Chuang Tzŭ*], in *The Sacred Books of the East*, vol. 39, ed. F. Max Müller and trans. James Legge (Oxford: Clarendon Press, 1891), 379; text slightly modified. Cf. the passage on page 188, beginning: "Under heaven there is nothing greater than the tip of an autumn down, and the Thâi mountain is small."

24. Excerpts from Dennis are found in Ashfield and de Bolla, *The Sublime*, and in Townsend, *Eighteenth-Century British Aesthetics*. The Lyotard reading is reprinted widely, including in *The Bloomsbury Anthology of Aesthetics*, ed. Joseph J. Tanke and J. Colin McQuillan (New York: Bloomsbury Academic, 2012).

25. Samuel Taylor Coleridge, *On the Sublime*, ed. David Vallins (New York: Palgrave Macmillan, 2003).

26. On the sublime in Greek and Roman antiquity, including an excellent discussion of Plato, see Porter, *The Sublime in Antiquity*, esp. 537–617. The Greek adjective (also used by Plato) *kalon* can refer to the beautiful, fine, admirable, or noble.

27. Martin Heidegger also deserves to be mentioned. Anxiety and wonder are core emotions in Heidegger's philosophy, and they bear similarities to the sublime. Although these emotions play crucial roles in Heidegger's phenomenological analysis, he never focuses on the sublime. Despite three published book-length studies on Kant and numerous essays and lectures that allude to Kant, Heidegger "does not devote any major discussion to the Kantian sublime" even though Heidegger frequently "invokes key terms from the discourse of the sublime." Jeffrey S. Librett, "Afterword," in *Of the Sublime*, 193–219, 194.

28. For example, Yi Zheng, *From Burke and Wordsworth to the Modern Sublime in Chinese Literature* (West Lafayette: Purdue University Press, 2010). Lap-Chuen Tsang, *The Sublime: Groundwork Towards a Theory* (Rochester: University of Rochester Press, 1998). Kin-yuen Wong, "Negative-Positive Dialectic in the Chinese Sublime," in *The Chinese Text: Studies in Comparative Literature*, ed. Ying-Hsiung Chou (Hong Kong: The Chinese University Press, 1986), 119–58. For a discussion of the Hindu Brahman in relation to Jean-François Lyotard and Paul de Man, see Vijay Mishra, *Devotional Poetics and the Indian Sublime* (Albany: State University of New York Press, 1998).

29. Ashfield and de Bolla desire to overthrow the established scholarly tradition that casts "the British discussion as a kind of dress rehearsal for the full-fledged philosophical aesthetics of Immanuel Kant and his heirs"; Ashfield and de Bolla, *The Sublime*, 2. See also de Bolla's study of the sublime, Peter de Bolla, *The Discourse of the Sublime: Readings in History, Aesthetics and the Subject* (Oxford: Basil Blackwell, 1989).

30. For a provocative study that discusses the Arabic tradition (and identifies Longinus as the third-century rhetorician Cassius Longinus), see Adnan K. Abdulla, *A Comparative Study of Longinus and Al-Jurjani: The Interrelationships between Medieval Arabic Literary Criticism and Graeco-Roman Poetics* (Lewiston: Edwin Mellen Press, 2004).

31. The dates and authorship of *Peri Hypsous* are controversial, and it is not necessary to take stance on this issue here. I simply refer to the author of that treatise as Longinus.

32. Augustine, *Confessions*, 7.10.16 (Pine-Coffin translation, 147). On horror, dread, or awe in the divine presence, see also *Confessions* 9.4.9; 11.9.11; and 12.14.17.

33. Bonaventure, *The Journey of the Mind to God* (ch. 2, no. 3), trans. Philotheus Boehner (Indianapolis: Hackett, 1993), 12, translation modified.

34. Bonaventure, *Journey* (ch. 7, no. 5), 46, translation modified. Bonaventure also refers to God's "sublimity and dignity" (*sublimitatem et dignitatem*); see *Journey* (ch. 1, no. 14), 10. He refers to being rooted and grounded in "charity" so that we can comprehend the "sublimity of majesty" (*sublimitas maiestatisi*); see *Journey* (ch. 4, no. 8), 27.

35. Thomas Aquinas, *Summa Theologiae*, 61 vols. (Cambridge and New York: Blackfriars and McGraw-Hill, 1964–80). See *Summa Theologiae*, II-II, 180, ad.3. "[A]dmiratio est species timoris consequens apprehensionem alicuius rei excedentis nostram facultatem. Unde admiratio est actus consequens contemplationem sublimis veritatis. Dictum est enim quod contemplatio in affectu terminatur." Thanks to Patrick Messina for assistance with the translation.

36. On these aspects during the medieval period, see the essays collected in *Magnificence and the Sublime in Medieval Aesthetics: Art, Architecture, Literature, Music*, ed. Stephen C. Jaeger (New York: Palgrave Macmillan, 2010).

37. For instance, Gen. 1:3: "And God said, Let there be light: and there was light."

38. Diderot is an often-overlooked figure in the history of the sublime. Due to space limitations and an already crowded group of modern texts, he could not be included in the present volume. See Denis Diderot, *Diderot on Art: The Salon of 1765 and Notes on Painting*, trans. John Goodman, *Diderot on Art*, vol. 1 (New Haven and London: Yale University Press, 1995). See also *Diderot on Art: The Salon of 1767*, trans. John Goodman, *Diderot on Art*, vol. 2 (New Haven and London: Yale University Press, 1995).

39. Exactly how the sublime has a basis or ground in reason, and what reflection here means, is a matter of considerable debate. There is a related dispute about what exactly Kant thinks the predicate "sublime" properly applies or refers to—ideas of reason, reason itself, the human moral vocation and calling, the capacity to set ends, freedom, and so on.

40. Johann Gottfried Herder, *Kalligone: Vom Angenehmen und Schönen* (Leipzig: Johann Friedrich Hartknoch, 1800).

41. Late nineteenth-century and early twentieth-century theorists such as Arthur Seidl and Hermann Stephani described aspects of the musical sublime in concrete technical terms. Arthur Seidl, *Vom Musikalisch-Erhabenen: Prolegomena zur Aesthetik der Tonkunst* (Regensburg: Druck von M. Wasner, 1887). Hermann Stephani, *Das Erhabene insonderheit in der Tonkunst, und das Problem der Form im Musikalisch-Schönen und Erhabenen* (Leipzig: H. S. Nachfolger, 1903). For a recent discussion of the sublime and music, see Adam Krims, "The Hip-Hop Sublime as a Form of Commodification," in *Music and Marx: Ideas, Practice, Politics*, ed. R. B. Qureshi (Chicago: University of Chicago Press, 2002), 63–80.

42. Sigmund Freud, *Civilization and Its Discontents*, edited and translated by James Strachey (New York: W. W. Norton & Company, 1961), 11.

43. Jacques Lacan, *The Ethics of Psychoanalysis, 1959–1960: The Seminar of Jacques Lacan, Book VII*, trans. Dennis Porter and ed. Jacques-Alain Miller (London: Routledge, 1992). Slavoj Žižek, *The Sublime Object of Ideology* (London: Verso, 1989).

44. E. F. Carritt, "The Sublime," *Mind* 19, 75 (1910): 356–72. He was criticizing the theory of A. C. Bradley.

45. Guy Sircello, "How is a Theory of the Sublime Possible?" *Journal of Aesthetics and Art Criticism* 51, no. 4 (1993): 541–50.

## Chapter 1

1. *Greek and Roman Aesthetics*, ed. Oleg Bychkov and Anne Sheppard (Cambridge: Cambridge University Press, 2010), xxv–xxvi.

2. James Arieti, in Longinus, *On the Sublime*, trans. James A. Arieti and John M. Crossett (New York: Edwin Mellen Press, 1985), xi.

# Notes

3. For an overview on authorship and dating, see Demetrio Marin, *Bibliography of the "Essay on the Sublime" (Peri Hypous)* (Leiden: Brill, 1967), 84–91. Marin is convinced that the author is the rhetorician Dionysios of Halikarnassos. See Marin, *Bibliography*, 87.

4. Marin, *Bibliography*, 1. See also Bernard Weinberg, "Translations and Commentaries of Longinus, *On the Sublime*, to 1600: A Bibliography," *Modern Philology* 47, no. 3 (1950): 145–51; and Gustavo Costa, "The Latin Translations of Longinus's *Peri hypsous* in Renaissance Italy," in *Acta Conventus Neo-Latini Bononiensis: Proceedings of the Fourth International Congress of Neo-Latin Studies, Bologna 26 August to 1 September 1979* (Binghampton: SUNY Press, 1985), 224–38.

5. Marin, *Bibliography*, 7.

6. Marin, *Bibliography*, 7. Cf. Weinberg, 146. Klaus Ley, *Longin – Von Bessarion Zu Boileau: Wirkungsmomente Der "Schrift Über Das Erhabene" in Der Frühen Neuzeit* (Berlin: Weidler, 2013) 190, 192. The text is manuscript Vat. Lat. 3441, Vatican Library. Ley's book includes a transcription of MS 3441 (pages 429–60), as well as a transcription of Falgano (Florence, 1575) (pages 461–501).

7. Marin, *Bibliography*, 10. A similar view is in *Translations of the Sublime*, trans. Caroline A. van Eck, et al. (Leiden: Brill, 2012), 8.

8. Bernard Weinberg, "Une Traduction Française Du 'Sublime' De Longin Vers 1645," *Modern Philology* 59, no. 3 (1962): 159–201.

9. van Eck, *Translations*, 1.

10. Arieti, in Longinus, *On the Sublime*, x.

11. Caecilius of Celeacte was an influential critic, active in the first century BC. Most of our knowledge of his views about sublimity has to be inferred from Longinus' refutation.

12. See Demosthenes, *Against Aristocrates* (23). 113.

13. This work no longer survives.

14. Longinus proceeds to discuss the first, second, third, fourth and fifth sources of sublimity in turn but, surprisingly, does not discuss emotion as a separate topic, despite the importance which he clearly attaches to it. The selection from his work presented here omits much of the rather technical discussion of figures, diction and word-arrangement.

15. Homer, *Odyssey* II. 315–17.

16. Encomia were formal speeches of praise.

17. In *Odyssey* II. 563 Ajax turns away from Odysseus in the Underworld without speaking.

18. Parmenio, one of Alexander the Great's generals, is reported to have said that if he were Alexander, he would stop fighting, to which Alexander retorted, 'So would I, if I were Parmenio.'

19. About six pages of the manuscript of *On Sublimity* are missing here.

20. Homer in *Iliad* 4.440ff. describes Strife as having her head in the sky and walking on earth. Longinus means that Homer too is a figure of cosmic dimensions.

21. Line 267 in the *Shield of Heracles*, a poem attributed to Hesiod.

22. *Iliad* 5.770–2.

23. Longinus here combines *Iliad* 21.388 and 20.61–5.

24. This passage conflates *Iliad* 13.18–19, 20.60, and 13.27–9.

25. *Iliad* 17.645–7.

26. *Iliad* 15.605–7.

27. These words are spoken by the aged Nestor in *Odyssey* 3.109–11.

28. Zoilus, a philosopher and rhetorician of the fourth century BC, was notorious for his severe criticisms of Homer.

29. Sappho, fr. 31.

30. The *Arimaspea* was a lost poem attributed to Aristeas of Proconessus, a prophet of Apollo in the seventh century BC. The Arimaspi are described by Herodotus (4.27) as one-eyed people perpetually attempting to steal a hoard of gold guarded by griffins.

31. *Iliad* 15.624–8.

32. Aratus, *Phaenomena* 299.

33. Several extant fragments by the lyric poet Archilochus relate to storms and shipwreck, but we do not know just which passage Longinus is referring to here. The passage of Demosthenes is the famous description of the panic at Athens when news came one evening in 339 BC that Phillip of Macedon had captured Elatea (*On the Crown* 169).

34. Plato, *Republic* 9.586a–b (slightly adapted).

35. It was widely believed in antiquity that the Pythia, the priestess of Apollo at Delphi, inhaled a vapor which sent her into a prophetic trance.

36. Ammonius was a second-century BC critic, a pupil of the famous Alexandrian scholar Aristarchus. He wrote a work on Plato's borrowings from Homer.

37. Hesiod, *Works and Days*, 24.

38. The first quotation comes from Euripides, *Orestes* 255–7, the second from Euripides, *Iphigenia in Tauris*, 291. Both are spoken by Orestes who sees the Furies (the Erinyes) pursuing him in vengeance for his killing of his mother, Clytemnestra.

39. Homer, *Iliad* 20.170–1.

40. These two passages come from Euripides' *Phaethon*, a play which told how Phaethon, on discovering that he was the son of Helios, the sun-god, asked to be allowed to drive the chariot of the sun across the sky, with disastrous consequences. Substantial fragments of the play survive.

41. This line may come from Euripides' lost play, *Alexandros*.

42. Aeschylus, *Seven against Thebes*, 42–46.

43. The first quotation comes from Aeschylus, *Lycurgus* fr. 58 Radt, the second from Euripides, *Bacchae* 726.

44. The first part of the sentence refers to the final scene of Sophocles' *Oedipus at Colonus*, the second perhaps to the appearance of Achilles' ghost in Sophocles' lost play, *Polyxena*.

45. Euripides, *Orestes* 264–5.

46. Demosthenes *Against Timocrates* (24).208.

47. Philip of Macedon defeated the southern Greek states, led by Athens and Thebes, at the battle of Chaeronea in 338 BC. The orator Hyperides played a leading role in Athenian opposition to Philip after the battle.

48. Eratosthenes, like Apollonius and Theocritus, was an Alexandrian poet of the third century BC. His lost poem, *Erigone*, told the story of the death of Icarius and the suicide of his daughter Erigone.

49. Hyperides' account of Leto occurred in a lost speech, the *Deliacus*. His Funeral Speech, on those who fell in the Lamian War, largely survives.

50. Hyperides' defence of Phyrne, a courtesan, is lost. His speech *Against Athenogenes*, a large part of which survives, concerns a contract for the purchase of slaves.

51. A line from the 'epigram on the tomb of Midas' ascribed to Homer.

52. It is disputed whether this refers specifically to the very large "Colossus of Rhodes" or just to any colossal statue. The Doryphorus of Polyclitus was famous for its beautiful proportions.


## Chapter 2

1. *Nāṭyaśāstra*, trans. Ghosh, 102.

2. Ibid., 107.

3. Kathleen M. Higgins, "An Alchemy of Emotions: Rasa and Aesthetic Breakthroughs," *Journal of Aesthetics and Art Criticism* 65 (2007): 43–54, 49.

4. *Nāṭyaśāstra*, trans. Ghosh, 102.

## Notes

5. Square and round brackets are reprinted as they appear in Ghosh's translation, unless otherwise noted. Ghosh's footnotes have been omitted.

6. A Sloka is a (sometimes poetic) saying or proverb; in the present case, it gives directions to actors.

## Chapter 3

1. Kin-yuen Wong, "Negative-positive Dialectic in the Chinese sublime," in *The Chinese Text: Studies in Comparative Literature*, ed. Ying-Hsiung Chou (Hong Kong: The Chinese University Press, 1986), 147, 152.

2. Kin-yuen Wong, "Negative-positive Dialectic in the Chinese sublime," 155, 158.

3. Sherman E. Lee, *A History of Far Eastern Art* (New York: H.N. Abrams, 1967), 348f.

4. The translator thanks Lauren Pfister and Jesse Ciccotti for their insights and revisions of this translation. The editor is grateful to Jonathan Johnson for his translation of Guo Xi's text.

5. While this could be taken as "peace" or "peaceful-distance," the translator has interpreted it here in a more aesthetic sense.

6. Or: quality, expression.

7. Since these phrases pertain to depiction of figures in landscape paintings, one could also use terms such as "small strokes" rather than "fine pieces."

8. It is helpful to recall that these three phrases are used in the context of a treatise on painting, in which the artist obeying the rules of perspective must paint figures using appropriate brushstrokes.

## Chapter 4

1. "Zeami—Introduction," in *Literary Criticism (1400–1800)*, ed. Michael L. LaBlanc, vol. 86 (Detroit, MI: Gale Cengage, 2003). Accessed June 1, 2017.

2. Graham Parkes, "Japanese Aesthetics," in *The Stanford Encyclopedia of Philosophy*, ed. Edward N. Zalta (Spring 2017 Edition) (Stanford: Stanford University, 2017).

3. Zeami, *On the Art of the Nō Drama: The Major Treatises of Zeami* (Princeton: Princeton University Press, 1984), 73.

4. A phrase often cited, in a slightly different form, in a variety of texts by Zen priests of the period, such as Musō Kokushi (AD 1275–1351).

5. Another Zen saying that appears, in various versions, in a number of texts circulated at this time in Japan, among them the Hsü-t'ang ho-shang yü (Jap. Kidō oshō goroku) (The Sayings of Preceptor Hsü-t'ang). Hsü-t'ang (AD 1185–1269) was a priest of the Ch'an (Jap. Zen) sect. The passage is located in Book 2.

6. A passage found in Section 13 of the *Pi-yen lu* (*The Blue Cliff Records*) compiled by Yüan-wu (AD 1036–1135) and widely circulated in Japan as the Hekiganroku. For a translation of the passage, see R. D. M. Shaw, trans., *The Blue Cliff Records*, 65–67.

7. The precise source of this quotation has not been determined.

8. The phrase is adapted from *The Blue Cliff Records*, Section 53. See R. D. M. Shaw, 177–78.

9. That is, what the world calls the Way of *nō* is Role Playing, yet the True Way represents the Two Basic Arts. The phrase is an adaption of the opening of section one of the *Tao Te Ching* of Lao Tzu. See Arthur Waley, trans., *The Way and Its Power* (New York: Grove Press, 1958), 141. Zeami has slightly changed the emphasis of the original.

10. A similar passage appears in Section 12 of *The Blue Cliff Records*. See R. D. M. Shaw, *The Blue Cliff Records*, 59–60.

11. A similar phrase appears in Section 27 of the *Shih-men wen-tzu ch'an* (Jap. *Sekimon moji zen*) [Zen of the Stone Gate Inscription], compiled by the Chinese Ch'an priest Hui-hung (AD 1071–1128).

12. The phrase does not originate in Confucius but in the writings of the Confucian scholar Hsün Ch'ing (Hsun-tzu), ca. 300 BC. See the following note.

13. See Homer H. Dubs, trans., *The Works of Hsüntze* (London: Arthur Probsthain, 1928), 35.

14. The phrase is based on one from the *Cheng-tao ke* (Jap. *Shōdōka*) [The Song of Enlightenment] by the Chinese priest Yung-chia (AD 665–713) of the T'ien-t'ai (Jap. Tendai) sect. For a translation of the passage, see Daisetz Teitaro Suzuki, *Manual of Zen Buddhism*, 121.

## Chapter 5

1. The name of the mountain appears as "Ventosus" in Latin documents as early as the tenth century, though originally it had nothing to do with the strong winds blowing about that isolated peak. Its Provençal form "Ventour" proves that it is related to the name of a deity worshiped by the pre-Roman (Ligurian) population of the Rhone Basin, a god believed to dwell on high mountains (cf. C. Jullian, *Histoire de la Gaule,* VI, 329; P. Julian, "Glose sur l'étymologie du mot Ventoux," in *Le Pélérinage du Mt: Ventoux* [Carpentras, 1937], 337 ff.).

2. In his *History of Rome* (xl. 21.2–22.7) Livy tells that King Philip V of Macedonia went up to the top of Mount Haemus, one of the highest summits of the Great Balkans (ca. 7,800 feet), when he wanted to reconnoiter the field of future operations before the Third Macedonian War, which he was planning to fight against the Romans (181 BC). Since Petrarca knew the exact location of this mountain from Pliny's *Natural History* (iv. 1. 3 and xi. 18. 41), it must have been a slip of his pen that made him substitute "Thessaly" for "Thrace."

3. Mela *Cosmographia* ii. 2. 17.

4. Cf. Cicero *De imperio Cn. Pompei* 21. 61, where he praises the courage of Pompey, who took over the command of the Roman armies in 77 BC though he was then but an "adulescentulus privatus."

5. Virgil *Georgica* i. 145–46; Macrobius *Saturnalia* v. 6.

6. Mt. 7:14 (Sermon on the Mount).

7. A typical metaphor familiar to ecclesiastical writers; cf., for example, Anselm of Canterbury *Letters* i. 43 (Migne, *Patrologia Latina,* CLVIII, 1113, etc.), where it is used as a friendly wish in salutations.

8. Ovid *Ex Ponto* iii. 1. 35.

9. Ps. 106 (107): 10; Job 34:22.

10. 1 Cor. 15:52; Augustine *Confessions* vii. 1. 1 (cf. Shakespeare, *Merchant of Venice,* Act. II, scene 2, line 183).

11. Though Petrarca was familiar with the idiom of southern France, he misinterpreted the Provençal word *fiholo*. There is still today a spring just below the summit of Mont Ventoux called "Font-filiole" and a ravine nearby by the name of "combe filiole," the word meaning a water conduit or a rivulet, but the summit can have received the name only secondarily (P. de Champeville, "L'ltinéraire du poète F. P." in *L'Ascension du Mt. Ventoux* [Carpentras, 1937], p. 41).

12. Hannibal is said to have made his troops burn down the trees on rocks obstructing their way and pour vinegar on the ashes to pulverize the burned material when he crossed the Alps in 218 BC (Livy *History of Rome* xxi. 37; cf. Pliny *Nat. Hist.* xxiii. 57). Later authors referred to this incident as an example of Hannibal's ingenuity in overcoming seemingly unsurmountable obstacles (Juvenal *Satire* 10, 153).

13. Petrarca is referring to Giacomo Colonna, bishop of Lombez, who had gone to Rome in the summer of 1333; cf. *Fam.,* I, 5 (4), and I, 6 (5).

14. *Confessions* ii. 1. 1.

15. Ovid *Amores* iii. 11. 35.

16. Two rival wills are struggling in Petrarca's breast, the old one not releasing him from his amorous servitude and blocking his spiritual progress, the other urging him forward on the way to perfection (cf. Augustine *Confessions* viii. 5. 10; x. 22–23, and Petrarca's Sonnet 52 (68).

# Notes

17. The small-sized manuscript codex of Augustine's *Confessions,* a present from Dionigi accompanied Petrarca wherever he went until the last year of his life, when he could no longer read its minute script and gave the book to Luigi Marsili as a token of his friendship.

18. Augustine *Confessions* x. 8. 15.

19. Seneca *Epistle* 8. 5.

20. Rom. 13:13–14, quoted by Augustine *Confessions* viii. 12. 29.

21. Mt. 19:21, quoted by Athanasius in his *Life of St. Anthony* (Latin version by Euagrius), chap. 2, and from there by Augustine *Confessions* viii. 12. 29.

22. Cf. Mt. 7:13–15.

23. Virgil *Georgica* ii. 490–92. [The ellipsis is in the translation. – Ed.]


## Chapter 6

1. Caroline A. van Eck, et al., eds., *Translations of the Sublime: The Early Modern Reception and Dissemination of Longinus' Peri Hupsous in Rhetoric, the Visual arts, Architecture and the Theatre* (Leiden: Brill, 2012), 3. On the development of modern aesthetics, see Paul Guyer, *A History of Modern Aesthetics* (Cambridge: Cambridge University Press, 2014), vol. 1.

2. Alfred Rosenberg, *Longinus in England bis zum Ende des 18. Jahrhunderts* (Berlin: Mayer & Müller, 1917); van Eck, et al., *Translations*, 8.

3. van Eck, et al., *Translations*, 8.

4. Ibid.; and James Porter, "Lucretius and the Sublime," in *The Cambridge Companion to Lucretius*, ed. Stuart Gillespie and Philip Hardie (Cambridge: Cambridge University Press, 2007), 167–85.

5. John Hall was a pamphlet writer for Cromwell; the poet Andrew Marvell drew on the sublime to write about the execution of King Charles I. The sublime's occasional connections to the political can be seen throughout the present anthology.

6. Quoted from Dilworth's translation in Boileau, *Selected Criticism*, 52. This definition from Reflection XII can be found, e.g., in Nicolas Boileau Despréaux, *Oeuvres de Nicolas Boileau Despréaux*, vol. 3 (Dresden: G. C. Walther, 1767), 323.

7. A Greek lexicographer of the tenth century AD in whose work are preserved fragments of many lost authors of antiquity.

8. Hermogenes, a Greek rhetorician of the second century AD, was born at Tarsus in Cilicia, went to Rome, and there became famous by the time he was fifteen.

9. Caecilius Calactinus, a teacher of rhetoric at Rome in the time of Augustus. His book on the sublime is lost. [Longinus is writing to rebut the views of Caecilius of Calacte. – Ed.]

10. In the sense of choice of words, and of ordering of words and ideas.

11. Isaac Casaubon, born in Geneva in 1559, died in London in 1614. This great Renaissance scholar and Calvinist theologian was called "the Phoenix of the learned" by Scaliger, who was at least his peer. He was buried in Westminster Abbey.

12. Boileau assumes, as did other people for some time to come, that this treatise *On the Sublime* was written by Cassius Longinus, a famous Neoplatonic philosopher, scholar, and critic of the third century AD. With the progress of knowledge we know now that our treatise was written by a writer unknown.

13. This Syrian Neoplatonic philosopher (ca. 233–304 AD) is best known for his works on the life and doctrine of Plotinus. He is said to have been also a pupil of Origen, and is known to have written fifteen books against the Christians.

14. *Lives of the Philosophers and the Sophists.* Eunapius, born at Sardis in Lydia about 347 AD, wrote the lives of the Neoplatonic philosophers after Plotinus.

15. Marc-Antoine Muret (1526–1585), poet, learned teacher, and priest.

16. According to the Latin form of Paolo Manuzio. He was the third son (1511–1574) of the great Aldus. He published an edition of Longinus, the second ever to be printed (the first was that of Robortello in Basel, 1554) in Venice in 1555.

17. Gabrielle dalla Pietra, whose Greek text with Latin translation appeared in Geneva in 1612. Brossette tells us that he was professor of Greek at Lausanne, and that he was alive in 1615.

18. Gerard Langbaine the elder (1609–1658), provost of Queen's College, Oxford. He reprinted, with notes, the edition of Petra, at Oxford in 1636 and 1638. Brossette, the *Dictionary of National Biography,* and the *Cambridge Bibliography of English Literature* are wrong in accrediting Langbaine with a translation of his own. See note by Dumonteil: Tome IV, page 17, in the Saint-Marc (1747) edition of Boileau; and B. Weinberg, "Translations and Commentaries of Longinus, *On the Sublime,* to 1600."

19. Tannegui Lefebvre (1615–1672), philologist and editor of classic texts, father of Madame Dacier, and teacher of her and her husband André. Lefebvre's edition, which reprinted the translation of Petra, was published in Saumur in 1663, as by Tanaquil Faber.

20. Literally "galimatias."

21. [This was the final paragraph in the first edition of the Preface (1674). – Ed.]

22. [This and the following paragraph were added to the 1683 edition, in response to criticisms by Pierre-Daniel Huet. – Ed.]

23. Pierre-Daniel Huet (1630–1721), learned in mathematics and ancient languages, as well as a frequenter of the Hôtel de Rambouillet, tutor to the Dauphin, and Bishop of Avranches.

24. "The gentlemen of Port-Royal," says Brossette, "and especially M. Lemaistre de Saci" (1613–1684: spiritual father at Port-Royal, and translator of works spiritual and profane).

25. Edition of 1683.

26. [These "Remarques" appeared in the same volume as Boileau's translation and preface. – Ed.]

27. See Note 19 [above, on Tannegui Lefebvre – Ed.]. Anne Lefebvre, Madame Dacier (1654–1720) was famous for her classical translations, commentaries, and editions. Her greatest triumph was her translation of Homer (*Iliad,* 1699; *Odyssey,* 1708).

28. Edition of 1701. [This final paragraph was added to the 1701 edition. – Ed.]

## Chapter 8

1. Vico quotes Horace, *de Arte Poetica*, 304–05. [Translation by Ben Jonson, *Horace, His Art of Poetrie* (1640), 19, 21. The ellipsis and modern spelling are found in the English translation. – Ed.]

2. Lucretius 1.73.

3. Lucretius 1.926.

4. To avoid giving the reader a sense of anachronism—this is, of course, from "Ulalume" by Edgar Allan Poe.

## Chapter 9

1. Tomohiro Ishizu and Semir Zeki, "A Neurobiological Enquiry into the Origins of Our Experience of the Sublime and Beautiful," *Frontiers in Human Neuroscience* 8 (2014), article 891: 1–10.

2. Richard Shusterman, "Somaesthetics and Burke's Sublime," *British Journal of Aesthetics* 45, no. 4 (2005): 323–41.

3. "A Description of the Events in Paris, 12–15 July 1789," in *The Morning Post* (July 21, 1789), page 2. Quoted in Robert R. Clewis, *The Kantian Sublime and the Revelation of Freedom* (Cambridge: Cambridge University Press, 2009), 200; and Duffy and Howell, *Cultures of the Sublime,* 163.

4. Edmund Burke, "Some Thoughts on the Approaching Executions, Humbly Offered to Consideration," in *The Works of Edmund Burke* (New York, 1834), vol. 2, 387. Quoted in *Cultures of the Sublime*, edited by Duffy and Howell, 162.

## Chapter 10

1. This overview draws extensively from Daniel Dahlstrom's notes and Introduction (ix–xxxix) in Moses Mendelssohn's *Philosophical Writings* (1997); and Daniel Dahlstrom, "Moses Mendelssohn," *The Stanford Encyclopedia of Philosophy* (Summer 2015 Edition), ed. Edward N. Zalta. https://plato.stanford.edu/archives/sum2015/entries/mendelssohn/

2. Caecilius was a Sicilian rhetorician working in Rome during the first century CE. His work on the sublime, mentioned by Longinus, has been lost entirely.

3. Longinus, *On the Sublime,* trans. W. Rhys Roberts (New York and London: Garland, 1987), 41.

4. Longinus' work is dedicated to Terentian. See *On the Sublime,* trans. Roberts, ch. 1, 41–43, and Introduction, 18–20.

5. Mendelssohn is referring to "Rhapsody," *Philosophical Writings*, 144–45 (in the volume edited by Dahlstrom).

6. Klopstock, *Der Messias,* Bk. I, Song IV, ll. 7, 10, page 65: "*Und* das Geschrey, *und* der tödtenden Wut, *und* der donnernde Himmel."

7. Longinus, *On the Sublime,* trans. Roberts, ch. 19, ch. 20, 98–99, 100–01.

8. The Roman general, Marcus Atilius Regulus (ca. 250 BC), was captured by the Carthaginians and then released for the purpose of conveying the Carthaginians' conditions for peace to Rome. After he argued for pursuing war further, he returned to prison in Carthage where he was tortured and killed.

9. Corneille, *Cinna* (Paris, 1640) and Johann Elias Schlegel, *Cannut* (Copenhagen, 1746).

10. Friedrick Nicolai, "Abhandlung vom Trauerspiel," *Bibliothek der schönen Wissenschaften und der freyen Künste* (Berlin, 1757) vol. I, Part I, page 56. (Nicolai's entire essay is to be found on pages 17–68).

11. Longinus, *On the Sublime*, trans. Roberts, ch. 7, 54–57.

12. Zeuxis was a Greek painter (fl. 400 BC) celebrated for his portrayal of human figures in superhuman proportions. Antinous (110–130 AD), a favorite of the Emperor Hadrian, was depicted in sculptures and on coins as a model of youthful beauty. [Dahlstrom translates *Bewunderwung* with either "awe" or "awe and admiration," and *Verwunderung* with "amazement." – Ed.]

13. "Behold a spectacle worthy of God's attention as he contemplates his work; behold what is worthy and fitting for God, a *brave man confronted with misfortune!*"; Cf. Seneca, *Moral Essays*, trans. John W. Basore (Cambridge, MA: Harvard University Press, 1970), vol. I, 10–11.

14. Horace, *Ars Poetica*, I.364: "that it does not fear a judge's critical insight." Cf. Horace, *Satires, Epistles and Ars Poetica*, trans. H. Rushton Fairclough (Cambridge, MA: Harvard University Press, 1966), 480–81.

15. Ibid., II.361–65.

16. *Iliad*, XVII.645.

17. *Der Messias*, Song IV, ll.5–12, vol. 1, 65. [A footnote by Dahlstrom here quotes the German text from *Der Messias*, but the German is omitted here and in the next footnote, also from *Der Messias*. – Ed.]

18. Ibid., Song V, ll. 217–23, vol. 1, 106.

19. Longinus, *On the Sublime*, trans. Roberts, ch. 10, 68–71.

20. Joseph Addison and Sir Richard Steele, *The Spectator,* No. 229 (Thursday, November 22, 1711); in *The Spectator*, ed. Gregory Smith (London: Dent, 1958), 180.

21. Longinus, *On the Sublime*, trans. Roberts, ch. 18, 96–97.

22. Demosthenes, *Phillipica* I.9–12. Cf. Demosthenes, *Works*, trans. J. H. Vince (London: Heinemann, 1930), 75.

23. [Like the present one, this essay was included in Mendelssohn's *Philosophical Writings* (1761). – Ed.]

24. Longinus, *On the Sublime*, trans. Roberts, ch. 7, 56–57.

25. Boileau, *Réflexions Critiques sur Quelques Passages de Longin* (Paris, 1693); the editors of [Mendelssohn's] Jubilee edition note, however, that the tenth and eleventh reflections stem from 1710, at which point Perrault was already dead; see Boileau *Œuvres* (Amsterdam, 1717), 276 n.

26. Charles Perrault, *Parallèle des Anciens et Modernes* (Paris, 1688).

27. Longinus, *On the Sublime*, trans. Roberts, ch. 7, 56–57.

# Chapter 11

1. But surely this is the case with *all* history during the dark ages. And the reason seems obvious; when the higher orders of society had no literary education, the consequence was that they thought little, and fought much. Hence politics in the present sense of the word, were little known. The sword was not only the *ultima*, but the *prima ratio regum*; and the success of battles depended more on individual strength and skill, than on scientific arrangement and combined movements. [Carter is referring to the phrase, *ultima ratio regum*, "the final argument of kings," that is, the resort to arms. In other words, the sword was not only the final, but also the first argument of kings. – Ed.]

2. [Carter's nephew and editor of the 1818 volume, Pennington, placed a note here expressing his wish that she had extended this claim into an argument for the soul's immortality. – Ed.]

3. [Carter is paraphrasing a letter by Horace (Quintus Horatius Flaccus) to Claudius Nero, in behalf of his friend Septimius (Horace, *Epistles* 1.9). "Only Septimius of course understands how much, Claudius, you make of me." Horace, *Satires, Epistles and Ars Poetica,* trans. H. Rushton Fairclough (Cambridge: Harvard University Press, 1966), 311. – Ed.]

4. [Carter is referring to a 1762 poem by Lord Lyttelton, "The Vision." Pennington included it in *A Series of Letters between Mrs. Elizabeth Carter and Miss Catherine Talbot* (London: Rivington, 1809), vol. 4, 371–73. – Ed.]

# Chapter 12

1. Domitian was the emperor of Rome from 81 to 96 CE. According to Suetonius, "at the beginning of his reign he used to spend hours in seclusion every day, doing nothing but catch[ing] flies and stab[bing] them [with] a keenly sharpened stylus"; *The Lives of the Caesars*, trans. John C. Rolfe, rev. edn. (London: 1930), Book 8, vol. 2, 345.

2. Pierre Bayle says of Kepler, "we may place him among those authors, who have said, that they valued a production of a mind above a kingdom"; article Kepler, in *The Dictionary Historical and Critical of Mr. Peter Bayle*, trans. Pierre Des Maizeaux, 2nd edn. (London: 1736), vol. iii, 659–60. The article on Kepler is not included in the modern volume of selections from Bayle edited by Richard Popkin (Indianapolis: Hackett, 1991).

3. The sublime, and the contrast between the beautiful and the sublime, were a constant theme in European letters after the republication of the ancient treatise *Peri Hypsous*, falsely attributed to the rhetorician Dionysius Cassius Longinus (ca. 213–73 CE); it was translated into English as early as 1652 and, famously, into French by Nicolas Boileau Despréaux as *Traité du Sublime* (Paris: 1674). The most famous work in the eighteenth century on the beautiful and the sublime was by Edmund Burke, *A Philosophical Enquiry into the Origin of our Ideas of the Sublime and Beautiful* (London: 1757, second edition: 1759). Burke's book became known in Germany immediately through the 1758 review by Moses Mendelssohn, "Philosophische Untersuchung des Ursprungs unserer Ideen vom Erhabenen und Schönen," *Bibliothek der schönen Wissenschaften*, vol. 3, Part 2. Kant would cite Burke several times in the *Critique of the Power of Judgment*, notably in the General Remark following §29 (5:277).

4. Virtually all of Book I of *Paradise Lost* offers a graphic description of the imagined terrors of Hell. Some sample lines are:

"The dismal situation waste and wild,

A dungeon horrible, on all sides round

As one great furnace flamed, yet from those flames

No light, but rather darkness visible

Served only to discover sights of woe,

Regions of sorrow, doleful shades, where peace

And rest can never dwell, hope never comes

That comes to all; but torture without end

Still urges, and a fiery deluge, fed

With ever-burning sulphur unconsumed:

Such place eternal justice had prepared

For those rebellious, here their prison ordained

In utter darkness, and their portion set

As far removed from God and light of heaven

As from the centre thrice to the utmost pole."

See *Paradise Lost*, Book 1, lines 60–74; from John Milton, ed. Stephen Orgel and Jonathan Goldberg (Oxford: Oxford University Press, 1991), 357.

5. Presumably Kant has in mind the description of Elysium that Virgil gives in the *Aeneid*, Book IV, beginning at line 853:

"His duty to the goddess done, they came

To places of delight, to green park land,

Where souls take ease amid the Blessed Groves.

Wider expanses of high air endow

Each vista with a wealth of light. . . .

Within a fragrant laurel grove, where Po

Sprang up and took his course to the world above,

The broad stream flowing on amid the forest.

This was the company of those who suffered

Wounds in battle for their country; those

Who in their lives were holy men and chaste

Or worthy of Phoebus in prophetic song;

Or those who better life, by finding out

New truths and skills; …

… None of us

Has one fixed home. We walk in shady groves

And bed on riverbanks and occupy

Green meadows fresh with streams."

See Virgil, *The Aeneid*, trans. Robert Fitzgerald (New York, Random House: 1981), Book IV, lines 853–903, pages 182–83.

6. Hera requested Aphrodite to help her reconcile the feuding Greeks and Trojans:

"'But if words of mine could lure them back to love,

back to bed, to lock in each other's arms once more...

they would call me their honored, loving friend forever.'

Aphrodite, smiling her everlasting smile, replied,

'Impossible – worse, it's *wrong* to deny your warm request,

since you are the one who lies in the arms of mighty Zeus.'

With that she loosed from her breasts the breastband, pierced and alluring, with every kind of enchantment woven through it. ... There is the

heat of Love, the pulsing rush of Longing, the lover's whisper, irresistible

– magic to make the sanest man go mad. And thrusting it into Hera's

outstretched hands, she breathed her name in a throbbing, rising voice:

'Here now, take this band, put it between your breasts – ravishing openwork,

and the world lies in its weaving!'"

See Homer, *The Iliad*, trans. Robert Fagles (New York, Viking: 1990), Book 14, lines 251–66, pages 376–77.

7. The example comes from *Bremen Magazine for the Propagation of the Sciences and the Arts and Virtue. Collected and Edited from the English Monthlies by Some Lovers of the Former* (in German), vol. 4 (1761), 539.

8. D. Friedrich Hasselquist, *Journey to Palestine in the Years 1749–1762* (in German) (Rostock: 1762), 82–94.

9. Kant refers to both the pyramids and St. Peter's in the course of his explication of the mathematical sublime in the *Critique of the Power of Judgment*, §26, 5:252.

10. This sentence anticipates Kant's later account of dependent judgments of beauty; see *Critique of the Power of Judgment*, §16, 5:230.

11. Albrecht von Haller, *On Eternity* (in German) (1736).

12. Kant attributes this statement to Oliver Cromwell, Lord Protector of Great Britain.

13. Achilles hated Agamemnon for having taken the girl Briseis from him, and refused to join in the fight against Troy for the recovery of Helen, when, after all, Agamemnon already had Briseis. Agamemnon sent ambassadors with gifts to recruit Achilles, but Achilles replied, "I hate that man like very Gates of Death/who says one thing but hides another in his heart." Homer, *The Iliad*, Book 9, lines 378–79. See the translation by Fagles, 262.

14. Jonas Hanway, *Mr. Jonas Hanway's Reliable Description. Together with an Impartial History of the Great Conqueror Nadir Kuli or Kuli Chams* (in German, where the author is called "Hanaway") (Hamburg and Leipzig, 1754), Part 11, 396.

15. William Hogarth (1697–1764), British painter and engraver, artist of such famous series as *The Rake's Progress*, and author of *The Analysis of Beauty: Written with a View of Fixing the Fluctuating Ideas of Taste* (London: J. Reeves, 1753).

16. Heraclitus of Ephesus, fl. ca. 500–480 BCE. "The legend of the 'weeping philosopher' is late and based on a combination of a Platonic joke, Heraclitus's theory of flux, and a misunderstanding of Theophrastus's word 'melancholia', which originally meant 'impulsiveness.'" Michael C. Stokes, "Heraclitus of Ephesus," in *The Encyclopedia of Philosophy*, ed. Paul Edwards (New York: Macmillan, 1967), vol. iii, 477–81, at page 477. For the standard work on Heraclitus, see Charles H. Kahn, *The Art and Thought of Heraclitus: An Edition of the Fragments with Translation and Commentary* (Cambridge: Cambridge University Press, 1979).

17. The argument that virtue depends on principles rather than feeling anticipates Kant's mature moral philosophy; the present reference to the special dignity of human nature should be compared to Kant's statement in the *Groundwork for the Metaphysics of Morals*, Section 2, 4:435.

## Chapter 13

1. See the introduction in *Cultures of the Sublime*, ed. Cian Duffy and Peter Howell (New York: Palgrave Macmillan, 2011), 127–28.

2. "Paradoxes of the Heart" is the subtitle of Noël Carroll's book, *Philosophy of Horror*, and is discussed in its last chapter, which mentions Aikin. See Further reading.

3. Aikin also addresses the issue in another essay in the 1773 volume: "An Enquiry into Those Kinds of Distress which Excite Agreeable Sensations," *Miscellaneous Pieces*, 190–215.

4. *Macbeth*, V.v.13. *supt*: supped (i.e., has had its full).

5. *Jaffeir and Belvidera*: characters in Thomas Shadwell, *The Humours of the Army* (1713).

6. *The fall of Wolsey*: from Shakespeare's *Henry VIII*.

# Notes

7. *The death of Shore*: Shore was mistress to Edward IV and the subject of a number of plays, including Thomas Heywood's *History of King Edward the Fourth* (1613) and Nicholas Rowe's *The Tragedy of Jane Shore* (1714).

8. William Collins, "Ode to Fear" (1746), ll. 44–45.

9. Milton, *Il Penseroso* [The brooding, pensive person], ll. 109–110. Milton's reference is to Chaucer's unfinished *Squire's Tale*, an orientalist and fantastical story of the Tartar King Cambuscan and his family.

10. In *Henry V*, V.i, Pistol is forced by the Welshman Fluellen to eat a raw leek after he mocked the tradition of wearing leeks on St. David's day.

11. Robert-François Damiens was executed in Paris for his attempted assassination of Louis XV in 1757. Descriptions of the gruesome execution were widely circulated, often as evidence of French barbarity.

12. A misquotation of Alexander Pope, *Essay on Man* (1733–34), III, 251: "power unseen, and mightier far than they."

13. Horace Walpole, *Castle of Otranto* (1764), one of the first novels in the modern Gothic tradition.

14. Tobias Smollett, *The Adventures of Ferdinand Count Fathom* (London: W. Johnston, 1753), an episodic story of the eponymous character's journey across Europe.

15. An adventurous story about "Sir Bertrand" here follows.


## Chapter 14

1. This quotation is not marked with inverted commas, because it is not exact. [Original footnote. – Ed.]


## Chapter 15

1. Kant followed the British tradition in distinguishing between the beautiful and the sublime in his 1764 *Observations on the Feeling of the Beautiful and Sublime*; but this work, especially the second half, focuses on issues such as the differences in the responses to the beautiful and sublime between the genders, different nations, and so on (see also *Logik Blomberg*, 24:47). Because Baumgarten did not address the sublime in his chapter on empirical psychology in the *Metaphysica*, Kant had far less to say about the sublime than about the beautiful in his anthropology lectures and the notes for them, so we have fewer sources for the development of his views on the sublime than for his views on the beautiful. Moreover, when he did address the sublime, Kant often said that because the sublime moves us or stirs our emotions, it is not the subject of an objective and universally valid judgment like the beautiful: see *Anthropologie Collins*, 25:198; *Anthropologie Parow*, 25:388–89, 391; and even *Anthropology from a Pragmatic Point of View*, §67, 7:241. The first of the anthropology notes that clearly reveal Kant's intention to organize the "Critique of Aesthetic Judgment" around the distinction between the beautiful and the sublime are Reflections 992 and 993, 15:436–39; both of these notes are from the late 1780s.

2. While not always consistent on the extent to which the feelings of pleasure and displeasure are analyzable, in some passages Kant explained pleasure as the feeling that expresses a condition that promotes life and its activity, while the feeling of displeasure expresses a hindrance to life or a check to its activity. This conception is presupposed by Kant's conception of the pleasure in the free play of the cognitive faculties.

3. For the complex character of the feeling of respect, see *Critique of Practical Reason*, 5:72–73.

4. It may sometimes seem as if Kant holds that only objects in nature may produce the experience of the sublime, but this passage at least tacitly acknowledges that there can be at least a representation of the sublime in art. See also §52, and *Anthropology from a Pragmatic Point of View*, §68, 7:243.

5. See also *Anthropology from a Pragmatic Point of View*, §68, 7:243, where Kant draws this distinction as that between responses to size and to intensity.

6. In §30, Kant will say that the judgment on the sublime does not need a separate deduction, because it makes a claim only about our own state of mind, not about any object in nature, and thus its exposition already is its deduction (5:280). So here he must mean only to refer to the further exposition of the sublime in the immediately following sections.

7. On the claim that all ordinary measurement is based on arbitrarily chosen units and is therefore "relative" rather than "absolute," see Reflection 5727 and 5729, 18:338–39, both from the 1780s.

8. Leibniz had famously established that there can be no greatest number; see for example, *New Essays Concerning Human Understanding*, book II, chapter xvii, §§1, 3; in the translation by Peter Remnant and Jonathan Bennett (Cambridge: Cambridge University Press, 1981), 157–58. Further statements on this issue can be found in *Die Philosophischen Schriften von G. W. Leibniz*, ed. C. J. Gerhardt (Berlin: 1875–90), I:338, II:304–5, V:144, and VI:629. These references are from Bertrand Russell, *A Critical Exposition of the Philosophy of Leibniz*, second edition (London: George Allen and Unwin, 1937), 109.

9. Claude-Étienne Savary (1750–1788), orientalist, Egyptologist, and translator of the Koran; his *Lettres sur l'Égypte*, to which Kant refers, was published in Paris in 1786. The passage reads: "Having arrived at the bottom of the pyramid, we circled it while contemplating it with a sort of terror [*effroi*]. When considered up close, it seems to be made of blocks of stones, but from a hundred feet, the size [*grandeur*] of the stones is lost in the immensity of the edifice, and they seem very small." See Claude-Étienne Savary *Lettres sur l'Égypte où l'on Offre le Parallèle des Moeurs Anciennes et Modernes de ses Habitants [...]*, 3 vols. (Paris: Onfroi, 1786), vol. 1: 189. [ – note modified by Ed.]

10. This is not to say, however, that Kant thinks there is no sublime in art, or at least no artistic representation of the sublime; see *Anthropology from a Pragmatic Point of View*, §68, 7:243 [excerpted in the present anthology – Ed.].

11. Kant gives a similar definition of the monstrous in *Anthropology from a Pragmatic Point of View*, §68, 7:243.

12. For Kant's account of how the imagination schematizes the concept of magnitude to produce determinate numbers, see *Critique of Pure Reason*, A 142–43/B182 and A 162–63/B 202–4.

13. In *Wiener Logik*, 24:892, Kant says that "one can also count with 4 numerals, as Leibniz did." In his note to the latter passage, editor Gerhard Lehmann says that Kant may be making a mistaken reference to Leibniz's dyadic system for counting, using 0 and 1; see 24:1022. However, in a transcription of early mathematics lectures made by J. G. Herder, and edited by Lehmann more than two decades after his edition of the logic lectures, Kant correctly ascribes the dyadic system to Leibniz and the tetradic system to Valentin Weigel (1533–88) (see 29:56); Kant presumably got the reference to Weigel from Christian Wolff's *Mathematisches Lexikon* (Halle, 1716). The translators owe this reference to Frank and Zanetti, pages 1332–33.

14. Compare this passage to Kant's *Universal Natural History and Theory of the Heavens* (1755), chapter 7, 1:307–8; in the translation by W. Hastie (reprinted Ann Arbor: University of Michigan Press, 1969), 137.

15. For this aspect of Kant's treatment of the feeling of respect, see *Critique of Practical Reason*, 5:78–79, 87–88.

16. See also *Anthropology from a Pragmatic Point of View*, §68, 7:243.

17. Kant frequently contrasted what he considered the craven attitude of fear of God's threats and hopes of his rewards with the more noble thought that moral rectitude is intrinsically honorable and therefore pleasing to God; see, among many such passages, *Moralphilosophie Collins*, 27:309–310.

18. Kant refers here to the *Voyages dans les Alpes, Précédés d'un Essai sur l'Histoire Naturelle des Environs de Genève*, 4 volumes (Geneva, 1779–86) by Horace-Bénédict de Saussure (1740–99), the Genevan geologist and physicist who made the second ascent of Mont Blanc in 1787. A German translation of the whole work was published in Leipzig from 1781 to 1788, and abbreviated as *Nachricht von einer Alpenreise des Herrn von Saussure* in Berlin in 1789.

19. In spite of this comment, Kant was also willing to say that while aesthetic experience does not actually improve (*verbessern*) a person it does refine (*verfeinern*) him; see *Menschenkunde*, 25:1102, and *Anthropologie Mrongovius*, 25:1332.

20. For comparison of this note to an earlier version of Kant's account of the bearing of aesthetics upon our moral development, see the section "On the Utility of the Culture of Taste" (*Vom Nutzen der Cultur des Geschmacks*) in *Anthropologie Collins* 25:187–96.

21. See *Critique of Practical Reason*, 5:23.

22. Kant's use of the four headings of the categories here to distinguish between the agreeable, the beautiful, the sublime, and the good differs strikingly from his use of the same four headings to organize the discussions of the aspects of the judgments on the beautiful and the sublime in the "Analytic of the Beautiful" and §24 of the "Analytic of the Sublime," respectively. For some other examples of the flexibility of Kant's use of this organizing scheme, see *Critique of Practical Reason*, 5:66, and *Religion within the Boundaries of Mere Reason*, 6:101–102.

23. To the foregoing argument, compare Reflection 1928 (1780s), 16:159; *Anthropologie Parow*, 25:388; *Menschenkunde*, 25:1102; *Anthropologie Mrongovius*, 25:1332; *Metaphysics of Morals*, "Doctrine of Virtue," §17, 6:443; and *Anthropology from a Pragmatic Point of View*, §69, 7:244.

24. At a number of places in his lectures, Kant says that beauty must be distinguished from usefulness but must also be compatible with the usefulness of an object. See *Menschenkunde*, 25:1100–101; *Anthropologie Mrongovius*, 25:332; and *Anthropologie Busolt*, 25:1510.

25. For Kant's comments on enthusiasm or *Enthusiasmus* and its distinction from fanaticism, see *Observations on the Feeling of the Beautiful and Sublime* (1764), 2:251n; "Essay on the Maladies of the Head" (1764), 2:267; *Anthropologie Friedländer* (1775–76), 25:528–31; *Anthropologie Mrongovius* (1784–85), 25:1262, 1287, 1373; *Critique of Practical Reason* (1788), 5:157; *Metaphysics of Morals* (1797), 6:408–9; *The Conflict of the Faculties* (1798), 7:85–87n; *Anthropology from a Pragmatic Point of View* (1798), 7:253–54, 269, 313–14. [ – note modified by Ed.]

26. See *Anthropology from a Pragmatic Point of View*, § 75, 7:253, where Kant says that "The principle of apathy— namely, that the sage man must never be in a state of emotional agitation, not even in that of sympathetic sorrow over his best friend's misfortune—is a quite correct and sublime moral principle of the Stoic school."

27. On astonishment, see *Anthropology from a Pragmatic Point of View*, §78, 7:261.

28. For other passages on the contrast between affects and passions, see Kant's handbook *Anthropology from a Pragmatic Point of View*, §§ 73–74, 7:251–53, and the following lecture transcriptions: *Anthropologie Collins* (1772–73), 26:212–18; *Anthropologie Parow* (1772–73), 26:414–26; *Anthropologie Friedländer* (1775–76), 26:589–92; *Menschenkunde* (1781–82), 26:1115–25; *Anthropologie Mrongovius* (1784–85), 26:1353–56; *Anthropologie Busolt* (1788–89), 26:1519–27.

29. Kant contrasts the affects of timidity and fortitude in *Anthropology from a Pragmatic Point of View*, §77, 7:256–58.

30. See *Metaphysics of Morals*, "Doctrine of Virtue," §34, 6:456–57, where Kant argues that feelings of sympathy are useful only when we can do something for another, for otherwise one just adds to the unhappiness in the world.

31. Kant frequently attacked the idea that human beings could please God by any forms of cult or prayer rather than by actions motivated simply by respect for the moral law itself; see for example, *Moralphilosophie Collins*, 27:325–32; *Moral Mrongovius*, 29:627–28; and *Religion within the Boundaries of Mere Reason*, 6:170–75.

32. Exodus 20, 4.

33. Kant's repeated use of this term in what looks like an English rather than a German form (*Enthusiasmus*), suggests a British origin. Locke contrasted assent based on reason to that based on enthusiasm in the *Essay concerning Human Understanding*, Book IV, Chapter XIX, and the first work in Shaftesbury's *Characteristics* is "A Letter concerning Enthusiasm" (in the edition by Robertson, vol I., pages 5–39).

34. By the "inscrutability of the idea of freedom," Kant usually means the doctrine that we can be certain of the reality of freedom on the practical basis of our awareness of our obligation to comply with the moral law, but cannot give any theoretical explanation of the reality of freedom. See *Groundwork*, 4:459–62; *Critique of Practical Reason*, 5:47, where Kant refers to the freedom that is deduced from the moral law as an "inscrutable faculty"; and *Religion*, 6:138, where he says that freedom, as the ground of the moral law, is "inscrutable to us . . . since it is *not* given to us in cognition."

35. Here Kant refers to Daniel Defoe's *Robinson Crusoe* (1719), which spawned many imitations in both British and German popular literature in the eighteenth century.

36. See Note 18 on Horace-Bénédict de Saussure (1740–99), above.

37. In Burke's original words: "if the pain is not carried to violence, and the terror is not conversant about the present destruction of the person, as these emotions clear the parts, whether fine, or gross, of a dangerous and troublesome incumbrance, they are capable of producing delight; not pleasure, but a sort of delightful horror, a sort of tranquility tinged with terror" (part IV, §vii; Boulton, 136).

38. Kant gives page references to Garve's 1773 translation of Edmund Burke's *A Philosophical Enquiry into the Origin of Our Ideas of the Sublime and Beautiful* (London: Robert Dodsley, 1757; second edition with new "Introduction on Taste," 1759). There are modern editions by J. T. Boulton (London: Routledge and Kegan Paul, 1958) and Adam Phillips (Oxford: Oxford University Press, 1990). Moses Mendelssohn published an extensive review of the first English edition in *Bibliothek der schönen Wissenschaften*, volume 3, part 2 (1758) (reprinted in Moses

Mendelssohn, *Ästhetische Schriften in Auswahl*, ed. Otto F. Best [Darmstadt: Wissenschaftliche Buchgesellschaft, 1974], 247–65), and the book was published in an anonymous German translation, actually by Christian Garve, in 1773. This translation here cites the modern edition edited by J. T. Boulton, which reprints Burke's second edition.

39. In Burke's original words, with their original context: "Beauty acts by relaxing the solids of the whole system. There are all the appearance of such a relaxation; and a relaxation somewhat below the natural tone seems to me to be the cause of all positive pleasure. Who is a stranger to that manner of expression so common in all times and in all countries, of being softened, relaxed, enervated, dissolved, melted away by pleasure?" (part IV, §xix; Boulton, 149–50).

40. Kant also made this claim about Epicurus (341–271 B.C.) in *Anthropologie Collins*, 25:202 (actually from the transcription *Hamilton*).

41. In the first edition (though omitted in the second), the heading "Third Book" stood over this title; however, Kant's manuscript had stated not "Third Book" but "Third Section: Deduction of Aesthetic Judgments." [While in the subsequent sections Kant proceeds to offer a deduction of judgments of beauty, this opening paragraph, §30, explains why his exposition of the judgments on the sublime in nature was at the same time their deduction. – Ed.]

## Chapter 16

1. "On the Pathetic" and "Concerning the Sublime" are also found in *Essays*, ed. Daniel Dahlstrom and Walter Hinderer.

2. [Ossian was the narrator and purported author of a cycle of epic poems published by the Scottish poet James Macpherson poet beginning in 1760. – Ed.]

3. [Kant quotes a version of this inscription; see the *Critique of the Power of Judgment*, 5: 316 n. – Ed.]

## Chapter 17

1. Walter Scott, in Anna Seward, *The Poetical Works of Anna Seward; With Extracts from Her Literary Correspondence*, ed. Walter Scott, 3 vols. (Edinburgh: John Ballantyne and Co., 1810), vol. 1, Preface, v.

2. Letter LXXXVII, in *Letters of Anna Seward,* vol. 3, 338.

3. Letter IV, *Letters of Anna Seward*, vol. 5, 27.

4. Letter LVII, *Letters of Anna Seward*, vol. 5, 324.

5. A modern edition can be found in *Ossian and Ossianism*, ed. Dafydd Moore (London: Routledge, 2004).

6. Letter LVI, *Letters of Anna Seward*, vol. 6, 316.

7. Letter LVI, in *Letters of Anna Seward*, vol. 1, 263.

8. The young poet Thomas Chatterton (1752–70) committed suicide.

9. Throughout this letter, Seward quotes Macpherson with some slight deviation from the original text. See James Macpherson, *Fingal: An Ancient Epic Poem, in Six Books* (Dublin: Peter Wilson, 1763), 6.

10. See Macpherson, *Fingal*, 21.

11. Seward appears to be quoting the English classicist Vincent Bourne (1695–1747).

## Chapter 18

1. *Cultures of the Sublime*, ed. Cian Duffy and Peter Howell (New York: Palgrave Macmillan, 2011), 146–48.

# Notes

2. *Madame Montoni*: Emily's aunt and recent bride to Montoni. She remains unmoved by the sublime scenery.

3. *campagna*: Italian for "landscape" or "countryside."

4. *Po and the Brenta*: rivers in northern Italy.

5. *Valancourt*: Emily's lover, with whom she had been forced to part by lord Montoni and her aunt when they removed her from France.

## Chapter 19

1. Williams, Letter XL, *A Tour in Switzerland* (London: Robinson, 1798), vol. 2, 270.

2. References to the pages in *A Tour in Switzerland* (1798, vol. 1) are here given in parentheses.

## Chapter 20

1. See William Wordsworth, *Wordsworth's Guide to the Lakes: Fifth Edition*, ed. Ernest de Sélincourt (London: Henry Frowde, 1906), which gives the following bibliographic information: Williams Wordsworth, *A Guide through the District of the Lakes* […] (Kendal: Hudson and Nicholson, 1835). References in this brief overview and headnote are to the Sélincourt edition, and placed in parenthesis, for instance: "(1835 edition, 87)."

2. *The Letters of John Keats, 1814–21*, ed. Hyder Edward Rollins (Cambridge: Cambridge University Press, 1958), vol. 1, 386–87.

3. The draft of the appendix begins with an ellipsis.

4. The editors Owen and Symser conjecture adding "hopes" here.

5. On Schaffhausen, see also Helen Maria Williams's conribution to the present volume.

6. According to Owen and Symser, presumably a loose quarter sheet was once here inserted and has since been lost.

## Chapter 21

1. Cian Duffy and Peter Howell, *Cultures of the Sublime: Selected Readings, 1750–1830* (Houndmills, Basingstoke, Hampshire: Palgrave Macmillan, 2011), 121.

2. Vijay Mishra, *The Gothic Sublime* (Albany: SUNY Press, 1994), 216.

## Chapter 22

1. Arthur Schopenhauer, *The World as Will and Representation* (New York: Dover Publications, 1969), vol. 2, 433; translation modified.

2. I am now all the more delighted and surprised, forty years after advancing this thought so timidly and hesitantly, to discover that St. Augustine had already expressed it: *Abusta formas suas varias, quibus mundi hujus visibilis structura formosa est, sentiendas sensibus praebent; ut, pro eo quod NOSSE non possunt, quasi INNOTESCERE velle videantur.* (*De Civitate Dei*, xi, 27)

   "The trees offer to the senses for perception the many different forms by which the structure of this visible world is adorned, so that, because they are unable to *know*, they may appear, as it were, to want to *be known*." [ – Tr.]

3. "I am all this creation collectively, and besides me there exists no other being." [ – Tr.]

## Chapter 23

1. G. W. F. Hegel, *Encyclopedia of the Philosophical Sciences in Basic Outline: Part 1: Science of Logic*, ed. and trans. Klaus Brinkmann and Daniel Dahlstrom (Cambridge: Cambridge University Press, 2010), 153. Hegel explains the dialectic at *Encyclopedia* §§79–82.

2. Georg Wilhelm Friedrich Hegel, *Aesthetics: Lectures on Fine Art*, trans. T. M. Knox (Oxford: Oxford University Press, 1975), vol. 1, Section 1, "The Symbolic Form of Art," 303.

3. Benedetto Croce, *Aesthetic as Science of Expression and General Linguistic*, trans. Douglas Ainslie (Boston: Nonpareil Books, 1978), 87–89.

4. E. F. Carritt, "The Sublime," *Mind* 19, no. 75 (1910): 356–72, 368.

5. [Parsis (or Parsees) are followers in India of the Persian prophet Zoroaster and immigrated to India to avoid religious persecution. Throughout Part II of his lectures on aesthetics, Hegel discusses the Parsis, Indians, and Egyptians. – Ed.]

6. Kant's distinction is made in §23. Thereafter he goes on to deal with the sublime in detail. – Tr.

7. Professor R. C. Zaehner [Robert Charles Zaehner (1913–74) – Ed.] translates the closing section of this passage as follows: "Know too that all states of being whether they be of Nature's constituent purity, energy, or lethargy proceed from me; but I am not in them, they are in me. By these three states of being inhering in the constituents the whole universe is led astray and does not understand that I am far beyond them and that I neither change nor pass away. For all this is my Maya, composed of the constituents, divine, hard to transcend. Whoso shall put his trust in me alone, shall pass beyond this my Maya" (R. C. Zaehner, *Concordant Discord: The Interdependence of Faiths* [Oxford: Clarendon Press, 1970], 124, 135). Professor Zaehner points out that at this stage of Indian thought "Maya" means creative power, not illusion. The "three properties" are the three "constituents" through which Nature acts. – Tr.

8. [Here the Suhrkamp edition reads "7" rather than "10." G. W. F. Hegel, *Vorlesungen über die Aesthetik I* (Frankfurt am Main: Suhrkamp, 1970), 473. There are also other minor differences between the Knox translation and Suhrkamp edition, concerning for instance the use of italics and the paragraph breaks. – Ed.]

9. [Mount Meru, in Hindu mythology, is a sacred mountain standing at the center of the universe. – Ed.]

10. [Rumi is considered one of the greatest mystic poets of Persian literature. – Ed.]

11. Friedrich Rückert, Poet and Orientalist, 1788–1866. – Tr.

12. Shamsud-Din-Mohammed, ca. 1320–89. – Tr.

13. Joseph, Freiherr von Hammer-Purgstall, Orientalist, 1774–1856. – Tr.

14. Goethe, who lived to be 83, was 64 when he published this in 1813. – Tr.

15. The idea is that the pearl is a raindrop that fell into the sea and was "ripened" in an oyster shell. – Tr.

16. For example, "God in my nature is involved, As I in the divine" (*Hours with the Mystics*, by Robert Alfred Vaughan, London, 1895, vol. ii, pp. 5 ff.). Angelus Silesius is probably the pseudonym of Johannes Scheffler, 1624–77. – Tr.

17. *On the Sublime*, IX. 9, quoting Gen. 1:3. – Tr.

18. Hegel's contrast between *Scheinen* (show) and *Erscheinen* (appear), a favorite one of his, has no English equivalent. – Tr.

19. The Argonauts passed safely through the Symplegades which were fated to come to rest if any ship passed safely through them. See Sir James Frazer's note to the Loeb edition of Apollodorus, I. ix. 22, for references. [James George Frazer, *Apollodorus: The Library*, 2 vols. (London: William Heinemann, 1921), 107. – Ed.]

## Chapter 24

1. Werner Herzog, "On the Absolute, the Sublime, and Ecstatic Truth," *Arion* 17, no. 3 (2010): 1–12, 8.

2. *Die Welt als Wille und Vorstellung*, II. 415.—Richard Wagner. [*The World as Will and Representation* - Ed.]

3. Ibid. 418.—Richard Wagner.—In the edition of 1879 the corresponding pages are 417 and 419–20. – Tr.

4. This "dream" hypothesis does not appear in the *The World as Will and Representation*, however, but in a lengthy essay on "Ghost-seeing" in vol. I. of the *Parerga and Paralipomena*, written after the publication of the larger work; so that the "connection" must be regarded in a purely subjective light, that is to say, as Wagner's own discovery. In fact our author, partly by re-arranging the "material supplied [elsewhere] by the philosopher," partly by his independent observations, has carried Schopenhauer's Theory of Music infinitely farther than its originator could ever have dreamt. – Tr.

5. Cf. "In lichten Tages Schein, wie war Isolde mein?" and in fact the whole love-scene in *Tristan und Isolde*, act ii. – Tr. [In day's bright shining, how could Isolde be mine? – Ed.]

6. Cf. Wagner, vol. II.—*Opera and Drama*—page 219. – Tr.

7. Cf. *Tristan und Isolde*, act iii. "Die Sonne sah ich nicht, nicht sah ich Land noch Leute: doch was ich sah, das kann ich dir nicht sagen." – Tr. [The sun I did not see; I saw neither land nor people: but what I did see, I cannot tell you. – Ed.]

8. To specify, I have done this in brief and general terms in an essay entitled "Zukunftsmusik" [Music of the Future – Ed.], published at Leipzig about twelve years ago, without, however, finding any manner of attention; it has been included in the seventh volume of these *Ges. Schr. u. Dicht.* [*Collected Writings and Poetry* – Ed.], and may here be recommended to fresh notice.—Richard Wagner.

9. "Die Erkenntniss flieht mit dem Bekenntniss ihres Irrthumes." Cf. *Parsifal*, act. ii.: "Bekenntniss wird Schuld und Reue enden, Erkenntniss in Sinn die Thorheit wenden." – Tr. [Confession will end guilt and remorse; knowledge will change folly into sense. – Ed.]

10. Wagner's essay continues for another 13 pages, containing various cultural criticisms from a German nationalistic point of view – Ed.

# Chapter 25

1. *Idea*: a key term for Hegel, according to whom the Idea develops through history and is ultimately comprehended by and through philosophical thought.

2. Friedrich Nietzsche, *Ecco Homo*, trans. Anthony M. Ludovici, in *The Complete Works of Friedrich Nietzsche*, ed. Oscar Levy, 18 vols., vol. 17, section 1, "The Birth of Tragedy," 69 (T.N. Foulis: Edinburgh and London, 1911), translation modified.

3. Friedrich Nietzsche, *Thus Spake Zarathustra,* trans. Thomas Common (T.N. Foulis: Edinburgh and London, 1911), 198–99, translation modified.

4. *Apollo*: in Greek mythology the son of Zeus and Leto (hence a half-brother of Dionysus), associated with the sun and prophecy.

5. *Lucretius*: Titus Lucretius Carus (99 BCE–55 BCE), Roman philosopher and poet, author of *De Rerum Natura* (*On the Nature of Things*).

6. *Hans Sachs*: an historical person and a character portrayed in Richard Wagner's opera *Die Meistersinger von Nürnberg*.

7. *The veil of Maja*: a phrase used by Schopenhauer to describe a screen which exists between "the world inside my head and the world outside my head," that is, the world of human representation which has no true objectivity.

8. *Sacaea*: a riotous Babylonian festival.

9. *Eleusinian mysteries*: secret ecstatic religious ceremonies.

   ". . . creator": this quotation comes from Schiller's poem, which provides the words for Beethoven's *Ode to Joy*.

10. *Head of Medusa*: In Greek mythology, Medusa was one of the three monstrous sisters called the Gorgons; her face could turn those who looked at it into stone.

11. *Doric art*: an older form of Greek art and architecture which arose in the seventh century BCE.

12. *Cithara*: a traditional stringed instrument.

13. *Requiem aeternam deo*: eternal rest for God.

14. *No dispute about taste and tasting*: a reference to the Latin adage *de gustibus non disputandem est* ("in matters of taste, there can be no disputes").


## Chapter 26

1. Rudolf Otto, *The Idea of the Holy* (London: Oxford University Press, 1972), 10–11; 13.

2. Leon Schlamm, "Numinous Experience and Religious Language," *Religious Studies* 28, no. 4 (1992): 533–51.

3. Otto, *The Idea of the Holy*, 63.

4. We are often prone to resort to this familiar feeling-content to fill out the negative concept "transcendent," explaining frankly God's transcendence by His "sublimity." As a figurative analogical description this is perfectly allowable, but it would be an error if we meant it literally and in earnest. Religious feelings are not the same as aesthetic feelings, and "the sublime" is as definitely an aesthetic term as "the beautiful," however widely different may be the facts denoted by the words.

5. [*unauswickelbar*: the German is given in the translation. With the phrase "unauswickelbarer Begriff," Otto takes himself to be paraphrasing Kant. For a recent edition based on the 1936 edition of Otto's book, see Rudolf Otto, *Das Heilige: Über das Irrationale in der Idee des Göttlichen und sein Verhältnis zum Rationalen* (Munich: C.H. Beck, 2014). – Ed.]

6. Neither Heterogony nor Epigenesis is genuine Evolution. They are rather just what the biologists call *generatio equivoca*, and therefore mere formation of an aggregate by addition and accumulation.

7. This numinous-magical character is specially noticeable in the strangely impressive figures of the Buddha in early Chinese art; and here too it affects the observer independently of "ideas" ["*ohne Begriff*" – Ed.], i.e., without his knowing anything about the speculative doctrines of Buddhism. Thus Sirén justly says of the great Buddha from the Lung-Men Caves (T'ang Dynasty):

   Anyone who approaches this figure will realize that it has a religious significance *without knowing* anything about its motif. . . . It matters little whether we call it a prophet or a god, because it is a complete work of art permeated by a spiritual will, which communicates itself to the beholder. . . . The religious element of such a figure is immanent; it is "a presence" or an atmosphere rather than a formulated idea. . . . It cannot be *described in words*, because it lies *beyond intellectual definition*. [Quoted in English by Otto on *Das Heilige*, 87, and with these italics. – Ed.]

   (Oswald Sirén, *Chinese Sculpture*, London, 1925, vol. i, 20.)

8. From an article by Otto Fischer on Chinese landscape painting in *Das Kunstblatt*, January 1920.

9. [Wilhelm Worringer, *Formprobleme der Gotik* (München: R. Piper, 1911), published in English as Wilhelm Worringer, *Form Problems of the Gothic* (New York: Stechert, 1912). – Ed.]

10. [*numen praesens*: present numen or divine power – Ed.]

11. [See, for instance, the cover image (a detail of a painting by Guo Xi) and his chapter in the present volume. – Ed.]

12. [In the German edition of 1936, Otto here cites a work by Lao Tzu: Laotse, *Tao te king: Das Buch des Alten vom Sinn und Leben*, translated with commentary by Richard Wilhelm (Jena: E. Diederichs, 1911), xx. See Otto, *Das Heilige*, 90. – Ed.]

13. The Jewish tradition has been, however, very well aware of the import of the matter. In the splendid New Year's Day Hymn of Melek Elyōn the words run: "All the mighty ones on high *whisper low*: Yahweh is King."

14. [Felix Mendelssohn (1809–47): the grandson of the philosopher Moses Mendelssohn. – Ed.]

15. [In the 1936 German edition, Otto both omits the Thomas Luiz passage ("And, if a final example may be cited . . .") and adds two sentences (just before the discussion of Mendelssohn) about Beethoven's *Missa solemnis*. See Otto, *Das Heilige*, 91. – Ed.]

# Notes

## Chapter 28

1. Francis de Sales, *Introduction to the Devout Life*, trans. Thomas S. Kepler (New York: World, 1952), 125. (Modified to conform to the French text, which reads, "l'abjection de soy-mesme.")

## Chapter 29

1. Fredric Jameson, *Postmodernism, Or the Cultural Logic of Late Capitalism* (London and New York: Verso, 1992).
2. David E. Nye, *American Technological Sublime* (Cambridge, MA: MIT Press, 1996), 23.

## Chapter 30

1. For essays by Jean-François Lyotard, Jean-Luc Nancy, Phillippe Lacoue-Labarthe, et al., see the collection *Of the Sublime*, ed. Jean-François Courtine (Albany: State University of New York Press, 1993).
2. Jean-François Lyotard, "Presenting the Unpresentable: The Sublime," trans. Lisa Liebmann, *Artforum* 20, no. 8 (1982): 64–69, 68. Lyotard calls this piece a "critical sketch" (69) of his ideas on representation.
3. Jean-François Lyotard, *Enthusiasm: The Kantian Critique of History*, trans. Georges Van den Abbeele (Stanford, CA: Stanford University Press, 2009), 30.
4. Lyotard, *Enthusiasm*, 31.
5. See Jean-François Lyotard, "The Works and Writings of Daniel Buren: An Introduction to the Philosophy of Contemporary Art," trans. Lisa Liebmann, *Artforum* 19, no. 6 (1981): 57–64.
6. Lyotard, "Presenting the Unpresentable," 64–65.

## Chapter 31

1. bell hooks, "Representing Whiteness in the Black Imagination," in *Cultural Studies*, ed. Lawrence Grossberg, Cary Nelson, and Paula A. Treichler (New York: Routledge, 1992), 338–46, 341.
2. Terry Eagleton, *The Ideology of the Aesthetic* (Oxford: Basil Blackwell Ltd., 1990), 75.
3. Edmund Burke, *A Philosophical Enquiry into the Origin of Our Ideas of the Sublime and Beautiful*, ed. James T. Boulton (London: Routledge and Kegan Paul, 1958), 147.
4. The force of aesthetic discourse for contemporary theories of cultural difference is engaged by Michael Taussig's critical use of several forms of the Burkean, Conradian, and postmodern sublime to inform his experimental ethnography. See Michael Taussig, *Shamanism, Colonialism, and the Wild Man: A Study in Terror and Healing* (Chicago: University of Chicago Press, 1987) and *The Nervous System* (New York: Routledge, 1992).
5. I am writing here of European aesthetics and by "forms of difference" I mean, primarily, foreign bodies: those whose flesh, features, and practices were imagined as radically other than those of Europeans. [...]
6. In other media, images of an exotic sublime would only grow in importance and complexity in the nineteenth century. I am thinking of the work of romantic orientalist painters such as Jean-Leon Gerome and Eugene Delacroix, or Victor Hugo's redefinition of the sublime as grotesque, precisely to the extent that the grotesque was also exoticized. See Hugo's "Preface to Cromwell" in *Prefaces and Prologues to Famous Books*, ed. Charles W. Eliot (New York: P. F. Collier & Son, 1910), vol. 39, 354–408.
7. The imagination of difference in romantic and orientalist discourse contributes to—is perhaps embedded within—existing aesthetic frameworks. The articulation of the "exotic," whether in terms of nation, culture, or gender is accomplished in part through a reimagination of the categories of beauty and sublimity.

8. For sustained discussions of the relationship between theories of ideology and aesthetic discourse, particularly with regard to deconstructive and Marxist theory, see Eagleton, *The Ideology of the Aesthetic*, and Forest Pyle, *The Ideology of Imagination: Subject and Society in the Discourse of Romanticism* (Stanford: Stanford University Press, 1995). [...] Part of the task of my essay is to read the imagination of foreign bodies and terrors in the aesthetic treatises of Burke and Kant as just such an ideological process of presenting and obscuring the thematic and performative aspects of stereotypes of race and gender *as they inform* the discursive relationships between "language, subjectivity, society" [Pyle, p. 4 – Ed.] in these texts and the material (bodies) from which their images arise.

9. Burke, *A Philosophical Enquiry into the Origin of our Ideas of the Sublime and Beautiful*. This text will be cited by the abbreviation *E* followed by a page number, in parenthesis.

10. In S. H. Monk's assessment, *The Sublime: A Study of Critical Theories in Eighteenth-Century England* (Ann Arbor: University of Michigan Press, 1960), this emphasis on the subjective also makes it possible for theories of the sublime such as Burke's to be interpreted as contesting neoclassical views. Walter J. Hipple, Jr., adds a qualification: "This program [Burke's] is not, as some moderns have seen it, a step from the objectivism of the neoclassic to a psychological and subjective view; ... all the aestheticians from Addison to Kant and onwards conceived of the sublime as a feeling in the mind caused by certain properties in external objects" (*The Beautiful, the Sublime and the Picturesque*, 84). Of course, Hipple's opinion of Burke and Kant is established without consideration of the particular bodies both use to establish the sublimity of racial and gendered differences.

11. Burke's *Enquiry* can be read as a performance of the kinds of feelings and distinctions which he deems part of any correct view of beauty or the sublime. In this sense, then, Burke's invocation of the black female as an example of the natural "effects of blackness" instantiates the act of distinction as in part also a willful blindness to its replication of other adjacent discursive practices, in this case terror inspired by race or gender. The *Enquiry* is a performance of aesthetic experience in many ways similar to that Judith Butler describes for identification with heterosexuality, in part because heterosexual practices provide the metaphorical basis of comparisons between the feminine and masculine in Burke's text. This is perhaps most striking to the extent that Burke is "educating" a suspiciously masculine passion/eye. [...] Butler refers to the enabling of certain identifications and the foreclosure of others as an "exclusionary matrix by which subjects are formed" which requires the production of the *abject,* a term which holds some kinship with the sublime. [...] (*Bodies That Matter: On the Discursive Limits of "Sex"* [New York: Routledge, 1993], 3). See also Butler's further discussion of the psychoanalytic importance of the abject in Note 2, p. 243. Butler's "abject" differs significantly from Julia Kristeva's in *Powers of Horror: An Essay on Abjection*, trans. Leon Roudiez (New York: Columbia University Press, 1982), particularly because Butler is interested in questioning Kristeva's association of the feminine/maternal with that which is "outside" or at the boundaries of the human. See the analysis of Kristeva and Irigaray on this point in *Bodies That Matter*, 36–49. [...] Burke's use of the black female as an illustration inadvertently threatens the premise that the "effects of blackness" are "natural," not cultivated through association. At the same time, this illustration disrupts Burke's argument and suspends its legitimacy.

12. Admittedly, what I am calling "cultural" would be somewhat foreign to Burke, who uses here the terms "custom" and "habit" interchangeably to indicate those objects and experiences to which we have become accustomed. "Custom" and "habit" are the subject of extended criticism in the *Enquiry* precisely because Burke wishes to locate beauty and the sublime as out of the ordinary, possessed of a novelty which is not merely curiosity but able to elicit higher passions (apparently of society and love). "Novelty" may be read as the site of Burke's ideological move to say both that beauty and sublimity are natural, beyond the contingencies of the merely cultural, and that aesthetic experiences of them are customary within the subject's identification with the roles dictated by what he calls "sex." [...]

13. See, for instance, part IV, sec. V–XIII, which speculate about the importance of the physiological effects of light rays on the eye, and the possibility that it is the quantity and intensity of vibration of light rays bouncing off sublime objects which produce the pain associated with it. Of course, if as Burke says, "Black bodies, reflecting none, or but a few rays, with regard to sight are but so many vacant spaces dispersed among the objects we view" (*E*, p. 147), it is hard to see how such physiological effects produce the sublime "effect of blackness" in the boy's vision of the black female offered in the Cheselden example. Burke explains, however, that in this case it is the shock the eye feels upon suddenly relaxing in such blackness which causes it to suffer "a convulsive spring" (*E*, p. 147).

14. "There is a chain in all our sensations; they are all but different sorts of feelings, calculated to be affected by various sorts of objects, but all to be affected after the same manner" (*E*, p. 120).

## Notes

15. See Sander Gilman, "Black Bodies, White Bodies: Toward an Iconography of Female Sexuality in Late Nineteenth-Century Art, Medicine, and Literature," *Critical Inquiry* 12 (1985): 204–42.

16. On the bearded lady, see Immanuel Kant, *Observations on the Feeling of the Beautiful and Sublime*, trans. John T. Goldthwait (California: University of California Press, 1960), 54. This text will henceforth be cited by the abbreviation *O* followed by a page number, in parenthesis.

17. The treatise begins, "The various feelings of enjoyment or of displeasure rest not so much upon the nature of the external things that arouse them as upon each person's own disposition to be moved by these to pleasure or pain" (*O*, p. 45).

18. For discussions of the growth of an idea of race, see Henry Louis Gates Jr., "Writing, 'Race' and the Difference it Makes," *"Race," Writing, and Difference, Critical Inquiry* 12 (1985): 1–20; Michael P. Banton, *The Idea of Race* (Boulder, CO: Westview Press, 1978); and Nancy Stepan, *The Idea of Race in Science: Great Britain 1800-1960* (London: Macmillan, 1982).

19. Here, Kant defers to Hume's racist challenge that one could not find "a single example in which a Negro had shown talents" and that "not a single one [negro] was ever found who presented anything great in art or science or any other praiseworthy quality" (*O*, p. 111).

20. Hugo, "Preface to Cromwell."

21. "The Indians have a dominating taste for the grotesque, of the sort that falls into the adventurous. Their religion consists of grotesqueries. Idols of monstrous form, the priceless tooth of the mighty monkey Hanuman, the unnatural atonements of the fakirs (heathen mendicant friars) and so forth are his taste. . . . What trifling grotesqueries do the verbose and studied compliments of the Chinese contain! Even their paintings are grotesque and portray strange and unnatural figures such as are encountered nowhere in the world" (*O*, p. 110).

22. See Meg Armstrong, "'A Jumble of Foreignness': The Sublime Musayums of Nineteenth-Century Fairs and Expositions," *Cultural Critique* 23 (1992–1993): 199–250.

23. See Fredric Jameson's remarks on the "hysterical sublime" in "Postmodernism, or the Cultural Logic of Late Capitalism," *New Left Review* 146 (1984): 53–92 [excerpted in the present volume – Ed.]; Arjun Appadurai, "Disjuncture and Difference in the Global Cultural Economy," *Public Culture* 2 (Spring 1990): 1–24; and James Clifford, *The Predicament of Culture: Twentieth-Century Ethnography, Literature, and Art* (Cambridge, MA: Harvard University Press, 1988), 1–17.

24. See also *0*, 48–49 on the sublimity of pyramids and deserts.

25. [The quote is from Fanon, whom Armstrong discusses in this section. Frantz Fanon, *Black Skin, White Masks,* trans. Charles Lam Markmann [New York: Grove Press, Inc., 1967], 112. – Ed.]

26. "It is hard to resist the thought that the 'great horror' at the black woman (in contrast to the mere 'uneasiness' at a black object) is as much owing to the clash of aesthetic and political sensibilities as it is to the mechanics of vision," in W. J. T. Mitchell, *Iconology: Image, Text, Ideology* (Chicago: University of Chicago Press, 1986), 131.

27. [A fifth, final section has been omitted. – Ed.]

## Chapter 32

1. Immanuel Kant, *The Critique of Judgment*, trans. James Creed Meredith (Oxford: Clarendon Press, 1969), 104/256. This and subsequent references are to this translation; pagination refers first to this version and then to the German edition.

2. I can mention here two other treatments of the sublime in film: "The Street Angel and the Badman: *The Good Woman of Bangkok*" *Photofile* 35 (1991): 12–15, in which Adrian Martin uses the notion of the sublime in an analysis of Dennis O'Rourke's avant-garde documentary, *The Good Woman of Bangkok.* (I am grateful to Philip Robertson for drawing this article to my attention and sending me a copy of it from Hong Kong.) Also Rob Wilson, "Cyborg America: Policing the Social Sublime in *Robocop* and *Robocop 2*," in *The Administration of Aesthetics: Censorship, Political Criticism, and the Public Sphere*, ed. Richard Burt (Minneapolis: University of Minnesota Press, 1994), 289–306.

3. See Jacques Derrida, *The Truth in Painting*, trans. Geoff Bennington and Ian McLeod (Chicago: University of Chicago Press, 1987), esp. 14–147, "The Parergon"; Jean-François Lyotard, *Lessons on the Analytic of the Sublime*

*(Kant's Critique of Judgment, sections 23-29)*, trans. Elizabeth Rottenberg (Stanford, CA: Stanford University Press, 1994); Slavoj Žižek, *The Sublime Object of Ideology* (London: Verso, 1989).

4. The term is used by Paul Crowther in *The Kantian Sublime: From Morality to Art* (Oxford: Clarendon Press, 1989), 155.

5. See Samuel H. Monk's explication of Burke in *The Sublime: A Study of Critical Theories in Eighteenth-Century England* (New York: Modern Language Association, 1935 [reprinted in 1960]), 96–97.

6. In this chapter, I will not be considering how work by cognitivist philosophers, such as Gregory Currie, *Image and Mind: Film, Philosophy, and Cognitive Science* (Cambridge: Cambridge University Press, 1995); or Noël Carroll, *The Philosophy of Horror, or Paradoxes of the Heart* (New York: Routledge, 1990), and *A Philosophy of Mass Art* (Oxford: Clarendon, 1998), would bear on the topic of the sublime.

7. See Roland Barthes, "The Face of Garbo," from *Mythologies;* reprinted in *Film Theory and Criticism*, ed. Gerald Mast, Marshall Cohen, and Leo Braudy (New York: Oxford University Press, 1992), 628–31.

8. One suggestion I have heard is that the sublime is simply the condition of cinema itself when films are viewed as they were meant to be, in a movie theater (Marty Fairbairn, H-Film Electronic Discussion List, December 14, 1995).

9. On this issue, see Derrida, *Truth in Painting*, 125–26, 140–43; and Lyotard, *Peregrinations: Law, Form, and Event* (New York: Columbia University Press, 1988), 40–43.

10. Here I am indebted to Jerrold Levinson's "Messages in Art," in *Art and Its Messages: Meaning, Morality, and Society*, ed. Stephen Davies (University Park: Pennsylvania State University Press, 1995), 70–83.

11. The subject occupies pages 90–204 of the Meredith translation. My account is indebted to various sources, including Crowther; Timothy Gould, "Intensity and Its Audiences: Toward a Feminist Perspective on the Kantian Sublime," in *Feminism and Tradition in Aesthetics*, ed. Peggy Zeglin Brand and Carolyn Korsmeyer (University Park: Pennsylvania State University Press, 1995), 66–87; Paul Guyer, *Kant and the Experience of Freedom* (Cambridge: Cambridge University Press, 1993); and John H. Zammito, *The Genesis of Kant's "Critique of Judgment"* (Chicago: University of Chicago Press, 1992).

12. "Two things fill the mind with ever new and increasing admiration and awe, the oftener and more steadily we reflect on them: the starry heavens above me and the moral law within me"; Kant, *Critique of Practical Reason*, trans. Lewis White Beck (New York: Liberal Arts Press, 1956), 166.

13. My point here is similar to that made by Peter Lamarque in "Tragedy and Moral Value," in *Art and Its Messages*, ed. Davies, 59–69. However, Lamarque does not invoke the notion of rupture or reflexive artistic features of a work in the way I do.

14. The film shows its black and Indian characters, and perhaps the women as well, as victims of the European (males) plans.

15. Ed S. Tan, *Emotion and the Structure of Narrative Film: Film as an Emotion Machine*, trans. Barbara Fasting (Mahwah, NJ: Erlbaum, 1996).

16. Tan comments, "Other aspects of the artefact, such as acting, may strike almost any viewer" (65).

17. Tan does seem to recognize this when he writes that "in a general sense, it may be that the more intense the emotion, the greater the likelihood the viewer will realize this is a special experience and be aware of what he or she is seeing is indeed an artefact" (65).

18. See the articles by Joseph LeDoux and Jeffrey A. Gray in *The Nature of Emotions: Fundamental Questions*, ed. Paul Ekman and Richard J. Davidson (New York: Oxford University Press, 1994).

19. See Antonio Damasio, *Descartes' Error: Emotion, Reason, and the Human Brain* (New York: Putnam, 1994).

20. Joseph LeDoux, *The Emotional Brain: The Mysterious Underpinnings of Emotional Life* (New York: Simon and Schuster, 1996).

21. LeDoux, *The Emotional Brain*, 19.

22. Damasio, *Descartes' Error*, 125–26.

23. An example of an attempt to begin using cognitive science in a way that recognizes these gaps is Ellen Spolsky's *Gaps in Nature: Literary Interpretation and the Modular Mind* (Albany: State University of New York Press, 1993).

24. Damasio criticizes standard views about the differentiation of lower from higher brain structures; see *Descartes' Error*, 128.

## Notes

25. See, for example, Mark Johnson, *Moral Imagination: Implications of Cognitive Science for Ethics* (Chicago: University of Chicago Press, 1993).

26. I am grateful to Peg Brand, Alan Richardson, and the volume editors [Carl R. Plantinga and Greg M. Smith – Ed.] for useful criticisms of earlier drafts. My colleague Anne Jacobson not only offered helpful comments but introduced me to a whole new literature of cognitive science on the emotions. I also thank the other participants at a colloquium on Philosophy and Film at the University of Colorado where an earlier version was read (Luc Bovens, Ted Cohen, Timothy Gould, Marian Keane, and Thomas Wartenberg).

## Chapter 33

1. Newman's "The Sublime Is Now" and Lyotard's "The Sublime and the Avant-Garde" are both reprinted in the present volume. This quote is from Lyotard's "Answering the Question: What is Postmodernism?" – Ed.

2. Clement Greenberg (1909–94), an American art critic. – Ed.

3. These are the opening words of Newman's essay. A slight misquote ("confused and identified" rather than "identified and confused") has been corrected here, and in this chapter, similar misquotations have been corrected silently. – Ed.

4. Ellipses have been added by the present volume editor.

5. The German is given by Danto, who is quoting from Kant's second *Critique*, Academy Edition vol. 5:161. These words could also be translated with "admiration and reverence." – Ed.

6. The comment in square brackets and ellipsis in this quote are from Danto. – Ed.

7. Danto's text reads "*Second Critique*'s." – Ed.

8. Actually, in this passage Kant implies that he is not speaking about the sublime as such, but about the *examples* he is using to illustrate pure aesthetic judgments: "In the transcendental aesthetic of the power of judgment it is strictly pure aesthetic judgments that are at issue, consequently the examples must not be drawn from those beautiful or sublime objects of nature that presuppose the concept of an end" (Academy Edition vol. 5:270). If so, there may be room for conceptually informed sublimity after all. – Ed.

9. *der bestirnte Himmel*: the starry heavens. It is important to note, however, that Kant preceded this passage about the ocean (cited by Danto in the block quote) with the claim that he is choosing his examples in light of the fact that "in the transcendental aesthetic of the power of judgment it is strictly pure aesthetic judgments" that are at issue (Academy Edition vol. 5:270), which could be read as implying the possibility of *impure* (or dependent) aesthetic judgments of the sublime, that is, judgments that partially take into account our knowledge of objects or their purposes. – Ed.

10. Since 1 Italian *braccio* equals about 0.7 meters, it would have been approximately 8.4 meters. Michelangelo's *David* stands 5.17 meters tall. – Ed.

11. *Piranesi*: Giovanni Battista Piranesi (1720–78), Italian artist and engraver. – Ed.

12. *aniconic*: without images or pictures. – Ed.

13. See Martin Heidegger, *Being and Time*, trans. Joan Stambaugh, revised by Dennis J. Schmidt (Albany, NY: SUNY Press, 2010). – Ed.

14. Danto, *The Abuse of Beauty*, 31–32. – Ed.

15. This is the end of the chapter as well as of *The Abuse of Beauty*. – Ed.

## Chapter 34

1. It is important to re-emphasize that this natural/man-made distinction is not a sharp one. For example, Mount Fuji is a dead volcano, but also, as "Mount Fuji," it is a symbolic achievement of the human spirit and this essay's author was acutely aware, while climbing it to the summit from Fuji Sengen-jinja (a famous Shinto shrine in Fuji-Yoshida at

the volcano's base), of the countless generations of awe- and aesthetic-awe-struck monks and priests who preceded him and built temples and shrines along the paths. The author's aesthetic awe and thrills at the summit were not a "mountain high," but in part caused by the sense of being privileged to follow in the footsteps of prior generations of monks in a distant land.

2. Panksepp (1995, 1998, pp. 278–79) has argued for the music-induced thrills to be regarded as reflecting the activation of our "ancient separation-distress response systems," on the grounds that his data show that "sad music" is a more powerful inducer of chills than "happy music," and that women—presumably the primary care-givers and thus more attuned than men to distress calls—are differentially more responsive to "sad music" than men. In addition, because his data show that women, unlike men, prefer the term "chills" to "thrills," Panksepp himself prefers the former term. However, there are indications that these generalizations may be limited to Panksepp's subject samples in Ohio. Because of the mixed results obtained in the present author's laboratory regarding these matters (Konečni 1995–2004), and the fact that Goldstein's (1980) early paper used "thrills" in the title, the terms "thrills" and "chills" are used interchangeably in the present paper.

3. As just two personal examples (in which unique associative and semiotic elements, in addition to the beauty of the space and the music, were involved), this paper's author can cite his experiences at Dom zu Salzburg and Thomaskirche in Leipzig. At the Salzburg Festival in 1991, Mozart's *Requiem* in D Minor (KV 626, completed by Franz Xaver Süssmayr) was performed by the Vienna Philharmonic at the Salzburg Cathedral, conducted by Carlo Maria Giulini. The performance poignantly marked the passage of two centuries since the composer's death in the place in which he had been baptized. At St. Thomas's Church, where Johann Sebastian Bach had been Kantor, the author sat literally at Bach's tomb while Bach's distant heir to the Kantor position in 1991 (241 years after Bach's death) played *Toccata* and *Fuga* D Minor (BWV 565) at the author's request—at 7:30 in the morning.

4. Tarozzi Goldsmith (1999) contends that the *new* in art maintains the (presumably essential) sublime in it despite the nihilistic onslaught from Nietzsche on. From this essay's standpoint, the view of the centrality of the new in the sublime is an only superficially attractive idea. To save the sublime in art from destructive deconstruction, the new must have an assured degree of continuity (or, more accurately, "continuality") and the series must be conceptually extended not only forward, but also backward, to the ancient artworks. Thus the continual new that manages repeatedly to recreate the sublime must maintain its ancient core. There is nothing new under the sun in aesthetics, or, rather, in the attributes of the stimuli that are capable of producing aesthetic awe.

# Chapter 35

1. Paul Crowther, *The Kantian Sublime* (Oxford: Clarendon Press, 1989); Jean-François Lyotard, *Lessons on the Analytic of the Sublime,* trans. Elizabeth Rottenberg (Stanford University Press, 1991); Kirk Pillow, *Sublime Understanding: Aesthetic Reflection in Kant and Hegel* (Cambridge, MA: MIT Press, 2000); Dabney Townsend, ed., *Eighteenth-Century British Aesthetics* (Amityville: Baywood Publishing, 1999); Andrew Ashfield and Peter de Bolla, eds., *The Sublime: A Reader in British Eighteenth-Century Aesthetic Theory* (Cambridge: Cambridge University Press, 1996).

2. Sircello, "How is a Theory of the Sublime Possible?" 541–50. References to Sircello's work will be inserted in parentheses in the body of the text.

3. Joseph Addison, "*The Spectator*, No. 412, Monday June 23, 1712," in *The Sublime: A Reader in British Eighteenth-Century Aesthetic Theory,* 62–70, quote from 62.

4. Anthony Ashley Cooper, Third Earl of Shaftesbury, "Characteristicks," in *The Sublime: A Reader in British Eighteenth-Century Aesthetic Theory,* 72–80, quote from 73.

5. Edmund Burke, "A Philosophical Enquiry into the Origin of Our Ideas of the Sublime and Beautiful," in *The Sublime: A Reader in British Eighteenth-Century Aesthetic Theory,* 131–44, quote from 132.

6. Jean-François Lyotard, *The Postmodern Condition: A Report on Knowledge* (Minneapolis: University of Minnesota Press, 1984), 81.

7. James Usher, "Clio, or a Discourse on Taste," in *The Sublime: A Reader in British Eighteenth-Century Aesthetic Theory,* 147–57, quote from 150–51.

8. Addison, "*The Spectator*," 62.

9. Burke, "A Philosophical Enquiry," 133.

10. Immanuel Kant, *Kritik der Urteilskraft* (Frankfurt am Main: Suhrkamp, 1974). I rely for English translation of this text on *Critique of Judgment,* trans. J. H. Bernard (New York: Hafner Publishing Co., 1972). References to the English version of the third *Critique* will appear in the text in parentheses, with section and page number; references to the German text will be provided in subsequent footnotes.

11. Kant, *Kritik der Urteilskraft,* 172.

12. Ibid.

13. Malcolm Budd, "Delight in the Natural World: Kant on the Aesthetic Appreciation of Nature. Part III: The Sublime in Nature," *The British Journal of Aesthetics* 38 (1998): 233–51, quote from 240.

14. Kant, *Kritik der Urteilskraft,* 172.

15. Budd, "Delight in the Natural World," 241.

16. As Paul Guyer has noted, "it is we ourselves who are sublime." See his "The Difficulty of the Sublime," presented to the American Society for Aesthetics Annual General Meeting, Providence, Rhode Island, October 2005, for the panel "Knowing the Sublime," 15.

17. Immanuel Kant, "Foundations of the Metaphysics of Morals," in *Kant Selections,* trans. Lewis White Beck (Upper Saddle River, NJ: Prentice Hall, 1998), 281, emphasis added. I have chosen this translation for its emphasis on the term "sublime." And see Kant, *Grundlegung zur Metaphysik der Sitten* (Frankfurt am Main: Suhrkamp, 1974), 75. Henry Allison, in *Kant's Theory of Taste: A Reading of the Critique of Aesthetic Judgment* (Cambridge: Cambridge University Press, 2001), offers a good discussion of the moral implications of the sublime, see 341–44.

18. Immanuel Kant, *Critique of Practical Reason,* trans. Lewis White Beck (Upper Saddle River, NJ: Prentice Hall, 1993), 92. And see Kant, *Kritik der praktischen Vernunft* (Frankfurt am Main: Suhrkamp, 1974), 211.

19. Budd, "Delight in the Natural World," 246.

20. Ibid.

21. My thanks to Mark Smith of Queen's University at Kingston for a discussion on this point.

22. William Wordsworth, *The Prelude 1799, 1805, 1850,* quoted in Sircello, 543.

23. Lao-tzu, *Tao te Ching,* quoted in Sircello, 544.

24. An early version of this article was presented at the American Society for Aesthetics Annual General Meeting, Providence, Rhode Island, October 2005, for the panel "Knowing the Sublime." I greatly benefited from the commentary provided by Jeffrey Wilson, Department of Philosophy, Loyola Marymount University, and from discussion by participants Paul Guyer, Kirk Pillow, and Melissa Zinkin.

## Chapter 36

1. Jane Forsey, "Is a Theory of the Sublime Possible?" *Journal of Aesthetics and Art Criticism* 65 (2007): 381–89. Henceforth I shall cite this paper in parenthetical citation to the page number.

2. In fact, Forsey poses the difficulty as a trilemma, with the third horn as offering mere descriptions of sublime experience. In a reply to an earlier version of this paper, Forsey suggests that I succumb to this third horn insofar as my attempt at a theory "appears to be an explicit phenomenology of the kind that . . . [she holds] in doubt: how are we to determine we are feeling the correct emotion? How does a feeling ground an analysis or theory? Why would a terrifying experience bring us pleasure?" (Jane Forsey, "The Sublime, Redux," in *The Possibility of the Sublime,* 102). In response to these worries, I hold that while *mere* phenomenological descriptions would obviously not amount to an actual "theory" of the sublime—and thus I think the third horn is a "straw horn"—I do think that phenomenological descriptions of prima facie sublime responses are *indispensable* in trying to theorize this area of aesthetics. For it is largely the phenomenology of such aesthetic responses—the thoughts and feelings of being humbled and exalted, overwhelmed, and uplifted—that forms the *object* of theorizing. This is why I think

it is important for aestheticians to pay close attention to the phenomenology, and why, in section II of this paper, I adduce three rich descriptions that authors have given of various sorts of sublime experience. Yet, aestheticians should not simply describe the phenomenology, they should try to make sense of it, and that is what I try to do here.

3. For fuller reconstructions of a theory of the sublime for contemporary environmental aesthetics, see Sandra Shapshay, "Contemporary Environmental Aesthetics and the Neglect of the Sublime," *British Journal of Aesthetics* 53, no. 2 (2013): 181–98. For a theory of the sublime for contemporary philosophy of art, see Sandra Shapshay, "The Problem and the Promise of the Sublime" in *Suffering Art Gladly*, ed. Jerrold Levinson (Palgrave Macmillan, 2013), 84–107. I have adapted much of the material from these papers for this commentary on Forsey's article.

4. I do not mean to suggest here that one needs to *proclaim* to have had a sublime experience in order to have had one. Also, I do not believe that a person needs to possess the category or concept of the sublime in order to have the experience. Many thanks to Robert Clewis for pressing me to be clearer on these points.

5. See Shapshay, "Neglect of the Sublime," for full argument.

6. I will leave aside the very interesting question about whether one might have a sublime response (let alone any aesthetic experience) without occurrent perception of an object or environment. Purely conceptual art raises this issue, and some might argue that a sublime response may be had to a particularly elegant mathematical proof. These present difficult cases for the account of aesthetic experience as fundamentally perceptual that I am assuming here.

7. Aristotle, *Nicomachean Ethics*, trans. W. D. Ross (Place undentified: Pacific Publishing Studio, 2011), 2 (Bk I, Ch. 3). Also available online at http://classics.mit.edu/Aristotle/nicomachaen.html (accessed July 13, 2017).

8. Carolyn Korsmeyer, *Savouring Disgust: The Foul and the Fair in Aesthetics* (Oxford: Oxford University Press, 2011).

9. Keltner and Haidt, "Approaching Awe, a Moral, Spiritual, and Aesthetic Emotion," 297–314, 306.

10. Ibid., 304.

11. Martha C. Nussbaum, *Upheavals of Thought: The Intelligence of Emotions* (Cambridge: Cambridge University Press, 2001), 54, n. 53. Cited in Katie McShane, "The Role of Awe in Environmental Ethics" in a special issue of the *Journal of Aesthetics and Art Criticism*, "The Good, the Beautiful, the Green: Environmentalism and Aesthetics," ed. Sandra Shapshay and Levi Tenen (2018), 76, no. 4.

12. Marjorie Hope Nicolson, *Mountain Gloom and Mountain Glory: The Development of the Aesthetics of the Infinite* (New York: W. W. Norton, 1963), 2.

13. John Conron, *American Picturesque* (University Park: Pennsylvania State University Press, 2000).

14. Bence Nanay, *Aesthetics as Philosophy of Perception* (Oxford: Oxford University Press, 2016), 156.

15. Yuriko Saito, *Everyday Aesthetics* (Oxford: Oxford University Press, 2007), Chapter 3.

16. Quoted in Nanay (157), who cites the following studies to support this view: Takahiko Masuda and Richard E. Nisbett, "Attending Holistically versus Analytically: Comparing the Context Sensitivity of Japanese and Americans," *Journal of Personality and Social Psychology* 81 (2001): 922–34. Li-Jun Ji, Kaiping Peng, and Richard E. Nisbett, "Culture, Control and Perception of Relationships in the Environment," *Journal of Personality and Social Psychology* 78 (2000): 943–55.

17. Lydia Goehr, *The Imaginary Museum of Musical Works: An Essay in the Philosophy of Music* (Oxford: Clarendon Press, 1992).

18. John Muir, *The Mountains of California* (Boston, MA: Houghton Mifflin, 1894), Chapter 10.

19. Donovan Webster, in Edward O. Wilson (ed.), *The Best American Science and Nature Writing 2001* (Boston, MA: Houghton Mifflin, 2001), 253–54.

20. Noël Carroll, "On Being Moved by Nature: Between Religion and Natural History," in *Nature, Aesthetics, and Environmentalism: From Beauty to Duty*, ed. Allen Carlson and Sheila Lintott (New York: Columbia University Press, 2008), 169–87, 170. Carroll's essay was originally published in Salim Kemal and Ivan Gaskell (eds.), *Landscape, Natural Beauty and the Arts* (Cambridge: Cambridge University Press, 1993), 244–66.

21. Edmund Burke, *A Philosophical Enquiry into the Origin of Our Ideas of the Sublime and Beautiful* (London: R. and J. Dodsley, 1759), Part III, section 27, 238. References to Burke's *Enquiry* will be to this (the second) edition.

22. Burke, *Enquiry*, Part IV, section 7, 257.

23. Joseph Addison, *The Works of the Right Honourable Joseph Addison* (London: H.G. Bohn, 1854) vol. IV, *Spectator* No. 489, page 7.

## Notes

24. Kant, *The Critique of the Power of Judgment,* trans. Paul Guyer and Eric Matthews (Cambridge: Cambridge University Press, 2000), 129 [Academy Edition vol. 5:245].

25. Burke, *Enquiry,* Part I, Chapter 7, 59.

26. In Kant and Schopenhauer's versions of thick sublime response, these reflections involve a felt recognition of human *rational and moral freedom* that is revealed precisely in the face of vast or powerful natural environments or works of art which threaten the subject either existentially or psychologically, with annihilation or with complete insignificance. Given the transcendental-idealist background for both of these philosophers, one cannot *know* that one is free because freedom belongs to the "supersensible substrate" of nature, or more specifically, to the intelligible character. But insofar as sublime experiences afford a felt recognition (albeit not genuine knowledge) of freedom they are very important systemically.

27. Robert R. Clewis, "What's the Big Idea?: On Emily Brady's Sublime," *The Journal of Aesthetic Education* 50, no. 2 (2016): 104–18.

28. Clewis, "On Emily Brady's Sublime," 112.

29. Ibid., 113.

30. Carroll, "On Being Moved by Nature," 170.

31. It is difficult to give a good account of what constitutes an aesthetic experience, but Nanay has recently utilized work in the philosophy of perception to illuminate some key features of these experiences, and I am following him here: "in the case of some paradigmatic instances of aesthetic experience, we attend in a distributed and at the same time focused manner: our attention is focused on one perceptual object, but it is distributed among a large number of the object's properties. This way of attending contrasts sharply with the most standard way of exercising our attention (which would be focusing on a limited set of properties of one or more perceptual objects). In other words, this way of attending is special and I argue that it is a central feature of some paradigmatic cases of aesthetic experience." Nanay, *Aesthetics as Philosophy of Perception,* 13.

32. Paul Crowther, *The Kantian Sublime: From Morality to Art* (Oxford: Oxford University Press, 1989), 162.

33. Crowther, *The Kantian Sublime,* 161.

## Chapter 37

1. Dacher Keltner and Jonathan Haidt, "Approaching Awe, a Moral, Spiritual, and Aesthetic Emotion," *Cognition & Emotion* 17, no. 2 (2003): 297–314, 307–08.

2. Vladimir Konečni makes this point in his contribution to the present volume. I briefly discuss the nature of the "aesthetic" in the Introduction to this volume.

3. For instance, in the Keltner and Haidt paper cited in the first footnote above, there is little attention to the possibility that awe might raise *conceptual* questions about its coherence, nature, causes, and evolutionary purposes.

4. Werner Herzog, "On the Absolute, the Sublime, and Ecstatic Truth," *Arion* 17, no. 3 (2010): 1–12, 2 (original ellipsis). Herzog writes that Kant's "explanations concerning the sublime are so very abstract that they have always remained alien to me in my practical work . . . Longinus . . . is much closer to my heart, because he always speaks in practical terms and uses examples" (9). After providing commentary on Longinus, he pulls back: "But I don't want to lose myself in Longinus, whom I always think of as a good friend. I stand before you as someone who works with film" (11).

5. Jane Forsey, "Is a Theory of the Sublime Possible?" *Journal of Aesthetics and Art Criticism* (2007) 65, no. 4: 381–89, 381; reprinted in the present volume. What is questioned (by Forsey) is neither the existence of experiences called "sublime" nor the veracity of the claim that people report such experiences, but that such reports can be theorized about in a coherent and consistent manner. (Forsey also questions whether people can communicate the experience, but in my view this is not the most fundamental point raised by her analysis.)

6. Andrew Chignell and Matthew C. Halteman, "Religion and the Sublime," in *The Sublime: From Antiquity to Present,* ed. Timothy Costelloe (Cambridge: Cambridge University Press, 2012), 183–202, 202.

7. E. F. Carritt, "The Sublime," *Mind* 19, no. 75 (1910): 356–72, 357. Although Carritt's analysis is valuable, I do not share his assumption that we should view a theory of the sublime as an attempt to specify the criteria that are sufficient and necessary for membership in a class ("sublime").

8. This line eventually raises questions concerning aesthetic properties and dispositional properties, but such complexities are beyond the scope of this paper. My account is not necessarily committed to what is called "realism" in the anti-realism–realism debate about aesthetic properties.

9. Guy Sircello, "How is a Theory of the Sublime Possible?" *Journal of Aesthetics and Art Criticism* 51, no. 4 (1993): 541–50.

10. Forsey, "Is a Theory of the Sublime Possible?" 383.

11. The problem can be seen in the following *modus ponens*. The object is transcendent and inaccessible. If the object is transcendent and inaccessible, it is not possible to comprehend and provide an adequate theory of it. Thus, it is not possible to comprehend and provide an adequate theory of the object.

12. Insufficient attention to the emotional and affective aspects of the experience likewise diminishes the value of some recent theories of the "technological" or "postmodern" sublime, inspired by the work of David Nye and Frederic Jameson. For example, Rowan Wilken, "'Unthinkable Complexity': The Internet and the Mathematical Sublime," *The Sublime Today: Contemporary Readings in the Aesthetic*, ed. G. B. Pierce (Newcastle upon Tyne: Cambridge Scholars Publishing, 2012), 191–212.

13. See Sandra Shapshay's contribution to the present volume.

14. The history of aesthetics, too, is replete with such accounts. Anna Aikin, Joseph Addison, Joseph Priestley, Thomas Reid, Moses Mendelssohn, and Immanuel Kant all gave versions of it.

15. Other related cognitive faculties, such as memory, may also be activated and stimulated, though I cannot develop this point here. Nor can I investigate the relationship between perception and imagination.

16. Alan Richardson's "neural" or "corporeal" sublime appears to be a quasi-epistemological account, since it is dependent on the notion of exposing perceptual illusions, hence on representing a kind of cognitive failure. However, it is debatable whether these tricks on the mind produce the *intense affective feeling* and emotional experience associated with the sublime conceived as an aesthetic experience. Alan Richardson, *The Neural Sublime: Cognitive Theories and Romantic Texts* (Baltimore: The Johns Hopkins University Press, 2010).

17. David Hume, *A Treatise of Human Nature*, II.i.viii, "Of Beauty and Deformity." References to the *A Treatise of Human Nature* are to the Book, Part, and Section. David Hume, *A Treatise of Human Nature*, ed. P. H. Nidditch (Oxford: Clarendon Press, 1978).

18. See Clewis, "A Theory of the Sublime Is Possible," 48, for quotations and references. While these examples of sublime discourse are expressions of the poet's sublime experience, they need not necessarily *evoke* the sublime. The latter is not always the poet's aim.

19. Even if the latter phrase avoided self-contradiction, in the end it would still raise the question of the metaphysical status of the "infinite."

20. The notion of an "object" is understood broadly. The class of sublime elicitors in principle includes great thoughts, ideas and concepts, events, artifacts of technology (e.g., the internet), not just natural objects like canyons, ravines, and ecosystems. It includes works of art—music, poetry, architecture, and so on. In the present discussion, however, I focus on non-mental, perceived objects since they are more concrete and readily accessible.

21. Stephen Pepper, *Aesthetic Quality: A Contextualist Theory of Beauty* (Westport: Greenwood Press, 1970) 61. As Pepper notes, novelty is not the same as uniqueness. He distinguishes "intrusive" (cultivated) novelty—which an artist might elicit through technique and skill—from "naïve" (child-like) novelty, which arises before we acquire habits. The former is naturally of more interest to aesthetics.

22. In his 1712 essays on the pleasures of the imagination, Addison suggested that the encounter with what is perceived to be new or uncommon plays a significant role in generating the emotional response that we would generally call the sublime.

23. Andrew Ashfield and Peter de Bolla, *The Sublime: A Reader in Eighteenth-Century Aesthetic Theory* (Cambridge: Cambridge University Press, 1996), 119.

24. Note that, contrary to widespread interpretations of the sublime inspired by Kant, Wordsworth refers to these unfamiliar shapes as huge and mighty *forms*. William Wordsworth, *The Portable Romantic Poets*, ed. W. H. Auden and N. H. Pearson (New York: Penguin, 1978), 207.

25. William Wordsworth, "The Sublime and the Beautiful," in *The Prose Works of William Wordsworth*, vol. 2, ed. W. J. B. Owen and Jane Worthington Symser (Oxford: Clarendon Press, 1974), 349; reprinted in the present volume. Thanks to Emily Brady for clarifying this point.

26. Quoted in Ashfield and de Bolla, *The Sublime*, 119; original emphasis.

27. Immanuel Kant, *Critique of the Power of Judgment*, trans. Paul Guyer and Eric Matthews (Cambridge: Cambridge University Press, 2000), §26, 5:252. References to Kant are to this translation, by section (§) and volume and page number in the Academy Edition of Kant's collected works.

28. Quoted from Kin-yuen Wong, "Negative-Positive Dialectic in the Chinese Sublime," *The Chinese Text: Studies in Comparative Literature* (Hong Kong: The Chinese University Press, 1986), 119–58, 143. See also Guo Xi's contribution to the present volume.

29. Emily Brady, "The Environmental Sublime," in *The Sublime: From Antiquity to the Present,* ed. Timothy Costelloe (Cambridge: Cambridge University Press, 2012), 171–82, 182; reprinted in the present volume.

30. Shapshay's thin/thick distinction should not be confused with a related one, my distinction between free and conceptual (adherent) sublimity. The latter is presented in Robert R. Clewis, "What's the Big Idea? On Emily Brady's Sublime," *The Journal of Aesthetic Education* 50, no. 2 (2016): 104–18, 111–13; and Robert R. Clewis, *The Kantian Sublime and the Revelation of Freedom* (Cambridge: Cambridge University Press, 2009), 96–108. For instance, when we learn the age of an ancient redwood, that information often plays a role in shaping our aesthetic experience and brings about what I have called an experience of adherent sublimity.

31. Both reflexivity in the sublime and empirical studies are discussed in Clewis, "A Theory of the Sublime Is Possible," 52–54. See Tomohiro Ishizu and Semir Zeki, "A Neurobiological Enquiry into the Origins of Our Experience of the Sublime and Beautiful," *Frontiers in Human Neuroscience* 8 (2014), article 891: 1–10; Michelle Shiota, Dacher Keltner, and Amanda Mossman, "The Nature of Awe: Elicitors, Appraisals, and Effects on Self-Concept," *Cognition and Emotion* 21, no. 5 (2007): 944–63. The studies' methods of determining *which* objects are considered sublime (rather than beautiful or ordinary) and of classifying the participants' feelings are explained in the "methods" sections of the papers. Studies by Ishizu and Zeki, and Shiota, et al., indicate that when experiencers and observers attest that they are experiencing sublimity or aesthetic awe, they report a diminishment of self-awareness (though not necessarily *vice versa*). Moreover, when subjects are reporting that they are experiencing the sublime, the areas associated with the imagination are stimulated and activated. It appears that the perceiver's imagination is being stretched by the engagement with a vast/powerful object, and that the areas associated with self-awareness are *deactivated*. The latter (deactivation) is in agreement with philosophical theories like Priestley's that downplay self-awareness in the sublime.

32. Criticizing Keltner and Haidt's model, Sundararajan emphasizes the elements of self-reflexivity in the experience of awe (she mentions neither the sublime nor sublimity). Louise Sundararajan, "Religious Awe: Potential Contributions of Negative Theology to Psychology, 'Positive' or Otherwise," *Journal of Theoretical and Philosophical Psychology* 22, no. 2 (2002): 174–97. It would be useful, however, to distinguish self-diminishment and self-admiration in theories of awe (and sublimity), as well as to explore the extent to which a feeling of self-diminishment or smaller self is a kind of self-reflexivity (i.e., whether it must involve explicit attention to one's own affective response).

33. I here agree with Tom Hanauer, "Pleasure and Transcendence: Two Paradoxes of Sublimity," in *The Possibility of the Sublime: Aesthetic Exchanges*, ed. Lars Aagaard-Mogensen, 29–43 (Newcastle upon Tyne: Cambridge Scholars Publishing, 2017), 39 n. 28. This issue raises fundamental questions about the nature of aesthetics that cannot be pursued here.

34. In "Religion and the Sublime," Chignell and Haltman explain what they mean by "epiphany."

35. See her contribution to the present volume.

36. Melanie Rudd, Kathleen Vohs, and Jennifer Aaker, "Awe Expands People's Perception of Time, Alters Decision Making, and Enhances Well-being," *Psychological Science* 23, no. 10 (2012): 1130–36. See also Robert R. Clewis, David B. Yaden, and Alice Chirico, "Awe and Sublimity: A Belonging-Rising-Imagining Model," unpublished manuscript.

37. Kant, *Critique of the Power of Judgment*, §27, 5:259.

38. See Burke's contribution to the present volume, Part II, Section I, "Of the Passion Caused by the Sublime."

39. Some empirical studies seem to suggest that the feeling of the sublime is linked to prosocial behavior. Yaden, Haidt, et al. "The Varieties of Self-Transcendent Experience," 143–60. See also Konečni's contribution to the present volume. The connection between a feeling of connectedness in the sublime and prosocial behavior deserves more attention.

40. Kant, *Critique of the Power of Judgment*, §24, 5:247. In light of Kant's intersubjective account, well known to Forsey, I remain puzzled by her remark, "I have said nothing so far about an *intersubjective* account of the sublime because there is almost no mention in the literature of this experience being culturally shared or even communicable. The sublime has been described as a wholly personal, even intimate experience without reference to others." Forsey, "Is a Theory of the Sublime Possible?" 387 (original emphasis).

41. Clewis, *The Kantian Sublime*, 15. I give an updated reading in Robert R. Clewis, "The Place of the Sublime in Kant's Project," *Studi kantiani* 28 (2015): 63–82.

42. Richard Rorty, "Habermas and Lyotard on Postmodernity," in *Habermas and Modernity*, ed. Richard J. Bernstein (Cambridge, MA: MIT Press, 1985), 161–75, 174.

43. Hans Ulrich Gumbrecht, *In Praise of Athletic Beauty* (Cambridge: Belknap Press, 2006), 206.

44. Gumbrecht, *Athletic Beauty*, 228–29, and 48, respectively.

45. Elias Canetti, *Crowds and Power*, trans. Carol Stewart (London: Phoenix, 2000), 20.

46. In his contribution to the present volume, Konečni adopts the pan-cultural view.

47. James Elkins, "Against the Sublime," in *Beyond the Finite: The Sublime in Art and Science*, ed. Roald Hoffmann and Iain Boyd Whyte (Oxford: Oxford University Press, 2011), 75–90; see esp. 75, 87–88.

48. Marjorie Hope Nicolson, *Mountain Gloom and Mountain Glory: The Development of the Aesthetics of the Infinite* (New York: W. W. Norton, 1963).

49. Richard Steele and Joseph Addison, *Selections from* The Tatler *and* The Spectator, ed. Robert J. Allen (New York: Holt, Rinehart, and Winston, 1970), 401.

50. See Burke's contribution to this volume, Part II, Section I, "Of the Passion Caused by the Sublime."

51. Moses Mendelssohn, *Philosophical Writings,* ed. and trans. Daniel O. Dahlstrom (New York, NY: Cambridge University Press, 1997), 195; reprinted in the present volume.

52. Brady, "The Environmental Sublime," 177.

53. Emily Brady, *The Sublime in Modern Philosophy* (Cambridge: Cambridge University Press, 2013), 201.

54. One might think that the emphasis on the pleasures of the imagination, and on vitality and vivifying mental activity, makes the sublime a form of beauty. But as noted in the previous section, the structure of the sublime contains a negative moment not readily found in beauty. Sublimity is a response to contra-purposive qualities perceived in the object.

55. Kant, *Critique of the Power of Judgment*, §25, 5:249.

56. Ibid., §28, 5:262.

57. Arthur Schopenhauer, *World as Will and Representation*, translated by E. F. J. Payne (Dover, 1969), 2 vols., vol. 1, 201; reprinted in the present volume.

58. John Muir, *The Mountains of California* (New York: The Century Co., 1907 [1894]), ch. 10, 256.

59. Schopenhauer, *World as Will and Representation*, 205 (for this and the following quote).

60. Carl Sagan, *Pale Blue Dot: A Vision of the Human Future in Space* (New York: Random House, 1994), 6–7. Sagan moves from describing the earth as a "very small stage in a vast cosmic arena" and "a lonely speck in the great enveloping cosmic dark" to a sense of responsibility "to deal more kindly with one another" and concern for our "home."

61. David Yaden, Jonathan Iwry, et al., "The Overview Effect: Awe and Self-Transcendent Experience in Space Flight," *Psychology of Consciousness: Theory, Research, and Practice* 3, no. 1 (2016):1–11.

62. I leave aside the differences between pleasure, contentment, satisfaction, and enjoyment.

63. Brady, "The Environmental Sublime," 176–77.

64. Joseph Margolis, "The Art of Landscape Reconceived," *International Yearbook of Aesthetics*, vol. 17 (Sassari: Edizione Edes, 2013), ed. Raffaele Milani and Jale Erzen, 21–31, 27.

65. Kant, *Critique of the Power of Judgment*, §28, 5:262.

66. Ibid., §23, 5:245.

67. John Onians, "Neuroscience and the Sublime in Art and Science," in *Beyond the Finite: The Sublime in Art and Science*, 91–105, 97. For Onians' neurobiological explanations of the source of the pleasure which draw from the work of Zeki, see 97–100.

68. See Wordsworth's contribution to the present volume.

69. Mendelssohn, *Philosophical Writings*, "Rhapsody," 145. The following quote is from "On the Sublime and Naive," 195; reprinted in the present volume.

70. Carritt, "The Sublime," 365, 363.

71. Several theories from the history of aesthetic theory and philosophy develop this account of the sublime as a kind of mental (imaginative) stretching, filling, or swelling in response to a powerful or massive object. For passages from Longinus, Addison, Hume, Baillie, Burke, Home (Kames), Duff, Reid, Priestley, Kant, and Lyotard, see Clewis, "A Theory of the Sublime Is Possible," 60–63. In her contribution to the present volume, Anna Aikin also offers a version of the exercise or "expansion of the imagination" theory.

72. Kant, *Critique of the Power of Judgment*, §28, 5:262; and "General remark on the exposition of aesthetic reflective judgments," 5:269.

73. The inferior frontal gyrus, which is activated in the sublime, "has also been found to be active when subjects imagine future events [...] hence emphasizing the *importance of the imagination* in neural terms, just as it has been emphasized in hypothetical terms in past discussions of the sublime" (Ishizu and Zeki, "A Neurobiological Enquiry," 8; emphasis added). See also Onians, "Neuroscience and the Sublime in Art and Science," 98–99, which emphasizes the role of the imagination in the sublime. For empirical evidence from psychology, see Clewis, Yaden, and Chirico, "Awe and Sublimity: A Belonging-Rising-Imagining Model," unpublished manuscript.

74. Joseph Priestley, in Ashfield and de Bolla, *The Sublime*, 119.

75. Vladimir Konečni, "Aesthetic Trinity Theory and the Sublime," *Philosophy Today* 55, no. 1 (2011): 64–73, 64. Under a family of terms such as "awe," "aesthetic awe," "elevation," and "peak aesthetic experiences," the sublime has been investigated by several independent psychological papers by Jonathan Haidt, Dacher Keltner, Vladimir Konečni, Michelle Shiota, and David Yaden, among many others. Over the last thirty years there has been a considerable amount of empirical work of sublime or quasi-sublime responses elicited by art, but most of these studies focused on music rather than visual stimuli or linguistic phenomena (e.g., narratives, poetry). I take the existence of these studies to be another reason to frame a philosophical theory so as to include *works of art* in the class of possible stimuli of the sublime. On music's stirring effects, see the studies listed by Konečni (in "Aesthetic Trinity Theory" and his contribution to this volume) and also Jeanette Bicknell, *Why Music Moves Us* (London: Palgrave Macmillan, 2009).

76. Anjan Chatterjee, "Neuroaesthetics: A Coming of Age Story," *Journal of Cognitive Neuroscience* 23, no. 10 (2010): 53–62, 59.

77. Judy Lochhead, "The Sublime, the Ineffable, and Other Dangerous Aesthetics," *Women and Music: A Journal of Gender and Culture* 12, no. 1 (2008): 63–74, 72.

78. See the contribution by Emily Brady in the present volume.

79. The author is grateful to many individuals for comments and/or discussion, including but not limited to: Emily Brady, Alice Chirico, Elanna Dructor, Abigail Friel, Norbert Gratzl, Tom Hanauer, Rebecca Gullan, Vladimir Konečni, Cornelia Kroiss, J. Colin McQuillan, Patrick Messina, Lara Ostaric, Amanda Pirrone, Amanda Wortham, and David B. Yaden.

## Chapter 38

1. Recent extended work on the sublime in philosophy includes Paul Crowther, *The Kantian Sublime: From Morality to Art* (Oxford: Clarendon Press, 1989); Andrew Ashfield and Peter de Bolla, eds., *The Sublime: A Reader in*

*British Eighteenth-Century Aesthetic Theory* (Cambridge: Cambridge University Press, 1996); Kirk Pillow, *Sublime Understanding: Aesthetic Reflection in Kant and Hegel* (Cambridge, MA: MIT Press, 2000); James Kirwan, *Sublimity: The Non-Rational and the Irrational in the History of Aesthetics* (New York: Routledge, 2005); Christine Battersby, *The Sublime, Terror and Human Difference* (London: Routledge, 2007); and Robert R. Clewis, *The Kantian Sublime and the Revelation of Freedom* (Cambridge: Cambridge University Press., 2009). There has always been interest in the sublime in literary studies and criticism, reaching as far back as Longinus's *On the Sublime,* which was probably written in the first century but only rediscovered in the sixteenth century. See Philip Shaw, *The Sublime* (New York: Routledge, 2006), and Chapters 1 and 6 of Timothy Costelloe, ed., *The Sublime: From Antiquity to the Present* (Cambridge: Cambridge University Press, 2012).

2. Mary Mothersill, *Beauty Restored* (Oxford: Oxford University Press, 1986).

3. Burke, *A Philosophical Enquiry into the Origin of Our Ideas of the Sublime and Beautiful* (London: R. and J. Dodsley, 1759), Part II, Section 1, 95–96.

4. Immanuel Kant, *Kritik der Urteilskraft,* in *Kant's gesammelte Schriften,* Königlichen Preussischen (later Deutschen) Akademie der Wissenschaften, 29 vols. (Berlin: Reimer [later de Gruyter], 1900–), vol. 5; *Critique of the Power of Judgment,* ed. Paul Guyer; trans. Paul Guyer and Eric Matthews (Cambridge: Cambridge University Press, 2000) (CJ).

5. Guy Sircello, "How Is a Theory of the Sublime Possible?" *Journal of Aesthetics and Art Criticism* 51, no. 4 (1993): 541–50, 542.

6. I follow Guyer's view that the two artifacts mentioned by Kant, St. Peter's basilica and the pyramids in Egypt, are not true examples of the sublime because they are too "finite to induce a genuine experience of the sublime." See Paul Guyer, *Values of Beauty: Historical Essays in Aesthetics* (Cambridge: Cambridge University Press, 2005), 158n16. Kant does not dismiss the possibility of artistic sublimity outright, but if there are cases of it in the *Critique of the Power of Judgment,* they are likely to be of a different type (e.g., impure rather than pure judgments). See Uygar Abaci, "Kant's Justified Dismissal of Artistic Sublimity," *Journal of Aesthetics and Art Criticism* 66, no. 3 (2008): 237–51, and Robert R. Clewis, "A Case for Kantian Artistic Sublime: A Response to Abaci," *Journal of Aesthetics and Art Criticism* 68, no. 2 (2010): 167–70.

7. The massive scale of some earthworks projects and other forms of environmental art, as well as of some pieces of music, are possible candidates for sublimity. The "technological sublime" also offers a new area of potentially sublime artifacts, for example, the turbines of wind farms.

8. See Marjorie Hope Nicolson, *Mountain Gloom and Mountain Glory: The Development of the Aesthetics of the Infinite* (Seattle: University of Washington Press, 1997 [1959]).

9. Denis Cosgrove, *Social Formation and Symbolic Landscape* (London: Croom Helm, 1984), 223.

10. Nicholas Entrikin, "Afterword: The Unhandselled Globe," in *High Places: Geographies of Mountains, Ice and Science,* ed. Denis Cosgrove and Veronica Della Dora (London: L.B. Tauris, 2009), 216–25, 222.

11. The metaphysical dimension in Romanticism is, arguably, pantheistic, whereas in Kant it is a metaphysical aspect associated with the autonomous self.

12. See, for example, Rachel Zuckert, "Awe or Envy: Herder Contra Kant on the Sublime," *Journal of Aesthetics and Art Criticism* 61, no. 3 (2003): 217–32. Zuckert argues that Herder offers a more plausible theory of the sublime in the form of a naive naturalism that combines the best aspects of the sublime in Burke and Kant. Herder agrees with Kant that the sublime is ultimately an elevated feeling in response to awe-inspiring objects but is critical of Kant's transcendental, a priori method and pursues instead an empirical approach, which recenters the sublime object and provides a more realist understanding of sublime feeling. In setting aside the metaphysical framework, Herder does not abandon the moral import of the sublime, but he does remove from it awareness of the ideas of reason and felt freedom that characterize the Kantian sublime.

13. For his earlier view on the issue, see Ronald W. Hepburn, "Contemporary Aesthetics and the Neglect of Natural Beauty," in *Wonder and Other Essays: Eight Studies in Aesthetics and Neighbouring Fields* (Edinburgh: Edinburgh University Press, 1984), 9–35.

14. Ronald W. Hepburn, "Landscape and Metaphysical Imagination," *Environmental Values* 5 (1996): 191–204, 193–94.

15. Hepburn, "Landscape and Metaphysical Imagination," 192.

16. Ibid.

## Notes

17. See Yuriko Saito, "Appreciating Nature on Its Own Terms," *Environmental Ethics* 20 (1998), 135–49; Ronald W. Hepburn, "Trivial and Serious in Aesthetic Appreciation of Nature," in *Landscape, Natural Beauty and the Arts,* ed. Salim Kemal and Ivan Gaskell (Cambridge: Cambridge University Press, 1993), 65–80; Hepburn, "Landscape and Metaphysical Imagination," 192; and Malcolm Budd, *The Aesthetic Appreciation of Nature* (Oxford: Oxford University Press, 2002).

18. Allen Carlson, "Environmental Aesthetics," *Stanford Encyclopedia of Philosophy* (2007), http://plato.stanford.edu/entries/environmental-aesthetics (accessed June 30, 2010).

19. Hepburn, "Landscape and Metaphysical Imagination," 194.

20. On this point, see Paul Guyer, *Kant and the Experience of Freedom: Essays on Aesthetics and Morality* (Cambridge: Cambridge University Press, 1996), 203–05, 208–09, and 210–14, who discusses the different and sometimes inconsistent ways Kant describes the relationship between pleasure and displeasure in the sublime, and Rudolf Makkreel, *Imagination and Understanding in Kant* (Chicago: Chicago University Press, 1994), 310, who maintains that the feelings of pleasure and displeasure are simultaneous. Budd, *The Aesthetic Appreciation of Nature*, 85, interprets the sublime as a state that oscillates between feelings of repulsion and attraction.

21. Emily Brady, "Reassuring Aesthetic Appreciation of Nature in the Kantian Sublime," *Journal of Aesthetic Education* 46, no. 1 (2012): 91–109.

22. Ronald W. Hepburn, *The Reach of the Aesthetic* (Aldershot: Ashgate, 2001), 80.

23. This point invites further discussion concerning similarities between how imagination functions in our responses to the sublime and in our responses to fiction in the arts.

24. John Dennis, *Remarks of a Book Entitled, Prince Arthur* (1696), in *The Sublime*, ed. Ashfield and de Bolla, 30–31, 30.

25. Kant, CJ 5:245. Kant uses the term "subreption" for the "substitution of a respect for the object instead of for the idea of humanity in our subject" (CJ 5:257).

26. See Christopher Hitt, "Toward an Ecological Sublime," *New Literary History* 30, no. 3 (1999): 603–23, 604.

27. Hepburn, "Landscape and Metaphysical Imagination," 201.

28. Ronald W. Hepburn, "The Concept of the Sublime: Has It Any Relevance for Philosophy Today?" *Dialectics and Humanism* 15 (1998), 137–55, 143.

29. Ronald W. Hepburn, "Nature Humanised: Nature Respected," *Environmental Values* 7 (1998): 267–79, 277.

30. Willam Cronon, "The Trouble with Wilderness; or, Getting Back to the Wrong Kind of Nature," in *Uncommon Ground: Rethinking the Human Place in Nature*, ed. William Cronon (New York: W. W. Norton, 1996), 69–90.

31. See, for example, Kate Soper, "Looking at Landscape," *Capitalism, Nature, Socialism* 12, no. 2 (June 2001): 132–38, 134; Hitt, "Toward an Ecological Sublime," 603; and Battersby, *The Sublime, Terror and Human Difference*.

32. Entrikin, "Afterword: The Unhandselled Globe," 222.

33. James Beattie, *Dissertations Moral and Critical* (1783), in Ashfield and de Bolla, *The Sublime*, 180–94, 186.

34. See Paul Guyer, "Eighteenth Century German Aesthetics," *Stanford Encyclopedia of Philosophy* (2007), http://plato.stanford.edu/entires/aesthetics-18th-german (accessed July 3, 2010).

35. Brady, "Reassessing Aesthetic Appreciation of Nature in the Kantian Sublime."

36. There is some dispute whether the Kantian sublime falls within the aesthetic or moral domain. In "Reassessing Aesthetic Appreciation of Nature in the Kantian Sublime," I defend an aesthetic interpretation of his theory. Cf. the contribution by Melissa McBay Merritt in Costelloe, ed., *The Sublime: From Antiquity to the Present*, 37–49.

37. See, for example, Jane Kneller, "Beauty, Autonomy, and Respect for Nature," in *Kant's Aesthetics,* ed. Herman Parret (Berlin: Walter de Gruyter, 1998), 403–14, and for a less anthropocentric reading of Kant's ethics, Onora O'Neill, "Kant on Duties Regarding Nonrational Nature," *Proceedings of the Aristotelian Society: Supplementary Volume 72,* no. 1 (2003): 211–28.

38. Clewis, *The Kantian Sublime and the Revelation of Freedom*, 143–44.

39. Other writers note this dual respect. See Arnold Berleant, "The Aesthetics of Art and Nature," in *Landscape, Natural Beauty and the Arts*, ed. Salim Kemal and Ivan Gaskell (Cambridge: Cambridge University Press, 1993), 228–43, and Hitt, "Toward an Ecological Sublime."

40. See Arnold Berleant, *Aesthetics of Environment* (Philadelphia: Temple University Press, 1992); Allen Carlson, *Aesthetics and the Environment* (New York: Routledge, 2000); Hepburn, "Contemporary Aesthetics and the Neglect of Natural Beauty"; and Emily Brady, *Aesthetics of the Natural Environment* (Edinburgh: Edinburgh University Press, 2003).

41. Interestingly, Kant suggests something similar, not explicitly in terms of an aesthetic relationship but as a preparation for morality: "The beautiful prepares us to love something, even nature, without interest; the sublime, to esteem it, even contrary to our (sensible) interest" (CJ 5:267).

42. Entrikin, "Afterword: The Unhandselled Globe," 223.

43. For a defense of the concept of otherness in the environmental context, see Simon Hailwood, "The Value of Nature's Otherness," *Environmental Values* 9 (2000): 353–72.

44. Jean-Francois Lyotard, "The Sublime and the Avant-Garde," in *The Lyotard Reader*, ed. Andrew Benjamin (Oxford: Blackwell, 1989), 196–211, 199. [Reprinted in the present volume. – Ed.]

45. Jean-François Lyotard, "The Communication of Sublime Feeling," in *Lyotard Reader and Guide*, ed. Keith Crome and James Williams (Edinburgh: Edinburgh University Press, 2006), 254–65, 260.

46. Ronald W. Hepburn, "Mystery in an Aesthetic Context," manuscript read to the Philosophy Department Research Seminar, University of Durham, 2003. See also David E. Cooper, *The Measure of Things: Humanism, Humility and Mystery* (Oxford: Clarendon Press, 2002).

47. Isaiah Berlin, *The Roots of Romanticism* (London: Chatto and Windus, 1999), quoted in Hepburn, "Mystery in an Aesthetic Context."

48. Hepburn, "Mystery in an Aesthetic Context."

49. As described by Budd, *The Aesthetic Appreciation of Nature*, and Carlson, *Aesthetics and the Environment*, respectively.

50. Stan Godlovitch, "Icebreakers: Environmentalism and Natural Aesthetics," *Journal of Applied Philosophy* 11, no. 1 (1994): 15–30, 26.

51. Hepburn, "Contemporary Aesthetics and the Neglect of Natural Beauty," 13.

52. Again, I have tried to interpret Kant in a way that does not commit him to this view. See Brady, "Reassessing Aesthetic Appreciation of Nature in the Kantian Sublime."

53. See also Berleant, "The Aesthetics of Art and Nature," 234–38, for a reconstruction of the sublime, although one that is critical of Kant's theory.

54. See Yuriko Saito, "The Aesthetics of Unscenic Nature," *Journal of Aesthetics and Art Criticism* 56, no. 2 (1998): 101–11.

# BIBLIOGRAPHY

## Selected filmography

*Aguirre: The Wrath of God* [*Aguirre, der Zorn Gottes*] (1972) Dir. Werner Herzog, West Germany.
*Blade Runner* (1982) Dir. Ridley Scott, USA.
*Children of Paradise* [*Les Enfants du paradis*] (1945) Dir. Marcel Carné, France.
*Fitzcarraldo* (1982) Dir. Werner Herzog, West Germany.
*Gone with the Wind* (1939) Dir. Victor Fleming, USA.
*The Passion of Joan of Arc* [*La Passion de Jeanne d'Arc*] (1928) Dir. Carl Theodor Dreyer, France.
*Queen Christina* (1933) Dir. Rouben Mamoulian, USA.
*2001: A Space Odyssey* (1968) Dir. Stanley Kubrick, USA.

## Bibliography

Aagaard-Mogensen, Lars, ed. *The Possibility of the Sublime: Aesthetic Exchanges*. Newcastle upon Tyne: Cambridge Scholars Publishing, 2017.

Abaci, Uygar. "Kant's Justified Dismissal of Artistic Sublimity." *Journal of Aesthetics and Art Criticism* 66, no. 3 (2008): 237–51.

Abdulla, Adnan K. *A Comparative Study of Longinus and Al-Jurjani: The Interrelationships between Medieval Arabic Literary Criticism and Graeco-Roman Poetics*. Lewiston: Edwin Mellen Press, 2004.

Abrams, Meyer H. *The Mirror and the Lamp*. New York: Norton, 1953.

Addison, Joseph. *The Works of the Right Honourable Joseph Addison*, vol. IV. London: H.G. Bohn, 1854.

Addison, Joseph, and Sir Richard Steele. "The Spectator, No. 229." In *The Spectator*, edited by Gregory Smith. London: Dent, 1958.

Aikin, Anna Letitia. "On the Pleasure Derived from Objects of Terror; with Sir Bertrand, A Fragment." In *Miscellaneous Pieces, In Prose*, 119–27. London: J. Johnson, 1773.

Aikin, John, and Anna Letitia Aikin. "An Enquiry into Those Kinds of Distress which Excite Agreeable Sensations." In *Miscellaneous Pieces, In Prose*, 190–215. Belfast: James Magee, 1774.

Albrecht, William Price. *The Sublime Pleasures of Tragedy: A Study of Critical Theory from Dennis to Keats*. Lawrence: The University Press of Kansas, 1975.

Almond, Philip C. *Rudolf Otto: An Introduction to His Philosophical Theology*. Chapel Hill: University of North Carolina Press, 1984.

Altmann, Alexander. *Moses Mendelssohn: A Biographical Study*. Alabama: University of Alabama Press, 1973.

Appadurai, Arjun. "Disjuncture and Difference in the Global Cultural Economy." *Public Culture* 2 (1990): 1–24.

Aquinas, Thomas. *Summa Theologiae*, 61 vols. Cambridge and New York: Blackfriars and McGraw-Hill, 1964–80.

Arendt, Hannah. *Lectures on Kant's Philosophical Philosophy*. Edited by Ronald Beiner. Chicago: University of Chicago Press, 1982.

Aristotle, *Nicomachean Ethics*. Translated by W. D. Ross. Place unidentified: Pacific Publishing Studio, 2011.

Armstrong, Meg. "'The Effects of Blackness': Gender, Race, and the Sublime in Aesthetic Theories of Burke and Kant." *The Journal of Aesthetics and Art Criticism* 54, no. 3 (1996): 213–36.

Armstrong, Meg. "'A Jumble of Foreignness': The Sublime Musayums of Nineteenth-Century Fairs and Expositions." *Cultural Critique* 23 (1992–1993): 199–250.

Ashfield, Andrew, and Peter de Bolla, eds. *The Sublime: A Reader in British Eighteenth-century Aesthetic Theory*. Cambridge: Cambridge University Press, 1996.

Ashmun, Margaret. *The Singing Swan: An Account of Anna Seward and Her Acquaintance with Dr. Johnson, Boswell and Others of Their Time*. New Haven: Yale University Press, 1931.

Auerbach, Erich. *Literary Language and Its Public in Late Latin Antiquity and in the Middle Ages*. Princeton: Princeton University Press, 1993.

Augustine. *Confessions*. Translated by R. S. Pine-Coffin. London: Penguin, 1961.

Augustine, *On Christian Doctrine*. Translated by D. W. Robertson, Jr. Indianapolis: Bobbs-Merrill, 1958.

Banton, Michael P. *The Idea of Race*. Boulder: Westview Press, 1978.

Bayle, Pierre. *Historical and Critical Dictionary: Selections*. Edited by Richard Popkin. Indianapolis: Hackett, 1991.

Bayle, Pierre. *The Dictionary Historical and Critical of Mr. Peter Bayle*. Translated by Pierre Des Maizeaux. London, 1736.

Barbauld, Anna Letitia. *Anna Letitia Barbauld: Selected Poetry & Prose*. Edited by William McCarthy and Elizabeth Kraft. Peterborough: Broadview Press Ltd., 2002.

Barnard, Teresa. *Anna Seward: A Constructed Life: A Critical Biography*. New York: Routledge, 2016.

Barnes, Brooks. "When Art of Decay Decays, what's a Curator to do? Aging Dung, Blood and Food Give Conservators Fits." *The Wall Street Journal*, October 28, 2003, p. 1.

Barthes, Roland. "The Face of Garbo." In *Film Theory and Criticism*, edited by Gerald Mast, Marshall Cohen, and Leo Braudy, 628–31. New York: Oxford University Press, 1992.

Battersby, Christine. *The Sublime, Terror and Human Difference*. London: Routledge, 2007.

Battersby, Christine. "Stages on Kant's Way: Aesthetics, Morality and the Gendered Sublime." In *Feminism and Tradition in Aesthetics*, edited by Peggy Zeglin Brand and Carolyn Korsmeyer, 88–114. University Park: The Pennsylvania University Press, 1995.

Beardsworth, Sara. *Julia Kristeva, Psychoanalysis and Modernity*. Albany: SUNY Press, 2004.

Beattie, James. *Dissertations Moral and Critical*. In *The Sublime: A Reader in British Eighteenth-century Aesthetic Theory*, edited by Andrew Ashfield and Peter de Bolla, 180–94. Cambridge: Cambridge University Press, 1996.

Beckley, Bill. *Sticky Sublime*. New York: Allworth Press, 2001.

Beiser, Frederick. *Diotima's Children: German Aesthetic Rationalism from Leibniz to Lessing*. Oxford: Oxford University Press, 2009.

Beiser, Frederick C. *Schiller as Philosopher: A Re-Examination*. Oxford: Oxford University Press, 2005.

Benedetto, Croce. *Aesthetic as Science of Expression and General Linguistic*. Translated by Douglas Ainslie. Boston: Nonpareil Books, 1978.

Berleant, Arnold. "The Aesthetics of Art and Nature." In *Landscape, Natural Beauty and the Arts*, edited by Salim Kemal and Ivan Gaskell, 228–43. Cambridge: Cambridge University Press, 1993.

Berleant, Arnold. *Aesthetics of Environment*. Philadelphia: Temple University Press, 1992.

Berlin, Isaiah. *The Roots of Romanticism*. London: Chatto and Windus, 1999.

Berlyne, Daniel E. *Aesthetics and Psychobiology*. New York: Appleton-Century-Crofts, 1971.

Betz, John. "Beyond the Sublime: The Aesthetics of the Analogy of Being (Part Two)." *Modern Theology* 22 (2006): 1–50.

Betz, John. "Beyond the Sublime: The Aesthetics of the Analogy of Being (Part One)." *Modern Theology* 21 (2005): 367–411.

Bharata-Muni. *The Nātyaśāstra Ascribed to Bharta-Muni*. Translated by Manomoha Ghosh. Calcutta: Asiatic Society of Bengal, 1951.

Bicknell, Jeanette. *Why Music Moves Us*. London: Palgrave Macmillan, 2009.

Blakemore, Steven. *Crisis in Representation: Thomas Paine, Mary Wollstonecraft, Helen Maria Williams, and the Rewriting of the French Revolution*. Vancouver: Fairleigh Dickinson University Press, 1997.

Blood, Anne J., and Robert J. Zatorre. "Intensely Pleasurable Responses to Music Correlate with Activity in Brain Regions Implicated in Reward and Emotion." *Proceedings of the National Academy of Sciences 98* (2001): 11818–23.

Boileau Despréaux, Nicolas. "Preface to his Translation of Longinus on the Sublime." In *Selected Criticism*, edited by Ernest Dilworth, 43–52. Indianapolis: Bobbs-Merrill, 1965.

Boileau, Nicolas (Despréaux). *Oeuvres de Nicolas Boileau Despréaux*, vol. 3. Dresden: G. C. Walther, 1767.

Boileau, Nicolas (Despréaux). *Oeuvres*. Amsterdam: David Mortier, 1717.

Boileau, Nicolas (Despréaux). *Réflexions Critiques sur Quelques Passages de Longin*. Paris, 1693.

Bonaventure. *The Journey of the Mind to God*. Translated by Philotheus Boehner. Indianapolis: Hackett, 1993.

Brady, Emily. *The Sublime in Modern Philosophy: Aesthetics, Ethics, and Nature*. Cambridge: Cambridge University Press, 2013.

# Bibliography

Brady, Emily. "The Environmental Sublime." In *The Sublime: From Antiquity to the Present*, edited by Timothy Costelloe, 171–82. Cambridge: Cambridge University Press, 2012.

Brady, Emily. "Reassuring Aesthetic Appreciation of Nature in the Kantian Sublime," *Journal of Aesthetic Education* 46, no. 1 (2012): 91–109.

Brady, Emily. *Aesthetics of the Natural Environment*. Edinburgh: Edinburgh University Press, 2003.

Bray, Matthew. "Helen Maria Williams and Edmund Burke: Radical Critique and Complicity." *Eighteenth-Century Life* 16, no. 2 (1992): 1–24.

Brody, Jules. *Boileau and Longinus*. Geneva: Droz, 1958.

Brown, Amber, and Vladimir J. Konečni. "Comparative Effects of Valenced Music and Recalled Life-events on Self-ratings and Physiological Thrills/Chills." Unpublished manuscript. University of California, San Diego. 2004.

Budd, Malcolm. *The Aesthetic Appreciation of Nature*. Oxford: Oxford University Press, 2002.

Budd, Malcolm. "Delight in the Natural World: Kant on the Aesthetic Appreciation of Nature. Part III: The Sublime in Nature," *The British Journal of Aesthetics* 38 (1998): 233–51.

Budd, Malcolm. *Music and the Emotions*. London: Routledge & Kegan Paul, 1985.

Budick, Sanford. *The Western Theory of Tradition: Terms and Paradigms of the Cultural Sublime*. New Haven: Yale University Press, 2000.

Burckhardt, Jacob. *The Civilization of the Renaissance in Italy*. Translated by S. G. C. Middlemore. New York: Macmillan, 1890.

Burke, Edmund. *A Philosophical Enquiry into the Origin of Our Ideas of the Sublime and Beautiful*. Edited by Adam Phillips. Oxford: Oxford University Press, 1990.

Burke, Edmund. *A Philosophical Enquiry into the Origin of our Ideas of the Sublime and Beautiful*. Edited by James T. Boulton. London: Routledge and Kegan Paul, 1958.

Burke, Edmund. *A Philosophical Enquiry into the Origin of Our Ideas of the Sublime and Beautiful. The Second Edition. With an Introductory Discourse concerning Taste, and Several Other Additions*. London: R. and J. Dodsley, 1759.

Butler, Judith. *Bodies That Matter: On the Discursive Limits of "Sex."* New York: Routledge, 1993.

Canetti, Elias. *Crowds and Power*. Translated by Carol Stewart. London: Phoenix, 2000.

Carlson, Allen. "Environmental Aesthetics." *Stanford Encyclopedia of Philosophy* (2007), http://plato.stanford.edu/entries/environmental-aesthetics (accessed June 30, 2010).

Carlson, Allen. *Aesthetics and the Environment*. New York: Routledge, 2000.

Carrier, David, Frank Ankersmit, Noël Carroll, Michael Kelly, Brigitte Hilmer, Robert Kudielka, Martin Seeland, and Jacob Steinbrenner. "Danto and His Critics: Art History, Historiography, and After the End of Art." *History and Theory* 37, no. 4 (1998): 1–143.

Carritt, E. F. "The Sublime." *Mind* 19, no. 75 (1910): 356–72.

Carroll, Noël. *A Philosophy of Mass Art*. Oxford: Clarendon, 1998.

Carroll, Noël. "On Being Moved By Nature: Between Religion and Natural History." In *Landscape, Natural Beauty and the Arts*, edited by Salim Kemal and Ivan Gaskell, 244–65. Cambridge: Cambridge University Press, 1993.

Carroll, Noël. *The Philosophy of Horror, or Paradoxes of the Heart*. New York: Routledge, 1990.

Carter, Elizabeth, and Montagu Pennington. *Memoirs of the Life of Mrs. Elizabeth Carter*. Cambridge: Cambridge University Press, 2011 [1807].

Carter, Elizabeth, and Montagu Pennington. *Letters from Mrs. Elizabeth Carter to Mrs. Montagu, Between the Years 1755 and 1800, Chiefly upon Literacy and Moral Subjects*, vol. 1. Edited by Montagu Pennington. London: F. C. and J. Rivington, 1817.

Carter, Elizabeth, Catherine Talbot, Elizabeth Vesey, and Montagu Pennington. *A Series of Letters between Mrs. Elizabeth Carter and Miss Catherine Talbot, from the Year 1741 to 1770: To Which Are Added Letters from Mrs. Elizabeth Carter to Mrs. Vesey, between the Years 1763 to 1787; Published from the Original Manuscripts in the Possession of the Rev. Montagu Pennington*. London: Rivington, 1809.

Cassirer, Ernst, Francis R. Johnson, Paul Oskar Kristeller, Dean P. Lockwood, and Lynn Thorndike. "Some Remarks on the Question of the Originality of the Renaissance." *Journal of the History of Ideas* 4, no. 1 (1943): 49–74.

Chakrabarti, Arindam, ed. *The Bloomsbury Research Handbook of Indian Aesthetics and the Philosophy of Art*. London: Bloomsbury, 2016.

Chatterjee, Anjan. "Neuroaesthetics: A Coming of Age Story." *Journal of Cognitive Neuroscience* 23, no. 10 (2010): 53–62.

Chen, Wangheng *Call for Papers*. The Wuhan University Aesthetics Conference on "Beauty and the Way of Modern Life." Wuhan, China. May 2004.

Chignell, Andrew, and Matthew C. Halteman. "Religion and the Sublime." In *The Sublime: From Antiquity to Present*, edited by Timothy Costelloe, 183–202. Cambridge: Cambridge University Press, 2012.

Chirico, Alice, David B. Yaden, Giuseppe Riva, and Andrea Gaggioli. "The Potential of Virtual Reality for the Investigation of Awe." *Frontiers in Psychology* 7 (2016), article 1766: 1–6.

Clarke, Norma. *British Women's Writing in the Long Eighteenth Century*, edited by Jennie Batchelor and Cora Kaplan. London: Palgrave Macmillan, 2005.

Clemente, Marie-Christine. "The Sublime Dimension of 9/11." In *The Sublime Today: Contemporary Readings in the Aesthetic*. Newcastle upon Tyne: Cambridge Scholars, 2012.

Clewis, Robert R. "A Theory of the Sublime Is Possible." In *The Possibility of the Sublime: Aesthetic Exchanges*, edited by Lars Aagaard-Mogensen, 45–68. Newcastle upon Tyne: Cambridge Scholars Publishing, 2017.

Clewis, Robert R. "What's the Big Idea? On Emily Brady's Sublime." *The Journal of Aesthetic Education* 50, no. 2 (2016): 104–18.

Clewis, Robert R. "The Place of the Sublime in Kant's Project." *Studi kantiani* 28 (2015): 63–82.

Clewis, Robert R. "Kant's Distinction Between the True and False Sublimity." In *Kant's Observations and Remarks: A Critical Guide*, edited by Susan Shell and Richard Velkley, 116–43. Cambridge: Cambridge University Press, 2012.

Clewis, Robert R. "A Case for Kantian Artistic Sublimity: A Response to Abaci." *Journal of Aesthetics and Art Criticism* 68, no. 2 (2010): 167–70.

Clewis, Robert R. *The Kantian Sublime and the Revelation of Freedom*. Cambridge: Cambridge University Press, 2009.

Clewis, Robert R., David B. Yaden, and Alice Chirico. "Awe and Sublimity: A Belonging-Rising-Imagining Model." Unpublished manuscript.

Clifford, James. *The Predicament of Culture: Twentieth-Century Ethnography, Literature, and Art*. Cambridge, MA: Harvard University Press, 1988.

Cochrane, Tom. "The Emotional Experience of the Sublime." *Canadian Journal of Philosophy* 42, no. 2 (2012): 125–48.

Cohen, Hermann. *Kants Begründung der Aesthetik*. Berlin: F. Dümmler, 1889.

Cohn, Jan, and Thomas N. Miles. "The Sublime in Alchemy, Aesthetics, Psychoanalysis." *Modern Philology* 74 (1977): 289–304.

Coleridge, Samuel Taylor. *On the Sublime*. Edited by David Vallins. New York: Palgrave Macmillan, 2003.

Conron, John. *American Picturesque*. University Park: Pennsylvania State University Press, 2000.

Cooper, David E. *The Measure of Things: Humanism, Humility and Mystery*. Oxford: Clarendon Press, 2002.

Corneille, Pierre. *Cinna ou la Clémence d'Auguste*. Paris: Toussaint Quinet, 1643.

Cosgrove, Denis. *Social Formation and Symbolic Landscape*. London: Croom Helm, 1984.

Costa, Gustavo. "The Latin Translations of Longinus's *Peri hypsous* in Renaissance Italy." In *Acta Conventus Neo-Latini Bononiensis: Proceedings of the Fourth International Congress of Neo-Latin Studies, Bologna 26 August 1 to September 1979*, 224–38. Binghamton: SUNY Press, 1985.

Costa, Mario. *Le Sublime Technologique*. Lausanne: Iderive, 1994.

Costa, Mario. *Il Sublime Tecnologico*. Salerno: Edisud, 1990.

Costello, Diarmuid. "On Late Style: Arthur Danto's *The Abuse of Beauty*." *British Journal of Aesthetics* 44, no. 4 (2004): 424–39.

Costelloe, Timothy M. *The Sublime: From Antiquity to the Present*. Cambridge: Cambridge University Press, 2012.

Courtine, Jean-François, ed. *Of the Sublime: Presence in Question*. Translated by Jeffrey Librett. Albany: State University of New York Press, 1993.

Crockett, Clayton. *A Theology of the Sublime*. London: Routledge, 2001.

Cronon, Willam. "The Trouble with Wilderness; or, Getting Back to the Wrong Kind of Nature." In *Uncommon Ground: Rethinking the Human Place in Nature*, edited by William Cronon, 69–90. New York: W. W. Norton, 1996.

Crowther, Paul. *The Kantian Sublime: From Morality to Art*. Oxford: Clarendon Press, 1989.

Currie, Gregory. *Image and Mind: Film, Philosophy, and Cognitive Science*. Cambridge: Cambridge University Press, 1995.

Dahlstrom, Daniel. "Moses Mendelssohn." In *Stanford Encyclopedia of Philosophy*, edited by Edward N. Zalta. Summer 2015 Edition.

Dahlstrom, Daniel. "Moses Mendelssohn." In *A Companion to Early Modern Philosophy*, edited by Steven Nadler, 618–32. Malden: Blackwell, 2002.

Dahlstrom, Daniel, ed. Moses Mendelssohn, *Philosophical Writings*. Cambridge: Cambridge University Press, 1997.

Damasio, Antonio. *Descartes' Error: Emotion, Reason, and the Human Brain*. New York: Putnam, 1994.

# Bibliography

Danto, Arthur. "Symposium: Arthur Danto, *The Abuse of Beauty*." *Inquiry* 48, no. 2 (2005): 189–200.

Danto, Arthur. *The Abuse of Beauty: Aesthetics and the Concept of Art*. Chicago: Open Court Publishing Company, 2003.

Danto, Arthur. *The Transfiguration of the Commonplace: A Philosophy of Art*. Cambridge, MA: Harvard University Press, 1981.

Davidson, Robert F. *Rudolf Otto's Interpretation of Religion*. Princeton: Princeton University Press, 1947.

de Bolla, Peter. *The Discourse of the Sublime: Readings in History, Aesthetics and the Subject*. Oxford: Basil Blackwell, 1989.

de Man, Paul. "Kant and Schiller." In Paul de Man, *Aesthetic Ideology*, 129–62. Minneapolis: University of Minnesota Press, 1996.

de Sales, Francis. *Introduction to the Devout Life*, trans. Thomas S. Kepler. New York: World, 1952.

Deligiorgi, Katerina. "The Pleasures of Contra-purposiveness: Kant, the Sublime, and Being Human." *Journal of Aesthetics and Art Criticism* 72, no. 1 (2014): 25–35.

Demosthenes. *Works*, 7 vols. Translated by J. H. Vince. London: Heinemann, 1930.

Dennis, John. *Remarks of a Book Entitled, Prince Arthur*. In *The Sublime: A Reader in British Eighteenth-century Aesthetic Theory*, edited by Andrew Ashfield and Peter de Bolla, 30–31. Cambridge: Cambridge University Press, 1996.

Dennis, John. *The Critical Works of John Dennis*. Edited by Edward Niles Hooker. Baltimore: The Johns Hopkins Press, 1939.

Dennis, John. *The Grounds of Criticism in Poetry*. London: Strachan and Lintott, 1704.

Derrida, Jacques. *The Truth in Painting*. Translated by Geoff Bennington and Ian McLeod. Chicago: University of Chicago Press, 1987.

Derrida, Jacques. *La Vérité en Peinture.*. Paris: Flammarion, 1978.

Desmond, William. *Art and the Absolute: A Study of Hegel's Aesthetics*. Albany: State University of New York Press, 1986.

Diderot, Denis. *Diderot on Art: The Salon of 1765 and Notes on Painting*. Translated by John Goodman. In *Diderot on Art*, vol. 1. New Haven and London: Yale University Press, 1995.

Diderot, Denis. *Diderot on Art: The Salon of 1767*. Translated by John Goodman. In *Diderot on Art*, vol. 2. New Haven and London: Yale University Press, 1995.

Doran, Robert. *The Theory of the Sublime from Longinus to Kant*. Cambridge: Cambridge University Press, 2015.

Dorr, Priscilla. "Elizabeth Carter (1717–1806) UK." *Tulsa Studies in Women's Literature* 5, no. 1 (1986): 138–40.

Dubs, Homer H. *The Works of Hsüntze*. London: Arthur Probsthain, 1928.

Duffy, Cian and Peter Howell, eds. *Cultures of the Sublime: Selected Readings, 1750–1830*. Houndsmills, Basingstoke, and Hampshire: Palgrave Macmillan, 2011.

Eagleton, Terry. *The Ideology of the Aesthetic*. Oxford: Basil Blackwell, 1990.

Ekman, Paul, and Richard J. Davidson, eds. *The Nature of Emotions: Fundamental Questions*. New York: Oxford University Press, 1994.

Ekman, Paul, Robert W. Levenson, and Wallace V. Friesen. "Autonomic Nervous System Activity Distinguishes among Emotions." *Science* 221 (1983): 1208–10.

Elkins, James. "Against the Sublime." In *Beyond the Finite: The Sublime in Art and Science*, edited by Roald Hoffmann and Iain Boyd Whyte, 75–90. Oxford: Oxford University Press, 2011.

Ellison, Julie. "Redoubled Feeling: Politics, Sentiment, and the Sublime in Williams and Wollstonecraft." *Studies in Eighteenth-Century Culture* 20, no. 1 (1991): 197–215.

Entrikin, Nicholas. "Afterword: The Unhandselled Globe." In *High Places: Geographies of Mountains, Ice and Science*, edited by Denis Cosgrove and Veronica Della Dora, 216–25. London: L. B. Tauris, 2009.

Faderman, Lillian. *Surpassing the Love of Men: Romantic Friendship and Love Between Women from the Renaissance to the Present*, 132–38. New York: William Morrow, 1981.

Fairbairn, Marty. H-Film Electronic Discussion List. December 14, 1995.

Fanon, Frantz. *Black Skin, White Masks*. Translated by Charles Lam Markmann. New York: Grove Press, Inc., 1967.

Ferguson, Frances. *Solitude and the Sublime: Romanticism and the Aesthetics of Individuation*. London: Routledge, 1992.

Fiore, Silvia Ruffo. *Giambattista Vico and the Pedagogy of 'Heroic Mind' in the Liberal Arts*. Paideia: Boston University, 1998.

Forsey, Jane. "The Sublime, Redux." In *The Possibility of the Sublime: Aesthetic Exchanges*, edited by Lars Aagaard-Mogensen, 93–106. Newcastle upon Tyne: Cambridge Scholars Publishing, 2017.

Forsey, Jane. *The Aesthetics of Design*. New York: Oxford University Press, 2013.

Forsey, Jane. "Is a Theory of the Sublime Possible?" *Journal of Aesthetics and Art Criticism* 65, no. 4 (2007): 381–89.

Frazer, James George. *Apollodorus: The Library*. London: William Heinemann, 1921.

Freeland, Cynthia A. *But Is It Art?* Oxford: Oxford University Press, 2001.

Freeland, Cynthia A. "Bill Viola and the Video Sublime." *Film-Philosophy* 3, no. 28 (1999): 1–7.

Freeland, Cynthia A., and Thomas E. Wartenberg. *Philosophy and Film*. New York: Routledge, 1994.

Freeman, Barbara Claire. *The Feminine Sublime: Gender and Excess in Women's Fiction*. Berkeley: University of California Press, 1995.

Freud, Sigmund. *Totem and Taboo*. London: W. W. Norton, 1989.

Freud, Sigmund. *Civilization and Its Discontents*. Edited and translated by James Strachey. New York: W. W. Norton & Company, 1961.

Freudenthal, Gideon. *No Religion Without Idolatry: Mendelssohn's Jewish Enlightenment*. Notre Dame: Notre Dame University Press, 2012.

Furniss, Tom. *Edmund Burke's Aesthetic Ideology: Language, Gender and Political Economy in Revolution*. Cambridge: Cambridge University Press, 1993.

Gasser, Reinhard. *Nietzsche und Freud*. Berlin: Walter de Gruyter, 1997.

Gabrielsson, Alf. "Emotions in Strong Experiences with Music." In *Music and Emotion: Theory and Research*, edited by Patrik N. Juslin and John A. Sloboda, 431–52. Oxford: Oxford University Press, 2001.

Gates, Henry Louis, Jr. "Writing, 'Race' and the Difference it Makes." *Critical Inquiry* 12, no. 1 (1985): 1–20.

Gaver, William W., and Mandler, George. "Play it Again, Sam: On Liking Music." *Cognition and Emotion* 1 (1987): 259–82.

Gerow, Edwin. "Indian Aesthetics: A Philosophical Survey." In *A Companion to World Philosophies*, edited by Eliot Deutsch and Ron Bontekoe, 304–23. Malden: Blackwell, 1997.

Gilbert-Rolfe, Jeremy. *Beauty and the Contemporary Sublime*. New York: Allworth Press, 1999.

Gilby, Emma. *Sublime Worlds: Early Modern French Literature*. London: Legenda, 2006.

Gilman, Sander. "Black Bodies, White Bodies: Toward an Iconography of Female Sexuality in Late Nineteenth-Century Art, Medicine, and Literature." *Critical Inquiry* 12, no. 1 (1985): 204–42.

Godlovitch, Stan. "Icebreakers: Environmentalism and Natural Aesthetics." *Journal of Applied Philosophy* 11, no. 1 (1994): 15–30.

Goehr, Lydia. *The Imaginary Museum of Musical Works: An Essay in the Philosophy of Music*. Oxford: Clarendon Press, 1992.

Goldstein, Avram. "Thrills in Response to Music and Other Stimuli." *Physiological Psychology* 8 (1980): 126–29.

Gould, Timothy. "Intensity and Its Audiences: Toward a Feminist Perspective on the Kantian Sublime." In *Feminism and Tradition in Aesthetics*, edited by Peggy Zeglin Brand and Carolyn Korsmeyer, 66–87. University Park: Pennsylvania State University Press, 1995.

Gracyk, Theodore A. "Sublimity, Ugliness, and Formlessness in Kant's Aesthetic Theory." *Journal of Aesthetics and Art Criticism* 45, no. 1 (1986): 49–56.

Green, Christopher D. "All that Glitters: A Review of Psychological Research on the Aesthetics of the Golden Section." *Perception* 24 (1995): 937–68.

Grube, George Maximilian Anthony. *The Greek and Roman Critics*. Indianapolis: Hackett Publishing, 1995.

Gumbrecht, Hans Ulrich. *In Praise of Athletic Beauty*. Cambridge: Belknap Press, 2006.

Gurney, Edmund. *The Power of Sound*. London: Smith, Elder, 1880.

Guyer, Paul. *A History of Modern Aesthetics*, vol. 1. Cambridge: Cambridge University Press, 2014.

Guyer, Paul. "The Post-Kantian German Sublime." In *The Sublime: From Antiquity to the Present*, edited by Timothy M. Costelloe, 102–17. Cambridge: Cambridge University Press, 2012.

Guyer, Paul. "Eighteenth Century German Aesthetics." *Stanford Encyclopedia of Philosophy* (2007). http://plato.stanford.edu/entires/aesthetics-18th-german (accessed July 3, 2010).

Guyer, Paul. *Values of Beauty: Historical Essays in Aesthetics*. Cambridge: Cambridge University Press, 2005.

Guyer, Paul. "The Perfections of Art: Mendelssohn, Moritz, and Kant." In *Kant and the Experience of Freedom: Essays on Aesthetics and Morality*, 131–60. Cambridge: Cambridge University Press, 1993.

Guyer, Paul. *Kant and the Experience of Freedom: Essays on Aesthetics and Morality*. Cambridge: Cambridge University Press, 1993 [reprinted 1996].

Hache, Sophie. *La Langue du Ciel: le Sublime en France au XVIIe Siècle*. Paris: H. Champion, 2000.

Haidt, Jonathan. Personal Communication with Vladimir Konečni. March 11, 2004.

Haidt, Jonathan. "The Positive Emotion of Elevation." *Prevention & Treatment* 3 (2000): 1–4.

Hailwood, Simon. "The Value of Nature's Otherness." *Environmental Values* 9 (2000): 353–72.

Hamilton, William D. "The Genetical Theory of Social Behaviour." *Journal of Theoretical Biology* 7 (1964): 1–52.

## Bibliography

Hanauer, Tom. "Pleasure and Transcendence: Two Paradoxes of Sublimity." In *The Possibility of the Sublime: Aesthetic Exchanges*, edited by Lars Aagaard-Mogensen, 29–43. Newcastle upon Tyne: Cambridge Scholars Publishing, 2017.

Hanauer, Tom. "Sublimity and the Ends of Reason: Questions for Deligiorgi." *Journal of Aesthetics and Art Criticism* 74, no. 2 (2016): 195–99.

Hanslick, Eduard. *On the Musically Beautiful*. Indianapolis: Hackett, 1986.

Hegel, Georg Wilhelm Friedrich. *Encyclopedia of the Philosophical Sciences in Basic Outline: Part 1: Science of Logic*. Edited and translated by Klaus Brinkmann and Daniel Dahlstrom. Cambridge: Cambridge University Press, 2010.

Hegel, Georg Wilhelm Friedrich. *Aesthetics: Lectures on Fine Art*, vol. 1. Translated by T. M. Knox. Oxford: Oxford University Press, 1975.

Hegel, Georg Wilhelm Friedrich. *The Philosophy of Fine Art*, vol. 2. Translated by Francis Plumtre Beresford Osmaston. New York: Hacker Art Books, 1975.

Hegel, Georg Wilhelm Friedrich. *Vorlesungen über die Aesthetik I*. Frankfurt am Main: Suhrkamp, 1970.

Heidegger, Martin. *Being and Time*. Translated by Joan Stambaugh, revised by Dennis J. Schmidt. Albany: SUNY Press, 2010.

Heiland, Donna. "Swan Songs: The Correspondence of Anna Seward and James Boswell." *Modern Philology* 90, no. 3 (1993): 381–91.

Helmling, Steven. *The Success and Failure of Fredric Jameson: Writing, the Sublime, and the Dialectic of Critique*. Albany: SUNY Press, 2001.

Hepburn, Ronald W. "Mystery in an Aesthetic Context." Manuscript read to the Philosophy Department Research Seminar, University of Durham, 2003.

Hepburn, Ronald W. *The Reach of the Aesthetic*. Aldershot: Ashgate, 2001.

Hepburn, Ronald W. "Nature Humanised: Nature Respected." *Environmental Values* 7 (1998): 267–79.

Hepburn, Ronald W. "The Concept of the Sublime: Has It Any Relevance for Philosophy Today?" *Dialectics and Humanism* 15 (1998): 137–55.

Hepburn, Ronald W. "Landscape and Metaphysical Imagination." *Environmental Values* 5 (1996): 191–204.

Hepburn, Ronald W. "Trivial and Serious in Aesthetic Appreciation of Nature." In *Landscape, Natural Beauty and the Arts*, edited by Salim Kemal and Ivan Gaskell, 65–80. Cambridge: Cambridge University Press, 1993.

Hepburn, Ronald W. "Contemporary Aesthetics and the Neglect of Natural Beauty." In *Wonder and Other Essays: Eight Studies in Aesthetics and Neighbouring Fields*, 9–35. Edinburgh: Edinburgh University Press, 1984.

Herbert, Zbigniew *Dušica*. Translated from Polish to Serbian by B. Rajčić. *Knjizevni Magazin*, Nos. 25–26, July–August (2003): 2–5.

Herder, Johann Gottfried. *Kalligone. Vom Angenehmen und Schönen*. Leipzig: Johann Friedrich Hartknoch, 1800.

Herzog, Werner. "On the Absolute, the Sublime, and Ecstatic Truth." Translated by Moira Weigel. *Arion* 17, no. 3 (2010): 1–12.

Higgins, Kathleen M. "An Alchemy of Emotions: *Rasa* and Aesthetic Breakthroughs." *Journal of Aesthetics and Art Criticism* 65 (2007): 43–54.

Hipple, Jr., Walter John. *The Beautiful, the Sublime and the Picturesque in Eighteenth-Century British Aesthetic Theory*. Carbondale: Southern Illinois University Press, 1957.

Hitt, Christopher. "Toward an Ecological Sublime." *New Literary History* 30, no. 3 (1999): 603–23.

Hoffmann, Roald and Iain Boyd Whyte, eds. *Beyond the Finite: The Sublime in Art and Science*. New York: Oxford University Press, 2011.

Holmqvist, Kenneth, and Jaroslaw Pluciennik. *Infinity in Language: Conceptualization of the Experience of the Sublime*. Newcastle upon Tyne: Cambridge Scholars Publishers, 2008.

Holmqvist, Kenneth, and Jaroslaw Pluciennik. "A Short Guide to the Theory of the Sublime." *Style* 36, no. 4 (2002): 718–37.

Hooker, Edward Niles, ed. *The Critical Works of John Dennis*, 2 vols. Baltimore: The Johns Hopkins Press, 1939.

hooks, bell. "Representing Whiteness in the Black Imagination." In *Cultural Studies*, edited by Lawrence Grossberg, Cary Nelson, and Paula A. Treichler, 338–46. New York: Routledge, 1992.

Homer, *The Iliad*. Translated by Robert Fagles. New York: Viking, 1990.

Horace. *Satires, Epistles and Ars Poetica*. Translated by H. Rushton Fairclough. Cambridge, MA: Harvard University Press, 1966.

Hu, Yunhua. *Chinese Penjing: Miniature Trees and Landscapes*. Hong Kong: Wan Li Book Co., Ltd., 1987.

Hugo, Victor. "Preface to Cromwell." In *Prefaces and Prologues to Famous Books*, edited by Charles W. Eliot, vol. 39, 354–408. New York: P. F. Collier & Son, 1909–14.

Hume, David. *A Treatise of Human Nature*. Edited by P. H. Nidditch. Oxford: Clarendon Press, 1978.

Hume, Nancy G., ed. *Japanese Aesthetics and Culture: A Reader*. Albany: State University of New York Press, 1995.

Huron, David. "Is Music an Evolutionary Adaptation?" *Annals of the New York Academy of Sciences* 930 (2001): 43–61.

Ishizu, Tomoshiro and Semir Zeki. "A Neurobiological Enquiry into the Origins of Our Experience of the Sublime and Beautiful." *Frontiers in Human Neuroscience* 8, article 891 (2014): 1–10.

Jaeger, Stephen C., ed. *Magnificence and the Sublime in Medieval Aesthetics: Art, Architecture, Literature, Music*. New York: Palgrave Macmillan, 2010.

James, Robin. "Oppression, Privilege, & Aesthetics: The Use of the Aesthetic in Theories of Race, Gender, and Sexuality, and the Role of Race, Gender, and Sexuality in Philosophical Aesthetics." *Philosophy Compass* 8, no. 2 (2013): 101–16.

James, William. *The Varieties of Religious Experience: A Study in Human Nature*. New York: Longmans Green, 1903.

Jameson, Fredric. *Postmodernism, or, the Cultural Logical of Late Capitalism*. London and New York: Verso, 1992.

Jameson, Fredric. "Postmodernism, or the Logic of Late Capitalism." *New Left Review* 1, no. 146 (1984): 53–92.

Ji, Li-Jun, Kaiping Peng, and Richard E. Nisbett, "Culture, Control and Perception of Relationships in the Environment." *Journal of Personality and Social Psychology* 78 (2000): 943–55.

Jin Shui [Shi Tie-sheng.] *Fate*. Translated from the Chinese by M. S. Duke. In *Contemporary Chinese Fiction*, edited by Carolyn Choa and David Su Li-qun. New York: Vintage Books, 2001.

Johnson, Mark. *Moral Imagination: Implications of Cognitive Science for Ethics*. Chicago: University of Chicago Press, 1993.

Kahn, Charles H. *The Art and Thought of Heraclitus: An Edition of the Fragments with Translation and Commentary*. Cambridge: Cambridge University Press, 1979.

Kant, Immanuel. *Anthropology from a Pragmatic Point of View*. Translated by Robert Louden. In *Anthropology, History, Education*, edited by Günter Zöller and Robert Louden, 231–429. Cambridge: Cambridge University Press, 2007.

Kant, Immanuel. *Observations on the Feeling of the Beautiful and Sublime*. Translated by Paul Guyer. In *Anthropology, History, Education*, edited by Günter Zöller and Robert Louden, 23–62. Cambridge: Cambridge University Press, 2007.

Kant, Immanuel. *Critique of the Power of Judgment*. Edited by Paul Guyer and translated by Paul Guyer and Eric Matthews. Cambridge: Cambridge University Press, 2000.

Kant, Immanuel. *Kant Selections*. Translated by Lewis White Beck. Upper Saddle River, NJ: Prentice Hall, 1998.

Kant, Immanuel. *The Critique of Practical Reason*. Translated by T. K. Abbott. Amherst, NY: Prometheus Books, 1996.

Kant, Immanuel. *Kritik der Urteilskraft*. Edited by Manfred Frank and Véronique Zanetti. Frankfurt am Main: Deutscher Klassiker Verlag, 1996.

Kant, Immanuel. *Critique of Practical Reason*. Translated by Lewis White Beck. Upper Saddle River, NJ: Prentice Hall, 1993.

Kant, Immanuel. *The Critique of Judgment*. Translated by James Creed Meredith. Oxford: Clarendon Press, 1986.

Kant, Immanuel. *Grundlegung zur Metaphysik der Sitten*. Frankfurt am Main: Suhrkamp, 1974.

Kant, Immanuel. *Kritik der praktischen Vernunft*. Frankfurt am Main: Suhrkamp, 1974.

Kant, Immanuel. *Kritik der Urteilskraft*. Frankfurt am Main: Suhrkamp, 1974.

Kant, Immanuel. "An Old Question Raised Again: Is the Human Race Constantly Progressing?" In *On History*, translated by Lewis White Beck, Robert Anchor, and Emil Fackenheim, 137–54. New York: The Liberal Arts Press, Inc., 1963.

Kant, Immanuel. *Observations on the Feeling of the Beautiful and Sublime*. Translated by John T. Goldthwait. Berkeley: University of California Press, 1960.

Kant, Immanuel. *Critique of Practical Reason*. Translated by Lewis White Beck. New York: Liberal Arts Press, 1956.

Kant, Immanuel. *Kritik der Urteilskraft*. In *Kant's gesammelte Schriften*, 29 vols., vol. 5. Königlichen Preussischen (later Deutschen) Akademie der Wissenschaften. Berlin: Reimer [later de Gruyter], 1900–.

Keats, John. *The Letters of John Keats, 1814–1821*, vol. 1. Edited by Hyder Edward Rollins. Cambridge: Cambridge University Press, 1958.

Keltner, Dacher. Personal Communication with Vladimir Konečni. February 13, 2004.

Keltner, Dacher, and Jonathan Haidt. "Approaching Awe, a Moral, Spiritual, and Aesthetic Emotion." *Cognition & Emotion* 17, no. 2 (2003): 297–314.

## Bibliography

Kemal, Salim, and Ivan Gaskell, eds. *Landscape, Natural Beauty and the Arts*. Cambridge: Cambridge University Press, 1993.

Kennedy, Deborah. *Helen Maria Williams and the Age of Revolution*. Lewisburg: Bucknell University Press, 2002.

Kick, Linda Lee. *A Feminist Sublime and Grotesque: Dorothea Schlegel, Mary Shelley, George Sand, and their Twentieth-Century Daughters*. Santa Barbara: University of California, 2011.

Kirwan, James. *Sublimity: The Non-Rational and the Irrational in the History of Aesthetics*. London: Routledge, 2005.

Klinger, Cornelia. "The Concepts of the Sublime and the Beautiful in Kant and Lyotard." In *Feminist Interpretations of Immanuel Kant*, edited by Robin Schott, 191–211. University Park: Pennsylvania State University Press, 1997.

Kneller, Jane. "Beauty, Autonomy, and Respect for Nature." In *Kant's Aesthetics*, edited by Herman Parret, 403–14. Berlin: Walter de Gruyter, 1998.

Konečni, Vladimir J. "Aesthetic Trinity Theory and the Sublime." *Philosophy Today* 55, no. 1 (2011): 64–73.

Konečni, Vladimir J. "The Aesthetic Trinity: Awe, Being Moved, Thrills." *Bulletin of Psychology and the Arts* 5, no. 2 (2005a): 27–44.

Konečni, Vladimir J. "On the 'Golden Section.'" *Visual Arts Research* 31, no. 2 (2005b): 76–87.

Konečni, Vladimir J. "Ancient and Contemporary Aesthetic 'Emotions.'" Invited Plenary Lecture at the Wuhan University Aesthetics Conference on "Beauty and the Way of Modern Life." Wuhan, China. 2004a.

Konečni, Vladimir J. "On Music and 'Emotion.'" Unpublished manuscript. University of California, San Diego. 2004b.

Konečni, Vladimir J. Personal Communication by Vladimir Konečni to Jonathan Haidt, March 11, 2004c.

Konečni, Vladimir J. "The Golden Section: Elusive, but Detectable." *Creativity Research Journal* 15 (2003a): 267–76.

Konečni, Vladimir J. Review of *Music and Emotion: Theory and Research*, edited by Patrik N. Juslin and John A. Sloboda. *Music Perception* 20 (2003b): 332–41.

Konečni, Vladimir J. "The Golden Section in the Structure of 20th-century Paintings." *Rivista di Psicologia dell'Arte*, *Nuova Serie* 22 (2001a): 27–42.

Konečni, Vladimir J. "The Vase on the Mantelpiece: The Golden Section in Context." *Empirical Studies of the Arts* 15 (1997): 177–207.

Konečni, Vladimir J. Unpublished Laboratory and Classroom Data on the Effects of Musical and Theatre Stimuli on (Physiological) Thrills. University of California, San Diego. 1995–2004.

Konečni, Vladimir J. "Psychological Aspects of the Expression of Anger and Violence on the Stage." *Comparative Drama* 25(1991): 215–41.

Konečni, Vladimir J. "Altruism: Methodological and Definitional issues." *Science* 194 (1976): 562.

Konečni, Vladimir J., Rebekah A. Wanic, and Amber Brown. "Emotional and Aesthetic Antecedents and Consequences of Music-Induced Thrills." *The American Journal of Psychology* 120, no. 4 (2007): 619–43.

Konečni, Vladimir J. and Cline, L. E. "The 'Golden Woman': An Exploratory Study of Women's Proportions in Paintings." *Visual Arts Research* 27 (2001): 69–78.

Korsmeyer, Carolyn. *Savouring Disgust: The Foul and the Fair in Aesthetics*. Oxford: Oxford University Press, 2011.

Krims, Adam. "The Hip-Hop Sublime as a Form of Commodification." In *Music and Marx: Ideas, Practices, Politics*, edited by R. B. Qureshi, 63–80. Chicago: University of Chicago Press, 2002.

Kristeva, Julia. *Powers of Horror: An Essay on Abjection*. Translated by Leon Roudiez. New York: Columbia University Press, 1982.

Krumhansl, C. L. "Music: A Link between Cognition and Emotion." *Current Directions in Psychological Science* 11 (2002): 45–50.

Krumhansl, C. L. "Topic in Music: An Empirical Study of Memorability, Openness, and Emotion in Mozart's String Quintet in C Major and Beethoven's String Quartet in A Minor." *Music Perception* 16 (1998): 119–34.

Krumhansl, C. L. "An Exploratory Study of Musical Emotions and Psychophysiology." *Canadian Journal of Experimental Psychology* 51 (1997): 336–52.

Kwang-dze. *The Writings of Kwang-dze*, in *The Sacred Books of the East*, vol. 39. Edited by F. Max Müller and translated by James Legge. Oxford: Clarendon Press, 1891.

LaBlanc, Michael L., ed. *Literary Criticism (1400–1800)*, vol. 86. "Zeami – Introduction." Detroit, MI: Gale Cengage 2003 (accessed June 1, 2017).

Lacan, Jacques. *The Ethics of Psychoanalysis, 1959–1960: The Seminar of Jacques Lacan, Book VII*. Edited by Jacques-Alain Miller and translated by Dennis Porter. London: Routledge, 1992.

Lamarque, Peter. "Tragedy and Moral Value." In *Art and Its Messages: Meaning, Morality, and Society*, edited by Stephen Davies, 59–69. University Park: Penn State University Press, 1995.

Langer, Susanne K. *Philosophy in a New Key*. Cambridge, MA: Harvard University Press, 1942.

Lao-tzu. *Tao te Ching*. Translated by Stephen Mitchell. New York: HarperCollins, 1988.

Laotse. *Tao te king: Das Buch des Alten vom Sinn und Leben*. Translated by Richard Wilhelm. Jena: E. Diederichs, 1911.

LeDoux, Joseph. *The Emotional Brain: The Mysterious Underpinnings of Emotional Life*. New York: Simon and Schuster, 1996.

Leibniz, Gottfried. *New Essays Concerning Human Understanding*. Translated by Peter Remnant and Jonathan Bennett. Cambridge: Cambridge University Press, 1981.

Leibniz, Gottfried. *Die Philosophischen Schriften von G. W. Leibniz*. Edited by C. J. Gerhardt. Berlin, 1875–90.

Lee, Sherman E. *A History of Far Eastern Art*. New York: H. N. Abrams, 1967.

Levinson, Jerrold. "Messages in Art." In *Art and Its Messages: Meaning, Morality, and Society*, edited by Stephen Davies, 70–83. University Park: Penn State University Press, 1995.

Ley, Klaus. *Longin – Von Bessarion Zu Boileau: Wirkungsmomente Der "Schrift Über Das Erhabene" in Der Frühen Neuzeit*. Berlin: Weidler, 2013.

Lin, Yutang. *The Chinese Theory of Art: Translations from the Masters of Chinese Art*. New York: Putnam's Sons, 1967.

Lintott, Sheila. "The Sublimity of Gestating and Giving Birth: Toward a Feminist Conception of the Sublime." In *Philosophical Inquiry into Pregnancy, Childbirth, and Mothering: Maternal Subjects*, edited by Sheila Lintott and Maureen Sander-Staudt, 237–50. London: Routledge, 2012.

Litman, Théodore A. *Le Sublime en France, 1660–1714*. Paris: Nizet, 1971.

Lochhead, Judy. "The Sublime, the Ineffable, and Other Dangerous Aesthetics." *Women and Music: A Journal of Gender and Culture* 12, no. 1 (2008): 63–74.

Loewenstein, George. "Because It Is There: The Challenge of Mountaineering...for Utility Theory." *Kyklos* 52 (1999): 315–44.

Lombardo, Giovanni and Francesco Finocchiaro. *Sublime Antico e Moderno: una Bibliografia*. Palermo: Università di Palermo, 1993.

Longinus. "On the Sublime." In *Greek and Roman Aesthetics*, edited by Oleg Bychkov and Anne Sheppard, 147–65. Cambridge: Cambridge University Press, 2010.

Longinus. *On the Sublime*. Translated by W. Rhys Roberts. New York and London: Garland, 1987.

Longinus. *On the Sublime*. Translated by James A. Arieti and John M. Crossett. New York: Edwin Mellen Press, 1985.

Lyotard, Jean-François. *Enthusiasm: The Kantian Critique of History*. Translated by Georges Van den Abbeele. Stanford: Stanford University Press, 2009.

Lyotard, Jean-François. "The Communication of Sublime Feeling." In *Lyotard Reader and Guide*, edited by Keith Crome and James Williams, 254–65. Edinburgh: Edinburgh University Press, 2006.

Lyotard, Jean-François. *Lessons on the Analytic of the Sublime: (Kant's "Critique of Judgment," sections 23–29)*. Translated by Elizabeth Rottenberg. Stanford: Stanford University Press, 1994.

Lyotard, Jean-François. "The Sublime and the Avant-Garde." In *Inhuman: Reflection on Time*, translated by G. Bennington and R. Bowlby, 89–107. Stanford: Stanford University Press, 1990.

Lyotard, Jean-François. *The Differend: Phrases in Dispute*. Minneapolis: University of Minnesota Press, 1988.

Lyotard, Jean-François. *Peregrinations: Law, Form, and Event*. New York: Columbia University Press, 1988.

Lyotard, Jean-François. "The Sublime and the Avant-Garde." Translated by Lisa Liebmann, Geoff Bennington, and Marian Hobson. *Paragraph* 6 (1985): 1–18.

Lyotard, Jean-François. *The Postmodern Condition: A Report on Knowledge*. Minneapolis: University of Minnesota Press, 1984.

Lyotard, Jean-François. "Presenting the Unpresentable: the Sublime." Translated by Lisa Liebmann. *Artforum* 20, no. 8 (1982): 64–69.

Lyotard, Jean-François. "The Works and Writings of Daniel Buren: An Introduction to the Philosophy of Contemporary Art." Translated by Lisa Liebmann. *Artforum* 19, no. 6 (1981): 57–64.

Macpherson, James. *Fingal: An Ancient Epic Poem, in Six Books*. Dublin: Peter Wilson, 1763.

Mair, Victor H. *The Columbia Anthology of Traditional Chinese Literature*. New York: Columbia University Press, 1994.

Makkreel, Rudolf. *Imagination and Understanding in Kant*. Chicago: Chicago University Press, 1994.

Mann, Bonnie. *Women's Literature and the Sublime: Feminism, Postmodernism, Environment*. New York: Oxford University Press, 2006.

Margolis, Joseph. "The Art of Landscape Reconceived." In *International Yearbook of Aesthetics*, vol. 17, edited by Raffaele Milani and Jale Erzen, 21–31. Sassari: Edizione Edes, 2013.

Marin, Demetrio. *Bibliography of the "Essay on the Sublime" (Peri Hypsous)*. Bari: Leiden, 1967.

Martin, Adrian. "The Street Angel and the Badman: *The Good Woman of Bangkok*." *Photofile* 35 (1991): 12–15.

Marx, Leo. *The Machine in the Garden: Technology and the Pastoral Ideal in America*. New York: Oxford University Press, 1964.

Maslow, Abraham H. *Toward a Psychology of Being*. New York: Van Nostrand Reinhold, 1968.

Maslow, Abraham H. *Religions, Values, and Peak-Experiences*. Columbus: Ohio State University Press, 1964.

Masuda, Takahiko and Richard E. Nisbett, "Attending Holistically versus Analytically: Comparing the Context Sensitivity of Japanese and Americans." *Journal of Personality and Social Psychology* 81 (2001): 922–34.

McCarthy, William. *Anna Letitia Barbauld: Voice of the Enlightenment*. Baltimore: Johns Hopkins University Press, 2009.

McQuillan, J. Colin. *Early Modern Aesthetics*. London: Rowman and Littlefield International, 2015.

McShane, Katie. "The Role of Awe in Environmental Ethics." *Journal of Aesthetics and Art Criticism* 76, no. 4 (2018).

Melissa, Raphael. *Rudolf Otto and the Concept of Holiness*. Oxford: Clarendon Press, 1997.

Mendelssohn, Moses. *Philosophical Writings*. Edited by Daniel O. Dahlstrom. New York: Cambridge University Press, 1997.

Mendelssohn, Moses. *Ästhetische Schriften in Auswahl*. Edited by Otto F. Best. Darmstadt: Wissenschaftliche Buchgesellschaft, 1974.

Meyer, Leonard B. *Emotion and Meaning in Music*. Chicago: The University of Chicago Press, 1956.

Miller, Geoffrey. "Evolution of Human Music through Sexual Selection." In *The Origins of Music*, edited by N. L. Wallin, B. Merker, and S. Brown, 329–60. Cambridge, MA: MIT Press, 2000.

Milton, John. *John Milton*. Edited by Stephen Orgel and Jonathan Goldberg. Oxford: Oxford University Press, 1991.

Milton, John. *The Poems of Mr. John Milton, both English and Latin*. London: Humphrey Moseley, 1645–46.

Mishra, Vijay. *Devotional Poetics and the Indian Sublime*. Albany: State University of New York Press, 1998.

Mishra, Vijay. *The Gothic Sublime*. Albany: SUNY Press, 1994.

Mitchell, W. J. T. *Iconology: Image, Text, Ideology*. Chicago: University of Chicago Press, 1986.

Monk, Samuel Holt. *The Sublime: A Study of Critical Theories in Eighteenth-Century England: With a New Preface by the Author*. Ann Arbor: University of Michigan Press, 1960.

Moore, Dafydd, ed. *Ossian and Ossianism*. London: Routledge, 2004.

Morley, Simon. *The Sublime*. London: Whitechapel Gallery, 2010.

Morris, David Brown. *The Religious Sublime*. Lexington: University Press of Kentucky, 1972.

Mosco, Vincent. *The Digital Sublime: Myth, Power and Cyberspace*. Cambridge, MA: MIT Press, 2004.

Mothersill, Mary. *Beauty Restored*. Oxford: Oxford University Press, 1986.

Muir, John. *The Mountains of California*. New York: The Century Co., 1907.

Muir, John. *The Mountains of California*. Boston, MA: Houghton Mifflin, 1894.

Munk, Reiner. *Moses Mendelssohn's Metaphysics and Aesthetics*. New York: Springer, 2011.

Myers, Mitzi. "Politics from the Outside: Mary Wollstonecraft's first *Vindication*." *Studies in Eighteenth-Century Culture* 6 (1977): 113–32.

Myers, Sylvia Harcstark. *The Bluestocking Circle: Women, Friendship, and the Life of the Mind in Eighteenth-Century England*. Oxford: Clarendon, 1990.

Nagatomo, Shigenori. "Zeami's Conception of Freedom." *Philosophy East and West* 31, no. 4 (1981): 401–16.

Nanay, Bruce. *Aesthetics as Philosophy of Perception*. Oxford: Oxford University Press, 2016.

Newman, Barnett B. "the sublime is now." *Tiger's Eye* 1, no. 6. (1948): 51–53.

Nicolai, Friedrich. "Abhandlung vom Trauerspiel." In *Bibliothek der schönen Wissenschaften und der freyen Künste*, vol. 1, part 1, 17–68. Leipzig: Dyck, 1757.

Nicolson, Marjorie Hope. *Mountain Gloom and Mountain Glory: The Development of the Aesthetics of the Infinite*. Seattle: University of Washington Press, 1997.

Nicolson, Marjorie Hope. *Mountain Gloom and Mountain Glory: The Development of the Aesthetics of the Infinite*. New York: W. W. Norton, 1963.

Nietzsche, Friedrich. *The Birth of Tragedy: Out of the Spirit of Music*. Translated by Ian Johnston. London: Penguin UK, 2003.

Nietzsche, Friedrich. *Ecco Homo*. Translated by Anthony M. Ludovici. In *The Complete Works of Friedrich Nietzsche*, vol. 17, edited by Oscar Levy, 1–143. Edinburgh and London: T. N. Foulis, 1911.

Nietzsche, Friedrich. *Joyful Wisdom*. Translated by Thomas Common. In *The Complete Works of Friedrich Nietzsche*, vol. 10, edited by Oscar Levy, 1–354. Edinburgh and London: T. N. Foulis, 1910.

Nietzsche, Friedrich. *Thus Spake Zarathustra*. In *The Complete Works of Friedrich Nietzsche*, vol. 11, edited by Oscar Levy, 1–402. Edinburgh and London: T. N. Foulis, 1911.

Norton, Rictor. *Mistress of Udolpho: The Life of Ann Radcliffe*. London: Leicester University Press, 1999.

Nussbaum, Martha C. *Upheavals of Thought: The Intelligence of Emotions*. Cambridge: Cambridge University Press, 2001.

Nye, David E. *American Technological Sublime*. Cambridge, MA: MIT Press, 1996.

Nykliček, Ivan, Julian F. Thayer, and Lorenz J. P. Van Doornen "Cardiorespiratory Differentiation of Musically-induced Emotions." *Journal of Psychophysiology* 11 (1997): 304–21.

O'Connell, Michael. "Authority and the Truth of Experience in Petrarch's 'Ascent of Mount Ventoux'." *Philological Quarterly* 62 (1983): 507–20.

Oliver, Kelly. *Ethics, Politics, and Difference in Julia Kristeva's Writings*. New York: Routledge, 1993.

O'Neill, Daniel I. *The Burke-Wollstonecraft Debate: Savagery, Civilization, and Democracy*. University Park: Pennsylvania State University Press, 2007.

O'Neill, Onora. "Kant on Duties Regarding Nonrational Nature." *Proceedings of the Aristotelian Society: Supplementary Volume* 72, no. 1 (2003): 211–28.

Onians, John. "Neuroscience and the Sublime in Art and Science." In *Beyond the Finite: The Sublime in Art and Science*, edited by Roald Hoffmann and Iain Boyd Whyte, 91–105. Oxford: Oxford University Press, 2011.

Otto, Rudolf. *Das Heilige: Über das Irrationale in der Idee des Göttlichen und sein Verhältnis zum Rationalen*. Munich: C.H. Beck, 2014.

Otto, Rudolf. *The Idea of the Holy, An Inquiry Into the Non-rational Factor in the Idea of the Divine and Its Relation to the Rational*. Translated by John W. Harvey. London: Oxford University Press, 1972.

Panksepp, Jaak. *Affective Neuroscience: The Foundations of Human and Animal Emotions*. Oxford: Oxford University Press, 1998.

Panksepp, Jaak. "The Emotional Sources of 'Chills' Induced by Music." *Music Perception*, 13 (1995): 171–207.

Panzarella, Robert. The Phenomenology of Aesthetic Peak Experiences. *Journal of Humanistic Psychology* 20 (1980): 69–85.

Parkes, Graham. "Japanese Aesthetics." *Stanford Encyclopedia of Philosophy* (Spring 2017 Edition), edited by Edward N. Zalta. Stanford: Stanford University, 2017.

Paul, H. G. *John Dennis: His Life and Criticism*. New York: AMS Press, 1966.

Pence, Jeffrey. "Cinema of the Sublime: Theorizing the Ineffable." *Poetics Today* 25, no. 1, (2004): 29–66.

Pepper, Stephen. *Aesthetic Quality: A Contextualist Theory of Beauty*. Westport: Greenwood Press, 1970.

Perrault, Charles. *Parallèle des Anciens et des Modernes, en Ce Qui Regarde les Arts et les Sciences*. Paris: Dialogues, 1688–97.

Petrarca, Francesco [Petrarch]. "Ascent of Mont Ventoux." In *Renaissance Philosophy of Man*, edited by Paul Oskar Kristeller, Ernst Cassirer, and John Herman Randall, Jr., 36–46. Chicago: University of Chicago Press, 1948.

Petrarca, Francesco [Petrarch]. "Familiar Letters." In *Petrarch: The First Modern Scholar and Man of Letters*, edited and translated by James Harvey Robinson. New York: G. P. Putnam, 1898.

Pezzotta, Elisa. *Stanley Kubrick: Adapting the Sublime*. Jackson: University Press of Mississippi, 2013.

Pillow, Kirk. *Sublime Understanding: Aesthetic Reflection in Kant and Hegel*. Cambridge, MA: MIT Press, 2000.

Pinker, Steven. *How the Mind Works*. London: Allen Lane, 1997.

Poland, Lynn. "The Idea of the Holy and the History of the Sublime." *The Journal of Religion* 72 (1992): 175–97.

Pollock, Sheldon, trans., *A Rasa Reader: Classical Indian Aesthetics*. New York: Columbia University Press, 2016.

Porter, James I. *The Sublime in Antiquity*. Cambridge: Cambridge University Press, 2015.

Porter, James. "Lucretius and the Sublime." In *The Cambridge Companion to Lucretius*, edited by Stuart Gillespie and Philip Hardie, 167–85. Cambridge: Cambridge University Press, 2007.

Prade, Claire and Vassilis Saroglou. "Awe's Effects on Generosity and Helping." *The Journal of Positive Psychology* 11, no. 5 (2016): 522–30.

Pyle, Forest. *The Ideology of Imagination: Subject and Society in the Discourse of Romanticism*. Palo Alto: Stanford University Press, 1995.

Rachwal, Tadeusz, and Tadeusz Slawek, eds. *The Most Sublime Act: Essays on the Sublime*. Katowice: Wydawnictwo Universytetu Ślaskiego, 1994.

Radcliffe, Ann. *The Mysteries of Udolpho: A Romance; Interspersed with Some Pieces of Poetry*. London: G.G. and J. Robinson, 1794.

Radden, Jennifer. *The Nature of Melancholy: From Aristotle to Kristeva*. New York: Oxford University Press, 2008.

Rancière, Jacques. *The Future of the Image*. London: Verso, 2009.

# Bibliography

Ratcliff, Carter. "The Sublime Was Then: The Art of Barnett Newman." In *Sticky Sublime*, edited by Bill Beckley, 211–39. New York: Allworth Press, 2001.

Richardson, Alan. *The Neural Sublime: Cognitive Theories and Romantic Texts*. Baltimore: The Johns Hopkins University Press,, 2010.

Richir, Marc. *Du Sublime en Politique*. Paris: Payot, 1991.

Rodgers, Betsy. *Georgian Chronicle: Mrs. Barbauld and Her Family*. London: Methuen, 1958.

Rogers, Deborah D. *The Critical Response to Ann Radcliffe*. Westport: Greenwood Press, 1994.

Rogers, Katharine M. *Feminism in Eighteenth-Century England*. Urbana: University of Illinois Press, 1982.

Rolfe, John Carew, trans. *The Lives of the Caesars*, vol. 2. London: 1930.

Rorty, Richard. "Habermas and Lyotard on Postmodernity." In *Habermas and Modernity*, edited by Richard J. Bernstein, 161–75. Cambridge, MA: MIT Press, 1985.

Rosenberg, Alfred. *Longinus in England bis zum Ende des 18. Jahrhunderts*. Berlin: Mayer & Müller, 1917.

Rowe, Nicholas. *The Tragedy of Jane Shore*. London: D.S. Maurice, 1714.

Rowton, Frederic. *The Female Poets of Great Britain: Chronically Arranged with Copious Selections and Critical Remarks*. Edited by Marilyn L. Williamson. Detroit: Wayne State University Press, 1981.

Rudd, Melanie, Kathleen Vohs, and Jennifer Aaker. "Awe Expands People's Perception of Time, Alters Decision Making, and Enhances Well-being." *Psychological Science* 23, no. 10 (2012): 1130–36.

Russell, Bertrand. *A Critical Exposition of the Philosophy of Leibniz*. London: George Allen and Unwin, 1937.

Ryan, Vanessa L. "The Physiological Sublime: Burke's Critique of Reason." *Journal of the History of Ideas* 62, no. 2 (2011): 265–79.

Sagan, Carl. *Pale Blue Dot: A Vision of the Human Future in Space*. New York: Random House, 1994.

Saint Girons, Baldine. *Le Sublime, de l'Antiquité à Nos Jours*. Paris: Desjonquères, 2005.

Saito, Yuriko. *Everyday Aesthetics*. Oxford: Oxford University Press, 2007.

Saito, Yuriko. "Appreciating Nature on Its Own Terms." *Environmental Ethics* 20 (1998): 135–49.

Saito, Yuriko. "The Aesthetics of Unscenic Nature," *Journal of Aesthetics and Art Criticism* 56, no. 2 (1998): 101–11.

Saito, Yuriko. "The Japanese Appreciation of Nature." *The British Journal of Aesthetics* 25, no. 3 (1985): 239–51.

Savary, Claude-Étienne. *Lettres sur l'Égypte où l'on Offre le Parallèle des Moeurs Anciennes et Modernes de ses Habitants*. 3 vols. Paris: Onfroi, 1786.

Scherer, Klaus R., and Marcel R. Zentner. "Emotional Effects of Music: Production Rules." In *Music and Emotion: Theory and Research*, edited by Patrik N. Juslin and John A. Sloboda, 361–92. Oxford: Oxford University Press, 2001.

Schiller, Friedrich. "Concerning the Sublime." In Friedrich Schiller, *Essays*, edited by Daniel Dahlstrom and Walter Hinderer and translated by Daniel Dahlstrom, 70–85. London: Continuum, 1998.

Schiller, Friedrich. "On the Pathetic." In Friedrich Schiller, *Essays*, edited by Daniel Dahlstrom and Walter Hinderer and translated by Daniel Dahlstrom, 45–69. London: Continuum, 1998.

Schiller, Friedrich, et al. *Du Sublime: (de Boileau à Schiller): Suivi de la Traduction de Über das Erhabene de Friedrich Schiller*. Edited by Pierre Hartmann. Strasbourg: Presses universitaires de Strasbourg, 1997.

Schlamm, Leon. "Numinous Experience and Religious Language." *Religious Studies* 28, no. 4 (1992): 533–51.

Schlegel, Johann Elias. *Cannut*. Copenhagen: Mumme, 1746.

Schopenhauer, Arthur. *The World as Will and Representation*, 2 vols. Translated by E. F. J. Payne. New York: Dover Publications, 1969.

Schopenhauer, Arthur. *Die Welt als Wille und Vorstellung*. München: G. Müller, 1912.

Schopenhauer, Arthur. *Parerga und Paralipomena*. Berlin: A.W. Hayn, 1851.

Schwarz, Susan L. *Rasa: Performing the Divine in India*. New York: Columbia University Press, 2004.

Seidl, Arthur. *Vom Musikalisch-Erhabenen. Prolegomena zur Aesthetik der Tonkunst*. Regensburg: Druck von M. Wasner, 1887.

Seneca. *Moral Essays*, vol. 1. Translated by John W. Basore. Cambridge, MA: Harvard University Press, 1970.

Seward, Anna. *Bluestocking Feminism: Writings of the Bluestocking Circle, 1738–1785: Anna Seward*. Edited by Jennifer Kelly. London: Pickering & Chatto, 1999.

Seward, Anna. *Letters of Anna Seward: Written Between the Years 1784 and 1807*, vols. 3–6. Edited by Archibald Constable. Edinburgh: George Ramsay & Company, 1811.

Seward, Anna. *The Poetical Works of Anna Seward; With Extracts from Her Literary Correspondence*, vol. 1. Edited by Walter Scott. Edinburgh: John Ballantyne and Co., 1810.

Shadwell, Thomas. *The Female Officer: Or, The Humours of the Army, A Comedy*. Dublin: James Hoey, 1763.

Shaftesbury, Anthony Ashley Cooper. *Characteristics of Men, Manners, Opinions, Times*. Edited by John M. Robertson. Indianapolis: Bobbs-Merrill, 1964.

Shapshay, Sandra. "Commentary on Jane Forsey's 'Is a Theory of the Sublime Possible'." In *The Possibility of the Sublime: Aesthetic Exchanges*, edited by Lars Aagaard-Mogensen, 69–80. Newcastle upon Tyne: Cambridge Scholars Publishing, 2017.

Shapshay, Sandra. "Contemporary Environmental Aesthetics and the Neglect of the Sublime." *British Journal of Aesthetics* 53, no. 2 (2013): 181–98.

Shapshay, Sandra. "The Problem and the Promise of the Sublime." In *Suffering Art Gladly*, edited by Jerrold Levinson, 84–107. Palgrave Macmillan, 2013.

Shapshay, Sandra. "Schopenhauer's Transformation of the Kantian Sublime." *Kantian Review* 17, no. 3 (2012): 210–479.

Shaw, Philip. *The Sublime*. London: Routledge, 2017 [2006].

Shaw, Ronald D. M. *The Blue Cliff Records*. London: M. Joseph, 1961.

Shell, Susan Meld. *The Embodiment of Reason: Kant on Spirit, Generation, and Community*. Chicago: University of Chicago Press, 1996.

Shelley, Mary Wollstonecraft. *Frankenstein*. Edited by Susan Wolfson. London: Pearson, 2007.

Shelley, Mary Wollstonecraft. *Frankenstein*. Edited by Johanna M. Smith. Boston: Bedford/St. Martin's, 2000.

Shelley, Mary. *Frankenstein; or, The Modern Prometheus*. London: Lackington, Hughes, Harding, Mavor, and Jones, 1818.

Shiota, Michelle, Belinda Campos, and Dacher Keltner. "The Faces of Positive Emotion: Prototype Displays of Awe, Amusement, and Pride." *Annals of the New York Academy of Sciences* 1000, no. 1 (2003): 296–99.

Shiota, Michelle, Dacher Keltner, and Amanda Mossman. "The Nature of Awe: Elicitors, Appraisals, and Effects on Self-Concept." *Cognition and Emotion* 21, no. 5 (2007): 944–63.

Shusterman, Richard. "Somaesthetics and Burke's Sublime." *British Journal of Aesthetics* 45, no. 4 (2005): 323–41.

Shweder, Richard A., and Haidt, Jonathan. "The Cultural Psychology of the Emotions: Ancient and New." In *Handbook of Emotions*, edited by Michael Lewis and Jeannette M. Haviland-Jones, 397–414. New York: Guilford, 2000.

Silverman, Hugh J. *Lyotard: Philosophy, Politics, and the Sublime*. New York: Routledge, 2002.

Silverman, Hugh J., and Gary E. Aylesworth, eds. *The Textual Sublime: Deconstruction and Its Differences*. Albany: State University of New York Press, 1989.

Sircello, Guy. "How is a Theory of the Sublime Possible?" *Journal of Aesthetics and Art Criticism* 51, no. 4 (1993): 541–50.

Sirén, Oswald. *Chinese Sculpture from the Fifth to the Fourteenth Century*, vol. 1. London: Ernest Benn, 1925.

Sloboda, John A., and Andreas C. Lehmann. "Tracking Performance Correlates of Changes in Perceived Intensity of Emotion During Different Interpretations of a Chopin Piano Prelude." *Music Perception* 19 (2001): 87–120.

Sloboda, John A. "Musical Structure and Emotional Response: Some Empirical Findings." *Psychology of Music* 19 (1991): 110–20.

Smith, Murray. *Film, Art, and the Third Culture: A Naturalized Aesthetics of Film*. Oxford: Oxford University Press, 2017.

Smollett, Tobias. *The Adventures of Ferdinand Count Fathom*. London: W. Johnston, 1753.

Soper, Kate. "Looking at Landscape." *Capitalism, Nature, Socialism* 12, no. 2 (June 2001): 132–38.

Spolsky, Ellen. *Gaps in Nature: Literary Interpretation and the Modular Mind*. Albany: State University of New York Press, 1993.

Stanislavsky, Constantin. *An Actor Prepares*. Translated from the Russian by E. Reynolds Hapgood. New York: Theatre Arts Books, 1936.

Stanislavski, Constantin, and Pavel Rumyantsev. *Stanislavski on Opera*. Edited and translated by E. Reynolds Hapgood. New York: Theatre Arts Books, 1975.

Steele, Richard, and Joseph Addison. *Selections from* The Tatler *and* The Spectator. Edited by Robert J. Allen. New York: Holt, Rinehart, and Winston, 1970.

Stepan, Nancy. *The Idea of Race in Science: Great Britain 1800–1960*. London: Macmillan, 1982.

Stephani, Hermann. *Das Erhabene insonderheit in der Tonkunst, und das Problem der Form im Musikalisch-Schönen und Erhabenen*. Leipzig: H.S. Nachfolger, 1903.

Stoler, John A. *Ann Radcliffe, the Novel of Suspense and Terror*. New York: Arno Press, 1980.

Stravinsky, Igor. *An Autobiography*. New York: Simon and Schuster, 1936.

Sundararajan, Louise. "Religious Awe: Potential Contributions of Negative Theology to Psychology, 'Positive' or Otherwise." *Journal of Theoretical and Philosophical Psychology* 22, no. 2 (2002): 174–97.

Suzuki, Daisetz Teitaro. *Manual of Zen Buddhism*. Kyoto: Eastern Buddhist Society, 1935.

Tan, Ed S. *Emotion and the Structure of Narrative Film: Film as an Emotion Machine.* Translated by Barbara Fasting. Mahwah, NJ: Erlbaum, 1996.

Tanke, Joseph J., and J. Colin McQuillan, eds. *The Bloomsbury Anthology of Aesthetics.* New York: Bloomsbury Academic, 2012.

Tarozzi Goldsmith, Marcella. *The Future of Art: An Aesthetics of the New and the Sublime.* Albany: SUNY Albany Press, 1999.

Taussig, Michael. *The Nervous System.* New York: Routledge, 1992.

Taussig, Michael. *Shamanism, Colonialism, and the Wild Man: A Study in Terror and Healing.* Chicago: University of Chicago Press, 1987.

Taylor, Barbara. *Mary Wollstonecraft and the Feminist Imagination.* Cambridge: Cambridge University Press, 2003.

Thampi, G. B. Mohan. "Rasa as Aesthetic Experience." *The Journal of Aesthetics and Art Criticism* 24, no. 1 (1965): 75–80.

Thorndike, Lynn, Francis R. Johnson, Paul Oskar Kristeller, and Dean P. Lockwood. "Renaissance or Prenaissance?" *Journal of the History of Ideas* 4, no. 1 (1943): 65–74.

Tolstoy, Lyov. *War and Peace.* Translated by C. Garnett. New York: The Modern Library/Random House, 1931.

Townsend, Dabney, ed. *Eighteenth-Century British Aesthetics.* Amityville: Baywood Publishing, 1999.

Townshend, Dale, and Angela Wright. *Ann Radcliffe, Romanticism and the Gothic.* Cambridge: Cambridge University Press, 2014.

Trivers, Robert L. "The Evolution of Reciprocal Altruism." *Quarterly Review of Biology* 46 (1971): 35–57.

Tsang, Lap-Chuen. *The Sublime: Groundwork Towards a Theory.* Rochester: University of Rochester Press, 1998.

Ueda, Makoto. "Zeami and the Art of the Nō Drama: Imitation, *Yūgen*, and Sublimity." In *Japanese Aesthetics and Culture: A Reader*, edited by Nancy G. Hume, 177–91. Albany: State University of New York Press, 1995.

Vaitl, Dieter, Wolfgang Vehrs, and S. Sternagel. "Prompts–Leitmotif–Emotion: Play it Again, Richard Wagner." In *The Structure of Emotion: Psychophysiological, Cognitive, and Clinical Aspects*, edited by Niels Birbaumer and Arne Öhman, 169–89. Seattle, WA: Hogrefe & Huber, 1993.

van Eck, Caroline, Stijn Bussels, Maarten Delbeke, and Jürgen Pieters, eds. *Translations of the Sublime. The Early Modern Reception and Dissemination of Longinus'* Peri Hupsous *in Rhetoric, the Visual Arts, Architecture and the Theatre.* Leiden: Brill, 2012.

Vandenabeele, Bart. *The Sublime in Schopenhauer's Philosophy.* New York: Palgrave Macmillan, 2015.

Vandenabeele, Bart. "Schopenhauer on Aesthetic Understanding and the Values of Art." *European Journal of Philosophy* 16, no. 2 (2008): 194–210.

Vandenabeele, Bart. "Schopenhauer, Nietzsche, and the Aesthetically Sublime." *Journal of Aesthetic Education* 37, no. 1 (2003): 90–106.

Vasalou, Sophia. *Schopenhauer and the Aesthetic Standpoint: Philosophy as a Practice of the Sublime.* Cambridge: Cambridge University Press, 2013.

Vaughan, Robert Alfred. *Hours with the Mystics.* London: Gibbings & Company, Ltd., 1895.

Vico, Giambattista. *On Humanistic Education (Six Inaugural Orations).* 1699–1707). Translated by Giorgio A. Pinton and Arthur W. Shippee. Ithaca: Cornell University Press, 1993.

Vico, Giambattista. "On the Heroic Mind." *Social Research: An International Quarterly* 43, no. 4 (1976): 886–903.

Vico, Giambattista. *Opere.* Edited by Fausto Nicolini. Milan: Riccardo Ricciardi, 1953.

Vico, Giambattista. *Opere.* Edited by Fausto Nicolini. Bari: Laterza, 1941.

Vico, Giambattista. *Scritti Vari e Pagine Sparse.* Edited by Fausto Nicolini. Bari: Laterza & Figli, 1940.

Vico, Giambattista. *Opere di Giambattista Vico*, vol. 1. Edited by Francesco Saverio Pomodoro. Napoli: Stamperia dei classici latini, 1858.

Virgil, *The Aeneid.* Translated by Robert Fitzgerald. New York, Random House: 1981.

Wagner, Richard. "Beethoven." In *Richard Wagner's Prose Works*, vol. 5. Translated by William Ashton Ellis, 59–126. London: Kegan Paul, Trench, Trubner, Trübner Co., Ltd., 1896.

Wagner, Richard. "Opera and Drama." In *Richard Wagner's Prose Works*, vol. 2. Translated by William Ashton Ellis. London: Kegan Paul, Trench, Trubner & Co., Ltd., 1895.

Wagner, Richard. *Beethoven.* Leipzig: E. W. Fritzsch, 1870.

Waley, Arthur. *The Way and Its Power: A Study of the Tao tê Ching and Its Place in Chinese Thought.* New York: Grove Press, 1958.

Walpole, Horace. *The Castle of Otranto: A Story.* London: Tho. Lownds, 1764.

Ware, Malcolm. *Sublimity in the Novels of Ann Radcliffe: A Study of the Influence upon Her Craft of Edmund Burke's "Enquiry into the Origin of Our Ideas of the Sublime and Beautiful."* Uppsala: Uppsala University, 1963.

Ware, Owen. "Rudolf Otto's Idea of the Holy: A Reappraisal." *Heythrop Journal* 48, no. 1 (2007): 48–60.

Waterman, Mitch. "Emotional Responses to Music: Implicit and Explicit Effects in Listeners and Performers." *Psychology of Music* 24 (1996): 53–67.

Weinberg, Bernard. "Une Traduction Française du "Sublime" de Longin Vers 1645." *Modern Philology* 59, no. 3 (1962): 159–201.

Weinberg, Bernard. "Translations and Commentaries of Longinus, *On the Sublime*, to 1600: a Bibliography." *Modern Philology* 47, no. 3 (1950): 145–51.

Weiskel, Thomas. *The Romantic Sublime: Studies in the Structure and Psychology of Transcendence.* London: The John Hopkins University Press, 1986.

White, Daniel E. "The 'Joineriana': Anna Barbauld, the Aikin Family Circle, and the Dissenting public Sphere." *Eighteenth-Century Studies* 32, no. 4 (1999): 511–33.

White, Luke, and Claire Pajaczkowska, eds. *The Sublime Now.* Newcastle upon Tyne: Cambridge Scholars Publishing, 2009.

Wilken, Rowan. "'Unthinkable Complexity': The Internet and the Mathematical Sublime." In *The Sublime Today: Contemporary Readings in the Aesthetic*, edited by G. B. Pierce, 191–212. Newcastle upon Tyne: Cambridge Scholars Publishing 2012.

Williams, Helen Maria. *A Tour in Switzerland; Or, A View of the Present State of the Governments and Manners of those Cantons: With Comparative Sketches of the Present State of Paris*, 2 vols. London: G. G. and J. Robinson, 1798.

Willliams, Helen Maria. *Letters Written in France, in the Summer 1790, to a Friend in England.* London: T. Cadell, 1790.

Wilson, Edward O. *Sociobiology: The New Synthesis.* Cambridge, MA: Harvard University Press, 1975.

Wilson, Edward O., ed. *The Best American Science and Nature Writing 2001.* Boston, MA: Houghton Mifflin, 2001.

Wilson, Rob. "Cyborg America: Policing the Social Sublime in *Robocop* and *Robocop 2.*" In *The Administration of Aesthetics: Censorship, Political Criticism, and the Public Sphere*, edited by Richard Burt, 289–306. Minneapolis: University of Minnesota Press, 1994.

Wittgenstein, Ludwig. *Tractatus Logico-Philosophicus.* Translated by C. K. Ogden. London: Routledge & Kegan Paul, 1922.

Witvliet, Charlotte V. and Scott R. Vrana. "The Emotional Impact of Instrumental Music on Affect Ratings, Facial EMG, Autonomic Measures, and the Startle Reflex: Effects of Valence and Arousal." *Psychophysiology Supplement* 91 (1996).

Wlecke, Albert O. *Wordsworth and the Sublime.* Berkeley: University of California Press, 1973.

Wollstonecraft, Mary. *The Works of Mary Wollstonecraft*, 7 vols. Edited by Janet Todd and Marilyn Butler. London: William Pickering, 1989.

Wollstonecraft, Mary. *A Vindication of the Rights of Men, in a Letter to the Right Honourable Edmund Burke; Occasioned by His Reflections on the Revolution in France.* London: J. Johnson, 1790.

Wong, Kin-yuen. "Negative-Positive Dialectic in the Chinese Sublime." In *The Chinese Text: Studies in Comparative Literature*, edited by Ying-Hsiung Chou, 119–58. Hong Kong: The Chinese University Press, 1986.

Wood, Theodore E. B. *The Word 'Sublime' and Its Context 1650–1760.* The Hague: Mouton, 1972.

Wordsworth, William. *The Portable Romantic Poets.* Edited by W. H. Auden and N. H. Pearson. New York: Penguin, 1978.

Wordsworth, William. "The Sublime and the Beautiful." In *The Prose Works of William Wordsworth*, edited by W. J. B. Owen and Jane Worthington Smyser, 349–60. Oxford: Clarendon Press, vol. 2, 1974.

Wordsworth, William. *Wordsworth's Guide to the Lakes: Fifth edition (1835).* Edited by Ernest de Sélincourt. London: Henry Frowde, 1906.

Worringer, Wilhelm. *Form Problems of the Gothic.* New York: Stechert, 1912.

Wurth, Kiene Brillenburg. *Musically Sublime: Indeterminanacy, Infinity, Irresolvability.* New York: Fordham University Press, 2012.

Xinhua/Reuters. "The Great Wall Getting Less Great." January 26, 2004.

Yaden, David B., Jonathan Haidt, Ralph Hood, Jr., David Vago, and Andrew Newberg. "The Varieties of Self-Transcendent Experience." *Review of General Psychology* 21, no. 2 (2017): 143–60.

Yaden, David B., Jonathan Iwry, Kelley Slack, Johannes Eichstaedt, Yukun Zhao, George Vaillant, and Andrew Newberg. "The Overview Effect: Awe and Self-Transcendent Experience in Space Flight." *Psychology of Consciousness: Theory, Research, and Practice* 3, no. 1 (2016): 1–11.

Yaeger, Patricia. "'The Language of Blood': Toward a Maternal Sublime." *Genre: Forms of Discourse and Culture* 25, no. 1 (1992): 5–24.

## Bibliography

Yaeger, Patricia. "Toward a Female Sublime." In *Gender and Theory: Dialogues on Feminist Criticism*, edited by Linda Kauffman, 191–212. Oxford: Blackwell, 1989.

Yang, Xiaoshan. *Metamorphosis of the Private Sphere: Gardens and Objects in Tang-Song Poetry*. Cambridge, MA: Harvard University Press, 2003.

Young, Julian. *Friedrich Nietzsche: A Philosophical Biography*. Cambridge: Cambridge University Press, 2010.

Young, Julian. "Richard Wagner and the Birth of *The Birth of Tragedy*." *International Journal of Philosophical Studies* 16, no. 2 (2008): 217–45.

Young, Julian. "Death and Transfiguration: Kant, Schopenhauer, and Heidegger on the Sublime." *Inquiry* 48, no. 2 (2005): 131–44.

Young, Julian. *Nietzsche's Philosophy of Art*. Cambridge: Cambridge University Press, 1992.

Zaehner, Robert Charles. *Concordant Discord: The Interdependence of Faiths*. Oxford: Clarendon Press, 1970.

Zammito, John H. *The Genesis of Kant's "Critique of Judgment"*. Chicago: University of Chicago Press, 1992.

Zeami. *On the Art of the Nō Drama: The Major Treatises of Zeami*. Translated by J. Thomas Rimer and Yamazaki Masakazu. Princeton: Princeton University Press, 1984.

Zheng, Yi. *From Burke and Wordsworth to the Modern Sublime in Chinese Literature*. West Lafayette: Purdue University Press, 2010.

Žižek, Slavoj. *The Sublime Object of Ideology*. London: Verso, 1989.

Zöller, Günter. "The Musically Sublime: Richard Wagner's Post-Kantian Philosophy of Modern Music." In *Das Leben der Vernunft. Beiträge zur Philosophie Immanuel Kants*, edited by Dieter Hüning, Stefan Klinger, and Carsten Olk, 635–60. Berlin and Boston: Walter de Gruyter, 2013.

Zuckert, Rachel. "Awe or Envy: Herder Contra Kant on the Sublime." *Journal of Aesthetics and Art Criticism* 61, no. 3 (2003): 217–32.

Zylinska, Joanna. *On Spiders, Cyborgs, and Being Scared: The Feminine and the Sublime*. Manchester: Manchester University Press, 2001.

# INDEX

# Index

# Index

holy 233–9
  complex category 236
  relational and non-rational element 236
Home, Henry (Lord Kames) 373 n.15
Homer 1, 20–5, 27–8, 29, 57, 59, 62, 65, 67, 83, 106, 108, 110, 158, 162, 164, 223, 226
horror 2, 63, 85–6, 93, 97, 107, 114–16, 118–19, 139, 144, 158, 167, 168, 185, 187–8, 189, 246, 274–5, 287, 300, 314, 332
Hudson River 297
Huet, Pierre-Daniel 264
humanist sublime 361
humanities 1, 5, 244, 341, 355
humanity 76, 111, 120, 132, 142, 157, 160, 167, 191, 260, 337, 353, 360–1
human nature 73, 105, 109, 111, 112, 136, 137, 141, 146, 153, 159, 187, 259, 296, 298
human regarding 360–1
Hume, David 7, 343, 373–4 n.15, 396 n.19, 403 n.17
humility 362
hysterical sublime 5, 254–7, 260, 277, 299, 316–17, 320, 329, 357

idea 124, 127, 128, 130–2, 133, 135–44, 149–60, 194–5, 197, 210, 212–16, 219–20, 236
*The Idea of the Holy* (Otto) 233–9
Iguacú Falls 316
*Iliad* (Homer) 22, 65, 108, 299, 376 n.20, 384–5 n.6
imagination 44, 62, 67, 81, 83, 85, 94, 95–6, 114–16, 118–19, 120, 123–45, 151, 153, 157–8, 159, 162, 170, 172, 184, 186, 196, 265, 272, 275, 277–8, 283, 285, 289, 298, 320
  expansion of 349, 360
  failure of 360
  metaphysical 349, 350, 355, 359–60
  power of 360
  reason and 139–40, 350
  as source of pleasure 349–52
  subjective movement of 346–7
immensity 91–2
immortality 154, 155, 172
independence 139
  abstract, of God 208
  moral 160
  from nature 150, 152
  satisfaction 139
individual will 216
industrialization 348
industrial revolution 256, 307
infinity 82, 127–30, 134, 151, 180, 181, 265, 277, 322.
  *See also* unconditioned
intellectual satisfaction 140–1
intensive immensity 91
*The Interest of Lofty Forests and Springs* (Guo Xi) 41–2
intersubjective validity 347
intersubjectivity 347–8
Irigaray, Luce 5
"Is a Theory of the Sublime Possible?" (Forsey) 319–28, 329
Ishizu, Tomohiro 404 n.31
Isis at Sais, Egypt, temple of 158

James, Henry 294
Japanese artists/writers 348
Japanese performing arts 44
Japanese version of sublime 348
Jewish Enlightenment 91
jouissance 251
*The Journey of the Mind to God* (Bonaventure) 10
joyfulness 134
*Joyful Wisdom* (Nietzsche) 222, 228–9
judgment 111, 114. *See also* reason
  aesthetic (*see* aesthetic judgment)
  moral 278
  power of 122–46
  pure 128–9, 145–6
  teleological 146

Kamo no Chomei 44
Kant, Immanuel 3, 4, 6–7, 8, 11–12, 13, 78, 91, 105–13, 122–47, 149–60, 177, 194, 197, 200, 202, 212, 233, 234, 236, 243, 255, 256, 259–60, 261, 263, 265–7, 268, 271, 272, 275–8, 280–6, 288–90, 292, 296–302, 305, 306, 311, 322–7, 329, 333, 335–9, 343, 344, 345, 346–7, 348, 349–51, 355–62
Kantian sublime 322–4. *See also* Kant, Immanuel
Keats, John 12, 177, 298, 361
Keltner, Dacher 340
Kirwan, James 372 n.3, 406–7 n.1
"Knowing the Sublime" 343
knowledge 17, 19, 65, 70, 71–6, 82, 140, 150–1, 178, 179–80, 186, 194–6, 198, 214, 216, 217, 226, 233, 271–2, 297, 298, 320, 334, 335–6, 337. *See also* cognition
Konecni, Vladimir J. 3, 7, 13, 304–18
Korsmeyer, Carolyn 5, 340
Kristeva, Julia 7, 12, 223, 246–52

Lacan, Jacques 7, 12, 246, 249, 251, 373 n.15, 375 n.43
land of oblivion 250
landscape 351
landscape art 351
landscape paintings 41–2
Langbaine, Gerard, the elder 381 n.18
*Late Capitalism* (Mandel) 256
*Lectures on Fine Art* (Hegel) 200
LeDoux, Joseph 288–9
Leibniz 387 nn.8, 13
Leopardi 1, 6
*Letters from Mrs. Elizabeth Carter to Mrs. Montagu* (Carter) 102–4
Letter to Rev. Dr. Gregory (Seward) 162–5
level distance/perspective 41, 42
*Library of Fine Sciences and Fine Arts* 91
life 187–92, 346, 350
  causes of 185–7
  feeling of 145 (*see also* vital forces)
  inner 202, 207
  social 257
light 22, 29, 59–60, 63, 66–7, 74, 81, 84, 85, 87, 100, 106, 185, 186, 196, 204, 208, 209, 229, 224, 228, 266, 267, 273, 278
Lintott, Sheila 5, 7

# Index

# Index

Reid, Thomas  7, 373 n.15, 403 n.14
religion  11–18, 60, 62, 64, 66–7, 73, 81, 86, 135–6, 142–3, 154,
    200–10, 233, 234, 235–6, 238, 290, 306–7
    Absolute (Hegel)  4, 200, 201, 202, 203, 210
    divine (*see* divine)
    God (*see* God)
    holy  233–9
religious feeling, sublime and  3, 233–9
religious ideas  3, 62–7
*Remarks on a Book Entitled Prince Arthur, an Heroic Poem*
    (Dennis)  62
Renaissance  7, 10, 49, 243–4, 294, 296, 298, 301, 332
representation  12, 71, 91, 92, 95, 97, 109, 156, 194–8,
    254, 255, 256–7, 283, 284, 287, 346, 350, 357.
    *See also* unrepresentable
respect  80, 109, 118, 119, 120–1, 123, 131–2, 133, 135, 136,
    142, 160, 284, 289
Reynolds, Frances  7
Reynolds, Joshua  102
rhetoric  2, 4, 9, 11, 17–18, 58, 69, 73, 82, 243, 244, 263, 265,
    332, 356
Rhine River  9, 29, 171, 181, 296
Rimer, Thomas J.  45
river  134, 152, 162, 167, 171, 172, 284, 296, 333, 358
    Danube  9, 29, 296
    Nile  9, 29, 76, 152, 296
    Rhine  9, 29, 171, 181, 296
Roberts, W. R.  17
Robinson, Edward Arlington  299
Robortelli, Francisco  17
Rolland, Romain  313
Romanticism  5, 260, 262–3, 348, 361, 363, 407 n.11.
    *See also* sublime, romantic
romantic sublime  119, 162, 167, 177, 200, 244, 262, 265, 267,
    272, 356–8, 394 n.6–7
Rorty, Richard  347
Rothko, Mark  294, 316
Royal Prussian Academy of Sciences  91

sacred art  207–8
sacred texts  6
"sad music"  399 n.2
safety  1, 134, 139, 154, 167, 334, 351. *See also* security
Sagan, Carl  350
Saito, Yuriko  332, 348, 408 n.17
Salzburg Festival  399 n.3
satisfaction. *See also* pleasures
    aesthetic judgment  140
    independence  139
    intellectual  140–1
    in sublime/sublimity  349
Savary, Claude-Étienne  128, 344, 387 n.9
Schelling, Wilhelm Joseph  194, 343, 373 n.15
schema  233. *See also* Otto, Rudolf; schematism
schematism  139–40, 236
schematization  236
Schiller, Friedrich  2, 12, 149–60, 194, 221
Schjeldahl, Peter  295

Schneider, Pierre  295
"The School of Paris"  294
Schopenhauer, Arthur  12, 194–8, 212, 213–15, 223, 224–5,
    329, 335, 343, 346, 348, 350
science  360
    cognitive  2, 280, 281, 288–90
    fine  91–100
    philosophical theory and  341
    social  1
Scott, Walter  162, 389 n.1
sculpture  244, 257, 258. *See also* architecture
sea  76, 93, 152, 153, 157, 179, 190, 197, 203, 322, 356, 357–8
security  154
    existential  304, 306, 308
    moral  154, 155
    physical  154, 155
self  112, 170, 216. *See* sublime
    abjection  248–9
    environmental sublime and  363–4
    moral  159–60
    noumenal  329, 337
    transcendent  324
self-admiration theory  62
self-affirmation  269
self-aggrandizement theory  170
self-awareness  289, 301, 353, 404 n.31
self-congratulatory culture  296
self-consciousness  200, 214, 215, 216, 329, 345. *See also*
    self-awareness
self-discovery  361
self-evident  244–5
self-preservation  78, 134. *See also* Burke, Edmund; life
    instincts  150, 151, 154, 155, 351
    passions belonging to  79–80
    pleasure in sublime and  351
self-reflection  362, 364
self-reflexivity  404 n.32
self-regarding  360
self-reproach  136
self-respect  151
self-sacrifice  3
sensuously perfect representation  11, 92, 94
*sensus communis*  268
sentiments. *See also* emotions
    description of  32
    Erotic  33, 34
    Heroic  33, 34
    Marvelous  34, 35
    Odious  34, 35
    States and  32
    Terrible  33, 34, 35
Seven Wonders  299
Seward, Anna  4, 11, 162–5
Sewell, Elizabeth  69
Shakespeare, William  1, 98, 220, 226
Shapshay, Sandra  4, 329–39
Shelley, Mary  11, 184–92
Shelley, Percy Bysshe  6, 184, 185, 373 n.14